NATIONALIST CHINA
DURING THE SINO-JAPANESE WAR,
1937-1945

To Mr. & Mrs. Nicholas Esposito

With best wishes and personal

regards.

[signature]

August 30, 1977

Nationalist China
During the Sino-Japanese War, 1937-1945

對日抗戰中之中國國民政府

Edited with an Introduction
by

Paul K. T. Sih

薛光前主編

AN EXPOSITION-UNIVERSITY BOOK

Exposition Press   *Hicksville, New York*

To
TERESA DONG SIH

Contents

Contents

Chapter X

Contributors

Dennis Chinn, Stanford University
Lloyd E. Eastman, University of Illinois
Chi-ming Hou, Colgate University
Chiao-min Hsieh, University of Pittsburgh
Akira Iriye, University of Chicago
John Israel, University of Virginia
Steven Levine, Columbia University
Yun-han Li, Academia Historica, Republic of China
Chin-tung Liang, Academia Sinica
Hung-hsun Ling, Academia Sinica
Jessie G. Lutz, Douglass College, Rutgers University
Chun-fan Mao, New York University
Ou Tsuin-chen, New Asia Institute of Advanced Chinese Studies
Dison H. F. Poe, St. John's University
Peter Schran, University of Illinois
Tsung-han Shen, JCRR, Republic of China
Lawrence Shyu, University of New Brunswick, Canada
Paul K. T. Sih, St. John's University
Anthony Tang, Vanderbilt University
William L. Tung, Queens College of the City University of New York
William W. Whitson, Congressional Record Service, Library of Congress
Hsiang-hsiang Wu, College of Chinese Culture, Taiwan

Introduction:
Reflections on the Conference

BY PAUL K. T. SIH

JOHN F. KENNEDY once remarked, "Life is unfair." This is particularly true with the political history of a nation. It all depends upon what viewpoint one takes. Su Tung-po (1036-1101), a Chinese poet, wrote in one of his poems that when you look at mountains from different sides, one side looks like rolling hills and the other side looks like rugged peaks　横看成嶺側成峯　. No historical study is valid unless we put the entire situation in proper perspective. In other words, we have to enliven realism with idealism, and to temper idealism with realism. It is vitally important, therefore, to balance ideals with realities, aspirations with actualities.

Generally speaking, those who are directly involved in a situation, and therefore labelled "insiders," tend to lay more emphasis on actual experiences at the expense of theoretical thinking, while those who make a judgment without the advantage of firsthand knowledge and are usually called "outsiders" tend to attach more importance to hypothetical thinking than solid facts.

As students of history, our task today, as always, is to determine where to draw the line between the attainable and the visionary. The danger of covering up shortcomings or faults in any political system is always present. Likewise, there is the illusion, ignoring the hard substance of basic facts, of confusing theory, however noble, with reality.

It is with this balanced perspective in mind that "The Conference on Wartime China, 1937-1945" was held from April 30 to May 2, 1976, at the University of Illinois, Urbana, Illinois, under the joint sponsorship of the Center for Asian Studies, University of Illinois, and the Center of Asian Studies, St. John's University, New York. Thanks to the sustained cooperation of Dr. Lloyd E. Eastman, Professor of the Department of History at the University of Illinois, who acted with me as coordinator of the Conference, we were able to conduct the three-day conference with fruitful results, as evidenced in the production of this volume entitled *Nationalist China During the Sino-Japanese War, 1937-1945*.

With a view to achieving, as far as we could, a balance between idealism and realism, we endeavored to organize the Conference with a combined component of "insiders" and "outsiders." Each presented his views based upon either his personal experiences as an "insider" or by drawing his source of information from academic research as an "outsider" with complete frankness. The "insiders" are not necessarily infallible, nor are the "outsiders" altogether unrealistic. Discussions were sincere; exchanges were candid. We have learned a good deal from one another.

One thing bears noting at the outset. I refer to the scope of the Conference. When the Conference was being organized, it was named, for the sake of brevity, as the "Conference on Wartime China, 1937-1945" with the implied understanding, however, that it would be limited to discussions on China's wartime efforts under the Nationalist rule. In other words, it would not cover any studies of her wartime operations in the Communist-occupied area.

This guideline, with the exception of two discussants, Dr. Jessie G. Lutz on education and Dr. Peter Schran on economy and finance, was closely observed by all the speakers and the rest of the discussants. For this reason, the comments made by Dr. Lutz and Dr. Schran in their respective fields relating to Communist China were not fully discussed, since they were beyond the Conference's considerations as originally contemplated.

On the opening day, April 30, 1976, I, as coordinator of the Conference, had the privilege and honor of addressing my fellow colleagues as follows:

In the study of history, Arnold J. Toynbee singled out two elements essential to a treatment of the nation's history:

(1) No single nation can show a history which is in itself self-explanatory. History naturally depends on the action of forces which are not exclusively national but proceed from wider causes, particularly external relations.

(2) These wider causes, which lead to the action of national forces, operate upon each of the parts of a broader society, and are not intelligible, unless a comprehensive view of these wider causes is taken in their operation throughout that society.

The British historian further noted that in any historical study it is impossible to grasp the significance of any particular member's behavior, under a particular ordeal, without taking some account of the similar or dissimilar behavior of its fellows, and without viewing the successive ordeals as a series of events in the life of the whole society.*

---

*A *Study of History* by Arnold J. Toynbee (abridgement of Volumes I-VI by D. C. Somervell), New York & London: Oxford University Press, 14th Printing, 1958, pp. 1-4.

It is based upon these premises that we are to deal with the study of wartime China under the Nationalist rule, 1937-1945.

Since the Opium War, 1839-1842, China has never been free from external pressures and forces. We can hardly understand Chinese history without reference to other parts or powers of the world. Unequal treaties imposed upon China by foreign powers, which impaired China's sovereignty politically, economically, and socially, were not totally abolished until January 11, 1943, in the closing years of World War II when the United States and Great Britain concluded with China new treaties on the basis of equality and reciprocity.

In China's external relations, Japan, Soviet Russia, and Great Britain were major antagonists. This trio of contestants, differentiating themselves from one another in the form of performance, were consistent in seeking their respective interests and privileges at the expense of China.

During the Sino-Japanese War, 1937-1945, Japan was China's arch enemy. It was easy to be identified. Not so with Soviet Russia. Soviet Russia pretended to be China's friend, as she wished China to fight against Japan, her potential threat on the Eastern flank. However, after Soviet Russia concluded the Pact of Neutrality with Japan on April 13, 1941, her relations with China became dubious. The year 1941 was crucial.

It was in January 1941 that the Chinese Communists suddenly shifted their policy from reconciliation to confrontation, as evidenced in the case of the new Fourth Army incident. It was also in December 1941 that the United States was attacked by Japan at Pearl Harbor. As a consequence, Soviet Russia no longer needed to depend upon the "old China" headed by Chiang Kai-shek but the "new China" ruled by Mao Tse-tung. Soviet Russia was sure enough that Japan would be well taken care of, and would be finally defeated, by the United States. It was a Communist China, not a Nationalist China, in which Soviet Russia was interested!

After the Japanese attack on Pearl Harbor, the United States and Great Britain became China's allies. However, Britain's major objective in being involved in Asia was primarily to save her imperialistic gains. Until the present time, Britain still keeps Hong Kong. Although the United States did not entertain any colonial interest, yet because of her historical relations with Britain, in particular their common Far Eastern policy, China's trust and confidence in the United States could not be entirely unlimited. This was particularly true during the war when Chinese nationalism reached its climax. No nation can stomach any foreign intervention at the very time when she desperately resists an outside invader!

We cannot forget for a moment that there was a puppet regime in Nanking under Japanese domination headed by Wang Ching-wei. In challenging Wang's position, the Chinese Nationalist leadership could not possibly tolerate external pressure, at least on the surface, without weakening her patriotic resistance to all forms of foreign domination. Any attempt, no matter how admirable the goal may be, to change conditions in other countries has to be made behind the scenes, because no sovereign nation can allow itself to be pushed around in public. This state of mind must be taken into account when we consider Chinese-

American relations during the war, with special reference to General Stilwell's mission to China and General Marshall's mediation in China's internal conflicts.

In international contacts, it is very difficult to draw a line of demarcation between "friendly advice" of an ally and "political intervention" of a domineering foreign power. With the hindsight of the published stories concerning the CIA's foreign operations, we realize today that American good-will missions were not altogether as altruistic, pure, and innocent as they appeared or were intended to be!

The second essential element of historical study, as referred to at the outset, is to appraise partial operations through a comprehensive view of the total situation. In other words, it is important to study the trees individually, but not at the expense of losing sight of the whole forest. When we use our finger, pointing to the moon, it is important to look at the moon, not at the finger. Otherwise, we will not only miss the moon, but also miss the finger itself!

The analogy can be well applied to our concern with the problems facing wartime China, 1937-1945. The first and foremost consideration of China during the war was national survival. Nothing short of this would be realistic. Militarily, China was no match for Japan's far superior strength. It was only through determined and effective national leadership that China could sustain the trials and tribulations throughout the war years. In war, no government can be popular. How could it be, when it asks the people to sacrifice their lives and to give up their food for military use?

Historical facts take on meaning only within an inclusive context, and also concepts in history become relevant only to the extent that they are presented in factual text. This comprehensive appraisal of the whole war situation must be kept in mind when we are to evaluate the development of a specific problem or the behavior of an individual person. The total objective of wartime China, 1937-1945, as we well understand, was to stay in the war and to fight to the very end. This was finally achieved in spite of insurmountable difficulties. During these eight years of fighting, the National leadership was resolute. It charted the ship of state with a combined skill of caution and determination. Effective leadership, as we all know, was a prerequisite for a strong government needed for national resistance and survival. Naturally, there were shortcomings and mistakes. However, the achievement of victory surpassed all of them in importance and in necessity.

We must bear this in mind when we are to consider the attempts at the democratization of China during the war, including attempts at organizing a coalition government. Whatever its eventual outcome, a coalition government would deprive wartime China of the leadership it needed. When a house is on fire, it is all the more important to let the fire chief hold the water hose extinguishing the flame. There is no time to discuss how the hose should be handled or whether the fire engine needs to be lubricated!

As to the change of political rule of mainland China from the Nationalists to the Communists in 1949, that is another story beyond the scope of our consideration for the period 1937-1945. We need another conference dealing with this specific period, 1945-1949.

Obviously we cannot possibly divide the historical current in separate compartments, as there is always a continuity linking the different periods. Nevertheless, we can hardly appreciate the cause and effects of historical development in an intelligible way without pinpointing some major issues which characterize each of the different periods.

The years 1937-1945 were war years which were marked by war operations. The years 1945-1949 were years of rehabilitation which focused on recovery efforts. The Nationalist government succeeded in the war operations and should be given credit for its part in the outcome. The same government failed in post-war rehabilitation and should assume the responsibility for its mistakes, although, as Toynbee remarked, a nation's history cannot be attributed to internal causes alone. It should be viewed in the light of external forces and should be judged not by a single episode but by a series of successive factors. The performance of any particular person cannot be judged without taking account of the behavior of others who helped to cause that person's action or reaction. Truth is found, not in an isolated event, but in a comprehensive view of an extended operation in its totality.

Only with such an approach that steers a delicate course between the Scylla of partial observation and the Charybdis of superficial appraisal, an approach that permits a precise understanding of the parts without losing a profound comprehension of the whole, can we arrive at the truth and establish the just verdict of history.

The first paper, entitled "The Origins of War: Background of the Lukouchiao Incident, July 7, 1937," was authored by Professor Yun-han Li 李雲漢 of the Academia Historica, Republic of China. He skillfully presented, in the words of the discussant Professor Akira Iriye of the University of Chicago, "background facts back to the 1920's, and weaves various episodes and incidents prior to July 7, 1937, into a concise story of Sino-Japanese tension" (p. 33).

Professor Akira Iriye agreed basically with Professor Li in stating that "Japanese ambitions in Manchuria and North China were the ultimate cause of the Sino-Japanese war." He maintained, however, that if the pro-Japanese elements of the Nationalist Government had been given the opportunity for conciliatory efforts, the Sino-Japanese conflicts would have pursued a different course of development. This is what Professor Akira stated:

> . . . the existence of these Chinese (Wang Ching-wei 汪精衛 , Huang Fu 黃 郛 (膺白), and other leaders who sought some sort of accommodations with Japan) was of crucial importance in encouraging the thought among prominent Japanese that compromise and conciliation between the two countries were possible short of Japan's completely giving up the points of its conquest (p. 34).

Again, he reiterated, "On the Chinese side, there certainly was a divergence of views as to how to cope with the Japanese imperialism, ranging from uncompromising opposition to opportunistic accommodation" (p. 34).

The points raised by Professor Akira Iriye are interesting indeed. However, we must not ignore the national sentiments of the Chinese people and the political realities that the Nationalist government faced before the war broke out in July 1937. Nationalism was rising to the highest point. Anti-Japanese feelings became a nationwide uproar. No national leadership or political leader could assume a pro-Japanese position without serious consequences. Men like Wang Ching-wei and Huang Fu were entrusted by the Chinese Government, particularly by Generalissimo Chiang Kai-shek, to deal with the Japanese counterparts for the sole purpose of using delaying tactics. China needed time for a more adequate preparation for national defense, for a more effective resistance against Japanese aggression. In her reminiscences based on her husband's diary entries, letters and memoranda, Mrs. Huang Fu recorded that Huang was a true and zealous patriot.* His anti-Japanese spirit and fortitude were no less than anyone's. So was Wang Ching-wei at that time. Wang did not become a Japanese tool and a traitor until the end of 1938.

Therefore, before the outbreak of the war in July 1937, there had developed already a solid and unified national spirit of fighting against Japanese invasion. Most of the important members of the Cabinet, including Chang Chun 張 羣 , Ho Ying-chin 何應欽 , Chang Kia-ngau 張嘉璈 and Wu Ting-chang 吳鼎昌 , had studied in Japan. Because of their knowledgeability of Japan's internal situation, they were better known as *Chih-Jih Pai* 知日派 (group of knowing Japan best), instead of *Chin-Jih Pai* 親日派 (a pro-Japanese group), and were more realistic in counteracting Japan's aggressive designs and conspiracies under the guidance of the National leadership. There existed no group of pro-Japanese elements whatsoever on the Chinese side. The immediate national goal was *survival.*

As Professor Li told the Conference very lucidly, one of the major causes leading to the Lukouchiao Incident was misjudgment of the situation in China on the part of Japan. This is what Professor Li stated in his oral presentation:

---

*Reminiscences of I-yun 亦雲回憶 by Mrs. Huang Fu (Taipei: Biographical Literature Publishing Co. 傳記文學社 , 1968); also see *Chronological Events of Huang Fu* 黃膺白先生年譜長編 by Shan Yun-lun 沈雲龍 (Taipei: Lien-ching Publishing Co., 1976 聯經出版公司).

In the latter part of the 1930's there were two radical changes in China. One was the rise of nationalism and the other was the marked progress of nation-building efforts. Most of the Western scholars and political scientists who appreciated China's gains in national reconstruction realized that in the autumn of 1936, China entered into a new era. There was a genuine national unity. With the only exception of the Communists, the entire nation gave its support to the government under the leadership of Generalissimo Chiang Kai-shek. This was particularly true after the Sian Incident. The political situation underwent a total change. None would like to submit himself to any foreign aggressions. On the other hand, there was a general demand for taking back the lost national rights and privileges from foreign powers.

However, the Japanese government and the military people were ignorant of China's change. They still treated China with the old "twenty-one demands" attitude. They continued the post-Mukden Incident policy. For instance, the solution of "local settlement" would be accepted by China if it were proposed in 1932, as China did not have any choice. Not so in 1937. When Japan proposed "local settlement" in 1937, the Chinese Government demanded the right for national negotiation and approval. This was so because the Chinese Government in 1937 had the capacity of exercising its sovereignty. If Japan had understood the situation and modified her attitude a bit, I believe that the war would not have been inevitable.

The second paper, with "Total Strategy Used by China and Some Major Engagements in the Sino-Japanese War of 1937-1945" as its theme, was delivered by Professor Hsiang-hsiang Wu 吳相湘 of the College of Chinese Culture, Yangmingshan, Taiwan. Professor Wu pointed out, "When the Sino-Japanese War of 1937-1945 broke out, the Chinese Army and people swore to fight against the Japanese by conducting a war of attrition with the strategy of Chiang-wei of retreating into the interior of the country under Generalissimo Chiang Kai-shek's leadership and then of gaining the final victory after eight years of hard and brave fighting" (p. 42).

Professor Wu describes the total strategy in three aspects: (1) retreat to the interior; (2) trade space for time; (3) fight to the bitter end without compromising. In this regard, he cited Generalissimo Chiang Kai-shek in these words, "Frankly speaking, our purpose in resisting Japanese aggression is to have the war ended with the war in Europe and the World War at the same time. In other words, it means that the Sino-Japanese problem will be solved as one of the world problems at the same time" (p. 60). "In fact," Professor Wu further noted, "Chinese armed resistance to Japanese aggression began two years before the outbreak of the war in Europe, and the Sino-Japanese War was not

ended until more than three months after the armistice in Europe"
(p. 61).

Among major engagements in the war,° Professor Wu attaches
special importance—and rightly so—to the battle of Changsha in January 1942 under the field command of General Hsueh Yueh 薛　　岳
"In battle," Professor Wu records, "there were 1,591 Japanese troops
killed in combat, 4,412 wounded, the loss being 2.5 times more than
what had been suffered in the battle for the occupation of Hong Kong"
(p. 67). Again, he notes:

> The Japanese troops won every battle after the outbreak of the Pacific
> War except this one. Its meaning to the Allied Forces was significant:
> American and British troops could not check the advancing of Japanese
> troops, but Chinese troops made the first record to defeat Japanese troops.
> The author of the "U.S. Army in World War II" stated: "To the Chinese
> and their friends, Changsha was a name to conjure with" (p. 67).

Truly, this battle of Changsha alone denies the contention that
Nationalist China did not fight and did not win the war; she just
happened to be on the winning side!

There were two discussants on Professor Wu's study: one was Dr.
William W. Whitson of the Congressional Research Service, Library of
Congress, and the other, Professor Chiao-min Hsieh 　　謝覺民　　of
the University of Pittsburgh.

Dr. Whitson in his comments proposed eight alternative strategies
hypothetically available to the defense of China. The choice among these
alternatives would ultimately be governed by three sets of facts: strength
relative to the enemy; mobility relative to the enemy; and a degree of
national unity. He largely agreed with Professor Wu by stating in his
concluding remarks: "Professor Wu's excellent paper portrays much of
the foregoing, especially in its description of the early rationale leading
to the national defensive-offensive" (p. 84). This was one of the eight
alternative strategies suggested by Dr. Whitson.

Professor Hsieh agreed in totality with Professor Wu by attributing
China's military success to the correctness of her good strategy of "trading space for time" and "accumulating minor successes for forcing a
major victory," and Japan's big mistake was her lack of knowledge of
Chinese history and geography (p. 85). This is how Professor Hsieh
concludes his comments:

> In 1937, when the Japanese military operation was carried on mainly
> on the coastal plains, the invaders advanced an average of twelve miles

---

°During the eight-year war, 1937-1945, there were altogether 38,931 combats,
including twenty-two major engagements between the Nationalist and the Japanese
armies (*Chiang Kai-shek's Diary*　　蔣總統秘錄　　, *Central Daily
News*, Taipei, Taiwan, November 10, 1976).

daily on Chinese territory; but in 1938, when the fighting had shifted to the rugged western land, the advance decreased to only six-and-one half miles daily. In 1939, when the Chinese were defending the mountainous interior, the Japanese advance was reduced to half a mile a day. Here the terrain became a real asset to China's political geography" (p. 87).

Chiang Kai-shek himself pointed out most lucidly that:

> In economic resources, industry, science, and technology as well as in the striking power of her armed forces and weapons, China was weak as compared with Japan. After the Mukden Incident of 1931, we had to be patient and to negotiate with Japan; and for six years thereafter we did not talk lightly of armed resistance.
>
> Once hostilities were forced on us in 1937, however, we did not hesitate to adopt the scorched-earth policy, to "fall back into the interior". . . . We held fast to this strategic principle throughout the eight years of war and, despite the intrigues of Soviet Russia and the insurrection of the Chinese Communists, we achieved victory in concert with the Allies in August 1945.*

"Education in Wartime China" is the third paper, presented by Dr. Ou Tsuin-chen 吳俊升 of the New Asia Institute of Advanced Chinese Studies, Hong Kong. Dr. Ou evaluates wartime China's educational operations, largely from his personal experience and with eminent scholarship, including the moving of universities and colleges from the Japanese-occupied area to the free zone, giving succor to homeless teachers and students, reviving education behind the front, developing education on every level and in every category, reforming and establishing new systems, encouraging scholarly research, providing national culture, fostering international exchange, and enlisting as well as training students to participate directly in the war efforts. He reminisces that the war education under the Nationalist leadership was a success in attaining its dual goal of providing support to the war and preparing for national reconstruction. "War education," Dr. Ou remarks, "while continuing its primary purpose of nurturing talents and experts for national reconstruction, had to meet all the special needs of the war so as to be in accord with the national policy that equal opportunity be given to national reconstruction and the war of resistance" (p. 93).

Dr. Ou attributes the success of wartime China's higher education to the determined policy set forth by the national leadership. The internal educational crisis on the issue between regular education and war education was settled by providing that students, especially university and

---

*Chiang Kai-shek, *Soviet Russia in China* (New York: Farrar, Straus and Giroux, Revised, Abridged Edition, 1965), p. 146.

college students, who wished to stay in school would receive regular education, combining usual courses with special training programs designed to meet war needs (p. 97).

Education in the Japanese-occupied area was not ignored by the Nationalist Government in spite of extreme difficulties. "Even those left behind in the Japanese-occupied zone were not neglected by the government. Many underground schools were kept open, supported and supervised by Educational Agents sent from Chungking. The hazards of underground operations were such that at least 343 Educational Agents lost their lives in the line of duty" (p. 119).

Summing up his study, Dr. Ou outlines the causes leading to successful performance of wartime education in China as follows:

(1) The policy decision was correct.
(2) To value education has always been a Chinese tradition.
(3) The education administration was given much power and authority.
(4) The war, a constant reality in the mind of everyone, fostered a spirit of unity, self-sacrifice, austerity, and forbearance.
(5) Patriotism was responsible for a generation of energetic, industrious and highly motivated students (p. 122).

Of course, there are shortcomings, as always, in any governmental operation. This is particularly true when a nation is involved in a life-and-death struggle for survival. Measured against the successes thus achieved, failures in certain areas should be considered as minimal.

As I pointed out above, the scope of the Conference was limited to the discussion on Nationalist China alone. However, Professor Jessie G. Lutz offers another dimension of a contrasting view between the operations of Nationalist China and those of the Chinese Communists in these words:

> It is true that the Chinese Communist Party emerged from the war strengthened whereas the Kuomintang emerged weakened and factionalized; this knowledge tends to enhance Yenan's image, including its philosophy for the education and use of intellectuals. Educational accomplishments were, however, not simply a function of educational policies, they were greatly effected by inflation, the activism of guerrilla warfare versus the stalemate in positional warfare, the ability to control corruption, the discipline and unity of the party leadership, etc." (p. 126).

A Chinese proverb goes: "One who succeeds is a king; one who fails becomes an insurgent"   成則為王敗則為寇   . In other words, one cannot use the measurements of success or failure to judge a hero　　不可成敗論英雄　　. We cannot simply hold that because of the loss of the mainland by the Nationalists to the Communists, everything done by the Nationalists was bound to be wrong and everything done by the Communists, including education, was bound to be right. A drastic contrast of achievements in the field of education between the Communists on the mainland and the Nationalists in Taiwan in the last twenty-eight years since the Communist domination of the mainland in 1949 presents a very interesting study.

The fourth paper, "Southwest Associated University: Preservation as an Ultimate Value," by Professor John Israel of the University of Virginia, provides, in the words of the discussant Professor Chun-fan Mao 毛春帆 of New York University, "a compactly and selectively structured panorama of a multiplex story" (p. 156). Although an "outsider," Professor Israel assesses some realities of the early war years, in agreement with the famous Pieta essayist, Chu Tzu-ching 朱自清 , and with measured insight, by saying: "Because the war itself provided a unifying cause, there was less reason for Nationalistic student protests that divided students from the faculty and faculty members from each other. United by the pursuit of learning and the common struggle for survival, Lienta students and teachers shared a community of interest. Few saw any reason to disrupt the harmony" (p. 140).

However, there are a few remarks by Professor Israel which seem difficult to reconcile. For instance, in one place he notes that Lienta's relevance to the War of Resistance was "more symbolic than tangible" (p. 143), and yet in another place he comments that "Lienta had been part and parcel of China's wartime destiny that had elevated the nation to new heights of promise and responsibility" (p. 150). In another instance, Professor Israel cites Pan Kuang-tan's 潘光旦 observation that: "Government loans were inadequate and most students worked part time or even dropped out of school for a year or two in order to earn money to continue their studies" (p. 140). Yet he maintains that government support gave rise to the dependence/resentment psychology that alienated the students from the government (p. 146). We realize that the Southwest Associated University was a government-operated institution. It was well understood that when the students entered into the University, they were psychologically prepared to accept government support. In fact, during the war years all the Chinese depended upon the government for almost everything. How could they survive otherwise?

As an "insider" Professor Mao served as the discussant of Professor Israel's paper. She was able to classify and explain the situation at Lienta under the headings: War and Education, External Circumstances and Internal Resources, Puzzlements and Questions, which include the following topics:

(1) National Government and Lienta;
(2) Scholastic Students of Lienta;
(3) Intellectual Elite;
(4) Dependence/Resentment Psychology;
(5) Voluntary Subjection.

Professor Mao remarks with a reassuring thought as she reminisces:

> . . . the members of the Lienta community had maintained a stoical approach to life which was rooted in the Confucius tradition that the superior people can still have joy in the midst of the difficult circumstances. Perhaps, the academic communities in a more affluent society could look to the Lienta experience for the inspirations to solve some of the problems confronting them (pp. 160-61).

It may be added that, as good trees bear good fruits, we note that Yang Chen Ning 楊振寧 and Lee Tsung-dao 李政道 , two Nobel Prize winners in Physics, were products of the Lienta and several eminent American scholars, notably W. Theodore deBary, Glen W. Baxter, Joseph R. Levenson, William Rhoads Murphy, Nicholas Bodman, James Crump, Richard B. Mather, Hans H. Frankel, and George W. Seidl, were all among the recipients of Chinese Culture Fellowships provided by the Nationalist Government during the war (p. 123, n. 20).

Dr. Tsung-han Shen 沈宗瀚 is the author of the paper entitled "Food Production and Distribution for Civilian and Military Needs in Wartime China, 1937-1945." As an experienced "insider" who personally participated in the program, he provides a detailed and fully documented account of the subject under consideration.

Dr. Shen remarks:

> Food production and distribution during 1937-1945 were fairly successful and contributed to winning the war in China, thanks to the prohibition of poppy growing, the collection of land tax in kind and the good cooperation between the government and the people. Many of the experiences we gained in improving agricultural production to meet military and civilian needs have proved valuable in later years, especially in the post-war rural reconstruction of Taiwan (p. 191).

There were two discussants, Professor Anthony Tang 唐宗明 of Vanderbilt University and Professor Dennis Chinn 陳興家 of Stanford University, who reviewed Dr. Shen's paper. Professor Tang's evaluation was that Dr. Shen spoke "with the authority and certitude of someone who was not only there to witness the unfolding drama but in the role of a leading agricultural expert who helped shape wartime food policies and implement the related programs" (p. 194).

In a similar tone, Professor Chinn notes that Dr. Shen "documents the changing food situation from the prewar period to the end of the war in 1945. . . . Dr. Shen's analysis leaves no doubt that the policies adopted played an important role in maintaining the war effort by doing precisely that. We are indeed fortunate to have the benefit of the insight and firsthand observations of one who played such an important role in the actual events" (p. 198).

The sixth paper, "Economic Development and Public Finance," was presented by Professor Chi-ming Hou 侯繼明 of Colgate University. Outlining the immense burden of the war on the part of the Nationalist Government, Professor Hou points out that "the Sino-Japanese war in 1937 required a level of expenditure by the Chinese government higher than the pre-war levels. But the tax base after the war was reduced sharply. Given the lack of substantial economic assistance from abroad, the central question was how to finance the war internally, or, more precisely, who should assume the burden of the war" (p. 233). Again, he stresses:

> In an underdeveloped economy such as the one in Free China, economic development is a long and painful process and cannot be expected to take place overnight even under the most favorable circumstances. Surely it would be an extremely difficult task to develop during a war when the industrial establishments and the transportation network are constantly under the pressure of the enemy's attack and when the government is totally absorbed in fighting the enemy (p. 233).

Professor Peter Schran, discussant of the paper, agreed basically with Professor Hou's observations of Free China's war economy and finance. He introduces, however, an account of the development of war in the Chinese Communist occupied area based upon Claire and William Bound's report. It blames the Nationalist war strategy for favoring technically modern solutions at the expense of guerrilla tactics, as employed by the Chinese Communists (pp. 239-40).

We realize that in a war, positional warfare and guerrilla operations should go hand in hand. They are interdependent. If there is no positional fighting to hold the front line, it will be most difficult for guerrilla operations in the rear. In fact, the real aim of the Chinese Communists' participation in the war was to sit upon the mountain seeing the fighting between two tigers 坐山觀虎鬥 —the Nationalist and Japanese armies. This provided the Communists with the great advantage of staying behind the Japanese occupied area and building up their strength for taking over the political power.

Chang Kuo-tao 張國燾 , one of the twelve founders of the Chinese Communist Party, who defected from the CCP in April 1938, recorded: "After the Lukouchiao incident (July 7, 1937), because of the development of hostilities, the Communist guerrilla tactics were given an opportunity for extensive self-expansion. This paved the way for Mao Tse-tung's success in taking over the throne from the Nationalists on mainland China. This was entirely out of anyone's predictions."[*]

Furthermore, as Professor Hou notes in his study, it was the Nationalist Government which had to assume the entire burden of the war. The Japanese never dropped any bombs in Yenan throughout the war years, but they did not spare Chungking! The Communists just picked the advantages. There was a lot dropping in their laps, largely thanks to the Japanese invasion.[†] In fact, there existed during the war close relations between the Communist New Fourth Army and Japanese General Okamura's staff in Nanking.[**]

It is with these facts in mind that William W. Lockwood, Professor Emeritus and Lecturer, Woodrow Wilson School of Public and International Affairs, Princeton University, made a very objective assessment of the Chinese Nationalist problem in his article, "Asian Triangle: China, India, Japan":

> In Nationalist China of two generations ago, despite earlier decades of frustration, this was still a possibility—until its embryonic infrastructure was undermined and its hopes destroyed by the Japanese Army after 1937 . . . . Some 20 years later, with uncommon frankness, Chou En-lai greeted a conservative Japanese politician in Peking by expressing gratitude to Japan for delivering China to communism.[‡]

Dr. Hung-hsun Ling 淩鴻勛 of Academia Sinica, Republic of China, was the author of "China's Epic Struggle in Developing Its Overland Transportation System During the Sino-Japanese War." Among

---

[*]*Chang Kuo-tao's Diary* (Hong Kong: Min Pao Publication Co., 1973), Vol. III, p. 1288.

[†]For a summary and documentary study on the Chinese Communists' destructive actions during the Sino-Japanese War, see "Chung-Kung Po-Huai Kang-Chan Wei-hai Kuo-chia Shih-Shih" 中共破壞抗戰危害國家史實 by Chow Chih-fen 郋志奮 , *Central Daily News*, Taipei, Taiwan, October 17-21, 1976. Also, "To Commemorate the July 7, 1937 War of Resistance Against Japan by Refuting Once Again the False Propaganda of the Chinese Communists" 紀念七七抗戰再駁中共虛僞宣傳 , by General Ho Ying-chin 何應欽 (*Ibid.*, July 7-9, 1972).

[**]For a detailed account, see *The Vladimirov Diaries, Yenan, China, 1942-1945* (New York: Doubleday, 1975), p. 503. Peter Vladimirov was a Comintern liaison officer stationed at Yenan from 1942 to 1945. He served as Soviet Consul General in Shanghai from 1948 to 1951 and Soviet Ambassador to Burma in 1952.

[‡]*Foreign Affairs*, Vol. 52, No. 4, July 1974, p. 820.

the most outstanding achievements in the construction of new railroads during the war, according to Dr. Ling's account, were:

(1) The completion of the 280-mile section from Chuchow to Lochang on the Hankow-Canton Railway;

(2) The completion of the 338-mile section from Yushan to Pinghsiang on the Chekiang-Kiangsi Railway;

(3) The building of the 384-mile section from Hangyang to Laipi on the Hunan-Kwangsi Railway;

(4) The building of the 143-mile section from Chennankuan to Nanning on the Yunnan-Kwangsi Railway; and

(5) The extension of the 83-mile section from Sian to Paoki of the Lunghai Railway in September 1937 and then the further extension of the 96-mile section from Paoki to Tienshiu in 1945.

All these, with the additional construction of new highways throughout the nation, provided significant contributions to China's total efforts in breaking Japan's blockade and bringing the war to final victory.

Being the discussant of Dr. Ling's remarkable paper, I, as an "insider" who worked in the Ministry of Railways and the Ministry of Communications as Ling's colleague during the war years, had the privilege to review the study with great admiration. In reminiscing, I have this to offer in my comments:

> All these changes [in international transport routes] were made in adjusting to the various war conditions. The task was not easy. Both manpower and construction materials were in short supply. China had to draft a total of 14 million men to maintain an army between 2.2 and 5.7 million during the war years. Population was sparse in the interior districts which made it difficult to secure sufficient labor. Materials for constructing roads relied largely upon imported supplies. Every scrap of material and rails used for building bridges and tracks was taken from the dismantled stock of other railroads and refabricated. Tunnels were cut through, not by machines or with the help of explosives, but by human hands. All these achievements were realized under severe Japanese air raids or serious military threats (pp. 268-69).

Also, as an "insider," I have the pleasure to supplement Ling's study by providing an account of a land-and-waterway joint transportation line linking three provinces—Hunan, Szechwan and Shansi—covering about 4,000 miles　　川湘川陝水陸聯運　　. Using primitive and traditional means of transportation 驛運 , China was able to help overcome the difficulties with which modern equipment could hardly cope.

The next paper, "China's 'Wartime Parliament': The People's Political Council, 1936-1945," was authored by Professor Lawrence N. Shyu of the University of New Brunswick, Canada. His study, in the words of the discussant Professor Dison H. F. Poe　浦薛鳳　of St. John's University, "covers the manifold aspects of the PPC, including its origin and development, its membership and alignment, its sessions and meetings, its functions and contributions, and its expectations and disappointments. It is comprehensive, thoroughgoing and thoughtful." In a spirit of "seeking faults with a view to achieving perfection 求全之毀　," Professor Shyu feels disappointed by the failure of the Nationalist Government in making democracy work in wartime China. To this, Professor Poe cites two passages to explain the situation. One was reflected by General Albert C. Wedemeyer:

> China's real need was for a government with the power to govern. As I saw it the worst ills of China—corruption, maladministration, inefficiency, and the like—were the result not of the dictatorial nature of its government but of its lack of power and authority to get its orders carried out. . . . The powers of the Chinese Nationalist Government, far from being totalitarian, were limited too much. It interfered with the individual too little, not too much. Its sins of omission, not of commission, were the cause of its eventual downfall (p. 316).

Professor Poe also quotes Professor Lloyd E. Eastman from one of the latter's writings:

> Because of the nature of Chinese society and of its political traditions, it is perhaps one of China's tragedies during the twentieth century, that, in the quest for a viable political system, attempts had been made to erect democratic institutions. In a profound sense, Anglo-American democracy was not suited to China (pp. 316-17).

Indeed, democracy in China, as elsewhere, cannot be made. Nor can it be legislated. It grows, and grows in stability and with peace.

Professor Lloyd E. Eastman's paper is concerned with "Regional Politics and the Central Government: Yunnan and Chungking." He provides a realistic assessment of Nationalist China's performances during the war. "China was not a modern nation-state," Professor Eastman remarks, "for it lacked a highly articulated, effective system of control over its miltary and administrative arms. . . . Judgments regarding China's achievements during the war—for example, its ability to marshal the material and human resources of the nation, or its record of fighting the Japanese—ought not be made with the same criteria we might use to judge, say, Germany or the United States" (p. 329).

However, in evaluating the relationship between Yunnan under the governorship of Lung Yun 龍　雲 and the Central Government, Professor Eastman tends to consider any attempt by the Central Government to assert its national authority as encroachments over Yunnan's "independence" (p. 338). The case of the control of Yunnan's tin, for instance, by the Nationalist Government gave rise to a serious issue with Lung Yun. The reason for this governmental action was for the purpose of securing a $75,000,000 loan from the United States. It was to satisfy the urgent needs of war for the total interest of the nation, yet Lung Yun considered this as a kind of political intervention in Yunnan's "economic autonomy." Herein lie, as Professor Eastman's narrative shows, "difficult problems involved in the relations between national leadership and local authorities."

Speaking of Lung Yun, Professor Eastman notes that ". . . he was by the standards of his day a relatively dedicated, progressive and uncorrupt provincial militarist" (p. 331). However, he tends to have a different view with regard to Yen Hsi-shan 閻錫山, a provincial militarist in Shensi. Compared to Lung, who was an opium addict, Yen seemed, in the eyes of the Chinese regardless of their political differences, to say the least, no less dedicated, progressive or uncorrupt. Yen did participate in a separatist movement against the Nationalist Government in May 1930. Yet his loyalty toward the Central Government and his commitment to fight against the Japanese invasion during the war were never questionable. The fact that Yen later became Premier of Nationalist China (June 1949 to March 1950) during the most crucial period of national crisis was strong evidence attesting to his political convictions and integrity.

Professor Eastman provides in his study a great deal of information about the activities of political dissidents, with Yunnan at its core during the war years. The existence of these alleged internal strifes, particularly at a time when the Central Government was in charge of a life-and-death struggle for survival and was overburdened with all kinds of difficulties, is understandable. The logistic supplies made available in China to the U.S. Forces there, for instance, created serious difficulties for the Nationalist Government in her relations with the local authorities, particularly Yunnan. This was what Henry Morgenthau, Jr., recorded about a statement made by H. H. Kung 孔祥熙, China's wartime Minister of Finance, at a meeting on "Financial Settlement with China":

> . . . We are on the verge of bankruptcy. Every dollar you spend in China, we issue that dollar; besides the large projects we had to face, it is a dollar toward inflation.
> You speak about large imports to your men in China. I don't know whether you gentlemen realize how much it costs China—last month it

cost China three hundred million dollars, alone, to feed your Army. Last year—in the winter of last year—it cost us something about ninety dollars to feed an American soldier a day.

We in China are vegetable eaters. The poor people don't have much to eat, but of course, your boys must have roast beef and must have eggs for breakfast, and so forth. In England, I understand, you have to make application beforehand. You may be allowed an egg or two a month. But in China your boys need six eggs a day, and now it is cut down to four eggs. But you eat a pound of beef a day. In Kunming alone we are keeping cows and oxen to supply you twelve thousand pounds, or catties— that is one-fourth larger than a pound—Is it catties or pounds, Adler?

Mr. Adler: Catties.

Dr. Kung: We are supplying you twelve thousand catties of beef alone every day. Now, China is not like America, because in this country you raise animals for the purpose of meat; in China we don't do that. In order to supply the meat, we are feeding our oxen, used for farming purposes. I had a protest from the Governor of Yunnan, he had protests from the Provincial Assembly, saying that the cows and oxen were killed at such a rate that very soon there wouldn't be any animals left to help the farmers farm their land. We went out from Yunnan to the next province. The Governor of Kweichow around the first of April, wired me—he had issued orders prohibiting exporting cows out of his province.°

No one is contending that the Nationalist Government was perfect, and there was no discontent or conspiracy against it whatsoever during the war. However, most of the information quoted by Professor Eastman in these instances, in his own words, has "no reference in Chinese sources." He states that "the reasons for discontent and the targets of the conspiracy were reported differently by the State Department's several sources."† As Professor William L. Tung 董 霖 of Queens College of the City University of New York, discussant of Professor Eastman's paper, puts it:

> His [Eastman's] sources are drawn chiefly from the reports of American diplomats then stationed in China; some of them had long been known to hold a bias against the Kuomintang (Nationalist Party) and its leader, Chiang Kai-shek. Lack of access to the first-hand information from the participants after a lapse of three decades makes it difficult to present balanced views on many controversial issues (p. 363).

°*Morgenthau Diary* (China), Vol. II (Washington, D.C.: U.S. Government Printing Office, 1965), p. 1170.

†In Professor Eastman's study, there are altogether ninety-five notes. Of these, about two-thirds are directly or indirectly based upon the State Department's various sources.

It may be added that the information gathered by foreign intelligence agencies or diplomatic field staff is intended, as far as I can see, primarily for internal study, subject to judicious analysis and assessment. If it is to be used as a basis for scholarly research, an independent judgment with factual support must be taken into consideration.

Professor Eastman gives an extensive account of the discontents of the so-called liberals during the war under the blessing of Lung Yun. But who were these "liberals"?

On this point, Professor Tung has these comments to make:

> In those days, there were quite a number of so-called liberals who received special consideration and protection from Lung Yun. Lo Lung-chi was only one of them. After all, who were the liberals and who were the reactionaries? To the Communists and their sympathizers, any uncompromising Kuomintang member was a reactionary and whoever was willing to cooperate with anti-government elements was a liberal. While many Chinese intellectuals then believed in and promoted the practice of democracy, a good number of self-styled liberals were simply opportunists fishing in troubled waters as revealed by later developments. These labels had confused many discerning Western observers of Chinese politics (p. 365).

To conclude his remarks, Professor Tung notes:

> In his consolidation of national power against the traditional dominance of local militarists, Chiang should not be blamed. Considering Chiang's inherent difficulties and the limited resources at his disposal, "it was not an inconsiderable feat," in the words of Professor Eastman, "even to survive the eight years of war." The present discussant fully shares his view that "historians should therefore be slow to criticize the Chungking government for not playing a more active role" during that eventful period, when it was confronted with a formidable enemy and the challenges of the uncompromising Communists and provincial militarists (p. 367).

As a matter of fact, in dealing with the intransigent Communists and provincial militarists, Chiang practiced a well-balanced exercise of measured authority and moral persuasion. He avoided the arrogance of power and was aware of the limitations of patient diplomacy. This was the reason why he succeeded in solving the Sinkiang problem in September 1944. The difficulties of Sinkiang during the war, complicated by Soviet intrigues, were far more serious than those existing in Yunnan or Szechwan. They were of such a monumental scope that it would take years of deliberate and determined efforts even to improve the situation. Yet Chiang was able to remove Sheng Shih-tsai 盛世才

Governor of Sinkiang, without any confrontation, mainly because of Chiang's sagacity and wisdom beyond any ordinary level.

Last but not least, Professor Chin-tung Liang 梁敬錞 of Academia Sinica of the Republic of China, author of *General Stilwell in China, 1942-1944: The Full Story,** presents his study on "The Sino-Soviet Treaty of Friendship and Alliance of 1945: The Inside Story." "His narrative provides," in the words of the discussant Professor Steven L. Levine of Columbia University, "an extremely clear view of the main stages in the negotiations and presents intriguing detail from the Presidential Papers of Chiang Kai-shek to which he has been given access. Professor Liang's major contribution, however, is his insistence that the Sino-Soviet negotiations which produced the treaty must be viewed in a broad multilateral perspective reflecting the new structure of the postwar international system" (p. 398).

Rightly so, Professor Liang points out that if the United States had been willing to participate in the Sino-Soviet negotiation and had concluded a multipartite treaty in accordance with the spirit of the Yalta agreement and the U.S. open-door policy in Manchuria, the post-war situation in China would have been completely different. To this, however, Professor Levine offers a different view:

> When Chiang Kai-shek attempted to substitute multilateral Big Four arrangements in place of bilateral Sino-Soviet ones, he was trying to make the Big Four perform a function that was foreign to its design. The apparent multipolarity of the postwar international system barely concealed an essentially bipolar division of power between the United States and the Soviet Union. Furthermore, policies of these two powers took into account only those concerns of their alliance partners or satellites which were directly congruent with their own interest (p. 403).

The international situation of 1945 was completely different from that of today. In bipolar division of power between the United States and the Soviet Union in 1945-1946, there was something of a Russian dream; it was not yet a reality. The United States was the omnipotent power. The fact that her firmness brought results was evidenced in the Iranian case. United States strong support to protect the sovereignty of Iran forced the withdrawal of 30,000 Soviet troops from the Iranian province of Azerbaijan in March 1947.†

Lack of determination, not lack of strength, paved the way for Russian encroachment on China's sovereignty in Manchuria. It is with a sense of regret that Professor Liang reminisces in his further observa-

---

*St. John's University Press, New York, 1972.

†James F. Byrnes, *Speaking Frankly* (New York and London: Harper & Brothers, 1947), pp. 118-121 and pp. 304-305.

tions: "The causes of the collapse of Nationalist China were many, but the failure on the American part to maintain its high principles was also, at least, one of the major factors. Twenty-seven years have gone by, and it is high time for us to re-examine the mistakes on both sides so that a lesson might be learned from history" (p. 408).

In reviewing Nationalist China's efforts during the Sino-Japanese War, 1937-1945, we are, of course, not completely satisfied with what she has done, but are satisfied with the efforts she has exerted. There were many mistakes and weaknesses and fallibilities of the Nationalist Government, yet they were compensated for by the strong will of the Chinese people and the determined and enlightened policy of the National Leadership conducive to the final victory.

China did not happen to be on the winning side, as some Westerners contended. China did fight, and fight hard, to the bitter end. The fact that during these eight years of war—a war of attrition—China suffered a total loss estimated to be (U.S.) $31,330,136,000, and there were 3,311,419 casualties in combat and more than 8,420,000 civilians who died because of the war is solid evidence of the heavy price and sacrifices sustained by the Chinese people and nation.[*]

Sir Thomas More said: "Let us not desert the ship in the tempest because you cannot control the winds." This admonition was what the National leadership precisely endeavored to practice during the Sino-Japanese War. It could not realistically discharge its responsibility as the Central power of the nation which was in great peril, if it tolerated a situation whereby its political and military authority was impaired by dissident elements which sabotaged the execution of the war. In war, there is no substitute for victory. In the case of China, the immediate concern was not victory, but bare *survival*. There was no justification whatsoever, for instance, for any provincial militarist or "liberals" to use "democracy," "freedom," or any other seemingly attractive terms as pretext for chipping the power from the Central government merely to satisfy self-centered desires. *Survival of the nation must come first!*

In an imperfect world, one cannot demand perfection as the price of confidence. I do not claim that we should maintain faith in any government where there is no reason for that faith. But I do believe we must recognize that decisions of national leaders, in the real world, are often made in circumstances where the facts at hand are ambiguous. Some minimal degree of understanding of the enormous complexities immediately at hand, and in the foreseeable future, must be taken into account. China surely deserved this kind of restrained consideration.

There is another issue which clouded the performance of the Nationalist Government and leadership during the war years on the international

---

[*]*Chiang Kai-shek's Diary, op. cit.*

level. It was "communication." This simple word represents a complicated, vital process that is essential in the understanding of government. Leadership in today's political systems depends on confidence, but this will mean little unless the government leaders can communicate effectively with the public and their allied forces. This is true with the American system, and was even truer with Chinese leadership, which could not discharge effectively its responsibility during the national crisis without popular support of the public and complete confidence of the Allied Powers, particularly the United States. Nationalist China understood the importance of communicating but did not effectively counter the maneuvers of her political foes in obtaining domestic and international attention. Opposition parties' negative arguments made the news frequently, or constituted the substance of "field reports" of foreign diplomatic and intelligence services, but the government's positive views rarely reached the internal or foreign media fully. When political foes cultivated courtship with American agencies, they did it in the name of pursuing "democracy," "freedom," and "national ideals." Yet if the government leaders made any effort to accommodate themselves to American interests for the total execution of the war, they were labelled "American stooges" or "running dogs."

Chiang Kai-shek himself acknowledged that

> By comparison [to the Chinese Communists' tactics] our propaganda lacked initiative and was not militant enough ideologically to counter this worldwide political and psychological offensive, nor was it strong enough to arouse righteous indignation at home and a sense of justice abroad. In consequence, our government was beset with difficulties both internally and externally. Although several times we decided to take firm action, we vacillated and did not press on.°

One thing is certain. In this interdependent world, a small and weak nation which happens to be an American ally and friend cannot govern effectively unless it enjoys complete confidence and support of the United States. The influence of the United States on the small nations has been strongest, almost irresistible, when it was the unconscious irradiation of its national ideals, as well as the presence of its military and economic might. This was particularly true with China. During the war China depended on the United States for loyal support. By observing too literally traditional Confucian virtues of patience, tolerance, and forbearance, Chinese government leaders tend to maintain silence on any allegations or accusations made by political foes. Even when the *United States Relations with China,* generally known as "The White Paper,"

° *Soviet Russia in China,* p. 150.

outlining the failures of the Chinese National Government to meet the crises confronting it, was issued by the United States Department of State in August 1949,* the Chinese government did not care to make any comments or to offer any explanation clarifying its position. When the Chinese government failed to communicate, and the American public and bureaucracy stopped listening and believing, its ability to lead effectively soon vanished. This is the lesson we have to learn from painful experience as a result of our difficult years in wartime China.

This book, with its distinctive new point of view as well as its detailed presentation of historical facts, judiciously covering a wide range of related subjects, will make a valuable contribution to the understanding of the problems and issues confronted by Nationalist China during the Sino-Japanese War, 1937-1945. This new study will add, I am sure, to scholars' knowledge of a period about which very few studies of a critical and objective nature have been made. It will also generate more interest for further investigation. This is a beneficial consequence that necessarily results from the discovery of new facts or the re-evaluation of old ones in our academic community. In this way we can mitigate the burden of John F. Kennedy's observation, cited at the beginning of this introduction, that: "Life is unfair."

As Editor of the volume and Coordinator of the Conference, I wish to express my deep appreciation to the Center for Asian Studies, University of Illinois, for their co-sponsorship of the Conference and for making available to the Conference all the needed facilities and accommodations. I am most grateful to Prof. Lloyd E. Eastman for his kind cooperation in organizing the Conference as fellow Coordinator. Thanks should also be given to the speakers and the discussants of the Conference whose valued contributions are amply evidenced in this publication; to Prof. Leonard B. Allen of the Center of Asian Studies at St. John's University for his assistance in the production of the book and the preparation of the index; to Mrs. Dorothy Canner and Mrs. Sandra Esposito for their secretarial help; and to Mrs. April Tsao Chang for inserting in the text all the Chinese characters.

This book was composed by the Editor during the first six months of convalescence, after he underwent major stomach surgery at Sloan-Kettering Memorial Hospital, New York, on July 6, 1976. He is most grateful to his beloved wife, Teresa Chuan-tsien Dong 薛童傳全 for her total devotion and loving care conducive to his steady recovery, without which this project would not have become a reality.

March 1977

**United States Relations with China* (Washington, D.C.: United States Department of State Publication 3573, 1949), p. XIV.

NATIONALIST CHINA
DURING THE SINO-JAPANESE WAR,
1937-1945

CHAPTER I

The Origins of the War: Background of the Lukouchiao Incident, July 7, 1937

BY YUN-HAN LI

THE SECOND SINO-JAPANESE WAR, 1937-1945, is now a matter of history. However, the actual cause of the Lukouchiao 蘆溝橋 (which is known as the Marco Polo Bridge in the Western world) Incident, which took place on July 7, 1937, and marks the beginning of the eight-year war, is still an issue of controversy. During the past three decades, a good number of works relating to this subject have been worked out by both Oriental and Occidental historians. Some of them portrayed the Incident as the consequence of a conspiracy designed by the Japanese militarists in North China and as a repetition of a pattern of aggression identical with that of the Mukden Incident of September 18, 1931.[1] Others, especially those who wrote their books based almost entirely on Japanese sources, have been painting a different picture.[2]

The purpose of this study is not to make further comment on any related work. What the author wants to explain is that historians who ignore the special position occupied by those Japanese militarists in politics and the uneasy situation created by the Japanese Garrison in North China, and who know little about China's political development and nationalism in the 1930's will never be able to touch the core of the Sino-Japanese dispute. With this idea in mind, the author intends to make an attempt to ascertain the main factors which led to the outbreak of the Lukouchiao Incident of July 7, 1937, and to analyze the elements that eventually propelled China into full-scale resistance against Japan.

3

I

Japan's China Policy, 1927-1937

The Tanaka Memorandum

In discussing Japan's China policy during the period from 1927 to 1937, one can scarcely overlook the role played by Tanaka Giichi, a shrewd and ambitious soldier-politician who had taken Wakatsuki Reijuro's place as Japan's premier. Shortly after his Cabinet took office on April 20, 1927, Tanaka convened an important policy-making conference by which the so-called "positive policy" towards China was worked out. According to Tanaka himself, the Conference lasted eleven days (between June 27 and July 7, 1927) and was attended by "all the civil and military officers connected with Manchuria and Mongolia."[3]

On July 25, the same year, the Japanese Seiyukai Premier reported this "positive policy" to the Japanese Emperor by presenting a memorandum which was known as the "Tanaka Memorandum."[4] "It was by divine will," Tanaka wrote in that Memorandum, "that I should assist Your Majesty to open a new era in the Far East and to develop the new continental empire." To substantiate his policy, Tanaka wrote:

> The (Chinese) Three Eastern Provinces are politically the imperfect spot in the Far East. For the sake of self-protection as well as the protection of others, Japan cannot remove the difficulties in Eastern Asia unless she adopts the policy of "Blood and Iron." But in carrying out this policy we have to face the United States which has been turned against us by China's policy of fighting poison with poison. In the future if we want to control China, we must first crush the United States just as in the past we had to fight in the Russo-Japanese War. But in order to conquer China we must first conquer Manchuria and Mongolia. In order to conquer the world, we must first conquer China. If we succeed in conquering China the rest of the Asiatic countries and the South Sea countries will fear us and surrender to us. Then the world will realize that Eastern Asia is ours and will not dare to violate our rights. This is the plan left to us by Emperor Meiji, the success of which is essential to our national existence.[5]

Although the Japanese claimed it was a forgery and some Western historians dispute the authenticity of this document, the Chinese possess enough evidence for testifying that it is really a Japanese governmental plan for expansion. Tsai Chih-kan, a Taiwanese who lived in Japan at that time, confessed that he himself was the person who first got a copy of the Memorandum from the Japanese Palace in 1928. Without going into discussion of its authenticity, we note that the policy which Japan pursued towards China since 1931 was in perfect line with Tanaka's plan.

As his first objective was the conquest of Manchuria, the Chinese Three Eastern Provinces, Tanaka naturally did not like to see that China was approaching unification under the Kuomintang's rule. This basic idea led to Tanaka's decision to dispatch troops to Shantung to check the northern advance of the Chinese revolutionary forces, which resulted in the Tsinan Incident of May 3, 1928. However, Tanaka failed to fulfill his aim when Chiang Kai-shek, Commander-in-Chief of the National Revolutionary Army, decided to bypass Tsinan and continue his march northward.

When the revolutionary forces reached the Peking-Tientsin area in the opening days of June 1928, Marshal Chang Tso-lin 張作霖 , a Chinese warlord who had occupied the leading position in the Peking regime since 1926, decided to evacuate his troops back to his homeland, Manchuria, instead of fighting Chiang. On his way back to Mukden, he was murdered on June 4, at Huang-ku-tun, a small railroad station near Mukden, by a group of officers of the Japanese Kwantung Army.[6] The purpose of the assassination was to get rid of the stubborn Marshal who had recently been acting with marked independence rather than cooperating with Japan, so as to clear the way for a Japanese takeover of Manchuria later. "Had the conspiracy been successful," a Japanese officer, Tanaka Ryukichi, confessed eighteen years later, "the Manchuria Incident would have started then rather than in 1931."[7]

It is true that the Kwantung Army officers who plotted and carried out the assassination of Chang Tso-lin were acting on their own accord without asking Tanaka's Cabinet for approval. This meant that the Tanaka Administration did not have full power for controlling those young extremists in the Kwantung Army. In order to enhance his Cabinet's prestige, Tanaka tried to put a check on those extremists by punishing those officers who were involved in Chang's assassination. But he found before long that he was in no position to take any disciplinary action, as the Chief of General Staff and other senior officers in the Army opposed any disciplinary measure on the ground that such action against those responsible would weaken the morale of the army. Because of his failure to act, Tanaka was forced to resign in July 1929.

From the Mukden Incident to the Tangku Truce 塘沽協定

As Tanaka's successor, Hamaguchi Osachi, president of the opposition Minseito Party, formed a new Cabinet and restored Shidehara Kijuro to the Foreign Ministry. The new administration adopted a conciliatory policy toward China which was labeled as "the era of the second Shidehara diplomacy." However, the fact that the Hamaguchi administration failed to curb those extremists in the Kwantung Army made all Shidehara's peace efforts in vain.

As a matter of fact, the great impediment to the establishment of better relations between Japan and China was the aggressive attitude of the Japanese Kwantung Army with its base in South Manchuria. In 1928, the Kwantung Army moved its headquarters from Port Arthur to Mukden, a more commanding location, signifying its aggressive plans against Manchuria.[8] The fact that two ambitious young extremists, Lieutenant Colonel Ishihara Kanji and Colonel Itagaki Seishiro, joined the Kwantung Army in the following year was another indication of this aggressive purpose.

On September 18, 1931, the Mukden Incident, or the Manchuria Incident as the Japanese used to call it, occurred. It was a well-planned conspiracy designed by Colonel Itagaki, Lieutenant Colonel Ishihara and other military extremists as well as those civilian expansionists.[9] It precipitated a full-scale Japanese invasion of Manchuria. On January 28, 1932, Japanese forces launched another attack on Shanghai but met the surprisingly strong resistance by Chinese troops.

Having occupied the entire territory of Manchuria, the Japanese Kwantung Army pointed their red spear southwestward. In mid-March 1933, they seized another Chinese province, Jehol, and their march was not temporarily checked until the signing of the Tangku Truce on May 31, 1933. Within a period of two and a half years, the Japanese Army seized from China a territory equal in size to that of Germany, France, Poland, Italy, Rumania, Bulgaria, Belgium, Austria, Czechoslovakia and Great Britain put together.

The military victory over China had two effects. One was the rise of military Fascism which destroyed the Japanese party politics and made the Japanese administration to be a "Government by Assassination."[10] The other was that, as the result of Japan's withdrawal from the League of Nations in March 1933, she found herself in a position of diplomatic isolation. Japan was condemned as an aggressor both by Secretary Stimson's Non-recognition Doctrine and by the Lytton Report of the League of Nations.[11]

In the year 1932, almost half a dozen Japanese high-ranking political leaders were assassinated by military extremists. Among those victims, the most important was Inukai Tsuyoshi, who was murdered on May 15, 1932, by the elements of a terrorist organization, the Blood Brotherhood. Inukai, the aged Seiyukai leader, was the only person who wanted to work out an amicable settlement concerning the Sino-Japanese disputes. After he succeeded Wakatsuki as Premier in December 1931, Inukai sent a trusted friend to China for the purpose of undertaking negotiations with the Chinese National Government. Unfortunately, Inukai was killed before he could carry out his plan. Thus, the assas-

sination of Inukai not only sealed the fate of the Japanese party government but also ended any conciliatory efforts towards China.

The Amau Statement

Shortly after the signature of the Tangku Truce of 1933, the Japanese
War Ministry and the Army General Staff conducted a China policy of
"destroying the actual influence of the Chinese National Party in the
North and extending this tendency to the South."[12] It is apparent that
the Japanese military authorities had decided to absorb North China
first and then South China. Facing Japan's immediate threat, the Chinese
National Government tried to strengthen its forces by seeking international assistance. Both the League of Nations and the United States
wished to offer China technical help.

It was against this background that the Japanese Foreign Minister,
Hirota Koki, who was the chief architect of China policy in the next
three years, issued a statement in January 1934, in which he stated that
Japan bore "the entire burden of responsibility for the peace of East
Asia."[13] Three months later, a decisive Japanese China policy was for-
mally declared on April 17 by Amau Eiji, Chief of the Intelligence
Division of the Japanese Foreign Office. This was the "Amau Statement"
which was considered the official declaration of the Japanese "Monroe
Doctrine" for East Asia.[14] The emphasis of the statement was to warn
Western nations which were offering China military, technological or
financial aid. The statement noted:

> However, supplying China with war planes, building aerodromes in China
> and detailing military instructors or military advisors to China or con-
> tracting a loan to provide funds for political uses, would obviously tend
> to alienate the friendly relations between Japan and China and other coun-
> tries and to disturb peace and order in East Asia. Japan will oppose such
> projects.

Amau's statement was tantamount to a "hands-off" China policy
proclamation. Both the Chinese and Westerners were shocked by this
document. American, British and Chinese Ambassadors in Tokyo immediately expressed their deep concern about Japan's intention. Two days
later, from Nanking, capital of the Republic of China, came a formal
statement challenging the Japanese declaration.[15] Unfavorable reaction
to Japan's policy from Western powers also reached Tokyo. Therefore,
Hirota, Japan's Foreign Minister, issued a second statement toning down
the first one.[16] It stated that "Japan has not infringed upon China's independence or interests," and that "Japan has no intention to trespass upon
the rights of other powers in China." In addition Hirota asserted that:

"Japan cannot remain indifferent to anyone's taking action under any pretext which is prejudicial to the maintenance of law and order in East Asia."

In response to Hirota's statement, the Chinese Ministry of Foreign Affairs issued its second statement on April 20 which stated that:

> China cannot stand any infringement made by any country under any pretext upon her sovereignty, independence, and territorial integrity.

> China cannot stand any interference exercised by any country, under any pretext, with the relations between China and various countries which are based upon international law and beneficial to the development and safety of China herself.[17]

Despite Japan's hands-off warning, the Chinese Ministry of Finance signed a contract with a local representative of the American United Aircraft Company for a good number of reconnaissance bombers on April 19, two days after Japan made her announcement.[18] Japan was so annoyed by China's action that some Japanese troublemakers began to seek another pretext for threatening China.

In June of the same year, the Kuramoto Affair took place in Nanking. Kuramoto Eimei, Japanese Vice Consul in Nanking, suddenly disappeared from his office on June 8. The Japanese Government immediately put the responsibility for this matter on China and threatened to bombard Nanking. Within a couple of days, Japanese gunboats arrived at Nanking and Japanese troops in Shanghai stood in readiness to march toward the Chinese capital. Thanks to the efforts made by the Chinese policemen who finally discovered the hiding place of Kuramoto and took him back to the Japanese Consulate-General in Nanking, the case was closed. The Japanese diplomats in Nanking could say nothing but expressed their reluctant apology.

Plans for Detaching North China

Shortly after the occupation of Manchuria, the Japanese field commander, General Honjo Shigeru, conceived another plan to dominate North China. In his reminiscences, Hallett Abend testified:

> As early as December 1931, General Honjo, then Commander of all Japanese forces on the Asiatic mainland, told me quite frankly that Japan could not rest without control of the Peiping-Tientsin area, and ownership of the important Peiping-Suiyuan Railway, running for more than 400 miles northwestward from the one-time capital into Chahar and Suiyuan provinces, through an area rich in enormous iron ore deposits. And the Peiping-Tientsin area would not be "safe" unless Japan controlled all of China north of the Yellow River, he added.[19]

Though Japan's march was temporarily halted by the Tangku Truce of May 31, 1933, the Japanese military authorities lost no time to work out a plan for detaching North China from China's Central (National) Government. Just about a month after the signing of the Tangku Truce, the Kwantung Army authorities decided to suppress the Chinese officials in North China in order to implement "the faithful fulfillment of the Truce in its broad sense," and to make "the North China regime suppress the National Party's anti-Japanese activities in North China and make the Party gradually reduce itself until its final dissolution."[20]

On April 18, 1934, the Japanese Mukden Army Special Service Agency submitted a document with the title of "Draft for Saving North China" to the Chief of Staff in Tokyo in which they confirmed that "the pressing need of the moment is the establishment of a new North China regime."[21] There is little doubt that this document cast a new light on the making of Japan's new China policy in North China. In conformity with the suggestion of the War Ministry, the Okada Cabinet stipulated, on December 7, 1934, that "for the time being, it is desirable that Japan seek to reduce to a minimum degree the influence of the Chinese Central Government in North China."[22] Thus, the year 1935 witnessed a long succession of Japanese encroachments on two North China provinces: Hopei and Chahar.

As the Japanese military authorities decided "to attain our object step by step," they evidently divided their schedule into two stages. The first stage began in January 1935 with Japan's attack on Eastern Chahar, and ended in July with the so-called Ho-Umetsu Agreement 何梅協定 . In this stage, Japan's main purpose was to force the Chinese Central Government to withdraw its influence from North China and to replace all the official posts in this area with persons acceptable to the Japanese. The second stage covered a period from early August to the end of the year. In this period, Japan's prime aim was to sever North China from the Central Government by creating a "North China Autonomy Movement." Two ambitious Japanese militarists, Tada Hayao, Commander of the Japanese North China Garrison, and Doihara Kenji, Chief of the Kwantung Army's Special Service Section, played important roles in carrying out this political conspiracy.

By the end of November 1935, the North China crisis reached its climax which not only brought China to the brink of a defensive war but also deeply surprised the world powers, especially Great Britain and the United States.[23] In order to cope with the urgent situation, Generalissimo Chiang Kai-shek decided to send General Ho Ying-chin 何應欽 to Peiping to discuss ways and means of dealing with the Japanese along with General Sung Che-yuan 宋哲元 and other Twenty-ninth Army leaders. Ho arrived at Peiping on December 3, and a series of meetings followed in the succeeding several days. A

resolution was made at last with which they agreed to organize a political council, in line with the Southwestern Political Council in Canton,
to take charge of political affairs of the two provinces, Hopei and
Chahar, and the two municipalities of Peiping and Tientsin. The Japanese military authorities in Tientsin gave its reluctant consent on
December 6. Then the Chinese National Government ordered the set-up
of the Hopei-Chahar Political Council with Sung Che-yuan as Chairman
on December 11. As the inauguration of the Council, in the eyes of the
Japanese, symbolized the stabilization of North China, the Japanese-
sponsored autonomy movement temporarily came to an end. Optimis-
tically speaking, the North China crisis of 1935 was over.

Though every attempt was made to induce Sung and the other
Chinese military leaders into their trap in the succeeding years, the
Japanese finally found that Sung and his followers were no less patriotic
than the leaders of the National Government. No one disputes the fact
that the conspiracy of dismembering China temporarily misfired. Joseph
C. Grew, American Ambassador to Japan during the period from 1932
to 1942, describes Japan's failure in the following words:

> Sufficient to say that the overt intention and efforts of the Japanese mili-
> tary to detach the five Northern provinces from the jurisdiction of Nanking
> largely miscarried; that the support of the Japanese military of the wide-
> spread smuggling operations not only became an international scandal but
> went far to bring down on Japan the censure of foreign countries including
> the United States and Great Britain; and that, far from cooperating with
> Nanking in an effort to control the anti-Japanese sentiment rapidly devel-
> oping throughout China, the Japanese have constantly intensified that
> sentiment by their truculent and aggressive attitude and tactics.[24]

The Hirota "Three-Point Principle"

On December 7, 1934, an important decision on international and
national policy was worked out by the Okada Cabinet. According to this
policy, the general principle of Japan's new China policy was twofold:
(a) in making China follow the policy of the Empire to ensure peace in
East Asia by cooperation and mutual aid among Japan, Manchukuo and
China, with the Empire as center, and (b) in developing Japan's commercial right in China.[25]

As the militarists were actually running the Government at the time,
this policy was naturally agreed upon by both the Cabinet and the
military authorities. But they had different opinions in dealing with the
question on how to achieve their purpose. It was generally known that
the Kwantung Army leaders advocated a "tiger-policy," which means to
subdue China by force, while the diplomats were in favor of a "duck-
policy" which can be best explained by describing the movement of a

duck on the water: on the surface there is quiet, but underneath there is great activity. Thus in the year 1935, we saw further Japanese encroachment in North China on the one hand, and Hirota's decision on the other hand to promote the Japanese Minister to China to the rank of Ambassador with a view to initiating negotiations with Nanking in line with his "Three Principles." The three principles were the following:

1. China must abandon her policy of playing off one foreign country against another;
2. China must respect the fact of the existence of the "Manchukuo"; and
3. China and Japan must jointly devise effective measures for preventing the spread of Communism in regions in the northern part of China.[26]

Hirota's three principles were formally adopted by the Japanese Cabinet on October 4 in the same year.[27] Three days later, Hirota informed the Chinese Ambassador to Japan, Chiang Tso-pin 蔣作賓 , that these three points were the prerequisites for the improvement of Sino-Japanese relations.[28]

Diplomatic negotiations between China and Japan formally started in November 1935. The Chinese National Government, however, considered Hirota's three points as too vague in their phraseology to serve as a subject for useful discussion. After paying a visit to Chiang Kai-shek in Nanking, Ariyoshi Akira, Japanese Ambassador to China, reported that the Chinese Generalissimo had agreed in general to Hirota's Principles. Thus Hirota, on January 21, 1936, in his speech to the Japanese Diet, definitely made the statement that Nanking had concurred in his three-point policy. But on the next day, an official denial from Nanking came.

According to the Chinese record, Chiang had told Ariyoshi that if the Japanese Government could check those military officers' illegal activities in North China, China would like to open negotiations based on some more substantial suggestions.[29] As a matter of fact, negotiations between Ariyoshi and Chang Chun 張羣 , newly-appointed Foreign Minister of China, lasted nearly a year but reached no conclusion. This was largely due to the fact that the Japanese militarists made every attempt to sever North China from the Chinese National Government and engaged themselves in large-scale smuggling operations.[30]

After the unusually bloody orgy of assassination in February 1936, Hirota became Premier but his Cabinet was no more than the tool of the radical military leaders. The person who had final say in policy-making in the Cabinet was not Hirota but General Terauchi, Minister of

War. With Terauchi's consent, the officers of the Japanese North China Garrison continued to put pressure on Chinese local authorities in that area. Their purpose was still the separation of the five northern provinces from the Chinese Government. Every attempt was made by the Japanese officers to induce General Sung Che-yuan, Chairman of the Hopei-Chahar Political Council and concurrently Commander of the Twenty-ninth Army, to surrender to them, but these attempts ended in failure. Sung remained loyal to Nanking and later became the first Chinese general who fought against Japanese troops in North China.

By November 1936, all Hirota's efforts to secure a definite acceptance of his three-point principle failed and negotiations were brought to an end by the Suiyuan Incident, when a contingent of Japanese-sponsored Mongolian troops invaded the eastern part of Suiyuan Province where they were defeated by the Chinese garrison.

The Hirota Cabinet fell in January 1937. After the short interval of the Hayashi Government, at the end of May, Prince Konoye Fumimaro formed the first of his three Cabinets with Hirota as the Foreign Minister. War with China broke out just about a month later.

II

China's Response to Japanese Encroachment

National Renaissance Movement

After the Mukden Incident of 1931, Chiang already sensed the threat of Japanese aggression. However, in order to offer effective opposition to external attack, Chiang had to pacify the internal situation first. This is the reason why from 1932 to 1935, Generalissimo Chiang Kai-shek engaged himself in the task of exterminating Communist insurrection and at the same time, he initiated the New Life Movement on February 19, 1934, in Nanchang.

The fundamental objectives of the Movement, as defined by the Generalissimo himself, were the revival of the ancient virtues in the Chinese cultural heritage, and their application to modern living. Basic among these virtues he specified "Propriety, Justice, Integrity and Conscientiousness," which are considered "the four pillars of the country." Thus, a Chinese scholar defined the nature of the Movement by saying that "as a matter of fact, the New Life Movement was a moral revitalization of the Chinese people."[31]

During the year of 1934, the New Life Movement had its most notable results in the province of Kiangsi which has been so badly ravaged by the Communists. In explaining its broad sense, Generalissimo Chiang

Kai-shek reminded his countrymen that: "We must reconstruct society by extraordinary means instead of merely sitting down and waiting for the process of natural evolution." In the Generalissimo's eyes, the explicit purpose of the Movement was the promoting of social and moral reform. Then he continued to emphasize that: "It is the gigantic task of the New Life Movement to wipe out the background conditions of society by a wild storm and to supply the community with vitality and the right spirit by a gentle breeze."[32]

When Chiang returned to Nanking at the end of 1935, the National Headquarters of the New Life Movement was moved from Nanchang to Nanking, capital of the Republic of China. A number of local units were soon established in various provinces and major cities. In addition, there were three branches in Japan and Korea and six in Java and Malaya. By the close of 1935, some of the Chinese shipping lines had taken up the Movement among their employees. Though the evaluation of the Movement was varied, it proved itself, in its first two years, to be a dynamic movement which rejuvenated the spirit of millions of Chinese people. As Paul K. T. Sih 薛光前 put it: "The influence upon the Chinese will and fortitude was later to be shown in their resistance to the Japanese invaders."[33]

On April 1, 1935, Generalissimo Chiang launched another movement, the People's Economic Reconstruction Movement, at Kweiyang, capital of the backward southwestern province of Kweichow, with a view to rehabilitating the people's economic life. In an interview given to foreign correspondents, Chiang explained the new program as follows:

> In order to educate the public mind, as well as the official mind, to understand the vital needs of the times, the People's Economic Reconstruction Movement has been devised and launched. Its aim is the rehabilitation of China, and its task is to awaken the nation to the deep necessity of advancing from the status of an almost purely agricultural state to an industrial one.[34]

According to Chiang, the New Life Movement was to make everybody practice the four principles of Propriety, Justice, Integrity and Conscientiousness, to have a self-reliant and noble character and to become modern good citizens so as to lay the spiritual foundation for the nation, while the People's Economic Reconstruction Movement was to make everybody discharge his social duty, to render labor service and to increase productive capacity so as to lay the material foundation for the nation.[35] In one word, both were aimed at the modernization of Chinese society and people so as to provide adequate capacity for national survival.

In Chiang's own words, "After the Mukden Incident of September 18, 1931, I initiated the New Life Movement and the People's Economic

Reconstruction Movement with the purpose of providing both spiritual and material preparedness for an anti-Japanese war on one hand, and to convince the Japanese, on the other hand, through great suffering to change their Chinese policy of armed aggression."[36]

China's Nation-Building Efforts

Since the establishment of the Chinese National Government in Nanking in 1927, modernization has become the central concern. Serious efforts were made to unify the military system, to reduce military expenditures for the use of national reconstruction, and to negotiate with foreign powers for the abolition of unequal treaties. The growing danger of Japanese invasion made it even more urgent and imperative to speed up the process of modernization and national reconstruction.

In the midst of the Manchurian crisis, the Chinese National Government established the National Economic Council on November 15, 1931. It was designed as a super-advisory and coordinating body to work with all the ministries and departments to coordinate economic policy. Under the chairmanship of T. V. Soong　宋子文　, the Council gave a quickening impulse to the nation's economy, and the period 1932-1935 saw a substantial start on the road to China's reconstruction.

Needless to say, China's nation-building efforts embodied various aspects: communication construction, political reorganization, military improvement, fiscal transformation, currency reform, agricultural and industrial development, educational progress and so forth. It is beyond the scope of this study to enumerate all the achievements in the above-mentioned fields. It is noteworthy to observe, however, that the period of 1927-1937, under the National Government at Nanking, has been considered the "Golden Decade" of modern Chinese history, as referred to by General Albert C. Wedemeyer in his sworn testimony before the Judiciary Committee of the U.S. Senate, 82nd Congress, 1st Session, September 19, 1951.

However, the more improvements China achieved in her nation-building efforts, the quicker the relations between China and Japan deteriorated. As C. T. Liang　梁敬錞　noted: "We are told that it was China's weakness that encouraged Japan's ambition, but we are also told that it was China's strength that begot Japan's aggression."[37]

Chiang's Appeal and Warning to the Japanese

Although Chiang Kai-shek spared no effort to make all needed preparations for opposing the Japanese invasion, he still tried to pursue a policy of patience and perseverance with a view to delaying Japan's attack and gaining more time for national reconstruction. In this connection, he made the first appeal to the Japanese by publishing an important and well-reasoned essay entitled "Foe or Friend?" 友乎敵乎 in the Spring of 1935. It appears under the name of Hsu Tao-lin 徐道鄰 who served as Chiang's personal secretary. According to Chen Pu-lei 陳布雷 , the essay was dictated by Chiang himself. It stressed two points: to warn the Japanese not to force the Kuomintang beyond its rational limits of endurance, and to advise his nation to endure humiliation unless forced beyond these limits.[38]

Addressing first the Japanese, the message emphasized that peace between the two nations was economically, politically and culturally desirable, indeed imperative, if viewed within the context of international politics. "To that end," Chiang asserted, "Japan should respect China's territorial and administrative integrity and, considering what had transpired between them, should take the initiative to make known her peaceful intentions." For its part the Chinese Government would insist on only two points: the general principle of non-aggression and the restoration of Manchuria. Desirous of friendly relations with Japan and basing its judgment, "squarely on the calculation of national interests," China would be concerned only with these "essential issues" at the time, making it amply clear that the Chinese Government was prepared to negotiate on all other issues that might be construed as non-essential. In concluding his essay, Chiang left the responsibility of solving the Sino-Japanese impasse upon the Japanese by saying that: "The best man to unbind a bell is the man who had the bell bound" 解鈴 還是繫鈴人 —an ancient Chinese idiom which means the best way to shoot trouble is to make the troublemaker take the initiative.

Another essay written by Chiang Kai-shek, entitled "The Turning Point of Sino-Japanese Relations," appeared in the September issue of a Japanese monthly, *Economic Dealings.* After making an analysis of the general situation in East Asia, Chiang outlined China's position on the improvement of Sino-Japanese relations. "The greatest problem pending, among numerous items, was the Manchuria issue," Chiang asserted. "It is impossible to work for an improvement of Sino-Japanese relations without a satisfactory solution of the Manchuria problem." At about the same time, the Generalissimo asked Chiang Tso-pin, China's Minister to Japan, to convey to the Japanese Government his viewpoint concerning the Sino-Japanese relations: "China's endurance has its limits. By the time China is forced beyond the limits, our country will lose no time to fight the aggressors at any cost. In case the Sino-Japanese conflict continues, it will develop into a world war through which both China and Japan will be destroyed."[39]

By 1935, the Chinese Government had already uprooted the Communist troops from south Kiangsi and was relatively free from internal worry. Troops had been sent to chase the retreating Communists into the remote northwestern provinces while the Generalissimo moved himself to Szechwan and set up an official military training corps in Omei just as he did in previous years. It is evident that China was not actually in a better position to oppose Japan than before. In the meantime the Japanese military authorities lost no time to further their expansion in North China. To deal with the urgent situation, the Kuomintang convened its Fifth National Congress in November 1935 in Nanking. Chiang was invited to deliver a speech in which he outlined China's position toward Japan by declaring that: "We shall not forsake peace until there is no hope for peace; we shall not talk lightly of sacrifice until we are driven to the last extremity."[40] It is clear that although a limit was set, in Chiang's speech, to its policy, the National Government was still bent upon the preservation of peace. Though most of the Chinese people actually believed in Chiang's determination for a final resistance, they were anxious to know what were actually the limits beyond which they had to resort to war. In another speech delivered at the Second Plenary Session of the Fifth Kuomintang Central Executive Committee convened in the middle of July 1936, Chiang clarified the situation by stating:

> What the National Government considers to be the absolute minimum in foreign relations is the maintenance of our territory and sovereignty intact. If any nation should seek to violate our territory and sovereignty, it would be absolutely impossible for us to endure it. We shall definitely refuse to sign any agreement that violates our territory and sovereignty, and shall definitely refuse to endure any actual violation thereof. To put it more plainly, if others should force us to sign an agreement violating our territory and sovereignty, such as that for the recognition of a puppet state, it would be impossible for us to remain passive any longer; it would be time for us to make sacrifices. This is one point. Next, as determined by the National Congress in November last year, if our territory and sovereignty are found violated by others, in the event all political and diplomatic means are exhausted and the violation is still not redressed, it will mean that the fundamental existence of our nation and our race is threatened; it will mean that it is impossible for us to endure any longer. When that time comes, we shall not hesitate to make sacrifices. This is what we mean by the absolute minimum.[41]

In view of the above explanation, China's stand in dealing with the Japanese aggression is quite apparent. It also meant Chiang's final warning to the Japanese Government. The Japanese, however, offered no positive response.

A Turning Point in the Sino-Japanese Struggle

In the fall of 1936, China, for the first time since the completion of the Northern Expedition, reached the final stage in the unification of the country. With the triumph of the Fifth Communist-extermination Campaign and the success in concluding a peaceful settlement of the Southwestern problem, Chiang Kai-shek's prestige and power had been lifted to a new height. He was regarded by both Chinese and foreigners who lived in China as the indispensable leader of a united China. A feeling of optimism was well reflected in the nationwide celebration of his fiftieth birthday in November, which was characterized by leading intellectuals at that time as China's "first popular election."[42]

In mid-November of 1936, a force dispatched by the puppet Mongolian regime attacked Suiyuan with the aid of Japanese airplanes. As a matter of fact, this was a Japanese-designed invasion. However, the invaders were soon driven back by the Chinese local armies of Suiyuan Province under command of General Fu Tso-yi 傅作義 with reinforcements from the Central Government. On November 24, Chinese troops launched a large-scale counterattack on the invaders and captured Pailingmiao 百靈廟 which had served as a base for operations for the insurgents. Thereafter the invasion collapsed. Encouraged by the most surprising and significant victory on the Suiyuan front, an anti-Japanese outcry arose throughout the country. The new situation had such a strong and immediate influence upon the National Government that Chang Chun decided to terminate his talks with Kawagoe Shigeru, Japanese Ambassador to China, in the early days of December.

Nelson Johnson, American Ambassador to China, considered that the Autumn of 1936 marked a turning point in the Sino-Japanese struggle. The American Ambassador himself seemed to have thought, in October 1936, that Chiang Kai-shek might abandon a policy of placating Japan. After a trip to Nanking in the middle of that month, Johnson wrote to Stanley Hornbeck that he had "gathered . . . that Chiang and all those with him were prepared to meet force with force."[43]

It was at this juncture that General Chang Hsueh-liang 張學良 , known as the Young Marshal who led his Northeastern Army stationed in Sian area, having conspired with Yang Hu-cheng 楊虎城 and the Communists, carried out the dramatic Sian incident 西安事 變 on December 12, 1936. The conspirators presented an eight-point demand to Chiang which met with his refusal. There were also persistent demands for Chiang's execution or for his public trial on the part of the Communists. Moscow, however, advocated an amicable settlement. In the light of the unfavorable situation, Chang Hsueh-liang finally decided on December 25 to set Chiang free and agreed to proceed to Nanking with the Generalissimo and assume full responsibility for the coup. On the eve of Chiang's return to Nanking, a nationwide jubilation and acclamation over his personal safety evidenced his increasing prestige and undisputed leadership. This naturally invited Japan's jealousy and hastened Japan's policy of crushing China as soon as possible before she became too strong.

III

The Background of the Lukouchiao Incident

As a matter of fact, hostilities between Chinese and Japanese troops in North China had started with the arrival of Japanese reinforcements in the Peiping-Tientsin zone in June 1936, a year before the occurrence of the Lukouchiao Incident. Before tracing the development of the hostilities, historians who are engaging in the study of this subject should bear in mind the outspoken words of a capable and experienced Japanese veteran diplomat, Shigemitsu Mamoru: "The Japanese military view with regard to China was uncompromising. Its spearhead was wielded by staff officers serving at the front. . . . Military designs on North China had created a situation that could not be resolved without inviting a head-on collision between Japan and China."[44]

From the Fengtai Conflict to the Lukouchiao Incident

As early as November 26, 1935, a small detachment of Japanese troops stationed in North China was sent to Fengtai 豐 台 , a strategic railway junction where a battalion of Chinese troops was stationed.[45] This was the first step for carrying out the "Outline for the Military Disposal of Various Railways in North China," an aggressive plan designed by Tada Hayao, Commander of the Japanese garrison forces in North China.[46] According to the provisions of the Outline, the Japanese army expected to dispose of the six railways in North China by inducing the Chinese operators to serve for the benefit of the Japanese or by seizing some strategic lines.[47] Among the six lines, the Peiping-Hankow Railway was the most important. The Japanese Commander considered "it would be necessary to occupy and seize it by Military Railway Units, etc., at the outset."[48] Based upon such a plan, the Japanese troops seized Fengtai in September 1936, and repeatedly disclosed their interest in controlling the north section of the Peiping-Hankow Railway.

Ignoring the Chinese protest, the Japanese constructed barracks and sent more troops to Fengtai. By the end of May 1936, its forces were increased to over 1,000 men. Since the Japanese camped themselves alongside the Chinese barracks, conflict was bound to be unavoidable. The first conflict took place on June 26, 1936, when a Chinese cavalry horse strayed into the Japanese barracks. As the Japanese refused to return the horse, several Chinese soldiers entered the Japanese barracks to seize the horse. This event resulted in a Japanese protest by Imai, Japanese Military Attaché in Peiping, on the ground that the Chinese soldiers' action "constituted an insult to the Japanese nation."[49] At the same time, Japanese demands were presented to Sung Che-yuan for (a) apology, (b) indemnity, (c) punishment of the local commanding officer, and (d) withdrawal of the Chinese troops from Fengtai.[50] Sung accepted the first three but rejected the final and most important one. However, he agreed to replace the Chinese unit and assured that things of similar nature would not be allowed to occur again.

Just two months later, another conflict took place at the same town. In the afternoon of September 18, 1936, a company of Chinese troops led by Captain Sun Hsiang-ting met a Japanese detachment proceeding in the opposite direction on its return from the drill ground. In the course of passage a mounted Japanese officer ran into the Chinese line and was pushed back by Chinese soldiers. Then the Japanese arrested Sun Hsiang-ting and maltreated him. The result was a skirmish. Both sides faced each other throughout the whole night. Meanwhile negotiations were carried on between Chinese and Japanese military authorities. The Japanese demanded a public apology and the withdrawal of Chinese troops from Fengtai, Langfang, and Changhsintien. With a view to avoiding further conflict, Sung Che-yuan agreed to leave the Japanese alone at Fengtai but refused to withdraw his troops from Langfang and Changhsintien.[51]

Although it did not cause a full-scale war, the Fengtai conflict constituted an impetus to the development of anti-Japanese feeling among the Twenty-ninth Army as well as the other units throughout the country. When the news of the clash became widespread, the whole country was indignant and urged the Chinese troops to resist the enemy immediately. In a joint letter written to Sung Che-yuan on September 20, two eminent southern military leaders, Li Tsung-jen　李宗仁　and Pai Chung-hsi　白崇禧　, frankly told Sung "the only way to salvation is resistance," and "national unification is being accomplished so as to put up an effective resistance."[52] With Fengtai securely in Japanese hands, every Chinese knew that Lukouchiao, the strategic bridge, would naturally be the next object of Japanese attack.

In November 1936, the Suiyuan victory over the Japanese-sponsored bogus Mongolian troops encouraged Sung Che-yuan as well as his soldiers. According to a secret report from Tientsin, Sung Che-yuan had at one time tried to restore Tungchow by using force.[53] Following a Japanese provocative field-drill in early November, the Twenty-ninth Army staged its own maneuver in the vicinity of Peiping. Such an action was considered as a signal of the determination of Sung's army for resistance.[54] At about the same time, Liu Ju-ming　劉汝明　one of Sung's division commanders and concurrently Chairman of Chahar Provincial Government, confiscated a large amount of Japanese ammunition which was secretly transported into Kalgan.[55] In view of the precarious situation in North China, observers had good reason to believe that conflict between Chinese and Japanese troops would become inevitable.

How the Conflict Developed

On January 8, 1937, an unprecedented large-scale parade was staged by the Japanese forces in Peiping and Tientsin.[56] In the eyes of the Chinese, such an action meant nothing but an alarm of the coming Japanese military operation. The Chinese authorities lodged a protest against the Japanese. Matters came to a head in early July when a unit of Japanese troops engaged in a series of unscheduled field exercises in the vicinity of Peiping. The walled city of Wanping, which is very close to Lukouchiao, was selected by the Japanese as a hypothetical point of attack.[57]

In the midnight of July 7, Wednesday, the Chinese authorities in Peiping were informed by Colonel Matsui, Chief of the Japanese Special Service Agency in Peiping, that a company of Japanese troops on night maneuvers near Lukouchiao had been fired upon, that one Japanese soldier was missing, and that they wanted to enter the city of Wanping in search of him. Chin Te-chun 秦德純 , Mayor of Peiping, rejected the Japanese demands but ordered Wang Leng-chai 王冷齋 , Administrative Commissioner and concurrently Magistrate of Wanping district, to investigate the matter with the representatives of Japanese troops on the spot.[58] Meantime, Chin ordered Chi Hsing-wen 吉星文 , Chinese regimental commander who was responsible for the defense of Wanping, to hold the city against any Japanese attack but not to fire first.[59] On the part of the Japanese, a battalion reinforcement was sent to Wanping from Fengtai. As the Chinese defenders refused to let the Japanese enter the city, the Japanese troops attacked them at dawn. This was known as the outbreak of the Lukouchiao Incident which marked the beginning of the eight-year Sino-Japanese War, 1937-1945.

As mentioned above, the excuse for the Japanese demand to enter the city of Wanping was to search for a missing soldier. Just a little while after the presentation of this Japanese demand to the Chinese local authorities, the alleged "missing soldier" returned. The Japanese, however, still demanded to enter the city for "investigation" and then launched an attack on it. It is evident that the purpose of the Japanese was to force the Chinese troops to withdraw from Wanping, just as they did at Fengtai ten months earlier. In their first attempt, they failed to take the city. In the afternoon of July 8, the Japanese launched a more massive attack on the Chinese defenders. The skirmish lasted until the next day when a provisional ceasefire was arranged.

Shortly after the Incident occurred, Hashimoto Gun, Chief of Staff of the Japanese North China Garrison who was de facto Commander of all Japanese troops—as their Commander, General Kanichito Tashiro, was seriously ill—dispatched Wachi Takaji to Tokyo for consultation. Tokyo decided to effect a local settlement, but on the same day, July 10, the Japanese General Staff decided to dispatch strong units from the Kwantung Army in Manchuria and from the Japanese garrison forces in Korea to reinforce their troops in North China and, in addition, to prepare to send three divisions from Japan itself. On the next day, the Japanese Government announced its general mobilization plans. However, a provisional agreement was reached between the Japanese and the Chinese military authorities in Peiping on the same day. Upon this, the Japanese government decided to stop the dispatch of the home divisions but not the forces from Manchuria and Korea.[60] From July 12 onwards, these reinforcements began to pour into North China. They included two brigades, one mechanized, from the Kwantung Army, as well as air units and a division from Korea.[61]

Sung Che-yuan's Efforts Toward a Local Settlement

General Sung Che-yuan, Commander of the Chinese Twenty-ninth Army and concurrently Chairman of the Hopei-Chahar Political Council, had been on leave at his hometown of Loling in Shantung since the closing days of May 1937. When the initial report about the Lukouchiao Incident reached Loling, Sung was full of indignation. According to Wang Ching-wei 汪精衛 , Chairman of the Central Political Council in Nanking, Sung immediately instructed the commanders on the Wanping front to "extirpate the enemies in front of you."[62] However, instead of proceeding to that ominous spot immediately, Sung went to Tientsin on July 11 and tried to settle the issue by peaceful negotiations. As soon as he arrived at Tientsin, Sung realized that a verbal agreement for settling the conflict had been concluded between the Japanese and his subordinates. According to the Chinese version, the agreement contained three points: 1. The troops of both sides should withdraw to their original lines; 2. Both sides should express regrets for the lives lost; and 3. Steps would be taken to prevent a recurrence of such incidents in the future.[63] However, the Japanese insisted that the Chinese authorities had accepted their demands for an apology, punishment, withdrawal of troops, and guarantee of non-recurrence.[64] To these conditions, Sung seemed unwilling to agree. In an interview with leaders of various local organizations on July 13, Sung declared that although desirous of an amicable settlement, he would not accept any demand presented by the Japanese.[65]

During his sojourn in Tientsin, Sung was really embarrassed by the Japanese military officers and the Chinese pro-Japanese elements. The former repeatedly submitted more demands to him, while the latter did their utmost to persuade him to come to terms with the Japanese.[66] On July 16, Tokyo instructed the Japanese Headquarters in Tientsin to demand that Sung should sign the settlement of July 11 and apologize in person; that he should dismiss General Feng Chih-an 馮治安 , Commander of the Chinese Thirty-seventh Division and that he should complete the execution of the agreement by July 11.[67] After painful negotiations, Sung finally agreed to adopt some measures to appease the Japanese. According to Sung himself, what he had agreed to was that: (1) He and the Japanese Commander express mutual regret for the deaths of Japanese and Chinese soldiers; (2) He would consider the question of punishment of Chinese officials involved; (3) He made no reference to the withdrawal of troops; and (4) He informed the Japanese that he had always followed a policy of anti-Communism and was opposed to anti-Japanese activities.[68] On July 18, Sung called on Lieutenant-General Katzuki Kiyoshi, the newly-appointed Commander of the Japanese North China Garrison, as a symbol of mutual apology. Then he left for Peiping on July 19.

Sung's concessions in Tientsin did not satisfy the Japanese. On the same day that Sung left for Peiping, the Japanese presented a number of terms which they considered a supplement to the third condition of the Agreement of July 11 to Sung's two subordinates, Chang Tzu-chung 張自忠 and Chang Yun-yung, and asked for a signature. According to the Japanese version, the terms read as follows:

1. A complete suppression of Communists.
2. To get rid of persons who are inimical to Sino-Japanese relations.
3. The dismissal of the persons who belong to various anti-Japanese organizations within the realm of the provinces of Hopei and Chahar.
4. The evacuation of those elements that belong to the Blue Shirts, the C. C. Clique, and other anti-Japanese organizations from Hopei and Chahar.
5. To suppress all the anti-Japanese institutions and organizations and their speeches, propaganda, as well as those anti-Japanese movements sponsored by students and the common people.
6. To stop anti-Japanese education in all the military units and schools.[69]

Despite such harsh demands, Sung was confident in his peace efforts. On July 20, Sung formally issued a statement saying that he had always been a strong advocate of peace and that he hoped "both parts, with the spirit of mutual trust, will seek an amicable settlement in the interest of peace in the Far East."[70] The terms of the Agreement of July 11 were re-

ported to the Central Government in Nanking on July 22 for approval.[71]
Sung also asked the Central Government to stop sending troops to the
North.[72] Sandbags and other barricades in some parts of Peiping were
removed. Furthermore, Sung showed his reluctance to act in conformity
with Chiang Kai-shek's directive which ordered him to move to Paoting,
on the grounds that there was no such necessity. In Sung's eyes, the issue
might be settled by accepting some minor Japanese demands in order to
give China more time to prepare for a full-fledged war.

Negotiations Between Nanking and Tokyo

When the first report on the Lukouchiao Incident reached Nanking,
Wang Chung-hui 王寵惠 , Minister of Foreign Affairs, lodged
a verbal protest against the Japanese challenge on July 8.[73] Two days
later, the Chinese Foreign Affairs Ministry formally issued a statement
demanding that the Japanese troops should be withdrawn to their original positions and reserved China's legal claims to compensation for the
Incident.[74] On July 11, the Chinese Ministry of Foreign Affairs again
declared through a statement that: "The policy of China is, internally,
economic reconstruction and externally, the maintenance of peace. So
far as our relations with Japan are concerned, our policy is to seek a
peaceful settlement, through diplomatic channels, of all standing issues
on the basis of equality and reciprocity."[75]

On July 11, Hidaka Shinroku, Counsellor of the Japanese Embassy
in Nanking, informed the Chinese Ministry of Foreign Affairs, upon
instructions from Tokyo, that the Japanese Government desired to bring
about a local settlement and warned Nanking to do nothing to interfere
with it. In answering this Japanese warning, the Chinese Foreign Ministry presented to the Japanese Embassy, for transmission to Tokyo, an
aide memoire proposing a "mutual cessation of military movements and
withdrawal of troops on both sides to their original positions," so that a
settlement could be negotiated.[76] The Chinese Government also informed
the Japanese authorities that no arrangement for settlement of the
Lukouchiao Incident would be valid without the sanction of the Chinese
Central Government.

Here a question arose: Why did the Japanese insist on a local settlement and strongly oppose the Chinese Central Government's "interference with a local settlement?" The answer to this question lies in the
fact that, as Japan had gained so much in the course of localized incidents
and negotiations during the past years, the Japanese hoped to continue
to force local Chinese authorities to make concessions which had prac-
tically nothing to do with the incident itself. Local resistance would
thereupon draw "punitive action" from the Japanese Army which was
ready to take hostile action at any moment. Under military threat the

Chinese local authorities were bound to accept a humiliating settlement in order to avoid a possible war. "It is not good for the Japanese Government to formally submit demands to the Nanking Government," General Sato said on his return to Tokyo from China, "for there are other measures which can be taken."[77] In view of Sato's words, one can easily understand what the exact meaning of the term "local settlement" in Japanese military minds meant. To put it more plainly, the Japanese-designed "local settlement" is nothing but a trick. In the light of the danger embodied in a local settlement, the Chinese Central Government insisted on having a voice in the negotiations about the Incident.

In order to achieve the end of a peaceful and reasonable settlement of the Incident, the Chinese Government tried to invite the friendly service of Sir Hugh Knatchbull-Hugessen, British Ambassador to China. Ostensibly at his own initiative, Sir Hugh Knatchbull-Hugessen forwarded the Chinese message on July 16 to James Dodds, the British Chargé d'Affaires at Tokyo, for immediate transmission to the Japanese Foreign Office. The British Ambassador told Dodds that Generalissimo Chiang Kai-shek had wished to state formally that the Chinese Government was prepared to stop all troop movements the next day (July 17), provided that the Japanese would agree to do likewise. In addition, the Chinese Government was ready to enter into an arrangement thereafter for the return of the troops on both sides to their previous positions.[78] After Dodds personally delivered Sir Hugh's message to the Japanese Foreign Office, the Japanese promptly informed Sir Hugh that they could not act on Chiang's "standstill" proposal because the entire issue of the Lukouchiao Incident was a matter for the consideration of the local authorities in North China.[79]

On July 17, Generalissimo Chiang Kai-shek declared, through a speech delivered before a large group of the nation's educational and intellectual leaders at Kuling, Kiangsi, that China's fundamental policy was: "We seek for peace, but we do not seek for peace at any cost; we do not want war, but we may be forced to defend ourselves."[80] In concluding his speech, the Generalissimo listed four points as minimum conditions for a settlement of the Lukouchiao Incident:

1. Any kind of settlement must not infringe upon the territorial integrity and sovereign rights of China.
2. The status of the Hopei-Chahar Political Council is fixed by the Central Government and there must not be any illegal alteration.
3. Central Government appointees such as Sung Che-yuan, Chairman of the Hopei-Chahar Political Council, must not be removed by outside pressure.
4. No restrictions on the stationing of the Twenty-ninth Army.[81]

On the very same date when Chiang declared China's "minimum conditions," the Japanese Government sent to Nanking its "last warning." It called upon the Chinese Central Government to "realize its wish" for peace by ceasing immediately its provocative activities and undertaking that there shall be no interference with the execution of the terms of settlement by the "local authorities." Furthermore, it requested the Chinese Government "to give promptly an adequate answer."[82]

Two days later, on July 19, the Chinese Government answered the Japanese by delivering an *aide memoire* to the Japanese Government. It expressed China's wishes "to reiterate its desire for a peaceful settlement of the Incident as well as its intention not to aggravate the situation," and suggested that:

1. The two countries should agree on a date when movements of their military forces would cease and they would be recalled to their original positions.
2. Diplomatic negotiations for the settlement of the dispute should be carried out.
3. The authorization of the Nanking Government is essential for any agreement concluded on the spot.
4. China is willing to accept any means of settlement recognized by international law and treaties.[83]

The Japanese considered the Chinese suggestions "insincere" and replied in the form of an official statement, issued on July 20, to China in these words: "The reason for the deterioration of the situation lies solely in the Nanking Government's interference with a local agreement, coupled with the continuous dispatch of Central troops to the North."[84] On the same day, the Japanese Cabinet decided to take "adequate self-defensive steps" in dealing with the North China conflict.

China's Decision for Resistance

While the Japanese Government blamed China for lack of "sincerity," General Katsuki, Commander of the Japanese North China Garrison, "ordered the preparation of a plan of operations for the Wanping region and began to deploy his troops to advantageous positions.[85] Despite the fact that the Chinese Central Government gave its approval to the Agreement of July 11 on July 22, an uninterrupted stream of Japanese troops and equipment was still pouring into North China.[86] According to reports received in Nanking, by July 23, in addition to the Kwantung Army, eight divisions of Japanese troops had arrived or were on the way.[87] On July 25, the first of a fleet of Japanese ships began to unload

100,000 tons of military supplies at Tangku.[88] All the signs in North China demonstrated, at least in the Chinese eyes, that a massive war was unavoidable.

With a view to safeguarding themselves, the Chinese Twenty-ninth Army soldiers began to dig trenches and to build shelters. It was under these circumstances that Generalissimo Chiang Kai-shek sent General Hsiung Pin 熊 斌 , Vice-Chief of Chinese General Staff, to Peiping to consult Sung Che-yuan on the critical situation. On the next day, Kuo Ting-yuan, former Secretary-General of the Hopei-Chahar Political Council, and Liu Chien-chun 劉健羣 , former Director of North China Propaganda Corps, arrived at Peiping to report to Sung the attitudes of the Central Government toward the Incident and to persuade Sung to move his Headquarters to Paoting.[89] The visit of Hsiung and others to Peiping was regarded by the Japanese as "an encouragement to resist."[90] Thus, the Japanese tried to secure more strategic points so as to put themselves in a more favorable position for fighting.

In the evening of July 25, a contingent of Japanese troops led by Lieutenant Gonoi, under the pretext of repairing military telephone lines, occupied the railway station of Langfang, a strategic spot situated midway between Peiping and Tientsin, where a unit of Chinese troops was stationed. The Japanese demanded a withdrawal of Chinese troops but met with a rejection.[91] Then the Japanese attacked the Chinese defenders and bombed the small town ruthlessly. In view of the Langfang conflict, Sung Che-yuan realized that a full-fledged war was inevitable. He ordered Liu Ju-ming, Commander of the 143rd Division, to return to his Headquarters in Kalgan immediately to prepare military operations.[92] At the same time, Sung informed Sun Tan-lin, presiding official of the Ministry of Foreign Affairs, that war was inevitable.[93]

Following the Langfang conflict an ultimatum from the Japanese military authorities in North China was delivered to Sung Che-yuan demanding a withdrawal of Chinese troops from the Lukouchiao area before noon of July 27 and from Peiping and its suburbs the day after.[94] "In case of failure to carry out Japanese demands," the ultimatum concluded, "the Japanese army must, to its greatest regret, take its own decisive measures."[95] Sung refused to yield more to the Japanese this time. In the evening of July 27, he issued a circular telegram to the Central Government and the public expressing his determination to resist the Japanese aggression.[96]

Bitter war occurred at Nanyuan, Tienanmen, and other points on the 27th and 28th of July. The most severe Japanese attack was on Nanyuan, the chief Chinese barracks and center of military training, on the 28th. As the Japanese launched a sneak attack together with air raids, about 5,000 Chinese soldiers and university students were killed.[97] Generals

Tung Ling-kuo 佟麟閣 , Deputy Commander of the Twenty-ninth Army, and Chao Teng-yu, Commander of the 132nd Division, were among the casualties.

An informal meeting of the leaders of the Twenty-ninth Army was held at the Moral Promotion Club in Peiping in the evening of July 28. After examining the grave situation, Sung decided to evacuate the bulk of his troops from Peiping and to nominate Chang Tzu-chung, Commander of the Thirty-eighth Division, as Acting Chairman of the Hopei-Chahar Political Council, who was ordered to remain in Peiping to maintain order. Sung went to Paoting that night. The Japanese occupied Peiping without fighting. Then the Peiping-Tientsin area fell into Japanese hands.

On July 29, Japanese Foreign Minister Hirota Koki declared that Japan would reject any foreign intervention in the North China dispute, should such be attempted. On about the same date, the Japanese General Staff ordered the mobilization of three divisions and requested the special session of the Diet for an emergency appropriation of 97,000,000 yen. The Japanese Diet approved it without debate and passed a resolution of thanks to troops in North China.[98]

The Japanese decision left China with no other alternative but putting up full-fledged resistance. Shortly after the fall of Peiping and Tientsin, Generalissimo Chiang Kai-shek delivered a message to the armed forces of the nation calling them to "drive out the invaders."[99] Meanwhile, the Generalissimo made the following public statement: "The Government has the responsibility of defending national territory and sovereign rights and of protecting the people. The only thing to do now is to put into operation its comprehensive plan to lead the entire nation in a struggle for the protection of the nation to the very bitter end."[100]

NOTES

1. See Yale Maxon, *Control of Japanese Foreign Policy* (Berkeley: University of California Press, 1957), pp. 120-124; Richard Storry, *The Double Patriots* (Boston: Houghton Mifflin, 1957), pp. 215-223; Shuhsi Hsu 徐淑希 , *How the Far Eastern War Began* (Shanghai: Kelly & Walsh Co., 1938), pp. 1-16.
2. James B. Crowley, "A Reconsideration of the Marco Polo Bridge Incident," *Journal of Asian Studies* (hereafter *JAS*) Vol. XXII: No. 3 (May, 1963), pp. 277-291.
3. For further information concerning the Conference, see Takeuchi Tatsuji, *War and Diplomacy in the Japanese Empire* (New York: Doubleday, 1935), pp. 247-248.

4. The full text of the Memorandum was first published in 1929 in Chinese. An English translation appears in Arthur Tiedemann, *Modern Japan* (New York: D. Van Nostrand Co., 1962, revised edition), pp. 127-133, reading No. 8.

5. Arthur Tiedemann, p. 131.

6. The inner story of how the Kwantung Army plotted and carried out Marshal Chang's assassination was not fully disclosed until the end of World War II. For details see Paul S. Dull, "The Assassination of Chang Tso-lin," *The Far Eastern Quarterly*, November, 1952, pp. 453-463.

7. *International Military Tribunal for the Far East* (hereafter *IMTFE*) Doc. No. 1822.

8. Immanuel C. Y. Hsu, *The Rise of Modern China* (New York: Oxford University Press, 1970), p. 642.

9. A mass of new historical materials brought out at the Tokyo War Crimes Trials have proved that the Mukden Incident was engineered by both military extremists and civilian expansionists such as Dr. Okawa Shumei (*IMTFE*, Doc. 1882). For detailed description about the Incident, see Yoshihashi Takehiko, *Conspiracy at Mukden* (New Haven: Yale University Press, 1963), and Chin-tung Liang, *The Sinister Face of the Mukden Incident* (New York: St. John's University Press, 1969).

10. This is the title of Hugh Byas' famous work, *Government by Assassination* (New York: Knopf, 1942). One Japanese diplomat, Itaro Ishii, in his work titled *Gaikokan no Ishii* or *A Diplomat's Life* (Tokyo: Yomiuri Shinbunsha, 1950), aptly called the Japanese Government at that time a "Government of assassination, by assassination and for assassination" (p. 237).

11. Edward Bing-shuey Lee, *One Year of the Japan-China Undeclared War* (Shanghai: Mercury Press, 1933), pp. 370-374.

12. *IMTFE*, Doc. 3147-c.

13. N. Wing Mah & C. F. Chang, *Sino-Japanese Relations Since the Tangku Truce, May 31, 1933* (Shanghai: China Institute of Pacific Relations, 1936), p. 8.

14. *Foreign Relations of the United States: Japan, 1931-1941* (Washington, D.C.: U.S. Government Printing Office, 1943), Vol. 1, pp. 224-225.

15. Mah & Chang, p. 7.

16. For full English text of the document see *Foreign Relations of the United States: Diplomatic Papers, 1934.* (5 Vols., Washington, D.C.: U.S. Government Printing Office, 1950), Vol. 3, pp. 140-141.

17. *Kuo wen chow pao* (The National Affairs Weekly) 國聞周報 , Vol. 17, No. 17, (Shanghai: Ta Kung Press, April 30, 1934).

18. Mah & Chang, p. 8. At about the same time, an American wheat and cotton loan negotiation was under way.

19. Hallett Abend, *My Life in China, 1926-1941* (New York: Harcourt, Brace and Company, 1943), p. 173.
20. *IMTFE*, Doc. 3147-c.
21. *IMTFE*, Doc. 1763-a. The document was worked out by a Japanese-sponsored "North China People's Patriotic Association" but the Japanese Mukden military authorities considered "it is worth referring to from the point of view of our scheme against China," and was filed in the column of "top secret."
22. James B. Crowley, *Japan's Quest for Autonomy* (New Jersey: Princeton University Press, 1966), p. 201.
23. For the two powers' responses to the North China crisis of 1935, see Dorothy Borg, *The United States and the Far Eastern Crisis of 1933-1938* (Cambridge: Harvard University Press, 1964), Chap. V.
24. Joseph C. Grew, *Ten Years in Japan* (New York: Simon and Schuster, 1944), p. 193.
25. *IMTFE*, Doc. 1634-a.
26. Shuhsi Hsu, pp. 87-89.
27. *IMTFE*, record, pp. 29621-31.
28. The Association for Foreign Affairs Research, *The Sino-Japanese Diplomatic Relations Prior to the Lukouchiao Incident* (Taipei: Research Association on Diplomatic Problems of the Republic of China, 1966), pp. 17-18.
29. *Ibid.*
30. Burka Inlow, "Japan's Special Trade in North China, 1935-1937," *The Far Eastern Quarterly*, Vol. 6, No. 2, (Feb. 1947).
31. Chang Chi-yun　張其昀　, *A Brief History of the Kuomintang* (Taipei: China Cultural Press, 1962), p. 1944.
32. Hollington K. Tong　董顯光　, *Chiang Kai-shek* (Taipei: China Publishing Company, 1953), p. 158.
33. Paul K. T. Sih　薛光前　, *Decision for China: Communism or Christianity* (Chicago: Henry Regnery, 1959), p. 86.
34. Hollington K. Tong, p. 202.
35. Tsiang Fang-cheng (ed.)　蔣方震（百里）　, "Utterances of the Generalissimo," (Chungking: *The Progress Anglo-Chinese Weekly*, 1940), pp. 1-24.
36. *President Chiang Kai-shek's Speeches on Party Politics*, (3 Vols.; Taipei, 1971), Vol. I, p. 150.
37. Paul K. T. Sih (ed.), *The Strenuous Decade: China's Nation-Building Efforts, 1927-1937* (New York: St. John's University Press, 1971), p. 28.
38. Chen Pu-lei, *Reminiscence* (Taipei: Biographical Literature Press, 1967), p. 97.
39. Hollington K. Tong, *Biography of President Chiang* (Taipei: Committee on Chinese Publication Enterprise, 1952), Vol. I, pp. 226-227.
40. Shuhsi Hsu, p. 56.

41. *Ibid.*, p. 58.
42. For a general survey of Chiang's popularity in the mid-1930's, see T. S. Young, "The Chinese Have Found Their Leader," *China Weekly Review*, November 28, 1936, p. 452.
43. Dorothy Borg, p. 188.
44. Shigemitsu Mamoru (Trans. by Oswald White), *Japan and Her Destiny: My Struggle for Peace* (New York: E. P. Dutton, 1958), pp. 136-137.
45. Chou Kai-ching   周開慶 , *The Sino-Japanese Relations Prior to the Resistance War* (Taipei: Liberty Press, 1962), p. 218.
46. Tada reported this Outline to Tokyo on December 2, 1935. An English text of this document appears in *IMTFE*, record, pp. 3475-3486.
47. The six lines are (1) Peiping-Shanhaikwan Railway, (2) Tientsin-Pukow Railway (North of Hsuchow), (3) Peiping-Hankow Railway (north of the Yellow River), (4) Peiping-Suiyuan Railway (whole line), (5) Shantung Railway (whole line), (6) Lunghai Railway (east of Hsuchow).
48. *IMTFE*, record, p. 3478.
49. Chou Kai-ching, p. 219; *CWR*, July 11, 1936, p. 200.
50. Shuhsi Hsu, p. 4.
51. Shuhsi Hsu, p. 5; *Foreign Relations of the United States*, 1936, Vol. IV, p. 303.
52. *CWR*, October 10, 1936, p. 201.
53. *Chung-jih wai-chiao shih-liao Tsung-pien* (Collections of Sino-Japanese Diplomatic Historical Documents, hereafter *CJWST.*) (Taipei: Research Association on Diplomatic Problems of the Republic of China, 1966), Vol. 5, pp. 431-432.
54. *CWR*, January 16, 1937, p. 231.
55. Liu Ju-ming, *Reminiscence* (Taipei: Biographical Literature Press, 1966), p. 183.
56. *CWR*, January 16, 1937, p. 231.
57. Shuhsi Hsu, "The North China Crisis," *China Quarterly*, Vol. 2 (August, 1937), p. 591.
58. Chin Te-chin, "A Factual Account of the July 7th Incident," *IMTFE*, exhibit, 198; Wang Leng-chai, "Factual Accounts of Lukouchiao's Case," *IMTFE*, Doc., 1790.
59. *Ibid.*
60. Affidavits of Tanaka Shinichi and of Kawabe Torashiro, *IMTFE*, record, pp. 20676-20678, 21987.
61. *IMTFE*, record, pp. 20629, 21986.
62. The Original Record of Lushan Discussions, July 1937.
63. *Foreign Relations of the United States*, 1937, Vol. III, p. 137; *IMTFE*, record, 2330.

64. The Japanese insisted that the agreement consists of (a) apology to be made by the representatives of the Twenty-ninth Army and punishment of those directly responsible; (b) Chinese troops to evacuate Lukouchiao and to be replaced by the Peace Preservation Corps for the purpose of keeping the Chinese troops sufficiently separated from the Japanese; and (c) adequate measures to be taken for curbing the activities of the Blue Shirts and Communists. See Foreign Affairs Association of Japan, *How the North China Affair Arose* (Tokyo: The Commercial Chamber, 1937), p. 6.

65. "Highlights of the North China Crisis," *The People's Tribune* (Shanghai: China United Press, 1937), No. XXVI.

66. Pan Yu-kuei　潘毓桂　, "Preface to the Sketch Record of Pacification Work in Peking After the Lukouchiao Incident" (Peking: Peking Municipal Government Publication Office, 1938).

67. *IMTFE*, record, pp. 21991-2.

68. *Foreign Relations of the United States*, 1937, Vol. 3, p. 219.

69. Hata Ikuhiko, *Nih-chu sen-so shi* (History of the Sino-Japanese War) (Tokyo: Kawade Shoho, 1961), p. 337.

70. *Ta Kung Daily News*, Shanghai, July 21, 1937.

71. Shuhsi Hsu, *loc. cit.*, p. 592.

72. Sun Lien-chung, *Reminiscence* (Taipei: Preparatory Committee on Celebration of Sun Lien-chung's Seventieth Birthday, 1962), p. 43.

73. *CJWST*, Vol. 4, pp. 210-211.

74. F. C. Jones, *Japan's New Order in East Asia* (London: Oxford University Press, 1954), p. 35.

75. *China Quarterly*, Nanking, 1937, Vol. 2, pp. 711-712.

76. *Foreign Relations of the United States*, 1937, Vol. III, p. 211.

77. *The People's Tribune* (Shanghai, 1937), No. XXVI, p. 156.

78. *Foreign Relations of the United States*, 1937, Vol. III, p. 181; Yu Te-jen, *The Japanese Struggle for World Empire* (New York: Vantage Press, 1967), p. 104.

79. *Foreign Relations of the United States*, 1937, Vol. III, p. 206.

80. *The Collected Wartime Messages of Generalissimo Chiang Kai-shek, 1937-1945*, compiled by Chinese Ministry of Information (New York: John Day Company, 1943), Vol. I, pp. 21-25.

81. *Ibid.*

82. Shuhsi Hsu, p. 10.

83. *CJWST*, Vol. 4, p. 203.

84. *The People's Tribune*, No. XXVI, p. 151.

85. James B. Crowley, p. 337.

86. T. A. Bisson, *Japan in China* (New York: Macmillan, 1938), p. 19.

87. Shuhsi Hsu, p. 13.

88. T. A. Bisson, p. 19.

89. Liu Chien-chun, *Reminiscence* (Taipei: Biographical Literature Press, 1966), p. 99.
90. *How the North China Affair Arose, op. cit.*, p. 16.
91. *CJWST*, Vol. 4, p. 202.
92. Liu Ju-ming, p. 186.
93. *CJWST*, Vol. 4, p. 202.
94. Hata Ikuhiko, p. 337; *CJWST*, Vol. 4, pp. 512-513.
95. *Ibid.*
96. *Ta Kung Daily News* 大公報 , Shanghai, July 29, 1937.
97. For a detailed description of the battle of Nanyuan, see Colonel David D. Barrett's Affidavit, in *IMTFE*, record, pp. 3355-3364.
98. David J. Lu, *From the Marco Polo Bridge to Pearl Harbor* (Washington, D.C.: Public Affairs Press, 1961), p. 17.
99. *The Collected Wartime Messages of Generalissimo Chiang Kai-shek, 1937-1945* (New York: John Day Co., 1943), pp. 36-40.
100. Shuhsi Hsu, p. 66.

Comments:

BY AKIRA IRIYE

This is a straightforward description of the origins of the Sino-Japanese War. Mr. Li skillfully presents background facts, going back to the 1920's, and weaves various episodes and incidents prior to July 7, 1937, into a concise story of Sino-Japanese tensions.

It is difficult to disagree either with the paper's overall framework or with most of its factual details. The author's basic argument, that Japanese militarism harbored aggressive intentions in China, looking to the eventual domination over the country, and that these designs were the ultimate cause of the Sino-Japanese War, cannot be faulted. My only reservation at this level would be to say that this is not a particularly novel, interpretative framework. As a broad generalization, it would today be accepted by virtually all historians except a handful of apologists for Japanese imperialism who have refused to change their views for thirty years. The question which has not been sufficiently explored is not the existence of militarism in Japan but its nature and socio-ideological characteristics. I shall return to this question later.

Regarding factual details, Mr. Li has reproduced a wealth of pertinent data covering the ten-year period 1927-1937. Here again, many of his facts are familiar to students of history and mostly indisputable. I would only question the choice of certain data for inclusion in the paper, and the exclusion of some other. For instance, the author starts with the Tanaka memorandum in whose authenticity he seems to believe, then goes on to mention the Mukden incident, the Amau statement, Hirota's "three-point principle," the Sian incident, and the Marco Polo Bridge incident, and concludes by discussing the extension of hostilities in July 1937. These episodes are treated with clarity and sufficient documentation. (I wish, however, that Mr. Li had done more to correlate Japanese and Chinese primary sources. Both Japan and China have published large quantities of diplomatic and military documents relating to their crisis during the 1930's, but few writers have attempted to compare and analyze the two sets of documents.) I find especially enlightening the discussion of Sino-Japanese clashes just prior to and following the July 7 incident, in particular the efforts exerted by Sung Che-yuan to prevent the crisis from escalating. Sung, in fact, emerges as a central figure in this study, a patriotic Chinese who tried desperately to maintain Chinese sovereignty without provoking extreme Japanese retaliation which would only cause disaster to China's efforts at modernization.

At the same time, certain *dramatis personae* seem to be missing in this account. The Chinese Communists are mentioned only casually, in connection with Chiang's campaigns against them, and with the Sian incident. Should they not be given greater prominence in view of their strategic role in bringing about the second United Front? For that matter, the second United Front is nowhere mentioned in the paper. Nor is there a discussion of the Seventh Comintern Congress of 1935 which made history by calling for the formation of a worldwide popular front against fascism. On the other side of the spectrum, the leader of the pro-Japanese group, Wang Ching-wei, is almost entirely ignored in this presentation. China's "pro-Japanese elements" is cited once, but without explanation (p. 21). Wang, Huang Fu, and other leaders who sought some sort of accommodation with Japan could be ignored only if one believed that their roles in the developing drama of Sino-Japanese relations were minimal. It would seen, on the contrary, that the existence of these Chinese was of crucial importance in encouraging the thought among some prominent Japanese that compromise and conciliation between the two countries were possible short of Japan's completely giving up the fruits of its conquest. The recently published autobiography of Matsumoto Shigeharu is the best source for this type of thinking before 1937. Perhaps it was all an illusion, but the whole story of the Sino-Japanese War would be incomplete without some attention paid to the efforts of those who tried to prevent its occurrence.

This brings me to my central point. I said earlier that I agreed with the paper's overall framework and with the factual details it presented. My problem is with the intermediate generalizations which are explicitly or implicitly made in the paper. The author assumes that Japanese policy was controlled by "military fascism," that the military were united in their ambitions to conquer China, and that even non-military officials went along with them. On the Chinese side, Mr. Li assumes that Chiang Kai-shek and his followers were unanimously determined to resist Japanese encroachment upon Chinese sovereignty. Thus both Japanese and Chinese are pictured as monolithic entities, each of which had well-defined goals and interests.

It does seem to me that such a view is too simplistic. On the Chinese side, there certainly was a divergence of views as to how to cope with Japanese imperialism, ranging from uncompromising opposition to opportunistic accommodation. Some sort of typology might have been developed to analyze this divergence. This paper, for instance, has some very revealing quotes on China's need for industrialization. Chiang is quoted as stressing the necessity for China's "advancing from the status of an almost purely agricultural state to an industrial one." Was this a goal everyone in China was agreed upon? If so, what was the relationship between this goal and Japanese imperialism? Given the world economic crisis of the 1930's which was discrediting the viability of Western capitalism and industrialism, it would not have been surprising to find some Chinese turning to Japan for economic collaboration so as to undertake China's industrialization. Japanese ideologies often justified their imperialism in the name of Asian regionalism, designed to promote the national interests of Japan and China without fear of subjugation by Western imperialism. Wang Ching-wei and his followers chose to opt for this kind of cooperation with Japan, whereas Chiang Kai-shek turned to the West for capital and technology needed for Chinese industrialization. Thus viewed, the division in China takes on some real significance; it was between those who believed Japan would promote China's modern development and those who denied that Japan could be so trusted.

On the Japanese side, too, the picture was far from monolithic. The author states that after the Manchurian incident, Inukai "was the only person who wanted to work out an amicable settlement" between the two countries, and that his assassination "ended any conciliatory efforts toward China" (p. 7). But then several pages later Ambassadors Ariyoshi's and Kawagoe's negotiation for improving Sino-Japanese relations are mentioned. These efforts, at any rate, were doomed to failure, Mr. Li argues, given the Japanese military's determination to control North China. It is now well established, however, that the Japanese military became seriously divided by the mid-1930's. Recent studies by Mark Peattie, Hata Ikuhiko, and others on Ishihara Kanji indicate, among other insights they offer, the importance of understanding that Japanese militarism contained an array of divergent, often conflicting, interests and viewpoints. After all, Ishihara, whom Mr. Li rightly regards as an architect of the Mukden incident, was adamantly opposed to the extension of hostilities in 1937. His maneuvering to bring about the formation of a "Manchurian cabinet," composed of those who shared his views on the future of Japanese-Manchukuo relations, did not materialize. And his movement for an "East Asiatic league" served to brand him as a subversive in the eyes of General Tōjō and his clique. From the reminiscences of Horiba, Imai, and others we learn that Ishihara had supporters within the military who, too, doubted the wisdom of a prolonged war with China.

All this is not to deny that Japanese ambitions in Manchuria and North China were the ultimate cause of the Sino-Japanese War. I am simply pointing out the desirability of going a step beyond such generalizations and raising additional questions about the nature of Japanese militarism and China's reaction to it. From this paper, and from others to be presented at this conference, it seems possible to say, for instance, that economic development and growth were the key concerns of the Nationalist leadership after 1927. If so, a fundamental problem facing Japanese militarism and foreign policy was how to cope with Chinese "modernization." Even Chiang Kai-shek's New Life Movement, Mr. Li shows, had a strong industrializing component, and the Japanese had to take with the utmost seriousness China's determination for economic reconstruction and development. Japan's militarists were in a sense those who sought to stifle Chinese industrialization which would make the country strong and deny its resources to Japan. Men like Foreign Minister Hirota also opposed Chinese industrialization if it were to be accomplished through Western technological and financial assistance. Then there were those like Ishihara who were not against China's modernization *per se,* but who wanted to integrate the two countries' economic efforts against their allegedly common enemies: decadent Western capitalists and Soviet communists. Such pan-Asianism was extremely repugnant to the Western governments, who had their own ideas about Chinese development. In this way the Sino-Japan war tensions became part of the history of the industrialization of the non-West, where conflicting assumptions and interests competed with one another for control over China's destiny. Viewed in such a perspective, Mr. Li's paper throws light on the military and diplomatic implications of China's efforts at economic growth and development. This, it seems to me, is a far more interesting phenomenon to discuss than diplomatic negotiations, military clashes, and the like.

CHAPTER II

Total Strategy Used by China and Some Major Engagements in the Sino-Japanese War of 1937-1945

I N THE LAST eighty-five years there were two wars between China and Japan. Their cause, course, outcome and influence on Asia and the rest of the world were quite different. However, the basic principle in ancient and modern military history not only remains unchanged but also proves once again that in any war, final victory belongs to the party who commits the fewer mistakes.

Sun Tze in ancient China, more than two thousand years ago, and the great strategists in Europe and America have emphasized that the art of war is of vital importance to the state. As war between any two countries or blocs is total struggle, each party must try to win the final victory with all its powers. Before the war, the supreme authority of a nation should, under her supreme national policy, consolidate various powers and utilize them in a coordinated action towards one general objective. This is the total strategy in which political, economic, diplomatic and military phases are closely coordinated. When the actual war breaks out, any mistake found in the original plan must be corrected under the total strategy. Thus the victory or defeat of a nation in war depends on whether her total strategy is correct. As to military strategy, it is merely one phase of the conduct of total war and it may play an important role or secondary role as the case may be. If a nation lacks the strategy or there are some mistakes in her strategy, even her superior tactics or combat ability in the field cannot save her from defeat.

Seventy years ago, when he commented on the Sino-Japanese War of

1894-1895, a Chinese scholar, Liang Chi-chao 梁啟超 (BDRC Vol. II, 346-351), pointed out that the main reason for the defeat of China in that war was that it was no more than a contest between Li Hung-chang 李鴻章 (ECCP 464-471) himself and Japan, inasmuch as the majority of the Chinese people were not involved in it. Ten years ago, a Japanese professor, Fujiwara Akire, expanded this same point by saying: "When Japan developed as a modern nation, China was still under the domination of a feudal emperor without a national army, except for the forces commanded by Li Hung-chang." He also pointed out that: "At the beginning of the Sino-Japanese War [1937-1945], provoked by the Japanese Army, the latter committed a serious mistake in facing simultaneously two enemies—China and Soviet Russia, hoping to cope with this situation single-handed."[1] Hata Ikuhiko went even further: "In the Sino-Japanese War of 1937-1945, the Japanese Army started the war, and in such a way, that it committed the mistakes of confusion, irresolution, halfheartedness, and uncoordinated political and military strategies that led later to a position of doing nothing and completely lacking in policy. The seven hundred thousand troops in the first year could not contain and annihilate the main body of the Chinese National Army in the Hsuchow engagement despite the 'tactical win.' "[2] Masanori Ito wrathfully accused the Japanese soldiers for provoking the Marco Polo Bridge Incident which was the beginning of the war that ruined Japan. After they fell into the quagmire in China for four years with 190,000 men killed and 950,000 men wounded, the Japanese warlords launched the attack on Britain and America. This war without stratagem can be called the greatest blunder in history, the result of Japanese stratocracy under militarism.[3]

I

Growth of Nationalism in China

The outcome of the two Sino-Japanese wars depended basically on the existence and soundness of a total strategy. It is worth pointing out that Japan, despite her modernization, had no comprehensive stratagem in the war with China in 1937-1945, mainly because, after 1895, she was misguided by her victory and looked down upon China. She launched attacks against China by taking advantage of China's traditional weakness without calmly taking into account the progress China had made.

In November 1894, Dr. Sun Yat-sen initiated the National Revolution and in 1898 Kang Yu-wei 康有為 (BDRC Vol. II, 228-233) and Liang Chi-chao launched the One Hundred Day's Reform Movement. These two national patriotic movements were inspired by the logical results of the Sino-Japanese War of 1894-1895. The success of the 1911 Revolution was symbolic of Chinese awakening. Unfortunately, Japan extorted some special rights from China as a condition for her diplomatic recognition of the Republic of China. In 1915 she forced the 21 Demands on China by taking advantage of World War I. This was another shock which woke up China. In May 1918, Japan compelled the Chinese Government in Peking to sign a Joint Defense Pact against Russia which provoked the strong objection of Chinese students in Peking. One year later the May Fourth Movement occurred, launched by students and strongly supported by businessmen and workers all over the country. In 1928 during the Northern Expedition of the National Revolutionary Army, Japan moved her troops to Shantung. When Chinese nationalism was rapidly mounting, the Japanese disparaged it as "five minutes patriotism." In 1932, the Japanese delegate stated openly at the League of Nations: "China is not an organized nation but a geographic term."

In 1934 Dr. Hu Shih 胡　適　　(BDRC Vol. II, 167-174) published an article in the *Independent Review,* of which he was publisher, in which he wrote: "Since the establishment of the Republic of China in 1912—although there are many signs of stagnation which give us no satisfaction—there has been much undeniable and valuable progress: (1) the overthrow of the monarchy, (2) innovations in education, (3) family reforms, (4) modernization of social customs, (5) new experiments in political organization, (6) promulgation of new statutes, (7) liberation of women." These types of progress have been developed in the wake of the 1911 Revolution. Hu Shih further pointed out: "We can say without hesitation that the leaders have been living in a new age in the past twenty or thirty years; their character is often greater than that of their counterparts in the old era; their mind is broader; their knowledge is more solid; their behavior is more vigorous and their personality is more refined. Compare Dr. Sun Yat-sen with Tseng Kuo-fan 曾國藩　　(ECCP 751-755); we can see striking differences between these two exemplary personages."

At the same time General Tsiang Fang-cheng 蔣方震 (BDRC Vol. I, 312-317) also pointed out: "Since 1894, the tremendous changes in Chinese society caused by the influence of circumstances are: (1) the close union between knowledge and military might, and some intellectuals have taken up military careers; (2) the soldiers have entered school to get knowledge; (3) collaboration between social and intellectual leaders and the statesmen in power. Both politics and national defense benefit from these changes accordingly."[4]

At that time, the Japanese aggressive actions in North China were becoming more and more overt. Based on his general study of the history of China and of the modern idea of total war, including the practice of general mobilization, Tsiang Fang-cheng stated the doctrine of integration: integration of living and fighting conditions. The realization of this doctrine depends first on the moral power of the people and their self-motivated discipline, and second, on the power of organization.

Tsiang Fang-cheng stated furthermore: "For the sake of world peace, a nation's means of survival should not be cut off. Otherwise that nation's will to survive will integrate the nation into a fighting body, which will struggle not only for its own survival, but also for the destruction of others."[5] This assertion not only implied the basic principle of Chinese national defense, but also was intended to warn Japan: Beware of China.

Hu Shih deemed that many people are not aware of progress and changes because of their lack of historical perspective. In other words, they do not realize that time brings changes and progress. On February 15, 1936, Ku Hsien-jung, a member of the House of Peers of Japan met Japanese General Matsui Iwane in Taipei, Taiwan. He emphasized that, as the situation of China was greatly changed, Japan had to appreciate Generalissimo Chiang's status, and only by cooperation with him could the security of East Asia be safeguarded.[6] However, his advice did not receive General Matsui Iwane's attention. (After the Sino-Japanese War broke out, General Matsui Iwane took the post of commander of the Japanese Army in the Shanghai Campaign, August 1937.)

As Fujiwara Akira has said: "The Japanese Army trained under the conventional Japanese Army education became peculiarly ingrown and narrow-minded, blinded largely by its own point of view."[7] The so-called old-China-hands of Japan, always looking down upon China, seldom studied the culture and history of China but stressed the fact that China was once ruled by Mongols and Manchurians, thereby seeking to learn some lessons about how the Han people could be ruled as subjects. Reading the Chinese classics without real understanding and listening to groundless intelligence data collected by Japanese spies in China, they had no true knowledge of China's evolution in the 1930's and of actual Chinese psychology. As Sun Tze said: "If you know yourself but not the enemy, for every victory gained you will also suffer a defeat."[8]

In the past thousands upon thousands of Chinese youths have gone to Japan to study there. Dr. Sun Yat-sen, Chiang Kai-shek, Liang Chi-chao, Tai Chi-tao 戴季陶 (BDRC Vol. III, 200-205), Tsiang Fang-cheng and Wang Peng-sheng (BDRC Vol. III, 391-393), all studied in Japan for a long time and investigated Japan carefully. The Shanghai Campaign and The Great Wall Campaign against Japan by the Chinese army 1932-1933 were the first opportunities to test the Chinese combat effectiveness since the Sino-Japanese War of 1894, which was helpful in "knowing one's situation and that of the enemy."

In the summer of 1934, when Generalissimo Chiang Kai-shek addressed the Lu Shan Officers Training Corps, he emphasized the following:

The best ways of winning the National War were: (1) To take initiative in operation, (2) Unity of command, (3) Spirit is more important than material, (4) To predict the future operational situation, get rid of old and new prejudices of Chinese and Western military science and research the most advanced tactics in order to defeat the enemy, (5) To prepare everything throughout the country in peace time, avail ourselves of material and manpower in order to resist Japanese aggression.[9]

This is the initial revelation of the principle of total war to resist the Japanese made by Generalissimo Chiang Kai-shek. In the summer of 1935 after Chiang's careful inspection in Szechwan, Yunnan, Kweichow and Shensi, the concrete approaches and schemes of carrying out the foregoing principles were finalized. The basic guiding policy was: "For the purpose of maintaining our territorial integrity, independent sovereignty, gaining our national existence and freedom and reconstructing a prosperous, powerful, peaceful and pleasant new China, we should urge that world peace be realized by collective security on one hand, and we should reinforce national defense and armaments and gain the final victory by fighting the war of attrition with our national power, in the event of the unavailability of peace."

Based on the foregoing policy, the various schemes were envisaged and pressed to complete the following objectives by the end of 1938: (1) Interior: to end the local and border troubles. (2) Foreign affairs: to ask the League of Nations to settle the dispute between China and Japan, to gain the support of the friendly countries, to build the international collective security relationship, so that world peace may be safeguarded. (3) Finance and economy: to renovate the monetary system, to carry out the legal tender policy and to attain self-sufficiency in food. (4) Education: to promote the New Life Movement, to carry out the national guard military training program so as to promote the national traditional morality, to cultivate national combatant spirit and develop the national economic construction in order to pave the way for long-term war. (5) Military: A. to construct permanent national defense works at the strategic points all over the country. B. to complete some main railways, highways in the Northwest, Southwest, and Southeast parts and the communication networks. C. to investigate and develop the quartermaster facilities, and to store military material. D. to unify the training of army, navy and air force, to reorganize the troops and enhance operational readiness. E. to establish the military service system. F. to carry out the Lu Shan and Omei training programs in order to promote spiritual consolidation.[10]

The foregoing measures were the prerequisites of total war strategy for resisting Japan—China should gain the final victory by the war of attrition with her whole national manpower and resources because she had the advantageous condition of boundless territory, a large population, high mountains and intricate rivers. The well-known "Trading Space for Time" dictum was the common expression of this strategy. In military science, this is the principle of retreating into the interior of the country.

In 2640 B.C. the battle in which Huang-ti　黃　帝　defeated Chih Yu's　蚩　尤　rebellious army of superior numbers with the strategy of retreating into the interior with an army of inferior numbers was the earliest precedent of this strategy in history. Sun Tze in *The Art of War* deals with this strategy also. According to Liu-Ho-Chu-Chih　劉後主志 in Hua-Yang-Kuo-Chi　華陽國志　(ECCP 418), Volume VII, written by Chang Chu 常　璩　, in the fourth century, Chiang Wei 姜　維　, the brave general, in the Three Kingdoms envisaged in 258 A.D. and carried out the withdrawal strategy to resist the strong army of Wei State. This withdrawal strategy of "tempting the enemy into a trap" is described in detail. However, after Chang Chu, Chen Shau 陳　壽　, the author of the *History of Three Kingdoms*, neglected the essential significance of Chiang Wei's: "Let the enemy invade the plain," in order to tempt them into the trap and then to fight the decisive battle against them. He therefore prefixed a word "not" before the clause "Let. . . ." (*The History of Three Kingdoms*, Volume XIV), and thereby gave the contrary meaning. According to "Hua Yang Kuo Chih," Szu-Ma Kwang 司馬光　in the Sung Dynasty clarified Chiang Wei's original meaning when he wrote a 294-volume *Chronicle*　資治通鑑　. Hu San-Sheng 胡三省 made its meaning more clear by noting: "Let the enemy invade the plain," after its text. Unfortunately, Szu Ma Kwang and Hu San-shen considered that "Chiang Wei withdrew from the strategic point by his own will and Shu State perished accordingly." *Tung-Chien-Chih-Lan* 通鑑輯覽　in the period of Chien Lung Emperor of the Ching Dynasty emphasized: "Chiang Wei did not defend the gate of the frontier but stationed his army in order to tempt the enemy for the purpose of counterattacking them when they withdrew; it was like opening the door to admit the thief." *The Collective Note on the History of The Three Kingdoms*　三國志集解　, published in Hupeh in 1937, further emphasized this assessment.

In spite of the fact that traditional Chinese scholars had different interpretations of Chiang Wei's strategy of withdrawal, when the Sino-Japanese War of 1937-1945 broke out, the Chinese Army and people swore to fight against the Japanese by conducting a war of attrition with the same strategy of Chiang Wei of retreating into the interior of the country under Generalissimo Chiang Kai-shek's leadership and then gaining the final victory after eight years of hard and brave fighting. Why? This is worth studying.

II

Retreat in the Interior

In 1901 when Dr. Sun Yat-sen was aware in Japan of the guerrilla tactics carried out by the brave Boers in the South African War to beat the English Army, he determined to adopt these tactics in the uprising to be led by the Chinese revolutionary party in the future.[11] Furthermore, the Chinese students studying military science in Japan learned Western military history enthusiastically. After studying Chinese and Western military experiences by the method of synthesis, some Chinese leaders suggested plans for their national defense.

Liang Chi-chiao published *Tseng Hu Chih-Ping Yu-Lu* 曾胡 治兵語錄 (ECCP 755) compiled in 1911 by General Tsai O 蔡 鍔 (BDRC III, 286-290). They commended effective tactics of offense and defense by maintaining that the attacker is the "guest" but the defender is the "host" who can beat the attacker by waiting in comfort for the exhausted enemy. Although modern military science has advanced day by day, this principle remains unchanged. Based on the experiences of the Boer War and the Moscow Campaign in 1812, Tsai O pointed out in the conclusion of this book: "In my humble opinion, if in several years we have to go to war with another country, to stake our victory on positional defense is not preferable to defending ourselves on chosen terrain and withdrawing in planned steps, so that our main force is intact and the enemy will lose their freshness. When they have gone so deep that their supporting line cannot be maintained, we shall fight the last battle for their extermination."[12] This is the earliest publication of the strategy of "trading space for time" against Japan.

Tsiang Fang-cheng, the schoolmate of General Tsai O, wrote "New Commentaries on Sun Tze," quoting from the famous works of Western military science and military history, hoping that Chinese soldiers would know the essentials of Western military science in order to enrich their knowledge. In 1922 Tsiang Fang-cheng pointed out in his article that: "Facing our aggressive neighbour state, the only way of winning the war is to be the opposite of the enemy in everything—if a quick decision is beneficial to them, we must rely on protracted sustenance, so as to exhaust them; while their forces are on the first line, we must put our forces on the second line of battle, so that they will have difficulty in finding room to exert their forces." Tsiang Fang-cheng mentioned again and again a tactic to drag Japan to its downfall in his recommendation to the National Government before the Sino-Japanese War 1937-1945 broke out.[13]

Tsai O and Tsiang Fang-cheng mentioned Karl Von Clausewitz in their articles, especially Tsiang who quoted from his famous book *On War* very often. Von Clausewitz has played an important role in Western military science. In the beginning of the twentieth century, Japan's Military Academy published the Japanese version of *On War* for Japanese students only. However, Chinese students succeeded in getting this book and studied it. Chiang Kai-shek stated: "After getting this book which is one of my favorite books, I read and underlined it with red pencil several times."[14] This book in Chinese translation was published in China in 1915.[15]

Chinese soldiers were interested in this book especially, because in addition to its influence on modern Western military science, some of its important ideas closely resemble Chinese military art.[16]

As pointed out in the first section of this article, since the establishment of the Republic of China, and especially since the completion of the Northern Expedition, Chinese nationalism and patriotism among the people and the fighting force rose steadily. After the Mukden Incident, when Japan launched the aggressive war against China again, the Chinese intellectuals urged repeatedly that all Chinese should prepare to fight for national freedom and independence at any cost, which strengthened China's determination to strive for national progress and to resist Japan unconditionally.

In August 1932, Professor Fu Ssu-nien   傅斯年   (BDRC Vol. II, 43-46), one of the leaders of the May Fourth Movement, advocated in his article published in the *Independent Review* 獨立 評論 , the policy of resisting Japan actively, saying: "Although we Chinese cannot beat Japan in the first round, we will sustain ourselves until final victory. The longer the time, the more we are favored. . . . The potential power of the Chinese people lies in the three or four hundred million farmers, not in the rulers or the leaders of large cities or towns. The destiny of China depends on struggling for survival, not on hoping for survival and fearing death. . . . History tells us that China is an unexterminable race and facts tell us Japan is not a useful and admirable nation." This is the earliest advocacy of a long-term war of resistance against Japan advocated by Chinese intellectuals.

In April 1933, when Japan declared her withdrawal from the League of Nations, Hu Shih urged in his article in the *Independent Review* that we should prepare to suffer great and terrible sacrifices and at the same time only if we are confident of victory can we suffer the great sacrifice. "The moral condemnation falls on our enemy and the final victory will belong to us undoubtedly."

When Japan carried out her scheme of concentrating on North China, Hu Shih wrote Wang Shih-chieh   王世杰   (BDRC Vol.

III, 395-397), Minister of Education in Nanking, on June 27, 1935, that China must determine to suffer great sacrifice saying:

> When we try to estimate the limit of this great sacrifice, we must determine to undergo the suffering of chaos, bitter fighting, losing territory and ruin for three or four years.
>
> We must prepare to suffer: 1. Ruin of seaports along our coast and the cities along the lower Yangtze, which will need the mobilization of the Japanese navy on a large scale. 2. The struggle in Northern China and the loss of Hopei, Shantung, Chahar, Suiyuan, Shansi and Honan, occupied and destroyed which will need the mobilization of the Japanese army on a large scale. 3. The blockade of the Yangtze, financial breakdown and Tientsin and Shanghai under occupation and destruction.
>
> We must prepare to fight against the enemy bitterly for three or four years. We shall have to fight for our national freedom alone and not have to look for other nations involved in our war, but we can only hope that when we fight to the ultimate condition and our army is exhausted, there will be international assistance from friendly countries.

It was Hu Shih's hope in his letter that Wang Shih-chieh would like to convince the leaders of the government and the military that the long-term bitter fighting was the imperative condition for national renaissance. Hu Shih further considered that Generalissimo Chiang Kai-shek's conception "that we would not become engaged in the war until we were well prepared" seems to fall short of the basic requirement never to turn back. Therefore, Hu Shih emphasized again in his letter that:

> If we would like to fight, we had to give up the wrong conception that we should not engage in the war until we were well prepared. We had to prepare to engage in military failure for three years with the alpha army defeated in the front line and the commercial centers as the battle fields. However, in spite of failure, we had to fight step by step from place to place because we had no alternative.[17]

Wang Shih-chieh replied in his letter of July 11, 1935, to Hu Shih that Tai Chi-tao, Sun Fo 孫 科 (BDRC Vol. III, 162-165) and Chu Cheng 居 正 (BDRC Vol. I, 469-475) agreed with Hu's counsel. But "it would be subject to Generalissimo Chiang's determination."[18] In fact, Generalissimo Chiang made a policy statement against Japan early in November 1932: "The powerful nation should place her national defense stress on the border and adopt the offensive, but the weak nation should understand defense in depth and adopt measures accordingly." He added: "In the event of war we should concentrate on the Yangtze Valley and control the Lung-Hai Railway line as our priority."[19]

Later, as Szechwan, Kweichow and other provinces were under the National Army's control, our domestic situation would gradually achieve stability. After deeply reconsidering the war against Japan in the future, Generalissimo Chiang decided: "The strategy of war against Japan should take the areas south of the Yangtze and west of the Peking-Hankow Railway as the main front and the line of Loyang, Hsiangyang, Fancheng, Chingchow, I-Chang and Changteh as the final front and the three provinces of Szechwan, Kweichow, Shensi as the nucleus and Kansu and Yunnan as the rear."[20] This is the basis of supreme strategy of the long-lasting war of attrition carried out with the national power mentioned in the first section of this article.

Hu Shih's letter and Generalissimo's plan were the top secret documents then. However, on July 21, 1935, Professor Ting Wen-chiang 丁文江 (BDRC Vol. III, 278-282) urged in his article published in *Ta-Kung Daily News* in Tientsin 天津大公報 that: "North China is our Ukraine; Hunan, Szechwan and Kiangsi our Urals and Yunnan, Kweichow our Kamchatka Peninsula. . . . Let's prepare to go to Kamchatka!"

Ting Wen-chiang's heroic advice expressed fully the determined policy of retreating into the interior at any cost as suggested by intellectuals. Professor Ting Wen-chiang was a well-known international geologist who travelled through the most part of China mainland. His wide knowledge and personal experiences won the admiration from the people all over the country. As soon as Ting's article was published, Hu Shih, Fu Ssu-nien and others seconded it, and it became the public opinion immediately. This advice paralleled Generalissimo Chiang's secret plan without previous consultation. Even the article "Long Lasting War" written by Mao Tse-tung, Chinese Communist, pointed out: "The war of resistance against Japan is to be placed on the interior line of operation. However, the relationship between the regular army and the guerrilla is that the regular army is to be placed on the interior line and the guerrilla will be placed on the exterior line. In strategy, the regular army on the interior line should retreat rearward but the guerrilla on the exterior line should march towards the enemy's rear persistently."[21]

Concord between government and people is the first essential to victory.

China possesses a natural advantage for defense. From East to West, China extends through more than sixty-five degrees of longitude. From North to South it includes the climates of the frigid, temperate and torrid zones. Rivers, mountains and deserts abound in China's interior and in the West; arctic cold alternates with tropical heat. Topography and climate are again combining against China's invaders as in the past.

No weapon in the world will be effective against this combination, reinforced by the firm determination and mighty strength of the Chinese people.

III

The Command Post of China, Szechwan

Ever since ancient times, Chinese geographers have compared Szechwan Province to a man's brain, Ching-Chow and Hsiang Yang in Hupeh Province to a man's breast and Kiangsu and Chekiang to a man's legs, as the topography of China is higher in the Northwest and lower in the Southeast, with plains, slope and the rivers on the whole running from the West to East. Szechwan Province is located in the west part of China proper. With its lofty mountains, beautiful rivers, good climate, plentiful harvests, great hydraulic engineering, plentiful rainfall, large, diligent population of fifty millions, rich cultural heritage, Szechwan can indeed be called a "Heavenly Country."

From the military point of view, the Province of Szechwan actually meets the requirements for resisting aggression. In 263 A.D., General Chiang Wei, Field Marshal of Shu Kingdom of the Three Kingdoms, failed in applying the strategy of retreating into the interior of the kingdom, simply because of the corruption in the government of Shu. But during the Southern Sung Dynasty, General Yu Chieh took advantage of the terrain of the mountain ranges of Szechwan to build more than ten fortified cities, and taught the people the austerity way of life warranted in wartime, in order to resist the Mongolian cavalry which had shaken Europe, and Yu's successor triumphed. As a result, the brave Mangu Khan, Field Marshal of the Mongolian cavalry, eventually was exhausted and died in Szechwan (1250 A.D.).

This brilliant success was derived from a combination in Szechwan of three elements: the time factor of Heaven, the geographical factor of Earth, and the cooperative factor among Men, in perfect conformity with modern geopolitics and with Clausewitz' concepts enunciated more than five hundred years later.[22]

The battle of defense, carried out by Yu Chieh's successor, prolonged the life of the Southern Sung Dynasty for twenty more years; but as the Southern Sung Dynasty had already moved its capital near the sea, the Mongols took advantage of the occupied land of Hupei and rolled down eastward, finally overpowering the Southern Sung Dynasty. So the best researcher on the geography of national defense in the Ming Dynasty, Ku Tsu-yu 顧祖禹 (ECCP 419-420), in his famous writing "The Essentials of the Historical Geography" lamented the fact that the Southern Sung Dynasty had failed to retreat to the Provinces of Szechwan, Yunnan, and Kweichow as a base of national recovery. The situation at the end of the Ming Dynasty was better than that of the Southern Sung, but unfortunately, the Province of Szechwan was ravished by Chang Hsieh-chung **張獻忠** (ECCP 37-38). Still Ku Tsu-yu wanted to rehabilitate broken Szechwan, in order to keep it from being used by the enemy, and to make it into the base of national recovery. Unfortunately the authorities of the Southern Ming had not seen this point and were eventually conquered.[23]

The peace and order of Szechwan is related to the peace and order of the whole country, as can be seen in many cases in Chinese history. In 1911, the landlords of Szechwan opposed the policy of the nationalization of the railways and ignited the Revolution of 1911, leading to the establishment of the Republic of China. In 1934, the troops of the Central Government of China entered Szechwan without trouble, turning Szechwan from "disorder" into "order." Since then the "Heavenly Country" began to undertake the great responsibility as the base of resistance to the aggression of Japan.

In 1935, after Generalissimo Chiang had made close inspections in the Provinces of Szechwan, Yunnan, Kweichow, and Shensi, the master plan was made for sustained resistance and "taking Szechwan, Kweichow, and Shensi as the core and Kansu and Yunnan as the hinterland." On August 11, 1935, Generalissimo Chiang gave a speech to the cadres on various levels of Szechwan, Kweichow, and Yunnan assembled in the Omei Training Corps: "I dare say, even if we would lose fifteen provinces of the eighteen provinces of China proper, with Szechwan, Kweichow, and Yunnan provinces in our control, we definitely will beat any enemy, and recover all the lost territory, for rehabilitation and completion of the revolution."[24]

Generalissimo Chiang declared his faith publicly like this in order to establish the "common faith" of the people of Szechwan, Yunnan, and Kweichow, and so for all the people and soldiers of the whole country.

In the spring and summer of 1935, Generalissimo Chiang took up residence at Chengtu. Then very often he discussed with the leaders at all levels in Szechwan in order to get proper ways for the reform of administration, reorganization of troops, changing of customs, development of the transportation system, and the unification of the currency. In the first place, a decision had been made to complete the four main highway lines: Szechwan to Shensi, Szechwan to Kweichow, Szechwan to Hunan, and Szechwan to Yunnan. Though there was no bulldozer or road building machinery, the workers just worked with their two hands and simple tools. These difficult works were completed within two years and were finished before schedule. And this exploded the old idea that "The road of Shu (Szechwan) was difficult." At the same time, military officers and civilian officials of Szechwan adopted the slogan of: "to support the Central Authorities and to unify Szechwan Province," and cancelled the Defense Area System, unified the Financial and Military System, pushing forward industrial and mining enterprises.

The work of reduction and reorganization of the troops of Szechwan was complicated. It had not been carried out according to schedule, and even some obstructions were met. On June 28, 1937, the Generalissimo's Chungking Headquarters proclaimed "The Sketch of the Military Forces Reorganization Committee for Szechwan and Sikang" and the list of the members of the committee. On July 6, the same year, Minister of War, Ho Ying-chin, went to Chungking by plane from Nanking to preside over the opening ceremony of the conference. On July 8, General Ho reported on the incident of the Marco Polo Bridge, and the all-out resistance to the aggression of Japan now became unavoidable. After that the conference went on smoothly. Finally a decision was made that all the troops of Szechwan and Sikang should be completely reorganized before August 10. On August 13, the Shanghai Incident took place, and the all-out resistance was carried out by the whole nation. The work of reorganization of the troops of Szechwan and Sikang was speeded up. After September 1, the troops of Szechwan marched along the highways on the east, north, and south of Szechwan to the battlefields to join the war. And the troops of the first echelon joined the battles of Shanghai and Taiyuan. After that, they continuously reinforced the frontlines, and in the battles of Hsuchow, Wuhan, and Changsha there were brave soldiers of Szechwan and Sikang who fought courageously against the enemy. Several high-ranking commanders died in action.

In November 1937, the National Government proclaimed the movement of its capital to Chungking. After that the "Heavenly Country," with plenty of production, a large population, and improved highways everywhere, became the command post of China in its stubborn resistance to Japan.

In the eight years of resistance to Japan's aggression, Szechwan offered sufficient manpower to work on the construction of highways, airfields, and to take part in military service. Meantime, the farmers worked hard on cultivation, to supply food for soldiers and people. Although there were some events of disorder and confusion in the eight years, generally speaking, the aggression of Japan had accelerated the reform of the military and political affairs of Szechwan. The noble concerns of the nation had superseded the private interests. This rapid and important transformation was not comprehended by the Japanese who had been used to focusing their attention on the shortcomings of China. In the winter of 1938, even the instigations made by Japanese and Wang Ching-wei to distract the minds of the military authorities of Szechwan ended in failure.

The heart zone of the resistance war against Japan was Szechwan with the Northwest provinces of China as the left flank and the Southwest provinces on the right flank, Kansu and Yunnan provinces being the major international thoroughfares of special military value. Since ancient times, Kansu and Szechwan always stood together whenever Szechwan was safe; on the contrary, Kansu would separate from Szechwan in time of danger. Therefore, the union and separation of Szechwan and Yunnan are closely related to the security and danger in these areas.

On the 7th of July, 1940, the 3rd Anniversary Day of the Resistance War of China against Japanese aggressors, Professor Chang Chi-yun 張其昀 (BDRC Vol. I, 24-26) of the National Chekiang University pointed out:

> We assume that after the Incident of Marco Polo Bridge, Japanese troops gave up their attack on Nanking, and concentrated their forces to initiate offensive actions against the provinces of the Northwest or Southwest. I am afraid that their action will mightily affect the reconstructions of our rear base. What a danger it is!
>
> Japan is much better materially than we, but the most important thing she lacked is far-sighted leadership. So far as we know, the method of the Japanese in studying Chinese history is like that of Western sinologists. They pay much attention to the partial proofs but do not understand the major arterials and sources of Chinese history. Since the Japanese don't really understand China, they, of course, can't conquer China. By this critical yardstick, this conclusion has been proven true.[25]

In September of 1940, after the 8th Route Army had launched "a major engagement of Army to Army" in the rear area of the Japanese troops in the Northern part of China, Chu-teh 朱 德 (BDRC, Vol. I, 459-465) pointed out: "This is to resist the attempt of the Japanese troops to invade the rear areas of the Northwest and Southwest parts of China, and also to harass and impede the operating plan of the Japanese aggressors in launching an offensive attack on Sian, Chungking, and Kunming."[26]

These are the concrete examples of the wholehearted support of Chiang Kai-shek in dealing with the rear constructions of the Northwest and the Southwest parts of China in carrying out our strategy against the Japanese, irrespective of political party affiliation or geographical divisions.

IV

Inducement of Japanese Troops to Change
Their "Combat Front" from Southward to Westward

After the conclusion of the Shanghai Incident in May 1932, there was a possibility of hostilities breaking out between China and Japan in the international metropolis. In September of 1936, as Chinese Minister of Foreign Affairs, Chang Chun 張 羣 (BDRC Vol. I, 47-52) met with the Japanese Ambassador to China, Kawagoe Shigeru, for a peace talk in Nanking. The encounters between the Chinese and Japanese in Chengtu, Peihai, and Hankow happened every so often. So the Japanese Navy showed its determination to "punish" China and to promote combat readiness against China. On September 25, 1936, the Japanese Navy and Japanese Army agreed unanimously: "In case of the outbreak of war: 1. The Japanese Navy and Army should make common efforts to occupy Hopei and Shantung; 2. The Navy and Army should cooperate to safeguard Shanghai; 3. The Japanese Air Force should bombard Chinese Military forces and key points often; 4. The blockade of the Chinese coast."[27]

As pointed out by the Japanese news reporter, Matsumoto Shigeharu, the deteriorating situation almost made the Sino-Japanese War break out earlier. Later the hostilities were slowed down because Chiang Kai-shek waived the conventional diplomatic protocol and met with Japanese Ambassador Kawagoe Shigeru. In other words, the patience of the Chinese government delayed the outbreak of the Sino-Japanese War more than ten months.[28]

Meanwhile Chinese authorities facing the actions of Japanese aggressors in Shanghai were inclined to take actions against them. In the winter of 1935, Chiang Kai-shek secretly ordered General Chang Chih-chung 張治中 (BDRC, Vol. I, 41-46) to prepare the entrenchments in the area of Shanghai and Nanking, hoping that in the event of unavoidable war we would be able immediately to use superior strength to launch a surprise attack on the Japanese troops in the war zone of Shanghai and annihilate them so as to recapture our important positions and to prevent their reinforcements. In the summer of 1936, we organized a special trip for military cadres and staff officers, and constructed the encircling entrenchments at the key points of Wusung and Shanghai. For example, the edifice of the Chapei Terminal of the Nanking-Shanghai Railway was specifically designed according to the requirements of military authorities. Simultaneously, we readjusted the military techniques of the Nanking-Shanghai Railway, built up necessary highways in the rear zone, improved signal equipment of the Yangtze River defense networks, organized the common people and gave them military knowledge for time of war.[29]

On July 11, 1937, four days after the Marco Polo Bridge Incident, the Japanese Cabinet decided to dispatch the Kwantung Army, Chosen (Korea) troops, and local Imperial Divisions for the reinforcements in Northern China; at the same time, the Japanese Imperial Staff Headquarters prepared a Japanese Armed Forces Operational Plan for Central China for the purpose of annihilating the Chinese Air Force. On the 16th of July, the Commander of the Japanese Fleet in Shanghai suggested that at the beginning of hostilities all Japanese Air Forces should be used to choke China to death. On the 28th of July 1937, when Japanese troops attacked Peiping, the Japanese government ordered the evacuation of all Japanese people living in the upper reaches of the Yangtze River and instructed the Japanese Navy to protect the interests of Japan in the Middle and the Southern parts of China. On the 8th of August, Japanese Military Authorities issued the order of action.[30]

The Chinese Government facing these actions by Japanese troops held a national defense conference on August 6, 1937, in which the attendants were the governors and military commanders including the Governor of Szechwan Province, Liu Hsiang 劉 湘 (BDRC, Vol. II, 395-398), Governor of Yunnan Province, Lung Yun 龍 雲 (BDRC, Vol. II, 457-459), and Commander-in-Chief of Kwangsi Military Forces, Pai Chung-hsi 湯恩伯 (BDRC, Vol. III, 51-56). At the conference Chiang Kai-shek announced: "Based upon the adopted national defense guidance for long-term attrition warfare, we concentrate all the strength of China to carry out this plan for winning final victory. Also prepared were operational principles for defensive warfare: 1. Part of National Armed Forces will concentrate in northern China for sustained resistance, and special attention will be given to the protection of natural fortifications in Shansi province. 2. The main force of the national troops will be concentrated in eastern China to attack the enemy in Shanghai so as to safeguard the fortress of Wusung in Shanghai for the protection of Nanking. Besides, a minimum force will be sent to defend the ports along the coast of southern China."

The Chinese fought in strict accordance with the strategy of fighting a war of attrition. One hand was used to obstruct the offensives of Japanese troops, so as to wear them out. And the other hand was used to keep the main force intact and to delay the time of the decisive battle. As the Chinese troops were weak in materiel, they had to avoid decisive battles on the northern China plains.

From the purely strategic point of view, the Japanese had the advantage of sea transportation and high mobility, enabling them to coordinate their Army, Navy and Air Force. But China, lacking these advantages, was wise to take the advantage of lakes and mountains along the Yangtze River valley.

There are records of many times when the troops from northern China carried out aggression against Yangtze River and Hansui areas in the last one thousand years. Now, if unfortunately history should repeat itself, Japanese troops would take advantage of its high mobility to advance along the Peiping-Hankow railway direct to Hankow and would dispatch a unit from Loyang to block Tung-kuan, then China would be cut in two from East to West. Then the troops, civilians, and materials in the area of the lower reaches of the Yangtze River would not be able to withdraw to the western part of China, and the work of preparation in the Southwest and Northwest would be in vain. The strategy of sustained resistance could not be carried out. So the Chinese troops must induce the main force of the Japanese troops to be used in eastern China, but not in the area of northern China.

Shanghai was not only China's financial center, but also an international metropolis. When Japan had occupied Peiping and Tientsin without resistance, if Chinese troops did not defend Shanghai, it would be a disastrous loss of face. The Government would not be able to rally the support of the people. So the sacrifice of Chinese troops was necessary in its defense.

On August 9, 1937, a Japanese soldier was killed as he attempted to enter the Hungchiao Airfield. Both Chinese and Japanese were under great tension. Late at night on the 11th, Chang Chih-chung was ordered at once to lead his crack troops of the 87th and 88th Divisions to be stationed along the Nanking-Shanghai railway pushing toward Shanghai. On August 13, the war at Shanghai broke out. The Chinese Army and Air Force took the offensive at once. And the crack troops of the Central Government came to reinforce them from different places continuously. The results were: (1) The stubborn resistance of Chinese troops inspired the enthusiasm and dedication of the whole Chinese nation in resisting Japanese aggression. (2) The warlords of Szechwan, Kwangsi, Hunan, and Yunnan abandoned the old idea of preserving their strength, and decided to join the nation's "holy war," bringing about a real unification of China as never before in the present generation.[31] (3) On October 12 of the same year, President Roosevelt received Hu Shih in the White House, and expressed the hope that China would keep up the resistance to await the support of the world opinion.[32] Mamoru Shigemitsu pointed out that Japanese troops who landed at Wusung were engaged in bitter fighting and, even with bitter fighting, there was no way to make any advance. They suffered heavy losses and stuck firmly to Shanghai. As this battle took place without declaration of war and centered around the international metropolis and was launched by the forces of Japan's Army and Navy, the result was to arouse criticism of Japan in world opinion.[33] (4) Most of the machines, skilled technicians, and essential materials in factories in Shanghai and Nanking were moved to Hankow and thence to Sian or Chungking and gave support to the war of resistance.[34]

Even more important was the fact that Japan had dispatched five divisions to Shanghai at this time and later on transferred three divisions and one detachment from along the Peiping-Hankow Railway. As recorded by the War History of Japanese Forces: In October of this year, the General Staff determined to transfer the main force from northern China to Shanghai.[35]

The transference of Japanese troops from north China to Shanghai gave the Chinese troops there the needed time to guard the natural fort of Shansi.

Shansi Province surrounded by mountains, with other mountains in its interior, is like the ridge of a roof with reference to north China. Shansi, the most important strategic point, has always been the key area that the strategists have had to fight for in order to control Hopei Province to the east and Central China to the south. After Peiping and Tientsin were occupied by the Japanese, Shansi constituted the most important position where the Chinese Army could threaten the right flank of the Japanese Army in Hopei.

Two corps of the Chinese Army led by General Tang En-pai 湯恩伯 (BDRC, Vol. III, 225-228) contained, from the mountain zone in South Chahar, the Japanese Army in Peiping and Tientsin. From August 8, 1937, they fought for the position along the line from Chu Yung Pass to Nan Kou for eighteen days. Unfortunately, as Changkiakow (Kalgan) had fallen into enemy hands, the flank of General Tang's force was threatened. Hence, they could not but withdraw toward Shansi. The Japanese Army marched on the front line along the Great Wall in North Shansi.

Shansi was the second theater of war in China, and the Chinese Army there was commanded by General Yen Hsi-shan 閻錫山 (BDRC, Vol. IV, 47-50). In the days prior to the Sino-Japanese War, the national defense works were constructed along Niang Tsu Pass, Ping Hsing Pass, Yen Men Pass, Pien Pass South of the Great Wall. On September 22, 1937, when the Japanese Army marched at dawn near the said line of defense, Yen Hsi-shan ordered General Fu Tso-yi 傅作義 (BDRC, Vol. III, 47-51) to command the army at the front line at Ping Hsin Pass. The operation plan was: one division would defend the original position and two divisions would launch the attack on the advancing Japanese Army. Lin Piao 林彪 (BDRC, Vol II, 374-377), the division commander of the 115th Division of the 8th Route Army, commanded his troops to attack the enemy's rear. The attack was launched against the enemy according to the operation plan in the morning on September 25, 1937, with support of the Chinese Air Force. Lin Piao's troops cut off the Japanese communication line between Ping-Hsing Pass and Lin Chiu at noon of the same day. The Japanese Army with their reinforced strength marched continuously against the Chinese Army, who, however, attacked the enemy bravely with the support of the Chinese Air Force. From the operation order captured from the corpse of a Japanese major killed in the field, the Chinese Army ascertained the Japanese Army's plan of breaking through Ping Hsing Pass to threaten the rear area of Yen Men Pass. The battles lasted for five days. Owing to the action taken by the Japanese Army elsewhere, Yen Hsi-shan ordered the Chinese Army to shorten the defense line and retreat from Ping Hsing Pass.[36]

Generalissimo Chiang decided to move four-and-a-half divisions from the line along the Peiping-Hankow Railway to reinforce the Chinese Army in Shansi on October 1, 1937. The former arrived at Hsin Kou on October 12, 1937, and attacked the Japanese Army marching from the north toward south Shansi, where the Japanese Army's action was stopped. The troops who had marched from Szechwan to North China on foot participated in the Niang Tsu Pass Campaign on October 24, but failed to stop the enemy's attack. When the Japanese Army pressed near Taiyuan, the troops defending Hsin Kou could not but retreat from there. Taiyuan fell to the enemy on November 8, 1937, when the Chinese troops in the Shanghai field retreated from there at the same time.

The Japanese Army estimated that Shansi could be captured without fighting, and Japan could realize her scheme of the "Specialization of North China." But the result was to the contrary. After Taiyuan fell, Yen Hsi-shan led his troops in retreat into the mountain region in the southwestern part of Shansi, where he contained the Japanese Army till the end of the war, as the Japanese Army could not attack Shensi across the Yellow River.

Sun Tze said: "The clever combatant imposes his will on the enemy, but does not allow the enemy's will to be imposed on him."[37] The strategy of the Chinese Army, which compelled the Japanese Army to change their main attack direction, realized the supremely important principle of "holding the initiative position in operation." As the Japanese Army created the war in north China, the Japanese Navy in contending for credit could not help provoking the upheaval in Shanghai. Thanks to the early anticipation made by the Chinese authorities, the strategic principle, as taught by Sun Tze, was followed, namely "by holding out advantages to him, he can cause the enemy to approach of his own accord; or by inflicting damage, he can make it impossible for the enemy to draw near."[38]

The Japanese troops landing at the Bay of Hangchow forced the Chinese Army to retreat. Generalissimo Chiang considered this merely a "neglect" in the local strategy which did not affect the whole situation of the war, because the Chinese Army had decided the total war strategy of "retreating into the interior" long before. The fruit gained in three months of the Shanghai Campaign could cover this loss.

Clausewitz said: "Unity of plan, concentration of force is the basic principle of operation." The operation of the Japanese Army in Shanghai and north China violated this principle totally. Especially the determined resistance made by the Chinese Army rendered Japan's ideas of "the strategy for speed decision by applying overwhelming forces against the enemy" and even "the strategy for conquering China without fighting" completely unobtainable.

V

Trading Space for Time

The Chinese Army retreated from Shanghai, according to plan, directly to Nanking.

After Nanking fell in December 1937, in order to allow time for the defense of Wuhan, Chiang Kai-shek immediately set up a course of combat actions: (1) To transfer the seasoned troops for control of Wuhan and the border areas of Honan and Anhwei provinces; (2) A part of well-trained troops to be transferred from north China and the banks of the Yangtze to increase the strength in the middle part of Shantung Province and in regions south of the Huai River, to consolidate Hsuchow and to induce the main forces of Japanese troops to concentrate along the Tientsin-Pukow Railway so as to delay their advance toward the upper course of the Yangtze; at the same time, efforts were made to protect the north of Honan Province and the south of Shansi Province, north of the Yellow River, to prevent Japanese troops from crossing the Yellow River to threaten Hankow directly, and to initiate extensive guerrilla warfare for holding and exhausting Japanese troops.

Along the southern section of the Tientsin-Pukow Railway there are many streams, and its northern section passes through hills and valleys; thus there was a wide battlefield with complicated combat characteristics while the Japanese troops in north and central China had no supreme command. For these reasons, the Chinese troops could take advantage of these weak points of the Japanese troops.

In February 1938, when the Japanese troops began to take military action, Chinese troops were in danger at first. But upon arrival of reinforcements at the front line, they began to launch counterattacks on Japanese troops, fought them back and forced them to retreat to the south bank of the Huai River. This indicated that Japanese troops had no aggressive design; on the contrary, part of the Chinese troops were picked out to transfer to the northern section of the Tientsin-Pukow Railway, which was one of the factors resulting in the great victory of the Tai-Erh-Chuang   台兒莊   Engagement.[39]

On April 7, 1938, the Japanese Imperial Headquarters in Tokyo formally ordered Japanese Armed Forces in north and central China to launch an attack on Hsuchow. The objective was that once the Japanese troops in north and central China were linked up to storm Hankow, the

Chinese main forces would be defeated one by one. However, Chiang Kai-shek resolutely decided to move a part of the crack troops into the strategic Hsuchow convex angle to exploit battle results. He kept another army at Kueiteh and Lanfong in the north of Honan Province to safeguard the rear area of the 5th operational theater, with Hsuchow as the center, in the hope of diverting the attention of the Japanese troops.

Facing the concentration of seasoned Chinese trooops in these areas, the Japanese troops attempted to leave the north of Anhwei and Honan provinces to encircle Hsuchow but Chinese troops used the mobile retreat tactics of "dividing the integral into the individual," to withdraw the small fighting units from the line of combat through the gaps of the encircling Japanese troops, including the German-equipped heavy artillery units under command of General Tang En-pai. Thus the Chinese could familiarize themselves with the geographical surroundings, and could be supplied with food. But because of their heavy equipment, the Japanese troops moved with difficulty in the territory of a hostile nation. On the 19th of May, the Japanese troops occupied Hsuchow, but their attempt to encircle and annihilate Chinese troops had completely failed.[40]

On May 31, 1938, the Chinese troops were also evacuated westwards to avoid fighting a decisive battle with the Japanese troops on the plains in the east of Honan. On June 7, the Chinese troops broke the dam of the Yellow River, and converted the country into a lake so that most of the personnel and equipment of the Japanese troops were affected by the flood. From then on, the Japanese troops could not advance southwards along the Peiping-Hankow Railway because of the changed course of the Yellow River, ending their menace from north of Hankow.[41] Thus the Chinese troops got five months for combat readiness.

As soon as the Japanese had captured Nanking and Shanghai, Wuhan immediately became the political and economic center. The machinery of arsenals and cotton mills was removed to Szechwan and Shensi Provinces. However, it took much time to ship these materials from I-chang to Chungking by wooden boats.

The Japanese Army used more than thirteen divisions to invade Wuhan with navy and air force support. In early June of 1938, the Japanese troops at Hofei in Anhwei Province came out to attack from the south and the north of Ta-Pei Mountain where they turned around. Meanwhile, the actions of Japanese troops took place north of the Yangtze River. On July 26, 1938, the Japanese troops occupied Kiukiang, after Chinese troops had made a stubborn resistance. Then the Japanese gradually increased their strength on the south bank of the Yangtze with a push westward on both sides of the river.

After all, the Japanese military authorities underestimated the combat strength of Chinese troops and misjudged the dispositions of the latter.

Only because of superior air force, Japanese troops could push forward slowly in complicated terrain and sweltering summer heat. Early in the Wuhan external operations, Chiang Kai-shek had instructed General Chen Cheng 陳　誠 (BDRC, Vol. I, 152-160), Commander-in-Chief of the Wuhan War Theater, as follows: "The Japanese troops try to annihilate the main strength of the Chinese Armed Forces to end the war, but we must fight to the bitter end." Therefore, General Chen used sixty per cent of this total strength to fight this attrition war and kept forty per cent of it to serve as a basis of sustained operations in the future. It was estimated by General Chen that after occupying Wuhan, the Japanese troops needed longer time to consider their future plans, while the Chinese Armed Forces would have enough time to recover their strength. General Chen was originally scheduled to retreat from Wuhan at the end of August 1938, but because of the hesitation of the Japanese, he delayed the date of retreat to the end of September, and again to October, and finally to October 20, 1938.[42]

Ten months and twelve days were gained from the fall of Nanking and five months and six days from the Hsuchow retreat. The most important thing was that Generalissimo Chiang's strategy of changing the Japanese direction of attack from north toward the south, from east toward the west was successful eventually. From then on, China would no longer worry over her territory being cut vertically into two parts, and resistance could be achieved as planned in July 1935.

On November 25, 1938, one month after the Wuhan withdrawal, Generalissimo Chiang pointed out at the first Nanyueh military council 第一次南嶽軍事會議 : "As China is weaker than Japan, we should not give the enemy a chance to hit us twice, so we do not make the unalterable, permanent plan, and envisage the accurate strategy and apply it properly." Again he stated: "If we had not hit the enemy, smashed their plot, and exhausted their power, based on these strategies, but had fought against them with our whole army in the Peiping-Tientsin area after the Marco Polo Bridge Incident and the enemy's occupation of Peiping and Tientsin, the Republic of China would have collapsed. However, today when we have fought for seventeen months, not only can the Chinese Army continuously resist the enemy until they fall into the quagmire, but also our national spirit is getting higher and higher, and our conviction of final victory is getting firmer and firmer."[43]

Sun Tze said: "Hence the skillful fighter puts himself into a position which makes defeat impossible and does not miss the moment for defeating the enemy."[44] This strategic supremacy was gained at a great cost to the Chinese Army. But for the Japanese Army, when they occupied Wuhan and Canton, their strategy had reached its climax and the terminal of military offensive; but their hope of ending the war by conquering China with military means was not served. Moreover, the Japanese Army confessed that they were falling into the trap of long-range warfare.[45]

VI

Kang-Chan-Tao-Ti (Fight to the Bitter End) 抗戰到底

In prosecuting a modern war, it is essential not only to have a thorough knowledge of the enemy and of oneself, but also to understand the trend of international developments. Therefore, in July 1934, when Generalissimo Chiang spoke at the Lu Shan Officer's Training Corps on the topic "The Strategy of Retreating into the Interior," he pointed out: "It will take at least one month for Japan to occupy one of our provinces. Therefore, it will take at least eighteen months for them to occupy our eighteen provinces as a whole. During this period the international situation is bound to change a great deal, not to mention the fact that it is impossible for Japan to occupy one province each month!" He added: "Moreover, Japan was in no position to beat the great powers. Japan could not conquer China, and she could not gain mastery over Asia as long as she could not conquer China."[46]

Seeing Japan's tyrannical action and the League of Nations' failure, many well-known people in Europe and America became pessimistic. The Sixth Session of the Institute of Pacific Relations held in America in August 1936 was full of this type of attitude of defeatism. Dr. Hu Shih therefore spoke on the topic "The Changing Balance of Forces in the Pacific" at many American universities and colleges and published his address in the form of an article in *Foreign Affairs* (January 1937), pointing out that this defeatism represented a wrong view of the Pacific situation. The supremacy of Japan in the Far East belonged to historical fact, but the current situation, because of Japan's aggressive action, had resulted in the rise of three powers: (1) Soviet Russia's return to the Pacific as a first-rate military power; (2) the rapid rearmament of all the non-Asiatic nations bordering the Pacific or having possessions there; (3) the growth of a nationalistic China's resolve to resist external aggression.

Hu Shih emphasized: "In the new balance Japan is merely one of several factors. She therefore cannot be the only nation there. Evidently if these new factors are not properly organized, they may lead toward a terrible international conflagration. It might begin with a war forced on China by Japan's continued aggression, and gradually it might involve Soviet Russia, Great Britain, and ultimately the United States. In the modern world, war is truly as 'indivisible' as peace. No nation bordering on the Pacific, or interested in its fate, can hope to escape being involved in any major Pacific conflict."

Unfortunately, not more than a half year after this article was published, Japan's aggressive war against China broke out.

On September 26, 1937, Hu Shih flew to the United States of America, where he emphasized in his talks with American government officials and in his public addresses during the war that China had planned to resist Japan's aggression with supreme hard efforts and at all costs in a long war of even twenty or thirty years.

In October 1940, Hu Shih wrote a long telegram himself and sent it to the Minister of Foreign Affairs in Chungking: "My opinion is to work hard to support the war and to wait for the change of the international situation which will come about in time, a change of the situation of the world which will be beneficial to China. What I expect especially is the naval battle of the Pacific and the destruction of the Japanese Navy. This seems like something that can happen only in a dream. However, according to the events of history, peace talk between China and Japan is more difficult than war. It will not be certain that the Pacific Peace Conference will be carried out any easier than the carrying out of the naval battle of the Pacific. . . . The Japanese power is entirely supported by its Navy, and at the present time maybe they don't dare to stake all on a single throw."[47]

But only slightly more than a year later, the Japanese Navy did carry out its surprise attack on Pearl Harbor, and this action made the prediction of Hu Shih come true. It was the greatest of the many mistakes made by Japan since 1937. And of course it was a benefit to China, as it strengthened their determination to resist Japanese aggression to the bitter end.

Early on August 14, 1937, Generalissimo Chiang had declared: "Once the resistance to Japanese aggression had been carried out by the whole nation, there was only one way for us to follow and that was to resist to the bitter end with absolutely no compromise in the middle of the way." In the winter of 1938, Generalissimo Chiang made it more clear that *Kang-Chan-Tao-Ti* (to resist to the bitter end) meant the restoration of the situation as it was before the incident of Marco Polo Bridge took place. In the autumn of 1939, as the war in Europe broke out, Generalissimo Chiang made further explanation on the meaning of resisting Japanese aggression to the bitter end:

> Frankly speaking, our purpose in resisting Japanese aggression is to have the war ended with the war in Europe and the World War at the same time. In other words, it means that the Sino-Japanese problem will be solved as one of the world problems at the same time. . . . It does not

mean that the people of Europe even the people of the whole world should face the terrible war, but it just makes the fact more clear that today's world problem unfortunately has to be solved by means of war. The Sino-Japanese problem is not simply the problem between China and Japan: it is a problem of the whole of East Asia and also of the whole world. Furthermore, today's China problem really is the center of the problem of the world, so the only way to have the problem of China solved is to let it be solved with the other problems of the whole of East Asia or the whole world. Then it will be truly solved. . . . So, with respect to time, especially in the solution of the last problem, we have to make China's resistance to Japanese aggression connected with the World War.[48]

It was a firm and clear expression: China is a part of the world, sharing peace and danger in common, as well as joy and sorrow. The real meaning of resisting Japanese aggression to the bitter end was not only not to compromise with the enemy in the midstream, but also not to negotiate with the enemy singly. In fact, Chinese armed resistance to Japanese aggression began two years before the outbreak of the war in Europe, and the Sino-Japanese War was not ended until more than three months after the armistice in Europe.

Japanese militarists just kept their superficial point of view. When they could not reach their purpose to conquer China with their troops, they even wanted to use Wang Ching-wei as their tool to work with their troops to force China to submit to them and thereby attempt to end the so-called China Incident at the end of 1940.[49]

Early in April 1939, the *Ta-Kung-Pao* of Chungking and Hong Kong had published the intelligence information: A secret agreement had been made between Wang Ching-wei and Japanese Prime Minister Hiranuma Kiichiro; Japanese troops would attack and occupy Sian, Nanning, Changsha and other strategic points. On August 9, Wang Ching-wei again made a radio broadcast in Canton expressing the hope that the Cantonese General Chang Fa-kuei (BDRC, Vol. I, 56-61) would join him in governing South China.[50] On September 3, the war in Europe broke out. On the 12th, the Japanese set up the General Headquarters of the China Expeditionary Force in Nanking to command all Japanese troops in North China, Central China, among these the 11th Army stationed at the Wuhan area, the basic field combating troops of Japan, with the strength of more than two hundred and thirty thousand officers and men.[51]

In the period from September 16 to 23 of that year, Japanese troops launched offensives in Kiangsi and Hunan. It was the first main operation since their setting up of the China Expeditionary Force. It was the First Battle of Changsha.[52] But the Japanese, in their *War History of the Japanese Army* published after the War, merely stated it with no emphasis and called it "The Battle of Kiangsi and Hunan." In fact, in the complicated area of mountains of the area between Kiangsi and Hunan, the Japanese did not have close coordination among their operations. They were approaching in various directions but had not attacked the same place at the same time. Chinese troops on the first line in the north of Hunan carried out stubborn resistance and even fought separately and carried out counterattacks against Japanese troops. Such a strong will to fight was beyond the estimation of the Japanese troops. And the Chinese troops already had destroyed the railways and highways in the area between the north of Hunan and Changsha, and the cultivated fields were full of water. There were only the passes about half a meter wide which could be used to pass through. Consequently Japanese troop movement was greatly obstructed. So the Chinese troops got the necessary time to transfer to the mountain area in the north of Hunan. Japanese troops observed that the Chinese troops "made a great distance retreat operation," so they knew that they could not get the chance to break the main force of the Chinese forces. So they moved back on October 1 and had not carried out the offensive against Changsha. The front line commander of the Japanese troops did not agree with the attitude of the GHQ of Nanking that it had failed to issue the order to occupy the strategic point [Changsha] and defend it.[53]

At the same time, the main forces of Chinese troops were stationed in Hunan to prevent Japanese troops from coming back and attacking the famous area of food production. Meanwhile the Japanese had shipped their troops from Chingtao and Taiwan and landed them at Chinchow Bay, Kwangsi, on November 15 and occupied Nanning on the 24th.

The meaning of this confirms what Clausewitz said: "In all circumstance we have to think of war not as an independent thing, but as a political instrument. And only by taking this point of view can we avoid falling into contradiction with the whole of military history."[54] This battle in southern Kwangsi is an adequate illustration.

1. The main force of the invading Japanese troops that attacked Nanning was the 5th Division of which Itagaki Seishiro had been the commander before he was called back to Tokyo, 1938. He was appointed the head of the Japanese Army Ministry to fiddle the peace conspiracy tune, trying to charm the Chinese government. After a while, he was appointed General Chief of Staff of Japan's China Expeditionary Force to handle Wang Ching-wei's puppet regime. That Tokyo sent a division having a close tie with him to invade Kwangsi Province apparently had political meanings; especially when it was clearly stated in their papers that though the Japanese navy joined in this task, the army was in charge of conspiracy.[55]

2. General Pai Chung-hsi, Commander of Generalissimo Chiang Kai-shek's Field Command in Kweilin, and General Chang Fa-kuei 張發奎 , Commander of the 4th Combat Zone, both had anti-Chiang Kai-shek records in the past. These two generals were both proud of their military talents and had their own ideas of winning a war. Furthermore, General Pai had hired Japanese military advisors in 1934 to help him train his troops. Japanese army officers who used to be aware of the weak points of the Chinese people thought they could make good use of these factors to stir trouble among the Chinese commanding generals, not knowing that General Pai and General Chang were firmly standing with Generalissimo Chiang to fight against the Japanese invasion. The Japanese had General Pai's former advisors go with their troops into Nanning. They even found their former servants and attempted to resume their disrupted relationship.[56] General Chang Fa-kuei was a goal which Wang Ching-wei aimed at with his radio transmitter to call for "cooperation." Generalissimo Chiang understood this Japanese political trick very well. He knew that the Japanese were hoping for a split among Chinese commanding generals because of their threat. However, the Japanese did not know that the result they were going to get was just the opposite of what they expected.[57]

3. The Chinese 5th Army, one of the best equipped and best trained, was ordered to move into Kwangsi Province from Hunan. Other well-equipped and well-trained troops stationed in Szechwan, Kweichow, Hupei and Kiangsi were also ordered to move down to the south. The 200th Division of the Chinese 5th Army was equipped with German-made heavy automatic weapons. Its commander, deputy commander and chief of staff were all talented officers trained in European military academies. The Chinese armed forces made up their minds firmly to stop the Japanese moving forward and to strengthen the defense of Liuchow which was the hub of transportation and traffic in the south-western provinces. The 200th Division was in charge of attack to take over Kun Lung Kwan 崑崙關 then occupied by Japanese troops. They fired more than 2,000 rounds of 150mm howitzer shells into the Japanese stronghold.[58] It was the first strong artillery fire that the Chinese army maneuvered since the Battle of Shanghai in August 1937.

4. The Japanese had planned to occupy this area for good. They established a puppet regime and installed permanent telephone and electrical lines. But the pressure from the Chinese army was really heavy and an international road between Kwangsi and Vietnam was built. There was no meaning to hold this area any longer. Therefore, the Japanese withdrew to Vietnam in an attempt to cut off the international highway of China. It was another mistake the Japanese made in China which was one of the major factors to cause the confrontation between Japanese and the U.S. force.

This battle in southern Kwangsi made the Japanese realize the fact that it was difficult for them to force Chungking to give in on battlefields. Therefore, they changed their policy. Tokyo wanted to undermine the high morale of the Chinese troops by means of feigned peace talks. Chungking, on the other hand, was willing to take this opportunity to play a mock game with the Japanese in the hope of delaying the time when Tokyo was going to recognize Wang Ching-wei's puppet regime in Nanking. There was even an arrangement of holding a "Changsha Conference" at which Chiang Kai-shek, Wang Ching-wei and Itagaki Seishiro would talk face to face "to solve all the problems." By the time the Japanese found out they had been tricked by Chungking agents, ten months had already passed.[59]

During this time the Japanese were alternately using their peace conspiracy. They also carried out their fatigue bombing on Chungking, attempting to force China to give in. But their heavy bombing did not create the effect they expected. Contrary to their wishful anticipation, guerrilla wars and clean-up actions against them in both north China and south China became more active and more frequent than ever before.

In July 1941, the Japanese decided to take up an offensive attack against Hunan in September that year with multi-purposes: to give the Hunan Combat Zone a "great big hit," to occupy the two cities of Changsha and Chuchow, and to grab food and other supplies. Through careful mock-exercises and several plan amendments, they finally decided to use forty-five infantry groups, twenty-six artillery groups and six air force groups together with navy ships and field tanks. Their offensive started on September 18.[60] Far beyond their imagination, the Japanese met strong resistance from the Chinese army on their way from northern Hunan down to the south. Roads were purposely destroyed by the Chinese. Not only did the Japanese troops have difficulty in getting their supplies but also their judgment on the deployment of Chinese troops was not accurate. They often ran across Chinese armies and entangled themselves in surprising skirmishes.[61] They had to give up their plan of attacking the key city of Ping Kiang.[62] As a matter of fact, Chinese troops at that time had already got themselves well ready to launch a side attack from the mountain area northeast of Changsha. A part of the Chinese troops crossed by ferry from the west bank of the Hsiang River and launched a counterattack.[63] The Japanese were forced to withdraw.[64]

Whenever the Japanese occupied a certain place, they would put out propaganda saying that they had swept the Chinese troops and "reversed the original situation." In fact, Clausewitz had already pointed out that: "Even if an enemy's army, from sheer lack of provisions, starts to retreat, yet this retreat is still caused only by the restraint in which our sword holds that army."[65]

VII

Good Example of Retreating to the Inland

On December 8, 1941 (Japanese time), the Japanese carried out a surprise attack against Pearl Harbor and at the same time, according to the prepared plan, they attacked Hong Kong. For the purpose of embarrassing Japanese operations, the Chinese sent two armies to Kwangtung from Hunan. On the 13th, the Japanese decided to attack Hunan to obstruct Chinese troop movements. General Hsueh Yueh 薛　岳 (BDRC, Vol. II, 153-155), Commander of the War Zone of Hunan, before the offensive operation was carried out by Japanese troops, had already made the decision to lure the Japanese troops to the suburbs of Changsha, in order to enable the main force of Chinese troops lying in ambush in the mountain area northeast of Changsha to attack the flank of Japanese troops, to envelop them and cut their communication lines.

At that time I was working with the Chief of Staff in General Hsueh's Headquarters. I knew the development of the battle situation from the very beginning to the very end. After the battle, according to documents and papers obtained from the Chinese Army and Japanese troops and information from Japanese broadcastings, I wrote a record of the third battle of Changsha. After the Sino-Japanese War, in a chapter on "The Battles of Hong Kong-Changsha" of the *War History of the Japanese Army*, comparisons and quotations were made from my work. It proved that my record was correct. Japanese troops were lured to move forward into the trap of Changsha.

On December 24, Japanese troops launched the offensive. The next day Hong Kong was occupied. Chinese troops that were going southward by train immediately moved northward. At the same time, Chinese troops in the north of Hunan still resisted Japanese troops obstinately. On the 27th, Japanese Prime Minister Tojo Hideki delivered a report to the Diet, claiming that the Chinese troop movement southward was given up because of the threat of the offensive carried out by Japanese troops. At the same time, Japanese observation planes reported Chinese troops were retreating to Changsha. Japan's 11th Army commander Anami Korechika, who directed the battle, in spite of the intelligence information and the insufficient preparation of supply, made the unique decision himself and ordered Japanese troops to proceed fast toward Changsha.[66]

During that time, the garrison troops of Changsha had already been stationed in the fortified works, and the 150mm howitzers brought along with them to the mountain range west of Changsha were aimed at Japanese troops moving on.[67] This strategy can be explained by Sun

Tze's military doctrine: "Thus one who is skillful at keeping the enemy on the move maintains a deceitful appearance according to which the enemy will act. . . . By holding out baits, he keeps the enemy on the march; then with a body of picked men he lies in wait for the latter."[68]

The Japanese officers and men wanted to get there first and moved forward without rest. At noon on January 1, 1942, the Japanese 3rd Division started to attack the south suburb of Changsha. In the morning of January 3, the Japanese 6th Division started to attack the north suburb of Changsha.[69] Chinese troops defended their important points with strong resistance, and they were in the fortified works with good preparation in psychology and material. The 150mm howitzers and pack howitzers of the Chinese artillery on the mountains of the west of Changsha fired on the Japanese troops. The Japanese troops were short of ammunition, and their advance was checked. The Chinese troops in ambush in the mountain area northeast of Changsha appeared on the rear of the Japanese troops and cut the Japanese troops into pieces and enveloped them. The only way now open to the Japanese troops was to try their best to attack the point of the river crossing in order to carry out the retreat.

The 3rd Division of Japanese troops selected crack units for night combat and formed a battalion with Major Kato as commander to attempt breaking into the patrol line of the Chinese troops. But they failed, and Kato was killed by a Chinese soldier. From his body a piece of combat order was seized. General Hsueh Yueh found out about the Japanese strategy and their lack of ammunition. Very gladly he said: "The gaining of this piece of paper is better than ten thousand machine guns in reinforcement." Immediately he ordered the various units enveloping the Japanese troops to intensify their attack.[70]

The Japanese attempted to get Kato's body back and continued their attack, but the fire-power of the 150mm howitzers was too great, especially in the impact on Japanese morale. On the night of the 4th under heavy stress, Anami Korechika ordered the Japanese troops to "reverse" at once.[71] But due to the envelopment made by the Chinese troops, all units of Japanese troops escaped only by "bitter fighting" and "deadly combating." In the battle many regimental flags of the Japanese troops were cut or captured by Chinese troops.[72]

After ten days of rushing and dashing to the east and to the west, the Japanese troops escaped the envelopment of Chinese troops and moved northward.

After the war, the Japanese discussed the result and meaning of this battle and recognized that from the very beginning to the end, due to many mistakes, Japanese troops fell into all kinds of trouble and that the main reason which caused it was "the mistake made in the estimation of their [Chinese troops] strength and ours [Japanese troops]. . . . So in spite of the intelligence information and because of the insufficiency of supply, they moved step by step into the trap of the Chinese troops." In the whole battle, there were 1,591 Japanese troops killed in combat, 4,412 wounded, the loss being 2.5 times more than what had been suffered in the battle for the occupation of Hong Kong.[73]

The Japanese troops won every battle after the outbreak of the Pacific War except this one. Its meaning to the Allied Forces was significant: American and British troops could not check the advancing of Japanese troops, but Chinese troops made the first record to defeat Japanese troops. The author of "The U.S. Army in World War II" stated: "To the Chinese and their friends, Changsha was a name to conjure with."[74]

American writers respect General Hsueh Yueh as the "Tiger of Changsha" or "Tiger of Hunan."[75]

Three months later on April 18, 1942, James H. Doolittle led American planes to bomb Tokyo and other places in Japan. It was a big shock to Japanese troops and people, but they could find no answer as to where the American planes came from. When they captured five American pilots near Nanchang in Kiangsi, they discovered American planes had taken off from an aircraft carrier and that after the bombing of Japan, they flew to the airfield of Chuchow in Chekiang Province and landed there.

For the purpose of keeping the homeland in safety and to prevent American planes from using this kind of "wonderful method," the Imperial Headquarters of Tokyo issued an order to the China Expeditionary Forces on April 20 to use forces immediately and to destroy all the airfields in Chekiang thoroughly.[76]

The Japan China Expeditionary Forces decided to use eighty-seven battalions in this action. It was equal to the total strength used in the operation against various places in Southeast Asia. They planned to make pincer movement along the Hangchow-Nanchang Railway. On May 16, the Japanese Army started to attack Chinese troops in Chekiang. And on May 31, the Japanese started to attack Chinese troops south of Nanchang.[77]

The battle of Chekiang and Kiangsi took place when China, the United States, and Britain united to defend Burma and failed, and the Japanese were near to the border of Yunnan. To Generalissimo Chiang, it was more important to keep the security of the hinterland of the Southwest and the international communication line than to defend Chekiang and Kiangsi. So it was decided to keep a few units of the fighting forces on the west of the Hangchow-Nanchang Railway to carry out resistance.

Hereafter the guidance of operation of the Japanese Army especially emphasized the destruction of Chinese field armies and blockage of

Sino-American Air Force activities. American planes improved continually in quality and striking power. B-29s from the newly built airfield at Chengtu in Szechwan could reach Japan proper, Manchuria, and Taiwan with ease, whereas the Japanese Army did not have the capability to attack Szechwan.

In early August 1942, China, the U.S., and Britain cooperated in training new armies in the Ramgarh Training Center. Officers and men were selected and air transported there for the training (a total of 25,000 persons). This was for the recovery of Burma and a general offensive.

Japanese troops tried to reduce Chinese troop strength and to contain Chinese troops in Yunnan. On November 2, 1943, they used sixty-two battalions to attack Changteh of Hunan, threatening Changsha, Heng-yang, and Szechwan. Due to Chinese stubborn resistance, it was not until after twenty days of combat on external points that Japanese troops reached the suburb north of Changteh, and they began to attack the city. The defense troops met them with counterattack at once, and two battalion commanders of Japanese troops were killed right there.[78]

Changteh is my birthplace, and I know it well. Its city wall is used mainly to protect the city from the flood of the Yuan River. It had never been attacked with modern weapons. Now there were 13,000 men of the Chinese Army, inside and outside this city wall, resisting the Japanese invasion. On November 25, Japanese artillery concentrated their heavy fire upon this city and Japanese airplanes joined in too. The Chinese Army, with close air support from the U.S. 14th Air Force, fought back calmly and firmly. By noon on November 28, the Japanese Army on the north bombarded and forced open the north city gate and some soldiers swarmed in. They knocked open the east city gate and swarmed in the next day. The Chinese soldiers hid in houses and continuously resisted the invading Japanese Army on the streets. The invading Japanese burned civilian houses, and the Chinese Army fought against them from house to house. On December 2, the Japanese forced the rest of the protecting force to the southwest corner of the city, but the spirit of the Chinese Army was still high enough to wound a Japanese regimental commander. At dawn the next day, the Japanese began their all-out attack on every spot held by the defenders. The whole city fell into Japanese hands by noon that day.[79]

While the street fighting was going on in Changteh, the Japanese Army tried every means to block the south area of Changteh, hoping to halt the Chinese Army advancing from Changsha from the south in its effort to rescue Changteh. Both armies fought furiously. Although two division commanders of the Chinese Army were killed in action, the rescue troops marched on continuously. On December 8, the Chinese Army took the city back from the Japanese.[80]

Back on November 25, when the Japanese army began their all-out attack on Changteh, the Chinese Air Force together with the United States Air Force raided Japanese Hsinchu Air Field on Taiwan. (The Cairo Conference was in session at that time.) This air raid made the Japanese aware that the day the Allied Air Force was going to attack Japan proper might be near. Therefore, they decided to enforce their plan of operations on the Chinese mainland in an attempt to destroy all the Chinese-U.S. airfields. As soon as the Japan's China Expeditionary Forces GHQ received the report of the capture of Changteh, its commander immediately ordered the commanding general in front to keep it secure. However, the Japanese Army was sick and tired, and its casualty list was high. Moreover, the Chinese counterattack force from the south of Changteh was really strong. Thinking the pressure was unbearable, the Japanese commanding general in this theater ordered a wholesale retreat under the cover of night on December 11. Both the Japanese headquarters in Nanking and in Tokyo became very angry and gave strict orders to stop the retreat. They wanted the Japanese Army in the front to make an immediate attack to seize Changteh city and keep it in their possession. The Army general staff in the Japanese Operations Division flew to Nanking trying to save the worsening situation but in vain.[81] The Japanese were not able to carry out the order given to them by their high echelon to retake Changteh city again. This is similar to what Clausewitz said in his famous book: "Even if at the end of his aggressive course, when the enemy falls a victim to the difficulties of his attack, when detachments and hunger and sickness have weakened and worn him out, it is always only the dread of our sword that can cause him to turn about and let everything go."[82]

VIII

China Was Able to Pass a Very Severe Ordeal

From the fall of 1943, the U.S. ships and airplanes were very active in the Pacific. The possibility of bombing Japan proper and cutting off Japanese transportation on the seas grew daily. For the sake of her own safety, Japan decided to redouble their efforts on the Chinese mainland, planning to take hold of all the three main railroad trunk lines— Peiping-Hankow Railway, Hankow-Canton Railway and Hunan-Kwangsi Railway; to destroy completely all the Chinese-U.S. airfields along these railroads and to block off all United States air force activities.[83]

In order to carry out these operations of hers, Japan moved her ground force and newest airplanes originally defending Tokyo to the Hankow-Wuchang area in central China. Her airplanes, heavy guns,

and railroad reconstruction material and equipment in Manchuria together with the infantry and engineering corps there were all moved into
North China.[84] According to the Japanese war history, the total force
was as follows: Personnel: 510,000; horses: 100,000; artillery: 1,500;
motor vehicles: 15,000.

As the Japanese pointed out, there were 600 more guns than Japan
used in the Fengtien (Mukden) engagement in the Japanese-Russian
War of 1904-1905, and the personnel was doubled. The diameter of the
operations was many times that of the previous war. It was really a big
battle never seen by them before.[85]

On April 18, 1944, the Japanese Army crossed the Yellow River in
Honan Province by means of a hastily built steel bridge, and the
prelude of a big battle thus began. The Japanese had a tank division,
an infantry division, a cavalry brigade, and some artillery battalions,
totaling 148,000 troops, stampeding across the big plain in the Province
of Honan. The Chinese Army, meanwhile, fought to resist this strong
enemy force only with light arms. It was certainly difficult for them to
halt the invading enemy successfully. The Japanese took over the whole
Peiping-Hankow Railway on May 8, and the battle in Honan Province
ended on May 25.

On May 27, the Japanese force in central China started the attack on
Hunan and deployed the following troops and weapons: personnel:
362,000; motor vehicles: 9,450; horses: 67,000; tanks: 103; artillery: 1,282.

Both the fire-power and the mobility of the Japanese force in that
field were far superior to those of the Chinese. The Japanese this time
adopted a roundabout strategy and attacked first the mountainous region
northeast of Changsha. At the same time they swept the water mines
in Tung-ting Lake and the Hsiang River laid by the Chinese force.
Japanese ships transported 150mm howitzers to the waterfront opposite
Changsha city. They fired against the Chinese artillery battalion, attempting to silence them and to seize the city. Changsha fell on June 18, and
the Japanese hurriedly turned to raid the Chinese airfield in Hengyang.

The Chinese defending force in Hengyang skillfully made use of
streams, hills and even city walls to make up their defending lines and
successfully warded off three Japanese general attacks of combined fire
from the air and on the ground. They used grenades to force back the
Japanese 58th Division's soldiers who were specially trained in street
fighting. After a 47-day-long bitter fight, the Japanese finally occupied
this city.[86] However, it was just as the author of "U.S. Army in World
War II" stated, that this "victory" hardly helped the Japanese solve their
problems,[87] because they had a worsening situation in the Pacific theater
as a whole.

There were some in the Japanese Army, therefore, who doubted the
purpose of this big operation. Because it was at a time when Japan was

vigorously preparing to fight a decisive battle with American forces in the Philippine Islands, it would be more logical, they thought, that Japan should avoid any embroilment in other places and concentrate all her attention to the hot battle which would soon come on the South Pacific Islands and surrounding waters. However, there were others in the Japanese Army who thought this large scale operation was a cheerful light in the dark stormy sky that would be soon over. Therefore, they expected very much from these widespread operations.[88]

The Japanese troops were never stopped long in their invasion of Kwangsi Province. They took Kweilin and Liuchow on November 10 and then turned to the Kwangsi-Kweichow Railroad trunkline. On December 2, they attacked and occupied Tushan in south Kweichow.

The Japanese occupation of Tushan looked like the doom of the China theater for the Japanese were marching on to Kweiyang, and Chungking was dangerously threatened. But when one looked farther and wider at the other theaters in Africa, Europe and Southeast Asia as well as the battles on the high seas, one would be convinced that it was the very turning point from which the situation on the Chinese mainland was to change for the better. British Prime Minister Sir Winston S. Churchill agreed to the suggestion offered by President Franklin D. Roosevelt that very day that two divisions of the Chinese Army in the Burma theater be airlifted back to China to reinforce the defending troops around Kunming.[89] It was an indication that the Chinese Army attacking the Japanese Army from both India and Yunnan Province of China had successfully accomplished their missions and the international highway would soon be opened for supplies into the China theater. General Albert Wedemeyer began actively his work of training new Chinese troops. Meanwhile, Japan lost completely her gamble on December 25 when her navy lost all operational functions on the seas. The connecting tie between Japan proper and other resourceful areas in Southeast Asia was cut as a result. Not only had Japan lost all the supplies she needed for a modern war but also her allies in Europe. The Germans were on the brink of disaster.

Examining the result of these battles, the author of the Japanese War History book stated: "It is an undeniable fact that our offensive operations in Hunan and Kwangsi provinces brought great heavy losses to China. However, the plan of destroying all the United States airfields in China to protect the safety on Japan proper, which we expected when we first conceived the plan of operations, finally turned out to be unfulfilled or futile because we lost all the sea battles on the Pacific waters. From the operational point of view, those battles we fought were meaningless. It is especially bad that at a critical time when the United States forces were pouring into the areas of the South China Sea and East China Sea, the main part of the Japan's China Expeditionary Force was deep in the southwestern corner of the China mainland in a very unfavorable situation facing the United States attacking force from the east. Whatever the reasons for the (Japanese) invasion to Kweilin, Liuchow and other places in Southwest China were, they are controversial."[90] But the Japanese military authority in China at that time certainly was not as objective as we now are. They continued to pass deep into the mountainous region in western Hunan in an attempt to destroy the Chinese Army there, but they got no result except the tired and weary looks they saw in their soldiers.

There are three ways to end a war: 1) destruction of the enemy's military force, 2) conquest of the enemy's country, and 3) the subjugation of the will of the enemy. None of the three ways stated above was tried successfully in China by the Japanese. Through a war longer than seven years with the large scale battles fought in the Hunan-Kwangsi area, only one thing was tested and proved true: that China was able to survive a very severe ordeal. The Japanese tried all the three ways to end the war without any success. The Chinese total strategy of retreating into the interior and trading space for time was proved correct and successful.

As Clausewitz indicated in his famous book *On War*,[91] it was proven true and wise in the Chinese situation in this war against Japanese aggression.

During all the eight years of the Sino-Japanese War, neither the weapons and the equipment nor the training and the staff work of the Chinese forces were as good as those of the Japanese. There were inevitable mistakes in military strategies and in tactics. However, the highest principle of the whole war and the total strategy of the war were correct without question. On the contrary, the Japanese had no total strategy or general policy. They fought only by massive armed force.

Both Sun Tze and many distinguished generals in the Western world indicated that the art of war is just like the skill of cooking.[92] Tasteful dishes are cooked with well-proportioned seasonings. Comparing the chop suey you had many years ago with the now skillfully cooked Chinese dishes in a restaurant in San Francisco or New York City's Chinatown, you will find they are quite different. From the delicious dishes in a Chinese restaurant you will learn to understand the changes and the progress of the Chinese people in the years between the first Sino-Japanese War (1894-1895) and the second Sino-Japanese War (1937-1945). The strategy of trading space for time, drawing the enemy into a stalemate deep in the interior, finally succeeded, coupled with the psychological power which the Chinese people used in their "all-people" war against Japanese aggression through eight bitter years.

NOTES

1. Fujiwara Akira, "The Role of the Japanese Army," in *Pearl Harbor as History: Japanese-American Relations, 1931-1941*, eds., Dorothy Borg and Shumpei Okamoto (New York: Columbia University Press, 1973), pp. 191-93.
2. Hata Ikuhiko　秦郁彦 , and Usui Katsumi　臼井勝美 , *Taiheiyo sensō e no michi*　太平洋戦争への道　(The Road to the Pacific War), *Nitchu Sensō*　日中戦争 (The Sino-Japanese War) (Tokyo: Asahi Shinbun Sha　朝日新聞社 , 1963), IV: 23, 24, 70.
3. Masanori Ito　臼井勝美 , *Gumbatsu kōbō shi*　軍閥興亡史 (The History of the Rise and Downfall of Japanese Militarists) (Tokyo: Bungeishuju Sha　文藝春秋社 , 1958), pp. 1, 11.
4. Tsiang Fang-cheng　蔣方震 , *Kuo fang lun*　國防論　(On National Defense) (Taipei: Chung-hua Book Co., 1962), p. 62. For the development of education in the military field, cf. F. F. Liu, *A Military History of Modern China: 1924-1949* (Princeton, New Jersey: Princeton University Press, 1956), pp. 81-90.
5. Wang Jan-chi　王冉之 , *General Chiang Pai-li* (Tsiang Fang-cheng) *and His Military Thought* (A Ph.D. Dissertation at St. John's University, New York, 1971), pp. 133-36.
6. *Ku Hsien-yung Chuan*　辜顯榮傳　(Life of Ku Hsien-yung) (Taipei: Publication of the Committee of Ku Hsien-yung's Biography　辜顯榮傳記刊行會 , 1939), pp. 247-48.
7. Akira, "The Role of the Japanese Army," p. 192.
8. Sun Tze, *On the Art of War*, trans., Lionel Giles (London: Luzac & Co., 1910), p. 24.
9. *Chiang Tsung-tung chi*　蔣總統集　(President Chiang's Works) (Taipei: National War College, 1971), I: 792-811.
10. *Chung-Jih chan-chen shih-lueh*　中日戰爭史略　(The Outline of the History of the Sino-Japanese War) (Taipei: Military of Defense, Republic of China, 1962), II: 158. Also *Kang-chan chien-shih*　抗戰簡史 (A Brief History of the Resistance War) (Taipei: Ministry of Defense, Republic of China, 1952), pp. 6-11.
11. Lyon Sharman, *Sun Yat-sen, His Life and Its Meaning: A Critical Biography*, with an introduction by P. Van Slyke (Stanford, Calif.: Stanford University Press, 1968), pp. 66-68.
12. *Tsai Sung-pu hsien-sheng i-chi*　蔡松坡光生遺集　(Collected Works of Tsai Sung-pu), compiled by Liu Ta-wu　劉達武 (Taipei: Wen-hsin Book Co., 1962), p. 63.

13. Wang Jan-chi, *General Chiang Pai-li*, pp. 144-46, 173-181.

14. *Chiang Tsung-tung chi*, II: 2477.

15. F. W. Huang, *Global Strategy and Military Science* (Hong Kong: Asia Publishing Co., 1957), p. 46.

16. (A) Clausewitz emphasized repeatedly that defensive war is more advantageous than offensive war while Chinese military science says that the defender is the host and attacker the guest: the attacker's morale is high at first but weak later, whereas, the morale of the host is weak at first but strong eventually.

   (B) *On War* deals in a whole chapter with the advantages of retreating into the interior of the country [Karl Von Clausewitz, *On War*, trans. O. J. Matthijs Jolles (Washington, D.C., 1950)], pp. 446-456.

   (C) Clausewitz repeatedly emphasized the moral quantities in the War: the incredible influence as exemplified by history (*On War*, pp. 125-126) is especially favored by Chinese who adore the doctrine that spirit is more important than material and who would like to say our "*Tao*" (Way) is not exclusively our own belief.

   (D) Clausewitz further pointed out that Russia, in the campaign of 1812, has taught us that a nation of great dimensions cannot be conquered, and, secondly, that the probability of final success does not in all cases diminish in the same measure as battles, capitals and provinces are lost. He told the story that Prussians supported their government in fighting for their existence, as an illustration, saying, "These events have all shown what an enormous factor the heart and the sentiment of a nation may be in its total political and military strength" (*On War*, p. 165). This parallels what Sun Tze said without previous consultation too: "The moral law causes the people to be in complete accord with their ruler, so that they will follow him regardless of their lives, undismayed by any danger" (Sun Tze, p. 2).

17. Hu Shih copied the whole text of this letter in his diary. Columbia University has the microfilm of his diary.

18. The copy of this letter was offered by Wang Shih-chieh 王世杰 .

19. Chang Chi-yun 張其昀 , *Chung-hua Ming-kuo shih-kang* 中華民國史綱 (An Outline of the History of the Republic of China) (Taipei: Chung-hua wen-hua ch'u-pan shih-yeh wei-yuan hui, 1954), IV: 134.

20. *Ibid.*, IV: 211.

21. *Mao Tse-tung hsueh-chi* 毛澤東選集 (Selected Works of Mao Tse-tung) (Peking: Jen-min ch'u-pan she, 1971), p. 461.

22. Yao Tsung-wu: (A) "The Great Expedition against Shu (Modern Szechwan) led by Emperor Hsien Tsung, or Mangu Khan, of the Yuan Dynasty; and his death at the battle of Tiao-Yu-Ch'eng near Hochow," in *Bulletin of the College of Arts* (Taipei: National Taiwan University, November 1965), No. 14. (B) "Yu Chieh: A Critical Biography," in *Essays Dedicated to Mr. Li Chi on His Seventieth Birthday* (Taipei: Tsing Hua Journal of Chinese Studies Press, 1967), Part II. (C) "Notes on the Battles of Tiao-Yu-Cheng between the Sung and the Mongols," in *Bulletin of the Institute of History and Philology* (Taipei: Academia Sinica, 1958), Vol. XXIX. Yao pointed out: "European scholars know very little about this war between the Southern Sung Dynasty and the Mongols, especially facts on the fortified cities built by Yu Chieh, and the truth of the death of the brave Mangu Khan on the battlefield of Tiao Yu Cheng, near Chungking." During the Sino-Japanese War many Chinese scholars visited the remains of Tiao Yu Cheng impregnable mountain fort near Chungking, which Mangu Khan was unable to carry. See Kuo Mo-Jo, "A Visit to the Old Site of Tiao Yu Fortress" (*Shuo-wen Monthly*, III, No. 7, August 15, 1942, Chungking) and Fan Hao, "A Survey of the Relic of Tiao Yu Ch-eng" (*The Eastern Miscellany*, XXXX, No. 13, July 15, 1944, Chungking).

23. Chang Chi-yun 張其昀, "Chan-lueh chih li-lun yu shih-chien hsin" 戰略之理論與實際性 (The Theory and Practicalness of Strategy) in *Chung-kuo chin-tai shih lun-tsung* 中國近代史論叢 (The Collected Works on Chinese Modern History) (Taipei: Cheng Chung Book Co., 1963), IX: 145-48.

24. Chiang Kai-shek, *Omei hsun-lien chih* 峨眉訓練集 (The Records of Omei Training Corp.), p. 16. Also, Huang Shao-hung 黃紹竑, *Wu-shih hui-yi* 五十回憶 (Reminiscences at Fifty) (Hangchow: Yun-feng Press 雲風出版社, 1945), pp. 306-7.

25. Chang Chi-yun, *Chan-lueh chih li-lun yu shih chien hsin*. Ku Tsu-yu traveled even more places in the end of the Ming Dynasty in China than the famous traveler Hsu Hsia-ko (ECCP, 314-16). Based on the records in books and the facts he gathered, he wrote the famous book *Tu-shih fang-yu chi-yao* 讀史方輿紀要 (Essentials of Historical Geography) (ECCP, 420). In the book he praised the skill of the Mongols in their use of strategy very much. Japanese scholars have done some basic work in this field. For instance, Hogama Sadao edited "The Index of Essential Historical Geography —The General Reading of Names of Places of China in Different Dynasties"; in the winter of 1938, the Japanese Government established the Asia Development Board, then translated the book *Sheng*

wu chi 聖武記 (ECCP 851) into Japanese and published it. But the skill of the Manchu (Ching Dynasty) in using strategy and military forces was far behind the Mongols.

26. *Pai-tuan ta-chan te-chi* 百團大戰特集 (Special edition of One-Hundred Regiment's Battle), ed., Political Department of the Eighth Route Army.

27. *Gendaishi shiryo* 現代史資料 (Source Materials for Modern History), comp., Usui Katsumi, Inaba Masao 稻葉正夫 (Tokyo: Misuzu Shobo みすず書房, 1964), VIII: 219-27.

28. Matsumoto Shigeharu 松本重治, *Shanghai jidai* 上海時代 (The Shanghai Period) (Tokyo: Chuokoron Sha 中央公論社, 1974), II: 261-68.

29. *Kang-chan chien-shih*, pp. 43-44.

30. *Gendaishi shiryo*, IX: 185-205.

31. *Kang-chan chien-shih*, pp. 11, 12, 45, 53. Also *Chung-jih chan-chen shih-hueh*, p. 169; Chen Cheng, *Pa-nien Kang-chan ching-ku kai-yao* 八年抗戰經過概要 (The General Sketch of the Eight-Year Sino-Japanese War) (Nanking: Department of Defense, Republic of China, 1947), p. 9; *Chen-fu Tsung-tung chi-nien chih* 陳副總統紀念集 (A Memorial Record of Vice President Chen) (Taipei: Committee for Vice President Chen's Funeral Service, 1965), p. 19 and *Wu-shih hui-yi*, p. 336.

32. *Chung-Jih wah-chiao shih-liao tsung-pien* 中日外交史科叢編 (Publication of Sino-Japanese Foreign Affairs Source Materials) (Taipei: Foreign Policy Council of Republic of China, 1966), IV: 362-63.

33. Shigemitsu Mamoru 重光葵, *Showa no doran* 昭和の動亂 (The Disorder of the Showa Era) (Tokyo: Chuokoron Sha, 1952), Ch. V.

34. Lin Chi-yung 林繼庸, *Ming-yung Chang-Kuang Nui-chien chi-yao* 民營廠礦內遷紀要 (A Brief Record of Inward Movement of Private Factories and Mines) (Chungking: National Resources Commission, Ministry of Economic Affairs, 1942).

35. *"Hokushi no chian sen (1)"* 北支の治安戰 (The Peace-Keeping Warfare of North China) in *Senshi sōsho* 戰史叢書 (The Series of War History), ed. by Nippon Boeicho Senshi Shitsu 日本防衛廳戰史室 (Tokyo: Asagumo Shimabun Sha, 1968), No. 18, p. 25.

36. *"Hokushi no chian sen (1),"* pp. 37-40. Also *Tai-yuan hua-chan* 太原會戰 (The Engagement of Taiyuan) (Taipei: Department of Defense, Republic of China, 1966).

37. Sun Tze, p. 42.

38. *Ibid.*, p. 43.

39. *Kang-chan chien-shih*, pp. 54-63. Also, *"Hokushi no chian sen (1),"* p. 61. With regard to this battle, Frank Dorn pointed out: "For the first time since their attempted invasions of Korea under Hideyoshi had resulted disastrously in 1592-98, the Japanese had been forced to swallow the bitter pill of a major defeat at the hands of a despised opponent." [*The Sino-Japanese War 1937-41: From Marco Polo Bridge to Pearl Harbor* (N.Y.: The Macmillan Co., 1974), p. 157.]

40. *Chung-Jih chan-chen shih-lueh*, II: 215-17. Mao Tse-tung remarked: "The mistakes made by Japanese troops were due to the fact that they made many envelopments but seldom broke the Chinese troops. Chinese troops tried to avoid any decisive battle with Japanese troops, as in the case of the retreat from Hsuchow, to make the Japanese plan to end the war fast in vain" (*Mao Tse-tung hsueh-chi*, p. 496). Cf. also *Chung-Kuo lu-chun Ti-shan Fang-mei Chun Kang-Chan chi-shih* 中國陸軍第三方面軍抗戰 紀實 (A Record of Operations Carried Out by the 3rd Army Group in the Sino-Japanese War) (Taipei: World Book Co., 1962).

41. After the Hsuchow battle, the North China Front Army, in accordance with ancient Chinese strategy, strongly proposed to attack from Cheng Chow down south along the Peiping-Hankow Railway. However, this plan was not carried out due to rejections by Imperial Headquarters and flooding of the Yellow River (Cf. Taiheiyo sensō e no michi, IV: 51). Also, Tsao Chu-jen 曹聚仁 , *Chung-Kuo Kong-chan Hwa-shih* 中國抗戰畫史 (Pictorial History of China's War of Resistance, Shanghai, China, 1947), p. 171; and *Tsai-fang Wai-Chi* 採訪外記 (A Side Report 香港創墾 社刊 , 1962), p. 202.

42. Chen Cheng, *Ti-chiu chan-chu Wuhan huei-chan Chan-tou hsiang-pao* 第九戰區武漢會戰戰鬥詳報 (A Detailed Report of Combat in the Battle of Wuhan, 9th War Zone), 1939.

43. *Chiang Tsung-tung chi*, I: 1058-59.

44. Sun Tze, p. 30.

45. *"Taiheiyo sensō no e michi,"* IV: 54, 58, 59.

46. *Chiang Tsung-tung chi*, I: 798.

47. Hu Sung-ping 胡頌平 , *Hu Shih-tse hsien-sheng nien-pu Chien-pien* 胡適之先生年譜簡編 (A Simplified Biography of Hu Shih) (Taipei: Academia Sinica, 1971), pp. 54-55; *Chung-Jih wah-chiao shih-liao tsung-p'en*, IV: 343-44. Mao Tse-tung, in the article "Long Lasting War," remarked: "In the third phase, the enemy would carry out the retreat movement and defensive measures, and we would carry out strategic offensive. To recover the lost land, it would not be enough to depend just on our

own force; we would still need the assistance of the international force and the internal change of the enemy; otherwise, we would not get the victory. So it put more weight on the work of international propaganda and foreign affairs" (*Selected Works of Mao Tse-tung hsueh-chih*, p. 455). In the preface of the English edition of "Long Lasting War," Mao emphasized the importance of international assistance very much. It could be seen that Chinese in all fields put their attention on the international situation and international aid. Hu Shih rendered much help in this field. He, on the one hand, made speeches in America and Canada to explain that "China is fighting to defend a way of life" and at the same time, he mailed letters and sent telegrams to the homeland to point out the idea of the people in the West: "To help the man who helps himself," and "It is not worthwhile to help the man who failed." So, many times he emphasized: "To bear hardship and wait for the change of the international situation." In the eight years of the Sino-Japanese War, Chinese forces retreated under the total strategy of "retreating into the interior," but all the time kept the organized resistance and strategic offensive.

48. President Chiang Kai-shek points out first in his speech: "We made a determination at first—from the beginning of the Sino-Japanese War till now and until the future when we get the final victory, from the first to the end—we have to struggle independently and to exist on our own force, without regard to the respect which we gained from nations by the spirit of self-reliance and independence, and the effort we put into world peace and righteousness. All nations which support righteousness and peace-loving, for the spirit of their own country, will come and support us" (*Chiang Tsung-tung chi*, II: pp. 1189-1192).

49. *"Taiheiyo sensō e no michi,"* IV: 63-65.

50. *Ta Kung Pao* (Hong Kong, April 6, 1939), p. 3; John Hunter Boyle, *China and Japan at War, 1937 to 1945: The Politics of Collaboration* (Stanford, Calif.: Stanford University Press, 1972), p. 231.

51. *"Hong Kong Chosa sakusen"* 香港長沙作戰 (The Battle of Hong Kong and Changsha) in *Senshi sōsho* (Tokyo: Asagumo, 1971), No. 47, pp. 342-52.

52. Chao Tseng-chou 趙曾傳 , ed., *Kang-chan chi-shih* 抗戰紀實 (The Records of the Resistance War) (Taipei: Commercial Press, 1961), II: 49-115. Cf. *Foreign Affairs Bibliography, 1952-1962* (New York: R. R. Bowker Co., 1964), p. 619. Also Frank Dorn, *The Sino-Japanese War*, pp. 269-283.

53. *"Hong-Kong Chosa sakusen,"* pp. 345, 355.

54. Clausewitz, *On War*, pp. 17-18.

55. *Gendaishi shiryo*, IX, p. 418.

56. Masanori Ito, *Gumbatsu kobo shi,* pp. 153-58.
57. Chang Chi-yun, *Chung-hua Ming-kuo shih-Kang,* V: 14.
58. *Kwei-nan huei-chan* 桂南會戰 (The Engagement in Southern Kwangsi) (Taipei: Department of Defense, Republic of China).
59. Gerald E. Bunker, *The Peace Conspiracy: Wang Ching-wei and the China War, 1937-1941* (Cambridge: Harvard University Press, 1972), pp. 240-43.
60. *"Hong Kong Chosa sakusen,"* pp. 382-83.
61. *Ibid.,* pp. 395-400, 420, 445-46, 455.
62. *Ibid.,* p. 423.
63. *Ibid.,* pp. 473-74. Also *Kang-chan chi-shih,* III: 132-38.
64. *"Hong-Kong Chosa sakusen,"* pp. 475-76; Frank Dorn, *The Sino-Japanese War,* pp. 363-70.
65. Clausewitz, *On War,* p. 346.
66. *"Hong Kong Chosa sakusen,"* pp. 581-84.
67. *Ibid.,* p. 586; *Kang-chan chi-shih,* IV: 179-82.
68. Sun Tze, p. 40.
69. *"Hong Kong Chosa sakusen,"* pp. 587-590.
70. *Ibid.,* pp. 594-95; *Kang-chan chi-shih,* IV: 184-90.
71. *"Hong Kong Chosa sakusen,"* pp. 599, 610.
72. *Ibid.,* pp. 613-38.
73. *Ibid.,* p. 658.
74. Charles F. Romanus and Riley Sunderland, *Stilwell's Command Problems* (Washington, D.C.: Office of the Chief on Military History, Department of the Army, 1956), p. 372.
75. Barbara W. Tuchman, *Stilwell and the American Experience in China, 1911-1945* (New York: The Macmillan Co., 1971), pp. 278.
76. *"Showa ju-shichi, hachi-nen no shina hakengun"* 昭和十七、八年の支那派遣軍 (China Expeditionary Forces in 1942-1943), *Senshi sōsho* (Tokyo: Asagumo Shinbun Sha, 1972), No. 55, p. 129.
77. *Ibid.,* pp. 117-212.
78. *Ibid.,* p. 465.
79. *Ibid.,* pp. 515-17.
80. *Ibid.,* p. 531; *Kang-chan chi-shih,* IV: 48-54.
81. *"Showa ju-shichi, hachi-nen no shina hakengun,"* pp. 526-37; Romanus, *Stilwell's Command Problems,* pp. 21-22.
82. Clausewitz, *On War,* p. 346.
83. *"Kanan no kaisen"* 河南の會戰 (Battle of Honan) in *Senshi shōsho* No. 4 (Tokyo; 1967), *"Konan no kaisen"* 湘南の會戰 (Battle of Hunan), No. 16, pp. 11-14, 19-22.
84. *Ibid.,* pp. 70-77.
85. *Ibid.,* pp. 48-51.
86. *Ibid.,* pp. 242-66, 353-91; *Kang-chan chi-shih,* IV: pp. 92-101.

87. Romanus, *Stilwell's Command Problems*, p. 405.
88. *"Kanan no kaisen,"* pp. 556-57.
89. Charles F. Romanus and Riley Sunderland, *Time Runs Out In CBI* (Washington, D.C.: Office of the Chief on Military History, Department of the Army, 1959), pp. 144-47; Albert C. Wedemeyer, *Wedemeyer Reports* (New York: Henry Holt, 1958), pp. 328-31. Winston S. Churchill, *Triumph and Tragedy: The Second World War* (New York: Bantam, 1962), pp. 171-71.
90. *"Koosai no kaisen"* 廣西の會戰 (Battle of Kwangsi) in *Senshi sōsho* No. 30 (Tokyo: 1969), p. 699.
91. Clausewitz, *On War*, p. 581.
92. Sun Tze, p. 36. Also, Andre Beaufre, *An Introduction to Strategy*, trans., R. H. Barry, with a preface by B. H. Liddell, (New York: Frederick A. Praeger, 1965), Ch. V.

❋   ❋   ❋

On page 38, note that ECCP refers to *Eminent Chinese of the Ch'ing Period*, ed., Arthur W. Hummel (Washington, D.C.: U.S. Government Printing Office, 1944) and likewise in other pages of the text. On page 38 note that BDRC refers to *Biographical Dictionary of Republican China*, ed., Howard L. Boorman (New York: Columbia University Press, 1968) and likewise in other pages of the text.

Comments (1):

BY WILLIAM W. WHITSON

Before commenting on Prof. Hsiang-hsiang Wu's paper on "Total Strategy Used by China and Some Major Engagements in the Sino-Japanese War of 1937-1945," it may be useful to set the stage with a brief discussion of alternative strategies hypothetically available to the defense of China and an even shorter reminder of the phases through which China's WW II defenders switched from one strategy to another.

Chart A portrays eight alternative strategies by which China might be defended. A national leadership's choice among these alternatives would ultimately be governed by three sets of factors: strength relative to the enemy; mobility relative to the enemy; and a degree of national unity.

CHART A

Model	Strategy	Defensive—Offensive	Offensive—Defensive
I	National Static		
II	National Mobile		
III	Regional Mobile		
IV	Regional Static		

A leadership which commanded the unquestioned loyalty of all regional leaders could choose among the four alternative national strategies labelled Models I and II on Chart A. A leadership which could not rely on the support of all regional leaders would be forced to focus on Models III and IV.

As long as a unified national leadership could control major lines of communication (railroads and waterways in China), a mobile strategy would be plausible. Once those lines were interdicted, a shift to regional models (II or III) or national static-warfare (Model I) would be necessary.

Faced by militarily superior invaders, either at the regional or the national level, a Chinese high command would be well-advised to employ a mobile defensive-offensive (D-O) strategy. That is, a preferred strategy would require a first phase strategic withdrawal aimed at overextending the invader's supply lines. The second phase would involve a massive counteroffensive after the defender had been able to stabilize a front, consolidate power and demoralize enemy will through a long war of attrition.

This is not to say that the strategy of national (regional) pre-emption (the offensive-defensive: O-D) would be totally foreclosed to a weak defender. Depending upon the invader's sense of confidence, the defender might attempt a bluff—an aggressive strike against the invader's weakest front in hopes of delaying the invader's schedule for invasion. Such a bluff would require confidence on the part of the defender: confidence based *at least* on a sense of national (or regional) unity plus control of interior lines of communication. In general, without such political unity *and* mobility, the defender would be well advised to avoid all four strategic options under the Offensive-Defensive column on Chart A.

Conversely, a Chinese force which was equal or marginally superior to the invader could be employed in all eight strategic alternatives. However, assuming political unity *and* mobility, the defender might make best use of available resources by avoiding *all* regional options in the early stages of the war, concentrating instead on one of the four national options. Indeed, armed with some surplus strength, the defender might be well advised to strike the invader's *main* attack with a pre-emptive, superior force. If successful, the pre-emptive, "spoiling" offensive might end the war immediately. If the attack failed, the post-attack options could still include six other strategic alternatives at the national and regional levels.

In these terms, what were the conditions confronting China's leadership in 1937? With respect to political unity, aside from a continuing measure of regionalism—if not outright residual warlordism, the Chinese Communist Party's concentration of adversary military and political power in northwest China diverted substantial resources from Nanking's available reserves. The post-Sian United Front agreements represented a very tenuous working alliance, providing no assurances to the national leadership in Nanking.

With respect to mobility, all Chinese military forces were constrained not only by a primitive rail net but also by a shortage of wheeled and tracked vehicles.

Finally, China's national army, in general, could not compare with that of Japan either quantitatively or qualitatively (unless one included all militia and local forces in China in 1937!).

Faced with those conditions, how did China's leadership, including Communist leaders in Yenan, choose among the alternative strategic defensive options?

First, it is clear that all four Offensive-Defensive options were rejected at the outset. Thanks to their temporary control of interior rail nets and waterways, and a temporary sense of national unity, the leadership logically chose Model II, the national mobile, defensive-offensive strategy. This strategy bought approximately two years of time for the Nanking leadership. By late 1939, however, all three of the major factors had changed and demanded a change in strategy.

Of the three factors, the most important was that of political unity. By late 1939, Communist and Nationalist leaders were barely on speaking terms. Their armed forces (both regular and guerrilla) cooperated rarely and had already fought each other in isolated actions. The Nationalist leaders were beginning to erect a blockade line along the Yellow River to attempt to control Communist access to military material. In East China, guerrilla competition for rural support was eroding the viability of the United Front.

With respect to mobility, by late 1939, all north-south rail lines were in Japanese hands or were so unreliable that a mobile strategy was largely precluded to the Nationalists.

Finally, Chinese military strength had increased substantially relative to the strength that the Japanese could mobilize nationally (although Japanese military superiority could be achieved regionally).

Under the circumstances, the autumn of 1939 brought a shift in strategy south of the Yellow River to Model IV, a regional static strategy in which local Nationalist War Zone commanders were held responsible (through a defensive-offensive) for holding the line in their respective regions. North of the Yellow River, the Communists also pursued a regional static strategy aimed at holding a line generally east of the Hopeh-Shansi provincial border, while recruiting and training an expanding regular army. By September 1940, the Red Army was capable of fielding over 400,000 men in the 100 Regiments Campaign in Shansi to attempt to block a Japanese offensive aimed at Shansi and threatening Yenan.

During the next fifteen months (Sept. 1940-Dec. 1941), the Communists paid for their audacious confrontations with the Japanese, who launched their "three-all Campaign." In December 1941, Yenan officially changed their defense strategy to a regional mobile strategy (Model III) requiring thousands of small-unit strikes against the Japanese. During the same period, the Nationalists successfully held the line, despite several major—and locally successful—Japanese offensives. Thus, Red Army weakness north of the Yellow River precluded their continued employment of Model IV and forced them to adopt the only strategy appropriate for the very weak: the regional, mobile defensive-offensive.

It was not until 1945 that conditions permitted both Nationalists and Communists to launch regional counter offensives against the Japanese occupier, seriously weakened by both the war on the China Mainland and the war in the Southwest Pacific.

Chart B summarizes the Chinese experience in the Sino-Japanese War.

CHART B

1937-1939:   National Mobile, Defensive-Offensive

1940-1941:   Regional Static, Defensive-Offensive

1942-1945:   Regional Static, Defensive-Offensive   (Nationalist)
             Regional Mobile, Defensive-Offensive   (Communist)

1945   : Regional Counter-offensive

Professor Wu's excellent paper portrays much of the foregoing, especially in its description of the early rationale leading to the national defensive-offensive.

The paper would perhaps be more balanced if more consideration were given to the critical period of 1940-41, when a changing set of circumstances forced Communist leaders north of the Yellow River to adopt a different regional strategy (mobile) from that appropriate for Nationalist leaders south of the Yellow River.

Comments (2):

BY CHIAO-MIN HSIEH

China has been invaded many times by her neighbors and has been conquered twice. But those invaders and conquerors were nomads who entered China by land. The first time that continental China was invaded by a sea power on a large scale was in 1937, when a naval attack by Japan started eight years of war, 1937-45, between the two countries.

At that time China had almost no navy, and her army was composed mainly of infantry, with few tanks, little artillery, and slight air support. Her coastline was totally blockaded; her industrial cities, most of them located on the coast, were overrun; and her railroads and navigable rivers fell into Japanese hands. Under these circumstances the Chinese could only fight and retreat. And so, they developed a policy of "trading space for time" and "accumulating minor successes for forming a major victory," and even planned to carry out a "scorched earth" type of resistance.

In August 1937, the Chinese defenders of Shanghai resolutely confronted the Japanese invaders in the bloodiest battle that the world has seen since Verdun in World War I. After inflicting as much damage as possible upon the enemy, China moved her government a thousand miles inland, from Nanking to Chungking, from which to carry on the seemingly hopeless fight. It was as if the United States had moved her capital from Washington to Omaha, Nebraska.

In this resistance against the Japanese, China had three assets—her space, her manpower, and her courage. As one military commentator has pointed out:

> The vast distances of China and the rugged character of the country are among the important points which favour its defense against invasion. Other major factors are the ability of the people to endure hardship, to be content with meagre rations, and to live in relatively self-sufficient economic groups. The prevalence of a philosophy which emphasized pride in race, love of family, and the desire to be revered by their children is another important asset.

The Japanese had been very shortsighted and had made a big mistake in their strategy. The coastal plains are the location of the great cities, which were economic and cultural centers; and large populations were concentrated there. The Japanese thought that if they could seize the cities of Peking and Tientsin in north China, Nanking and Shanghai on the Yangtze River, and Canton on the Si River, China would immediately bow to her. Therefore, according to the Japanese plan, the war in China would end within three months, and the Japanese would win. But the Japanese knew little of Chinese history. They had not learned how the Mongols in the thirteenth century and the Manchus in the sixteenth had conquered China by entering the interior of China and using an encircling strategy. If the Japanese at the beginning had landed on Hainan Island, penetrated southwest China, and entered Szechwan, the Chinese would have had no stronghold for resistance and would have had no place to which they could retreat. China would have had no hope for resistance but would have had to surrender.

When China moved her capital to Chungking in 1939, she established her stronghold in the interior of the country. The Szechwan basin was then the base for resistance. Szechwan Province, as big as Poland, is very rich in agricultural production—especially the Chengtu plain, which is one of China's rice granaries. With 70 million people living in the basin, there was no difficulty in recruiting soldiers.

The interior of China is very rugged; this configuration was a great obstacle for the mechanized Japanese Army. When the Japanese were checked at Tungkwang at the bend of the Yellow River in north China, at the Yangtze Gorge at I-chang, and by the north-south range of mountains on the border between Indochina and southwest China, the Szechwan basin—surrounded by the mountains—was a really protected place; and the Japanese found great difficulty in attacking that stronghold. The only thing the Japanese could do was to blockade the coastline and try to cut off China's supplies from the outside world. Fortunately, there were two transportation lines, which kept China from being totally isolated from the rest of the world and allowed her to receive the necessary war supplies. In the northwest there was a 2,000-mile-long supply route connecting China with the Soviet Union. In the southwest, from the province of Yunnan to Burma, was the Burma Road, which connected China with the Indian Ocean. By this route China could receive aid from the United States, Britain, and other Western countries.

As is noted above, the rugged terrain of western China was indeed a handicap for the Japanese. At the beginning of the war, the Japanese with tanks and other mechanized equipment captured the plains along China's east coast. In November 1938, after sixteen months of invasion, the major cities along the three great rivers—the Yellow, the Yangtze, and the Si—were all in Japanese hands.

Later, when the Chinese had retreated westward to the mountainous interior, the Japanese could not easily occupy much additional land, although they did seize railroad lines. The river gorges and mountain passes defended by the Chinese became formidable obstacles. During this stage, the Japanese were unable to seize railroad lines; however, they were able to capture certain strategic cities.

In the last stage of the war, the Japanese were able neither to occupy any extensive areas, nor to control any long railroad lines, nor to seize any points (cities). All they could do was to make air raids on cities. In other words, the Japanese could control no *area,* nor any *line,* nor any *point;* they had to try to control the *air.* Chungking, the war capital of China, became perhaps the most bombed city on earth. But even in the matter of air raids, the weather around Chungking favored the Chinese defense. In the winter season the Szechwan basin, where Chungking is located, is covered by fog in the morning, which made it difficult for the Japanese to send airplanes there before ten o'clock. Also, Chungking is built on a massive rock base, so that the people easily built shelters. The Japanese would send 20 to 30 airplanes to circle in the skies over the cities and bomb them, expecting to tire the people out. However, the inhabitants of Chungking and of other cities stayed in the shelters sometimes for days; and when the raid was over, they came out and went to work. Thus the Japanese bombing strategy was in vain.

In 1937, when the Japanese military operation was carried on mainly on the coastal plains, the invaders advanced an average of twelve miles daily on Chinese territory; but in 1938, when the fighting had shifted to the rugged western land, the advance decreased to only six-and-one half miles daily. In 1939, when the Chinese were defending the mountainous interior, the Japanese advance was reduced to half a mile a day. Here the terrain became a real asset to China's political geography.

CHAPTER III

Education in
Wartime China

BY OU TSUIN-CHEN

IT IS A REAL PLEASURE to be with you to review the wartime efforts of China. A sentiment of nostalgia and melancholy in the reminiscence of the wartime experience is bound to prevail. Not a few members of this conference have shared with me in the Sino-Japanese War the feelings of bitterness, agony, excitement and the sense of relief, and sometimes disillusion and disappointment. Now when we pass on review the heroic moments of wartime China, the revival of those sentiments would be both a pleasure and a sadness.

In this mental setting I would first apologize for the fact that, not simply as a pure historian, but also as an educator and educational administrator personally involved in the educational work during the war, I am afraid that I cannot treat the wartime education with complete objectivity, although personal experience is sometimes a good thing to add intimacy, vividness and understanding to things recounted. Among members present there are my ex-colleagues in the government or in the higher institutions during the war, who have contributed so much to the war efforts. I hope they can weigh with me what the balance is between the advantages and disadvantages of the personal involvement in a work to be treated as objectively as a historical event should be.

The contents of my paper are mostly based on the government documents, particularly the *Second Yearbook of Chinese Education* published by the Ministry of Education immediately after the termination of the War. This book was prepared by the Ministry staff, most of whom had participated in educational administration during the war. Judging by my own experience, it is a comprehensive and generally reliable work. Besides the said yearbook, I have freely used the material from *Memoir of Wartime Educational Administration* by the then Minister of Education, Dr. Chen Li-fu 陳立夫 . To this writing I have contributed a

89

modest part. I have also referred to my own memoir, "My Educational Experience of Sixty Years" and other relevant essays and articles of mine. A special issue of *Chung-Hwa Educational World*, namely "The General Review of the Ten-Year Education of China Since the War Began" has also been used as source material for this paper.

In education as in other wartime efforts, not only a short paper, but some volumes of books can be written. Because of the limitation both of time and space my paper has only treated the general aspects of educational efforts in wartime China. Among the events treated, educational policy decision, educational and cultural immigration, higher education and academic research have particularly been stressed. This is so because those things are more important and maybe more interesting to the members of the Conference, even if they are described in a sketchy form. Much could and should be added if more time and space were given.

Among the things which should have been elaborated are, above all, the conditions of life as actually lived by individuals in the higher institutions of learning. Besides the record of individual colleges and universities, there are numerous memoirs, recollections, even some novels, written by faculty members and students telling their suffering, adventures and hard work in the struggle for the survival of their academic life. In this connection I would mention with appreciation the fine paper to be presented later by my friend Dr. Israel on Southwest Associated University. The paper serves as a concrete illustration for my general description of the academic life of the higher institutions in wartime China. I have heard that a book on another Chinese university, namely the National Central University, by another American scholar, is also being prepared. When published, it will serve as another illustration of the hardship, efforts and accomplishments of Chinese colleges and universities.

My paper covers almost all aspects of Chinese education during the war, each aspect being touched with different degrees of emphasis. As has been mentioned above, policy decision, educational and cultural migration, and higher education occupied dominant positions in Chinese wartime education. Owing to the wise decision of the wartime educational policy, Chinese education was not only maintained as in peacetime, but also developed to a great extent both quantitatively and qualitatively. This was a remarkable event. In addition to maintaining the regular program unaffected, there were various temporary measures in response to war needs.

During wartime, Chinese education was meant to attain a dual goal, namely: support the war and prepare for national reconstruction. This dual goal was dictated by a higher principle that: "While peacetime should be seen as wartime, wartime should be seen as peacetime." As a result of this policy, an extensive educational and cultural migration took place. The migration involved a movement of huge numbers of teachers and students, books and equipment, and invaluable cultural treasures. It not only safeguarded the cream of the intelligentsia and the cultural heritage of the nation, but also made possible the educational and cultural interflow in the interior of wartime China. The spectacular migration on such an extensive scale was unprecedented in Chinese history or in the history of the world.

After the migration, education returned to normal in the interior. There was also development in all levels of education. With the shortage of both facilities and personnel and the continuous threat of enemy attacks and air raids, the quantitative advance of the wartime education in general and higher education in particular was an extraordinary performance.

Attention was also given to the improvement of the quality of education. Some administrative measures to improve the quality of higher education along with its sustainment and expansion bear special mentioning. As stated in my paper such measures as the reorganization of curriculum, the certification of teachers, and the unified entrance examination were adopted with psychological resistance from some parts of the academic field. Since these measures were to meet the actual needs of the time and were adopted after consultations and discussions with the academic circles, the psychological obstacles were at last overcome. All the measures have survived the war and are still in force as permanent institutions in Taiwan. With the said measures of quality improvement and unfailing efforts and devotion of the faculty and students, a generally acceptable academic performance was maintained.

International cultural exchange flourished considerably during the war. A great number of graduates were sent abroad to further their studies. The exchange of professors, scholars, and students with some of the Allied nations and the creation of Chinese studies fellowships for students in American, British, and Indian universities enhanced international cultural cooperation and understanding.

Wartime China did not neglect its fundamental education. For the first time in Chinese educational history, different kinds of national secondary schools were created by the Ministry of Education. They were created to meet the need of relocating the teachers and students migrated from the war zone. With standard curriculum and better teaching methods and efficient administration, these national secondary schools set good examples for local schools to live up to. Hence there was general improvement of secondary education at large.

All elementary education in wartime, as before the war, was run by local governments, but with the financial assistance from the provincial and central governments according to a nationwide development plan. Elementary education was more prosperous in wartime than before the war. It became compulsory in attendance and free of tuition, and at the same time almost universal.

Social education was graded on two levels. The higher level concerned national cultural heritage, which was taken care of by the world-famous national museums and libraries safely removed from the war zone and partly open to the public in the interior. The lower level of social education was practiced through various education halls, social corps, theaters, conservatories and symphony orchestras, educational films and radio programs and the like. All these contributed to the education and entertainment of the general public and also to the enhancement of the war spirit. One remarkable accomplishment of the wartime social education was the elimination of the great part of illiteracy in the nineteen provinces and municipalities in the interior.

To meet wartime needs, particular attention was also given to some special programs, such as education in border regions and overseas Chinese education. For the former the Ministry of Education took the initiative in establishing model national schools in border regions. For the latter all the displaced teachers, along with their students, from the overseas Chinese schools were relocated in the interior with new teaching positions, and new overseas schools were created. Even the faculty members and students of Hong Kong University were taken care of as well as those from Chinese institutions of higher learning.

In my paper there is a discussion of war-stricken students and their direct contribution to the war. We evacuated a huge number of students of all levels. We fed, lodged and clothed them and educated them with a regular program with only minor adjustment to the war needs. When the war became intensified and there developed a great need for direct participation of the college youth in war efforts, we did not hesitate to draft part of them to be enlisted in the army to fight in the front. The historic "One-Hundred-Thousand Youth for One-Hundred-Thousand Troops Movement" was started by the combined effort of the government and colleges and universities. It resulted in the formation of several special divisions of student soldiers. They fought as bravely and successfully as soldiers drafted among the unschooled youth.

So far I have sketched Chinese wartime education in its normal official aspect. A special aspect concerning the education practiced under the Chinese Communist regime during the wartime was omitted. This is for two reasons: first, so far no sufficient, reliable material has been available. Secondly, this aspect of wartime education should be left to some special authority to treat in order to do justice to its significance.

In conclusion, I would like to say something about the evaluation of Chinese wartime education in my paper. I have considered the wartime education in China as a success in attaining its dual goal of providing support to the war and preparing for national reconstruction. Apart from the success, I have also indicated its shortcomings. In evaluating the situation I did my best to take a purely objective view as an "insider." However, owing to my personal involvement in educational work during the wartime, as I mentioned at the beginning of this talk, there may be, without my noticing, some overestimating of the accomplishments and some overlooking of the defects of the education in wartime China. Any further clarification of the education difficulties and achievements during those years—of which the "insider," in spite of his subjective feelings, may be more knowledgeable than an "outsider"—will be highly appreciated.

I

Introduction

In such operations as the moving of universities and colleges to the free zone, giving succor to homeless teachers and students, reviving education behind the front, developing education on every level and of every category, reforming and establishing new systems, encouraging scholarly research, promoting national culture, fostering international exchange, and enlisting as well as training students to participate directly in the war efforts, much was accomplished in China during the Sino-Japanese War. As a result of these accomplishments national education not only survived the ravages of the war but grew immensely both in quantity and quality. Wartime education, while continuing its primary purpose of nurturing talents and experts for national reconstruction, had to meet all the special needs of the war so as to accord with the national policy that equal importance be given to national reconstruction and the war of resistance.

On the other hand, as victory over the enemy had priority over everything else, severe limitations in manpower and material resources could not but result in inadequacies in some aspects of education. Moreover, the exigencies of war called for concentration of power and on certain procedural priorities. Under these circumstances deliberation, consultation, and division of power, while quite appropriate during normal times, were sometimes curtailed. Some educators were unhappy over these unusual but necessary limitations. On the whole, however, one might say that Chinese education during the war fulfilled its mission.

Chinese Education on the Eve of the War

Chinese education continued to progress ever since a new educational system was adopted toward the end of the Ching Dynasty. The aim and purpose of education was gradually shifted from emphasis on the classics and the national heritage to the promotion of the modernization of China. At first the new school system was directly borrowed from Japan and indirectly inspired by French and German models. Later the American model prevailed. Emphasis was also shifted from the education of the elite to mass education. Education at every level and of every category was quantitatively expanded. But due to the change in polity, disorders created by the warlords, and the deficiencies in manpower and financial resources, the expansion was at first rather slow. The whole field of education began to change rapidly after 1927 when the National Government was formed. The details of this expansion are as follows:

1. *The Reformulation of the Aim of Education.* In 1929 the national government reformulated the aim of education as follows:

> The aim of education in the Republic of China is to enrich the life of the people, to maintain and develop social life, to promote the livelihood of the citizens, and to foster national life, in accordance with the Three People's Principles, ultimately aspiring to the independence of the nation, the universal assertion of the people's rights, the development of the people's livelihood, and the realization of world peace.

This aim, combining nationalism, democracy, socialism, and world unity, is truly a progressive aim. It has been upheld by the Chinese government throughout the war down to this day.

2. *The Reorganization of the School System.* The organizational chart for the school system, issued by the central government in 1922, follows more or less the American system. The Nationalist Government revised it slightly in 1928. The system is as follows: The elementary school was divided into lower and upper forms, extending over four and two years respectively. The first four years constituted what was known as compulsory education.

The middle-level education was divided into three categories: middle, normal, and vocational. Any given middle school could concentrate on one category or combine several categories. (In 1932 a decision was made that each middle-level school be limited to one category of instruction.) The middle school was divided into the junior and the senior schools, each requiring three years. The junior school could be an independent institution. The normal and the vocational schools took graduates of the junior middle school and gave them three years of training.

The undergraduate education in universities and colleges was a four-year program, except for medical school, which required five years of study. Technical colleges offered two-year or three-year programs. There was no time limit for graduate schools. The entire school system coincided generally with that of America.

3. *Chinese Education at Each Level Just Before the Outbreak of the War.* Elementary education was managed by the counties and municipalities in compliance with the elementary school statutes promulgated by the central government and in accordance with the standards set by

the Ministry of Education. Due to disparate local economic and cultural levels, progress for a while was not impressive. In 1935 the Ministry of Education proclaimed a timetable for the gradual completion of mass and compulsory education. Monitored by the Ministry and subsidized by the central government, the program was a success. During the 1936 school year (from August 1936 to July 1937) the elementary schools in the country enrolled 18,364,956 students, compared with the figure of 11,720,596 for the 1931 school year.[1]

Middle-level education was managed by the provinces, counties, and municipalities in compliance with the statutes governing the middle school, the normal school, and the vocational school, promulgated by the central government. The standards were set by the Ministry of Education. There was an increase in the numbers of students and schools during the early 1930's. According to the report of the Chinese Association for the Advancement of Education, in 1923 there were 547 middle schools with 103,385 students; 275 normal schools with 38,277 students; 164 grade A industrial schools (comparable to the vocational schools in the 1928 school system) with 20,360 students.[2] When the war broke out in 1937 there were 1,956 middle schools, 814 normal schools, and 494 vocational schools, with 482,522 students, 87,902 students, and 56,822 students respectively. A comparison between the two sets of figures will show that considerable advance was made in secondary education in the decade before the war.[3]

So far as higher education was concerned, national universities, colleges, and technical colleges were managed directly by the Ministry of Education. Provincial and private universities and colleges were managed by the provincial governments and private organizations. All institutions were run in accordance with the university statutes, technical college statutes, and relevant regulations. After the establishment of the Nationalist government in 1927 the Ministry of Education found in some of the existing institutions of higher learning unsatisfactory conditions such as duplication, lack of discipline, and low standards. Most of these were subsequently corrected. The number of institutions of higher learning was increased from seventy-four in 1928 to 108 in 1937; students grew from 25,198 in 1928 to 41,922 in 1937.[4]

From the above brief description one can see that Chinese education reached a considerable rate of growth just before the outbreak of the war. The Japanese invasion in 1937 put a stop to our efforts and plunged Chinese education into a grave crisis.

Crisis in Education After the Outbreak of the War

Chinese education met an unprecedented crisis when the war broke out. There were two aspects of this crisis: the external and the internal. The external crisis was brought about by the outbreak and the spread of the war: the deliberate destruction of educational and cultural institutions by the enemy. After the war broke out on July 7, 1937, educational centers such as Peiping, Tientsin, Nanking, and Shanghai fell one after another. All the educational and cultural institutions there were severely damaged. Subsequently, as the war zone expanded, many of the cities on the coast and along the Yangtze River were lost to the enemy. More educational and cultural institutions were in ruins. Many teachers and students were evacuated. The foundation that the Nationalist government had built with respect to education was more than half destroyed. As war continued to rage, even the educational and cultural institutions that survived in the free zone were frequently rendered inoperative by the bombing of enemy airplanes. So much for the external crisis.

Next let us look at the internal crisis. On September 18, 1931, Japan devised the so-called Mukden Incident and proceeded to occupy the Three Eastern Provinces (also known as Manchuria). Subsequently Japan sent more forces to its military bases in north China and instigated activities on the part of Chinese collaborators in Hopei and Chahar. Against this background of deepening crisis and menace of war, much discussion developed among Chinese educators and government leaders on how to recast education on a national scale so as to meet the unprecedented new challenge. Some advocated the implementation of a wartime system, which would consist of the suspension of all senior high schools, colleges, and universities, so that the students and teachers could enlist in the armed forces. Others would not go so far but suggested that a number of schools and universities be kept open with curriculum and teaching method reorganized to suit the exigencies of the war. After the fall of Nanking in late 1937 such demands became even more clamorous and constituted the internal crisis of Chinese education.

At that time some other educators held a different opinion with regard to wartime education. They took a long view and believed that education should respond to the war only in a limited and temporary way and that the long-term programs should not be interrupted.[5] Fortunately the government, in view of the diversity of opinions, took the matter under careful consideration. The final decision supported the belief of the last-mentioned group and was based on the following reasons.

1. Since the war was going to be a protracted one, trained personnel of every category would be needed, either directly or indirectly, in the war effort.

2. Higher education had never been much developed in China. For every ten thousand citizens there was only one college student, a figure much below that for advanced European and American countries. To

build up self-reliance, to keep up the war effort, to prepare for national reconstruction, we must maintain the current level of higher education.

3. It follows from the above that college students should be exempted from the draft. Moreover, with our massive population base, manpower supply for the armed forces was quite adequate.

The policy decision thus was: "wartime should be seen as peacetime." There were, of course, various temporary measures adopted in response to war needs, but the fundamental principle was that regular, peacetime education be retained.[6] This government policy was reformulated in January 1938 by Dr. Chen Li-fu, the newly appointed Minister of Education, in his "Letter to the Youth," issued on his assuming office. He formally notified all the youth of the nation that those who wanted to join the armed forces could do so with the encouragement of the government; those who wanted to stay in school (who turned out to be the majority) would receive regular education, combined with special training programs designed to meet war needs. Consequently every young man could decide his own course of action as he wished, and stability returned to all campuses where regular education was carried on without interruption. Similarly, education at other levels also proceeded in an orderly fashion.

The basic policy was subsequently reiterated at various party and government meetings as well as at conferences on education. The speech on the policy and goal of Chinese wartime education made by Generalissimo Chiang Kai-shek at the Third National Conference on Education was most decisive and effective in dissolving the internal educational crisis. He said:

> The current educational issue that has been attended by the most heated debate is the issue of wartime education versus regular education. In other words, should we do away with all the system of regular education, or should we retain the system of regular education but add to it measures dictated by the state of emergency? With regard to this issue, I hold the view that the solution is quite simple. In recent years I have often said: "Peacetime should be treated as wartime, and wartime should be treated as peacetime." I also said, "Wartime life is modern life. In modern times, without practicing a life of war no individual or nation can survive or avoid destruction." If we understand this idea, there will be no need for the so-called dispute between regular education and wartime education. It is precisely because we in the past were incapable of seeing peacetime as wartime that so many people today are incapable of seeing wartime as peacetime. These two errors are interconnected. We absolutely cannot say that education can leave this world and become independent of the needs of the nation, or close its door to the outside world, take a business-as-usual stance, and remain at ease even when a foreign enemy is march-

ing in. But neither can we say that because of war we may cast aside all school systems, curricula, and education laws and statutes, or that because of war we may unconditionally drive out all modern youth from laboratories and libraries into another environment where they engage in emergency work without aim or choice. We need soldiers; when necessary we may perhaps draft professors or college students. We need various kinds of cadres for war. We cannot but initiate various types of training programs outside of the regular educational system. But we also need technical personnel of all sciences and disciplines, research scholars, and experts. Especially during the time of war we need to emphasize all types of basic education.[7]

The instructions of Generalissimo Chiang Kai-shek, accepted and complied with by the entire educational world, completely dispelled the internal educational crisis caused by the dispute over the relation between peacetime and wartime education.

II

The Great Educational and Cultural Migration

As a result of the expansion of the Sino-Japanese War and the policy decision made by the Chinese government to support education, an educational and cultural migration on a scale unprecedented in Chinese history took place.

The educational and cultural institutions evacuated from the war zone were mostly universities, colleges, and technical institutes. Under the unified direction of the Ministry of Education these schools were ordered to move, as speedily as possible, teachers, staff, students, equipment, and archives to the rear. Schools at middle and elementary levels received their instructions and assistance from local governments, which tried their best to move the schools in the war zone to areas of relative safety, and to assist others to go underground. Teachers, staff, and students from schools which could no longer be operated in their original locale were collected by the Ministry of Education at various reception centers near the front and then transported to schools in the rear.

Other institutions originally located in areas now ravaged by war, institutions such as the national libraries and museums, were also moved in an orderly fashion to various designated points in the free zone, where they resumed operations as soon as books, collections, and staff arrived. The unprecedented scale of the movement, the hardship, self-sacrifice, and heroism attendant on this human effort cannot be fully narrated in a short report, nor could they be exhausted even by volumes of books. I shall sketch a brief outline of this great migration.

Within several months after the outbreak of the war, north China, the coastal cities, and the lower Yangtze valley were lost to the enemy. All these areas had harbored many centers of higher education. The most urgent mission of the central education administration at this time was to move the teachers, staff, students, libraries, equipment, and archives of the schools to the rear and to assist them to resume operations. Later when the war spread to the central plains, more schools were evacuated. The indiscriminate and ruthless bombing by Japanese airplanes, which frequently sought out educational and cultural institutions as primary targets, made necessary further evacuation to rural or hilly shelters.

According to the 1939 statistics published by the Ministry of Education, there had been 108 institutions of higher learning when the war broke out. Of these 108 schools fifty-two were moved to the rear, twenty-five were moved to foreign concessions in Shanghai or to Hong Kong, seventeen ceased operation, and the remaining were either schools originally situated in the rear, in Shanghai, or schools which on account of their missionary connections could manage to continue in the occupied zone.

With the outbreak of the Pacific War all schools which had survived in Shanghai foreign concessions, Hong Kong, or the occupied zone ceased operation. Some of these schools moved their teachers, staff, and students to the free zone and reestablished themselves. Even those schools which had been, from the very beginning, situated in the free zone may have had to move to more sheltered areas to escape from enemy air raids. Only one school—the Sinkiang College in Sinkiang—stayed throughout the war in its original location.

Limited by space I shall not describe the actual circumstances of moving. Only a few examples will be given. Several schools were moved from place to place until after much hardship a final site was found. For instance, the National University of Chekiang was first moved from Hangchow to Chien-te in Chekiang, then to Chi-an, then to Tai-ho in Kiangsi, then to I-shan in Kwangsi, and finally to Tsun-i in Kweichow, with a branch in Mei-tan. National Sun Yat-sen University was moved from Canton first to Lung-chou in Kwangsi, then to Cheng-chiang in Yunnan, then to Ping-shih in Kwangtung. The most peripatetic of them all was Kwangtung Provincial College of Arts and Sciences, which was moved from Canton to Wu-chou in Kwangsi, then to Teng-hsien, then to Jung-hsien, then to Ju-yuan in Kwangtung, then to Lien-hsien, then to Chu-chiang, then back to Lien-hsien, then, at long last, to Lo-ting.

The schools that travelled the farthest were Peking University and

Tsing Hua University in Peiping and Nankai University of Tientsin. The trio were first moved to Changsha, where they were reorganized into one entity under the name of Changsha Provisional University. Then it was moved to Meng-tzu and Kunming in Yunnan and renamed National Southwestern Associated University. About three hundred among the teachers, staff, and students went by foot from Changsha to Yunnan. It took them sixty-eight days to cover a distance of 3,300 *li* or 1,100 miles. No school was moved with greater speed and less loss than National Central University. All the teachers, staff, students, books, laboratory equipment, and archives went up the Yangtze by boat directly to the new campus. Only a portion of the cattle belonging to the College of Agriculture could not be shipped. They were driven over a land route and arrived safely in Chungking to rejoin the operation.[8]

As for the moving of schools at middle and elementary levels, because of their large number, only a few could be assisted. Some schools managed to survive in the occupied zone; others went underground under the secret direction of resistance workers sent behind enemy lines by the Ministry of Education. The teachers and students who were evacuated were quite numerous. They were registered and settled in various areas by the Ministry of Education. From the 1937-38 school year to 1945, 6,976 middle school teachers and 11,631 elementary school teachers were registered.[9] Some of them were recruited into the newly organized Middle and Elementary Teachers Service Corps. Others were assigned to national middle schools or provincial and municipal educational institutions in the free zone. In all cases they resumed the career for which they had been prepared. Since most of them came from educationally advanced areas on the coast or along the Yangtze, their relocation in the free zone was often a boon to the local schools.

Another important event during the war was the timely and carefully planned moving to the free zone of all national libraries and museums. Thus the cultural treasures of China escaped the ravages of war. What can be seen and admired in Taiwan today are essentially those items that survived the Sino-Japanese War in the free zone. Since the preservation of these treasures mean so much to the Chinese national heritage and to world culture, I shall dwell somewhat on this topic.

When the war broke out, the National Central Library was still in its planning stage. In 1937 the planning board and its acquisitions were moved to Chungking where the library was officially founded. Its excellent holdings were not only safely preserved throughout the war but significantly enlarged by the purchase, through secret negotiations in Shanghai, of a large number of rare books. Their safe delivery across the enemy line was certainly a great achievement in itself. Photolithographic reprints were made of many of the rare editions under the aegis of the library so as to insure wide circulation. After the war the library was moved back to Nanking. Today the library continues to serve the public at its present site in Taipei with all the original holdings intact.

Shortly before the war broke out the National Peking Library shipped its collection of rare editions to the United States and Hong Kong for safekeeping. Before the fall of Peking the library was moved to Changsha, then to Kunming. After the war the library was moved back to Peking. Its rarities were returned to China from Hong Kong and the United States. At present the collection is housed in the National Central Library and the National Palace Museum in Taipei.

The National Palace Museum is the inheritor of the cultural treasures that have been handed down through successive dynasties. Its holdings are admired by the world. After the Mukden Incident, Peiping was in the shadow of war, so a portion of the Museum's holdings were shipped to Shanghai, then to Nanking to be housed by a branch museum. When the war finally broke out the evacuation was accelerated. Eventually all the collections and personnel arrived safely in Chungking by way of Hupeh and Shensi, together with a collection of antiques then in the custody of the Ministry of Interior. An office of the museum was set up in Chungking, but in view of frequent air raids all the holdings were dispersed to other areas for safekeeping.

After the war the entire collection was shipped back to Nanking, where a center of the museum was established. The National Palace Museum that now functions in Taipei has in its custody all the important items that survived the war in the free zone.

III

Quantitative Advances
in Chinese Wartime Education

The most conspicuous and the most difficult achievement in Chinese wartime education was the quantitative advance. In spite of serious problems such as loss of territory, the spread of war, and relentless enemy air raids, Chinese education at all levels did not shrivel but managed to advance. The number of schools, students, and faculty grew most remarkably at the level of higher education. Middle, elementary, normal, and vocational education also made notable advances. In turn contributions were made to the improved literacy of citizens, the nurture of talents for national reconstruction, and the supply of technical personnel for the war effort.

We shall first show the quantitative advances in wartime education by statistics. The following is a tabulation of two sets of figures, one representing the first year, and the other the last year, of the war.

Item	The School Year of 1936	The School Year of 1944	Change
A. Higher Education			
Number of Schools	108	145	+37
Teachers	7,560	11,201	+3,641
Students	41,922	78,909	+36,987
Graduating Students	9,154	12,078	+2,924
B. Graduate Education			
Number of Schools	22	49	+27
Programs	35	87	+52
Students	75	422	+347
C. Middle Education			
Number of Schools	1,956	2,759	+803
Teachers and Staff	41,180	67,477	+26,297
Students	482,522	929,297	+446,775
Graduating Students	76,864	212,783	+135,919
D. Normal Education			
Number of Schools	814	562	−252
Teachers and Staff	10,222	13,347	+3,125
Students	87,902	157,806	+69,904
Graduating Students	24,162	26,808	+2,646
E. Vocational Education			
Number of Schools	494	424	−70
Teachers and Staff	8,645	9,811	+1,166
Students	56,822	76,010	+19,188
Graduating Students	10,294	14,030	+3,736
F. Elementary Education			
Number of Schools	320,080	254,377	−65,703
Teachers and Staff	724,871	655,611	−87,260
Students	18,364,956	17,221,814	−1,143,142
Graduating Students	2,166,377	3,871,688	+1,705,311

(Source: *The Second Yearbook of Chinese Education*)

The above tabulation shows that the number of colleges and universities, students, and the size of graduating classes grew a great deal through the war years. This was largely due to the fact that the Ministry of Education encouraged colleges and universities to move to the free zone and that the Ministry established new institutions.

As for middle-level education, the numbers of teachers, staff, and students also grew, except for normal and vocational schools. The growth in secondary education was the result of the increase in the number of provincial and municipal schools operating in the nineteen provinces and municipalities under Chinese control, and the establishment of national middle, normal, and vocational schools.

Elementary education was completely operated by the provinces and municipalities in the free zone. Occupation by the Japanese of much of Chinese territory resulted in the decrease in the total number of elementary schools. But the number of teachers, staff, and students showed only a moderate decrease, thanks to the massive promotion of elementary education in the free zone and the resultant higher percentage of school-age children attending schools. The large size of the 1945 graduating class was the result of including graduating students from shortened programs.

From the above tabulation we can see that wartime education in the free zone really thrived. This was in fact due to the emphasis placed on education by the government at both central and local levels and the massive promotion of education by government agencies. Credit should also be given to educators at all levels who did not shrink from wartime hardships but strived unceasingly to write a glorious page in the history of Chinese education and the War of Resistance.

IV

Higher Education Sustained and Expanded

During the war all the colleges and universities—whether they were moved from the war zone, dispersed to rural areas to escape from the air raids, or newly established—had to struggle very hard just to survive from day to day. Due to severe limitations in material resources, housing and equipment were quite inadequate and students and teachers eked out a bare living. The hardship that they sometimes had to endure defies imagination. Most of the buildings consisted of no more than thatched roofs over mud walls. Libraries and laboratories were poorly equipped. They remained unsatisfactory in spite of repeated subsidies from the government.

Although most of the schools were far from the battle front, they could not escape from the enemy air raids. Classes were held in spite of physical danger and material deprivations. Morale remained high throughout the war years. Teachers and students were resolute in their determination to confront all adversities and to overcome all difficulties. It was their high spirit and strong will that maintained the academic level of wartime higher education. The following description of campus life during the early years of the war, written by a college student, typifies the general condition of college life during the war.

The Southwest Associated University has up to now been in Yunnan for some two years. During these two years there was not a day that the university did not grow amidst hardships and setbacks. To sum up, the first hardship is "poverty." The equipment of the school deteriorated after each setback. Although additional funds were spent on the libraries and laboratories, the increase could not keep up with the growing need. The teachers and staff also suffered from poverty. Their monthly salary was, at the highest, equivalent to the price of four piculs of rice at the Kunming market; at the lowest, not quite one picul. How could they support a family? The students, except for a few, fared even worse. Generally speaking, everybody was pallid. Of course they did not expect the level of affluence they had enjoyed before, but the numerous current hardships were enough to destroy their spirit.

Another hardship had to do with housing. As each dark and small room in the dormitory had to accommodate half a dozen or more students, it is needless to say that the place was seldom quiet. On one occasion more than half of the students in one room came down one after another with scarlet fever, yet the others sharing the room had no place to move to. The problem of housing was not limited to dormitory space. The mud house that the university built in 1938 in the northwest suburb of Kunming later had to accommodate the freshman class of more than a thousand students.

Only the school of engineering, housed in the two *landsmanshaften* on the east side of the city, escaped chaos; all the other units of the university were moved around about once every other month. The cause of this unwanted mobility was that the University had no fixed campus: it simply leased buildings from several high schools which had been evacuated to the countryside to avoid air raids. As each high school returned to the city the university had to find new housing for some of its units.

The above is only a part of the hardship that confronted the Southwestern Associated University. It is impossible to describe all the difficulties that the school had to cope with. But the university grew and thrived in adversity. Many students who had participated in the war effort now have come back to school. Many high school graduates from the Japanese-occupied area, especially north China, have travelled a long way to Kunming hoping to be admitted into the Southwestern Associated University. Now although the university has taken many students from the southwestern provinces, it is still a stronghold of northern youth. The total enrollment reached 3,019 at the beginning of 1939. We must admit that the school is flourishing.

With the stabilization of the war front, curricular activities have become more serious. Students are more attentive in class. The laboratories are occupied from morning to night, even during the summer. The library is always full. The walls everywhere are covered with student-edited hand-written newspapers. There are more than twenty of them, dealing with political, economic, legal, historical, and social topics as well as current events. The students also enthusiastically participate in social service such as street theatre, rural propaganda, winter relief, and air raid first aid. It is incredible that students who suffer from cold and hunger are capable of doing so much.

Tempered by adversity, we believe that the best reply to the Japanese is to do our work well. The Southwestern Associated University has been bombed twice already. The first bombing occurred on September 28, 1938. About a dozen fragmentation bombs were dropped on the Kun-hua Normal School which was leased to the University. Two students who had just arrived from Tientsin were killed. The second bombing took place on October 13, 1939. The Japanese dropped more than one hundred bombs of all types on the main campus intending to finish off our school once and for all. The Teachers College was totally wrecked. Students lost all their belongings. The center of the university community bounded by Wen-hua Street and Wen-lin Road was also completely destroyed. Materially speaking, the greatest possible blow was dealt us by the Japanese, but the very next day classes were held as usual. Some of the professors after a night of sleep in the open came to lecture in the morning. Some students did not go to look for their belongings among the ruins until they had attended the classes. All the staff continued their work in the roofless, debris-strewn buildings. The university did not cease operations even for one day.[10]

During the war the central government not only maintained a high level of support for all the existing colleges and universities but, responding to the needs of the times, expanded higher education by establishing several new schools. As there was no institution of higher learning in Kiangsi, a new university—the National Chung-cheng University—was set up there. After Chekiang University was moved away, there was no longer a university in Chekiang. To fill the gap, National Ying-shih University was established in that province. Recognizing teacher training to be the foundation of all education, the government, besides adding schools of education to several universities, created two independent national teachers colleges, one for men and the other for women. Later Kweiyang Teachers College, Nan-ning Teachers College, and Hupeh Teachers College were set up. The School of Education in the Northwestern Associated University was granted autonomy and renamed Northeastern Teachers College. All these schools were intended for training teachers for secondary schools.

Responding to the wartime need of medical personnel, the government established several new schools. Chungcheng Medical College and

Wuchang Medical College, under planning since before the war, now came into existence. The latter, to tally with its new location, was renamed Kweiyang Medical College. Kiangsu Medical College, hitherto under provincial jurisdiction, and the private Hsiang-ya Medical College now joined the ranks of national colleges. Hupeh and Fukien each gained a provincial medical college.

The war years also saw the emergence of schools devoted to other applied sciences, such as the National Northwestern Agricultural College in Kansu and National College of Engineering in Shensi. Other new national schools were the College of Asian Languages, Fukien Conservatory, the Coast Guard Academy, the College of Border Affairs, the Central Polytechnic Institute, the Tzu-kung (Szechwan) Industrial Institute, the Northwestern Institute of Agriculture, the Sikang Polytechnic Institute, Institute of Physical Education, the College of Martial Arts and Physical Education, the Chungking Merchant Marine Academy, the College of Social Education, and National Conservatory. In addition, there were many new provincial and private schools, which I shall not record.

V

Administrative Measures to Improve Higher Education

Chinese higher education during the war years underwent not only quantitative advances but also qualitative improvements. Before the war the League of Nations Education Mission to China had criticized our higher education. The members of the Mission thought that the geographical distribution of Chinese universities favored only a few provinces and municipalities; the curriculum, relying entirely on foreign models, was not suitable to Chinese needs; the qualifications of professors were uneven; and the students were very varied in their accomplishments. The Mission also made several sound recommendations. The Ministry of Education considered adopting some of the recommendations but before anything could be done the war broke out. Subsequently the central government, taking into consideration these recommendations as well as the exigencies of the war, took important corrective measures on matters of geographical redistribution of schools, reorganization of curriculum, setting standards for faculty certification, and unifying entrance examinations.

When these measures were first adopted they met two types of psychological resistance. The first can be called permissiveness. In the past higher education in China was most lax. There were no regulations or common standards with regard to curriculum, faculty qualification, credit-granting, or school administration. Every school had its own way. Under such circumstances good universities, of course, could develop at will, but substandard schools also thrived in the laissez-faire situation. When the government tried to set minimum requirements in some areas of college education so as to improve efficiency and raise standards, some educators raised objections and condemned the proposed government actions as violations of academic freedom and disrespect to the lofty position of professors. These objections constituted the greatest psychological resistance.

Academic independence and institutional autonomy are, of course, the fundamental principles of higher education. But when funds are supplied by society and government, they then are entitled to set certain goals and call for an occasional accounting. Moreover, wartime has its exigencies. Any nation at war may set limits to the exercise of freedom in any sector of public life. Chinese higher education during the war was no exception. Therefore it was both reasonable and necessary that the government should have exerted some limited and appropriate control over higher education during the war years.

The second psychological resistance I would call exoticism, by which I mean an adoration of everything Western, combined with contempt for everything Chinese, a mental state bequeathed by the New Cultural Movement. This mental state was a great obstacle to the reform of university curriculum. As pointed out by the League of Nations Education Mission to China, several questionable practices prevailed in Chinese college instruction. Many basic courses were taught in foreign languages; textbooks, materials, and examples were all imported from abroad. This was true not only in natural sciences but also in history and social sciences.[11] The then Minister of Education deplored this state of affairs and referred to some Chinese universities as "cultural foreign concessions."[12]

To reclaim these "foreign concessions" it was necessary to reform the curriculum; the first step in the reform was the implementation of required courses and the production of textbooks emphasizing Chinese traditions and realities. These measures at first ran into resistance. Some took the emphasis on Chinese culture and Chinese materials to be conservative, antiquated, and obstructive to China's modernization. To overcome such resistance, the Ministry of Education tried every means other than simply promulgating regulations and statutes. Democratic processes and persuasion were adopted to induce voluntary compliance.

To this end the Ministry established the Committee on Academic Standards, of which half the members were elected by the heads of universities, the other half were appointed by the Ministry. The Committee was charged with the duties of certifying college teachers, reorganizing curriculum, stimulating research, as well as other matters related to the improvement of higher education. A group of professors and experts who held no office in the Ministry of Education were asked to draft a complete and detailed plan for the reorganization of curriculum, which in turn was reviewed and amended by subcommittees made of professors from each discipline. The final version of the plan did not become law until it was further reviewed and approved by the Committee on Academic Standards. Consequently the members of the higher education profession were won over. Since they believed that their own representatives participated fully in the decision-making processes, they accepted the decisions with alacrity. The following are a few of the measures adopted to improve higher education.[13]

The Reorganization of Curriculum

There were four steps in reorganizing curriculum: 1. formulation of guidelines for reorganization; 2. preparation of lists of required courses for each department and faculty; 3. preparation of syllabi for the required courses; 4. production of college textbooks.

In the spring of 1938 the Ministry of Education laid down three guidelines for the reorganization of college curriculum:

1. A unified standard must be established. This begins with regulating required courses for each academic department. Regulation aims at elevating the level of college courses and bringing them into full accord with national cultural and developmental policies.

2. Basic training must be emphasized. A common program of basic courses in humanities, natural sciences and social sciences should be required of every student before specialization is permitted. A broad intellectual foundation was advocated to prevent parochialism or one-sidedness.

3. Essential subjects should be emphasized. The content of all the courses offered by each academic department should be limited to the essentials of the discipline, so the student can steep himself fully in the proper subject matter without wasting time on extraneous facts or trivial details. Academic courses inconsistent with this guideline were to be discontinued.

To strengthen these three guidelines additional points were made, such as emphasis on Chinese and foreign languages; adoption of the academic year system with a rational method for granting course credits; incorporating into each course in addition to lectures, homework, discussion, self-study, and laboratory sessions; inclusion in the graduation examination of at least five important subjects distributed over the four years of college work. After professors and experts were consulted, these principles and points, together with a draft proposal on required common courses for each faculty (letters, sciences, and law) were presented by the ministry to the First Conference on Curriculum and obtained its approval. The proposal on required common courses stipulated that every student, in addition to the basic course required by his faculty, must take one of the required courses of each of the two other faculties. After this program was put in effect, the programs of required common courses for the colleges of agriculture, engineering, medicine, and education were also successively determined and proclaimed.

Subsequently, through similar procedures and processes, lists of required courses for each academic department in each faculty or college were also determined and promulgated. Now for the first time, similar departments and similar faculties or colleges in all universities throughout the country had identical sets of required courses. This enabled all students in any particular discipline to share a common minimum foundation and to reach a set level of proficiency. On the other hand, no restrictions were imposed on the offering of selective courses. In this area each school was free to develop its unique strengths and each student was permitted to follow his own inclinations.

The next step was the preparation of syllabi for required courses. Several hundred professors took part in the drafting of the syllabi and each draft syllabus was repeatedly reviewed and amended at committee sessions. After two years of work, syllabi for forty-two required courses were brought to completion in 1943. The use of the syllabi was completely at the discretion of the instructor, who remained free to select and organize course materials as he saw fit.

To alleviate the hardship caused by the wartime shortage of textbooks and the lack of appropriate teaching materials for some required courses, such as the history of Chinese law, politics, and economy, the Ministry of Education appointed experts to prepare books for the use of college students. By 1943 a total of 163 books were completed. A number of them pertain to natural sciences. This action contributed much to the Sinification of learning as well to the reclamation of foreign cultural concessions. But the use of these textbooks at the college level differed from the use of textbooks at the middle or elementary level: professors were not obligated to adopt the books prepared by the ministry; their use, either as texts or reference books, was entirely optional. Even so, some scholars considered the very existence of such books as an indication of violation of academic freedom.[14]

Certification of Teachers

Before the war qualifications of college faculty were very uneven: many of the professors were simply incompetent and devoid of credentials. Both Chinese public opinion and the report of the League of Nations Education Mission to China had criticized this situation. The

Ministry of Education had prepared regulations for certifying college teachers, but the war broke out before they could be put into effect. During the war the Ministry of Education again tried to tackle this urgent problem. The year 1940 saw the promulgation of a provisional regulation governing the qualification, rank, privileges, and remuneration of college faculty.

According to this regulation the college faculty were divided into four ranks: professor, associate professor, instructor, and teaching assistant. The qualification for each rank was defined in terms of education, effectiveness as a teacher, publications, and length of service. A procedure for promotion was also provided. Certification of individual faculty members was handled exclusively by the Committee on Academic Standards. Each case was first examined by an ad hoc board of experts selected from the discipline, and the Committee made the final decision. From 1940 to the end of the war, 7,000 applications were reviewed, and some 5,800 were approved.

One salutary feature of the regulation was the fact that teaching assistants and instructors could expect promotions to the rank of full professor through effective teaching, scholarly contribution, and seniority. In the past the avenue of advancement was often closed to those who did not study abroad, no matter how much they may have accomplished. Now the prospects of upward mobility offered much inducement to the college faculty in the lower ranks to become better teachers and scholars. At the same time, the new regulation helped in solving the problem of the shortage of college teachers caused by a proliferation of new institutions. Moreover, certification entitled teachers to such benefits as reappointment, sabbatical leave, and research grants. Professors of unusual achievements could be elected by their confreres to a Ministry Professorship.

All in all the 1940 provisional regulation contributed much to the elevation of the quality of college teaching. As it combined a fair and objective procedure for certification with provisions for benefits and privileges, it met with universal acceptance.[15]

Unified Freshman Admissions

Before the war each university and college processed its own applications for admission. The decision on each applicant was based mainly on his performance on the entrance examinations. Standards for admission varied widely from school to school. The League of Nations Education Mission to China recommended a uniform entrance examination for all schools. After the war broke out high school graduates, many of them homeless and penniless, found it nearly impossible to travel to widely scattered universities to take the entrance examination for their preferred schools. The Ministry of Education, mindful of the plight of the college-bound high school graduates and hoping to improve secondary education, decided to conduct, beginning with the 1938 school year, a unified college entrance examination. This continued for three years, with the procedure improved each year. The last one had the largest scale and the strictest management.

Established within the Ministry of Education, the Board of Unified Admissions for All Public Colleges and Universities took charge of matters such as preparation of tests, deciding standards for admission, and school assignment. The country was divided into several regions, each with its own Regional Board of Unified Admissions, which was responsible for matters such as registration, proctoring, grading and reporting the test scores to the Central Board. Entrance examinations were held in each region on the same day with the identical set of tests. The test results were reported back to the Central Board, which evaluated all the examinees from different regions by a uniform standard. Successful applicants were then assigned to schools and departments on the basis of their choice and grades.

The advantages of this procedure were many. Applicants were spared long, arduous, and costly travels. They could apply for several distant schools and yet took the entrance examinations nearby. Colleges and universities could save much labor and unnecessary duplication. Standards for admission could be uniformly maintained, and the government could exercise some control over the size of particular departments of disciplines in adjustment to the changing national needs. The effectiveness of each secondary school could be measured each year on the basis of how its graduates fared in the national examinations.

The herculean labor and great cost incurred by the System of Unified Admissions, combined with the severe constraints imposed by the war, finally put a stop to this unprecedented undertaking. Beginning with the academic year of 1940 universities and colleges coordinated their admission operations on a regional basis. Although the national uniform standard could no longer be maintained, applicants could still enjoy some convenience.[16]

VI
Academic Research, Graduate Education
and International Exchange

Academic Research

After the war broke out research units of various universities were moved to the rear along with other units of the schools. Two independent research institutions, the Academia Sinica and the Peiping Research

Institute, were also moved to the free zone. Other research organizations affiliated with government agencies also participated in the great migration. The ingenuity and resourcefulness of the research workers overcame most of the wartime privations: local products were used as substitutes for imported items; equipment was repeatedly repaired or even duplicated. Many contributed to the war effort and other applied fields while pure research was not neglected. The English scientist Joseph Needham made several detailed eye-witness reports on the indomitable spirit and substantial achievements of Chinese research workers.[17] *The Second Chinese Yearbook of Education* also recorded the wartime accomplishments of Chinese research institutions.[18]

Graduate Education

Graduate education had existed on a limited scale in prewar China. It became dormant after the outbreak of the war until 1938, when the Ministry of Education allocated funds for the resumption of graduate education. As a result new graduate programs were established in some of the better universities. By the academic year of 1944 there were forty-nine graduate programs with eighty-seven subjects and 422 graduate students. Requirements for the Master's degree were two years of course work and a thesis. The Committee on Academic Standards reviewed each candidacy before the degree was granted. During the war about 200 M.A. degrees were awarded.

To encourage artistic and scholarly pursuits the Ministry of Education, beginning in 1941, made yearly awards to those who contributed the most in the fields of writing, scientific invention, and fine arts. Each year there were more than 100 applicants. The final judge was the Committee on Academic Standards. A total of 200 awards were given in four years. Among the winners was the late historian Chen Yin-ko.

Resourcefulness on the part of the research workers could not overcome all the shortages. In view of the importance of basic research, the Ministry of Education granted U.S. $1,000,000 to the universities for purchasing in the United States books and laboratory equipment. The delivery in 1942 of all the acquisitions gave great impetus to research.

Efforts were also made abroad to solicit the donation of books. From 1940 to 1941 such efforts resulted in 4,000 books collected from England and more than 300 cases from the United States.

International Exchange

One cannot but admit that the balance of international exchange during the war years was in China's favor. To promote such exchange, a section was established by the Ministry of Education in its Department of Higher Education. This section was in charge of sending students abroad for advanced education and other matters regarding cultural exchange.

Dictated by the shortage in foreign currency, the policy of the government toward study abroad was a rather restrictive one during the early years of the war. In 1939 the Ministry of Education stipulated that study abroad be limited to holders of the Bachelor's degree with two years of work experience, who majored in scientific or technical subjects useful to the war effort. Consequently very few students left China for advanced education. Those who went were mostly supported by government scholarships, the Boxer Indemnity fellowships, or financial aid from the foreign universities that they attended.

In 1942 the government, anticipating postwar needs, lifted some restrictions. Students who passed the Study-Abroad Examination were allowed to purchase foreign currency at the official rate, which meant that in reality they were granted substantial financial support. Three hundred and twenty-seven students passed the examinations in 1943 and 195 in 1944. Most of the students, whether on scholarship or self-support, completed their studies. Many have since distinguished themselves in various fields, both in the West and in Taiwan. The most notable among them are the Nobel laureates Yang Chen Ning　楊振寧　and Lee Tsung-dao　李政道　.

Cultural exchange was maintained during the war years in spite of many difficulties. Lecturers and research scholars were exchanged with England, the United States, and India. From 1941 to 1943 fourteen foreign scholars came to China; among them were Joseph Needham and Sarvepalli Radhakrishnan, who later became President of India. During the same period twenty-five Chinese scholars went abroad.

Sino-Indian cultural relations were very close during the war. At the invitation of the Indian government an official Education and Culture Mission, consisting of high officials from the Ministry of Education and university professors, was sent to India. Following the recommendations of the Mission, China assisted one of the Indian universities to set up a chair professorship on Chinese culture and exchanged ten students with India.

During the war the English and American governments stationed cultural officers in Chungking. The American officers were Mr. and Mrs. John K. Fairbank. The English officer, Prof. Joseph Needham, was to write the multi-volume work entitled *Science and Civilization in China*. The foundation for this masterpiece was laid in wartime China. Dr. Chen Li-fu, the Minister of Education, took a personal interest in his project and opened to him the doors of all Chinese institutions. In recent years Dr. Chen has headed the project of translating Needham's book into Chinese. Eight volumes so far have been published in Taiwan.[19]

In return for the generosity of foreign universities in their assistance to Chinese scholars and students, the Chinese government set up Chinese Culture Fellowships at Oxford and London Universities in England; Harvard, Yale, Chicago, Columbia, and California in the United States; Calcutta and International Universities in India. There were five fellowships at each school, each fellowship was worth $1,500 per year. The fellowships were maintained into the late 1940's. Many of the recipients later distinguished themselves in the field of Sinology.[20]

VII

Progress in Fundamental Education

Secondary and elementary education is the fundamental education of a nation. In China fundamental education has been under the jurisdiction of local governments. During the war, with the loss of territory, many secondary and elementary schools ceased operation or were taken over by the Japanese and Chinese collaborators. Fortunately the Ministry of Education assumed a strong leadership in assisting local governments in the free zone to sustain and develop fundamental education. In addition, the Ministry of Education took direct responsibility for a group of secondary schools.

Secondary Education

Before the war the Ministry of Education had not involved itself directly in the management of secondary schools. But after the war broke out, it was necessary to settle the teachers and students evacuated from the war zone. To that end the Ministry created thirty-three national middle schools, twenty-eight national normal schools, and fourteen vocational schools. These were distributed widely over the provinces in the free zone and the border regions. These schools insured the resumption of educational life for the refugees as well as serving as exemplars for certain regions.

Furthermore, the Ministry enacted a number of plans, guidelines, and laws to strengthen secondary education. Among them were:

1. All the provinces were instructed to draw up plans for a redistribution of middle schools, normal schools, and vocational schools in each province. The redistribution was to accord with demographical, economic, and cultural factors of every district; overconcentration or duplication was to be avoided.

2. The Ministry undertook a reorganization of curriculum for all types

of secondary schools, bringing it in line with wartime needs. Specifications were made with regard to subjects, contact hours, and levels of proficiency.

3. The National Bureau of Compilations and Translations, under the Ministry's direction, prepared a complete series of textbooks for secondary and elementary education. Critics then and later deplored this undertaking as "thought control" or "unfair competition with private business." But the truth of the matter was that during the later years of the war there existed a serious shortage of textbooks. After the reorganization of the curriculum no private publisher had the resources to prepare a new set of texts in line with the changes. Reacting to the serious situation, provincial and municipal commissioners of education jointly petitioned the Ministry of Education for a solution on the national level. It was largely in response to such requests that the Ministry finally decided to undertake this huge and demanding task. The printing of the new textbooks was contracted to commercial concerns, which were assisted by the government with loans and a special allotment of paper ration to meet the massive demands in the free zone. The preparation of the textbooks went through several stages. Pilot projects were set up to test the early drafts of each text. The final version was the result of several modifications, taking into account the opinions and recommendations of experts and classroom teachers.[21]

Elementary Education

Elementary education was always completely under the jurisdiction of local governments. It was the most backward sector in Chinese education. In 1936 only 53 per cent of the school-age children were actually attending schools. After the war broke out only a limited number of elementary school teachers and students were evacuated. During the war the government at every level paid more attention to elementary education, aiming at enrolling every school-age child and putting in effect compulsory education. To that end the central government promulgated the Citizen's Education Act. For its implementation a timetable based on three five-year plans was issued in 1940.

By 1944 the number of elementary schools in the free zone reached 254,377, exceeding the goal set for that year in the first five-year plan. Currently 70 per cent of school-age children were now attending schools, a figure considerably higher than that for 1936.

To further elementary education the government promulgated more laws with regard to the regulation of kindergartens, standards for the subjects of elementary schools, and standards for moral education. The central government regularly subsidized local agencies in their effort to improve teacher training and remuneration.[22]

Special Programs

1. Social education. Social education in time of war was an indispensable part of the war effort. The ethnic and geographical complexities of China's vast border regions made it necessary that special educational methods and procedures be devised. Similarly, special attention had to be paid to the educational aspirations of the numerous and widely distributed overseas Chinese.

In maintaining civilian morale, promoting patriotism, and inducing the widest possible participation in the war effort, social education played an important role. To carry the work behind the enemy line, the Ministry of Education organized a Social Education Service Corps. In the free zone there were several threatrical troupes organized by the government to bring to a vast and varied audience plays and skits embodying the spirit of resistance. To nurture theatrical talents the ministry reorganized and supported two academies of dramatic arts. Music similarly contributed to the war effort. Under the auspices of the Ministry, massive choral performances of patriotic works were held in Chungking and other cities. Several conservatories and a symphony orchestra were established by the Ministry.

The value of film and radio also received ample recognition. In the expansion of its Department of Social Education, the Ministry of Education added a section of film and radio. An agency for promoting film and radio education was established in every municipality and province. Educational films, made under the aegis of the government, were shown to a wide public through the effort of fifty-two roving teams of technicians.

But the war effort was not the only concern of social education. Parts of the above activities were not directly related to the war. Under the sponsorship of the government, there were other undertakings whose primary purpose was cultural and educational. Among the organizations of this nature, established by the government during the war years, were the National Center for Social Education in Chungking, the National Northwestern Library, the National Kansu Museum of Science in Lanchow, the National Teng Kuang Institute in Teng Kuang, the National Academy of Rites and Music, and the National Museum of Fine Arts in Chungking.

The local governments were also encouraged to engage in social education. In response nine provinces and municipalities established museums of science which in turn initiated science education programs for the populace. Continuation education programs, under local control, proliferated after the enactment of the Continuation School Law, which made it possible for participants in continuation education programs to receive suitable credits for their school work and thereby to earn diplomas or certificates equivalent to those awarded by the regular school system.

The chief goal of social education has always been the complete eradication of illiteracy. According to the figures of 1944 the number of illiterates decreased by some 55,918,000 during the war.

2. *Education in Border Regions.* Vast in area and complex in ethnic composition, Chinese border regions always present great challenges to educational planning and execution. After the outbreak of the war the border regions gained new importance as bases for the war of resistance. Educational policy hence became inseparable from military and political considerations.

Education in the border regions largely followed the guidelines and stipulations contained in the two documents: *Proposal for Strengthening Education in the Border Regions* passed by the 1936 National Education Conference and the *Plan for the Education of Youth in Border Regions* proclaimed by the Executive Yuan in 1941. The goal of education as defined in the latter document was the fostering of patriotism and improvement of livelihood. The Ministry of Education was ordered to assume full responsibility for education in border regions.

During the war the Ministry took all the border schools hitherto under the jurisdiction of other government agencies. New schools of every level were added. The Ministry, in an unusual move, established and took direct control of seventeen national border elementary schools, which were to serve as models for other schools. Altogether the Ministry managed directly in the border regions forty-three schools of various levels, which accommodated a total of 5,858 students.

To gather firsthand information, the Ministry sent several groups of experts to the border regions. In the summer of 1941 under the Ministry's auspices the Students Voluntary Service Corps was organized and sent to the border areas of west Szechwan. In addition to making a survey and study of the two local ethnic minority groups, members of the Corps rendered social service such as education, health, and medical care to the local people. The report of the Corps eventually came out in a book form.

To advance knowledge of the border regions and to alleviate the shortage of trained personnel, Departments of Border Affairs were established at National Central and Northwestern Universities. New courses dealing with similar subjects were offered in other universities. Because of the linguistic multiplicity of the minority groups, there was a dearth of textbooks in non-Han languages. The Ministry financed a printing firm and purchased presses equipped with special keys to facilitate the production of bilingual texts.

Although the Ministry involved itself directly in most aspects of border regions education, the ultimate goal, as envisioned by the Ministry, was self-sufficiency and autonomy in education in the border areas. To this end subsidies were granted to the regions which undertook to manage their own education, while monitoring and assistance were continued by the ministry throughout the war.

3. *Overseas Chinese Education.* Overseas Chinese supported our war effort with exemplary enthusiasm. After the outbreak of the Pacific War, many overseas Chinese returned to China from the countries of their domicile now under Japanese occupation. To meet the special needs of overseas Chinese youth the Ministry of Education assisted more than twenty schools which had moved in from Hong Kong, Indochina and Burma so that they could resume operations in free China. Emergency grants were provided for needy Chinese overseas students. Those who received direct aid from the government numbered 14,286. Chinese overseas teachers stranded in South Asia after having fled from the Japanese were given free passage to China. Furthermore, the Ministry established five new overseas schools and gave financial aid to Chinese schools in countries untouched by war.

When more and more overseas Chinese came back to China as the warfront in South Asia broadened, the government established five national schools at the secondary level specifically for the overseas youth. They could also join special university-affiliated college preparatory programs designed specially to ease their transition to Chinese college life. Admissions quotas for overseas youth were mandated at most national universities, and in unusual cases entrance requirements were suspended. Mindful of the long tradition of patriotism and service on the part of the overseas Chinese, the government spared no effort in trying to repay their past contributions. Other efforts were the preparation of textbooks for overseas Chinese schools, and establishment of the National College of Asian Languages and the Southeast Asia Institute.[23]

IX

Students and the War: Evacuation, Aid, Training, and the Draft

The most fundamental task in wartime Chinese education was to keep the youth on our side. Without the youth we could not have waged the war, nor could we have prepared for national reconstruction. The first step of this task was to evacuate to the rear as many youths as possible. But even those left behind in the Japanese-occupied zone were not neglected by the government. Many underground schools were kept open, supported and supervised by Educational Agents sent from Chungking. The hazards of underground operations were such that at least 343 Educational Agents lost their lives in line of duty.

Those youths who fled from the enemy were met and collected at reception centers near the front. To receive, retrain, and resettle them, the Ministry of Education in 1941 established the Commission on Refugee Youth. Up to 1943 a total of 154,896 homeless youths were processed through the Commission. Food, shelter, and clothing were provided for them. Employment was found for a number of them; many others joined the armed forces. But more than half chose to continue their education. Many national secondary schools and temporary classes were founded for them.

Many college students, with their families or on their own, joined the great migration from the coastal areas to the rear. For their benefit a convenient unified transfer system was designed and administered by the Ministry of Education so that thousands of youth could painlessly resume their studies with advanced standing in a comparable school in the free zone.

Most students arrived in the free zone totally destitute. For them tuition was free. In addition, the Ministry of Education made generous loans to them to cover all the expenses. Later on, in view of serious inflation and the impoverishment of the middle class, financial aid was given to almost every student. Eventually all students in the national secondary schools and national universities were given full scholarships covering tuition, room, and board. This free universal education system was unprecedented in world history. Aid to students eventually accounted for nearly half of the total national expenditure for education. Those who completed college during the war entirely on government aid numbered more than 128,000.

Earlier I have outlined the debate during the early days of the war on whether college students should be exempted from the draft. Although the final decision resulted in deferment for the students, exceptions to the rule occurred as war needs rose. The first group that were drafted were medical students. During the early stage of the war, a portion of the medical school graduates each year were drafted to serve in the Medical Corps and the Red Cross hospitals. After 1939 all graduates were obligated to serve in military and public hospitals. Engineering students were also called from time to time. After the entry of England and the United States in the Pacific War the need for military interpreters was such that all male juniors and seniors who majored in English were drafted for that purpose. In 1944, 10 per cent of the law graduating class were drafted to serve as judge advocates. In total 6,371 college students were drafted during the war. This figure of course does not include those who volunteered for military service.

As the fighting on the front intensified more and more students enlisted in the armed forces. In 1942 the Ministry of Education called upon the students to volunteer. The response was most enthusiastic and by the end of 1943 some 15,000 students joined the armed forces. By 1944 the response grew into a broad movement which resulted in the formation of several special divisions of student soldiers.[24]

X

An Evaluation of Chinese Wartime Education

First of all let us review the wartime education policy. It can be simply phrased as equal emphasis on war effort and national reconstruction. In retrospect this policy must be recognized as a sound one. The consequence of this policy was that much direct and indirect contribution to the war was made by education while the nurture of talents needed in national reconstruction was not neglected. Overemphasis of either at the expense of the other would have caused great losses to the nation.

What, then, were the accomplishments of Chinese wartime education under the above policy? First of all, the great cultural and educational migration, systematically planned and generously supported by the government, was a great success. For this success credit should also be given to all cultural and educational workers as well as the student masses. Secondly, following the quick resumption of education in the free zone there were expansions, new undertakings, and large-scale innovations. Considering the wartime constraints and privations, the vigor and exuberance manifested in the education sector were truly extraordinary. There were people who thought that educational expenditure was excessive, but in a sense every measure was necessary, just as explained by Chen Li-fu, the wartime Minister of Education:

> Looking back I believe that nothing in wartime education was undertaken which did not meet a current or long-range need. When hundreds of thousands of students and teachers, homeless and penniless, flooded into the free zone, we could not but establish new schools to accommodate them. When technical skills and expertise were needed in the war effort, we could not but open new schools or add new programs to train people. In order to exhort the masses of people to participate in the war of resistance, innovations had to be attempted in social education. In order to stabilize the border regions and to assist the returning overseas Chinese students, we could not but expand special programs. In order to revive our cultural heritage and to catch up with Western science and tech-

nology, we could not but try to strengthen scholarly research. In order to develop expertise for national reconstruction, we could not but lift restrictions on study abroad. These undertakings covered almost all aspects of education. Superficially, we might be accused of extravagance and overreaching; but examined carefully, everything we did would appear to have been done out of necessity.[25]

Another way to evaluate Chinese wartime education is to see how much it contributed to the war effort and national reconstruction. The main contribution of higher education to the war effort was the training of huge numbers of students who were to participate either directly or indirectly in the war with their acquired skills and expertise. Just to give one example, thousands of engineering graduates took part in the construction in west Szechwan of a large and up-to-date airfield to accommodate long-range American heavy bombers. In a similar way, our research institutions solved many military problems and improved military technology. Fundamental education provided the military with thousands of youth whose literacy enabled them to serve as cadres in all branches of the armed forces. Social education did much in enhancing civilian morale and heightening patriotic spirit among the populace. Education in border regions in promoting ethnic harmony insured that no diversion of the military forces from the front would ever be necessary. In short, wartime education was in every way closely involved with the war.

In regard to national reconstruction, the goal of wartime education was the fostering of talented students in all useful fields who would subsequently, by their acquired expertise and skills, rebuild China from the war-inflicted shambles. Judging by the performance of the generation of scientists, professors, engineers, administrators, and business executives who had received their training in wartime China, we must admit that they had been well prepared. Most of the middle-age leaders in Taiwan today were the products of Chinese wartime education. Many of the graduates of wartime universities are even now playing important roles in science and technology on the Chinese mainland.

But the most objective measure of the quality of Chinese wartime education is to be found in the performance of its products in the United States. Most Chinese students who came to the United States to attend graduate school in the 1940's stood comparison with their American classmates.[26] Many of that generation of Chinese students have since distinguished themselves in various fields in America. From this sampling we could conclude that Chinese wartime education was as successful in quality as in quantity.

Next let us look at the reasons for the success of Chinese wartime education. The following are some of them:

1. The policy decision was correct. It was implemented with firmness and consistency.

2. To value education has always been a Chinese tradition. No matter how poor a family is, priority is always given to the education of the young. Similarly, in the government expenditure during the war, the allocation for education was only second to that for defense.

3. The education administration was given much power and authority. The educational leadership was strong.

4. The war, a constant reality in the mind of everyone, fostered a spirit of unity, self-sacrifice, austerity, and forbearance. In such a milieu all constructive endeavors, including education, thrived.

5. Patriotism was responsible for a generation of energetic, industrious, and highly motivated students. With such material to work with, education could not but succeed.

Wartime education also had its share of shortcomings. Because of severe limitations on budget, libraries and laboratories were inadequate and students undernourished. As a result, efficiency in learning and research was reduced. Furthermore, under the emergency situation caused by the war, the government could not but impose certain limits on all activities. Education was no exception. Certain government measures responding to the war situation may have caused inconvenience to some educators. This was both regrettable and unavoidable. Fortunately understanding was eventually reached by all and the mission of wartime education was completed through the joint effort of everyone.

NOTES

1. *Ti-erh-tzu Chung-kuo chiao-yu nien-chien* (Second Yearbook of Chinese Education) (Nanking: Ministry of Education, 1948), p. 1462. Henceforth abbreviated as CYNC.
2. Chen Chi-tien, *Tsui-chin Chung-kuo chiao-yu shih* (History of Modern Chinese Education), Chapter 18.
3. CYNC, p. 1429.
4. *Ibid.*, p. 1400.
5. Cf. Ou Tsuin Chen, "Lun kuo-nan chi nei te chiao-yu" in his *Chiao-yu yu wen-hua lun-wen hsuan-chi* (Selected Essays on Education and Culture) (Taipei, 1972).
6. Cf. CYNC, p. 101.
7. *Ibid.*, p. 53.
8. Cf. Lo Chia-lun, "Cha-tan hsia chang-ta te Chung-yang ta-hsueh," *Chiao-yu tsa-chih* (Journal of Education), Vol. 31, No. 7 (July, 1937), p. 67.

9. CYNC, p. 1373.
10. Cha Liang-cheng, "Kang-chan i-lai te Hsi-nan lien-ta," *Chiao-yu tsa-chih,* Vol. 31, No. 1.
11. *Kuo-lien chiao-yu kao-cha-tuan pao-kao-shu—Chung-kuo chiao-yu chih kai-chin* (Report of the League of Nations Education Mission to China: Reform in Chinese Education) (Nanking: Bureau of Compilations and Translations, 1932).
12. Chen Li-fu, *Tsung ken chiu chi* (Salvation from the Root), p. 65.
13. Cf. Ou Tsuin Chen, "Chiao-yu sheng-ya i chou chia," *Chuan-chi wen-hsueh* (Biographical Literature), No. 162.
14. CYNC, Part 5, Chapter 1, Section 3.
15. Cf. Chen Li-fu, *Chan-shih chiao-yu hui-i* (Memoirs on Wartime Educational Administration) (Taipei, 1951). Henceforth abbreviated as CCH.
16. Cf. CYNC, Part 5, Chapter 1, Section 3.
17. Joseph Needham's reports on science in wartime China were published in the following issues of *Nature:* 1943: 152, 9; 152, 36; 152, 64; 152, 343; 152, 372.
    1944: 153, 288.
    1945: 156, 496.
    1946: 157, 175.
18. CYNC, Part 6, Chapter 2.
19. Chen Li-fu, CCH, pp. 52-53.
20. Among the recipients of Chinese Culture Fellowships established by the Republic of China were: W. Theodore de Bary, Glen W. Baxter, Joseph R. Levenson, William Rhoads Murphy, Nicholas Bodman, James Crump, Richard B. Mather, Hans H. Frankel, George W. Seidl.
21. See the report made by Lu Tien-yang, Chairman, Committee on Secondary and Elementary School Textbooks, National Bureau of Compilations and Translations.
22. Chen Li-fu, CCH, Chapter 9.
23. *Ibid.,* pp. 37-46.
24. CYNC, Part 5, Chapter 7, Section 6.
25. Chen Li-fu, CCH, p. 64.
26. Tung-li Yuan, *A Guide to Doctoral Dissertations by Chinese Students in America 1905-1960* (Washington, D.C., 1961).

Comments:

BY JESSIE G. LUTZ

China is big; her history is long; and the difference between the life style of the masses and that of the ruling class has been great. In no history more than that of China is it imperative to attempt a conscious definition and delimitation of one's subject. Which China are you analyzing? The dusty northern plains or the steamy green hills of the south? The bent and hungry peasants, landed officials in the provincial cities, or elitist literati in the metropolitan centers of the east? Are your sources indicative of official policies and goals or of implemented reality? What is your time period and what changes occurred during these years?

Admittedly, our sources are inadequate for precise answers to these questions. But the attempt must be made even if it requires going beyond our traditional documentary materials, even if it makes broad generalizations untenable. It must be attempted even if the major result sometimes seems to be recognition that China's history is distorted because much is missing.

Defining the China which is the subject of our history becomes crucial when discussing wartime China, 1937-1945. Or rather, when discussing the wartime Chinas, for it might be said that from 1938 to 1945 there were four Chinas. There were those sectors known as free China and occupied China; within free China were territories under Kuomintang dominance and those under the Communists; in occupied China the Japanese might control the cities and the communication links, but the world of tiny peasant villages was beyond their effective grasp, and woe betide the lone Japanese soldier who ventured to enter this world.

Conditions in these four Chinas showed significant variations. Government policies differed, with Yenan's educational philosophy almost a mirror image of Chungking's. In all areas the gap between official goals and educational practice was considerable. Such might be due to government inefficiency and corruption, to poverty and inadequate communications, to popular opposition, or to a combination of these and other factors. The shortfall might be less or greater in any of the four Chinas but everywhere it was palpable enough so that no description of government policy conveys reality; no study based on official sources can be adequate. The 1942 rectification campaign of Yenan, the Kuomintang use of secret police, and the concern of the puppet governments over their failure to achieve legitimacy all attest to difficulties in implementation.

Attention must be given to chronology even during the short time span of the war years. The exhilaration which greeted the courageous military resistance at Shanghai, Hsuchow, and Wuhan in 1937-38 and the determination of Chiang Kai-shek to trade space for time is a far cry from the war-weariness of Chungking in 1945. Yenan's emphasis on united front opposition to Japan in 1937 had by 1945 given way to preparations for the power struggle awaiting postwar China.

To write a paper on China between 1937 and 1945 is to undertake a task fraught with pitfalls. As I question Professor Ou's definition of China in his paper entitled "Education in Wartime China," let me acknowledge that criticism is easier than historical composition and let me first remind you of several important findings by Professor Ou. Dr. Ou recalls the epic migration of many of China's institutions of higher education to the interior; this migration announced to the world that China would survive as a sovereign nation; in this confidence the government rejected accommodation with Japanese imperialism and trained scholars for the postwar reconstruction. Surprisingly, the number of teachers and of students enrolled above the elementary level increased during the war. Though it remained true that only a minority of eligible youth were attending school, the growth at the higher levels registered the continuing value placed on education by Chinese; it also reflected a persistent emphasis on higher education as preparatory to state service. The fact that college students enjoyed immunity from the draft and that most received a government rice subsidy was relevant as well.

Dr. Ou discusses the efforts of the ministry to standardize middle and higher education. Criticism of the specificity of the government regulations on curriculum, budget, textbooks, degree requirements, etc., was not lacking; many objected to their restrictive nature and to their use for surveillance purposes. Professor Ou rightly points out, however, the indiscriminate variations in both government and private schools. Lack of regulatory control had allowed small poverty-stricken institutions with only the most rudimentary library and laboratory facilities to assume the title university; any number of one and two-man departments existed in colleges; even the length of the bachelor's program might vary. Too many youths had frittered away time and money as a result of inadequate preparation before going abroad to study. Though Chinese educators and students complained about the loss of freedom at the hands of the party and arbitrariness in enforcement, few denied the need for some sort of minimal standards.

A study of Kuomintang educational policy in unoccupied China provides, however, an incomplete picture of wartime education. Even if one chooses to concentrate on education in southwest China during the war years, comparison with education in other sectors provides perspective. Some of the most interesting and unorthodox training was occurring in the Communist controlled areas of the north. Yenan deliberately abandoned fixed standards and levels; the goal was discreet educational programs rather than a hierarchy of degrees, and the length of the course might vary according to the backgrounds of the students and the exigencies of the war effort. Not general cultural education, but the knowledge and skills necessary for the prosecution of the war, for the growth of production in the northwest, and for the expansion of Communist Party influence received emphasis; theoretical instruction was, in fact, often combined with the practical activities of warfare, production, and mass-line administration. Whereas the Kuomintang elected to exempt scholars from military service and to continue orthodox education in order to stockpile talent for reconstruction of postwar China, the Communist Party tailored its training to immediate needs. Military instruction, political orientation, and, if necessary, the elemental skills of reading, writing, and arithmetic formed the core of the curriculum. Only the smallest possible number of courses essential to each program were to be offered.

There is not time here to evaluate the relative success of Kuomintang and Communist Party educational policies. John Israel has shown that survival as the ultimate value proved insufficient to sustain morale at Southwest Associated University. Certainly, the feeling of isolation and anomie characteristic of many institutions in southwest China in 1944-45 contrasts with the sense of involvement and commitment reported by numerous visitors to Yenan. Without further research, it would be difficult, nevertheless, to determine the extent to which the antithetic educational policies contributed to the difference in mood. It is true that the Chinese Communist Party emerged from the war strengthened whereas the Kuomintang emerged weakened and factionalized; this knowledge tends to enhance Yenan's image, including its philosophy for the education and use of intellectuals. Educational accomplishments were, however, not simply a function of educational policies; they were greatly affected by inflation, the activism of guerrilla warfare versus the stalemate in positional warfare, the ability to control corruption, the discipline and unity of the party leadership, etc.

More profitable is analysis of some of the reasons for the policy differences. *The Liberation Daily* (Chieh-fang jih-pao) of May 27, 1944 (trans. in P. Seybolt, *Revolutionary Education in China*, pp. 355-364), provides a clue. Modern education, according to the article, was not suited to the situation in the base areas because it was the product of capitalist countries at an advanced stage of economic development, the product of peacetime, and the product of the large cities. The perception as well as the environment of the Kuomintang and the Chinese Communist Party differed. The Kuomintang assumed its legitimacy for both the present and the future; it set goals, therefore, in long-range nation-wide terms. Education should prepare for the coming era of peace when industrialization would be a primary aim; it should prepare leaders for a China which included the great metropolitan complexes of the east along with the present centers under Kuomintang administration; it should cultivate talent for a modern China, which party leaders often identified with an urban China.

Chinese Communist Party leaders, on the other hand, assumed that they must make a revolution if they were to attain legitimacy and authority; increasingly, they saw the war as part of the revolutionary process. They, therefore, devised their educational goals and methods in terms of the present; otherwise, there might be no future. Their power base was a poverty-stricken area almost devoid of cities; just as they developed political and military techniques appropriate to peasant China, so they evolved educational programs for training activist peasants and former students from east China in revolutionary warfare. The task of developing talent for an urban industrialized China would be faced only if there were success in the present. For the moment all effort could be pointed toward winning a chance to become spokesman for China.

In some ways Kuomintang responsibilities seemed more complex; their territory was larger and more varied; they sought to represent China both nationally and internationally and so had to staff numerous and diversified positions; they tried to live in the future as well as the present. With a party membership several times that of the Chinese Communists, maintenance of unity and discipline was much more difficult.

The contrast in the perceptions and policies of the Kuomintang and the Chinese Communist Party makes all the more fascinating the fact that both regimes underwent a crisis of confidence regarding intellectuals and educational policies during the early 1940's. They even asked some of the same questions. Why do students look upon education as a means of personal advancement rather than preparation for national service? How is it that schools concentrate on training people to progress to the next educational level even though only a minority actually continue their studies? Why do students elect general programs and resist specific vocational and professional training? Why is modern education so far divorced from Chinese reality? What is necessary to make intellectuals loyal and dedicated instruments of the party?

Even though the questions might be asked in a somewhat different context, their similarity indicates the persistence of traditional attitudes and the gap between government policy and implementation. Also germane was a change in outlook regarding the war. As the emergency stretched into years and as the Sino-Japanese conflict became part of a world war with decisive battles and decisions occurring outside China, the united front disintegrated; the Kuomintang and the Chinese Communist Party increasingly prepared for the power struggle in the postwar period. Should educational policies and party relations with intellectuals be altered? Education in imperial China had been the means to political influence, economic reward, and social status; all these were associated with government office. Despite the many changes of the twentieth century, students continued to look upon education as preparation for state service; thus, the emphasis on higher education; thus, the elitism of intellectuals and their readiness to assume the role of opinion-makers, their reluctance to accept party direction, their preference for theoretical, general education rather than professional training. Poverty and primary commitment to other goals undercut government implementation of educational policies. Recognizing their fiscal limitations, both Yenan and Chungking chose to concentrate on training the leadership, but even the institutions of higher education operated on the fringes of financial disaster. Education as planned in Chungking and even in Yenan was a giant step from the actual education in the schools. The frequently expressed hope for a return to prewar standards is but one indication of conditions in southwest China.

Responsibility for elementary education was relegated to the provincial governments or lower administrative units with the result that there was lack of control by the center, economic privation, and anarchy in standards. Plans drawn up by the Ministry of Education sometimes bore scant resemblance to conditions at the village level. It has been said that at the beginning of the war there were more pupils studying under old-style tutors than enrolled in new-type elementary schools. According to Professor Ou there were, in 1936, 437 elementary students for every college or university student, and in 1944 the proportion was still 218 to one. The central government, the intellectuals, and therefore the source materials most readily available emphasize higher education. We know little about what went on below the college level and not much has been done to find out. But the history of higher education in China is only the tip of the iceberg.

Perhaps partly because they had little choice under wartime conditions, Yenan and Chungking made no attempt to assume responsibility for elementary education after their reassessments of the early 1940's. The Kuomintang reaffirmed its policy of nurturing elite talent for postwar reconstruction and stepped up its efforts to control dissident elements. Yenan devised guidelines for mass education and promised advice and know-how to villagers but popular education was to be staffed and supported at the local level. The Communist Party stated quite frankly that there was a limit at present to what it could do for the masses in the educational realm. The training of cadres, however, underwent significant change. Emphasis was on strengthening commitment to the party and to its revolutionary ideals. Many cadres from elite backgrounds had initially been attracted to Yenan by its anti-Japanese, united front stance. Their concept of guerrilla warfare had now to be rectified; they must learn to view every action, every thought within the framework of a Marxist-Maoist revolution. New and old cadres must above all acquire the ability to rouse peasant energies, to reorganize and increase production, and to redefine power and community at the village level. The flexibility with which the Communist Party responded to the challenges of the early 1940's contrasted with the conservatism of the Kuomintang.

Meanwhile, a large portion of the Chinese people were living in occupied China and education continued in their sector. Though writers during and after war have emphasized the great migration by the prestigious universities, only thirty-four, out of 108 institutions of higher education, accompanied by one-third of their staff and students, moved to the interior before 1941; twenty-five institutions congregated in the International Settlement of Shanghai or in Hong Kong, and fourteen remained in their original location, as Professor Ou points out. The Japanese founded or took over several schools and a number of private colleges continued to operate, but much of the higher education took place in Christian institutions which sought protection from Japanese interference by flying the United States flag or by conducting their classes in areas under Western control.

The Christian colleges found themselves in the paradoxical position of serving Chinese youth by stressing their foreign connections and extra-territorial rights. Their role was not an easy one; the possibility of misunderstanding was always present; uncertainty about Japanese actions was an unremitting worry, and the suspicion of collaboration was never completely absent from the minds of those in free China. Many Chinese, nevertheless, appreciated the opportunity to continue education in east China, especially as the conflict stretched into years. Enrollments at Fu Jen and Yenching in Peiping, at the Associated Christian Colleges in Shanghai, and at the Hong Kong-Canton centers skyrocketed, often expanding more rapidly than facilities or staff. After Pearl Harbor, several of the Christian institutions joined the trek to the interior and a few closed down, but a number continued to operate, sometimes underground with unfortunate consequences for academic standards, sometimes in the open despite necessary accommodation with the puppet governments.

Higher education in occupied China actually survived in a variety of settings and many institutions acceded to pressures to increase their enrollments. The war lasted eight years and not all Chinese desirous of higher education could or did make the journey to the interior. There is, nevertheless, a tendency to identify higher education in wartime China with education in free China.

About middle and elementary education in occupied China, even less has been written. Statistics would seem to indicate that there was some decline, but we know that many schools remained open. We know that the Japanese insisted on rewriting texts and revamping curricula in order to cultivate appreciation of things Japanese while the regime of Wang Ching-wei emphasized the issue of Western imperialism and of cultural aggression through education. We know that here too there was a gap between policy and accomplishment.

The subject of education in wartime China is particularly significant as we consider the significance of the differing educational experiences for postwar China. We know that relations between those who had remained in occupied China and those streaming eastward after 1945 were often strained and charged with mistrust. The differing wartime experiences continued to influence party policies and relations between the parties and intellectuals after 1945. In order to pursue these topics, however, we need to learn much more about education in wartime China. Professor Ou's paper provides us with a good foundation, but we must revise our definition of China as we continue the task.

CHAPTER IV

Southwest Associated University: Preservation as an Ultimate Value

BY JOHN ISRAEL

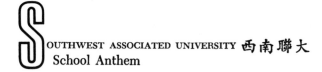

OUTHWEST ASSOCIATED UNIVERSITY 西南聯大
School Anthem

Ten thousand mile long march,
Farewell to Peiping's palaces of five dynasties;
In Hunan we rested on the slopes of Mt. Heng,
By the waters of the Hsiang,
Then again we moved on.
We were like promising timber
Transplanted on the outermost frontier,
While the blood of multitudes
Covered our native land.
Loud the flutes sound, songs resound, in Kunming
Together our spirits are bound.
Eternal shame will be washed white as snow,
The work of rebirth calls for heroes;
Though reduced to only three families, we shall remain
Stouthearted, indestructible;
Tempered by numerous hardships, countless sorrows,
A new national destiny is forged,
Heavy of heart, yet we remain
True to ourselves
In emulation of the sages,
Looking to the day when we have driven out the enemy,
Restored the sacred capital,
And reinstalled the triumphal tablet
In Peiping.

131

During the night of July 28 and the early dawn of July 29, 1937, the last students and teachers evacuated Nankai University 南開大學 in Tientsin. Several hours after the final departures, low-flying Japanese airplanes bombed the deserted campus into ruins. The next afternoon the enemy moved artillery to point-blank range and leveled the remains. On the morning of the 30th a military detachment moved through the ruins on foot, using mines and kerosene to complete the obliteration of the nation's leading private Chinese-supported university. When 62-year-old Chancellor Chang Po-ling 張伯苓 received word that a lifetime's dreams and efforts lay in ashes, he reportedly said, "The enemy can destroy the body of my Nankai; he cannot destroy its soul."[1]

In Peiping, which had been occupied without resistance, universities were desecrated rather than devastated. The old brick buildings of National Peking University, proud fountainhead of the May 4 movement, and the modern structures at American-endowed Tsinghua University 清華大學 , were converted into barracks for the Japanese Imperial Army. In the course of the war, Tsinghua's buildings served the occupying forces as hospital, bar, brothel, and stables. Peita 北大 was converted into a puppet university, and the basement of its College of Arts was used for the torture of prisoners. Such was the fate of these bastions of China's prewar anti-Japanese student movement.

For students who had not dispersed for the holidays, the summer of 1937 was a time for decision. Several hundred of them training with the 29th Army at the Southern Barracks outside Peiping, however, would have no further choices. Committed to battle by their commander in a brave but futile gesture of defiance, these lightly-armed recruits were mowed down by Japanese firepower.

More fortunate youngsters were able to join the war effort by escaping over Peiping's city wall or by making their way via the railroad to Tientsin's International Settlement, a point of embarkation for areas to the south. Some students ultimately joined guerrilla groups in the hills and mountains of Hopei, Shansi, and Shantung. Others moved one step ahead of the enemy to still unoccupied cities, carrying on propaganda, assisting in auxiliary activities in support of front-line soldiers, or recruiting groups to join the Communists in Yenan. Still others, home on vacation, braved tearful admonitions from concerned relatives before setting out to join the war effort.

I

Changsha Linta 長沙臨大

Though thousands of youths marched off to war, a majority of college students and an overwhelming majority of their teachers were determined to get on with education and scholarship. Fortunately preparations for the emergency were already in progress. In the spring of 1937 Hunan Commissioner of Education Chu Ching-nung 朱經農 invited Tsinghua to move to the provincial capital, Changsha, in the event of hostilities. As war clouds gathered over Peiping, construction got underway in Changsha, and Tsinghua administrators, together with their Peita and Nankai counterparts, laid contingency plans for evacuation to a joint campus in that city. On September 8, 1937, the Ministry of Education announced that Changsha Temporary University (Chang-sha lin-shih ta-hsueh *or* Linta) soon would open. During September and October refugee students and professors straggled in, and on November 1 classes began.

The situation at Linta was chaotic. Changsha's inadequate facilities compelled the College of Arts to move a hundred miles south to a separate campus at Hengshan 衡 山 . Professors, their notes left behind in Peiping and Tientsin, had to extemporize from classroom podiums. In some cases this spurred lecturers to unprecedented heights of creative thought; in others it left listeners bewildered. Students, who frequently arrived with only the clothes on their backs, depended upon uniforms of government-issued khakis and black overcoats, the latter doubling on rainy days as foul weather gear and at night as blankets. The official-looking uniforms gave them some sense of security in the military-dominated provincial capital. Linta had scarcely any books. Nankai's library had been bombed, looted, and burned; Tsinghua's and Pieta's were intact but inaccessible.[2]

On December 13, when the Temporary University had been in operation for barely six weeks, the fall of Nanking filled the refugee intellectuals with anxiety, foreboding, and confusion. With the nation's capital in enemy hands and the entire central Yangtze region vulnerable to attack, Hunan no longer offered a secure refuge. The pressing question for individuals and institution alike was what to do next.

II

War and Education

The sudden sense of vulnerability and the prospect of a prolonged countrywide conflict prompted many patriotic youngsters to cast aside their books and plunge bodily into war. For these individuals there was no shortage of options. Some went to Yenan for the short course of wartime education and Marxist ideology offered at Resistance University (Kangta) 抗 大 . Others enlisted in one of several war area service corps that were recruiting volunteers in Changsha. One group, headed by the famous woman writer Ting Ling 丁 玲 , entertained soldiers of the Communists' Eighth Route Army on the Shansi front. Students and graduates of Linta's neighboring college, Yale-in-China, organized a nursing corps. Many students joined the service corps attached to the First Army of Hu Tsung-nan 胡宗南 , who enjoyed a heroic reputation for his stubborn resistance to the Japanese at Shanghai. Among Hu's recruits were leftist activists Chen Chung-ching and Wu Cheng-ming, both of whom gained prominence in post-1949 China.[3] Other youngsters headed for Wuhan, temporary capital of the government and hub of united front activities. There they joined troop-cheering units, first aid teams, dramatic propaganda troupes, and a host of newspapers and magazines eager to recruit the talents of energetic young literati.

Even professors spoke of mobilizing for war. From the moment of arrival at Linta, a favorite topic of faculty conversation had been the conflict and their roles in it. Some had even gone to Nanking or Wuhan to attempt to offer their services. One of them, Professor of Chinese Wen I-to 聞一多 , recalled their state of mind:

> We had our heads filled with the European and American concepts of contemporary nations. We thought that once this kind of war had begun, the entire nation would have to mobilize. Of course we were not exceptions to this rule. So, many of us waited for government orders to go to the front or to apply ourselves to wartime production in the rear, or at least to exert a little effort to educate the soldiers or the general populace. The facts proved that this vision was, in the last analysis, no more than a vision. So we gradually sank back into the work appropriate to our station, preparing our lectures as before, teaching the same old stuff that we had always taught.[4]

Thus, even as the national crisis intensified, education fell back into well-tested molds. But not without dissent. During the chaotic 1937-38 academic year a lively debate was waged over the problem of "wartime education." The controversy, in fact, had started in Peiping before the Marco Polo Bridge incident as an outgrowth of the patriotic student movement of December 9, 1935. Students, especially leftists, argued that a curriculum of "dead books" was criminally irrelevant to the national crisis. They demanded instead a special curriculum geared to war and to popular mobilization. Most notable among faculty advocates of change was the prominent Peita chemistry professor Tseng Chao-lun 曾昭倫 , whose course on Wartime Chemistry, first developed in Peiping, was again offered in Changsha. Tseng lectured on subjects such as the formula for T.N.T. and the nature of poison gases, their composition, and the means of protection against them. As a practitioner of wartime education, however, Tseng was a minority of one on the Peita faculty, and even his course, according to a former student, had but a tenuous application to wartime needs.[5]

A more sweeping model of wartime education appeared in a *National Salvation Handbook*, written by Chien Chun-jui and Chiang Chun-cheng and published in January 1938. Among "research topics" listed in this publication were making and repairing machinery, the manufacture of cheap and effective protective devices against poison gas, the development of gasoline substitutes, and the rationalization of production. Another part of the curriculum was devoted to "wartime common sense," such as measures against air raids and gas attacks, methods of training the masses, work in mass literacy education, and various kinds of knowledge necessary for collective life, including information on organizing meetings, hygiene, scheduling, and the relationship between organization and individual. Considerable attention was given to the history of Japanese aggression against China and the principle of all-out resistance to the aggressor. Some academic subjects with a Marxist orientation, "the economic structure of modern capitalism" and "imperialism and the colonies," were included in the course of study.[6]

However, the wartime education movement lacked leadership and direction, especially from the government. Wary of leftist schemes for mass mobilization, the Kuomintang was also strongly influenced by western-trained scholars whose acceptance of the regime had always been contingent in large measures on official support for a modern system of higher education. According to a Communist critic, when students demanded wartime education, chancellors Chiang Monlin 蔣夢麟 of Peita and Wang Hsing-kung 王星拱 of Wuhan University 武漢大學 retorted, "All the years we were abroad we never heard that term. If you want wartime education, how will our professors teach it?"[7]

The Kuomintang, to be sure, was not entirely satisfied with the educational system promoted by westernized academic liberals, and was not averse to using the emergency and the slogan "wartime education" to its own ends. Party radicals such as Peng Wen-kai, editor of *Ching-nien chien-hsien* 青年前線 (Youth Front) "called for the replacement of regular schoolwork by propaganda, training, and organizing of the masses [and by] instruction in methods for increasing production, guerrilla warfare, espionage, first aid, fire fighting, and other subjects."[8]

However, the policy finally adopted by the KMT followed much less daring lines. Wartime education, stated the report of an emergency Kuomintang congress held in March 1938, meant "that we should remedy the fundamental defects of the educational system in the midst of national crisis. It does not mean that education in wartime is in any sense different from education in time of peace."[9] The ruling party's program looked back to the Six Arts of the Chou dynasty and advocated greater emphasis upon character training, physical education, the national and local problems of China, and practical subjects such as agricultural and industrial training.[10]

By the time of the KMT Congress, Changsha Linta was en route to a new campus in Kunming to continue under the name Southwest Associated University (Hsi-nan lien-ho ta-hsueh *or* Lienta). However, the decision to remove the university from the war zone to a remote refuge in Yunnan was hotly contested. News that school authorities were abandoning Hunan's facilities precipitated a debate over the relationship of the refugee scholar community to the national crisis. This argument went far beyond curricular disagreements over wartime education by focusing on the fundamental issue of the role of China's educated elite in the resistance against the invader. Was it morally justifiable to move to Yunnan, critics asked, when leadership was so desperately needed to mobilize the people of Hunan for the impending life and death struggle? The decision to move seemed to imply that selfish desires to continue prewar higher education would take priority over the patriotic imperatives of national salvation. Arguing that there was work to be done in Changsha, the Student Self-Governing Association sent representatives to Hankow to petition the Ministry of Education against moving, a position which elicited support from local newspapers.[11]

The issue was joined by two eminent visiting speakers. The first was General Chang Chih-chung, Hunan's governor who had initially offered hospitality to the refugee institutions. Chang used shock tactics. Dispensing with preliminary remarks, he lashed out at his student audience: "During this national crisis what the hell are you young people doing lying around here instead of going to the front?" So effective was this oratorical assault that his listeners, though stunned, were not offended. However, Chang was less persuasive than General Chen Cheng who argued in favor of the move. Chen meticulously analyzed the situation and cited opinions of leftist patriots Kuo Mo-jo 郭沫若 , Chou En-lai 周恩來 , and Chen Tu-hsiu 陳獨秀 on the responsibility of youths. Linta's students, he said, were national treasures. Even though China was in the midst of a crisis, it was vital that they complete their education, for a decade hence the nation's destiny would be in their hands. The combination of reason and flattery was devastating, and the fact that a majority of Linta's approximately 1,500 students moved to Kunming may be attributed in large measure to his influence.[12] Nonetheless an estimated 350 to 500 of them stayed to organize and mobilize the populace of Changsha.[13]

III

Chungking Policy and Kunming Practice

By moving to Kunming university administrators signified their approval of the fundamental KMT line for higher education: continuation through relocation. Geographically, however, Kunming was far removed from China's wartime capital of Chungking. The ruling power in Yunnan was Governor Lung Yun, who was pleased to allow Lienta's independent-minded intellectuals free rein to criticize the Chungking government and resist its centralizing policies. Lienta's freedom of action was enhanced by the enormous prestige of its constituent institutions, their faculties, and the governing committee of chancellors Mei Yi-chi 梅貽琦 , Chiang Monlin, and Chang Po-ling. Hence the university enjoyed considerable latitude to obey Ministry of Education edicts when it was convenient to do so and to temporize or resist when it was not.

The wartime curricular philosophy enunciated by the KMT's emergency congress of March 1938 would have placed greater emphasis upon moral cultivation and scientific research. In implementing these guidelines, Lienta educators took pains to preserve the university's liberal educational heritage. The course in the Three Principles of the People featured visiting lectures by eminent professors rather than systematic indoctrination in the philosophy of the ruling party. Only at the Normal College was there a flag-raising ceremony each morning, sometimes accompanied by moral exhortations from College Dean Huang Yu-sheng and Dean of Students Cha Liang-chao 查良釗 .

Promotion of science, similarly, was interpreted in its broadest sense. The emergency congress had called for the training of technical personnel, and Chiang Kai-shek had stated that "the aim of our education is economic development and enhancement of our military strength."[14] Some higher educational institutions, in keeping with these utilitarian precepts, established special courses in such subjects as explosives, air defense, automotive engineering, first aid, war finance, war sociology, and military psychology.[15] However, with some exceptions in the College of Engineering, little of this permeated the walls of Lienta, where the traditions of liberal education were carefully preserved from the baneful influence of mundane matters. Resistance to the utilitarian view of wartime education was voiced by Lienta philosopher Chin Yueh-lin: "If we return to some of the intrinsic purposes of education . . . the preservation of knowledge and the encouragement of knowledge, and the building-up of human character . . . we can easily see that too much . . . diversion of young men into one or two even admittedly useful lines will not give us the kind of citizens that some of us want."[16] Nor was the preservationist instinct limited to professors of the humanities. As physicist Wu Ta-yu 吳大猷 notes:

At the beginning of the war, my view was that we should minimize all expenditures in order to conduct an all-out war of resistance, and that research work could wait until after the war. But as the war dragged on, my view changed, and I gradually came to feel that if we were going to keep up the spirits of those who devoted themselves to research, we could not allow them to become despondent because they felt that there would

be no way to carry on their work for a long time to come. To develop and
train the human talent needed for research work that would go into postwar recovery, we should make provisions for research within the limits
imposed by the situation.[17]

Thus, as Lienta settled into its new home, there was an emerging consensus that the university's purpose was to preserve intact the prewar
system of higher education until the war was over. With Chen Li-fu as
Minister of Education, however, there was bound to be considerable
pressure to change. It was Chen's brother, Kuo-fu　陳果夫　, who
in 1932 had advocated a decade-long shutdown of all colleges of arts, law,
and fine arts and a monolithic emphasis upon the practical fields of
agriculture, engineering, and medicine. In fact, during the 1943-44 academic year, the Ministry began to exploit its power of the purse to steer
students into utilitarian disciplines. To incoming matriculants in public
normal, medical, pharmaceutical and engineering colleges it disbursed
Class "A" scholarships, providing free tuition and board plus an expense
allowance. Class "B" scholarships, for board only, were granted to 80
per cent of the freshmen in colleges of science, 60 per cent of those in
agriculture, and 40 per cent of those in arts, law, and commerce. However, after a year of this experiment, the Ministry reverted to scholarships
based solely upon need.[18]

Lienta's structure, as well as its tradition of pure scholarship, placed
the university at loggerheads with official priorities. There was no college
of medicine, agriculture, or pharmacy, and the College of Engineering
was located on the other side of Kunming from the main campus. The
Normal College, not an organic part of the original amalgamation but
established in 1939 by order of the Ministry of Education,, was regarded
with some condescension by other branches of the university. Nonetheless, Lienta's impoverished students had ample reasons to enter practical fields of study. Wartime economic conditions dictated that they
choose their majors with an eye on the job market. This produced large
enrollments in the economics department, which did not receive special
attention from the government, as well as in the officially-favored College
of Engineering.

Just as Nanking politicians had tried in vain to transform Peiping's
higher educational system between 1927 and 1937, Chungking's Ministry
of Education quickly discovered that it could not issue fiats to the proud
Peita, Tsinghua, and Nankai professors in Kunming. The Ministry's attempt to impose a standardized curriculum on higher educational institutions and its requirements for the registration of faculty members, a
comprehensive graduation examination, and the teaching of Sun Yat-sen's
Three People's Principles were ignored, sabotaged, or accepted only
insofar as they coincided with Lienta's own needs.

IV

The Quest for Purpose

Even though most politically active students had joined the war effort early in the conflict, a sense of uneasiness persisted among some of their schoolmates who had followed the universities into the interior. In "A University Student's Regrets," written on August 13, 1939, the second anniversary of Japan's attack on Shanghai, a Chungking youth lamented:

> August 13 is, I fear, a most appropriate day for writing "My Regrets."
>
> I recall that for ten days after the Marco Polo Bridge incident, I was constantly on the move southward, finally ending up coming to Chungking. I have now been here a year and a half, and I ask myself what contributions have I made to the state and to the nation? I have been living at the university on my parents' money, reading westernized books, eating six dollars a month's worth of food. Now the War of Resistance is in a new stage, at the front the military situation is relatively quiet, and in the rear things are more "stable" than at the front, and, precisely because the rear is more "stable" than the front, I have gradually lost touch with current realities.
>
> I am continually devising ways to continue life as normal. Is the curriculum that the school gives us not the same as prewar? Don't the professors teach just as they did before the war? We attend lectures, we take exams, we run after girls—isn't it all the same?. . . . We don't remember the troubles of the nation. Aside from occasional air raids, I can live exactly as I did before.[19]

As China's war dragged on year after year without a clear direction, the quest for a sense of purpose became more urgent. In 1943 a visitor to the Lienta campus noted that "the absence of a feeling of active partnership with other public and private bodies in molding the destiny of the Chinese nation is a terrific problem."[20] His concern was shared by a growing portion of the student body, even by a student of aeronautical engineering, a subject with obvious relevance to the war effort. The young man confessed: "I envy the youth in America and Britain and Russia. They all seem to be right in the thick of things, taking an active part in the war. Here in China we cannot help feeling that we are left altogether outside the national effort. Frankly, many of us are puzzled and bewildered."[21]

The faculty, however, had neither the desire nor the capacity for change. Only an occasional voice called for fundamental restructuring of higher education to meet the needs of the wartime environment. Such a voice was that of Lienta eugenicist Pan Kuang-tan   潘光旦   . Pan advocated a program of work-study education that would meet both wartime and postwar needs. Government loans were inadequate, he observed, and most students worked part time or even dropped out of school for a year or two in order to earn money to continue their studies. Would it not be better to allow students to take as few credits as they wished and to work part time even if that meant seven or eight years for graduation? Pan's program emphasized productive labor, especially the raising of livestock and vegetables to supplement student rice allowances. In addition, he urged dispersal of colleges and universities to the countryside. This, he argued, would remove them from the Japanese air raids which had an adverse psychological impact on their ability to study. Dispersal to the countryside would also help to end the tragic isolation of the urbanized educated class from rural China.[22]

Pan's proposals fell on deaf ears. His discontent with the educational status quo and his restless search for alternatives were not widely shared on the Lienta faculty. More typical were the views of the famous Peita essayist Chu Tzu-ching   朱自清   . Looking back with horror to the prewar December 9 period when students used the school as a launching pad for mass movements and obstructed its educational functions, Chu noted with satisfaction that relations between the generations had greatly improved during the war. Continued harmony, he argued, could be assured if the middle-aged academic establishment led by example, diligently pursuing scholarship, unflinchingly carrying out the school's regulations, providing the younger generation with moral leadership and the best possible intellectual, technical, and ethical training. For the present the leaders of the future had best remain subservient to the benevolent guidance of their elders.[23]

Chu's views reflected some realities of the early war years. Because the war itself provided a unifying cause, there was less reason for nationalistic student protests that divided students from the faculty and faculty members from each other. United by the pursuit of learning and the common struggle for survival, Lienta students and teachers shared a community of interest. Few saw any reason to disrupt the harmony.

V

The Heroics of Preservationism

Though scholars might justify their ivory towers as storehouses for the nation's future, as patriots they required reassurance that their efforts were also related to the anti-Japanese struggle. Peita classicist Lo Chang-pei, who spent several months in Japanese-occupied Peiping before joining his colleagues in Free China, later recalled:

> During this period, though my work was pressing I felt extremely uneasy! After the fall of the Ancient Capital, was it right to continue to shut oneself up in one's room every day and to bury one's head in this kind of pure academic research? Whether or not this was criminal behavior is a question not easily answered. But at that time I thought I could not instantly change my pen for a sword and throw myself onto the field of battle, and there was no opportunity to martyr myself for the country. So, rather than spend the entire day in lamentation with no plan of action, why not overcome my rising feelings of grief and indignation by throwing myself into my unfinished work? If in this occupied city I could manage to write several books, might I not in some way pay back the great benefits that the country had placed upon me in maintaining me as a scholar? Thus, even if the enemy should thrust his knife into my belly, I should die with a smile on my face, knowing that I had done right by myself, by my school, and by my country![24]

This was the spirit that maintained Lienta through its years in exile. By occupying, burning, and defiling China's finest universities, the enemy had dared the nation's scholars to keep the light of learning burning during the tempest of war. Business as usual was, therefore, seen as a gesture of defiance.

More than anything else, one event early in the war transformed the will to survive into a heroic epic. This was the "Long March," as Lienta chroniclers call it, a grueling 1,000-mile, 68-day trek across wild, bandit-ridden tribal territory from Changsha to Kunming. Though only a handful of faculty members and fewer than 300 students made the hike (more than twice as many traveled by train and ship via Hong Kong and Haiphong), the Long March made an indelible impression on the first generation at Lienta and became an enduring part of the institution's tradition. Like other wilderness myths, it gave new meaning to the more settled era that followed. As legend and epic, Lienta's Long March added a heroic dimension to the undramatic work of preservation.

Although the Long March placed the Lienta community a seemingly safe distance behind the front lines, safety was a relative concept. From the fall of 1938 until December 1941 the tranquil campus environment was disrupted by air raids. It was impossible to build shelters due to Kunming's high water table, and the only way to escape the bombs was to evacuate to the surrounding countryside. The academic schedule was adjusted to the rhythm of enemy attacks, with classes from 7 to 10 A.M. followed by lunch, with the middle of the day left free for dispersal. Classes resumed from 3 to 6 P.M. and sometimes continued into the evening. For the new arrival, the hikes into the countryside (always on lovely days, since the enemy never bombed in foul weather) were a novelty; for the pleasure-loving it was a welcome diversion; for the general population it was a monotonous routine. Most of the time the planes were en route to other targets, and students and teachers crouched down among the hills north of the city making wry comments about the anomalies of war. Some lightheartedly speculated that the bombing missions were part of a training program for Japanese air cadets whose graduation requirement included certification of a round-trip to Kunming.[25]

Whatever jokes might be told, there was a grim reality to the air raids. On several occasions bombs wrecked classrooms, laboratories, dormitories, and faculty housing. Though human casualties were rare, the bombers' wanton destructiveness reinforced the consciousness of mission in the Lienta community. As a student wrote after one such raid, "This proves how important culture is in the War of Resistance and in national construction. That is why the enemy is unwilling to let it be. From now on we will take up the heavy responsibility of national revival in a still more positive manner. We particularly want to sound the first note on the victory trumpet for the new students who are yet to arrive."[26] Putative evidence that China's cultural institutions were primary targets of Japanese aggression nourished the belief that preservation of these institutions constituted an act of patriotic defiance.

Though Chennault's Flying Tigers after 1941 deterred further air attacks except for a brief resumption in the spring of 1943, there was a recurring sense of danger over the ground war. In November 1939 the Japanese landed at Peihai on the southwest Kwangtung coast and advanced to the important junction of Nanning in the province of Kwangsi adjacent to Yunnan. This threat plus a shortage of space in Lienta's borrowed facilities prompted the Ministry of Education to order the university to prepare to move to Szechwan. The vulnerability of Kunming was underscored in the summer of 1940 when the enemy occupied Tongking and persuaded the British to close the Burma Road. Lack of a suitable site for the 5,000-strong academic community and realization of the waste in time and money that moving would incur, however, led to a scaling down of the relocation plan. During the 1940-41 academic year a separate campus for Lienta's freshmen and Preparatory Division operated in Hsuyung 敍 永 in southern Szechwan. By the summer of 1941, the military situation had stabilized, and the entire university was reunited on the outskirts of Kunming. In mid-1942, as the Japanese drove allied forces from Burma and the streets of Kunming were flooded with refugees, there was considerable uneasiness if not panic, but Mei Yi-chi (Lienta's de facto president) steadfastly announced that the university would remain in Kunming.[27] Thereafter, refusal to contemplate moving became a point of pride and enhanced the ethos of institutional survival as an end in itself.

In contrast to the purely physical dangers posed by earlier Japanese attacks, the Ichigo offensive generated violent shock waves that weakened China's political and psychological underpinnings. The campaign began in April 1944 and continued until February 1945, slicing through Chinese positions, overrunning laboriously-constructed U.S. air bases, and threatening China's interior cities. Among other things, Ichigo precipitated a reexamination of the decision to keep educated youth out of the war. In a dramatic reversal of earlier policies, the central government moved to channel the patriotic energies of the nation's dedicated but increasingly disenchanted college and high school students. A massive recruitment effort added a hundred thousand such young men to the army. Lienta, which had already sent a small number of students to serve as interpreters for American armed forces, now supplied some 300 enlistees for the Chinese army. By V-J Day, a total of 443 Lienta students were on active duty.[28]

The recruitment drive served as a momentary spur to patriotic zeal, but it came too late to restore the sense of struggle in a common cause that had forged spiritual links between government and academia early in the war. In fact, as recruits sent back bitter stories of mismanagement and irrationality in China's armed forces, the growing gulf between Kunming intellectuals and the Chungking government widened further still. Moreover, the recruitment of several hundred students did little to change the purpose and structure of the institution they left behind. Lienta's relevance to the War of Resistance continued to be more symbolic than tangible.

VI

The Struggle for Livelihood

For the overwhelming majority of the Lienta community the tribulations of daily living overshadowed the direct impact of war. The low Kunming prices which delighted those who arrived in 1938 did not last long. In spite of frequent adjustments, salaries failed to keep pace with the cost of living index which, by November 1943, had multiplied four hundred and ten times over its July 1937 level. Professors sold treasured books and clothing, took on outside jobs, and finally cut back on their basic diet. Without the accustomed servants to help out, proud male chauvinist academicians soon found themselves running errands and helping to care for children. In some ways those who had left families behind in Peiping or Shanghai were better off; at least they did not wake up each day to the cries of a hungry family.[29]

For Lienta students the economic crisis provided a very real, though extracurricular, wartime education. Cut off from families and funds, they were thrown upon the mercy of government "loans" (actually scholarships). As these proved increasingly inadequate to sustain a balanced diet, malnutrition became endemic. To supplement meager resources students took part-time and summer employment and sometimes dropped out of school to earn enough to continue their education. The jobs they took ranged from menial labor to white collar positions in banks and offices. One student was responsible for shooting off the cannon on the city wall to announce the noon hour. If he was a few minutes late getting out of class, noon was slightly delayed.[30]

Classrooms and housing were as inadequate as the students' diet. By the summer of 1940, after two years of makeshift accommodations, the school had completed its move onto the so-called "New Campus," a conglomeration of one-storied mud and wattle huts whose thatched roofs were in constant need of repair. Living conditions were described in a doggerel verse by foreign-languages-major Hsu Kai-yu 許芥 昱 :[31]

> When it pours outside
> It drizzles inside;
> When it stops raining outside
> It still drips inside.

Each of the barracks-like dormitories accommodated some forty students in crude double-decker beds. The only other furniture was a wooden crate between each set of two bunks; these held the students' meager possessions and served as occasional desks and writing tables. But little studying was done in these drafty ill-lit quarters. Students preferred to crowd outside the library in hopes of getting a seat when the doors opened, and large numbers flocked to the tea houses where for a few pennies they could nurse a cup of tea while studying or chatting with friends.

By 1943 a visitor noted "a deterioration of scholastic standards" due to the grinding force of poverty, lack of adequate sleep and nourishment, and declining levels of health: "The students seem fatigued when they turn up for their seven o'clock classes in the morning. There is no freshness or vitality in their approach to problems presented to them during the day. Their grasp, as well as their memory, is slipping."[32]

These impressions of a transient foreigner must be weighed against testimony of alumni, who generally recall good health during their student years. They attribute this to their own youthfulness, Kunming's salubrious climate, a survival-of-the-fittest process that had weeded out less hearty schoolmates during childhood, and the virtues of a low-meat, low-fat diet. Memories, however, may have romanticized realities, for contemporary evidence shows that the Lienta community was troubled by serious health problems. As early as 1939, trachoma, typhoid, scarlet fever, and malaria were common, and lack of medical supplies had led to fatalities during epidemics.[33] In December of that year, Minister of Education Chen Li-fu visited Lienta, was shocked by the inadequate student diet and resulting malnutrition, and ordered funds appropriated to remedy the situation.[34] Governmental and private relief efforts may temporarily have alleviated this crisis, but there is little doubt that deteriorating nutritional standards contributed to student ailments later in the war. In the single month of November 1944, the Lienta infirmary treated 2,189 people. The most frequent complaints involved internal disorders (1,033 patients), followed by eye trouble (573 patients). Diagnoses held inadequate nutrition and poor lighting responsible for the prevalence of these maladies.[35]

Whatever the impact of physical deprivations on student health, material conditions had but a marginal effect on their consciousness. Being reduced to a working class standard of living did not endow students with a working class world view any more than raising their own vegetables, as many did, caused them to think like peasants. The proletarianization of living standards seemed, in fact, to reinforce their dogged determination to get an education. They remained an intellectual elite, though more threadbare and less energetic, perhaps, than the eager and better-nourished undergraduates who had arrived in Kunming in 1938.

VII

The Psychology of Dependence

Economic proletarianization combined with other forces wrought some striking psychological and social changes in Lienta's young intellectuals. Before the war Chinese students had led a relatively secure and sheltered life as sons and daughters of a privileged urban elite. Though family finances might be vulnerable to forces of international depression, Japanese imperialism, and agrarian crisis, students by and large were sheltered from the economic facts of life. Enjoying a detachment from the struggle for livelihood that was the lot of their fellow countrymen, they could devote attention to the larger national and international issues.

During the war all of this changed. Generally cut off from parents and dependent upon governmental support, students of the 1940's became wards of the state. As such, they joined their teachers as part of a salaried class that suffered most acutely the effects of inflation.[36] For some, government subsidies engendered a sense of gratitude, a sentiment still voiced thirty years later by occasional alumni on Taiwan. But others were frustrated and outraged as they strove to stay alive while well-placed insiders and war profiteers waxed rich. Student gratitude for governmental largess was outweighed by increasingly bitter resentment against political and military mismanagement, official corruption, and social inequities.

Only the most tenuous bonds united the authoritarian ruling party and the officially-subsidized university that proudly proclaimed itself the "bastion of democracy." In the early war years the latent contradictions in this relationship were less important than the common struggle against the Japanese aggressor. Potential dissent was further dissipated when radical activists fled the campus and went underground after the New Fourth Army incident of January 1941. No longer challenged by the left-wing Chun she (Society of the Masses), the San-min chu-i ching-nien tuan (Three Peoples Principles Youth Corps)   三民 主義青年團   was able to dominate student political life. By 1943, however, disillusionment with Chungking was beginning to find literary and political outlets.[37] In March of that year, the publication of Chiang Kai-shek's manifesto, *China's Destiny*   中國之命運   , deepened the intellectual gulf between Lienta's intellectuals and Kuomintang ideologues. Chiang anathematized liberalism along with Communism, arguing that both were noxious manifestations of the May 4 movement that had led to widespread adulation of things foreign and denigration of things Chinese. By promoting these alien theories, he said, educators had aided and abetted "cultural aggression."[38] In 1944 and 1945 Lienta reaffirmed its role as guardian of the liberal heritage of the New Culture by staging the most impressive May 4 observances since the founding of the university.[39] By this time, the ties that held Kunming's intellectuals to the Chungking government were growing frayed, and many were ready to establish new bonds with Chiang Kai-shek's less-than-loyal opposition.

The dependence/resentment psychology that became increasingly apparent in students' attitudes toward Chungking also began to affect their feelings toward the United States. American ties were nothing new for Kunming intellectuals. More than 50 per cent of Lienta's professors had studied in the United States, and the highest aspiration of Tsinghua's students and young instructors had been to win a Boxer fellowship to the promised land across the Pacific. But the march into the interior threw the university back upon its own resources and, though indemnity funds continued to flow into Lienta via its Tsinghua component, the pre-war stream of students going abroad for study diminished to a trickle.

The first break in the valiant but lonely self-reliance of the early war period came in December 1941 when the Flying Tigers drove Japanese bombers from the skies. By 1943 Kunming was becoming a major American base, and by 1945 there were some 50,000 Americans in the urban area. The riches of an affluent ally helped to transform the once sleepy provincial capital into a crowded, bustling metropolis where once-prohibitively-priced consumer goods could be bought for sums that many Lienta students could afford. Alumni, returning from service with American forces in Burma, added to the supply of sturdy boots, field jackets, and other items of American wearing apparel—even sunglasses —that were making inroads into the nondescript and threadbare wartime student wardrobes. American-educated engineering professors organized a group to contract for construction of U.S. military facilities, also providing jobs for students. The market for interpreters absorbed growing numbers of English-speaking students and alumni. On visits from Chungking, John K. Fairbank of the Office of War Information renewed friendships from prewar days at Tsinghua, made available English-language scholarly materials, and proposed that hard-pressed Lienta professors be hired to lecture American troops on Chinese culture. In downtown Kunming students crowded into the reading room of the United States Information Service to scan *Time, Life, Newsweek,* and *The Readers' Digest* for Chinese news that had been censored out of the local press. In wake of the Stilwell incident, American periodical reports critical of China's leadership were translated for campus wall newspapers.

Lienta students' high opinion of the American press did not extend to the behavior of American servicemen in China. Seen in their off-duty hours in pursuit of booze, sex, and other diversions, G.I.s became the objects of increasing censure in proportion to their proliferating numbers and public visibility. Though a few daring coeds accepted invitations to socials attended by American soldiers, the G.I.-jeep-and-girl phenomenon was roundly denounced by political conservatives and radicals alike. In March 1945, a Kunming newspaper columnist noted that an English-language sign had been affixed to a Yunnan University girls' dormitory gate warning male visitors to keep out. "Those who do not understand English," he remarked, "obviously are excepted."[40] The social conduct of G.I.s, however, failed to dim the allure of America's democratic political ideals.

By V-J Day increasing numbers of students were devising schemes to go abroad, ostensibly to further their education, actually to escape the seemingly insoluble problems of their own country. "As the war dragged on and conditions became harder," noted an American missionary, "one idea became dominant in minds of the more adventurous: 'Let's get out of all this and go to America.' The suggestion was, of course, phrased more politely in public: 'The country needs educated men. I have little talent to offer now; but if I can get my Ph.D., I shall return far better equipped to serve my country.' "[41]

America meant much more, however, than military support, economic sustenance, and political refuge for Lienta's beleaguered intellectuals. The United States also represented the values for which the war was being fought: democracy, peace, progress, and international cooperation. "We depend on you for spiritual guidance, just as our armies depend on you for planes and equipment," Chiang Monlin told an American reporter—and his sentiments were echoed by Mei Yi-chi.[42] Students and teachers alike were excited by the Rooseveltian vision of a postwar world in which a democratic and prosperous China would play a major role. As the display of American military power became ever more impressive, wishful thinking became common: If the American government wanted democracy in China, it would oppose authoritarian rulers and support democratic alternatives. If it wanted a prosperous China, it would underwrite postwar recovery with unlimited resources. If it wanted a peaceful China, it would take steps to prevent civil war.

The vision became still more compelling as the war neared its conclusion; men and women who had endured eight soul-searing years were not prepared to conclude it had all been for nought. As worldly conditions deteriorate, God-fearing people trust in the Lord. Similarly, as conditions in China became increasingly dismal, Lienta liberals placed increasingly desperate hopes on American intervention. In July 1944, when Vice-President Henry Wallace visited the campus, he was bombarded with appeals for American support against censorship, repression, and other manifestations of the fascism that students saw emanating from Chungking.[43] Neither Wallace nor any other American, however, would turn the tide of Chinese history. By the end of 1945 Kunming's 50,000-strong American community had been reduced to a number small enough to share a Christmas dinner in the consular dining room. No intervention, divine or human, would save Lienta's intellectuals from the realities of postwar China.

VIII
From the Pinnacle of Defeat
to the Abyss of Victory

Such might be the title of a book about wartime China, from her finest hour when a defiant Chiang Kai-shek symbolized a nation alone but united against the Japanese juggernaut, to the moment of victory as a tired, corrupt, and inflexible government prepared to lead a war-weary people into civil conflict. China's tragedy was shared by the Lienta refugees who nearly eight years earlier had trekked across a rugged wilderness to insure the survival of their ideals and institutions only to find both threatened with annihilation in the wake of national victory.

V-J Day brought but a brief moment of relief. The short-lived mood of confidence was reflected in the marketplace where, for the first time since 1937, prices fell and the value of the Chinese dollar rose. As Mao and Chiang toasted each other across a Chungking banquet table, people dared to think that civil war might be avoided. Throughout southwest China refugees talked about going home and beginning life where they had left off in 1937, but with no Japanese armies to disrupt the peace.

The Lienta community was soon wakened from these reveries. On October 3 General Tu Yu-ming 杜聿明 , commander of the central government's Kunming garrison, unleashed his troops against Lung Yun, the bulk of whose forces had been sent to accept Japan's surrender in northern Vietnam. On October 10, Chiang and Mao signed an inconclusive agreement that failed to address the real issues between them. Apprehensive that Chiang would settle the issue by force, Lienta students and professors began to mobilize an anti-civil-war movement. Kunming's new rulers made it clear, however, that the Lung Yun administration's tolerance for dissident intellectuals would not be continued. An evening rally scheduled for November 25 at Yunnan University was prohibited. The meeting was transferred to the nearby Lienta campus, where the electricity was cut, shots were fired over participants' heads, and *agents provocateurs* engaged in disruptive acts. When the next day's official *Chung-yang jih-pao* (Central Daily News) 中央日報 attributed the gunfire to a bandit incident outside the city, indignant students responded by calling a school strike and organizing a campaign to win over public opinion. Following clashes between students and police, plainclothesmen, and troops on the streets of Kunming, soldiers stormed the campus and killed four people with grenades. This "December 1 Incident" gave rise to China's most serious uprising since the anti-Japanese December 9 Movement of 1935-36.

Although the entire community was shocked and outraged, the united front against barbaric repression soon was shattered by a prolonged strike. Professors who deplored the interruption of the academic routine were denounced by student activists who summed up their own sentiments in the title of a scathing critique: *I Love My Teacher, but I Love Truth Even More.*[44] After the resumption of classes at the end of December, a siege mentality continued as people from miles around came to pay homage to the four martyrs whose bodies lay in state in the Lienta library. Only after March 17, when authorities finally permitted a funeral procession, did the situation quiet down. By then Lienta was preparing to redivide into constituent schools and return north. A closing ceremony on May 4, 1946, officially ended the eight-year history of Southwest Associated University.

IX

Conclusion

Throughout the war years Lienta had been kept alive by a sense of purpose and by a dream—that one day Peita, Tsinghua, and Nankai, proud, free, and unsullied, would return to campuses freed of the invader's yoke. In the summer of 1946 the dream seemed fulfilled. As professors and students prepared to head north, they erected a stele to commemorate the ideals for which Lienta had stood and the historical mission that it symbolized.

On three earlier occasions in the course of China's history, proclaimed the inscription, governments had fled south; this time was the fourth. But now there was an unprecedented sequence to the southern exile: within ten years the north had been recovered and the country reunified. China had emerged from the war like the ancient state of Chou, old yet with "a mission of renewal," prepared to play a leading role in the world. Lienta had been part and parcel of China's wartime destiny that had elevated the nation to new heights of promise and responsibility.

Lienta had demonstrated that people and institutions with divergent characteristics and histories could work as one, enhancing rather than destroying each other's individualities. The whole had proved greater than the sum of its parts: "The five colors blended into a light that grew in brightness; the eight notes played in concert sounded harmonious and peaceful." Furthermore, Lienta had provided a model of tolerance and democracy for contemporary society: "Within the campus walls it established a model of academic freedom; outside it won acclaim as the bastion of democracy. It spurned the praises of a thousand sycophants for the honest criticism of a lone scholar."[45]

Such a scholar was Lienta poet and classicist Wen I-to who carved these words upon the stele. An enthusiastic participant in the long march from Changsha, Wen had endured enormous hardships to eke out a wartime livelihood. His fingers, famous for calligraphic masterpieces, were ruined for this fine art by the arduous labor of carving seals to feed his poverty-stricken family. Already radicalized by his own experience and further politicized by the realities of Chinese government and society, Wen became an outspoken critic of the status quo. The KMT's moves toward resumption of civil war and its resort to brute force to suppress dissidents turned him into a virtually full-time political activist and an implacable enemy of the regime. His experience capsulizes, albeit rather hyperbolically, the political transformation of some Lienta professors and many students. Wen was regarded then, as now, as a symbol of the university and the embodiment of its spirit of independence and integrity.

Wen I-to stayed behind to conclude his affairs after most of his colleagues and students had returned north. He was still in Kunming on July 11, 1946, when Li Kung-pu　　李公樸　, his friend and comrade in the Democratic League, was assassinated. Wen delivered the eulogy at a July 15 memorial meeting, concluding with these words: "We are not afraid of death; we are constantly ready to follow Li Kung-pu's footsteps. The moment we step out the door, we don't think of stepping back."[46] Approximately three hours after leaving the meeting, Wen I-to was shot to death.

From Wen's assassination until the founding of the Chinese People's Republic some three years later, not a month passed without further evidence of the incompatibility between the dreams of Lienta and the realities of China. Lienta's brief history had been a glorious one, but the paradigm it represented—the independent liberal university unscathed by the grinding forces of politics, war, and revolution—had no place in China during the late 1940's. Feng Yu-lan　　馮友蘭　, the Neo-Confucian philosopher who composed the elegant and measured classical prose for the stele, chose to work with the Communists rather than flee to Taiwan with Chiang Kai-shek. In his late middle age he was about to undertake an agonizing reappraisal of a lifetime of thought and scholarship. The academic system for which he had worked so faithfully during the war years would be subjected to irresistible pressures. Traditional philosophers would be toppled from the pinnacle of his intellectual universe to be replaced by Mao Tse-tung. As Feng sang the praises of this prophet of eternal struggle, he might well have reflected upon the vision of harmony that had inspired him to conclude his tribute to Lienta:

Thus the stele is completed by engraving the words of our School Anthem. It tells of how we sadly moved south, bidding farewell to Peiping's palaces of five dynasties, how we rested in Hunan on the slopes of Mt. Heng and by the waters of the Hsiang, and then again moved on. It speaks, moreover, of the long march through precipitous mountains, of looking back to the blood-soaked central plain, and of how we arrived at the outmost frontier and continued our lectures. Our books of poetry and history were lost, but we still had our tongues. The song of the native flute drew us together.

China's eternal shame has finally been washed white as snow and the enemy has vanished like a mist. From northeast to southwest one sees a golden vessel without a crack, the great unity unbroken. In the work of restoration we will continue the glory of the past. The three schools are like brothers, tightly bound together, sharing hardships and pleasures. Now that our union has come to an end, our mission has been fulfilled, the sacred capital has been recovered, and we are returning to Peiping, we erect this tablet to set forth our firm principles, record our joy, and make all of these things known for men of wisdom in ages to come.[47]

NOTES

1. Wang Wen-tien, "Chang Po-ling hsien-sheng yu nan-kai" (Chang Po-ling and Nankai), *Chuan-chi wen-hsueh* (Biographical Literature) 13:1 (July 1968), p. 19.

2. For a vivid account of Changsha Linta, see Yu Chen-yung, "San-shih nien hou i chang-sha" (Recollections of Changsha after Thirty Years), *Ching-hua hsiao-yu tung-hsun* (Tsinghua Alumni Bulletin), 26/27 (January 3, 1969), pp. 10-12. My account draws upon alumni interviews in addition to written sources.

3. John Israel and Donald W. Klein, *Rebels and Bureaucrats* (Berkeley: University of California Press, 1976), pp. 77-78, and alumni interviews.

4. Wen I-to, "Pa-nien ti hui-i yu kan-hsiang" (Recollections and Sentiments of Eight Years), in Hsi-nan lien-ta chu-hsi fu-kan, ed., *Lien-ta pa-nien* (Eight Years of Lienta, Kunming: Hsi-nan lien-ta hsueh-sheng chu-pan she, 1946), p. 3. Hereafter *LTPN.*

5. Interview with chemistry major, Peita class of 1939, Taipei, November 17, 1973.

6. *Chiu-wang shou-tse* (National Salvation Handbook, Shanghai: Sheng-huo shu-tien, 1938), p. 85.

7. Shih-shih wen-ti yen-chiu hui, ed., *Kang-chan chung ti chung-kuo chiao-yu yu wen-hua* (Chinese Education and Culture during the War of Resistance, n.p.: K'ang-chan shu-tien, 1940), p. 88.

8. "Ching-nien tan-tso" (Young People's Roundtable), *Ching-nien chien-hsien*, no. 4 (Feb. 15, 1938), p. 20, cited in John Israel and Donald W. Klein, *Rebels and Bureaucrats*, p. 162. Quotation is from the Israel and Klein text, not the original source.

9. Ku Yu-hsiu, "Education," in *The Chinese Year Book, 1938-39 Issue* (Shanghai: Commercial Press, 1939), p. 642.

10. *Ibid.*, pp. 642-647. The congress summarized its concept of wartime education in these words: "Both the educational system and teaching material shall be revised. A program of wartime education shall be instituted with emphasis on the cultivation of the people's morals, and the enhancement of scientific research, and the expansion of necessary facilities shall be effected." See "Program of Armed Resistance and National Reconstruction," article 29, *China Handbook, 1937-1945* (New York: Macmillan, 1947), p. 18.

11. Cha Liang-cheng, "Kang-chan i-lai ti hsi-nan lien-ta" (Southwest Associated University since the War of Resistance), in Cha Liang-cheng and others, ed. and contr., *Kang-chan i-lai chih kao-teng chiao-yu* (Higher Education since the War of Resistance, Hong Kong: Lung-men shu-tien, 1966). Reprint of a special issue of *Chiao-yu tsa-chih* (The Chinese Educational Review) 31:1 (Jan. 10, 1941).

12. *Ibid.* and Yu Chen-yung, "San-shih nien hou i chang-sha" (Recollec-

tions of Changsha Thirty Years Later), *Ching-hua hsiao-yu tung-hsun* (Tsinghua Alumni Bulletin), 26/27 (January 3, 1969), p. 10.

13. Chiang Monlin. *Tides from the West* (New Haven: Yale University Press, 1947), p. 222; Israel Epstein, *The People's War* (London: Victor Gollancz, 1939), p. 151.

14. "Program of Armed Resistance and National Reconstruction," article 30, *China Handbook, 1937-1945,* p. 81; William P. Fenn, *The Effect of the Japanese Invasion on Higher Education in China* (Kowloon, Hong Kong: China Institute of Pacific Relations, 1940), p. 34.

15. *Ibid.,* p. 35.

16. Harley Farnsworth MacNair, ed., *Voices from Unoccupied China* (Chicago: University of Chicago Press, 1944), p. liii.

17. Wu Ta-yu, "Kang-chan chi-chung chih hui-i" (Recollections of the War of Resistance Period), part 2, *Chung-yang jih-pao* (Central Daily News), Sept. 5, 1964.

18. Chiao-yu pu chiao-yu nien-chien pien-tsuan wei-yuan-hui, ed., *Ti-erh-tzu chung-kuo chiao-yu nien-chien* (Second Yearbook of Chinese Education, Nanking: Commercial Press, 1948), p. 52; "Scholarships Instead of Loans for Students," *Quarterly Bulletin of Chinese Bibliography,* new series 3:3-4 (September-December 1943), p. 37.

19. Wang Chao, "I-ko ta-hsueh-sheng ti tsan-hui" (A University Student's Regrets), *Hsin-hua jih-pao* (New China Daily), August 26, 1939, in Shih-shih wen-ti yen-chiu hui, ed., *Kang-chan,* p. 88.

20. Ernest O. Hauser, "Poverty Campus," *The Saturday Evening Post* 216:19 (November 6, 1943), p. 93.

21. *Ibid.*

22. "Shuo kung-tu lien-ying" (On Work-Study), in Pan Kuang-tan, *Tzu-yu chih lu* (The Road of Freedom, Shanghai: Shang-wu yin-shu kuan, 1946), pp. 207-220.

23. Pei Hsuan (Chu Tzu-ching), "Chung-nien-jen yu ching-nien jen" (Middle-aged People and Young People), *Ching-nien kung-lun* (Youth Opinion), 1:2 (April 1, 1939), p. 12.

24. Lo Chang-pei, "Chi-chi shih-pien hou pei-ta ti tsan-chu" (The Tragic Situation at Peita after the July 7th Incident), *Chuan-chi wen-hsueh* 17:6 (December 1970), p. 94. Originally published in *Pei-ching ta-hsueh wu-shih chou-nien chi-nien te-kan* (Commemorative Volume for the Fiftieth Anniversary of National Peking University, no publication data, 1948).

25. Fei Hsiao-tung, "Chiao-shou sheng-huo chih i-chang" (A Chapter in the Life of a Professor), *LTPN,* p. 56.

26. Tsai Lien, "Shih-fan hsueh-yuan" (The Normal College), *Lien-ta ching-nien* (Lienta Youth), 1:2, October 16, 1941, p. 30.

27. Letter from a Peita professor to a British friend, May 17, 1942, in the Records of the Office of Strategic Services, RG 226, no. 105632, located in the National Archives.

28. *Hsi-nan lien-ho ta-hsueh hsiao-yu lu* (Southwest Associated University Alumni Register, no publication data, April 1946), p. 192.
29. See report by Kiang Wen-han in *Federation News Service,* April 1945, p. 6, and Kai-yu Hsu, "The Life and Poetry of Wen I-to," *Harvard Journal of Asiatic Studies,* vol. 21 (1958), pp. 134-179.
30. For descriptions of students' efforts at self-support, see *LTPN,* 96-102, and Lang Chang-hao, "Hsien-hua kung-tu" (Chat About Work-Study), *Lien-ta ching-nien* (Lienta Youth), 1:2 (October 16, 1941), pp. 23-25.
31. Kai-yu Hsu, interview, Tiburon, California, October 4, 1973.
32. Hauser, "Poverty Campus," p. 92.
33. Wu Yu, letter from Kunming, *China Weekly Review,* August 26, 1939, p. 397; Gilbert Baker, "A Student Church in Kunming," *Chinese Recorder,* February 1940, p. 88.
34. *New York Times,* January 6, 1940; "Students Lead Spartan Lives," *China at War,* 4:2 (March 1940), p. 61.
35. *Kuan-cha pao* (The Observer Daily, Kunming), Dec. 31, 1944. Nutritional conditions in Kunming were not atypical of those in other wartime cities. See Tsai Chiao, "Problems of Nutrition in Present-Day China," in MacNair, ed., *Voices,* pp. 16-25.
36. Wu Chi-yuen, "China's Social Environment and Her Economic Future," China Paper No. 3, Tenth Conference of the Institute of Pacific Relations (Stratford-upon-Avon, England, September 1947), p. 10.
37. For examples, see *LTPN,* pp. 47-51, 139 ff.
38. Chiang Kai-shek, *China's Destiny and Chinese Economic Theory* (New York: Roy Publishers, 1947), pp. 98-100.
39. *LTPN,* pp. 20-33.
40. *Kuan-cha pao,* March 20, 1945.
41. Gilbert Baker, *The Changing Scene in China* (London: S.C.M. Press Ltd., 1946), pp. 55-56.
42. Hauser, "Poverty Campus," p. 94.
43. For examples see U.S. State Department archives no. 893.00/7-1144. For faculty views expressed to Wallace see Records of the Office of Strategic Services, RG 226, no. XL 823.
44. *Wu ai wu shih wu yu ai chen-li* (Kunming: Hsueh-sheng chu-pan she, May 1946).
45. "Kuo-li hsi-nan lien-ho ta-hsueh chi-nien pai" (National Southwest Associated University Memorial Stele), photograph of rubbing, courtesy of Professor Wu Hsiang-hsiang.
46. Kai-yu Hsu, "The Intellectual Biography of a Modern Chinese Poet: Wen I-to (1899-1946)" (Ph.D. dissertation, Stanford University, 1959), p. 178.
47. "Kuo-li hsi-nan lien-ta chi-nien pai." My appreciation to Richard Bush, upon whose translation this one is based.

Comments:

BY CHUN-FAN MAO

"Lienta," "Kunming," "War of Resistance," for alumni and faculty of the National Southwest Associated University, the very sight and sound of these words would invariably conjure up visions of that unique period of life in that southern city surrounded by mountains and perched on the Yun-Kuei Plateau adjacent to Southeast Asia, during China's eight-year struggle against Japanese invasion. These visions would appear as clearly as scenes on a television screen; however, when one tries to capture them in writing and organize them into a coherent story, they would become as fleeting as morning mists or as elusive as a springtime dream. Things remembered, it seems, tend to present themselves a little more sweetly or a little more bitterly, a little more magnificently or a little more dejectedly, than they really were. One wonders whether this could serve as an explanation for the fact that though there is no scarcity of personal recollections, the story of Lienta remains to be told.[1] Perhaps, it is more fitting for a Western scholar, uninvolved in, yet greatly fascinated by, the life of this unique wartime institution of higher learning to tackle such a task!

About two years ago I met Professor John Israel at a dinner party given by Lienta alumna Feng Te-fu. At that time he had just come back from an extended trip to Taiwan and Hong Kong to collect materials for his book about Lienta. This is the very thing many Lienta alumni have wanted to do yet left undone. The hostess and nearly all the guests of about ten people at that party were Lienta alumni/ae. Naturally, they felt at once envious of and grateful to Professor Israel. In an atmosphere of envy mingled with gratitude, I proposed to make him an honorary alumnus.[2] The proposal was duly passed and happily accepted. Thus, as far as Lienta is concerned, John Israel is no longer an outsider but an "insider"—an "insider" of latter-day in this New Hemisphere.

Last November, when the annual reunion dinner meeting of the Lienta Alumni Association in Greater New York was held in Manhattan, N.Y.C., honorary alumnus John Israel and his wife journeyed from Charlottesville, Va., to attend. In replying to my question about his book on Lienta, he said, "It's coming along fine. But I take good time to write it. You know, it's a labor of love."

I have just finished reading his paper, "Southwest Associated University: Preservation as an Ultimate Value," which, I gather, is a microcosm of the opus on which he has been at work. If this paper is an indication, the larger work is bound to be a labor of love.

Prefaced with an English translation of the Lienta school anthem and beginning with the last departures of students and teachers from Nankai University in Tientsin in the summer of 1937, the paper takes the reader through the dissociation of Lienta into the three constituent schools (National Peking University, National Tsinghua University and Nankai University) in May 1946, and concludes with a long quotation from the stele commemorating Lienta's heroic struggles and glorious triumph. The paper succeeded in giving us a compactly and selectively structured panorama of a multiplex story. Instead of commenting on every facet of Lienta life touched upon in the paper, I believe it would be more fruitful to confine my comments to a few salient aspects which Professor Israel has put forward.

The story of Lienta was concomitant with China's eight-year war of resistance against Japan. Something must be said of Japan's invasion and China's resistance, for without taking account of them neither can the uniqueness of Lienta as an institution of higher learning be grasped nor can the insurmountable Lienta spirit and sense of humor in the face of adversities be understood. History shows us that it was the First World War that made Japan, a country with a long tradition of militarism, an upstart world power. She has harbored imperial designs on East Asia and even grandiose dreams of world conquest since then. The logical target of her designs as well as the springboard to realizing her dreams was the complete subjection of China. The Chinese revolution of 1911 overthrew the decaying Ching Dynasty and made China a Republic, the first one in Asia. After a century of humiliation under the impact of Western imperialism, the young Republic of China began to reassert herself as both her nationalism and self-confidence continued to gain momentum. Moreover, after the National Revolutionary Army of the Kuomintang (The Nationalist Party), led by Chiang Kai-shek and guided by the philosophy and program of *San Min Chu I*, had brought most of the country under control in 1927 and moved the seat of the National Government from Canton to Nanking, the Chinese accelerated their momentum to build up their country and to reclaim their rightful place under the sun. The antithesis between Japan's scheme to appropriate China as a colony and China's determination to emancipate herself from foreign domination inevitably led to the climax, the outbreak of the Second Sino-Japanese War in the summer of 1937.[3]

The Lukouchiao Incident that ignited the outbreak was no more and no less than its appellation, a mere incidental pretext that could be easily fabricated by Japan at will. China was compelled to make a decision. In theory, there was a choice: to surrender or to resist. In reality, there was none. What would the consequences have been had China surrendered and turned herself into a collaborator with the aggressor towards "the fulfillment of the ideal of Sino-Japanese cooperation" as Hirota Koki, Japan's foreign minister, proclaimed in his speech to the Diet in January 1938?[4] Mention might be made that in the same speech Hirota conveyed to the Western Powers, with a note of menace, the idea that Japan expected their recognition of the new conditions in China as well as their cooperation for a new order in the Far East. What would the outcome have been and what would Asia and the whole world have been like had the Chinese National Government stooped to collusion?

War and Education

Lienta was a product of China's resistance to aggression and subjection and her fight for self-preservation and independence; it was also a product of rational design by a community of scholars encouraged and supported at once by the Central Government to meet the exigencies of an extraordinary period and to keep the wheels of knowledge turning. This the narrative of Professor Israel's paper clearly confirms. That there was a diversity of opinion about education at that time is understandable. China was at war with a formidable invader, the end of the strife seemed a long way off. For the many patriotic youths of action who chose to postpone or forego a college education, there was no shortage of options to get themselves more directly involved, Professor Israel informs us very movingly (p. 133). Among the faculty members there was no lack of debate about curricular changes and mass mobilization. Professor Israel laments over the program adopted by the Kuomintang congress in March 1939 as old-fashioned—a program that "looked back to the Six Arts of the Chou Dynasty and advocated greater emphasis upon character training" (p. 135). On the other hand, he considers, based upon his interpretation of Chiang Kai-shek's philosophy of wartime education, the concentration on the immediate economic and military problems as narrowly utilitarian (p. 137). Even this emphasis exerted incredibly little influence on Lienta where "the traditions of liberal education were carefully preserved from the baneful influence of mundane matters" (p. 137).

Professor Israel seems to take the view that liberal arts education and applied sciences education are mutually exclusive, or at least incompatible. Therefore, the adoption of one necessitates the exclusion of the other, the development of one must be at the expense of the other. Both in theory and in fact, the two branches of learning are neither mutually exclusive nor incompatible. Among the six classic arts, archery and chariot-driving (in modern parlance, the art of war and mechanical engineering) are definitely utilitarian and practical in function. Furthermore, I suspect that Professor Israel has misread the wartime education program adopted by the Extraordinary Kuomintang National Congress

in March 1939, and misinterpreted Chiang Kai-shek's philosophy of wartime education, the text of which he quoted from William Fenn's book,
The Effect of the Japanese Invasion on Higher Education (note 12). A
closer scrutiny of Articles 29-32 of the Program of Armed Resistance and
National Reconstruction would reveal that the guiding principle was to
effect a well-balanced development of the several disciplines of learning.[5]
But as the war went on, in many cases readjustments were made to meet
wartime demands; e.g., the emphasis on applied sciences, a policy begun
in the early 1930's in the period of energetic national construction prior
to Japan's invasion. However, it did not mean at the expense of liberal
arts, rather it was a redress of the balance to insure a more harmonious
educational program.

The dialogues among Chinese leaders concerning education in wartime began in the summer of 1937, immediately after the Lukouchiao
Incident when the clouds of war were gathering. In the emergency
conference called by Chiang Kai-shek at the summer resort of Kuling,
Hu Shih expressed that "education in wartime is not extraordinary
education; it is regular education."[6] If there is a Chinese philosophy of
wartime education, this is it, defined succinctly and clearly by an
educator-philosopher. That the purpose of this philosophy of wartime
education is a naive "business as usual" (by blindly ignoring the existence of a war) is absurd and need not concern us. The exponents of such
a philosophy were positively not that naive. We are concerned, rather,
with the spirit and motive of this philosophy and the effects of its application. As the Chinese saying goes, it takes ten years to grow a tree, a
hundred years for a sound system of education to take root. Hu Shih's
advice is rooted in a long-range view of education that has been the
backbone of Chinese society for centuries.

The program finally adopted by the Central Government, no doubt,
was a mirror of this view, steadfastly looking forward to the difficult task
of national reconstruction and continuing the training of future leaders.
The sad fact that China's educational institutions, especially Lienta in
Kunming, had been the targets of ruthless Japanese bombings, obliquely
testified to the wisdom of this educational philosophy and the strength
of the program based on it. To keep the flame of learning glowing in the
midst of a war was but the other side of China's resolve to demonstrate
her resistance to foreign invasion.

External Circumstances and Internal Resources

The hardships that Lienta students and faculty members had faced
would have seemed insuperable to less resourceful and less confident
men and women. Under the subheading, "The Struggle for Livelihood,"
Professor Israel describes vividly how they coped with their daily prob-

joy in the midst of difficult circumstances. Perhaps, the academic communities in a more affluent society could look to the Lienta experience for inspiration to solve some of the problems confronting them.

Puzzlements and Questions

Being a member of the Lienta community, with the expected permission of latter-day alumnus John Israel, I would like to raise a few questions about some of the things which he has presented and which, at times, appear as puzzlements to me. I suggest to do this in the spirit of our teashop dialogue, seeking for clarification and better understanding.

National Government and Lienta. In his discussion under the subheading, "Chungking Policy and Kunming Practice," and elsewhere, Professor Israel seems to hold the view that there were fundamental differences between the National Government in Chungking and the National Lienta in Kunming. I find it difficult to appreciate such a view. At that time, the overall issue for the whole nation was the resistance against Japan for national independence. The National Government in Chungking was both the leader and symbol of this resistance. In the midst of war, the National Government, instead of tightening its grip of power, sought to enlarge the base of participation through the People's Political Council (PPC). Many Lienta faculty members were selected for PPC membership, and they were happy to be so honored. Was not this an indication that Lienta and the National Government were on friendly terms? I do not have the sources on hand to show how many Lienta faculty members had served as PPC members. But Lienta graduates of the political science department to this day still relish the fact that nearly all the teachers in that department were "elected" as PPC members, in the parlance of Lienta days, as "philosopher-kings."

As stated earlier, Lienta was a wartime institution of higher learning supported by the National Government for the purpose of carrying out the educational mission of the three constituent schools during the war period and of passing it on to them after the conclusion of the war. Thus, it was predestined to be an "interregnum," the fate of which was inextricably intertwined with the fate of the National Government in a time of national crisis.

Scholastic Standards of Lienta. When it comes to the rating of Lienta, in the absence of a systematic study, it would be difficult to ascertain one way or the other. However, during the War of Resistance, there was a tacit agreement that it was the number-one university in China. All youngsters looked longingly to that gate of the modest "New Campus" as the Mecca of high education. Just to get in that gate was quite a feat. Professor Israel cites the observations of an American visitor in

1943 that there was a deterioration of scholastic standards due to the grinding forces of poverty and difficult circumstances (p. 144). Was the visitor knowledgeable enough to make such a judgment?

No doubt the exhaustion of a protracted war left its imprint everywhere and on people of all walks of life, including undergraduate students, not just during the war period but beyond it. In 1948, a former Lienta professor, while teaching at Harvard, told some of his former students with a sigh that the postwar students were inferior to their wartime counterparts.

Intellectual elite. I am rather puzzled by the fact that whenever Professor Israel mentions the word "elite," he says it in an apologetic tone. China, at that time, had no policy of open admission for college education and has not had one since. Lienta teachers, liberal as they were, and kind in many instances, never intended to put the cap of scholarship to the head just for the asking. The Chinese have for centuries put a premium on education. The educated have always been inseparable from leadership. This is an historical fact. And it is still true today. Why apologize?

Dependence/Resentment Psychology. The account of students' frustration and resentment as a result of being recipients of government grants (p. 146) is too impressionistic and too sweeping for this reader. The primary purpose of Lienta students, similar to that of students elsewhere, was to get a good college education. They really fought to get in "The University" (as some British visitors called it) in wartime China out of their own volition. Why should receiving grants from the government to tide over a period of difficulty be considered a source of resentment?

Professor Israel's statement that out of this dependence/resentment psychology the students were increasingly looking toward America across the Pacific as the promised land needs clarification. Lienta students, generally speaking, were voracious readers of newspapers and periodicals and were well abreast of current affairs. The fact that the Central Government was bearing the brunt of the Japanese attacks and was withstanding the assault entirely alone for four years could not be unknown to them. The memory that for four years China had fought alone, with only world opinion and lip service on her side, was to remain fresh to all thinking Chinese, including college students.

True, feelings of resentment and frustration in a protracted war were rampant, but they were directed against the cause—the invaders. Even today, some four decades after the Lukouchiao Incident, such feelings would flash into their minds whenever anything reminded them of the war—with possibly one exception—the Chinese Communist leaders, who have never openly acknowledged the Japanese invaders as their *de facto* resuscitators. Without the Japanese invasion, they would never have had the chance to sit on the throne in the Purple Forbidden City.

It is not clear to me what Professor Israel means by "the promised land": a land of modern sciences and new ideas for those who care to seek them, or a land of escapism? As we know, the educated Chinese are intensely patriotic. They always have China in their hearts, though not always in their mouths.

Voluntary Subjection. Here comes the insoluble puzzlement. Professor Israel tells us that Lienta students and teachers believed that the United States could do anything it wished. If the American government wanted democracy in China, Chinese could be democratic. . . . If it wanted a peaceful China, it would bring about peace (p. 148). Could it be a reasoned belief of Lienta students and teachers who were considered by many as the cream of the Chinese society?[9] Only a Chinese of otherworldly innocence or hopeless stupidity about international politics would hold such a view, if it could be called a view. Could the United States really do anything it wished? Granted it could, was it able to make any country democratic? Was democracy some kind of concrete goods to be given or withheld at will? Even if the United States were a community of saints ruled by Almighty God, it could not perform such miracles.

Let's consider things from the Chinese side. Ever since the clarion call for a demonstration of militant national will against the invader (Chiang's July 19, 1937, speech at the summer resort of Kuling), the Chinese had fought alone for more than four years and after Pearl Harbor joined forces with Allied Powers as an equal. China needed the Allies, but they also needed China. That at the conclusion of the war China would docilely invite another foreign master was utterly unthinkable. Why did China resist Japan to begin with if she would not mind being dominated by some other outside power, and cared nothing about her independence?

The paper begins with a poem and concludes with a poem, both written by Professor Fung Yu-lan, now once again repenting in mainland China. One could almost hear the sighs of Professor Israel when he wrote the following: "As Fung sang the praises of this prophet [Mao Tse-tung], he might well have reflected upon the vision of harmony that had inspired him to conclude his tribute to Lienta," (p. 151). How well Lienta students remember their poet-philosopher teacher (dubbed as "Modern Confucius"), with his flowing beard, leisurely gait, and the ubiquitous eight-diagram cloth-wrapper (which he used as a briefcase). While he was teaching at Lienta, he was at the prime of his life. Material hardships did not deter him from writing some of his best works. His *New Philosophy* of 1942 won the first prize awarded by the Ministry of Education of the National Government in Chungking.

I shall conclude my comments with a prayer: May Lienta's "Modern Confucius" be given an opportunity to write freely his mature thoughts so the whole world may be benefited.

Further Comments:

BY CHUN-FAN MAO

Dr. Sih has kindly sent me the latest revised sections of Professor Israel's paper relating to diet, health and scholastic standards of Lienta students. Having read these sections in conjunction with an earlier revised version and the original paper, I am inclined to think my earlier views are still valid, but would like to take this opportunity to make some further comments.

Eating patterns, it seems to me, are largely determined by cultural backgrounds and economic realities, with ample room for variations. Is there really a so-called scientific, standard diet which is universally applicable? How much agreement in this respect can there be between those who rely mainly on a meat-and-fat diet and those who rely mainly on a rice-and-vegetable diet? How much difference is there between the simple fares of wartime Lienta students and the sophisticated meals of present-day wealthy people who, for reasons of health or vanity, draw their sustenance stoically from cucumber sandwiches and garden-fresh(!) vegetable salads? In the light of recent studies, mankind will be increasingly oriented toward a vegetarian diet. Chinese, in general, and the Lienta community members, in particular, are vanguards indeed.

There were doubtlessly health problems in the Lienta community during the war years, especially trachoma (which was prevalent in China, not just limited to school communities). But there were no outbreaks of life-threatening epidemics. The alumni who took advantage of the student clinic would remember the school physicians fondly as aspirin or eye-wash doctors. It may be appropriate here to point out that Chinese students, at least before and during the war years, were not in the habit of storing aspirin or like medicine; they went to the school clinic for such supplies as the need arose. This practice undoubtedly accounts for the high frequency of clinic visits. The multifarious extracurricular activities (e.g., drama, opera, wall posters, bulletins, excursion trips, etc.) in the Lienta community definitely indicated that there was no lack of energy and imagination. Some students, teachers and faculty wives had even enterprisingly tried their hands at arts and crafts, and light industry with considerable success.[10] As indicated earlier, Lienta, the mecca of learning during the Sino-Japanese War period, was the most sought-after university in China. Lienta students were positively not conscripts; they were free to leave. Those who chose to enter and stay were prepared for the intellectual discipline and wartime students' life. This is clear to Prof. Israel when he says that "material conditions had but a marginal effect on their consciousness." (p. 145).

In my earlier comments, I refrained from explicitly criticizing the wording of the topic, "Survival As An Ultimate Value."* Once again, in the spirit of Lienta teashop dialogue, I shall express my opinion candidly. I think the topic is a misnomer. "Survival," rightly viewed, is a process leading to some goals (be they ultimate or otherwise), or a state of continuing existence. In the former sense, it is a condition toward something else; in the latter sense, it is inadequate for rational human beings who are forever pursuing something beyond mere existence. Lienta, a wartime university, was destined to be coeval with China's War of Resistance Against Japan. No one had entertained any illusion of permanency. In an epic period led by the National Government that extolled patriotism and sacrifice for the country, members of the Lienta community envisioned a China independent, strong, and a leading member of the family of nations. Thus motivated, Lienta teachers and students had immersed themselves in the mission of maintaining and nourishing the roots of knowledge for post-war national construction.[11]

One never can tell how a poet reaches the truth with neither the long, winding reasoning of a philosopher nor the painstaking analysis of a scientist. Can it be that poetry, being the spontaneous flow of noble sentiments, transcends both logic and data? On the wall by my desk there hangs a pair of elegantly penned and beautifully mounted scrolls, a gift from a teacher, Prof. L. C. Cha, Lienta's beloved Dean of Students.[12] The couplet, jointly composed by two Lienta teachers, Prof. Cha and Prof. T. C. Huang, epitomizes both the Lienta spirit and the styles of the three constituent institutions. The two lines of verse run:

自然	自由	自在	Be Natural Be Liberal Be Spontaneous
如雲	如海	如山	Like Cloud Like Ocean Like Mountain

NOTES

1. There are many recollections about Lienta days, most of which appeared in *Tsinghua Alumni Bulletin* and *Biographical Literature* published in Taipei, Taiwan. In the summer of 1968, after the National Southwest Associated University Alumni Association in Greater New York was organized, a general letter was sent to alumni and teachers soliciting articles for a proposed special memorial edition. A five-member editorial committee was elected, with Mao

Editor's note: In the final revised topic the author has changed the word "Survival" to "Preservation."

Chun-fan as editor to take care of the expected flow of manuscripts. This expectation proved too optimistic. A score of personal letters written by the editor to alumni and teachers from a selected list succeeded in attracting six pieces of writing plus many, many promises. The manuscripts are in the care of the editor.

2. .In accordance with the rules of the Alumni Association constitution.

3. This interpretation is based mainly upon my recollection of some lectures given by Professor Nathaniel Peffer at Columbia University in the early 1950's.

4. Nicholas R. Clifford, *Retreat from China.* University of Washington Press (printed in Great Britain), 1967, p. 52.

5. *China Handbook,* 1937-1943. New York, the Macmillan Co., 1943, p. 378.

6. Hu Shih, *Excerpts of Diary* (Sources of Contemporary History, Taipei, 1955). The quotation is translated from Wu Hsiang-hsiang's book, *The Second Sino-Japanese War, 1931-1945.* Taipei, Tsung Ho Book Co., 1974, Vol. II, p. 677.

7. Wang Li-chang, *Exactly This Is Lienta.* (One of the manuscripts.) See Note 1.

8. *Ibid.*

9. Lienta students and teachers were dispersed to the surrounding countrysides during air raids. While enemy planes were flying overhead, local inhabitants would remark that Heaven and Holy Buddha would protect them because the best of China were all there.

10. Yeh Chai, *Lienta Intermezzo.* (One of the manuscripts.) See Note 1. (Prof. Yeh was Lienta's Chairman of Electrical Engineering.)

11. I also have reservations about the topic Prof. Israel has tentatively chosen for his book on Lienta: "Elite In Exile: Hsi-nan Lienta: 1938-46." The word "exile" is suggestive of punishment. May I suggest some topics as "Hsi-nan Lienta: A Wartime University, Typical Yet Unique," or "Hsi-nan Lienta: A Wartime University, the Mecca of Learning."

12. Prof. Cha, a youthful octogenarian and an active figure in Taipei's cultural circles, still retains his genius of being at more than one place at the same time and of eating split meals. Optimistic as ever, he loves to reiterate his unswerving conviction that soon we will "regain our sacred capital and reinstall the triumphal tablet there." My English rendition of the couplet is not nearly so elegant as the original.

CHAPTER V

Food Production and Distribution for Civilian and Military Needs in Wartime China, 1937-1945

BY TSUNG-HAN SHEN

I

Introduction

FOOD ADMINISTRATION BECOMES both more difficult and more mandatory in wartime than in normal peaceful years. The statement, obvious as it may appear, takes on great significance in China when full-scale war came in the summer of 1937 with the Japanese invasion—an invasion that was preceded by years of constant struggles in China to overthrow the Manchus, to consolidate the Republican movement against the war-lords and the Communist insurgents, and to cope with a series of earlier limited-objective Japanese incursions.

On the eve of the Sino-Japanese War which later ushered in World War II, the country was further weakened by a series of poor harvests. In the 1920's several droughts plagued north and northwest China, and there was a big flood in the lower Yangtze valley in 1931. Large imports of wheat and rice were made by the government to relieve the resulting famine. There were also droughts in 1936 and 1937 in Szechwan whose picturesque, somnolent provincial center, Chungking, was later to become Free China's wartime capital, following Japanese occupation first of Nanking and later of Hankow in 1937-1938. Had these natural disasters taken place during the war, the war might not have been won because no food could have been imported as the Japanese forces imposed a virtually complete blockade on a Free China gradually deprived of all significant accesses to the outside world.

Actually, the government made great efforts to improve food production before and during the war; and, through proper administration of food collection and distribution, sufficient quantities were made available to the armed forces and the civilian population in 1937-1945. People in occupied China as well as in government-controlled provinces doubtless suffered from a low level of food consumption, but there has been no conclusive evidence of *general* malnutrition due to food shortage for the country as a whole.

The exceedingly difficult economic problems faced by Free China can be seen from the fact that 50 million refugees had migrated from the war zones into the interior by 1940, increasing the population of Free China from a prewar 180 million to 230 million, or by about 25 per cent.[1]

II

Famine Prevention

The great famines of 1920-1921 and 1928-1929 in north and northwest China and the Yangtze flood of 1931-1932 made the National government aware of the urgent need for water control. Thus the government began to undertake various public works for both flood prevention and irrigation to stabilize food and agricultural production.

A significant development in water control was the unification of the various government water conservancy units in 1934 under the National Economic Council at three levels. While the National Economic Council was the administrative organ at the national level, provincial departments of reconstruction directed the conservancy work in their respective provinces, and hsien (or county) governments handled the work on the local level. The work of provincial and hsien governments was placed under the supervision of the National Economic Council.

Irrigation development was emphasized during the prewar period both by the National government and the provincial governments. Before 1937, a total of thirteen irrigation projects were completed, benefiting an aggregate area of more than six million *mou* (1 mou = 0.06 hectares) of land. They all had to do with the construction of canals. The most important canals built during this period were the Minsheng Canal in Suiyuan province completed in 1932; the Kinghui Canal in Shensi province completed in 1932; and the Lohui Canal in Shensi province completed in 1935. These irrigation canals later contributed much to Free China's critical wartime production of grain and cotton.[2]

III

Prohibition of Poppy Growing in West China

At the invitation of the National Resources Commission, the writer served as head of an agricultural survey team to study agricultural conditions in northwest China in 1934. Dr. John Lossing Buck of the University of Nanking and Mr. James Thorp of National Geological Survey joined the team focusing their attention on the rural economy and soil survey, respectively. Starting in summer from Sian, capital of Shensi province, the team traveled to Lanchow, capital of Kansu province, and to Kokonor Lake in Tsinghai province. From Kokonor Lake, the team split into two groups, one taking the northern route to Ninghsia and Suiyuan provinces, and the other taking the southern route to the southern part of Shensi province. Both groups returned to Nanking in the winter. A part of the team later made another trip to the southwestern provinces of Szechwan, Kweichow and Yunnan in the winter of 1935.

Based on their observations and the materials they had gathered on the spot, the team members made recommendations for the development of agricultural resources and the improvement of rural conditions in the western provinces, which were backward as compared with those along the seacoast. Three of their most important recommendations were land tenure improvement, soil conservation, and strict prohibition of poppy growing not only by farmers but also by local warlords, who depended on opium as one of their main sources of revenue. All these recommendations were accepted by Generalissimo Chiang Kai-shek and high-ranking government leaders and put into execution.

IV

Prewar Improvement
of Food Production and Marketing[3]

Some of the agricultural colleges were among the first to start research work on food crop improvement. In 1932 the government took measures to increase food and cotton production on an extensive scale. Three institutions were founded under the Ministry of Industry: the National Agricultural Research Bureau (NARB) in 1932, the National Cotton Improvement Bureau in 1934, and the National Rice and Wheat Improvement Institute (NRWII) in 1935. The writer served as technical director

of the NARB and head of the wheat division of the NRWII. These institutions were under the same administration and were largely responsible
for the breeding of improved varieties of crops, for determining demand
and supply of chemical fertilizers, for the study and control of diseases
and insects, and for collecting and reporting of crop and other agricultural statistics.

As adulteration of wheat, cotton and rice with water and foreign
matter in marketing was rather common before the war, especially in
the Yangtze region, the government established the Cotton Inspection
Bureau in 1934, the Wheat Inspection Bureau and the Rice Inspection
Bureau in 1937 and appointed the directors of the three improvement
Bureaus as directors of the respective inspection agencies. The latter
agencies set up offices in the wheat, cotton, and rice marketing centers
and inspected moisture and foreign matter contents as the first step
toward quality standardization. These agencies were suspended after
the war broke out in the winter of 1937. However, during the war the
Food Ministry kept up the inspection work in its grain storage operation.

V

Adjustment of Crop Production
at Start of the War

Japan launched its general attack on China in July 1937. The Chinese Government, as an emergency measure, established in August the
Fourth Department under the National Military Council   軍事
委員會   . Minister of Industry Wu Ting-chang 吳鼎昌   was
appointed concurrently as Minister of the Fourth Department. There was
a Food Division under the Fourth Department, of which the writer
served as deputy head in charge of food production and Mr. C. C. Chang
of the Bank of China was the head in charge of food storage and financing. Because the coastal provinces of Hopeh, Shantung, Kiangsu,
Chekiang, Fukien and Kwangtung did not produce sufficient food and
depended upon imports in prewar years, their crop patterns had to be
changed to give emphasis to food crops instead of cash crops. The
Fourth Department approved plans for crop adjustment in these provinces submitted by the writer.

The first plan dealt mainly with winter crop changes to be effected
immediately in August and September 1937. The planting season of
winter food crops such as wheat and barley was from September to
October from north to south. The goals of increasing winter wheat
acreage for the provinces were as follows:

Table 1

GOALS OF INCREASING WHEAT ACREAGE IN 1937

Unit: 1,000 *mou**

Province	Wheat acreage in 1935	Goal of increase in 1937	Expected wheat acreage in 1937
Kiangsu	32,108	10,000	42,108
Anhwei	19,829	6,000	25,829
Hupeh	17,072	7,000	24,072
Shensi	14,594	3,500	18,094
Honan	61,425	7,000	68,425
Shantung	51,730	5,000	56,730
Shansi	18,394	2,000	20,394
Szechwan	16,221	6,000	22,221
Chekiang	7,480	4,000	11,480
Hunan	3,765	1,000	4,765
Kiangsi	5,189	1,000	6,189
Total	247,807	52,500	300,307

*1 mou=0.06 hectares.

The experience of Shantung province could be taken as an example. In prewar years cotton and tobacco were the province's main cash crops, which were largely shipped to Shanghai for processing. As the war spread in the summer of 1937, shipment of these crops became increasingly difficult and their prices (at the farm level) became very low. The writer went to Shantung and assisted the provincial agencies and farmers in planting an additional five million *mou* of wheat (as shown in Table 1) in the winter of that year, replacing cotton, tobacco and soybean. This was accompanied by a plan to increase the planting area of kaoliang, millet and sweet potato so as to replace 80 per cent of the cotton and tobacco acreage in the spring of 1938.

Administratively, the Provincial Department of Reconstruction had charge of this project in cooperation with other agencies concerned. The Department invited and organized agricultural specialists of the Provincial Credit Cooperative Bureau, the Provincial Agricultural Experiment Station, the Provincial Tobacco Improvement Station, and the Experimental Farm of (private) Cheeloo University to serve as county agents for agricultural extension work. Each agent was responsible for helping a county government implement its food production projects. The magistrate of the county had the duty to persuade the local farmers, with the help of village heads, to grow more food crops. Banks were directed to extend farm credit only for the production of food crops, not cotton and tobacco.

The adjustment of crop production in other provinces near the war area followed the same policy. Farmers in northern Anhwei had difficulty in getting money to buy wheat seed for planting in the winter of 1937 because the private Shanghai Commercial and Savings Bank had stopped extending credit to them. To solve this problem, I called on Mr. Wang Leng-pae 汪樱伯 , chief inspector of the Bank of China, a government bank serving rural credit needs. He asked whether I could assure him the repayment of the proposed wheat loans in the following summer after wheat harvest. I replied, "If the area is still under governmental control, the farmers are honest and will repay the loans. If the area should fall into the hands of the Japanese, the farmers would not be able to repay the loans but would always remember the generosity of your bank and the kindness of our government to them."

Mr. Wang accepted my recommendation and extended one million Chinese dollars to the wheat growers. In the spring of 1938, the Japanese army occupied that area and the local soldiers carried on guerrilla war against the Japanese with the assistance of farmers. In the winter of 1938, General Lau 駱 , a guerrilla leader in that area, came to Kweilin, Kwangsi province, and told the Bank of China and me that there had been a good harvest of wheat there and the farmers were grateful for the bank loans and gave strong assistance to the guerrilla war. The bank realized that even though one million dollars had been lost, it had won the support of more than one million farmers for the government.

Shensi province offered a good sample of crop production adjustment in the war-free area. Cotton was a major cash crop but poppy was also planted in large areas of good land in prewar years. During the war the cotton belt in north China was directly affected by the hostilities. Shensi was the only province then that produced good long staple cotton which was greatly needed by cotton mills in the war-free area. My recommendation to Shensi provincial authorities was to encourage farmers to grow cotton and wheat but strictly prohibit poppy growing.

Shensi had several droughts and famines in prewar years but was fortunate to have a great hydraulic engineer, Mr. Li Hsieh 李仪祉 儀祉 as Director of the Provincial Water Conservancy Bureau. He had built seven irrigation systems which provided water to around 1.38 million *mou* 市畝 in 1946.[4] He was worshipped by the farmers. On behalf of the Fourth Department and as a good friend, I asked him to assume chairmanship of the Food Production Committee in Shensi province. He accepted it with enthusiasm. Due to enemy bombing, the railway from Nanking to Shensi was disrupted and I could not go there to help him in organization.

However, with his patriotism and able administration, the program for increase of wheat and cotton production and prohibition of poppy growing was carried out very effectively. He told the people that food was as important as soldiers and that the development of irrigation and agricultural extension service were prerequisites for food production. Under his authority as director of the water conservancy bureau, poppy planting in irrigated areas was strictly proscribed under the penalty that plants found would be destroyed and irrigation water supply stopped. During the war the food and cotton production program of Shensi was highly successful under his leadership.

VI

Reorganization of the Agricultural Bureaus

After the outbreak of war in 1937, the various government agencies were moved inland and consolidated in 1938. The new Ministry of Economics Affairs was established, which was put in charge of industry, agriculture, water conservancy and commerce. The National Cotton, Rice and Wheat Improvement Institutes were merged into the National Agricultural Research Bureau under the Ministry of Economics Affairs, and I was appointed deputy director of the Bureau in early 1938. The Bureau carried on its work in the interior in cooperation with provincial agricultural improvement institutes.

In December 1937 Mr. Wu, Minister of Industry and concurrently Minister of the Fourth Department, was appointed Governor of Kweichow province. As my old boss, he asked me to assist him in reorganizing the agricultural institutes in Kweichow. The province was mountainous and strategically important in Southwest China. In the prewar years poppy had been a major cash crop while food was imported from Szechwan and Hunan provinces. Drawing on the agricultural survey of Southwest China made by the National Resource Commission as mentioned before, and also on my personal visits to the existing experimental stations of crops, horticulture, sericulture, forestry, and animal husbandry, I submitted my recommendations to Governor Wu in January 1938 with the following salient features:

Purpose: To increase food production for the war.

Recommended Measures:

    A.   Improving agricultural infrastructure and incentive:

        (1)   To carry out a land census for increasing the revenue from land tax, replacing opium revenue;

(2) To reduce excessive land rent to give farmers incentive for high production;

(3) To enforce soil conservation work and develop grassland for cattle;

(4) To dig ponds and build farm irrigation systems;

(5) To establish agricultural cooperative banks for extending production credit;

(6) To allow a grace period of ten years for land reclamation loans; and

(7) To prevent the burning of forests.

B. Improving agricultural production:

Consolidation of Agricultural Experiment Stations: There were several small stations existing separately for crops, horticulture, sericulture, and animal husbandry. They were scattered in the suburbs of Kweiyang, and staffed mostly with graduates of agricultural vocational schools. No scientific experiments were conducted, and they had only some collections of crop varieties, chickens, ducks, fruit trees and vegetables. Nothing was worthy of extension to farmers. I recommended: (1) to consolidate these small stations into a big one under one able director and provide it with an adequate budget and a staff of college graduates; (2) to request the National Agricultural Research Bureau to assign a team of crop specialists to work in the Provincial Agricultural Improvement Bureau, and (3) to extend improved varieties of rice, wheat, and corn with a view to increasing the yield per unit area; control of cattle rinderpest and hog cholera, plantations of tung oil trees and tea on slopeland, and rehabilitation of sericulture.

After studying my plan, Governor Wu invited me to a dinner in the evening of January 21, 1938, at his residence. He gave me enough time to explain my plan. Then he voiced his fear that if the director of the proposed big station was incompetent, the new setup would be a failure. On the other hand, he said, if the five stations were allowed to remain, there would probably be some directors competent enough to do a good job. My reply was that it would be less difficult to select one competent director of a big station than to select good directors of small stations because a competent director is rare. At last Governor Wu smiled and said, "Your plan will be considered favorably." In February 1938 he gave orders to have the stations reorganized into the "Provincial Agricultural Improvement Station," according to what I had recommended. He was an eminent statesman and one of my esteemed superiors.

Governor Wu wanted to appoint me director of the new bureau. I was interested and hoped to develop this bureau as a model for other provinces. But in March 1938 Wong Wen-hao   翁文灝 , Minister of Economic Affairs, appointed me vice director of the National Agricultural Research Bureau in Chungking, the wartime capital, and he wanted me to help push agricultural improvement programs in the war-free areas.

Subsequently, all other war-free provinces including Szechwan, Hunan, Hupeh, Shensi, Yunnan, and Kansu followed the example of Kweichow and consolidated their small stations into the provincial agricultural improvement bureau. The National Agricultural Research Bureau developed a good and efficient program for cooperation with the provincial agricultural improvement bureaus in increasing food and cotton production. My colleagues at NARB and I visited the provincial bureaus regularly and provided them technical assistance where necessary. We gained practical experiences in planning, organization, and extension services for improving agricultural production in the war-free provinces. These experiences have been very useful in agricultural development in Taiwan.

VII

Establishment of Ministry of Agriculture and Forestry in 1940

In the early period of war, in view of the fact that a large portion of the cultivated land had fallen into the hands of the Japanese, resulting in a great reduction of food supply, and that the civilian and military needs for food were great and urgent, the Central Government established the Ministry of Agriculture and Forestry in July 1940 to take care of the work formerly undertaken by the Ministry of Economic Affairs. The NARB, now a subsidiary unit of the new Ministry, continued to assist the provinces in food and agricultural production. In order to expand the food production program, the Ministry established a Food Production Commission in 1941, which, with its own budget and extension staff, worked in close cooperation with NARB.

The new Commission had branch offices in various provinces, which cooperated with the provincial agricultural improvement stations in extending to the farmers improved varieties, fertilizers, pesticides, and improved methods of crop culture. The specialists of NARB could then devote themselves to research for solving practical problems.

Many measures were planned and carried out in order to increase food production. Fields which were unutilized during certain seasons were brought under cultivation, winter plowing was adopted in some areas, and land reclamation efforts were stepped up in order to increase the total cultivated area. The interplanting system for rice was extended in southwestern China where many of the fields used to lie fallow after rice was harvested. For increasing wartime food production, special efforts were made for extending this system as well as the planting of regenerated rice in Szechwan province.

Crop varieties were improved and extended. More than ninety improved rice and wheat varieties and also a number of varieties of corn, millet, and potatoes were obtained through selection and hybridization. In 1942 the use of improved varieties of rice, wheat, and miscellaneous food crops was extended to almost 1.9 million *mou* of land according to figures of the Ministry of Agriculture and Forestry.[5]

On the basis of soil-fertility surveys, the use of fertilizer was extended in some provinces. A ten-year soil-fertility survey revealed that 80 per cent of the total planted area was deficient in nitrogen, 40 per cent in phosphorus, and 15 per cent in potash. Because chemical fertilizers were lacking during the war, the primary fertilizers were bone meal and oilseed cakes. In 1942 fertilizer use was increased on 4.5 million *mou* of land. Technical advice was also given to the farmers in growing green-manure crops and in processing compost manure.

In addition to measures to increase cultivated acreage and productivity, efforts were also made to control losses due to diseases and insects. Application of improved methods of controlling loose smut of wheat and rice stem borer and of pesticides for controlling vegetable insects was extended to a total area of 5.5 million *mou* in 1942.

Thus, although government efforts were severely hindered by communication and transportation difficulties, shortage of labor, and lack of chemical fertilizers, appropriate measures were undertaken and significant success in increasing food production was achieved. In addition, the farmers in many areas had been introduced to improved materials and methods of farming which increased the impact of future extension work in China.

VIII

Irrigation Development

Irrigation development was emphasized by the government during the war as much as in the prewar years. Following the establishment of the Ministry of Agriculture and Forestry in 1940, the National Government set up the National Water Conservancy Board in 1941, whose work was also formerly undertaken by the Ministry of Economic Affairs. Its functions were to improve and develop irrigation canals to increase food and agricultural production, to keep navigable waterways in a serviceable condition to facilitate river transportation, and to regulate river courses and erect dykes to minimize dangers of flood.

In this study, owing to limited space, only some major irrigation projects will be mentioned. It would be appropriate to point out that the efforts made in the war period had benefited roughly four million *mou* of land[6] in nine provinces. Outstanding efforts in Shensi, Kansu and Szechwan provinces are briefly described in the following paragraphs.

Shensi Province

During the war irrigation had been best developed in Shensi province in a semi-arid area under the leadership of Mr. Li Hsieh, a German-trained hydraulic engineer. He was a native of Shensi and served as director of the Provincial Water Conservancy Bureau in 1922-1938. He died in 1938, but his work was continued by his deputy and his plan was followed up faithfully. By early 1947 a total of seven irrigation canals were completed, which irrigated a combined area of 1,381,000 *mou*. Furthermore, under construction were five other canals for a total area of 1,030,000 *mou*.[7] Tables 2 (a) and (b) show the periods of construction and irrigated areas of the first seven canals and the second five canals, respectively.

The benefits of irrigation were many. The land price was about one dollar per *mou* before irrigation, and jumped to over 100 dollars after irrigation. The wheat yield per *mou* was only one or two Chinese bushels before irrigation, and it later increased about ten times after irrigation; and that of cotton only twenty to thirty catties before, but over 170 catties afterwards.[8] The construction of irrigation facilities was financed by bank loans extended to the local irrigation associations. The associations were able to repay the loans with the water fee payments from their farmer-members whose income had been greatly increased because of the rise in both land prices and crop yields.

Instead of drought and famine as in 1928-1930, irrigation had increased and stabilized the food and cotton production to support the people and the war. Furthermore, when General Chu Shao-liang 朱紹良 , Commander of the Eighth War Area in Northwest China (1938-1940), led Nationalist forces in combating the Communists, he stated that the irrigation systems developed by Li Hsieh had increased farmers' production and improved their living so that they supported both the Nationalist government and Nationalist army and did not listen to the Communists' propaganda. In a way, Li's irrigation work had been stronger than the defense army of 100,000 soldiers who fought against the Communists. Therefore, irrigation can be considered as both an economic and a political weapon.

Table 2

(a)   THE FIRST SEVEN CANALS IN SHENSI PROVINCE

Name of Canal		Actual irrigated area in 1946 (mou)	Period of Construction
King-Wei	涇惠渠	661,277	1930-1935
Wei-Wei	渭惠渠	354,885	1935-1937
Mei-Wei	梅惠渠	82,696	1936-1938
Heh-Wei	黑惠渠	91,998	1938-1942
Han-Wei	漢惠渠	63,141	1938-1942
Per-Wei	褒惠渠	124,664	1939-1942
Ken-Wei	泔惠渠	2,283	1943-1944
	Total	1,380,944	

(b)   PLANNED AREAS OF THE SECOND FIVE CANALS
IN SHENSI PROVINCE

Lo-Wei	洛惠渠	500,000	1934-1947
Ting-Wei	定惠渠	40,000	1941-1947
Feng-Wei	灃惠渠	230,000	1941-1947
Hsu-Wei	湑惠渠	160,000	1941-1947
Lao-Wei	澇惠渠	100,000	1943-1947
	Total	1,030,000	

Source: Soong-Hsi-shang   宋希尚 , *Biography of Li Hsieh* 李儀
祉傳(Taipei: Chung-Young Publishing Co., 中央文物供應
社 1954), p. 36.

Kansu Province

Water Conservancy projects were undertaken in Kansu province by the provincial government. Topographically, Kansu province can be divided into two parts, namely, the Kansu Plateau and the Kansu Corridor. The Kansu Plateau is high land, and the irrigation development on this area is difficult, owing to the lack of vast plain land to irrigate and the difficult engineering works in constructing irrigation canals. In April 1941, the Kansu Incorporation for Agricultural Development was formed and jointly supported by the Provincial Government and the Bank of China. Dr. Shen Yi 沈 怡 , a German-trained hydraulic engineer, was appointed as the Director of the Incorporation, who implemented an irrigation development program in this arid region of northwest China. By 1945, four new canals irrigating 110,000 *mou* were completed and another five new canals capable of irrigating 290,000 *mou* were under construction in the Kansu Plateau.

The Kansu Corridor is topographically quite different. It is a great plain land extending from Wuwei 武 威 to Yuemen 玉 門 . In this area, there were many abandoned irrigation canals which had been constructed many centuries ago. In two years time from 1941 to 1942, the Incorporation, using a Central Government Subsidy amounting to ten million Yen (dollars) yearly, rehabilitated forty-four canals, restoring 1,000,000 *mou* back to irrigation, which resulted in a food production increase of 1,500,000 piculs 市 石 yearly. Another new irrigation system named Su-fung canal 肅豐渠 , located at Kiuchuean 酒 泉 , was also completed in 1945 irrigating 100,000 *mou*.

Summing up, in the Kansu province in war time, there were altogether ten new irrigation projects constructed for irrigating 500,000 *mou*, and forty-four abandoned canals rehabilitated for irrigating 1,000,000 *mou*, totaling 1,500,000 *mou* as shown in Table 3.

Szechwan Province

Except the plain area of Chengtu 成 都 , which was very well irrigated by the Tu-Chiang-Yen 都江堰 irrigation system, most other farmlands in Szechwan province were not irrigated but rainfed and weather dependent. During the war, the urgent need of increasing food production necessitated a program to construct new irrigation systems, which was executed by the Szechwan Provincial Water Conservancy Bureau.

As estimated in 1942, facilities for 351,710 *mou* had been completed and were in use, those for 148,500 *mou* were under construction, and those for 113,000 *mou* were under planning.[9] Important projects were the

Table 3

THE IRRIGATION DEVELOPMENT IN
KANSU PROVINCE IN WAR TIME (BY 1945)

Irrigation Development	Description	Irrigation Area (mou)	Total
A. Completed canals in Kansu Plateau	Tao-Wei	35,000	
	Wong-Wei	30,000	110,000
	Pu-Chi	35,000	
	Nan-Wei	10,000	
B. Canals under construction in Kansu Plateau	Yung-Fong	24,000	
	Yung-Lo	46,000	
	Chen-Fong	20,000	290,000
	Lan-Fong	120,000	
	Pei-Fong	80,000	
C. Canals rehabilitated from abandoned irrigation systems in Kansu Corridor			1,000,000
D. Su-Fung Canal in Kansu Corridor			100,000
		Grand Total	1,500,000

Source: The Table was supplied by Shen Yi.

Cheng Cheh Canal in Santai　三臺縣鄭澤渠　, Lung Si
Canal and Tien Shing Canal in Mienyang　綿陽縣龍西渠
及天星堰　, Li Chuang Canal and Shi Lai Canal in Meishan
眉山縣醴泉渠及西來圳　, Chin Po Chun Canal
in Mouhsien　茂縣青坡村　, Chin-Mao Canal in Chingtang
金堂縣青茅堰　, Hung Hua Canal in Chingshen 青神
縣鴻化堰　, as well as many irrigation ponds scattered all over
the province. Other projects for improvement or construction of many
small irrigation works in the plain areas of river valleys had been undertaken and were continued in the war period.

Food Situation in the War-Free Provinces in 1940-1941

In the beginning of the war, government leaders assumed that the
enemy would overrun North China and the coastal provinces and stop
at a line east of the Canton-Hankow railway. It was hoped that fourteen
provinces (i.e., Shensi, Kansu, Ninghsia, Tsinghai, Szechwan, Yunnan,
Kweichow, Hunan, Hupeh, Honan, Kiangsi, Kwangsi, Sikang and
Sinkiang) would remain free. But in the second year of the war it was
realized that Hunan, Hupeh, and Kiangsi could not be entirely held.
In a normal crop year these fourteen provinces had been self-sufficient
in food supplies to varying degrees,[10] but expanded production later
became necessary to provide for the large concentration of troops and
sudden inflow of refugees that developed as the war proceeded apace.

It has been estimated that 50 million refugees migrated from the war
zones into the interior by 1940, increasing the population of Free China
from a prewar 180 million to 230 million or by about 25 per cent.[11]
Although detailed population surveys were of course not possible due
to wartime conditions this figure is the estimate of a most reliable observer, Dr. Chang Kia-ngau　張嘉璈　. The population of Szechwan
province was estimated at 46.8 million[12] and that of Chungking at
297,000 in 1934, the latter reaching perhaps 600,000-700,000 in 1941.[13]
Szechwan province was the most important supplier of rice during the
war. The area around Chengtu, the provincial capital, was known as the
rice bowl, where there were excellent irrigation facilities.

Fortunately, following two poor crops in 1936-1937, the first two war
years were blessed with good rice crops in 1938 and 1939 as shown in
Table 4.[14] So rice price remained stable: $9.90 per picul (1 picul = 50
kg.) at Chungking and $10.80 at Chengtu in April 1938, and $6.70 at
Chungking and $9.80 at Chengtu in October 1938. In 1939, though the
rice crop was good, its price fluctuated as a result of a general rise in
prices of other commodities. The rice price rose to $11.40 at Chungking
and $14.80 at Chengtu in October 1939. It may be noted that Chungking
with its swollen wartime population drew its food supply from its sur-

rounding rice bowl centering on the Chengtu area. The lower Chungking
rice price was due to government procurement and price policy in favor
of the wartime capital.

Table 4
RICE PRODUCTION OF SZECHWAN PROVINCE

Year	Area (1,000 mou)	Production (1,000 piculs)*
1936	35,997	119,402
1937	27,676	78,668
1938	33,785	155,862
1939	33,692	151,088
1940	28,367	88,616

Source: The National Agricultural Research Bureau.

*20 piculs=50 kilograms.

Unfortunately, the rice crop in Free China in 1940 was poor partly
due to spring drought, although the harvests of wheat and other crops
were good. Consequently the output of food crops during 1940 fell by
an overall amount of 10 per cent. The Chungking price index for rice,
the most important single item in the price structure, rose by roughly
four times from May to December in 1940.[15] The prices of other food
crops also rose greatly and so did wages. This marked the beginning of
China's hyper-inflation, as shown in Table 5.

The jump in rice price in 1940 was triggered by hoarding by big
landlords and merchants. In that year the writer, who was living in a
rented house in the country, discovered that his landlord put his own
rice in storage and bought rice from the market for home consumption,
expecting further increases in price.[16] The significance of the role of the
landlords can be seen from the fact that in Szechwan, tenants formed
52 per cent of the farm population.[17] As the tenants paid the rent in
kind, large quantities of rice were placed in the hands of landlords. A
survey team of the National Agricultural Research Bureau sent by the
writer in autumn 1940 found that rice hoarding by landlords was prevalent throughout the province. These landlords used to hoard opium
before the war whenever monetary instability occurred. As poppy growing was stopped during the war, they hoarded rice instead when profitable.

As Free China, with its swollen population, government apparatus,
and army, was gradually compressed into an ever-shrinking ring of
interior provinces whose total economic base had been at best pre-

cariously balanced in prewar years, the inflationary pressures naturally mounted, as the war progressed. The severing under Japanese pressure of the two remaining outside supply lines—the rail connection between Yunnan and Hanoi and the famed Burma Road—aggravated the then gathering inflationary forces. As inflation gathered momentum, hastened on by the short rice crop of 1940, a general inflationary psychology began to spread among the people. Housewives started to spend money as soon as they received it on any commodity that was storable and easily salable. They bought soap, candles, rice, etc., by the cases and piculs. The wealthy landlords and merchants were of course in a preeminent position to profiteer through speculative hoarding and turnover. Such a self-feeding tendency of a runaway inflation is well known. In wartime China, this tendency was aggravated by the practice of continuing to collect the land tax on the basis of a prewar nominal rate per unit of land area, resulting in rapid declines in real taxes collected and further eroding the government's fiscal capability to meet fast-rising wartime budgetary requirements. The government's resolution of this problem is discussed in the following paragraph.

Table 5

PRICE INDEX FOR PREWAR SHANGHAI
AND WARTIME FREE CHINA

Year	Shanghai	Free China
1930	100.0	
1931	110.3	
1932	98.0	
1933	90.5	
1934	84.7	
1935	84.0	
1936	94.6	
1937	112.7	100
1938		131
1939		220
1940		513
1941		1,296
1942		3,900
1943		12,541
1944		43,197
1945		163,160

Source: Chang Kia-ngau, *The Inflationary Spiral,* (New York: Wiley & Technology Press, 1958) Appendix A. Table A-1 and Table A-2, p. 371.

IX

Collection of Land Tax in Kind[18]

The critical problem of spiraling rice prices existed not only in Szechwan but also in some other provinces owing to hoarding by landlords. To get rice from landlords and in general to raise the nation's fiscal capability, the government ultimately resorted to the method of collecting land tax in kind. Fukien was the first province in wartime China in which the new ruling for the payment of land tax in kind was enforced. This new system was well planned and implemented under the direction of Mr. C. K. Yen 嚴家淦 , then the Commissioner of Finance of the Fukien Provincial Government and now President of the Republic of China. From the sixty-three counties and special districts in the province, the Fukien authorities hoped to collect annually 2,000,000 piculs of rice and other grains.

An inspection party of the provincial government investigated conditions relating to the enforcement of the new system, and reported that it was working successfully. Then Commissioner Yen recommended to the provincial government that, judging from the popular response and the smoothness with which it was carried out, the new system, started in October 1940, should stay in force in the province.

Land tax in Fukien was classified into nine categories with rates ranging from a few cents to ninety cents per *mou* (1 *mou* = 0.06 ha.) or an average of fifty cents per *mou*. The average quantity of rice or grain collected from each *mou* under the system was estimated at 4.5 per cent of the crop. The prewar tax rate, which had remained unchanged, and the prewar rice price (i.e., in 1936) were used as the basis for calculating the quantity of rice or grain to be collected. For instance, if the prewar price was $5 per picul, then the provincial government could collect an average of ten catties (1/10 picul) of rice from each *mou*, which was the exact equivalent of the fifty cents paid before the war. The average yield of each *mou* was 230 catties.

In view of the increase of agricultural prices, one might consider the new system as amounting to a means to raise the tax rates. Actually this was not the case, as Yen pointed out. What the land produced had been essentially the commodity involved in the transaction of farm owners. If in prewar days an owner had to sell ten catties of rice to pay the fifty cents in tax, he now simply paid ten catties. The fact of the matter was that during the period of price rises the land tax in real terms steadily declined until the introduction of Yen's new system.

Prior to its enforcement, the plan for the system of collecting land tax in kind was submitted by the governor of Fukien to the Supreme

National Defense Council and the Ministry of Finance for approval. Generalissimo Chiang Kai-shek, chairman of the council, endorsed it as a means of accumulating a food reserve for the army and the civilian population in July 1940. Because of its successful implementation in Fukien, the Executive Yuan subsequently ordered other provincial governments to make preparations for the enforcement of the same system. Since the National Food Administration was responsible for the control, transportation, and distribution of foodstuff, its workers were made responsible for the inspection of the quality and the storage of the grain collected.

X

History of Collecting Land Tax in Kind

Though the collection of land tax in kind was introduced as a new measure during the war, it had been developed and practiced in ancient China before the economy was monetized. In times long past, the taxes were paid in kind and the salaries of government officials and soldiers were also paid in kind.[19] Consequently, the government built and established a system of government warehouses to store the collected grain called "Soldiers' and Officers' Food Stores" 軍公糧倉 , as recorded in history as early as the Period of the Warring States (722-484 B.C.) 春秋戰國 . The practice of payment in kind was discontinued in 1436 during the Ming Dynasty.[20] During the Sino-Japanese War, the government resorted to the old measure, the collection of land tax in kind, and also established a grain warehouse system similar to the ancient "Soldiers' and Officers' Food Stores" in principle.

XI

Food Conference's Resolutions

Sixty-three resolutions were adopted at the National Food Conference convened in Chungking on February 20-25, 1941. Generalissimo Chiang Kai-shek attended the meeting on the 24th and gave a 40-minute speech calling on food administrators to do their best in dealing with the prevailing food problems.

Of the sixty-three resolutions,[21] twenty-five dealt with food administration, twenty-two with transportation and supply, four with the increase of food production, and twelve with laws and regulations relating to food. They provided for more systematic investigation and survey of food stocks, stricter control over transportation and distribution, government intervention in food markets, economy in food consumption, increase of food production, the building-up of the army food reserve, and the introduction of new food policies and regulations including the collection of land tax in kind, the strengthening of cooperative societies guilds and government-owned food companies, and the study of food rationing. Food control measures, experimented with in a number of provinces in 1940, would be extended to the entire country through the provincial food control bureaus.

Fifteen free China provinces in six groups—the Szechwan-Hupeh, the Hunan-Kwangtung-Kiangsi-Kwangsi, the Yunnan-Kweichow, the Fukien-Chekiang-Anhwei, the Honan-Shensi-Kansu, and the Sikang districts—would raise their food production by 32,851,250 piculs in 1941. This would be done by increasing cultivation areas and yield per *mou* through the introduction of scientific farming, according to a report made to the conference by the Ministry of Agriculture and Forestry.

Fourteen provinces had prohibited the manufacture of wine and sugar with rice, wheat, *kao-liang*, millet, and corn since the war, according to the Ministry of the Interior. The ban would save approximately 40,000,000 piculs of foodstuffs each year.

XII

Finance Conference's Resolutions[22]

In early 1941, the rice situation in Szechwan worsened after the poor rice harvest in 1940. The price of rice in Szechwan in June 1941 was more than thirty times that of September 1940, and there was a corresponding upward movement in commodity prices generally. Accordingly, Premier H. H. Kung　孔祥熙　convened a National Finance Conference in Chungking on June 16-24, 1941. Generalissimo Chiang Kai-shek also attended the opening meeting on the 16th and delivered a long speech on the need and justification for collecting the land tax in kind and making the tax a source of national revenue instead of provincial revenue as had been the case in the past.[23] The National Government would return part of the land tax collected to the provincial governments according to the needs of different provinces. This change facilitated the centralization of food collection and monetary payment. It was one of the most important measures taken by the government to improve the food supply situation and thereby enhance the national strength to win the war.

The conference approved the following measures:

1. The land tax, which had been relinquished to the provinces in 1928, was to be restored to the Central Government, which would in turn subsidize the local government to compensate for their loss of revenue.

2. Beginning with the second half of 1941, all land tax was to be paid in kind.

3. The tax rate was fixed at one-fifth of a picul of unhusked rice for every dollar of land tax levied before the war. In regions where little rice was produced the land tax in kind was to be collected in wheat, sorghum, barley, or other foodstuffs.[24] In areas where the tax was excessive, relative to crop yields, a certain proportion, to be determined by representatives of the Central Government, could be paid in money.

XIII

Measures of Food Administration Since 1941

Farmers made up over 80 per cent of the population of China. In other words, 80 per cent of the people were producers, feeding the other 20 per cent. It was an enormous task to collect grains from the millions of farmers and landlords scattered all over the country. Food supply was not a problem in the first two years of war. But in 1940 several food producing provinces fell to the invading Japanese army, and communications between Szechwan and the mid-Yangtze provinces were disrupted after Ichang, west of Hankow, was lost, and the shipping of food and other supplies was affected.

In addition to these facts, there was a short period of drought in that summer which had the psychological effect of uneasiness on some people. The food situation was very serious, especially in Szechwan in 1940. The government established in August 1940 a National Food Bureau at Chungking. However, the supply of food in the capital and other big cities was often not enough and the food price began to rise rapidly out of government control, leading to serious inflation. After the Finance Conference, the bureau was abolished in July 1941 and in its place a powerful Ministry of Food was established, with Mr. Hsu Kan 徐 堪 , who had been a vice minister of finance, as minister.

Under the food supply measure taken by Minister Hsu, military personnel were given the first priority; civil servants, police and students the second priority; and ordinary citizens the third priority.[25] In fact the military food requirement took from one-half to two-thirds of the total amount collected by the government. This was to assure enough supplies for military consumption, keep a sufficient stock to meet emergency needs at times of crop failure or famine, and prevent the soldiers from requisitioning food from the local people so as to maintain good relations with them. The food ration for the military was 0.75 kg. of rice per person per day; for civilians, it was 0.50 kg. of rice.[26]

Two food collection measures were adopted by the Food Ministry.[27] The first was to collect land tax in kind as first practiced in Fukien province. The rates of land tax varied from province to province. Since the collection of grain was not enough to meet the government's need, the second measure was to purchase from landowners an additional compulsory amount of grain, equal to the land tax, at a price slightly lower than the market price. In order to avoid inflation half of the price was paid in cash while the other half in food debentures. The total collection of rice and wheat by both the land tax in kind and the purchase amounted to 52 million piculs in 1941 (about 6.1 per cent of Free China's total output of staple crops) and 67 million piculs in 1942 (about 7.4 per cent).[28] The farmers, however, retained most of their total output on the farm for seed and household consumption purposes and marketed only the excess over those requirements. Thus, while the government collection program accounted for only 6 or 7 per cent of total output of staple crops, it accounted for a much larger part of the total crop marketed, and was therefore an effective measure for combating hoarding and speculation on the part of landlords.

The main portion of the foodstuffs so collected was to stabilize the supply for the army and government employees. A second purpose of the program was to build up a stock for stabilization in years of poor harvest. Underpinning the program was the government's objective to shift the incidence of the cost of the food program in the direction of landowners by (1) restoring the land tax in real terms to the prewar level, and (2) imposing what amounted to a temporary land tax surcharge through the compulsory purchase at low official prices. By thus removing a significant portion of each year's harvest from the control of the landowners and merchants, the government hoped to dampen hoarding and profiteering and to stabilize prices.

Political actions[29] had also been taken to supplement those economic measures, such as, taking census of owners possessing surplus amount of food, registration of food merchants, control of business transactions through organization of food merchant guilds, strict prohibition of hoarding and profiteering in foodstuffs and banning the making of sugar and liquor by using staple foodstuffs as raw material. Since the enforcement of the aforementioned measures, substantial results were apparently achieved as may be inferred from the price statistics shown opposite.

The Chungking prices were evidently official prices. This fact explains the sudden jump in rice price in Chungking from $232 to $340 between March and April 1942. No similar jumps were observed in Chengtu and other major cities for which prices were reported. This in turn can be attributed to the Central Government's special effort to hold down prices in the wartime capital. It was necessary, however, to bring Chungking's prices in line periodically with those prevailing elsewhere.

There were bumper crops of rice and wheat throughout the free provinces in 1944, many of which were record yields in over ten years. Consequently, the prices of rice, wheat and other food crops declined 23 per cent in northern Kwangtung province, 25 per cent in western Hupeh province, and 42 per cent at Chengtu, Szechwan province. There was no difficulty in collecting 95 million piculs of rice and wheat for military and civilian needs in 1944. Together with the improvement of rice and wheat storage to reduce loss, the abundant food supply contributed to winning the war in 1945.

The land tax was relinquished again to the provinces not long after the war. Mr. Hsu Kan served as the Minister of Food until November of 1946.[30] The Ministry of Food was combined into the Ministry of Finance in March 1949.

		Chungking	*Chengtu*
		(Unit: NC$ per picul)	
1941	June	225	361
	July	232	336
	Aug.	232	263
	Sept.	232	226
	Oct.	232	268
	Nov.	232	310
	Dec.	232	273
1942	Jan.	232	251
	Feb.	232	225
	Mar.	232	307
	April	340	355
	May	340	374
	June	340	427
	July	340	425
	Aug.	340	409
	Sept.	340	411

Source: *The Chinese Year Book 1943*, prepared by the Council of International Affairs, Chungking (London: W. Thacker & Co.), pp. 568-569.

XIV

Lasting Value of Wartime Experiences and Achievements

A large number of Chinese agricultural scientists who had done good research work in prewar years obtained valuable experiences in agricultural organization, administration and extension services during the war in 1937-1945. These experiences in research and extension have been very useful to Taiwan's agricultural development, and the crop varieties improved during that time are still being used on the Mainland. *In Mainland China:* One instance is recorded in a work published in 1958 by the Seed Administration Bureau of the Communist Ministry of Agriculture under the title of "Improved Crop Varieties in the People's Republic of China,"[31] which includes a detailed list of all existing superior crop varieties with a description of the origin, major characteristics, areas of distribution, and the results of extension of each variety. Of particular relevance to the National Agricultural Research Bureau is the inclusion in this Communist publication of, among other things, four wheat varieties, "Li-ying 1," "Li-ying 3," "Li-ying 4," and "Li-ying 6," developed by Shen Li-ying, a plant breeder of NARB during the war. There are many other varieties of crops mentioned in that publication, which were grown in 1958 and probably in later years. *On Taiwan:* A considerable number of trained and experienced agricultural scientists from the Mainland together with those who were brought up here have contributed to Taiwan's successful agricultural development. It may be of interest to note that when the Sino-American Joint Commission on Rural Reconstruction (JCRR) was established in Nanking in October 1948, the National Agricultural Research Bureau served as the prime source from which JCRR drew its initial supply of senior agricultural specialists. As I was then Director of NARB and was concurrently JCRR Commissioner, ten experienced specialists of the Bureau were recruited to join the JCRR staff.

One of them was Dr. Y. S. Tsiang   蔣彥士   , who later became JCRR's Secretary General and Commissioner, and now Minister of Education. Other NARB specialists who came to Taiwan after joining JCRR first became Division heads and then were either reassigned to be Dean of the Agricultural College, National Taiwan University, or appointed Commissioner of the Taiwan Provincial Department of Agriculture and Forestry. Staffed initially with the experienced personnel and then with the enlistment of new blood in Taiwan, JCRR has been able to implement its plans and projects for rural reconstruction in the last quarter of a century and help make it possible for the Republic of China to achieve an average 6 per cent annual growth rate of agriculture in Taiwan during the period from 1952 to 1968.

XV

Conclusions

1. Although in the first few years of war there were localized shortages of food grains due to inadequate means of transportation and war

dislocations, there was no general shortage problem due to prewar investments.

2. The irrigation development in West China during the war not only increased and stabilized the food and agricultural production but also won the support of farmers for the National Government.

3. As the war progressed, Japanese control over food producing areas was extended, transportation routes were cut, and large numbers of refugees moved into the interior provinces, thus worsening the food situation. The additional factor of the extremely poor rice crops in 1940 and 1941 created a general situation of insufficient supply in Free China.

4. In response to this problem and the consequent rising food prices, the Chinese government adopted the measures to improve the technology and organization of food production and marketing detailed earlier.

5. Among those measures the collection of land tax in kind and the compulsory food grain purchases proved to be the most immediately effective in that they counteracted speculative behavior and hoarding, and supplied military and civilian requirements.

6. The measures to increase output were instrumental in raising food production in the final years of the war and after.

In conclusion, food production and distribution during 1937-1945 were fairly successful and contributed to winning the war in China, thanks to the prohibition of poppy growing, the collection of land tax in kind and the good cooperation between the government and the people. Many of the experiences we gained in improving agricultural production to meet military and civilian needs have proved valuable in later years, especially in the postwar rural reconstruction of Taiwan. A fact worthy of note is that a number of improved varieties of wheat and other crops, which were the results of research done under difficult wartime conditions, were grown in 1958 and probably in later years on the Mainland.

NOTES

1. Chang Kia-ngau, *The Inflationary Spiral,* (New York: Wiley & Technology Press, 1958), p. 25.
2. Ho, Franklin L., "Comments" in Paul K. T. Sih (editor), *The Strenuous Decade: China's Nation-Building Efforts, 1927-1937* (New York: St. John's University Press, 1970), p. 236.
3. Shen, T. H., *Agricultural Resources of China,* (New York: Cornell University Press, 1951), pp. 192-194.
4. Soong Hsi-shang   宋希尚 : *Biography of Li Hsieh* 李儀 祉傳 (Taipei: Chung-Young Publishing Co. 中央文物 供應社 , 1954).

5. See Chinese Ministry of Information, *China Handbook 1937-1943* (The Macmillan Company, New York, 1943), table 49, for figures relating to the results of the various food increase measures in 1942.

6. Based on the statistics of Chapter 3, "Irrigation Development in the Anti-Japanese War Period" 抗戰時期之灌溉工程, of the unpublished manuscript entitled "History of Water Conservancy Development in China" 中國水利史, edited by Shen Po-shien et al. 沈伯先

7. Soong Hsi-shang, p. 35.

8. *Ibid.*, p. 39.

9. Shen Po-shien et al, *ibid.*

10. Chang Kia-ngau, p. 213.

11. *Ibid.*, p. 25.

12. Tao, L. K. 陶孟和, "Population," *The Chinese Year Book 1943*, prepared by the Council of International Affairs, Chungking (London: W. Thacker & Co.), p. 42.

13. *Essays of Hsu Kan* 徐可亭先生文存 (Taipei: Szechwan Literary Association 四川文獻社, 1960), p. 119.

14. Shen, T. H., "Food Supply and Prices in Szechwan Province," *Ta-Kung Newspaper* 大公報, Chungking, Nov. 17, 1940; and also in *Autobiography Vol. II* 中年自述 (Taipei: Cheng-Chung Book Co. 正中書局, 1957), pp. 197-207.

15. Chang Kia-ngau, p. 34.

16. Shen, T. H., *Autobiography Vol. II* 中年自述, pp. 126-127.

17. Shen, T. H., *Agricultural Resources of China*, p. 96.

18. "Collection of Land Tax in Kind," *China at War*, published monthly by the China Information Publishing Company, Chungking, China, April 1941, Vol. VI, No. 4, pp. 44-45.

19. Chu, T. S. 曲直生, *Introduction to China's Food Warehouse System* 中國糧倉制度概論 (Taipei: Chung-Young Publishing Co. 中央文物供應社, 1954), pp. 1-7.

20. Chang Kia-ngau, p. 141.

21. "Food Conference's Resolutions," *China at War;* Vol. VI, No. 4, p. 45.

22. Chang Kia-ngau, pp. 140-141.

23. "Opening Speech by KMT Director-General Chiang Kai-shek," *Proceedings, the Third National Finance Conference* (Taipei: Hsueh-Hai Book Co. 學海書局, 1972), Section I, p. 12.

24. Shen, T. H., "Collection of Land Tax in Kinds Including Rice or Wheat in South, and Wheat or Millet in North," Section II, pp. 19-21.

25. *Essays of Hsu Kan*, p. 122.

26. *Ibid.*, p. 125.
27. *Ibid.*, p. 127.
28. Hsu Kan, "Food Administration," *The Chinese Year Book 1943*, p. 557.
29. Hsu Kan, "Food Administration," *The Chinese Year Book 1943*, p. 567.
30. *Essays of Hsu Kan*, p. 184.
31. Seed Administration Bureau, Communist Ministry of Agriculture: *Improved Crop Varieties in People's Republic of China* 全國農作物優良品種 (Shanghai: Agricultural Publishing Co., 1958), p. 198.

Comments (1):

BY ANTHONY M. TANG

It is probably a valid generalization to say that anyone who agrees to be a discussant of Dr. Shen's scholarly writings is asking for frustration. The truth is that when Dr. Shen expounds on a subject, he usually leaves little unsaid. And what he says is said with authority, i.e., with facts and theory on his side. The essay which he is presenting at this Conference is worse than typical—worse from the standpoint of his hapless discussant. It is tough enough to embellish on his writings on contemporary settings. But in the present paper he is dealing with a truly heroic period in China's long history about which many of us, unfortunately, have either little or no direct knowledge. At the same time, Dr. Shen can and does speak with the authority and certitude of someone who was not only there to witness the unfolding drama but in the role of a leading agricultural expert who helped shape wartime food policies and implement the related programs. Having thus prefaced my remarks that are to follow, I hope you will understand (1) why I was so slow in producing this discussion paper and (2) why you may find what I have to say to be inconsequential or trivial.

In an all-out war in which the aggressor country aims to subjugate another people there is no substitute for victory or peace with honor. Such was the war which Japan started in China without provocation in July 1937. In such a struggle for national survival, people and resources are subject to mobilization by a purposeful government for the attainment of the overriding goal. Civil liberties are curtailed, and the government intervenes massively in the economic domain. Administrative decisions and resource allocation by command are adopted, displacing or limiting the role normally played by markets and prices. Price control, rationing, direct or indirect measures to bring about hard work and austere living by the people, allocation of key commodities by decree instead of by prices, coercive procurement of critical goods and resources at arbitrary (low) prices, etc., are all familiar measures adopted by governments, whatever their political and ideological persuasions, in times of war involving goals for which there are no trade-offs. Prices are shunned as the premier allocative device because they are either parochial or entailing distributive and equity consequences that are ethically unacceptable.

194

It is clear thus that the test which matters, insofar as wartime food policies are concerned, is whether they promoted the central war aim of the country. Put somewhat differently, the test is whether the policies permitted the agricultural sector to produce and deliver sufficient quantities of output to fuel the war industries and to feed and clothe the troops as well as civilians so as to maintain morale and otherwise meet war requirements in a manner consistent with winning the war. *Ex ante,* what is the performance needed to achieve all this is difficult to gauge. But *ex post,* we can all agree that inasmuch as China emerged victorious in the end, the agricultural or food policies adopted by its leaders were equal to the task. In this regard, one needs to accept Dr. Shen's essential conclusion about the success of the wartime policies regarding the production and distribution of food.

The task had not been an easy one. Although figures on the economic base and production vary from one source to another, largely because of the variant definitions of the geographical scope of Free China, Chang Kia-ngau's data are as good as any.[1] The interior provinces which made up Free China were for all practical purposes completely sealed off from the outside world in terms of commercial relations during the last four years of the war, 1942-45. Agriculturally, the provinces produced about half the prewar food output of the country.[2] Thus, the addition by mid-1940 of some 50 million refugees to their prewar population of 180 million, bringing their wartime population to about one-half of the nation's total, did not appear at first blush as a strain.[3] This, however, reckoned without acreage diversion needed to raise the output of such non-food crops as cotton whose prewar production in the interior provinces amounted to only about 18 per cent of the total. A near doubling in 1940 of the size of the wartime army from perhaps 2.5 million to 4.5 million men, each of them requiring a substantially larger ration of food and other necessities than per capita civilian requirements, added further to the demand. The loss of industrial production in the enemy held areas where a disproportionately large capacity was located forced a lowering of living standard in Free China, while putting still more demand pressure on the food supply.[4] With food looming as the only wage good of consequence and its supply precarious in relation to demand, a couple of poor harvests in 1940 and 1941 were all that was needed to start the inflationary spiral going. The initial role of Dr. Shen's subject of food production and distribution is thus clear.

In what remains I shall address the distribution aspect since, on the aggregate side, it is likely that there was not much more that the government could have done, under the severe resource and time constraints, to boost output. The government began to address the distribution question in earnest in 1941 with the restoration of the land tax in kind to central authorities, coupled with a further compulsory levy in kind of an almost confiscatory character on large landowners. While these central levies on landholders stabilized the distribution to the military and government sector, the regional and local supply and demand imbalances remained unaddressed. This problem may have been a key factor responsible for massive welfare losses suffered by the people in various localities and for leaving China in a generally exhausted state, economically and psychologically, even as the war was being won.

Dislocations among areas came about for a variety of reasons: (1) a highly inadequate transportation system even in terms of peacetime requirements was rendered intolerable by war-related expansion in transport needs, by enemy obstruction of important arteries; (2) government levies on internal trade in an attempt to make up for losses in customs duty, salt impost, and other key traditional sources of revenues; (3) localization of war-related activities; thus, the construction of the Burma Road brought about a large influx of laborers and others into Yunnan creating a local inflation. Similarly, location of new military bases around population centers aggravated local dislocations. (4) enemy harvest offensives.

As a reflection of the seriousness of local dislocations, a 1945 NPA study reported a recent tragedy in the Ninth War Area involving the death of 78 per cent of "a levy of conscripts" of dysentery traceable to malnourishment.[5] D. K. Lieu, whose analysis of wartime inflation stressed the role of local bottlenecks, gave the following account. Kunming received an addition of perhaps a quarter of a million people from the war zones in 1939 which led to a ten-fold increase in rice price while neighboring Szechwan's price remained stable. Lieu figured the gaping price differential just about represented the transport cost between the two points. In further illustrating the transport bottleneck effect, Lieu gave the price of 20 yuan per gallon of gasoline in the producing area of Kansu and 500 yuan in Chungking.[6]

Transport cost of such magnitude effectively prevents significant movement of goods between areas in response to differential local scarcities. The welfare losses, often in terms of death and debility, were no doubt large. In such a situation, society can ill-afford to leave distribution of such key commodities as food to the private traders who are naturally bound by cost considerations that are real and relevant to them. But given seasonal rural underemployment and the modest incremental ration for transport work (over idleness or low-energy work), much labor can be mobilized by government to equalize supplies between regions while incurring little or no opportunity cost (i.e., without causing much, if any, loss in other productive endeavors).

Chang Kia-ngau was no doubt right in suggesting that the real bottleneck in the 1940 build-up of the Chinese Army after much attrition in 1937-39 was not manpower but equipment. The subsequent build-up in manpower from 2.5 to 4.5 million probably did little by way of contribution to combat strength, while its local effect on production and supply-demand imbalance was obvious enough. One wonders in retrospect what might have been the effect on the war and subsequent postwar developments if the new troops had been employed in transport work? After all, manpower alone can go a long way toward shoring-up transport gaps. Witness the supply job done on the Ho Chi-min trail in the Indo-Chinese war—a road network of veritable trails traversed by men carrying supplies on their backs during most of the long war.

NOTES

1. Chang Kia-ngau, *The Inflationary Spiral: The Experience of China, 1939-1950,* (New York: Wiley and Technology Press, 1958). For his definition of Free China, see note 1, table 59 p. 213.
2. *Ibid.* p. 213.
3. *Ibid,* p. 25.
4. For a distribution of prewar production of a key sample of industries between the occupied zone and Free China, see *ibid.,* pp. 213 ff. For troop numbers and rations, see pp. 127-28.
5. National Planning Association, *China's Relief Needs,* Planning Pamphlet No. 40 (Washington: January 1945), p. 25.
6. D. K. Lieu, *China's Economic Stabilization and Reconstruction,* (New Brunswick: Rutgers University Press, 1948), pp. 69-70.

Comments (2):

BY DENNIS CHINN

Dr. T. H. Shen has written an excellent exposition of food and agricultural policy in wartime China, both in terms of administrative and organizational aspects and in terms of specific policy measures. He documents the changing food situation from the prewar period to the end of war in 1945. From rough prewar self-sufficiency the situation changed to one of localized shortages in the early war years due primarily to poor transportation facilities and wartime dislocations. And by the early 1940s, due to increased requirements of wartime mobilization, the war dislocation of supply channels, massive movements of population into the interior provinces, and the extremely poor harvests of 1940 and 1941, a potentially serious general shortage had developed. Unless production in the interior was substantially increased, and speculation and hoarding were controlled, the cumulative effects of these factors would have severely hindered the war effort. Dr. Shen's analysis leaves no doubt that the policies adopted played an important role in maintaining the war effort by doing precisely that. We are indeed fortunate to have the benefit of the insight and firsthand observations of one who played such an important role in the actual events.

My only complaint as a discussant is that there is little to find fault with in the paper's organization, detail, or clarity of exposition. In terms of substance, for what it is worth, my secondhand reading of the statistical record thirty-five years later agrees with Dr. Shen's firsthand analysis and interpretation of the situation. It seems appropriate here to present some additional parts of that record to supplement aspects of Dr. Shen's analysis. Most of my comments concern the data in the two tables presented below.

My first comment concerns the loss in foodgrain producing capacity due to the Japanese occupation of the outer provinces. A rough idea of the magnitude of that loss can be obtained from Table 1. In the prewar period 1931-1937 an average of 267 million *mou* of land was devoted to rice and 302 million *mou* to wheat. The fifteen interior provinces (listed in Table 1) accounted for 211 million *mou* of the rice acreage and 110 million *mou* of the wheat acreage. Thus, by around 1940-1941, 20 per cent of prewar rice acreage and over 60 per cent of total wheat acreage were under Japanese control. Except for small amounts of foodgrains which were competitively purchased in occupied areas the output of the occupied provinces, including that of the surplus regions bordering on the Yangtze River, was lost to Free China. As the population in the interior swelled, efforts to increase effective acreage devoted to food production in the interior provinces by reducing production of non-essential crops, land reclamation, winter plowing, and the expansion of irrigation systems assumed critical importance as means of compensating for the loss in total acreage.

My second comment concerns the magnitude of the production short-falls in 1940 and 1941, and the role of food imports during this period. Table 4 in Dr. Shen's paper documents the severity of the rice crop failure in Szechwan Province in 1940. Concurrent but less severe crop failures were experienced in most of the other interior provinces. Table 1 shows that for the fifteen interior provinces as a whole, rice production in 1940 fell to 619 million piculs, some 15 per cent below prewar (1931-1937) levels or 19 per cent below the 1939 level. The 1941 harvest was roughly 11 per cent below prewar levels. The data in the table also show that even though wheat acreage expanded between 1940 and 1941, wheat output fell substantially by 18 per cent to 165 million piculs in 1941, further worsening the already serious food shortage. Although the overall production shortfall in foodgrains did not approach the 40 per cent shortfall of rice output in Szechwan Province, the food situation in Free China as a whole did become critical after 1940. In addition, imports of rice amounted to 9 per cent of total rice production in 1941, but by 1942 imports of all staple foods had virtually ceased.[1] The degree of success achieved by the policies implemented during this difficult period in helping to maintain the war effort is a tribute to Dr. Shen and his colleagues.

My third comment concerns the government foodgrain procurement policies. Dr. Shen emphasizes the collection of land tax in kind and the compulsory purchases at below market prices as most immediately effective in combating hoarding and speculation. There is little question that this emphasis is justified. As Dr. Shen noted, from the point of view of food price stability, the relevant supply consideration is total marketed output, rather than total production. This distinction is quite important. John Lossing Buck reported that for the period 1929-1933 only 15 per cent of total rice production in twenty-two provinces of China was sold. Of the remaining 85 per cent, 56 per cent was consumed by the farm household, 21 per cent was used to pay rents, and small amounts were used for seed or added to carryover stocks.[2] Thus, although the government procurement program accounted for only 6-7 per cent of total output, it did account for a much larger proportion of total marketed output, and hence did play a significant role in retarding the rate of increase in food prices as well as in supplying military and civilian needs.

Table 1

RICE AND WHEAT PRODUCTION IN CHINA

	22 Provinces 1931-37 (acreage)	1931-37 (acreage)	15 Interior Provinces* 1938	1939	1940	1941
Area *(1,000 mou)*						
Rice	267,448	210,868	206,341	207,048	198,714	198,258
Wheat	302,311	110,023	111,029	114,742	118,870	125,069
Production *(1,000 piculs)*						
Rice	911,918	726,315	747,569	763,649	618,863	643,519
Wheat	434,858	169,160	202,911	198,188	201,110	165,120

Source: Chinese Ministry of Information, *China Handbook 1937-1943* (New York: The Macmillan Company, 1943), pp. 561 and 567.

----

*15 interior provinces as in 1938-42; Ninghsia, Tsinghai, Kansu, Shensi, Honan, Hupeh, Szechwan, Yunnan, Kweichow, Hunan, Kiangsi, Chekiang, Fukien, Kwangtung, and Kwangsi.

It may also be useful to point out that the contribution of the procurement policies varied between provinces. Table 2 presents data on government rice collection for selected provinces for which data on both components of the procurement program were available. The table accounts for only about half of the 52 million piculs collected in total in 1941 reported by Dr. Shen. Nonetheless the data do indicate that the proportion of total rice output procured by the government varied considerably between provinces with the greatest amount being collected in Szechwan Province where the shortage was most severe. Also it appears that the compulsory purchases of rice were roughly as important as the collection of land tax in kind.

My final comment concerns the lasting value of the Chinese wartime experience with food and agricultural policy. The difference between mobilization for war and mobilization for development seems to be primarily one of degree. In Taiwan after 1950, as on the mainland earlier, the policies described by Dr. Shen were highly successful in raising agricultural output. This suggests that while historical experiences are not transferable between countries, particular policies may be. The fact that the agricultural development experience of Taiwan today serves as a model for other developing countries in Asia is indirectly a result of the experience gained in wartime China.

Table 2
GOVERNMENT RICE COLLECTION
FOR 1941 IN SELECTED PROVINCES

Province	In-kind collection of land tax		Compulsory rice purchases	
	(1,000 piculs)	*Percent of total output*	*(1,000 piculs)*	*Percent of total output*
Szechwan	6,781	7.5	6,566	7.3
Kweichow	998	6.4	724	4.7
Hunan	2,402	2.7	4,220	4.7
Hupeh	652	3.0	800	3.7
Kwangsi	1,364	2.2	1,159	1.9

Source: Computed from tables in Chinese Ministry of Information, *China Handbook 1937-1943* (New York: The Macmillan Company, 1943), pp. 567, 651, 653.

NOTES

1. National Government of China, Directorate of Statistics, Directorate General of Budgets, Accounts and Statistics, *Statistical Abstract of the Republic of China 1947* (Nanking, July 1947), pp. 36-37.
2. John Lossing Buck, *Land Utilization in China* (Chicago: University of Chicago Press, 1937), p. 236.

CHAPTER VI

Economic Development and Public Finance in China, 1937-1945

BY CHI-MING HOU

I

Introduction

N THE EVE OF THE Lukouchiao Incident, the Chinese economy may be described as an underdeveloped and dualistic economy. There coexisted a small modern sector and a vast traditional sector. The modern sector was brought about by an interplay between a Western economic challenge (foreign trade and investment) on the one hand and an intricate Chinese response on the other.[1]

Under the protection of a treaty-ports system and because of a rather effective Chinese resistance, foreign economic influence was primarily limited to the coastal areas. Foreign investment in manufacturing was legally confined to treaty ports; foreign investment in mining and railways had to be negotiated with the Chinese government which was usually not receptive, as witnessed, for example, by the restrictive mining regulations. Foreign investment in agriculture was nil.

The concentration of foreign investment in treaty ports in the coastal areas and along the navigable rivers was augmented by Chinese-owned modern enterprises. They, too, clustered in these ports at least in part because of the infrastucture created by foreign firms (banking facilities, public utilities, labor force, law and order in foreign concessions, etc.).

This treaty-ports and Western-technology-based modern sector grew rather rapidly before the 1930's. According to John Chang's index (which does not include handicraft), the average annual growth rate of industrial production was 9.4 per cent from 1912 to 1936 (8.3 per cent from 1926 to 1936 or 9.3 per cent from 1931 to 1936).[2]

Yet, the modern sector remained small. For example, in 1933 modern nonagricultural sectors contributed no more than 13 per cent to net domestic product.[3] The Chinese economy remained primarily traditional. In Tawney's phrase, the modern sector was merely a fringe stitched along the hem of an ancient garment.

It was this dualistic nature of the economy which presented enormous difficulties and challenges to the Chinese government and people when the Sino-Japanese war broke out in 1937. The immediate results of the war were an increase in government expenditures and an imposed demand for resources to be devoted to war needs. But at the same time much of the coastal areas where the modern sector of the economy was primarily situated was rapidly occupied by the Japanese forces. Since the modern sector had provided much of the revenue of the government as well as modern industrial goods, the economic base of fighting a prolonged war was seriously curtailed. China had to fight a large-scale modern war on the basis of a vast traditional economy. The present essay deals with the course of development by which the war demands were met. The economic consequences of the war will also be examined.

II

The Economic Base of Free China

In the initial phase of the war, the Chinese military strategy was to trade space for time. By October 1938, when Hankow fell, the Japanese forces had overrun North China and the coastal provinces. China could count on only fourteen provinces as a base to fight the war.[4] Even of these provinces, China was not in full control; a large part of Kiangsi, Honan, and Hupeh was under Japanese occupation. It is true China also retained control of parts of provinces other than the fourteen (such as Chekiang, Fukien, and Kwangtung). But by and large, the fourteen provinces may be regarded as the core area of Free China.

The Share in 1937

There are no data on the total share of national income which originated in these fourteen provinces before the war. But the following pieces of information may be suggestive.

Excluding Manchuria, Mongolia, and Tibet, a little more than half of the Chinese population lived in the fourteen provinces in the 1930's, with about the same percentage of total cultivated land of the country. These provinces were quite adequate in the production of rice, accounting for nearly 65 per cent of total production in China (excluding Manchuria). Their share in wheat and other food crops was probably much less (less than 40 per cent in the case of wheat). (Rice consumption provided about 50 per cent of all calories from food crops, taking the country as a whole.) (See Table 1.)

In manufacturing the share of the fourteen provinces in the national total was considerably less than that for population or agricultural production; in fact, it was unbelievably small. For example, in 1933 the output of cloth made in factories in the fourteen provinces was only 5 per cent of the total for the country as a whole. In Ninghsia, Kansu, Kweichow, Yunnan, Tsinghai, and Sinkiang, there was no factory making cloth at all. Of spindles for cotton spinning, Free China had only 17,000 as compared with about five million for China proper in 1936.[5]

For factories in all industries in 1937, the fourteen provinces accounted for no more than 13 per cent of the national total in terms of paid-up capital, and 19 per cent in terms of workers (Table 1). Most of the modern factories in China before 1937 were concentrated in six cities along the coast: Shanghai, Tientsin, Wu-han, Wu-hsi, Canton, and Tsingtao. Altogether, they accounted for nearly 70 per cent of the national total (excluding Manchuria) in terms of gross value of production and 54 per cent in terms of the number of workers employed.[6]

The overwhelming majority of the factories in the fourteen provinces were small. There were only a handful of large factories: one power plant, one cement mill, five flour mills, one paper mill, and two machine factories in Szechwan; one paper mill in Kweichow; and one machine shop in Kiangsi.

As for the fuel, the fourteen provinces accounted for about 25 per cent of coal production in China proper in 1936 (Table 1). But their share in iron ore (by modern mines) was virtually nil, if Hupeh is excluded. However, their native mines accounted for about 27 per cent of the national total for both iron ore and pig iron (Table 1). They had virtual monopoly in the production of copper, lead, zinc, tungsten, and tin.

As for modern transportation, the bulk of Chinese railways were located in Manchuria and the coastal provinces; very few in the fourteen provinces. In auto transportation, although the fourteen provinces accounted for 42 per cent of total mileage of highways in China proper, they accounted for only 8 per cent of the total in terms of number of automobiles (of all types) (Table 1).

As for trading stores and restaurants, the fourteen provinces accounted for about 36 per cent of the national total in terms of number of establishments (Table 1).

Taking China as a whole, in 1933 the value added in the traditional sector was about 87 per cent of total net domestic product, leaving 13

Table 1
THE ECONOMIC SHARE OF THE 14 PROVINCES (FREE CHINA)
(1930's)

	Population[1] (1930's) millions	%	Cultivated area per capita[2] (Mou)	Rice Production[3] (1933) %	Mileage of Highways (1933)[4] %	Number of Motor Vehicles[5] %	Number of Trading Stores and Restaurants[6] %	Factories (1937)[7] Paid-up Capital Ch$ millions	%	Workers 1,000's	%
Ninghsia	1.0	0.2	2.50		4.2	0.1					
Kansu	6.5	1.4	4.49		1.1	0.1	0.6	0.3	0.1	1.2	0.3
Shensi	9.7	2.1	5.57	0.2	1.9	0.6	1.9	2.8	0.7	4.6	1.0
Honan	36.3	7.8	3.39	0.7	3.4	0.5	1.2	8.6	2.3	13.3	2.9
Hupeh	27.3	5.9	3.08	8.2	3.0	2.6	4.7	20.0	5.5	30.1	6.6
Hunan	33.4	7.2	2.37	15.8	2.3	0.9	14.4	4.8	1.3	7.5	1.7
Kiangsi	16.5	3.5	2.61	5.8	3.8	0.6	4.1	4.4	1.2	2.4	0.5
Kwangsi	16.6	3.6	2.59	5.1	6.5	0.7	2.9	0.9	0.1	0.2	0.1
Kweichow	12.6	2.7	1.78	3.1	1.9	0.2	0.7	0.1		0.2	0.1
Yunnan	15.9	3.4	2.26	4.9	2.2	0.2	0.5	4.2	1.2	6.4	1.5
Szechwan	55.4	11.9	2.33	20.1	6.6	1.5	4.9	2.1	0.6	13.0	2.9
Sikang	3.8	0.8	1.21		1.0						
Tsinghai	1.3	0.3	6.00		1.9						
Sinkiang	2.7	0.6	5.93		2.2	0.2	0.1				
14 Provinces	239.0	51.4	2.82	64.2	42.1	8.2	36.1	48.3	12.9	78.9	17.3
China Proper[*]	465.3	100.0	2.79	100.0	100.0	100.0	100.0	373.4	100.0	457.0	100.0

Sources:

[1] Ta-chung Liu and Kung-chia Yeh, *The Economy of the Chinese Mainland: National Income and Economic Development 1933-1959* (Princeton: Princeton University Press, 1965), p. 178.

[2] Computed from data on population and cultivated area given in *Ibid.*, pp. 178 and 278.

[3] *Ibid.*, p. 290.

[4] Ou Pao-san, *1933 Chung-kuo kuo-min so-te* (China's National Income, 1933), 2 Vols. (Shanghai: Chung-hua Book Co, 1947), Vol. 2, p. 202.

[5] *Ibid.*, Vol. 2, p. 202.

[6] *Ibid.*, Vol. 1, p. 102.

[7] Chen Chen, Ed., *Chung-kuo Chin-tai kung-yeh-shih tzu-liau* (Source material for *History of Modern Industry of China*) (Peking, 1961), Vol. IV, Section 1, p. 97.

[*] Manchuria, Mongolia, and Tibet excluded.

	Output of Cotton Weaving Industry: Factory, 1933[8]		Coal Production (1936)		Iron Ore (1934)[9]		Pig Iron[10]	
	Ch$ millions	%	1,000 metric tons	%	Metric tons	%	Metric tons	%
Ninghsia			15					
Kansu			100	0.4				
Shensi			200	0.8	180		50	
Honan			2,266	10.2	25,000	6.1	8,000	5.8
Hupeh	1.5	1.9	563	2.5				
Hunan	.2	0.3	919	4.1	12,800	3.1	5,052	3.6
Kiangsi	.2	0.3	346	1.6				
Kwangsi	.1	0.2	100	0.4	11,500	2.8	3,350	2.4
Kweichow			80	0.4	300		75	
Yunnan			123	0.6	1,500	0.4	500	0.4
Szechwan	2.0	2.6	663	3.0	60,000	14.7	20,000	14.4
Sikang								
Tsinghai								
Sinkiang			100	0.4				
14 Provinces	4.0	5.2	5,475	24.6	111,280	27.2	37,027	26.7
China Proper*	76.6	100.0	22,250	100.0	409,530	100.0	138,727	100.0

[8]Ou Pao-san, *op. cit.*, Vol. 2, p. 97.
[9]Production of native mines, *The Chinese Year Book 1944-1945*, p. 655.
[10]Production of native mines, *The Chinese Year Book 1944-1945*, p. 655.

per cent located in the modern sector. Assuming that half of the value added in the traditional sector and 15 per cent of the value added in the modern sector were from the fourteen provinces, it follows that the latter accounted for no more than 46 per cent of total net domestic product of China proper. Such an estimate is, of course, rough and has a large margin of error; but it does seem to be in accord with our general impressions.

Inward Migration

Recognizing that the industrial centers were in extreme danger of being occupied by Japan after the war broke out, the Chinese government took actions to move modern factories from the coastal areas to the inland immediately. In August 1937, large quantities of industrial equipment accompanied by hundreds of workers were moved from Shanghai to Hankow. In July 1938, when Wuchang and Hankow were threatened, another move was made westward eventually to Szechwan by way of Ichang.

Government measures in assisting private enterprises for such removal included financial subsidies, loans, reduction of freight rates, allotment of land for building plants. Aside from government plants, more than 600 factories were removed to the interior together with 116,000 tons of equipment and materials, and more than twelve thousand skilled workers (see Table 2). They were largely moved to Szechwan and Hunan; 70 per cent of them resumed operation by 1940. They played a key role in industrial development in Free China.

Table 2
MIGRATED FACTORIES AND WORKERS OF
COASTAL AREAS TO FREE CHINA

Industry	Number of factories	Number of workers
Iron and Steel	2	360
Machine-making	230	5,968
Electrical manufacturing	41	744
Chemical	62	1,408
Textile	115	1,688
Food	46	580
Educational supplies	81	635
Mining	8	377
Others	54	404
Total	639	12,164

Source: *The Chinese Year Book 1944-1945*, p. 645.

III

Industrial Development

The government played a key role in industrial development in Free China. Many new enterprises were established under government ownership and operation. And, especially in the last few years of the war, some private enterprises were taken over by the government. Measures were also adopted to assist private firms. The main focus of development was on basic and national defense industries and daily necessities.

State Enterprises

The National Resources Commission of the Ministry of Economic Affairs was the main agency in charge of the development of state-owned enterprises emphasizing such basic industries as electric power, coal, iron and steel, copper, lead, zinc, minerals for export (tungsten, antimony, tin, mercury), machinery, electrical manufacturing, liquid fuel, and chemical industry.

In 1937 the National Resources Commission had only twenty-three working units; by 1945 the number increased to 130.[7] In 1944 it employed a staff of 12,000 persons and 160,000 workers.[8] Its chief source of funds for industrial development was provided by government appropriations and by loans made by government-controlled banks. Very little foreign exchange was used to purchase materials from abroad.

The funds provided in the government budget for the Commission was quite modest, usually about 1 per cent and never exceeding 3 per cent of the total central government budget in any year. At pre-war prices, the Commission's annual budget was only Chinese $11.1 million in 1941, the highest during the war years, as compared with seventeen million in 1937. For other years, it was eight or nine million before 1942; thereafter it dropped sharply to around two million (Table 3).

The working capital of the enterprises under the Commission was provided largely by bank loans, especially since 1943, by the Bank of China and the Bank of Communications. From 1943 to 1945, these two banks provided a total of nine billion Chinese dollars (in current prices) for industrial development.[9]

It is difficult to judge how successful the Commission's enterprises were financially; the Commission's accounting records are not available. In a period of rapid inflation any calculations of profit rates are subject to serious difficulties for well-known reasons. For example, because profits are in current prices whereas equity capital in lower prices, the rates of return on investment are often overstated. Yet for the available 154 finan-

Table 3
ANNUAL BUDGET OF
THE NATIONAL RESOURCES COMMISSION
(1937-1945)

	Commission's Budget (in 1936 prices)[1] Ch $1,000's	Commission's Budget as percentage of total central government's budget[2]	Payment of interest and dividends to the government, as percentage of Commission's Annual budget[3]
		%	%
1937	16,984	1.2	
1938°	6,665	1.0	
1939	7,892	1.2	
1940	9,257	2.8	
1941	11,062	2.2	1.32
1942	7,095	1.6	2.83
1943	2,041	0.9	4.29
1944	1,739	0.9	3.69
1945	3,607	0.7	

Sources: For 1 and 2, Chen Chen, *op. cit.*, Vol. III, Section 2, p. 892. For 3, *Ibid.*, p. 1391.

°half year.

cial statements of the Commission's enterprises from 1937-1945, no less than 28 per cent showed a loss; 25 per cent a profit rate of less than 5 per cent; 20 per cent a profit rate of 5-20 per cent and 27 per cent a profit rate of more than 21 per cent.[10] Thus, more than 50 per cent of the financial statements reported a result of operation which could hardly be described as profitable. Possibly some of the enterprises were operated without profit motive, but some enterprises did score very high profit rates (more than 300 or 400 per cent for some of the mining enterprises). In one case, it was nearly 2,000 per cent. All this seems to suggest the need for further research on the efficiency of operation of government-operated enterprises.

Aside from the National Resources Commission, there were also other branches of the government which operated industrial enterprises: the Ministry of Military Affairs, ammunition and war supplies; the Ministry of Communications, fuels, repair and machine shops; the Ministry of Food, food processing; the Ministry of Education, paper and printing, educational supplies; the government banks, in a wide variety of industries. A number of industrial enterprises were also undertaken either solely or jointly with private capital, by provincial governments.

There is little doubt, however, that the enterprises under the National Resources Commission were predominant. According to one estimate, the total paid-up capital of all government enterprises was Chinese $0.8 billion at the end of 1941, of which 0.6 billion (or 75 per cent) were for the Commission's enterprises.[11]

In relation to private enterprises, state enterprises enjoyed a dominant position in Free China especially when compared with the pre-war situation. For example, at the end of 1935, total paid-up capital of all factories in China proper was estimated to be Chinese $250 million, of which only 11 per cent belonged to state-operated factories. At the end of 1941, the share increased to 50 per cent in Free China.[12] The relative importance of state enterprises in various industries in 1942 is given in Table 4.

Table 4

SHARE OF PUBLIC AND PRIVATE ENTERPRISES:
BY INDUSTRIES, 1942[1]

(%)

	Paid-up Capital			Workers			Number of Factories		
	Tot.	Pub.	Pri.	Tot.	Pub.	Pri.	Tot.	Pub.	Pri.
Total[2]	100.0	69.6	30.4	100.0	32.0	68.0	100.0	17.5	82.5
Water & Electricity	7.4	6.6	0.8	1.9	1.0	0.9	3.3	1.6	1.7
Metallurgical	15.6	14.2	1.4	7.2	2.8	4.4	4.1	1.2	2.9
Metal Works	1.2	0.1	1.1	3.4	0.7	2.7	4.3	0.2	4.1
Machinery	17.4	12.7	4.7	13.1	4.1	8.9	18.1	1.3	16.8
Electrical Mfg.	4.8	4.2	0.6	3.0	2.1	0.9	2.6	0.6	2.0
Lumber & Construction	0.3	0.0	0.3	0.8	0.2	0.6	1.3	0.1	1.2
Chemicals	28.8	21.7	7.1	15.0	3.3	11.7	22.0	3.3	18.7
Food & Drinks	4.3	1.0	3.3	4.7	1.1	3.7	9.6	0.9	8.7
Textiles	15.0	7.4	7.6	38.6	14.3	24.3	21.0	6.5	14.5
Ornaments & Clothing	0.6	0.1	0.5	3.8	0.4	3.4	3.9	0.2	3.7
Educational Supplies	1.1	0.2	0.9	3.0	1.1	1.9	6.0	0.9	5.1
Miscellaneous	0.2	0.0	0.2	1.1	0.0	1.1	0.6	0.1	0.5

[1]Chen Chen, *op. cit.*, Vol. III, Section 2, p. 1422.

[2]The actual amounts: Total paid-up capital, Ch $1,939 million; number of workers, 242,000; number of factories, 3,758. See Chen Chen, *op. cit.*, Vol. I, p. 95.

As measured by capital and the number of workers, the state-operated enterprises were predominant in heavy industries such as metallurgical industry, water and electricity, machinery, electrical manufacturing, and chemical industry. But they were also important in textiles (machine-spun yarn and factory-made piece goods).[13]

As a rule, the state-operated enterprises were larger in scale and more capital intensive. For example, in 1942 the average paid-up capital for state enterprises was two million Chinese dollars, whereas for private enterprises only $0.2 million. The state enterprises employed about 100 workers per factory whereas private enterprises 50.[14]

Government Assistance to Private Enterprises

The Industrial and Mining Adjustment Administration of the Ministry of Economic Affairs was in charge of government programs to assist private industries. The assistance consisted primarily of granting loans (directly by the Ministry or indirectly through government banks), supplying certain raw materials (especially from abroad), and training of skilled workers.

The scale of assistance was of some significance. For example, in the year from July 1943 to June 1944, the Administration loaned directly to factories a total of Chinese $55 million and negotiated for these loans totaling Chinese $290 million through government banks. All this may be compared with the budget of the National Resources Commission which totaled Chinese $508 million in 1943 and $1,344 million in 1944.

During the same period (that is, July 1943 to June 1944), a total of 1,800 skilled workers were graduated from training classes held by the Administration. Another 1,800 were being trained.[15]

The functions of the Industrial and Mining Adjustment Administration were taken over by the War Production Board, established in November 1944, in response to mounting economic difficulties faced by industrial enterprises. It had broad power over production and distribution of goods for war and essential civilian needs; placing orders with government and private enterprises for military supplies and other materials; purchasing products for stockpiling in order to meet emergencies; leasing equipment to manufacturing and mining firms; granting short-term financial assistance; providing technical help; securing of raw materials and equipment. It was also given the power to determine priorities of transportation for various materials and supplies.[16]

Loans from government banks were main sources of financing of the Board's activities. Coincidental or not, there was a general economic recovery after the establishment of the Board.[17]

Geographical Distribution

An important feature of industrial development in Free China was its lack of concentration on a few localities. Except Sikang, Tsinghai, and

Ninghsia, all other provinces participated in the development in varying degrees. However, Szechwan, being the largest and richest province in Free China, and Chungking, the wartime capital, were more dominant than other provinces and cities. The geographical distribution of industrial establishments, capital, and workers is given in Table 5.

Industrial Production

Based on the industrial production index prepared by the Ministry of Economic Affairs, a few observations may be made on the pattern of industrial growth in Free China. (See Table 6.) First, the rate of industrial growth (as measured by industrial production) was very impressive, averaging 27 per cent a year from 1938 to 1945. Second, the rate of growth of consumers goods was substantially faster (averaging 41 per cent a year) than that of producers goods (averaging 20 per cent a year). Third, the differential rates of growth of producers, consumers, and all products imply predominance of producers goods as compared

Table 5
GEOGRAPHICAL DISTRIBUTION OF FACTORIES
IN FREE CHINA, 1944

	Number of Factories	Capitalization Ch$ millions	%	Number of Staff	Workers Number	%
Kiangsu	11	600	—	17	79	0.2
Chekiang	55	56,985	4.1	524	3,081	5.9
Anhwei	17	5,735	0.4	154	599	1.2
Kiangsi	51	58,594	4.2	865	3,916	7.5
Hupeh	5	4,872	0.3	67	252	0.5
Hunan	112	207,308	14.9	1,198	8,165	15.7
Szechwan	170	455,719	32.7	2,191	12,533	24.2
Sikang	4	19,365	1.4	53	238	0.5
Fukien	12	15,170	1.1	183	823	1.6
Kwangtung	16	18,620	1.3	223	1,077	2.1
Kwangsi	53	33,048	2.4	475	1,520	2.9
Yunnan	35	176,150	12.6	672	5,787	11.2
Kweichow	27	25,400	1.8	213	673	1.3
Honan	6	1,810	0.1	41	174	0.3
Shensi	85	73,492	5.3	779	4,880	9.4
Kansu	49	19,383	1.4	297	1,486	2.9
Chungking	230	222,482	16.0	1,517	6,401	12.3
Total	928	1,394,733	100.0	9,471	51,883	100.0

Source: *China Handbook 1937-1945*, p. 363. These figures were based on a nationwide registration of both government and private factories since March 1941.

Table 6
INDEX AND ANNUAL RATES OF GROWTH OF
INDUSTRIAL PRODUCTION IN FREE CHINA
(MONTHLY AVERAGE, 1938=100)

	Total[1]		Producer's Goods		Consumer's Goods	
	Index	Growth rate[2]	Index	Growth rate[2]	Index	Growth rate[2]
1939	133.46	33.5	129.66	29.7	145.63	45.6
1940	214.45	60.7	181.13	39.7	306.27	110.3
1941	275.56	28.5	230.61	27.3	404.07	31.9
1942	372.93	35.3	272.12	18.0	658.88	62.9
1943	520.41	39.5	316.07	16.2	1,010.61	53.4
1944	495.70	—4.7	324.95	2.8	920.36	—8.6
1945[3]	473.58	—4.5	333.41	2.6	826.83	—10.2
Average		26.9		19.5		40.8
1944:						
Jan.-June	521.27		334.97		990.79	
July-Dec.	470.12		319.42		849.94	
1945:						
Jan.-Mar.	474.42		331.76		833.95	
Apr.-June	488.26		345.11		849.04	
July-Sept.	458.05		323.35		797.51	

Sources: *China Handbook 1937-1945*, p. 369; *The Chinese Year Book 1944-1945*, p. 675.

[1]Minerals for export not included.
[2]Previous year as base.
[3]Jan.-Sept. taken to represent whole year.

with consumer goods. (Note that the growth rate of the general index was much closer to that of producers goods.) Fourth, there was a rapid and continuous expansion of industrial production from 1938 through 1943. The general index increased at 40 per cent a year; producer goods at 26 per cent, and consumer goods at 61 per cent from 1938 to 1943. Thereafter, there was a decline. For consumer goods, the peak was reached by the end of 1943, and the decline thereafter was much sharper than that for producer goods. For the latter the peak was not reached until June 1944.

The rates of growth varied tremendously among producer goods, with silicon, iron, steel, generators, and motors among the highest. Iron production increased the least. (See Table 7.) For consumer goods, fastest growth took place in gasoline, alcohol, electric bulbs, printing ink, and cigarettes. For cigarettes the growth rate was 244 per cent a year from 1938 to 1944.

Factors accounting for the rapid expansion of industrial production from 1938 to 1944 cannot be easily quantified. But as a general explanation, the following may be suggested.

First, effective demand for industrial products was never lacking—government expenditures for war requirements and the influx of people from the coastal provinces meant an increase of demand for both producer and consumer goods. Government expenditures to expand basic and national defense industries not only stimulated the production of producer goods, they also stimulated demand for consumer goods through the familiar multiplier effect. What is surprising was the ease with which aggregate supply was expanded.

In the first six months of the war, China was almost completely cut off from the outside world by sea routes except through Canton. When Canton fell in October 1938, China was completely isolated from the world by sea route. The only indirect sea route available to Free China was the French-owned Tungking-Yunnan railway in the Southwest China border connecting Kunming and Haiphong. This route was cut off in June 1940. Thus, the Burma-Yunnan highway (the Burma Road) was the only land route by which China could get supplies from her Western allies before April 1942. The traffic capacity of this highway was very limited, however, enabling China to get no more than half of the needed external supplies. Russian aid in war materials came over land through the trans-Sinkiang highway before 1941.

In U.S. dollars, total imports to Free China dropped from $86 million in 1938 to $39 million in 1939. They were $67 million in 1940. This may be compared with $264 million for all China in 1937 (Manchuria excluded).[18]

The effective Japanese economic blockade was tantamount to protection for industries in Free China. But any increase in industrial production would imply an increase of use of inputs, labor, and raw materials. Since raw materials were largely agricultural and mining products and since both agricultural and mining were quite labor-intensive, an increase in the production of raw materials would also require an ample supply of labor. In an economy such as that in Free China, the existence of disguised unemployment or surplus labor may be expected. A mobilization or greater utilization of such labor may thus be deemed as an important source of industrial expansion in Free China.

Industrial production may also be stimulated by the usual wage-lag during inflation when wage increase tends to fall behind productivity increase. There are no data to enable us to calculate unit labor cost for industries in Free China, but one fact stands out clearly: worker's money

Table 7

INDEXES OF INDUSTRIAL PRODUCTION:
BY INDUSTRIES MONTHLY AVERAGE 1938=100

	1939	1940	1941	1942	1943	1944 Jan.-June	1944 Jul.-Dec.	1945 Jan.-Mar.	1945 Apr.-June	1945 July-Sep.
Producers' goods	129.66	181.13	230.61	272.12	316.07	334.97	319.42	331.70	345.11	323.35
Power	135.88	205.01	261.04	291.65	340.77	375.60	389.33	352.98	363.09	347.53
Coal	109.15	119.50	169.87	207.10	213.96	209.37	87.93	141.66	155.02	142.50
White iron	116.67	150.00	106.50	82.00	56.84	56.68	66.68	40.00	35.72	27.64
Grey iron	118.75	648.63	1,299.75	3,134.25	4,058.21	1,725.37	3,532.83	2,486.57	3,302.99	4,273.13
Steel	211.11	350.56	875.00	2,214.44	4,973.33	6,520.00	9,113.33	12,426.67	12,520.00	11,260.00
Electrolytic copper	100.00	283.75	159.50	127.23	122.22	236.11	155.55	175.00	180.56	102.78
Machine tools	204.52	296.39	367.47	340.66	514.29	514.29	314.29	350.00	325.00	225.00
Steam engine	100.00	492.32	747.25	581.15	464.00	414.00	788.00	394.00	258.00	214.00
Internal combustion engine	151.09	529.09	392.09	706.36	504.35	604.35	393.48	304.35	339.13	306.52
Generator	71.18	1,217.47	1,809.61	1,747.16	2,466.67	4,516.67	2,650.00	3,275.00	4,925.00	3,475.00
Motor	10,360.71	14,820.24	26,059.52	12,332.14	13,628.57	7,600.00	7,114.28	5,714.29	12,171.43	9,828.57
Transformer	81.78	127.31	236.04	351.16	271.80	251.70	235.77	174.15	368.15	266.58
Cement	230.80	246.50	124.18	193.83	173.65	222.07	182.97	192.94	285.91	191.44
Soda ash	132.42	115.57	66.95	160.06	248.10	332.91	454.43	356.12	257.27	250.25
Caustic soda	—	100.00	300.48	359.81	441.18	488.24	855.88	776.47	529.41	423.53
Bleaching power	—	100.00	348.30	448.98	425.00	400.00	700.33	883.33	541.67	508.33
Sulphuric acid	72.94	251.76	367.65	391.76	371.43	550.00	364.29	378.57	185.71	50.00
Hydrochloric acid	72.93	152.53	131.31	181.82	387.50	387.50	475.00	450.00	425.00	337.50
Consumers' goods	145.63	306.27	404.07	658.88	1,010.61	990.79	849.94	833.95	849.04	797.51
Gasoline	103.96	1,669.23	4,029.46	37,679.17	65,496.54	68,377.37	97,930.25	59,021.71	105,339.72	100,822.63
Alcohol	264.71	1,489.77	1,767.37	2,566.43	2,427.22	2,102.51	2,825.82	4,148.57	6,440.89	6,409.95
Cotton yarn	124.37	277.25	387.52	718.97	734.92	780.05	672.56	521.39	428.65	427.06
Wheat flour	127.29	214.09	298.08	322.54	272.97	227.92	214.14	184.16	153.07	107.15
Soap	120.69	341.34	489.02	390.24	430.75	403.95	167.35	208.30	221.45	147.64

Matches	101.05	123.51	126.51	488.96	69.77	76.53	69.17	47.20	54.67	47.57
Paper	106.83	134.06	257.47	691.06	582.98	644.88	613.32	637.41	751.22	722.93
Leather	107.42	122.61	140.87	281.25	330.06	298.68	228.29	242.51	240.02	225.02
Lamp bulbs	295.29	998.96	897.56	1,252.86	2,043.06	2,781.41	1,985.74	1,582.92	1,716.41	1,351.14
Printing ink	727.05	2,795.29	2,952.94	2,941.18	4,829.52	2,412.29	2,354.09	1,465.54	1,756.07	1,694.92
Pencils	124.94	121.16	80.20	92.28	131.24	148.39	125.82	53.87	112.88	21.47
Cigarettes	194.82	1,058.75	1,072.86	2,142.86	20,123.40	19,431.91	14,185.10	15,800.00	14,185.11	12,936.17
Minerals for export										
Tungsten ore	91.65	75.98	98.69	95.06	71.32	51.25	0.29	—	—	—
Antimony regulars	140.21	103.70	97.63	56.64	7.83	4.07	—	—	—	—
Tin	94.49	629.60	1,600.34	1,328.06	712.50	232.29	466.67	210.42	295.83	141.67
Mercury	100.00	70.59	71.77	95.88	71.43	64.23	64.28	50.00	42.86	14.29

Source: *The Chinese Year Book 1944-1945*, pp. 675-677.

wage rate did not increase as fast as prices. For example, taking the period January-June 1937 as 1, the price index of manufactured goods in Chungking rose to 141 while index of wage rates to eleven in 1942. Thus, the price of manufactured goods rose nearly thirteen times as fast as wages. (During the same period, the price index of raw materials rose from 1 to 37.) Even if allowance is made for a wide margin of error, these figures clearly indicate that the profit margins widened sharply. (Table 8).

Another stimulating factor to industrial production was the low rates of interest. The rates of interest were kept low by the government in the expectation that lower interest charges would lower production costs and commodity prices, and hence arrest inflation. Thus, the interest rate charged on loans by government banks to approved industrial enterprises was fixed below 10 per cent, substantially below the market rate of interest. The latter itself increased much more slowly than the rate of inflation. It is calculated that the market rate of interest constituted the following percentages of annual increase of wholesale price indexes: 48.0 in 1938; 17.3 in 1939; 5.1 in 1940; 2.3 in 1941; 1.2 in 1942; 0.8 in 1943; 0.3 in 1944; and 0.08 in 1945 (January-June).[19] This low interest

Table 8
INDEXES OF PRICES, WAGE RATES, AND INTEREST RATES IN FREE CHINA
JAN.-JUNE, 1937=100

	1937	1938	1939	1940	1941	1942	1943	1944
(1) Raw materials	0.9	0.9	1.4	4.5	13.3	37.0	114.0	383.9
(2) Semi-finished goods	1.1	1.5	2.5	6.3	17.5	60.4	169.4	504.1
(3) Finished goods	1.2	2.3	5.1	13.0	28.2	141.4	398.1	1,333.5
(4) Wage Rates	1.0	1.4	2.3	3.5	6.0	10.6	19.7	38.4
(5) Market Rate of Interest°: %	12.0	14.4	15.6	18.0	23.0	33.6	72.0	102.8
(6) Market Rate of Interest Index	1.0	1.2	1.3	1.5	1.9	2.8	6.0	8.6
(7) Ratio of (3) to:								
(1)	1.3	2.6	3.6	2.9	2.1	3.8	3.5	3.5
(2)	1.1	1.5	2.0	2.1	1.6	2.3	2.4	2.6
(4)	1.2	1.6	2.2	3.7	4.7	13.3	20.2	34.7
(6)	1.2	1.4	3.9	8.7	14.8	50.5	66.4	155.1

Source: Yu-kwei Cheng, *Foreign Trade and Industrial Development of China* (Washington, D.C.: The University Press of Washington, D.C., 1956), pp. 105, 121.

°annual rates in Chungking.

rate policy, though probably wrong as a means to combat inflation, surely produced enormous profits for some industrial enterprises and stimulated their production.

Thus, the increase in aggregate demand imposed by the war, the decline of imports, the existence of a large pool of under-utilized labor, and the growing disparity between prices and costs may be regarded as the leading forces contributing to the industrial boom in Free China from 1938 to 1944.

This boom was brought to an end first in the production of consumer goods toward the end of 1943 and then in producer goods in the middle of 1944. The reasons are not clear, but the following explanations may be relevant.

First, the Japanese blockade of Free China became complete following the Japanese occupation of Burma in early 1942. China could only resort to the very limited "Hump" airlift from India to Yunnan for carrying war material for the Chinese army. Shortage of parts and accessories of foreign machinery and scarce raw materials from abroad created bottlenecks in industrial production.

Second, crop production in 1940-1943 was at a low level as compared with 1939. The index of crop production dropped from 110 in 1939 to ninety-six in 1941 and ninety-eight in both 1942 and 1943. It did not recover until 1944 when the index reached 108. (The average in 1931-1937 was 100.) (See Table 9.) There was a severe drop in cotton production in 1942. (Taking 1931-1937 as 100, the index of cotton production reached 121 in 1939, 126 in 1940, 111 in 1941, and then dropped to

Table 9

INDEXES OF CROP AND LIVESTOCK PRODUCTION
AND TOTAL ACREAGE IN 15 FREE CHINA PROVINCES
1931-1937=100

	Total Crops	Winter Crops°	Summer Crops °°	Total Crop Acreage	Livestock Production (1937=100)
1938	106	111	103	99	97
1939	110	116	106	101	99
1940	102	115	93	102	99
1941	96	99	94	103	90
1942	98	115	86	106	87
1943	98	111	90	108	84
1944	108	129	94	109	85

Source: *China Handbook 1937-1945*, pp. 435-436.

°Include wheat, barley, field peas, broad beans, rape seeds, oats.
°°Include rice, glutinous rice, kaoliang, millet, corn, soybeans, sweet potatoes, cotton, peanuts, sesame, tobacco.

ninety-four in 1942. It recovered in 1943 when the index was 107.[20] Many crops, especially cotton, were chief raw materials for the production of consumer goods. The problem of shortage of raw materials due to decline in crop production was aggravated by an inefficient transportation system, which intensified such shortage in the cities—the industrial centers.

Third, as inflation accelerated in 1940 and 1941, a comprehensive price control program was eventually introduced in 1942. Price and wage ceilings were imposed by the government and a program known as "government purchases and sales of goods at equitable prices" was enforced. But the prices were fixed in such a way that disparity between prices and costs existed for a number of industries such as coal mining and textiles. It was suggested by some observers that some enterprises were forced out of business because of the low government purchase price relative to costs. It was also suggested that the price of cotton was fixed so low that farmers shifted to other crops, and hence a cotton shortage resulted.[21] There is little evidence, however, to ascertain how serious or widespread such undesirable consequences of price controls were.

Fourth, as prices rose at an accelerated rate, especially after China was completely isolated from the outside world by land and sea routes in early 1942, inflationary psychology became dominant. Some manufacturers found it more profitable to speculate in buying, hoarding, and selling than in manufacturing especially when there was a risk of enemy bombing or uncertainty of availability of raw materials.

But all this should not be exaggerated. After all, the general index of industrial production suffered no more than a 5 per cent decline a year both in 1944 and in 1945 (up until September).

IV

Agricultural Production

The Chinese government was keenly aware of the importance of agriculture in a prolonged war against Japan. In an isolated economy, agriculture is the source of supply of both food and raw materials. But agriculture is also a sector which cannot be changed or improved overnight.

The agricultural policy of the government was rather straightforward. It was designed to increase food production by an increase in cultivated area, extension of multiple cropping, improvement of seeds, insect and disease control, use of fertilizers, improvement in irrigation systems, and protection of farm animals. There were some positive results of all these measures, but in total, the achievements were rather marginal.

There was a steady increase of acreage of about 1 per cent a year from 1938 to 1944. But the index of total crop production (1931-1937 = 100) after rising to 106 in 1938 and 110 in 1939 began to decline. It was 102 in 1940; ninety-six in 1941, and stayed at ninety-eight in 1942 and 1943. It went up to 108 in 1944.[22] The index of livestock production (1931-1937 = 100) never reached the pre-war level, gradually declining from ninety-nine in 1939 (the peak year) to eighty-five in 1944 (Table 9).

V

War Finance and Inflation

The loss of the coastal provinces to Japan had an immediate adverse effect on government finance: By 1939, expenditures increased by 50 per cent from the 1936-37 level while revenue was cut by more than 60 per cent during the same period. The Chinese government was simply not able to raise enough revenues to meet war expenditures and had to resort to printing money or borrowing. This, of course, was the basic cause of inflation in Free China.

Table 10

CASH EXPENDITURES AND RECEIPTS OF THE
CENTRAL GOVERNMENT, 1938-1945
(CH $ MILLIONS)

	Cash Expenditures	Cash Receipts[1]	Deficits as percent of cash expenditures
1937-38[2]	2,091	1,314	37
1938 (2nd half)	1,169	341	71
Calendar Year			
1939	2,797	580	79
1940	5,288	1,589	70
1941	10,795	2,024	81
1942	25,149	6,254	75
1943	67,234	20,768	69
1944	193,619	61,046	69
1945	1,257,733	216,519	83

Source: Arthur N. Young, *China's Wartime Finance and Inflation, 1937-1945* (Cambridge: Harvard University Press, 1965), p. 20.

---

[1]Nonborrowed cash revenue plus proceeds from sales to the public of bonds, foreign currencies, and gold.
[2]Year ending June 30.

Government Expenditures

The Chinese strategy of fighting the war was one of prolonged resistance. Thus, the government adopted a dual policy of military expansion and economic development. The armed forces increased from about 2.5 million men in 1940 to nearly 4.5 million in 1941 and probably 5.7 in 1944.[23] Thus, military expenditures always constituted a high proportion of total government expenditure, about 60 per cent as minimum. The high was nearly 80 per cent (1940). (See Table 11.)

Expenditures for development were never high in proportion to the total budget. They were primarily for economic reconstruction and development of communications. (See Table 12.)

Table 11

EXPENDITURES OF THE CENTRAL GOVERNMENT
(1937-1945):

BY USES (IN PERCENT)

	Military	Development	Loan Service	General and Administrative	Total
1937-38	66	12	18	8	100
1938					
(2nd half)	60	13	21	7	100
1939	66	11	16	5	100
1940	78	10	7	4	100
1941	51	8	5	34	100
1942	56	8	5	30	100
1943	61	6	5	28	100
1944	61	10	2	27	100

NOTE: Figures for years before 1941 (inclusive) are from Chang Kia-ngau, *The Inflationary Spiral: The Experience in China, 1939-1950* (Cambridge: Technology Press of the Massachusetts Institute of Technology and John Wiley & Sons, Inc., New York, 1958), p. 125.

Figures for 1942-1944 are computed by adding proceeds from land tax in kind to Chang's figures. Seventy per cent of the proceeds from land tax in kind are assumed to have been spent for military purposes and hence are added to that column and to total expenditures. The other 30 per cent are assumed to have been used for general and administrative purposes and have already been included in Chang's figures. Hence, no adjustment is necessary.

The land tax in kind began to be collected in the second half of 1941, but the amount is not known. Chang's figures for 1941 do not include proceeds from land tax in kind and hence underestimate the share of military use for 1941.

The figures for proceeds from land tax in kind are taken from Arthur N. Young, *op. cit.*, p. 29.

Table 12

PERCENTAGE DISTRIBUTION OF DEVELOPMENT
EXPENDITURES OF THE CENTRAL GOVERNMENT

	Economic	Rural	Communi- cations	Development of Northwest	Total
1937-38	62	4	34		100
1939	33	2	65		100
1940	16	4	80		100
1941	22	6	72		100
1942	21	6	73		100
1943	15	8	65	12	100
1944	13	7	73	17	100

Source: Chang Kia-ngau, *op. cit.*, p. 129.

Expenditures for administrative and general purposes were small before 1940, amounting to only 4 per cent of total expenditures in 1940. In 1941 when land tax was collected in kind, there was an increase in administrative expenses in collecting the new tax. The central government also had to compensate the local governments for their loss in the land tax which now became a tax of the central government.

External Financing

A war may be financed externally or internally. Externally foreign goods and services may be imported for war or civilian use by using existing foreign exchange reserve, overseas remittances, foreign investment or loans, or simply foreign aid. In the Chinese case, foreign exchange reserve was limited when the war broke out; overseas remittances were never large, amounting to, for example, U.S. $27.1 million in 1940 and $17 million in 1941.[24] Foreign direct investment virtually stopped during the war. The major external sources of financing were foreign loans and aid.

But foreign aid was far from adequate. Before Pearl Harbor, China had to fight the war alone, utilizing no more than U.S. $350 million of foreign credits and lend-lease. From 1941 to 1945 (August), the total was U.S. $1.2 billion.[25] Foreign assistance was mainly in the form of military supplies.

China's share in total American lend-lease aid was only about 1.5 per cent in 1941 and 1942; about half of one per cent in 1943 and 1944; and in 1945 about 4 per cent up to the end of the war.[26]

Internal Financing

Internally, a war may be financed by taxes or borrowing from the public without inflationary effects. But Shanghai, the principal financial market was lost after the early months of the war. There was no effective securities market in the interior. At any rate, the credit standing of the government was too poor to borrow substantially from the public. The proceeds from internal borrowing in 1937-1941 produced about 5 per cent of total government expenditure, and much of this was in the first year of the war (Table 13). The proceeds from internal bonds went up in 1942 and 1943, accounting for about 10 per cent of total expenditure in 1943. These bonds were backed by U.S. dollars.[27]

In the pre-war years, about 85 per cent of the revenue of the Chinese government (at the central level) was from the customs revenue, the salt tax, and the commodity tax. Though China was an agricultural economy, the central government received no revenue from the land tax—a tax based on obsolete assessments and belonging to local and provincial governments.

Table 13

SOURCES OF FINANCING THE EXPENDITURES
OF THE CENTRAL GOVERNMENT, 1937-45
(IN PERCENTAGES)

	1937-38[1]	1938[2]	1939	1940	1941	1942	1943	1944	1945
Revenues in Cash:									
Indirect taxes	20.6	17.5	5.1	3.7	4.8	8.1	8.3	10.1	5.5
Direct taxes	0.9	0.7	1.0	1.3	1.4	5.1	8.0	3.5	1.1
Other	5.2	7.3	8.3	19.8	2.3	1.4	0.6	0.5	3.1
Sales of foreign exchange & gold	23.8	2.2	5.4	2.5	4.9	—	0.1	8.3	3.9
Borrowing from the public	12.3	1.5	1.0	2.7	5.4	5.3	5.1	1.8	0.4
Revenues in kind	—	—	—	—	—	20.1	28.3	23.6	18.2
Deficit covered by bank credit	37.2	70.8	79.2	70.0	81.2	60.0	49.6	52.3	67.7
Total	100.0	100.0	100.0	100.0	100.0	100.0	100.0	100.0	100.0

Source: Arthur W. Young, *op. cit.*, p. 33.

[1]Year ending June 30, 1938.
[2]Second half.

When the war broke out, the customs revenue which in 1928-1935 contributed more than 50 per cent of total government revenue was reduced to a trickle as the coastal provinces were occupied by Japan. (During 1923-1936 about 60 per cent of the customs revenue was collected at Shanghai, Tientsin, and Tsingtao.)[28] The government had to rely more upon the salt tax and the commodity tax and to raise new taxes.

To raise revenue from indirect taxes, a number of measures were adopted: more commodities were included; specific levy was replaced by *ad valorem* taxes, and tax rates were raised (in 1941); government monopoly in the distribution of salt, tea, rolled tobacco, matches, and sugar was adopted (in 1941) in lieu of the commodity taxes.

A major reform of the tax system took place in 1941 when the land tax (on agricultural land) was transferred from the provincial governments to the central government, and a procedure of collection in kind was introduced. In addition to land tax, a system of compulsory loans and purchase in kind was also introduced in 1942. The land tax and compulsory loans and purchase in kind yielded the government substantial collections in rice and wheat. The rice collections (both tax and loans) constituted 3.4 per cent of total rice production in Free China in 1941-42; 4.6 per cent in 1942-43; 8.8 per cent in 1943-44; and 7.1 per cent in 1944-45. The proportions were smaller (from 2 to 6 per cent) for wheat collection.[29] The value of the collections in kind were about equal to the amount of total cash receipts of the government in 1942-1945.[30]

About two-thirds of the grain collected went to the army (1.9 million metric tons in 1941 and 2.2 million in 1942). The rest was about equally divided between civil officials and the public (through sale at official prices).[31]

Direct taxes were introduced in China as late as in 1936 when income tax was levied on business profits, salaries, and professional fees, and interest and dividends. In 1938 and 1943, the government adopted measures to increase the scope and the rates of direct taxes. Excess profits, house rents, and income from lease of property were included. Tax rates on profits of business enterprises (including excess profits) were progressive according to the rates of returns on equity capital.

For income tax on business profits there was no tax when the rate of return was less than 10 per cent. When it was over 70 per cent or above, the marginal tax rate was 20 per cent. The tax rates on excess profits were also progressive. No excess profit tax was levied when the rate of return on capital was 20 per cent or less. The highest marginal rate was 60 per cent when the rate of return on capital was 200 per cent or higher.[32]

These then were the major changes on government revenues. Evidently they were not enough to produce a revenue large enough to meet all government expenditures, but they were able to narrow the government deficit as Table 13 shows.

The Extent of Inflation

War expenditures went up and had to be met right away at the start of the war, and could not wait for any tax reform or any growth of the tax base. The Chinese government simply met such expenditures by increasing note issue. And the inflationary spiral began.

The retail market prices in the cities in Free China rose by 14 per cent from August to December 1937. The rate of increase accelerated after the loss of Canton and Hankow in October 1938, and after the fall of Ichang in 1940. By 1943, it reached 245 per cent a year. After a slowdown in 1944, it went up to 250 per cent for the first eight months. (See Table 14.) For the period 1938 to 1944, the average annual rate of increase was 163 per cent.

Such an increase in prices could not be accounted for entirely by the increase in the volume of money. The average rate of increase of currency and bank deposits rose at only 82 per cent per year from 1938 to 1944. The rate of increase of currency or note issue was 94 per cent a year and that of bank deposits 72 per cent a year for the same period.

In terms of the familiar equation of exchange, $MV = PQ$, we have no data on Q, but in view of our discussion on crop production and industrial production, perhaps it may be assumed that Q did not change much at all. Thus, part of the forces pushing up prices was an increase in the velocity of circulation of money.

This is, of course, what should be expected in a period of rapid inflation. People would simply lose confidence in the currency as a store of value and would try to exchange money for goods as fast as possible, thus further driving up prices.

VI

Combating Inflation

The Chinese government employed a variety of weapons to fight against inflation, especially after 1939 when the latter began to accelerate. The anti-inflation policies included fiscal policy, monetary policy, incomes policy, and trade and exchange controls. Some aspects of the fiscal policy (increasing government revenues) have been noted above.

Monetary Policy

The monetary policy followed by the government aimed to achieve two objectives which were not entirely consistent. On the one hand, the monetary authority wanted to promote production by adopting a low rate of interest policy, on the ground that interest expense is a cost to business firms. Interest rates charged by all groups of banks (the Central Bank, the government banks, the modern commercial banks, the native banks, and the pawnshops) were all subject to control after 1943. At least partly because of such control, interest rates did not rise as fast as prices. In fact in Chungking, in the eight years from 1937 to 1944, there were only two years, namely 1937 and 1938, when the real interest rates were positive.[33]

Table 14
PRICE LEVEL, NOTE ISSUE AND BANK DEPOSITS
1937-1945

	Retail Market Prices[1] (Jan.-June, 1937=1)		Note Issue Outstanding		Bank Deposits[3]		Note Issue & Bank Deposits:
	Index (Dec.)	Annual Rate of Increase (%)	Year-end Ch$ billions	Annual Rate of Increase (%)	Year-end Ch$ billions	Annual Rate of Increase (%)	Annual Rate of Increase (%)
1937	1.18		2.1		3.3		
1938	1.76	49.2	2.7	32.7	4.2	25.6	28.3
1939	3.23	83.5	4.8	75.2	6.1	45.9	57.5
1940	7.24	124.1	8.4	75.8	7.8	29.3	49.9
1941	15.95	120.3	15.8	87.5	13.8	76.3	82.1
1942	66.20	315.0	35.3	123.4	23.0	66.2	96.7
1943	228.00	244.4	75.4	113.4	35.7	55.7	90.7
1944	755.00	231.1	189.5	151.3	105.4	194.8	165.3
1945[2]	2,167.00	187.0	556.9	193.9			
Average:							
1937-45		169.3		106.7			
1937-44		166.8		94.2		70.5	81.5

Sources: For retail market prices and note issue outstanding, Arthur N. Young, *op. cit.*, pp. 160 and 303.
For bank deposits, Chang Kia-ngau, *op. cit.*, p. 191.

[1]In fourteen to sixteen cities for years before May 1944; eight to nine cities thereafter.
[2]Index of June for retail market prices; note issue outstanding as of August 31.
[3]Largely demand deposits; some time deposits, and savings accounts.

Low interest rates, of course, would stimulate business borrowing, increase aggregate demand, and hence accelerate inflation. To mitigate this, a system of credit control was adopted: loans by both government and private commercial banks had to be screened and approved by the Joint Board of Administration of the Government Banks. Guidelines were issued regarding the type of loans which could be made. As a rule, priority was given to loans for national defense industries and for production and distribution of daily necessities. Such control was probably quite effective; for example, in the period 1942-1945 commercial bank loans increased only at half of the rate of increase in price levels.[34]

Other policies in counteracting the pressure of rising aggregate demand included attempts to increase bank savings and gold sales. Gold was nationalized in 1939 and private gold transactions were prohibited. This restriction was lifted in 1943; the Central Bank began to sell it for the purpose of reducing the volume of money in circulation. But it did not take long before the gold reserve was exhausted. Gold sales were discontinued near the end of 1944.

Table 15

INDEXES OF OFFICIAL AND MARKET EXCHANGE RATES,
MERCHANDISE IMPORTS AND EXPORTS

	Official Rate for US$[1]	*Official Rate with Supplements*[1]	*Average Market Exchange Rate for US$ (June 1937=1)*[1]	*Imports (US$ millions)*[2]	*Exports (US$ millions)*[2]
1937	1.00		1.01	279.9	245.8
1938	1.00		1.82	86.4	59.5
1939	1.00		3.98	39.1	21.3
1940	1.00		5.23	67.1	14.9
1941	5.60		8.65	136.0	20.0
1942	5.95		14.50	41.5	32.1
1943	5.95	8.93	25	48.9	25.9
1944	5.95	11.90	170	17.3	18.3
1945	5.95	11.90	870	7.0	8.8

Sources: For exchange rates, Arthur N. Young, *op. cit.*, p. 264. For imports and exports, Yu-Kwei Cheng, *op. cit.*, pp. 134 and 151.

---

[1]Rates are for averages in December except 1945 when the averages in July are used. Also the 1941 market exchange rate refers to the month of November.

[2]Amounts were yearly totals except 1945 when they were for January-August. Open market exchange rates were used in converting export values while import values were converted at rates set by Customs authorities.

Trade and Exchange Controls

Trade and exchange controls were adopted early in 1938 after a large trade deficit occurred (chiefly due to decline in exports). A series of complicated measures of trade restrictions and exchange controls were introduced, but the essence was rather simple. Essential goods such as iron, steel, and all metals, cotton and cotton goods, rice, wheat, and other food products were banned from exports. Proceeds from exports had to be surrendered to the government banks, and foreign exchange could be bought from them only for certain specified purposes, principally goods for national defense and daily necessities. Official exchange rates were set at a level which grossly overvalued the Chinese currency. To the extent that large sums of foreign exchange were provided for imports at such artificial rates, this foreign exchange policy performed a function in alleviating inflationary pressure. To the extent that such official exchange rates exerted pressure on market exchange rates, the latter also became overvalued. (See Table 15.) Exports in general would be adversely affected and receipts from overseas Chinese remittances would also be reduced. All this, too, would tend to have an anti-inflationary effect. But such a policy could not be maintained for long or at any large scale if foreign exchange reserve is limited as indeed it was in the case for China's international reserve. The net result was a lower level of both exports and imports. (See Table 16.)

Incomes Policy

The first set of regulations of price and commodity controls were promulgated in December 1937 and were revised and augmented in later years. Briefly, the government tried to control prices through the following measures.

(1) Price Ceilings. The Ministry of Economic Affairs was empowered in December 1937 to fix "equitable prices" for all commodities, but this power was not exercised until the end of 1938 when a price regulating committee was set up in Chungking comprising representatives from the government, the Chamber of Commerce, and the guilds of various trades.[35] Other cities were urged to follow suit and local governments were required to set up commissions to supervise price fixing. But this was carried out only in Chengtu, aside from Chungking. In Chungking effective rent control was also introduced in 1940.

The National General Mobilization Act was enforced in May 1942, and the Program for Strengthening Price Control was adopted in October 1942. Price ceilings based on the prices prevailing on November 30, 1942, were imposed, starting from January 15, 1943. After adoption of this Program, price ceilings were fixed for important necessities and transpor-

Table 16

INDEXES OF REAL INCOME OF THE GOVERNMENT

AND OTHER GROUPS, 1937-1944

(1937=100)

	Central Government[1]				Teachers and Government Officials[2]	Laborers[3]	Industrial Workers (Chungking)[3]	Rural Workers (Szechwan)[3]	Farmers (Szechwan)[4]
	Revenue		Expenditures						
	Cash	Cash & in kind	Cash	Cash & in kind					
Fiscal Year ending June 30									
1937	100		100						
1938	124		147						
1938 (2nd half)	50		127						
Calendar Year									
1937					100	100	100	100	100
1938					85	143	124	111	82
1939	27		99		53	181	95	122	67
1940	35		85		23	147	76	63	88
1941	19		76		23	91	78	82	108
1942	17	36	52	65	19	83	75	75	119
1943	17	38	40	56	21	74	69	58	86
1944	15	29	35	45					
1945	13	30	56	69					

[1]Fiscal 1937=100. Figures for 1938 (2nd half) are at annual rate by doubling original half year figures. See Arthur N. Young, op. cit., p. 30.

[2]Indexes are for December of each year. Four groups are included: college teachers, middle school teachers, primary school teachers, and government officials. The index is computed from data given in Ibid., p. 321.

[3]Chang Kia-ngau, op. cit., p. 63.

[4]Based on prices received and paid by farmers. China Handbook 1937-1945, p. 470.

tation charges and were enforced in most parts of Free China. Commodities placed under control varied from locality to locality; eight commodities were considered essential (food, salt, cooking oil, cotton, cotton yarn, cotton piecegoods, fuel, and paper).

In connection with price ceilings, hoarding of, and profiteering from, important daily necessities were strictly prohibited. Black markets were forbidden.

(2) Wage Ceilings. The Program for Strengthening Price Control also imposed wage ceilings fixed at levels prevailing in November 30, 1942. These ceilings applied to workers in the production of daily necessities, machinery, building materials, and in transportation.

(3) Government Purchases and Sales. At the end of 1938, the Ministry of Economic Affairs was empowered to create a bureau to purchase and sell daily necessities at equitable levels for the purpose of stabilizing commodity prices. This program became quite extensive as inflation worsened. In addition to the eight essential commodities as noted above, the government also acquired control of sugar, matches and tobacco, and coal and charcoal.

(4) Consumer Rationing. The Program for Strengthening Price Control began in October 1942 also provided that large cities should gradually adopt rationing for foodstuffs and other commodities so that a balance between production and consumption could be achieved and wasteful consumption be avoided. Production, transportation, and sale of luxuries and "unnecessary goods" should be suppressed.

But this was not generally carried out. When government began to collect land tax in kind and acquired large stocks of rice and wheat in 1941, the army was allocated food instead of procuring it on the market. Employees of the central government were given a fixed quota of rice or flour beginning in July 1941 and so were the employees of provincial and county governments in 1943. (The quota was 120 pounds of rice or wheat per annum for people over thirty-one; ninety-five pounds for the age group 26-30; and seventy pounds for those below twenty-five.)[36]

But there was no general rationing program for the civilian population except schoolteachers, students, and war orphans. Workers in essential industries were also supplied with government rice.

VII

Effects of the Inflation

Eight years of accelerated inflation had profound effects upon income distribution, efficiency of the government, social morale, and eventually the political support of the government both during the war and for the future.

Distribution of Income

Any inflation tends to redistribute income in favor of the industrial entrepreneurs, businessmen, and speculators whose income consists largely of profits. In the case of China, prices of manufactured and semi-manufactured goods rose at a much faster rate than that of raw materials and wages, thus leaving a wider margin for profits. Low interest rates (relative to rate of inflation) also helped the businessmen since they were the principal debtors.

The farmers' position, as reflected in the prices received and paid by them, dropped below the 1937 level in 1938-1940 and in 1944 and 1945. It rose beyond the 1937 level only in 1941 and 1942. (See Table 16.) Since crop production showed no appreciable increase during the war period and since the land tax was probably higher than in 1937 because of the collections in kind and the compulsory purchase, farmers' real income after tax declined, though moderately, for most of the war years.

The workers suffered. Money wages rose at a slower rate than prices. The real wage of workers in Chungking, for example, was higher than the 1937 (January-June) level only in 1938, during the entire war period. The index of real wage of industrial workers in Chungking declined from 100 in 1937 (January-June) to forty-one in 1944 (April).

The position of the college teachers, middle school teachers, primary school teachers, and government officials was even worse. The Nankai University indexes indicate that the index of the average real income of the above four groups declined from 100 in 1936-37 to eighteen by the end of 1943. Their lot was alleviated to some extent by rice allowances in kind, but there is little doubt that they were among the hardest hit by the inflation, especially the college teachers whose real income declined the most among the four groups (Table 16).

Government Revenue and Expenditure

The Chinese government took the easiest road to finance the war; that is, by inflation (via printing money). It worked for a brief period in 1938 when both its revenue and expenditure rose above the 1937 levels in real terms (Table 16). But starting from 1939, its expenditure in real terms began to decline, suggesting that even the money printing machine no longer could be relied upon as an effective means of transferring the nation's resources from private uses to the government. This downward trend of decline of expenditure in real terms continued even after land tax was collected in kind. By 1944 real expenditures were no more than 45 per cent of that in 1937. Real revenue (both cash and in kind) in 1944 was only 29 per cent of that in 1937.

The continuous decline of real revenue is difficult to explain in view of the fact that there was no corresponding decline in the tax base (as reflected in crop production and industrial production). It is not entirely impossible that the inflationary process played a part. Between assessment and collection of a tax there was a time lag which would reduce the real value of the tax. Although direct taxes were introduced and broadened in scope, their share in total government was no more than 20 per cent between 1942-1945 despite the apparently enormous increase in business profits.[37] There was widespread evasion of these taxes. Inflation redistributed income in favor of those classes who found it easy to avoid and evade taxes.

VIII

Concluding Remarks

The Sino-Japanese war in 1937 required a level of expenditure by the Chinese government higher than the pre-war levels. But the tax base after the war was reduced sharply. Given the lack of substantial economic assistance from abroad, the central question was how to finance the war internally, or more precisely, who should assume the burden of the war.

The burden of a war may be alleviated by an increase of gross national product. But in the absence of mass unemployment or idle resources, an increase in agricultural and industrial production usually takes time. In an underdeveloped economy such as the one in Free China, economic development is a long and painful process and cannot be expected to take place overnight even under the most favorable circumstances. Surely it would be an extremely difficult task to develop during a war when the industrial establishments and the transportation network are constantly under the pressure of enemy attack and when the government is totally absorbed in fighting the enemy.

Under the government leadership and the interplay of market forces, there was a rather rapid industrial development in Free China. But it started from a very low base, and industrial production was still very small in absolute terms. It is estimated that in 1943, a peak year of industrial production, the aggregate value of the principal industrial products in Free China was only 12 per cent of the total value of the same products produced in China before 1937.[38] As for agricultural production, the average level of production in 1938-1945 was only 2.6 per cent higher than its pre-war level in Free China.

Thus, in the absence of any significant increase in industrial and agricultural production the burden of the war would have to be assumed by sacrifices in living standards. As it turned out, it was the burden of the war, and more precisely, its inequitable distribution that proved to be fatal to the National Government.

It is not difficult to understand why the government had to resort to the printing machine as a means of financing the war. The urgency of the war expenditures and the nature of the tax system left the government very little choice especially during the initial years of the war. But inflation, when started, has its own way of getting out of control. China was certainly no exception.

The redistributive effects of the inflation were, of course, disastrous. The workers, the government employees, and the intelligentsia suffered the most. The farmers probably also suffered though to a much lesser extent. The only group who benefited, and enormously, were the industrialists, the merchants, and the "profiteers" (or speculators). To the extent that the anti-inflation policies and controls adopted by the government created opportunities for corruption, some government officials became beneficiaries of the inflation.

The government itself also suffered from the inflation. Both its revenue and expenditures declined substantially in real terms. Before the war government expenditures were supported by an economic base comprising all China. The war reduced the economic base by more than half; the provinces later known as Free China contributed no more than 46 per cent of national income of all China in the 1930's. It is of interest to note that by 1944 real expenditures of the government were reduced to no more than 45 per cent of those in 1937.

With hindsight the Chinese government should have drastically reduced its expenditures from the very beginning in 1938 or 1939 when it was forced to retreat to the hinterland. It would have avoided all the undesirable consequences of inflation without cutting down expenditures more than inflation did.

Or, the government should have entirely avoided deficit-financing, and introduced drastic reforms so that the war burdens could have been distributed among the people on an equitable basis. Such reforms might have proven to be unpopular, or offending to vested interest groups, but they could hardly have produced more disastrous effects than what inflation did.

The real damage of inflation did not manifest itself until after the Resistance War against Japan. The inflationary spiral, begun during the war, intensified after 1945. The sense of disaffection and discontent which was already intense during the war on the part of the intellectuals, government employees, workers and others whom every government has to count as basic supporters, was once again stirred up and deepened as the post-war inflation accelerated. The practice of corruption induced and developed during the war became more widespread and further demoralized the supporters of the government. Thus, all the destructive forces which owed much of their origin to financing the Sino-Japanese war exploded and eventually led to the collapse of the Nationalist Government. Inflation or hyper-inflation, though an economic phenomenon, is always political in consequences!

NOTES

1. For an analysis of this development, see Chi-ming Hou, *Foreign Investment and Economic Development in China 1840-1937* (Cambridge: Harvard University Press, 1965).
2. John K. Chang, *Industrial Development in Pre-Communist China: A Quantitative Analysis* (Chicago: Aldine Publishing Company, 1969), p. 71.
3. Ta-chung Liu and Kung-chia Yeh, *The Economy of the Chinese Mainland: National Income and Economic Development, 1933-1959* (Princeton: Princeton University Press, 1965), p. 89.
4. They were: Ninghsia, Kansu, Shensi, Honan, Hupeh, Hunan, Kiangsi, Kwangsi, Kweichow, Yunnan, Szechwan, Sikang, Tsinghai, and Sinkiang.
5. *The Chinese Year Book 1944-1945*, p. 669.
6. Foreign enterprises not included in the total; nor is Manchuria, see Chen Chen, Ed., *Chung-kuo Chin-tai kung-yeh-shih tzu-liao (Source Material for History of Modern Industry of China)* (Peking: 1961), Vol. IV, Section 1, p. 95.
7. *The Chinese Year Book 1944-1945*, p. 670.
8. *China Handbook 1937-1945*, p. 364.
9. Chen Chen, Vol. III, Section 2, p. 892.
10. Computed from *Ibid.*, pp. 1392-1396.
11. *Ibid.*, p. 1421. It is not stated what is included in capital; most probably it refers to paid-up capital.
12. *Ibid.*, p. 1420.
13. *The Chinese Year Book 1944-1945*, p. 703.
14. Chen Chen, Vol. III, Section 2, p. 1421.
15. *China Handbook 1937-1945*, p. 377.
16. *Ibid.*, p. 366.
17. *The Chinese Year Book 1944-1945*, p. 682.
18. Yu-kwei Cheng, *Foreign Trade and Industrial Development of China* (Washington, D.C.: The University Press of Washington, D.C., 1956), p. 134.
19. *Ibid.*, p. 105.
20. *China Handbook 1937-1945*, p. 435.
21. Chen Chen, Vol. I, p. 157.

22. On the average, crop production in 1938-1944 was 2.57 percent higher in 1931-1937. For a detailed discussion on agricultural development during the war, see Dr. T. H. Shen's paper for the Conference.

23. Chang Kia-ngau, *The Inflationary Spiral: The Experience in China, 1939-1950* (Cambridge: The Technology Press of Massachusetts Institute of Technology and John Wiley and Sons, Inc., New York, 1958), p. 127.

24. Shun-hsin Chou, *The Chinese Inflation 1937-1949* (New York: Columbia University Press, 1963), p. 164.

25. Arthur N. Young, *China's Wartime Finance and Inflation, 1937-1945* (Cambridge: Harvard University Press, 1965), p. 121.

26. *Ibid.,* p. 121.

27. *Ibid.,* p. 87.

28. Shun-hsin Chou, p. 43.

29. *Ibid.,* p. 58.

30. Arthur N. Young, p. 29.

31. *Ibid.,* p. 27.

32. *China Handbook 1937-1945*, pp. 189-190.

33. Shun-hsin Chou, p. 251.

34. Chang Kia-ngau, p. 251.

35. *Ibid.,* p. 345.

36. *Ibid.,* p. 347.

37. *Ibid.,* p. 139.

38. Yu-kwei Cheng, p. 265.

Comments:

BY PETER SCHRAN

There are basically two ways in which a critic can comment on an author's paper: on the one hand, he can ask whether the author answers the questions which he raises to the critic's satisfaction; on the other hand, he can wonder whether the author poses the questions which the critic would like to see discussed. In my comments on Chi-ming Hou's paper on "Economic Development and Public Finance in China, 1937-1945," I shall emphasize the second approach, since I find little fault with what Professor Hou has written, as well as because I read his paper with a study of comparable experiences in the Chinese Communist base areas fresh on my mind. Needless to say, the author may not share the critic's perspective and therefore may encourage him to answer such questions himself.

In his introduction, Professor Hou outlines the overall situation and problem. He describes China on the eve of the war as an underdeveloped and dualistic economy, whose modern sector—small as it was—was concentrated in the coastal regions, thus making it vulnerable in the event of war. I find no fault with this description and would only add that John Chang's index as quoted refers to China inclusive of Manchuria (the growth rates for the twenty-two provinces being substantially lower). I also agree that the principal problem of the national government was its dependence on this modern sector which was lost almost entirely during the initial phase of the war. However, I wonder whether ". . . China *had to* fight a large-scale modern war on the basis of a vast traditional economy . . ." (italics added), given the fact that part of China fought in very different ways. In other words, I believe that the national government had some choice with respect to the methods of warfare, public finance, and government generally. On such a premise, the principal economic problem was that of adapting effectively in terms of methods and organizations to the resource constraints of the backward interior.

Professor Hou takes the actual choice of the national government, i.e., "large-scale modern war," as given and proceeds to describe the initial state in the interior as improved by the crash program to relocate industry from the coastal areas. I was struck by the omission of references to cotton growing and to handicraft production. I was also surprised by the apparent confidence with which national government statistics are used, when there is little doubt that most resources are more or less severely understated. (I can demonstrate as much for one of the most backward parts of the interior, the Shensi-Kansu-Ninghsia Border Region).

Professor Hou next describes the rapid development of a state-operated industrial sector under the direction of the National Resources Commission. I would find it useful to hear more about the relations with the rest of the world than the statement that ". . . very little foreign exchange was used to purchase materials from abroad" (p. 209). I don't see much point in discussing the sector's profitability in the absence of meaningful opportunity costs (p. 209), and I miss a reference to the fact that private industry stagnated most of the time. For the same reasons, I am also not convinced that the explanation of industrialization on pp. 213-14 ff. is fully relevant.

Professor Hou summarizes very briefly the official reports on the development of agricultural production, which is really the topic of Dr. Shen, and then turns his attention to problems of wartime finance and inflation. Again, I have no basic disagreement with the description of the situation. In the section on "external financing" (p. 223), I would find it helpful to see a reference to the fact that because of the isolation, foreign exchange could not be used to add significantly to the real resources in the interior. In the section on "internal financing" (p. 224), I would note that the shares of rice and wheat collections—small as they were—probably overstate the actual percentages because of the likely under-reporting of both crops. The same may be suspected generally of the national government's share in Free China's income and expenditure.

As a last topic, Professor Hou reviews the extent of inflation due to note issue and the government's efforts to combat it. It might be useful to point out in the section on "trade and exchange controls" (p. 229) that the principal cause of the decline of foreign trade was the isolation due to enemy action, not the manipulation of exchange rates. Similarly, it might be helpful to indicate that the rationing system was so limited in scope because the vast majority of the people resided in self-supplying farm households, and that the actual rations were so inadequate because the government collected so little in kind.

In his concluding remarks, Professor Hou finally poses two of "my" questions—without answering them. He says:

> With hindsight the Chinese government should have drastically reduced its expenditures from the very beginning in 1938 or 1939 when it was forced to retreat to the hinterland. It would have avoided all the undesirable consequences of inflation without cutting down expenditures more than inflation did.
>
> Or, the government should have entirely avoided deficit-financing, and introduced drastic reforms so that the war burdens could have been dis-

tributed among the people on an equitable basis. Such reforms might have proven to be unpopular, or offending to vested interest groups, but they could hardly have produced more disastrous effects than what inflation did.

I agree. And I would add that in one respect at least the problems of public finance appear to have been not so extreme. By retreating into the interior, the government added at most 5 per cent to the indigenous population of that region. It therefore had to acquire a similar or somewhat larger share of the region's output in order to feed, clothe, and house its employees (soldiers, administrators, teachers, workers in state enterprises, etc.). In order to reduce this burden, the government could cut the size of its staff as much as possible and divert those who were not needed to productive activities which would add to the output of the region. In the extreme, it could even involve the remaining members of its staff in part-time production in order to achieve some degree of self-sufficiency within the public sector—apart from the involvement in armaments production, that is.

To meet the demand of both public and private sectors in real terms, of course, it was also necessary to replace and supplement imports from the coastal regions and from abroad. The region's technical backwardness imposed limits on the methods by which this could be accomplished. If it was impossible to relocate and develop enough industrial capacity on short notice, import substitution could be promoted in technically retrogressive forms, by the reactivation of various handicrafts. Similarly, some increases and improvements in agricultural production could be achieved by comparably old-fashioned methods in the absence of adequate modern inputs.

I further would note that such responses to the problems of isolation in the interior not only appear reasonable with hindsight but were actually proposed and dismissed at the time. The Chinese government was advised to reduce the size and reform the organization and operations of its military and civilian personnel. It was encouraged to sponsor the Chinese Industrial Cooperatives among others and could have activated the farmers' associations to do similar things. Moreover, it could convince itself of the effectiveness of such approaches easily by studying the development policies of the Chinese Communist movement and their effects on the Chinese Communist base areas in substantially more trying circumstances.

The latter contrast was certainly apparent to Claire and William Band, who had spent two years in Chinese Communist territory after their escape from Peiping on their way to Chungking. After lauding the work of the National Resources Commission, they observed:

The pity of it was that this industrial reconstruction was not all being used. There was little if any demand for the results of their industry, their products remained chiefly museum pieces, in ones and twos instead of being produced in thousands. Undoubtedly the country needed the goods, but there was no money to buy them; economically the public were not in a position to afford the kind of luxuries which the industry offered.

There was a marked contrast here with the reconstructive work going on in the Communist areas. There every improvement, although simple and elementary, was directly related to the needs and demands of the population, and was at once turned into wide-scale operation. Here in Chungking, which the Communists thought of as a reactionary centre, the industrial revolution was so revolutionary that it was above the heads of the common people. The material upheaval in their way of life that was being promised by industry in Free China was so great that in fact the country was not quite prepared to accept it. Their industrial exhibits were fantastically remote from anything that the average Szechwan resident had ever dreamed of seeing, let alone of using in his everyday life. In a sense the scientists of Chungking were far more revolutionary than the Communists, their promise for the future more vast and visionary; but their actual influence upon the real progress of the country as a whole was disappointingly small.

To turn all this industrial skill and promise into positive use for the war effort was the problem of the moment, a problem which seemed to have baffled the national leaders. . . . (Band, pp. 309-310)

Similarly, in their comments on the work of the farmers' associations, which they applauded as an idea, the Bands felt moved to conclude:

What should theoretically become an excellent medium through which peasant life and culture might energetically be stimulated for the benefit of the nation, has been almost completely frustrated by the Kuomintang clique's insistent demand to keep all possible checks and controls in operation to prevent the movement from getting out of hand. Only in this way could the party gain approval from its reactionary supporters for such a revolutionary scheme. In practice the officers of the farmers' associations have to spend their time in dealing with busybodies and jealous petty officials from this or that party or government organization, including others not listed above. Intelligent patriotic leadership such as has achieved such remarkable results in the "mass associations" in the guerrilla areas, has here been squandered in futile dealings with bureaucracy. (Band, pp. 312-313)

The same contrast appears with respect to the Chinese Industrial Cooperatives, and not only in the view of protagonists such as Nym Wales. The CIC was evidently accommodated much more readily by the Chinese Communists, and it became relatively more effective in the Shensi-Kansu-Ninghsia Border Region.

All such observations, just like Professor Hou's questions, point to a mistaken strategic orientation on the part of the Chinese government which by all indications resulted in a substantially inferior mobilization and utilization of the available resources. Because this orientation was seemingly well considered, since it was upheld so ardently against well-meant advice, I would ask next for the reasons which caused such a determination: The bias of the progressive scientists in favor of technically modern solutions? The fear of the conservative politicians that any change in social organization would benefit the Communists? Bureaucratic inertia on the grounds that the approach had been workable before in the coastal areas? Or the leadership's confidence that it did not really matter because in the end the Pacific War would be won by the Americans in island Asia?

Let me stop at this point with the invitation to answer these and other conceivable explanations for the failure of the national government to adapt to the interior conditions, which Professor Hou has demonstrated convincingly.

CHAPTER VII

China's Epic Struggle in Developing Its Overland Transportation System During the Sino-Japanese War

BY HUNG-HSUN LING

I

Introduction

ONSTRUCTION OF AN overland transportation network is vital to a developing country when it is being attacked by a militarily superior neighbor. The network will facilitate the movement of troops and war material and sustain the country's wartime economy. Additionally, adequate transportation facilities will enable the removal of industrial equipment from areas threatened by the enemy as well as the evacuation of tens of thousands of refugees from the war zones. This is especially true when the enemy approaches from the direction of the sea. In the absence of adequate coastal defense, the country must develop a transportation network in the hinterland to receive aid supplies from friendly neighbors.

It is equally important for the aggressor that in addition to sealing off the victim's coast, he should seek to destroy the existing network of land communication as well as road projects under construction so as to paralyze the victim's economy, weaken his power of resistance, and cut off the flow of aid supplies from his friendly neighbors.

The validity of this strategy was demonstrated again and again throughout the Sino-Japanese War from 1937 to 1945.

China and Japan, being neighbors, have had a long history of ethnic and cultural ties. With the advent of the Meiji era, however, Japan made territorial expansion a part of its national policy. The declaration of war with China by Japan in 1894 over the Korean Incident marked the beginning of a long period of hostility between the two nations. In 1931, the Japanese captured Mukden and occupied the vitally strategic and potentially the most industrial Northeastern Provinces. Although sorely provoked, China was not yet in a position to wage a major war against Japan. It was not until the Lukouchiao Incident near Peiping in 1937, when Japan intensified its aggression, that China began its all-out war of resistance.

China in 1912 was well aware of Japan's intentions and had in fact wasted no time in getting ready to meet the situation. The preparation work was not easy because of China's vastness and its geographical characteristics. Peiping, then the capital and the cultural and political center of the country, is some 1,200 miles north of Canton, the center of commerce and import-export activities. In addition to the distance, differences in the environment and the mode of living created political barriers between the two population centers. These barriers became even more apparent following the founding of the Republic of China in 1912.

The vast area of China's coastal region is traversed by several rivers flowing from west to east, including the Yellow River in the northern and the Yangtze River in the central regions. These two river basins had been linked by two north-south railways, namely, the Peiping-Hankow Railway and the Tientsin-Pukow Railway, even before 1912. But the central region is separated by an east-west mountain chain from the metropolis of Canton at the mouth of the West River in the south. Through north-south communication, therefore, depended on the completion of the 660-mile Canton-Hankow Railway.

This trunk line of vital political, economic and strategic importance had been planned by the Ching Dynasty to link up with the Peiping-Hankow Railway and the rail system in the Northeast, but its construction was interrupted as a result of the suspension of loan negotiations following the outbreak of World War I. Only 230 miles at the northern end and 140 miles at the southern end had been completed by 1915. Work on the most difficult 280-mile section across the mountain range in the center was suspended for fifteen years. Transportation links between north and south depended solely on the shipping lines between Hong Kong and Shanghai, and the political differences between the two population centers in the north and the south became more intensified with the evolution of time. Japan, waiting on the sidelines, had taken the lack of political unity and the incomplete vital communication system as a golden opportunity to launch its war of aggression against China.

Although the government and people of the Republic of China were well aware of the ambitions of Japan, the sprawling country must first be united before it could effectively face an aggressor. Political unity remained elusive due to the wide geographical differences described earlier. Even after the founding of the Republic of China and the removal of the national capital to Nanking, Kwangtung Province remained largely a semi-autonomous state. A Ministry of Railways was therefore established in 1928 to supervise the construction of trunk lines and to plan a basic network of railroads. An east-west trunk line and a north-south trunk line were then under active consideration. The east-west trunk line was to extend the existing Lunghai Railway which was already running between Haikow (Haichow) in the east and Tungkwan in the west, a distance of about 570 miles. The projected construction would extend it further westward to Sian, the capital of Shensi Province, and on to Lanchow in the heart of the Northwest. This extension is about 500 miles. The north-south trunk line was the completion of the 280-mile middle section of the Canton-Hankow Railway.

The writer was in charge of extending the Lunghai Railway further westward when he was transferred in 1932 by the Ministry of Railways to head up the project of completing the Canton-Hankow Railway. The rationale behind this transfer was that the extension of the Lunghai Railway would take considerable time, while the completion of the Canton-Hankow Railway would give the country a badly needed north-south artery, and therefore should merit a higher priority. Thus work on the middle section of the Canton-Hankow Railway was resumed in 1933, to be completed in four years.

II

Completion of the Canton-Hankow Railway 粵漢鐵路

The resumption of work on this railway did not go unnoticed by the Japanese. Shortly afterwards, they were actively spying all along the route. An engineer who had studied in Japan was repeatedly queried by the Japanese Consul in Canton as to the progress of work and the expected completion date.

In addition to having already occupied the Northeast Provinces, Japan continued to exert pressure in northern China for special political favors, creating various "incidents" to justify its demands. China was then ill-prepared to challenge the might of Japan, and had no choice but to concede to a number of unequal treaties with Japan, and to bide its time.

A few months after the resumption of work in the middle section of the Canton-Hankow Railway, Dr. Koo Meng-yu 顧孟餘 , then Minister of Railways, confided in the writer the view that the pressure exerted by the Japanese in northern China presaged some large-scale aggression. The Canton-Hankow Railway would be essential in meeting this aggression. Could it be rushed into completion ahead of the scheduled four years? The writer, while promising to shorten the construction time by at least six months, planned to complete the project one full year ahead of schedule. The line was actually completed in April 1936. It was open to military traffic in August and to passenger and freight traffic in September.

Thus, the age-old suspicions between the north and the south were gradually eliminated and the political and military unity between the two regions was greatly strengthened. Less than ten months after the Canton-Hankow Railway was opened to traffic, the Japanese created the so-called Lukouchiao Incident. China finally decided to make a determined stand against its aggressor. The Canton-Hankow Railway not only served to promote political unity; it also proved its crucial military importance by serving as a vital means of transportation in that part of China.

III

Linking Up the Canton-Hankow
& Canton-Kowloon Railways 廣九鐵路

The completion of the Canton-Hankow Railway left one more major problem to be solved before this north-south trunk line could reach directly an international port, that of linking up with the Canton-Kowloon Railway. When construction was initiated many years ago, these two railways had their separate terminals in Canton. The terminal of the Canton-Hankow Railway was in the western part of the city while the terminal of the Canton-Kowloon Railway was in the eastern part. Although Canton was the commercial center of South China, the business community there feared that a direct link between the two railways would make the city a mere passing station instead of an entreport and that Canton would therefore lose its importance. This provincial view persisted even after the completion of the Canton-Hankow Railway.

When Japan stepped up its aggression in July of 1937, the Chinese Government concluded that protracted hostilities would be unavoidable and the international port of Kowloon must be fully utilized. It was decided that a connecting line was to be built outside the city to link up the two railways. This link was completed in two weeks, and on August 20, 1937, the first train travelled directly from Wuchang to Kowloon by way of Canton. In the same month, Japan launched its offensive against Shanghai and shipping on the Yangtze River was brought to an abrupt halt. Thus the newly completed Canton-Hankow Railway was called on to bear a major share of the difficult task of transporting troops and materiel in support of the war. In the sixteen months between the Lukouchiao Incident and the fall of Wuchang and Canton to Japan, this railway was responsible for the movement of over 2,100,000 troops in 2,341 trips and transported over 539,000 tons of war materiel and over 700,000 tons of construction supplies into the interior. This not only enabled the Chinese to make a year-long stand in the Wuchang-Hankow area, but also to strengthen its position in the Southwest. If Japan had initiated its all-out attack one year earlier, the course of the Sino-Japanese War would have taken a much worse turn.

IV

Completion of
the Chekiang-Kiangsi Railway 浙贛鐵路

The completion of the Chekiang-Kiangsi Railway was of equal importance. It was a major link south of the Yangtze River between Shanghai and the Canton-Hankow Railway by way of Hangchow. The Chekiang-Kiangsi Railway was started by the local authorities to develop Chekiang Province. A 205-mile section from Hangchow to the western part of Chekiang bordering on Kiangsi Province had been completed by 1934, the Shanghai-Hangchow section having been completed earlier. The railroad planners realized then that if this railway was extended further westward through the central part of Kiangsi Province, it would not only be a vital east-west artery south of the Yangtze River, but be able to link up Canton with Nanking and Shanghai, since the Canton-Hankow Railway was near completion, and a branch line had already been built into the western part of Kiangsi Province.

While the early railways were mostly financed by the National Government or by foreign loans, the Chekiang-Kiangsi Railway was largely financed by Chinese banks and the Chekiang and Kiangsi Provincial Governments, setting a new example in railway financing. The entire route of 550 miles was standardized and in operable condition by the time of the Japanese invasion in 1937. The eastern terminal of this railway, however, was separated by the 4,000-foot-wide Chientang River from the terminal in the city of Hangchow and the railway running to Shanghai and Nanking. Construction was therefore started in 1934 for a bridge across the river to carry both highway and rail traffic and to link up the Chekiang-Kiangsi Railway with the terminal in the City of Hangchow. The bridge was completed in October 1937, three months after the Lukouchiao Incident and two months after Shanghai had been occupied. The Japanese invaders were then already on their way towards Hangchow. The Chinese had no choice but to dynamite the bridge that had cost so much money and labor to build. The one consolation was that before its destruction, hundreds of locomotives and rolling stock as well as large quantities of equipment were able to be evacuated from Peiping, Tientsin and Shanghai to the southwestern part of China.

Although the Chekiang-Kiangsi Railway had been disrupted time after time in the course of the war, connections were made with certain highways along the railroad, and troop reinforcements from Kwangtung and Kwangsi were speeded to the beleaguered provinces. While most of the southeastern part of China had fallen into Japanese hands during the eight-year Sino-Japanese War, the Chinese Government was able to hold on to the border region between Chekiang and Kiangsi provinces largely on account of this railway.

V

Construction of
the Soochow-Kiahsing Railway 蘇嘉鐵路

Since the Japanese had invaded Shanghai in August 1937, how did the Chinese Government manage to remove the railway cars and other equipment from North China and the Nanking-Shanghai area to the south via the Chientang Bridge? It is necessary to recapitulate and to relate how the direct line between Soochow and Kiahsing was rushed to completion. In their long term policy of aggression in China, the Japanese had instigated hostilities in Shanghai as early as January 1932. China had to try to localize the hostile incidents and make concessions to the Japanese in order to buy time, as it was not yet in a position to put up all-out resistance. China was not allowed to station troops in Shanghai, nor transport troops by way of Shanghai.

To meet communication needs in time of war, the Chinese Government decided to build a direct line from Soochow on the Nanking-Shanghai Railway to Kiahsing on the Shanghai-Hangchow Railway so as to by-pass Shanghai. This 46-mile railway was completed in July 1936, one year before the outbreak of the Lukouchiao Incident. This short cut permitted trains to proceed from Nanking to Hangchow without going through Shanghai. Thus it was possible to evacuate a large number of railway cars and quantities of equipment from North China to the rear by way of the Chientang Bridge. The construction of this railway was another example of how the Chinese Government, while being forced to accede to one Japanese demand after another, was at the same time directing its every effort to prepare itself for the war of resistance.

VI

The Yangtze River Train Ferry 揚子江輪渡

Nanking became a transhipment center after the Tientsin-Pukow Railway and the Nanking-Shanghai Railway were opened to traffic. But Nanking and Pukow were separated by the Yangtze River, 670 feet wide at its narrowest point, and it was difficult to move freight across and inconvenient for passengers.

A bridge across the Yangtze River had been contemplated back in 1927 when Nanking was chosen as the national capital. The construction cost would be very high because the Yangtze River must be open to ocean-going vessels and warships at this point, and the river was 172-feet deep at low tide, with a tidal variation of twenty-four feet.

So it was decided in 1930 that a ferry should be built first. Wharfs which may be raised and lowered along steel towers were built on both banks. The ferry was 360 feet long, with three lines of rails on deck, each accommodating seven railway cars. It was custom built in England at a cost of £256,000 plus over one million Chinese dollars. The boat was delivered in the autumn of 1933 and the first ferry run was made on December 22 of the same year, ending the need of freight and passenger transfer.

When the Sino-Japanese War broke out in 1937, a vast quantity of locomotives and rolling stock was moved from North China to the south by this ferry which made as many as twenty-seven runs each day. The role played by this ferry at that time may be compared to that played by the Chientang River Bridge.

VII

Construction of the Hunan-Kwangsi Railway 湘桂鐵路

The Japanese moved large numbers of troops from the Northeast to the South and blockaded all the major Chinese ports following the Lukouchiao Incident in July 1937. With the fall of Kowloon and Hong Kong shortly after the Pearl Harbor attack, China was deprived of the last communication link with the outside world. It then became imperative for China to establish communication links with neighbors bordering its hinterland.

French Indochina and British Burma southwest of China were not yet in direct conflict with Japan, so the Chinese Government first sought to establish a communication link with Indochina. Although there was already in existence the so-called Yunnan-Indochina Railway, which had one of its terminals in Kunming, capital of Yunnan Province, Kunming was many hundreds of rugged miles from the important wartime city of Kweiyang and the wartime capital of Chungking. Construction of a railway linking up these cities was not an easy matter and could not have been completed in time to meet urgent wartime needs. There also was a highway linking Hanoi with Langson and Chennankwan on the China-Indochina border, and the same highway was connected with Nanning, Liuchow and Kweilin in Kwangsi Province, but the volume of highway transportation was grossly inadequate to meet wartime needs.

Indochina, however, had an excellent seaport in Haiphong capable of handling ocean shipping. There were shipping routes from Haiphong to Hong Kong in the east and to India and Rangoon in the west. There was also a railway extending from Haiphong via Hanoi and Langson to Dong Dang, which was only two miles south of Chennankwan on the Chinese border. Extension of this railway to Chennankwan would not be difficult and would furnish a most direct route from a foreign seaport to the rear of wartime China.

The war had not yet spread to the middle reaches of the Yangtze River at that time. If the so-called Hunan-Kwangsi Railway could be constructed within a relatively short period of time, it would be possible to link up Hengyang on the Canton-Hankow Railway with Haiphong in Indochina via Chennankwan. Such a link would be a tremendous asset in the war of resistance against Japan. The Chinese Government had intended to build a railway linking Hengyang and Kweilin, provincial capital of Kwangsi, after the completion of the Canton-Hankow Railway. Soon after work began, however, hostilities broke out in North China and the Chinese Government proceeded in 1938 to build the entire railway from Chennankwan to Kweilin via Nanning and Liuchow in an effort to establish communication links with the outside world.

Half a century earlier, Great Britain and France were vying for special rights to China's southwest, including the right to build railways. France, in particular, was interested in such provinces as Szechwan, Yunnan and Kwangsi. In 1888, China was pressured into letting France extend its existing railways and those yet to be completed in Indochina into Chinese territory. In 1896, China again granted a French company the right to construct a railway from Chennankwan to Lungchow and to extend it to Dong Dang to link up with railways in Indochina. In 1898, France took advantage of China's defeat in the first Sino-Japanese War to demand the right to build the Yunnan-Indochina Railway and other lines. It had long been the ambition of France to include in its sphere of influence the western part of Kwangtung, the provinces of Kwangsi and Yunnan, and even the province of Szechwan.

At the time, the Manchu Dynasty and the Chinese people were

indignant over these French demands, regarding them as economic aggression and even territorial aggrandizement. But now, it was China, struggling for its very survival, which requested French cooperation in the construction of the same vital railways in order to establish a link with the outside world!

The Chinese initiated negotiations with France in January 1938 for the completion of the two-mile section from Dong Dang to Chennankwan as well as for the cooperation in constructing the section from Chennankwan to Nanning. Although these projects suited the French quite well, the Chinese felt it necessary to enter into some form of economic cooperation with the French to ensure their wholehearted support and the use of the port of Haiphong. A number of French banks had long had extensive business dealings with several railways in North China, and the banking, industrial and commercial circles in France had more than a casual interest in the China market.

Thus, agreement was reached for a consortium of French banks to underwrite the purchase of the necessary materials; for the Chinese Government to be responsible for the labor cost; and for the Kwangsi Provincial Government to supply the work force. The Nanning-Chennankwan section was started in April 1938. Since the railway in Indochina was of the narrow one-meter gauge, the section on the Chinese side was also constructed temporarily at the same gauge so that trains could run across the border.

The Kwangsi Provincial Government had had considerable experience in recruiting labor for the construction of highways and airfields, so that the building of railway roadbed proceeded at a rapid rate. The railway was extended from Indochina across the border into China in May 1939 and steadily shortened the distance over which supplies from abroad must be transported by highways.

The Japanese noticed the effect of the progress of this railway on China's war effort and proceeded to occupy Hainan Island as well as to send carrier-based aircraft off Peihai for daily bombing raids against the construction crew. Eventually, the Japanese landed in Peihai to cut off this international route. Before the Japanese took Nanning in December 1939, China had completed over 50 miles of the railway from Chennankwan towards Nanning.

At the same time, construction of the 106-mile section from Kweilin to Liuchow and of the 160-mile section from Liuchow to Nanning was underway, utilizing the materials and supplies evacuated from the central part of China. The Kwangsi provincial government recruited workers for the construction of the railway roadbed. The recruitment also served to facilitate the mobilization of all the able-bodied men in the province towards the war effort. Over 600,000 men had been recruited during this two-year period.

While the Japanese were landing in Peihai to invade Nanning, the section between Kweilin and Liuchow was already in operation, enabling a large number of Chinese troops to be rushed south to confront the enemy and to stop it from making further inroads to the north. This is another memorable event in the wartime railway construction work.

VIII

The Hunan-Kweichow Railway 湘黔鐵路

The Japanese increased their pressure in North China following their occupation of the Northeast Provinces and the setting up of the Manchu puppet regime. All the major railways in North China were in danger of being taken. The Chinese Government thus promptly shifted its attention to the planning work in Central China and the southwest provinces. Since the Canton-Hankow Railway had already been completed in 1936 and the Chekiang-Kiangsi Railway was scheduled to be open soon, it was decided to construct the Hunan-Kweichow Railway. This railway would enable the developing of the rich mineral resources in the western part of Hunan and would provide rail links between Nanking, Shanghai or Hankow with Kweichow Province.

Railway construction bonds were issued and a loan was negotiated with a German firm for the purchasing of materials and supplies. The entire railway extended some 600 miles. The eastern section, the 130-mile section linking up with the Canton-Hankow Railway, was under construction by the spring of 1937. This section was to link up, in Kweichow Province, at Tuyun on the Kweichow-Kwangsi Railway then already under construction, and eventually with Kweiyang, the capital of Kweichow Province. Unfortunately, fighting had already spread to the Yangtze River Basin and it became impossible to extend this railway westward. About 100 miles of rails had already been laid in the eastern section by the time work was suspended in March 1939. The rails and bridges in the completed section were then dismantled and, together with other supplies and equipment not yet used, were evacuated for the use of the Hunan-Kwangsi Railway.

IX

The Kweichow-Kwangsi Railway 黔桂鐵路

The section of the Hunan-Kwangsi Railway between Hengyang and Liuchow had already been rushed into completion by 1939. To further develop rail communication in the Southwest, the Chinese Government decided to construct the Kweichow-Kwangsi Railway extending from Liuchow northwestward to Kweichow to meet military transportation needs. The Kwangsi Provincial Government again took on the responsibility of recruiting the necessary labor for the earthwork. Materials, supplies and rolling stocks were to come from those evacuated from North China, south of the Yangtze River, and from Central China.

Construction work was started in April 1939 when the war of resistance was at its most difficult stage. The difficult construction work on this section was compounded by the shortage of supplies and equipment as well as labor. It should be borne in mind that by this time, the Japanese had landed in Peihai, posing a serious threat to the southern part of Kwangsi. The frequent bombings that took place made a difficult job even more difficult. The section from Liuchow to Chinchengkiang had been completed by February 1941. Further progress was impeded by bridge work. Chinchengkiang thus served for more than a year as the connecting point between railway and highway traffic involving the transportation of troops and military supplies at a time when the fighting was most intense. By the spring of 1944, rails had been laid to as far as Tuyun, over 280 miles from Liuchow. Further work had to be suspended, however, as the Japanese were already deep into Kwangsi Province, poised to invade Kweichow Province.

X

The Hsufu-Kunming Railway 敍昆鐵路

The Yunnan-Indochina Railway mentioned earlier was built back in 1897 under French pressure. It was 280 miles long, of narrow gauge, and extended from the border of Indochina to Kunming, the capital of Yunnan. Following the loss of the coastal areas to the Japanese and before the completion of the Hunan-Kwangsi Railway, a considerable quantity of war materiel and construction supplies was transported on this railway from Hanoi and Haiphong to Kunming and then to the rear. If this railway could be extended from Kunming to Hsufu (Yipin) in the upper reaches of the Yangtze River, it would be possible to link up the wartime capital Chungking by river traffic to this international lifeline.

The Chinese Government, determined to wage the war of resistance over the long haul, considered it vitally important to develop all possible routes of communication. Its policy was to develop the vast area in the Southwest, and to lay equal emphasis on waging the war of resistance and on carrying out various construction projects. The implementation of this policy would offer employment to a large number of qualified workers who had retreated from the war zone, or had escaped from the occupied territory.

Towards the end of 1937, the Chinese Government and the Provincial Governments of Szechwan and Yunnan jointly organized the Szechwan-Yunnan Railway Company to build the one-meter gauge Hsufu-Kunming Railway. The supplies and equipment were to be purchased with a French loan which took a long time to negotiate and was finally available by March 1940. By that time, France itself was faced with invasion by Germany, and, while France was purchasing the agreed upon supplies, Japan occupied Indochina and cut off the Yunnan-Indochina Railway, making it impossible to ship supplies to Kunming.

Construction, however, had already begun on the 100-kilometer railway from Kunming to Chucheng since December 1938, but the occupation of Indochina by the Japanese forced the Chinese Government to destroy the Hokou Bridge of the Yunnan-Indochina Railway on the border. The Chinese also dismantled over 90 miles of track material and used them to lay the section between Kunming and Chucheng. Locomotives and railway cars of the Yunnan-Indochina Railway were pressed into service and this section was opened to traffic in March 1941. Although another 100 miles of roadbed had been completed, further construction work was impossible due to lack of supplies.

XI

Westward Extension
of the Lunghai Railway 隴海鐵路

As early as 1912, when the Republic of China was founded, the Chinese Government decided to construct the Lunghai Railway from the east coast south of the Yellow River to Sian and Lanchow, traversing the Yellow River Basin. Some 1,100 miles in length, this railway would be the longest trunk line in China. Sian, the famed capital of the Han and Tang Dynasties, was an important cultural center, while Lanchow was the geographic center of China as well as a strategic base for the administration of the Northwest frontier region.

Although the Yellow River runs also in an east-westerly direction, it is not navigable. The Lunghai Railway therefore would mean a great deal in terms of facilitating transportation in the Yellow River Basin area. The construction was financed by a banking consortium from Belgium which then entertained no political ambitions in the Far East, and the Chinese Government was more than happy to accept its investment and cooperation. Shortly after work was started, however, Belgium was dragged into World War I which broke out in 1914, and bonds of this railway could no longer be floated in the European market, causing suspension of its construction.

Thereafter northern China came increasingly under the threat of Japanese aggression. By 1931, when Japan occupied China's Northeast Provinces, the Lunghai Railway was completed only from the east coast to Tungkwan on the border of Honan and Shensi Provinces, less than half of the entire projected route. When Japan attacked Shanghai in January 1932 and threatened Nanking, the Chinese Government temporarily moved its capital to Loyang on the Lunghai Railway. Developing and opening up of the Northwest became more urgent and the need to extend the Lunghai Railway further westward became more imperative. Since the Belgian banking consortium was no longer able to offer assistance, the Chinese Government had to devise other means to complete the project.

The writer was engaged in the construction of the Lingpao-Tungkwan section and the Tungkwan to Sian section when he was reassigned in 1932 to complete the Canton-Hankow Railway. The section from Tungkwan to Sian was later completed in 1934, and another section from Sian west to Paoki was completed in 1937, two months after Japan launched its full scale offensive in northern China. Although the line temporarily terminated at Paoki, it went a long way towards the opening up of the Northwest.

Shortly after the Lukouchiao Incident, Japanese troops overran most of the coastal provinces. Some proceeded westward on the Lunghai Railway from Chengchow and began to threaten Tungkwan. Others advanced along the Chengtai Railway and the southern section of the Tungpu Railway soon reached Fengling Ferry, separated from Tungkwan only by the wide Yellow River. Historically, Tungkwan had always been a military redoubt. The Lunghai Railway from Lingpao to Tungkwan along the southern bank of the Yellow River contained a number of tunnels. There was even a 3,000-foot tunnel right under the City of Tungkwan. The Japanese army, entrenched along the northern bank of the Yellow River, shelled Tungkwan day and night. Should this strategic redoubt be lost, Japanese troops could advance unhampered along the railway westward towards Sian, and if Sian was lost, the entire Northwest would be left defenseless.

Furthermore, large quantities of railway supplies and railway cars which had been evacuated westward along the railway would have no more place to go. It was decided, therefore, to construct the ninety-eight-mile section from Paoki to Tienshiu. This section ran along the narrow gorge of the Wei River, and required the boring of over 120 tunnels. The writer was in charge of the construction of this section, which was completed in 1945 under the most difficult circumstances. Japan, by then, had already surrendered some four months earlier.

XII

Highways

A railway carries far more cargo than a highway, but also requires far more stringent methods of construction. Selecting a route for a railway over mountainous terrain is more difficult; the construction is more costly and often requires material and equipment not readily available during wartime. A railway also takes longer to build, and thus often cannot meet wartime exigencies. Selecting a route for a highway is far easier and improvements can be made at almost any time. A highway can be open to traffic before it is paved, or even before its gravel base is completed. Bridges can be built of wood on a temporary basis and ferries may be used to cross wider rivers.

In spite of its lower freight-carrying capacity, higher attrition rate of the motor vehicles, and the difficulties in obtaining spare parts, fuel and lubricants, a highway plays a more prominent role during wartime construction because of the all-important time element. In a race against time, construction is often started even before the entire route has been defined; transportation of the cargo can begin without any dispatching organization, and before the establishing of repair facilities, stockpile of spare parts, or even warehouses for the cargo. Although the volume of traffic is limited at its initial stage, improvements made along the way enable the highway system to contribute significantly towards the transportation needs during a war. Such was the case during the eight-year Sino-Japanese War. While the Chinese Government gave top priority to the construction of railways, it was also rushing the construction of highways to link up major cities in the interior, and to link up the neighbors bordering the Southwest and Northwest.

Before the outbreak of the Sino-Japanese War, China had about 72,000 miles of highways, 35 per cent of which were gravel surface. Following the temporary removal of the national capital to Chungking, China's Southwest and Northwest assumed increasing importance in the war. There were already highways linking Chungking with such provincial capitals as Kweilin, Changsha, Kweiyang, Kunming, Chengtu, Sikang, Sian and Lanchow. Improvements were constantly being made on most of these roads, but more urgently needed was the construction of highways to link up with China's neighbors not only to facilitate the inflow of war materiel and other necessary supplies from abroad, but also to permit the outflow of surplus agricultural and mineral products to earn much needed foreign exchange. The principal international routes included the Kwangsi-Indochina Highway, the Yunnan-Burma Highway, the China-India Highway and the Kansu-Sinkiang Highway, each with its network of auxiliary roads.

The Kwangsi-Indochina Highway 湘越公路

The first to come into use, the Kwangsi-Indochina Highway was also the most direct international route since there was already a major highway running from Hunan to Kwangsi, going through Nanning and connecting with the highways in Indochina by way of Chennankwan on the Chinese border. This highway played a crucial role in China's war of resistance in the two-and-a-half years from the outbreak of war to the Japanese invasion of Kwangsi. When Indochina fell into Japanese hands in 1940, supplies were no longer permitted to be transhipped to China. This highway, along with the Yunnan-Indochina Railway, lost its importance. Thenceforth, military supplies had to be imported via the Yunnan-Burma Highway.

The Yunnan-Burma Highway 滇緬公路

Yunnan Province is adjacent to Burma which was then under British rule. An existing railway ran from the Burmese capital of Rangoon northward to Mandalay, then branching into two, one extended north to Myitkyina while the other extended to Kunlong northeast of Lashio. Both of these terminals are close to the Yunnan border, and there was even a highway running from Lashio to Wanting on the Chinese border.

Following the Japanese occupation of the Canton-Hankow Railway and the disruption of the Kwangsi-Indochina Railway, the Chinese Government sought to establish another international link by building a highway from Yunnan to Burma, then using the existing railway there to reach the seaport of Rangoon. After a series of Sino-British studies and negotiations, two routes were defined. One was to go from Kunming through Paoshan and Tengchung to Bhamo in Burma, then along the Irrawaddy River to Rangoon. The other was to go from Kunming through Paoshan and Lungling to Wanting, connecting with the Burmese highway to Lashio. Eventually the second route was deemed more preferable. Thus began the construction of the Yunnan-Burma Highway, cutting across some very difficult terrain in the western part of Yunnan.

Several mountain ranges had to be traversed and river gorges crossed in going from Kunming to Lashio. The Chinese were to construct the 575-mile section from Kunming to Wanting and the Burmese were to improve the 117-mile section from Wanting to Lashio. The much longer Chinese section contained much greater construction demands. All the earthwork for the roadbed had to be moved by manual labor. Yunnan was not a densely populated province to begin with, and it was virtually impossible to find labor within 100 miles along the proposed route. Peasant laborers often had to walk 200 miles to reach the construction site.

In response to the recruitment campaign in the war against Japan, most of the able-bodied men had already joined the army. Those who had not were hard pressed to keep the important agricultural sector of the economy going, so that among the labor recruits for the highway were large numbers of aged, women, and even children. While the majority of the laborers were Chinese, a sizable number were illiterate aborigines and Tibetans to whom Chinese was virtually a foreign language. Work camps were not readily available and the laborers had to build their own crude shelters with branches and straw. The weather was severe and constantly changing, many of the laborers often contracted colds, bronchitis and even pneumonia. Poor sanitary conditions and the lack of potable water caused a variety of intestinal diseases. Although the casualty rate was high, so was the morale. Few, if any, of the laborers asked to be relieved of their duties.

Started in 1937, the section from Kunming to Wanting was opened to traffic in about two years. The section between Lashio and Wanting was completed, and it was paved with asphalt.

Several shipments of Russian war supplies for China arrived in Rangoon by the end of 1938; this represented the first consignment of war materiel supplied to China by foreign countries. Early in December of the same year, the first batch of war supplies was transported by rail from Rangoon to Lashio, transhipped to Wanting by trucks, and then via the newly constructed highway to Kunming. A consignment of tungsten, bristles, etc., was carried on the return trip and exported by way of Rangoon, marking the beginning of the Yunnan-Burma Highway as an international route.

Although there was a rail link between Rangoon and Lashio, the freight volume of its northern section never exceeded 10,000 tons per month under the most favorable conditions. A highway also linked Rangoon with Lashio, but very little use was made of it in the initial stage. Even new motor vehicles were shipped from Rangoon to Lashio by rail. Until 1941, when the United States started to supply China with a large quantity of motor vehicles under the Lend-Lease Act, they were transported from Rangoon to Kunming by trucks via the Yunnan-Burma Highway, as the railway was already carrying its maximum capacity in freight. Lashio, being the transhipment center between railway and highway, often had a tremendous pile-up of material due to the enormous disparity in freight capacity between the incoming trains and outgoing trucks. Each railway car could carry thirty or forty tons, and each train could carry up to 1,000 tons, while each truck could only carry three tons. China purchased 200 new trucks in Rangoon in 1939, and an additional 300 in 1941. Another 100 trucks were donated by the overseas Chinese in Burma. Some 3,000 overseas Chinese were recruited to serve as drivers and mechanics. Thus the truck freight to Kunming could also average 10,000 tons per month, matching the freight capacity of the railway.

This highway continued to serve as China's vital international lifeline until the occupation of the northern part of Burma by the Japanese in 1942 and 1943. It has the distinction of having served the longest period of time and on the largest scale as China's international route during the Sino-Japanese War. When Lashio fell to the Japanese, part of the function served by the Yunnan-Burma Highway was taken over by the China-India Highway.

China-India Highway 中印公路

When the Japanese advanced on northern Burma and the western part of Yunnan following their occupation of Rangoon in 1942, that section of the Yunnan-Burma Highway south of Paoshan could no longer be used to link up with the railway system in Burma. The United States was then in the process of establishing a supply base at Ledo in northern India which was connected by rail to Calcutta, and by April 1942 began to airlift gasoline and other supplies from Ledo to Kunming over the "hump." Later, agreement was reached between the United States and China to construct a highway from Ledo to link up with the Yunnan-Burma Highway.

Work was to be started by the U.S. Army Corps of Engineers from the Ledo end. The Chinese sent their Tenth Regiment of Army Engineers, numbering 2,700 men, to join in the construction work. The 103-mile section between Ledo and Hsinpingyang was completed first, and following the recapture of the western part of Yunnan by the Chinese, the 167-mile section between Hsinpingyang and Myitkyina was also opened to traffic in the autumn of 1944. On the Chinese side, the original plan was to build a highway from Lungling toward Myitkyina, but since it would be shorter to go from Paoshan to Tenchung and across the border to Myitkyina 70 miles away, work was begun in 1944 in the vicinity of Paoshan. The eastern and western sections of the highway were connected on January 19, 1945, and the entire China-India Highway was open to traffic on January 21. The first convoy of trucks from Ledo arrived in Kunming on February 4. Until the surrender of Japan six months later, this highway served as a vital supply line.

The Kansu-Sinkiang Highway 甘新公路

In the Northwest, China's backyard of Sinkiang borders with Russia through a vast expanse of desert with no natural boundaries. During the Czarist days, Russia had already taken over a considerable part of the territory that rightfully belonged to China. But since the bordering region is so remote from China's geographical center of Lanchow, its control by the Chinese Government was often only nominal.

As early as in the Han Dynasty, a route had wound its way from

Lanchow northwestward between two mountain ranges. This was known as the Northwest Corridor. The geographical and racial make-up as well as the religion and customs in this area were quite different from those in the more developed central China. Local insurrections occurred frequently and there were times when China's control over this area was tenuous at best. Kansu and Sinkiang were plagued by a series of insurrections in the middle of the 19th century and Russia took advantage of the situation to extend its control over that part of Asia, occupying the town of Ili.

In 1876 the Manchu Government sent an expeditionary force under the command of Tso Tsung-tang to reassert Chinese control over Sinkiang. After several years of arduous campaign, Sinkiang was made a province of China and Ili was retaken. Thus there remained two centers of international commerce in the northwest corner of Sinkiang, Chuguchak (Tahcheng) and Ili; all traffic between Russia and China must pass through them.

In 1933, the Chinese Government appointed Sheng Shih-tsai military governor of Sinkiang and relations with the Soviet Russia were greatly improved. The Turkestan-Siberia Railroad was then already in existence and a highway had already been constructed from Alma Ata to Khorgos on the Chinese border and on to Ili. This highway was further extended across Sinkiang Province to Hsinghsinghsia on the Sinkiang-Kansu border via Tihwa (Urumchi) and Hami, and was already opened to traffic at the outbreak of the Sino-Japanese War in 1937. From Hsinghsinghsia into Kansu Province, Lanchow is about 730 miles away along the Northwest Corridor. Except for a few towns along the way, this route traverses a wide expanse of barren hardpan. The annual precipitation in this area is near zero, so no paving was required and no definite route was followed by the travellers. There was no scheduled commercial traffic along this route before the outbreak of the Sino-Japanese War and maintenance of the road and the drainage system was undertaken by the troops stationed along the way.

Following the outbreak of the Sino-Japanese War, China concentrated on developing the communication system in the Southwest to link up with those in Indochina and Burma, but also paid special attention to the back door in the Northwest. A Sino-Soviet barter trade agreement was then in force. The Soviet Union was to supply the Chinese with one thousand 2½-ton trucks in exchange for tungsten, wool, etc. The trucks were delivered to Hami in Sinkiang Province in October 1937, and were to be taken over by the Chinese. But the 800-mile route from Hami to Lanchow needed improvements, and there were no service nor food and lodging facilities along the way. Drivers had to be trained, and road signs and communication systems had to be set up. In the end, the Russian drivers were permitted to continue on from Hami to Lanchow.

The first convoy arrived in Lanchow on November 11, 1937. Later, Chinese drivers were sent to Hami to receive the trucks.

It was at this time that a rich oil reserve was discovered in Yumen, some 500 miles northwest of Lanchow, and a refinery had been set up. But the output at the beginning was too low and the trucks had to carry their own fuel supplies from Hami to Lanchow. A small number of these trucks were consigned to the route between Lanchow and Sian while the majority were used to run between Lanchow and Chungking.

The work of maintaining and improving this lengthy Kansu-Sinkiang Highway was undertaken by the troops stationed in the area and by technicians sent by the government. As this route was relatively free from enemy harassment, the traffic volume was on the increase constantly and a considerable quantity of Soviet arms aid was carried on this road to the fighting front. The opening of this back door in the Northwest during the initial stage of the Sino-Japanese conflict gave a great lift to the morale of the Chinese defenders.

XIII

Conclusion

Japan invaded the Northeast Provinces of China and set up the puppet Manchu regime in 1932. Her ambition to conquer China by military and political means became obvious to the entire world and the Chinese people were well aware of what Japan's next step would be. While Japan was well prepared for massive military actions and had little regard for world opinion, China was ill-prepared in every way. She had yet to achieve complete political unity and did not even have what might be described as a rudimentary network of communications.

No one realized this situation better than Generalissimo Chiang Kai-Shek. He therefore made many humiliating concessions with the enemy in North China in order to gain time. He also placed top priority on the completion of the north-south Canton-Hankow Railway and the east-west Chekiang-Kiangsi Railway to facilitate bringing about political unity and to consolidate China's military position south of the Yangtze River. Had these two railways not been rushed to completion while there was still time, the Japanese, having already entrenched themselves in North China, might well have realized their boast of bringing the Chinese to their knees within a matter of months.

The Chinese Government declared at the time that it would not abandon peace as long as there was a last shred of hope and that it would not resort to war as long as it could be avoided. When the Japanese created the Lukouchiao Incident in 1937, China was forced to gird herself for protracted warfare in its own defense. To make its intention unmistakably clear, the Chinese Government moved the national capital from Nanking to Chungking and concentrated on the development of communication systems for the defense of the wartime capital and the linking up of the provincial capitals in the Southwest. China thus fought alone against Japan for four long years before the Pearl Harbor attack which triggered the outbreak of the Pacific War. China by then was in the midst of undertaking the enormous construction program of developing a transportation network in its interior and of establishing links with her friendly neighbors in the Southwest.

The lack of construction materials from abroad, due to the complete blockade of the coastal area and the sustained enemy bombing of the limited transportation system, cast doubts not only among foreign observers, but also among the policy-makers in China, and even those directly responsible for the construction. How was China to complete the various railways and highways and to keep open domestic as well as international communications during the war? The writer participated in the construction work during those eight years and wishes to relate some of the more memorable events.

The construction of railways requires large quantities of steel rails, sleepers, locomotives, cars, wagons and various tools and materials of construction as well as vast human labor resources. As the Japanese aggressors steadily advanced from North China to the south, locomotives, cars and wagons were evacuated to various provinces in the rear, carrying with them the materials salvaged from the dismantled railways. Sometimes, even steel rails were spirited piece by piece out of the areas under Japanese occupation. Thus the railways in the interior of China were extended for additional hundreds of miles. Sleepers evacuated from occupied areas were augmented by cross ties produced from wood locally available. Scarce modern explosives, such as TNT, were substituted by locally manufactured black powder. Cement substitute supplanted the limited quantity of cement produced, and old steel rails were sometimes used to build bridge piers. Engineers and trained technicians were plentiful among those who had retreated from the war zone and the supply of unskilled labor was adequate. Factories were set up to produce automobile spare parts. Alcohol was used as a substitute for gasoline.

In the four years when China fought single-handedly against Japan, human endurance was pushed to the limit and a number of miracles were produced. When fighting broke out in the Pacific and the United States entered the war, China was able to obtain some supplies via the international routes in the Southwest and this alleviated some of the difficulties experienced in the earlier years.

China suffered incalculable losses in property and human lives during the eight years of fighting with Japan. All was not in the loss column, however, as the Chinese people, taxing their endurance and resourcefulness to the limit, successfully implemented the twin national policy of resisting the enemy while at the same time engaging in the work of construction. Thus the often forgotten interior was developed, and tens of thousands of peasants learned a special trade as a result of their being mobilized into the construction force.

The Sino-Japanese War was not merely for the survival of China and her people as a nation. If the Chinese people had not had the determination to surmount the indescribable difficulties during the first four years of the war, it was entirely possible that Japan would have conquered not only China, but the whole of Southeast Asia as well. In that event, the shape of the world would have been affected and even modern history might have to be rewritten.

MAP I
Railway and Highway
Construction Prior to,
and After, 1937 (1)

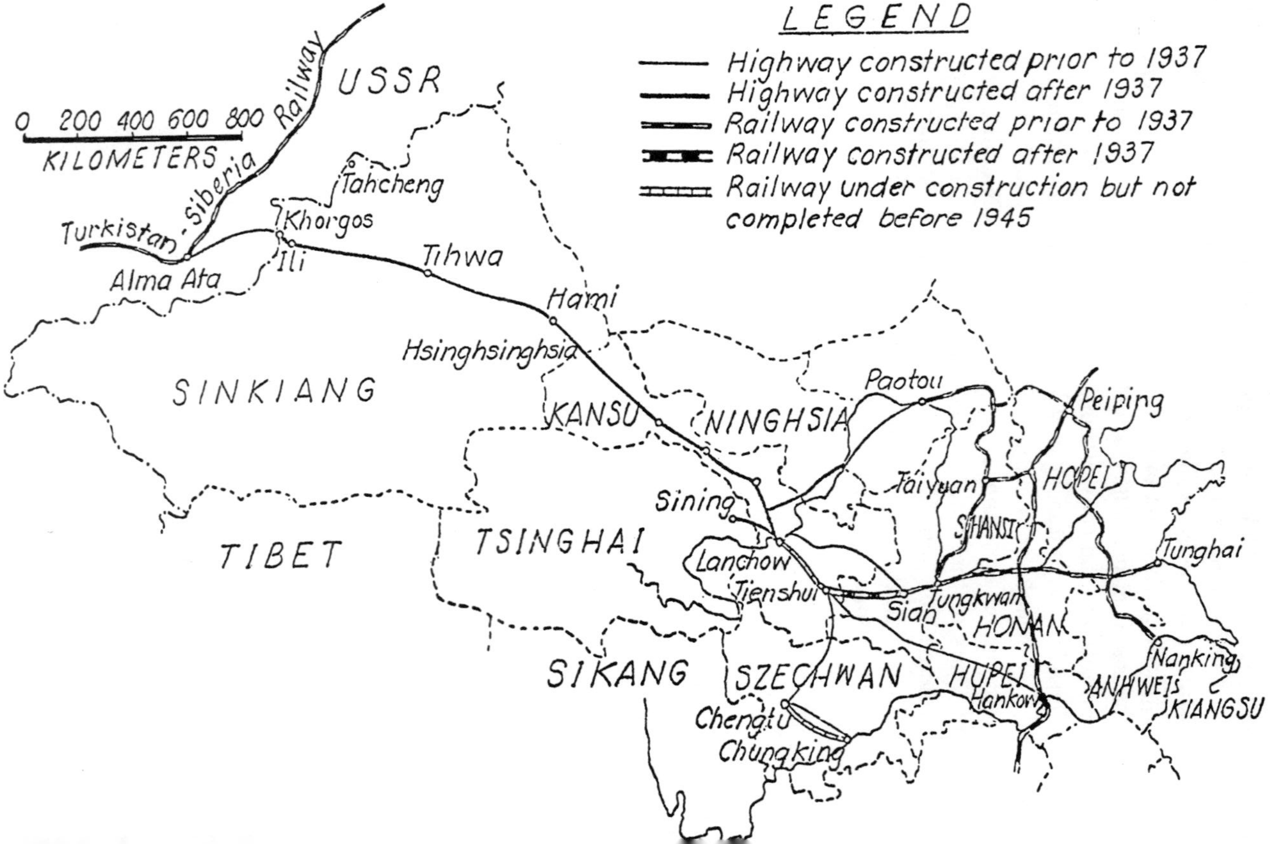

LEGEND

Highway constructed prior to 1937
Highway constructed after 1937
Railway constructed prior to 1937
Railway constructed after 1937
Railway under construction but not
  completed before 1945

MAP II
Railway and Highway
Construction Prior to,
and After, 1937 (2)

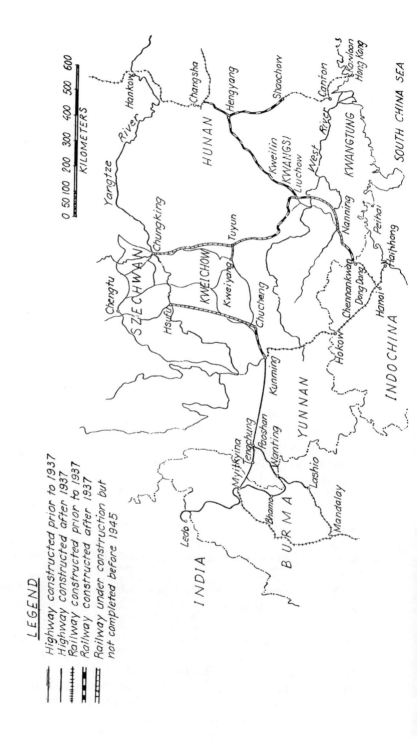

LEGEND

Highway constructed prior to 1937
Highway constructed after 1937
Railway constructed prior to 1937
Railway constructed after 1937
Railway under construction but
not completed before 1945

Comments:

BY PAUL K. T. SIH

The author of this paper, Dr. H. H. Ling, is a renowned scholar as well as an eminent public official who has served his country with great distinction. For over half a century, he has been devoted to governmental service in China's communication and transportation system.

Dr. Ling progressed in his railroad career from junior engineer in 1918, to engineer, and then to senior engineer in various government-operated railroads. He served as Director and Engineer-in-Chief of the extension of the Lunghai Railroad, in the completion of the Lunghai Railroad, in the completion of the Canton-Hankow Railroad, in charge of building the Hunan-Kwangsi Railroad, and directing the railroad and highway transportation system in the northwestern provinces of China before and during World War II.

It seems to me that there is no other person who could be more competent or qualified than Dr. Ling to prepare this study based principally upon his personal experience. This is particularly true with the three major railways, the Lunghai line, the Canton-Hankow line and the Hunan-Kwangsi line, all of which were constructed under his personal direction and supervision, and which played an important part in military operations during the Sino-Japanese War, 1937-1945.

China had no railroads before 1866. From 1866 to 1942, China constructed 12,036 miles of railroads. Of these, 3,726 miles were lost in 1931 because of the Japanese invasion of Manchuria. Another 6,566 miles were lost during the first five-and-a-half years of the Sino-Japanese War. This left only 1,744 miles of railroads, of which 1,001 miles were built during the war.[1]

In December 1935, less than two years before the war broke out, the Ministry of Railways of the Chinese Government was headed by Dr. Chang Kia-ngau 張嘉璈（公權）. In the spring of 1938, after Nanking, China's capital, was taken over by the Japanese, the Government merged the Ministry of Railways with the Ministry of Communications, still with Dr. Chang as the head of this combined Ministry. Chang served in this capacity until 1942. It was under his leadership that the transportation systems made valued contributions to the war effort against Japan's invasion.[2]

In reviewing Dr. Ling's study, the book, *China's Struggle for Railroad*

Development (New York: John Day Company, 1942) authored by Minister Chang, was of great benefit to me. As a matter of fact, when Chang was Minister of Railways (1935-1938) and Minister of Communications (1938-1942), I had the good fortune to serve the two Ministries as Senior Secretary to the Minister and Chief of the Bureau of Research, Planning and Statistics. During the latter part of the war, I served concurrently as Deputy Director of the National Highway Administration which had supervision over the Burma Road and Director General of the Joint Transportations (overland and waterways) of Hunan, Szechwan, and Shensi Provinces. This provided me with ample opportunity of acquainting myself with the operations of both overland and waterway transportation systems in wartime China. With this background and experience, I feel confident and doubly pleased to discuss this paper.

Ling's account is lucid and complete as it is and needs no further explanation or elaboration. What I wish to single out is the difficult conditions under which the transportation systems developed and operated during the war period.

China fought the war for eight years, 1937-1945. In the first four years, China faced the powerful enemy single-handedly. It was not until 1941 after the attack on Pearl Harbor by Japan that China was able to fight hand in hand with the Allies. In the first four years, 1937-1941, China was completely isolated. Neither the United States nor Great Britain was in a position to extend a helping hand to her. In fact, the United States was still exporting, at that time, scrap iron, steel, and petroleum products to Japan.[3] This was not stopped until January 1940 when the U.S.-Japanese Treaty of Commerce and Navigation came to an end.

Under these conditions, China had to pursue a policy of self-reliance. This was particularly true with the railway system. The war in China was characterized by the struggle over the railways. In the first phase of the war, from the Marco Polo Bridge Incident in July 1937 to the fall of Hankow in November 1939, Japanese strategy was concentrated upon the utilization of Chinese railway lines for military expansion and control. During these twenty-one months, over eighty percent of China's railways built before the war had either fallen into the hands of the Japanese or been destroyed.[4]

From that time on, the railroads ceased to play an important part in China's defense. China concentrated her military efforts on counterblockade and guerrilla fighting while her transportation policy was concentrated on the development of highways and waterways.[5]

Among the most outstanding achievements in the construction of new railroads during the war were:

(1) The completion of the 280-mile section from Chuchow

株 州 to Lochang 樂 昌 on the Hankow-Canton Railway;

(2) The completion of the 338-mile section from Yushan 玉 山 to Pinghsiang 萍 鄉 on the Chekiang-Kiangsi Railway;

(3) The building of the 384-mile section from Hengyang 衡 陽 to Laipin 藍 平 on the Hunan-Kwangsi Railway;

(4) The building of the 143-mile section from Chennankwan 鎮南關 to Nanning 南 寧 on the Yunnan-Kwangsi Railway; and

(5) The extension of the 83-mile section from Sian 西 安 to Paoki 寶 鷄 of the Lunghai Railway in September 1937 and then further extension of the 96-mile section from Paoki to Tienshui 天 水 in 1945.

All these provided significant contributions to China's total efforts in breaking Japan's blockade and bringing the war to final victory. In the words of Dr. Chang Kia-ngau, "Japan had hoped for China's surrender as soon as the loss of most of the railroads forced the Chinese Government into regions without any modern transport facilities. . . . But China still fought on. This caused Japan to give up her blitzkrieg tactics and to make blockade her main weapon in a prolonged war of attrition. China had to break this blockade wherever possible by developing new international routes."[6]

As soon as the war broke out in July 1937, Shanghai was attacked in August. Three months later, Nanking, China's capital, fell into the hands of the Japanese. China's international route had to shift from Shanghai to the south and southwest seacoast of China with Hong Kong and Haiphong as the ports. This is the reason why the newly-built sections of the four railways—the Hankow-Canton Railway, the Chekiang-Kiangsi Railway, the Hunan-Kwangsi Railway, and the Chennankwan-Nanning Section—served the immediate need for military operations.

After Haiphong was lost in 1940 and Hong Kong fell into Japanese hands in 1941, China had to rely upon Burma for her outside connections. Fortunately, the Burma Road had been completed in 1939. At the time, China received Soviet aid via the Kansu-Sinkiang Highway. However, after the conclusion of the Neutrality Pact between Soviet Russia and Japan in April 1941, this source of supply became insignificant. Again, after northern Burma and Rangoon were lost in 1942, China had to seek another new international link with India. Hence the construction of the China-India Highway.

All these changes were made in adjusting to the various war conditions. The task was not easy. Both manpower and construction materials were in short supply. China had to draft a total of a million men to maintain an army of between 2.2 and 5.7 million during the war years. Population was sparse in the interior areas which made it difficult to secure sufficient labor. Materials for constructing roads relied largely upon imported supplies. Every scrap of material and rails used for building bridges and tracks were taken from the dismantled stock of other railroads and refabricated. Tunnels were cut through, not by machines or with the help of explosives, but by human hands. All these achievements were realized under severe Japanese air raids or serious military threats.

Besides railroads, highways and waterways also played an important part in China's war of resistance. Before the war, China already built a network of highways linking up seven leading provinces. After the hostilities began, further intensive efforts were made to develop highway transportation systems in both the northwest and southwest regions. Improvements of the road surface and maintenance services were provided with great effort and under most difficult conditions. Most important of all was the construction of the Burma Road. The mountainous 575-mile section from Kunming to Wanting was completed in two years, mobilizing more than 200,000 laborers. This seemed almost a miracle!

In dealing with the highways, Dr. Ling does not mention the Szechwan-Sikang Highway 川康公路 from Chengtu 成都 to Kangting 康定 (210 miles), and from Kangting to Sichang 西昌 (180 miles). This is understandable as this road was not fully completed and did not provide significant use during the war. However, undertaking of constructing this road itself, leading to the interior part of China in the western region, did bolster to a great extent the morale of the people, particularly when the massive Ichigo operation 横山勇（一號作戰）兵略 launched the last and desperate attack from Liuchow toward Kweiyang from April 1944 to February 1945, thus seriously threatening the safety of Chungking, China's war capital. Just imagine, without this project linking Chungking with the farthest western region of Sikang as the last base of operation, what the state of mind and national morale would have been at that critical time!

It is understood that Dr. Ling, as the title of his paper indicates, is concerned primarily with overland transportation systems. Thus he has not covered the means of transport systems, other than railroads and highways. However, I wish to offer, as a kind of footnote, the operation of the so-called stage transportation which played an equally important role during the war.

As a traditional way of communication in ancient China, the stage transportation 驛運 , using highways and waterways and largely depending on manual labor, proved to be most useful, particularly at a time when all China's seacoasts were closed and when international routes could move only a very limited amount of imported material for modern transportation purposes.

In the fourteen-page account of China's wartime transportation in his outstanding book, *The History of the Sino-Japanese War, 1937-1945,* Professor Hsiang-hsiang Wu devoted more than two pages to describe this traditional means of transportation employed during the war.[7] Of the two pages, one entire page is concerned with the joint line linking three provinces—Hunan, Szechwan and Shensi—covering about 4,000 miles 川湘川陝水陸聯運 . I am especially happy to see this historical account, as I happened to be the Director General of this line, responsible for its total operation.

As Professor Wu put it very clearly, there were six routes linking Hengyang in Hunan to Chungking in Szechwan, with different means of transportation for varying distances. The shortest route was from Hengyang to Changteh 常 德 (43 miles), Yuanlin 沅 陵 (140 miles), Liya 里 耶 (356 miles), Miaochuan 妙 泉 (8 miles), Lungtan 龍 潭 (114 miles), Penghsui 彭 水 (1,900 miles), Fulin 涪 陵 (140 miles), and Chungking 重 慶 (180 miles), totalling 3,340 miles. With the exception of the sections between Miaochuan and Lungtan which used motor trucks, and between Lungtan and Penghsui, which used human carriers, all the remaining sections used waterways. This route was important in that it moved rice, tea, tung oil, raw minerals for making mercury, and tungsten from Hunan to Szechwan in exchange for salt on the return trip. From Chungking, this route was linked with Kwangyuan 廣 元 in Shensi by the Chialing River 嘉陵江 , about 700 miles long. From Kwangyuan there were highways leading to Kansu 甘 肅 and the Soviet border. With this network, China was able to maintain communication lines from the central part of the country all the way to the northwestern region leading to an international outlet.[8]

It was estimated that in the month of December 1942 alone, the route from Hunan to Szechwan moved commodities amounting to 800,000 ton-miles. Of this, 200,000 ton-miles were operated by motor trucks, 100,000 ton-miles by steamships, 540,000 ton-miles by wooden boats and 50,000 ton-miles by human carriers.[9] More than one-third of the commodities was tea exported to Soviet Russia for international barter.

The most difficult feature of this system of transportation was the large amount of human manpower required. For instance, in the 140-mile waterway between Penghsui and Fulin, there existed thirty-two groups of wooden boats. Each group consisted of eight boats with a capacity of fourteen tons each, and each boat required sixteen boatmen to operate it, totalling 128 men for each of the thirty-two groups, or 4,000 men for the entire operation. In the case of the 1,900-mile section between Lungtan and Penghsui, transports were made by human carriers. Each man could carry a limited amount of commodities, and could not travel more than thirty miles a day on this mountainous route, if the weather was favorable. From these instances we can imagine the complexities and problems involved in such primitive means of transportation—primitive it seemed to be, yet it was most successful in overcoming the difficulties with which modern transportation could hardly cope. With this experience in mind, we can readily understand why and how the Ho Chi-minh Trail was able to survive the intense American bombing and to serve a very important function in guerrilla fighting in the Vietnam War!

NOTES

1. Chang Kia-ngau, *China's Struggle for Railroad Development* (New York: John Day Company, 1942), p. 20.
2. "During the first five and a half years of war (July 1937 to December 1942), China depended upon her railroads for the movement of 21,582,000 troops and 4,433,000 tons of supplies, an achievement unprecedented in her history." (Chang Kia-ngau, p. 228.)
3. In 1937, for instance, U.S. exports to Japan amounted to $288,558,000. Of this, $42,747,000 was for crude and refined oils and $37,418,000 was for scrap iron and steel. *Pearl Harbor as History: Japanese-American Relations, 1931-1934*, ed. by Dorothy Borg and Shumpei Okamoto (New York: Columbia University Press, 1973), p. 371 and p. 372.
4. Chang Kia-ngau, p. 193.
5. For a general study of railway, highway and waterway transportation systems in wartime China, cf. *The Second Sino-Japanese War, 1931-1945*, two volumes, ed. by Hsiang-hsiang Wu (Taipei: Publishers of the *Scooper Monthly*, 1973), Vol. II, pp. 663-676.
6. Chang Kia-ngau, p. 18.
7. Hsiang-hsiang Wu, pp. 672-674.
8. *Ibid.*, p. 674. For an account of the "stage transportation system" in the northwestern part of China, from Kwangyuan in Szechwan to Hami in Sinkiang, see "Stories about the Establishment and Development of the Stage Transportation in the Northwest" by Chao Yao-yi. *Biographical Literature Monthly*, Vol. 27, No. 6, December 1975, pp. 29-30.
9. Hsiang-hsiang Wu, p. 674.

CHAPTER VIII

China's "Wartime Parliament": The People's Political Council, 1938-1945

BY LAWRENCE N. SHYU

T HE MAJOR PUBLICATIONS on wartime China in recent years have foci of attention in the areas of foreign relations and aid, the politics of collaboration, the rise of the Communist power, government finance and inflation, and military developments. Still largely unavailable are substantial scholarly works on the wartime economy, society, and internal political development of China. This article on the People's Political Council (PPC) is a preliminary effort to look into certain aspects of political, economic and social problems of China during the War of Resistance against Japan.

Since the Council had such a wide range of interests and activities as well as a relatively long life span (1938-1947), it is impractical to touch upon all aspects within the limited space of an article. Three questions will thus be singled out for discussion, namely, wartime national unity, the mobilization of manpower and resources, and constitutional movement. The Council played significant roles in all three areas, and yet its accomplishments varied greatly.

Further limitation will be imposed on the time span. Although the PPC ended formally only in 1947, its main functions were completed with the end of the war in 1945. Therefore the discussion in this article will not go beyond 1945. For the sake of clarification a brief description of the establishment, the structure, the powers, and the membership of the PPC will be made first.

I

The Origins and the Establishment of the PPC

The Chinese name of the People's Political Council, "Kuo-min tsan-cheng-hui," was first mentioned in a Plenary Session of the Kuomintang's Central Executive Committee (CEC) in December 1932. Japan's invasion of Manchuria and the fighting in Shanghai in 1931 created a crisis in China that made the continued policy of one party's monopoly of government unpopular. As a gesture of conciliation to the public opinion that urged national unity and resistance to Japan, the Kuomintang's highest organ resolved to establish a people's representative council in 1933 known as Kuo-min tsan-cheng-hui.[1] The resolution was supposedly also taken as a further step in the direction of Sun Yat-sen's theory of political tutelage.

But the Party's CEC failed to implement the resolution in the following year. The idea of Kuo-min tsan-cheng-hui was allowed to rest when it decided to call a national party congress to consider whether to create a national assembly without regard to the details of the tutelage program. The Fifth Party Congress met in November 1935 and resolved to call the National Assembly in the following year to bring to an end the work of tutelage.[2] As it happened, this proposed National Assembly which had received no support from the non-Kuomintang elements never had a chance to meet. The war broke out before the completion of the election process of its membership.

The eventual establishment of the People's Political Council as a wartime representative body in 1938 bore no connection with its namesake originally planned six years previously. It was created entirely out of the necessity of circumstances.

In the early 1930s Japan's encroachment on Inner Mongolia and North China following her aggression in Manchuria stimulated a powerful surge of anti-Japanese sentiment among the most active segments of the Chinese society—the intellectuals, the students, and the news media. Incessant anti-Japanese demonstrations were held by the students. Many merchants and workers responded to the patriotic call by boycotting the sale, purchase, and transportation of Japanese goods. There were differences of opinion even among the Kuomintang (KMT) leaders regarding the proper policy to meet the Japanese challenge. But both Chiang Kai-shek, the military strongman in the Nanking Government, and Wang Ching-wei, who served as President of the Executive Yuan from January 1932 to November 1935, insisted that armed resistance to Japan must be postponed until the internal Communist rebellion was suppressed and China's military power sufficiently strengthened.

A selected group of Chiang's trusted supporters from among the Whampoa graduates were busy trying to indoctrinate the nation with totalitarian ideology in their Blue Shirt Movement to "attain the goals of re-igniting the revolutionary spirit within the Kuomintang," and to create a rejuvenated state under the absolute control of the Leader.[3] Almost at the same time, the New Life Movement was inaugurated to facilitate the militarization of the Chinese society, to promote personal hygiene and to regenerate the moral life of the Chinese people.[4] Both movements, however, failed to reach the population mainly because of their neglect of social and economic welfare and their curbing of overt anti-Japanese expressions. Expectedly, Nanking's policy in those years produced frustration and dissatisfaction in the people, while the clamor of the hard-pressed Chinese Communist Party (CCP) for an end of the civil war and the formation of an anti-Japanese front appealed strongly to popular sentiments. The CCP's anti-Japanese propaganda affected especially the rank and file of the Tungpei Army ringed around the new Communist base area in northern Shensi. In December 1936, the dramatic episode of the Sian Incident took place. It abruptly ended the "Bandit Extermination Campaigns" and laid the groundwork for an anti-Japanese united front including the Communists.

Even before the Sian Incident there were signs pointing to the toughening of Nanking's stand vis-à-vis Japan, reflecting perhaps Chiang's increased sense of confidence in achieving internal unity. This shift in government policy was warmly received by the aroused public opinion. It explains the nation's great concern with Chiang's safety during the Sian kidnapping and the immense popularity Chiang enjoyed in the years between 1936 and 1939.

As a further step in promoting national unity, the Generalissimo invited prominent public figures to a series of informal meetings at the summer resort at Lushan for exchange of views on national problems. The Lushan talks of June-July 1937 were the first sign of political reconciliation between the ruling party and non-KMT elements in China which resulted in a tentative agreement to broaden the base of the National Government.

When fighting broke out in Shanghai in August following the Lukouchiao Incident, there was an urgent need for greater national unity and the wholehearted support of the populace. The anti-Japanese united front was finalized following the conclusion of a formal agreement with the CCP in September, the pledges of allegiance by various provincial military leaders, and an exchange of letters with the representatives of two other minor parties, the China Youth Party and the National Socialist Party, in the spring of 1938.[5] At the same time, an Advisory Council under the Supreme National Defense Conference was created in Nanking for the purpose of giving advice to the government on policy for furthering the cause of the war. The majority of its twenty-four members were leaders of other parties and prominent public figures.[6]

Although the creation of the Advisory Council helped to promote national unity, its official nature and the extremely limited power and membership could not represent a united front. Many people pressed the government to expand or reorganize the Council to include more delegates from all segments of the society. The government agreed in principle to such demands and proceeded to negotiate with the leaders of other parties and groups on this matter. The negotiations, however, were delayed by the rapidly deteriorating war situation in the lower Yangtze region, and reached a conclusion only in the spring of 1938 when the Government found a temporary respite in Wuhan. It was agreed that the name of the council was to be changed; its functions and power expanded; its membership enlarged to include both those "elected" by the provinces and those appointed by the Central Executive Committee of the Kuomintang.[7] This agreement was included as an item in the agenda of the KMT's Extraordinary National Party Congress convened in March-April 1938. It was this Congress that resolved to transform the Advisory Council into the People's Political Council as the permanent, highest, representative body of the people in wartime.[8] The resolutions of the Extraordinary Congress were confirmed by the Party's CEC which met in the same month to draft and promulgate an organic law and prepare a preliminary membership list for the PPC.[9]

The resolutions adopted by the Extraordinary Congress and the CEC in the spring of 1938 marked the culmination of the liberal trend in the Kuomintang policy. This was clearly precipitated by the military and international situation. After eight months of fighting, China suffered severe military reverse. Her best army units were badly mauled in the defense of Shanghai. She had lost all important cities in north China and the Yangtze delta to the Japanese. The much expected intervention or mediation by Western powers failed to materialize. China was isolated except for some limited aid from the Soviet Union who had otherwise scrupulously followed her policy of neutrality in the Sino-Japanese war. The gloomy outlook required the National Government to seek whatever support it could get from the people, therefore the resultant liberal internal policy.

II

Power and Membership of the PPC

When the PPC met in its first session in July 1938, the general atmosphere was quite favorable to its growth into a "wartime parliament."

In their addresses delivered to the PPC during its opening session, both Wang Ching-wei, who served as its Speaker, and Chiang Kai-shek, the country's highest military commander, had expressed their wishes to see the PPC laying a foundation for a democratic government in China.[10] The Council, from the outset, was given the power to approve the government's important policy plans put forth to it; the power to make proposals to the government; and the power to hear government reports and to put interpellations to the government. Later on, the PPC's power was further extended to include the right to organize investigating committees when requested by the government and the right to examine the government budget.[11] If all these powers were to be unobstructively exercised by the Council, the PPC could indeed develop into a full-fledged parliament. But in practice the power of the PPC was under a number of explicit and implicit limitations, and its future role was left largely to the discretion of the highest authority in the wartime government.

First, the Council did not enjoy the status of a representative body with the power of legislation. That power was exercised by the Legislative Yuan, another contemporaneous organ of the government. The proposals and resolutions passed at the Council were not in the form of bills with binding power. They were treated by the government merely as recommendations to be referred to various departments for consideration. Their adoption was left solely at the will of respective government ministers or commissioners.

Second, the government was free to interpret what were "important policy plans" and what were not; therefore it was not under explicit obligation to put forth its policy decisions for the approval of the Council. Moreover, the Chairman of the Supreme National Defense Conference was given the emergency power to issue decrees which would have the same effect as the PPC-approved policy plans.[12]

Third, the investigation committee of the PPC did not enjoy the same status and power as parliamentary investigation committees, and they were formed only at the request of the government. The result of the investigation was first reported to the Council, and then made into recommendations to the government. Again it was left to the discretion of the government whether to implement the PPC recommendations.

Fourth, the right of the PPC to examine government budgets was nothing more than an attractive promise with little significance. This power was added to the PPC as late as the Fourth Council in the summer of 1945, when the war was approaching its end. The Council was given only "the right to examine" the government's budget proposal, not "the power to change" it. Moreover, China's wartime budgetary procedure was so complicated and irregular as to render it ineffective. In the end, the national budget was always arbitrarily fixed by the highest government authority, without being hindered by any other source.

Fifth, although stipulated in its organic law to have quarterly sessions, the PPC in practice met just twice a year during 1938-1941, and only once a year after 1941. Until 1944, each of the sessions lasted only ten days. The infrequent sessions of short duration were another weakness which severely retarded its evolution into a parliamentary institution. The Council never had sufficient time to deliberate on all items on the agenda, and most of the proposals were rushed through the sessions without ample discussions.[13]

In summary, of all the powers designated to the PPC only the power of hearing reports, of interpellation, and of investigation carried any weight. The tasks that the PPC performed with varying degrees of success came mainly through its exercise of these powers. Interestingly, the power to hear reports from the government and to question the reports had a rather obscure beginning because the PPC Organic Law did not stipulate explicitly the nature and the scope of this power. But, probably due to this obscurity, the Councillors were able to take full advantage of it. Like officials liable to impeachment by the censors in imperial China, the government ministers and commissioners were made more responsible by the fact that they were susceptible to "public opinion" as expressed by the Councillors. It would be a great "loss of face" if a minister came under fire at the PPC and the criticism found its way to the news media.

Aside from the powers officially designated to it, the PPC also played a not unimportant role as a mediator to try to keep the wartime KMT-CCP alliance alive. The Council was a meeting ground for people from different backgrounds and political persuasions. In the PPC the members of the minor parties and the "independents" were often the most vocal when discussing issues of political nature. For common interest and better coordination, they decided to join force in 1939 in the creation of the United League for National Construction which was the predecessor of the Democratic League, a major third voice in wartime China. With the deterioration of relations between the KMT-dominated government and the CCP, the League increasingly took upon itself the role of a mediator.[14] Since many members of the League were PPC Councillors, the PPC became indirectly involved in this task and received tacit recognition from both sides in the conflict to serve as a forum of mediation.

During its nine-year existence, the PPC had thirteen sessions divided into four councils. The total membership of the PPC increased from 200 during the 1st Council to 362 in the final session of the 4th Council. The term of membership was set for one year, but subject to extension when deemed necessary by the government. Officials of the government could not hold membership in the PPC, but this restriction did not apply to the presiding officers of the Council.[15] As it stood during the 1st Council, eighty-eight members were chosen from the provinces and municipalities. They were the so-called "elected" category by geographical divisions. Actually, since most of the wartime provincial governments and assemblies were dominated by the Kuomintang, the "elected" Councillors turned out to be largely KMT members. Six members each were to represent the two special regions of Mongolia and Tibet, and the overseas Chinese communities. They were nominated by the respective government agencies in charge of their affairs, and the final selection was made by the Party's CEC. Again, most of those chosen from these two categories were KMT members.[16]

The fourth category consisted of 100 appointed members, fully half of the PPC membership in the first session. They were chosen from among "prominent people active in political, economic, cultural and educational affairs." In theory, the Supreme National Defense Conference was to make the nomination and the Party's CEC, the final selection. But in practice the choice of members in this category was subject to negotiations and bargaining between the KMT authorities and leaders of other political and professional groups prior to the convocation of the PPC. Probably due to the national crisis in early 1938, the government leaders made a conscientious effort to broaden their base of support, and became willing to compromise on the issue of PPC representation. Each political and professional group was actually assigned a quota. It was up to these groups to decide on their own candidates within the designated quota, and to submit the lists to the Kuomintang CEC for publication. The government also reserved a fair representation in this category to independent public figures and professional people who had no party affiliation.[17]

As a result of this arrangement, possibly over half of the 200 members of the 1st Council did not belong to the KMT. Virtually all political parties and interest groups were represented. There were delegates of the CCP, the China Youth Party, the National Socialist Party, the Third Party, the National Salvation Association, the Vocational Educational Society, and the Rural Reconstruction Association, etc. A large number of non-KMT Councillors were known as "independents"—not affiliated with any political group. By professional division they included successful lawyers, bankers, businessmen; noted scholars, educators, journalists, church leaders; retired senior politicians and gentry leaders of Szechwan. The membership presented an impressive list of prominent public figures outside of the National Government. In the words of the PPC's first Secretary-General, "The Council can really speak for almost all the articulate groups and regional interests of the nation."[18]

In spite of the heterogeneous background and diverse political persuasions, the non-KMT and non-CCP Councillors shared a certain broad common interest. First, they all supported the government's policy of all-out war of resistance against Japan and were therefore concerned with any development which might jeopardize or obstruct the nation's war efforts. Secondly, although conceding the necessity of the leadership of Chiang Kai-shek and the KMT during the war, they preferred an open democratic form of government to that of one party's monopoly of political power. They were opposed to arbitrary infringement on the civil liberties of the people. In short, they favored political liberalism and desired real unity in the country. They were fully prepared to support the National Government as long as it upheld their aspirations. Real or apparent, they tended to look upon themselves as representing the politically uncommitted "silent majority" in wartime China.

III

PPC and Wartime Unity

Of all interests shown and efforts made by the PPC Councillors during the war, nothing was more important than the task of holding the nation together in this life-or-death struggle against the vicious invader. The Japanese design, following the outbreak of the war, was to "crush the Chinese in three months, and they will sue for peace."[19] China could then be induced to cooperate with Japan and Manchukuo in the name of pan-Asianism and anti-Communism. When this expectation did not come, Tokyo was prepared to increase military pressure on China and to launch a simultaneous "peace offensive" to bring the "China Incident" to an end. The fact that the Nationalist unification was brought about by the inclusion into its ranks of the residue of warlordism rendered the Chinese government seemingly vulnerable to Japan's tactics. Furthermore, there were a remnant number of politicians and militarists of the old school who were left out of Nanking's power structure and were therefore prone to Japanese persuasion for collaboration. Even among the Kuomintang leaders the policy of an all-out war of resistance against Japan was not accepted with the same degree of determination.

During the first years of the war, the most immediate concerns of the PPC were to solicit support for the government, to strengthen the people's will of resistance, and to help prevent defections of Chinese troops and politicians to the enemy camp as well as the expansion of the influence of existing puppet regimes in China. The puppet regimes created by the Japanese military authorities in north and central China in the early stage of the war had little success in winning the cooperation of the populace. Only the Inner Mongolian regime under Teh

Wang achieved some degree of stability and prestige because of the greater autonomy it enjoyed and the attraction of pan-Mongolism to the ethnic Mongols in the region.[20]

Some Japanese leaders then toyed with the idea of either seeking a peace settlement with the National Government or securing a more prestigious Chinese to head a "united" regime in China which could show some resemblance of independence and yet at the same time would be willing to cooperate fully with Japan. Their peace overture to Chiang in the form of German mediation failed to go through. By the summer of 1938, both Wu Pei-fu, the noted former Peiyang warlord, and Tang Shao-i, the senior diplomat-statesman who had served as the first premier of the Chinese Republic, were approached by Japanese agents as possible candidates to head a government separate from Chungking. But for various reasons, both attempts failed to carry through in the latter part of the year.[21]

When the PPC met at Wuhan in July 1938, the existing puppet regimes in China had obviously failed to stir up any excitement in the Chinese political scene, and did little to conciliate the people. Japan's approaches to Wu and Tang were still veiled in a thick mist. To show their strong support to the National Government, the Councillors issued a joint manifesto to condemn the puppet leaders as traitors to their country and tools of Japanese aggression. The manifesto defended China's struggle as a just war made solely in self-defense and accused Japan of spreading baseless slanders and rumors about the imminent "sovietization" of China. It warned Japan that all China had rallied to the National Government under the leadership of Chiang Kai-shek, and that the war was to continue as long as China's sovereignty and territorial integrity were violated by the invader.[22] Until this time, in spite of serious military setback, China's internal unity was not much affected.

The first real test of China's wartime unity came at the end of 1938 in the form of an open demand for a peace settlement with Japan made by the number-two ranking leader in the KMT hierarchy, Wang Ching-wei. Earlier, Japan had made public a program of a "New Order in East Asia" based on "a tripartite relationship of mutual aid and coordination between Japan, Manchukuo, and China in political, economic, cultural and other fields." Prime Minister Konoe Fumimaro also announced a new peace policy toward China based on the twin principles of close economic cooperation between the two countries and a joint effort to combat Communism. This new policy showed some moderation in not demanding territorial concession and war indemnity from China. Possessed with the prior knowledge of Konoe's intended public statement and obviously believing Konoe's sincerity, Wang Ching-wei suddenly left Chungking and flew to Hanoi on December 21st. A week later, he sent a circular telegram to Chinese government leaders from his undisclosed residence in Hanoi urging the Chinese government to accept the latest Japanese proposal as a basis for negotiation leading to the restoration of peace in China.[23]

The Government was caught unprepared by this sudden turn of events, and many people were stunned by the news. Because of his position as the Speaker of the PPC and a certain prestige and popularity he enjoyed as an eloquent orator and capable leader in the Council, Wang's surprise action created a furor among the PPC Councillors. When the third session of the PPC opened in February 1939, several Councillors questioned the new Speaker, Chiang Kai-shek, about this matter. But without knowing Wang's real intention, even the Chungking Government could not do much. Wang was dismissed from all official posts he held, and expelled from the Party. Chiang issued a statement denouncing the Konoe proposal as a smokescreen for the Japanese design to dominate China. The strongest action the PPC could take at this moment was to pass a resolution in support of Chiang's statement, and to express the Councillors' strong objection to Wang's action.[24] Although the normal functions of the Council were not hampered by this development, because only three Councillors were found connected with Wang's move and were ultimately expelled from the Council, the mere fact that Wang served as its Speaker until his defection must have embarrassed the Councillors. For the next few months the PPC Vice-Speaker, Chang Po-ling, made a deliberate effort in his public speeches to dissociate the PPC policies from Wang's views and to clarify any misconception that the public might have had on this point.[25]

A more serious concern of the PPC was the damaging effect Wang's action might have had on China's internal unity and war effort. Fortunately for Chungking, none of its important military leaders followed Wang and only a handful of the upper echelon of party members were won over by him. Moreover, Wang's negotiations with Japan for the creation of a new government headed by him and with a high degree of autonomy in Japanese-occupied China proved to be slow and arduous. It took the two sides fifteen months to reach a formal agreement. By then the shocking effect of Wang's desertion had largely disappeared. The government at Chungking showed no sign of collapse as had been anticipated by some Japanese leaders. Even the expected desertion of some regional militarists in south China failed to materialize. As soon as Wang's real intention was made known, the PPC condemned him and his followers as traitors and called upon the soldiers and people of China to overthrow the puppet Nanking regime and to resist Japanese aggression to the last.[26] The Council never wavered in its support of the policy of continued resistance to Japan for the preservation of China's sovereignty and independence as against those who were willing to compromise this principle to buy peace.

Behind this resolute stand taken by the National Government and the PPC there was, nevertheless, visible distress and anxiety in unoccupied China. Aside from the precarious isolation and economic hardship resulting from three years' exhausting war, Wang's collaboration with Japan cast a shadow over the political future of Chungking because his action conferred a certain legitimacy upon the collaboration movement. The creation of a rival KMT regime at Nanking, the seat of the original National Government, which adopted the policy of anti-Communism, anti-Western imperialism, and close cooperation with Japan as an outgrowth of pan-Asianism succeeded in confusing the people and in blurring the image of the KMT-led Chungking Government. It deepened the CCP's distrust and suspicion of the KMT and gave additional ammunition to the Communist campaign to win the people's allegiance because the Communists could now convince the masses that they were more patriotic and nationalistic than the Kuomintang. The removal of Wang and his followers from the National Government resulted in the further concentration of power into fewer hands and seemed to have set in motion a more conservative trend in the government, which in turn affected the Government's relations with the CCP and other parties and groups in the PPC.

Even before the storm of Wang's defection calmed down, China's precarious wartime unity was threatened by another more ominous development. An issue of far greater consequence to China's future was the relationship between the KMT-led National Government and the CCP. Earlier, it was the Japanese threat that necessitated the two rival parties to abandon the enmity against each other. This entente was soon transformed into an anti-Japanese united front following the outbreak of the war. The CCP, in its declaration of September 22, 1937, pledged to abandon its policy of armed revolt and sovietization, to abolish the Central Soviet Government and the Red Army and to abide by the Three Peoples' Principles and a Common Program for the Anti-Japanese National United Front.[27] The KMT reciprocated with the relaxation of its internal political control and allowed greater freedom of speech, assembly, and the press. This liberal philosophy was written into the Program of Armed Resistance and National Reconstruction adopted in April 1938 and remained, in theory, in force throughout the war.[28] At least until the end of 1938, this liberal policy was generally upheld.

But under the facade of apparent accord lay seeds of their potential conflict. The united front formed in 1937 was, to a large extent, a more delicate one than the earlier experience of 1924-1927. First, this collaboration was much more limited in scope. The CCP members never joined the KMT as they did in 1924, and none of them was appointed to central government posts of any importance. The Red Army, although it was nominally reorganized and put under the Government's command, maintained its independence and was never integrated into the Central Armies. With the bitter memory of the previous decade, neither side could really trust the other.

The second and a more serious difficulty in this collaboration was the sharp ideological differences, and the diverse interpretations of the war-time united front. In its national policies the KMT of 1937 was generally more conservative than it had been during the first united front. The KMT leaders, after being in power for a decade, were still determined to maintain the Party's dominant position in the country and were not yet ready to share the political power with other parties. The formation of the wartime united front was interpreted as a nationwide consensus for the leadership of the KMT in the national exigency created by the war. Therefore, it was only natural for the National Government to demand wholehearted support and obedience from all other parties and groups.[29] The CCP, on the other hand, considered the wartime united front a necessary strategic retreat, not an abandonment of the Party's goals, nor a surrender of its own political, social, and economic pro-grams. The Communist leaders were equally determined to maintain their party's independence and the freedom of action of their armed forces.[30]

The cooperation between the two parties and the prevailing spirit of solidarity were necessitated by the onslaught of the superior Japanese war machine which threatened the very survival of China as an inde-pendent country in the first two years of the war. But when Japan turned to seek a political settlement in China after 1938, the war gradually moved toward a stalemate, and there were all indications that it would become a long, protracted struggle with no end in sight. Such a gloomy prospect boded ill for the National Government. It had sustained the brunt of the war in this first stage by losing the best-equipped army units and the most advanced regions of the country to the enemy. Its power was much weakened, and its territories reduced.

On the other hand, the Chinese Communists suffered very limited loss in the same period. Their ideology gave them a cohesiveness which the more diffuse KMT lacked; and this, combined with superior organization and the experience of guerrilla warfare learned in the previous decade, made them much more capable of undertaking a protracted struggle with a superior enemy. Their base area in the remote and desolate northern Shensi was hardly worthy to be a main target of Japanese offensive. Taking advantage of the thinness of the Japanese occupation in China, the CCP sent troops and cadres in small groups to infiltrate the countryside behind the enemy lines, and succeeded in getting support from an increasingly aroused peasant populace. The CCP's influence expanded most rapidly in north China where the KMT was the weakest. But even in central China the KMT found it difficult to compete with the

Communists. Frictions developed in which the KMT forces often were the victims. A keen observer put the change persuasively: ". . . Left without a positive policy, the KMT adopted a negative one: to restrict as much as possible the areas of CCP control, and to suppress Communist activities in areas controlled by itself."[31] This led inevitably to antagonism and conflict between them.

Beginning in 1939, military clashes between the two sides happened in Shantung, Hopei, Honan and Shansi provinces. Chungking countered the Communist expansion by re-enforcing a military blockade along the southern and western edge of the Communist Shen-Kan-Ning Border Region. Matters became serious enough for the Generalissimo to call a meeting with Chou En-lai and Yeh Chien-ying, the CCP representatives in Chungking, to seek an end to the clashes.[32] Since neither side was willing to give in, the direct talks dragged on for months without a settlement. The situation deteriorated further in the following year, the year in which the CCP made notable gains in north and central China mainly at the expense of KMT-controlled areas.

It was at this time the PPC Councillors became fully aware of the grave situation, and those who belonged to the minor parties and groups in the PPC were prompted to action in the interests of national unity. The initiative was taken by Councillor Liang Shu-ming whose personal interest and experience in rural educational works in Shantung led him to make an extensive tour of the guerrilla regions in north China during the spring and summer of 1939. Liang became convinced, at the end of his tour, that the united front was in jeopardy. He began immediately to explore the possibility of a political organization in the PPC that could assist in preserving national unity. Largely out of his effort, the United National Construction League was formed in November which had received the Government's approval and had an initial membership of more than thirty. All of them were drawn from the minor parties and independents in the PPC.

The League soon found itself in the position to offer mediation between the KMT and the CCP because fresh armed clashes developed in Hopei in the spring of 1940. Liang Shu-ming, on behalf of the League, proposed to the PPC that the KMT-CCP differences be settled within the PPC, and that a special committee be set up in the PPC for the purpose of regulating inter-party relations. The majority of the Councillors agreed that the conflict should not be allowed to continue and that the PPC should be chosen as the forum for both sides to put forth and to exchange their views. After studying Liang's and a few other similar proposals, the PPC, during its fifth session, passed a resolution calling for the formation of this special committee and asking the Speaker to appoint certain Councillors to it.[33] The inter-party special committee so formed in the PPC had eleven members who were entrusted with the responsibility of finding a formula to end the conflict. After much deliberation, the committee made a number of recommendations to the Government designed to supplement the direct KMT-CCP negotiations then proceeding, and to bring about a speedy settlement.

The PPC committee's effort seemed to have made some progress in late 1940 when an understanding to re-deploy Communist military units was said to be reached between the two sides. It would have let the Communists move their Eighth Route Army to the area north of the Yellow River, and would have permitted the transferral of their New Fourth Army to areas north of the Yangtze. However, before these military arrangements could be satisfactorily implemented, the "New Fourth Army Incident" occurred in January 1941, which aggravated the KMT-CCP relations to the brink of complete break. Whatever the immediate causes of this complicated and controversial incident were, the Communists suffered a crushing defeat, and the subsequent activities of the weakened New Fourth Army were largely confined to the north of the Yangtze.[34]

Political pressure and the curtailment of civil liberty accompanied the increasing fury of internal military clashes. Government censorship was more rigidly imposed upon all publications, and the "special service police" greatly expanded their operations to suppress not only the Communist-suspects, but anyone who openly criticized the policies of the Government. All these were ominous signs to a country still engaged in a desperate struggle for survival and which needed unity and support from the people more than anything else. Opinions of the news media showed deep concern with these trends. Overseas Chinese leaders and even the press of friendly foreign powers advised the Chinese Government to use restraint and tolerance in dealing with the problem of internal political differences and criticism.[35] These pressures, together with the grave outlook of the international situation in early 1941, convinced the leaders of the two sides that it was foolish to push the matter any further. An open civil war in China was avoided at the last minute, and yet the KMT-CCP relations were so strained that great efforts had to be made to maintain even a semblance of a united front.

The PPC viewed this development with particular alarm. The League members in the PPC and many other independents who were personal acquaintances of leaders of the two major parties proceeded immediately to mediate. The Second Council was scheduled to meet on March 1st. There was an imminent threat of the Communist boycott of the Council meetings. The CCP demanded harsh guarantees for the Communist Councillors' further attendance at the PPC meetings which were unlikely to be acceptable to the Government.[36] The mediators sent urgent appeals to both sides for moderation, and they were unanimous in their wish to see the continued CCP participation in the Council. When the Communist Councillors failed to turn up in the meetings, the PPC passed a resolution with unanimous support stating that the attendance of the PPC should not be made conditional by any Councillor, and that the CCP Councillors be urged to return to the PPC for the sake of national unity.[37] The Council's effort, coupled with the strong public concern over the prospect of unity, succeeded in cooling down the heated feelings on both sides. Chiang Kai-shek adopted a conciliatory stand when he stated in his speech delivered to the PPC on March 6th:[38]

> . . . I need scarcely assert that our Government is solely concerned with leading the nation against the Japanese invaders and extirpating the traitors, and is utterly without any notion of again taking up arms to "suppress the Communists." It desires never again to hear of that ill-omened term which now has a place only in Chinese history . . .

He further asserted that the Government would be ready to follow the PPC's advice in the settlement of all outstanding questions with the Communists. The CCP also retreated from its unyielding position by sending Councillor Tung Pi-wu back to the PPC meetings during the second session in November. Tung remained in attendance throughout the Third Council, sometimes accompanied by Teng Ying-chao. Tung was always elected to the Recess Committee, even during the absence of the Communists from the PPC.

Although the mediation of the PPC Councillors failed to bring about a quick settlement between the two parties, it made it possible for the antagonists to resume direct talks. Since the immediate issue involved was of military nature, the talks were conducted more frequently by professional military men on both sides. The Government was represented by Defense Minister Ho Ying-chin; the CCP, by Yeh Chien-ying and later Lin Piao.[39] The talks were often bogged down on specific issues such as the disposition, size and command of the Communist troops or the status of Communist-dominated regional governments, and little real progress was made during the next two years. Nevertheless, no serious military clashes between the two sides were reported in the rest of 1941 or in 1942. Only by the spring of 1943, when the Communists re-established guerrilla bases in north China after their temporary setback during the Japanese "mopping-up campaigns" of the previous year, did the KMT-CCP military relations become grave again.

In their effort to preserve the united front in 1941, the PPC mediators experienced great limitations of their influence. They attributed this impotence to the lack of organizational unity among themselves. Moreover, they felt that the autocratic and repressive trend of the ruling party could best be checked if they exerted a collective voice to put pressure on the government leaders. So they decided to expand the League to include all minor parties and groups in the PPC. The Federation of Chinese Democratic Parties was born in the spring of 1941. It adopted a program urging the end of one-party rule and the democratization of the National Government. Its members began to view themselves as part of an independent political force standing between the KMT and the CCP.[40]

In contrast to its earlier favorable attitude toward the League, the Government reacted to the birth of the Federation with great hostility. The KMT leaders openly criticized the attitude of the minor parties, and the Federation's activities were often obstructed by the Government. To seek a more favorable surrounding for free expression of opinions, the Federation established a propaganda center in Hong Kong and began the publication of the newspaper *Kuang-ming* (The Light) in September. When Hong Kong was overrun by the Japanese army, its personnel returned to southwest China and began to publish a journal *Min-hsien* (The People's Tribune) in Chungking. Yet despite this independence of action, the Federation continued to function mainly within the PPC and its main task continued to be the mediation between the Government and the Communists.[41]

To show its displeasure with the Federation, the KMT effected a re-apportionment of the PPC membership. Beginning from the Third Council in October 1942, the elected membership increased from ninety to 164, while the appointed category was reduced from 138 to sixty. The Government claimed that it had acted for the sake of "strengthening the democratic nature of the Council."[42] But in reality it was a means to tighten the rein on the future meetings of the PPC. Some of the outspoken critics of the Government were dropped from the Council while the KMT achieved a solid majority by this re-apportionment. Without a comparable democratization in the electoral procedure in the provinces, the re-apportionment of 1942 was indeed a setback to the PPC as a potentially viable representative body of the wartime government.

In the next two and a half years, it was largely the tactless attitude and policies of the KMT leaders that further alienated the majority of Federation members and drove them increasingly to seek protection and patronage from some regional military leaders in southwest China, as well as closer coordination with and support of the CCP. The Communists had nothing to lose in improving their relations with the Federation. By joining camp with the minor parties in criticizing the Government of being undemocratic and incompetent, the CCP increased its popularity without doing any harm to its own organization and power.

In the mediation effort members of the Federation in the PPC did their best to press both sides for a political settlement. They succeeded in September 1943 in bringing Chiang Kai-shek and the KMT's CEC to such a view when both conceded publicly that "the Chinese Communist problem is a purely political problem and should be solved by political means."[43] It is remarkable to note that such a statement was made in spite of fresh outbreaks reported in the previous months. When the second session of the Third Council opened later in the same month, the PPC endorsed the ruling party's resolution of seeking political settlement with the Communists, and urged the CCP to uphold the same principle for the sake of national unity.[44] Early in 1944 preliminary arrangements were made for a formal KMT-CCP negotiation which opened in May. This phase of the wartime KMT-CCP negotiations was the best known to the outside because its progress was fully reported to the following session of the PPC by representatives of both sides. It was a seeming victory for the PPC to be recognized by both parties as a proper place to present their cases, a development that had long been desired by the Council.

As for the talk itself, a wide gulf still existed between the two sides regarding the size and disposition of the Communist units, the relationship between Communist-controlled regional governments and Chungking, and problems relating to civil liberties and the legalization of the CCP. But the mere fact that the two parties were willing to settle their differences at the conference table instead of in the battleground, coupled with the frankness and sincerity demonstrated by the representatives in their reports, gave encouragement to the PPC that a peaceful final solution of the problem might be achieved.[45] Leaders of the Federation, however, warned the two sides that a settlement must be quickly reached before the end of the war. They argued that once the war ended, the pressure for national unity would be much weakened, and the two strongly armed adversaries would have less incentive to come to a peaceful general settlement.[46]

They decided also to create a new, more effective political organization to extend their influence and activities outside of the PPC. On October 10th, the formation of a full-fledged political party, the China Democratic League, was announced. The basic aims of the League remained the same as those of the Federation, only the goals were now more clearly announced to the general public, and the League definitely thought of itself as the "Third Force" between the KMT and the CCP, the spokesman for a large number of "uncommitted" in China. Its membership was on an individual basis and included many political activists both inside and outside of the PPC. Since many of its members were intellectuals engaged in teaching and writing, the League sponsored a number of newspapers and periodicals to publicize its cause. As a result, it enjoyed influence out of proportion to its size and even attracted the close attention of foreign governments.[47]

After having heard the reports of the early talks, the PPC Presidium, which had replaced the Speaker and the Vice-Speaker since the Second Council in 1941, suggested that a Yenan Observation Team be formed to help promote mutual understanding and bring about a speedy settlement, and that some politically neutral Councillors be chosen to serve in the Team.[48] This suggestion was approved in the PPC, but the Team's visit to Yenan was postponed due to the rapid progress of a new development—the American mediation of the same problem.

The effort of the United States to end the KMT-CCP conflict and to bring internal peace to China during 1944-1946 is a well-documented and an amply studied subject which needs no recount here. In short, the presence of General Patrick J. Hurley in Chungking in the fall of 1944, with the backing of the prestige of the United States and a special mission to bring unity and internal peace to China, made unnecessary further action by the PPC in this direction at that particular time. But still the PPC's effort during the following year complemented that of the American endeavor.

When the Hurley Mission ran into some difficulty and the KMT-CCP talks reached an impasse in the early spring of 1945, a PPC group, known as the Committee of Six, which included several members of the original Observation Team formed in 1944, was urged by the Government to approach the Communists for the resumption of talks. This group flew to Yenan on July 1st and brought back the new CCP proposal, thus clearing the way for a top-level talk in Chungking between the two parties shortly after the Japanese surrender.[49] The top-level talk and subsequent discussions between the two sides produced an agreement to hold a Political Consultative Conference. This Conference was finally convened on January 10, 1946. Since it was to be attended by leaders of various parties and was aimed at the settlement of all outstanding political issues in the country, it represented a triumph for the PPC peace promoters and was regarded as a high water mark of post-war KMT-CCP relations.

A close study of the Political Consultative Conference is beyond the scope of this article, but it is extremely interesting to note a few facts pointing to the close affinity between the Conference and the PPC. First of all, the major items on the agenda of the Conference were mostly unresolved problems that had been much discussed in the PPC. Particularly on the questions of the national assembly and the constitution, the draft documents used for deliberation in the Conference were the products of the PPC. Furthermore, of the thirty-eight delegates that attended the Conference, twenty-two were PPC Councillors. The remaining included seven who were high government officials and could not have qualified themselves as PPC Councillors. Therefore, to some extent the Political Consultative Conference of 1946 could be considered as an extraordinary committee of the PPC created to meet the urgent task of arranging a peace settlement between the Government and the Chinese Communist Party.[50]

IV

PPC and the Mobilization of Manpower and Resources

An issue of almost equal importance to that of national unity for wartime China was how best to mobilize the country's manpower and economic resources to sustain the war. The devastating impact of the war was the basic cause of China's economic difficulty after 1938. Japan's occupation of the most advanced part of China produced economic dislocation, material shortage, and high inflation in unoccupied China. Despite great efforts made by the Chinese War Production Board to salvage industrial facilities from the lower Yangtze valley and to boost industrial production in the interior, the wartime industry of unoccupied China was faced with the nearly insurmountable problems of the lack of heavy industrial base, the scarcity of raw materials, the primitive condition of transportation, and the unstable prices. Foreign imports through aid and trade were slow in coming and became virtually impossible with the tightening of the Japanese blockade. The total isolation and the scarcity of industrial products, combined with the ever-increasing government military expenditures, resulted in a rapid rise in commodity prices. The situation was further aggravated both by a crop failure in west China in 1940, which resulted in widespread hoarding and speculation in food, and by the irresponsible monetary policies of the wartime government.[51] Within four years the cost of living in unoccupied China multiplied a phenomenal one hundred times.

The hardest hit by the material shortage and hyper-inflation were the salaried personnel, particularly the military, the government officials, and the school teachers, because their income fell far behind the rising cost of living. In the army, while the higher officers could resort to dishonest irregular practices as a means of support, the common soldiers and low-ranking officers had to survive on whatever meager food rations and cash allowances they received. Many soldiers were insufficiently clothed, undernourished, and half-starved, conditions that nurtured a high rate of desertion and mortality, and seriously affected the army's morale, discipline, and efficiency. To compensate for the misery of their lives, the soldiers often turned on the civilian populace. Their looting and exploitation sometimes produced tragic consequences.[52] On the whole, the economic situation made a demoralizing and disrupting impact on the military and the National Government.

As the government's financial and economic policies failed to check the inflation and to improve the economic situation, the PPC Councillors became increasingly concerned with these problems. From 1940 on, economic and financial matters always occupied greatest attention in the deliberations of the PPC, and quantitatively the largest number of proposals made by the Councillors belonged to this category. The numerous proposals in this category could be divided into the following groups:[53]

1) Criticism of the official method of forced purchase of grain for military purpose which imposed hardship on the rural population, and suggestions for the improvement of the system and the prevention of abuses.

2) Criticism of the government's arbitrary measure of fixing prices to combat inflation. Recommendations to rationalize the approach and to treat small shop-keepers and merchants with fairness in the policy of price control.

3) Criticism of the government's monopoly of the production and sale of salt, tung oil, cotton cloth, coal, and several other minerals. The monopoly tended to kill individual incentive and efficiency in production and resulted in the decline of production as well as irregularities in management. Recommendations either to change or to modify the policy of monopoly.

4) Recommendation concerning means to promote native industry and handicraft manufacturing in unoccupied China.

5) Proposals urging the government to develop and improve the means of transportation in the southwest and the northwest.

Since the PPC had no power to supervise the implementation of its proposals, the Councillors could only pursue the issues when hearing reports from various government ministers. So the use of the power of questioning often complemented that of making proposals. Here again the majority of the recorded questions submitted during hearings after 1941 were in the areas of economy and finance. While it is almost impossible to appraise the effectiveness of every single PPC proposal, records indicate that the Council was able to have some of its recommendations implemented by the government.[54]

In general, the government seemed to be more cooperative and willing to implement PPC resolutions on financial, economic, and educational matters than military, political and administrative ones. As a rule, the government ministers of finance, economic affairs, transportation, and internal affairs were often invited to attend the meetings of two of the Council's standing committees: one on finance and economy, and the other on resources and prices. The purpose was to achieve a higher degree of cooperation between the Council and the government, and to make the PPC proposals more practical and easily acceptable to the respective government branches.

Further efforts to promote the better use of economic resources were made by the PPC in two other ways. One was the dispatch of inspection teams to study local conditions in various regions of unoccupied China to seek means for improvement. The other was the creation of special commissions designated by the government to draft plans for economic development. The Council's activities in these two areas were not limited solely to economic affairs but were concerned also with social welfare, local administration, etc. In 1938 some Councillors occasionally joined government officials or civic groups in visiting areas affected by war or famine. The purpose was to comfort the troops at the front and to bring relief funds and supplies to civilian refugees.

In February 1939 the PPC established a 29-member Commission for the Promotion of Economic Construction in Szechwan and Sikang, and organized an inspection team chosen from the Commission to investigate the local conditions of the two provinces. The Team made a three-month extensive fact-finding tour in the following spring that covered over a hundred districts (hsien). A lengthy report was submitted to the PPC by the Team upon the completion of its mission. The report listed 206 items delving into areas of local administration, military conscription, public peace, the opium problem, livelihood of the people, economic development, local education, and minority nationalities. Some problems mentioned were common to all regions but others were peculiar to certain districts. It not only pointed out the problems but discussed the ways for improvement.[55]

In all fairness the report was an excellent piece of work produced by some conscientious, dedicated Councillors. The report was well received in the PPC and highly praised by Chiang Kai-shek who was then the Speaker of the Council. It was made into a PPC proposal to the government and seemed to have received proper attention in the government for its implementation.[56]

To follow up its work, the Commission was authorized to establish a standing committee which was to meet at least once every three months, and five regional offices entrusted with the responsibility of periodic investigation of the respective regions in the two provinces. All recommendations made by the Commission were submitted to Chiang Kai-shek, who served concurrently as its chairman, the Speaker of the PPC, as well as the key leader in the KMT and the government. In this capacity the Commission became, in effect, a high advisory council to the supreme wartime leader on economic policies in the most important province in unoccupied China. Its recommendations were often accepted as a general guideline for the government's economic policies in Szechwan.[57]

Later in the same year a North China Inspection Team was created in the PPC with six members appointed by the Speaker. Its tour of Shensi, Honan, and Hupei provinces lasted from January 30 to March

17, 1940. Its mission was not only to comfort the troops and civilians in the war and famine-affected areas, but also to investigate the complex political-military situation developing in Honan and Hupei where a triangular struggle was brewing between the Central armies, the Communist units, and the newly created puppet Nanking troops. In its report submitted to the Council in April, the Team members urged the government to settle political issues with the CCP, to take immediate action to check front region smuggling, to correct the abuses of the forced purchase of grain, and to send relief to Honan where starvation was widespread.[58]

In October 1942 the Commission for the Promotion of Economic Construction in Szechwan and Sikang was reorganized and enlarged into a Commission for the Promotion of Economic Mobilization. The scope of its work was made more explicit and its responsibility was extended to cover all provinces under the control of Chungking. The main duty of the new commission was "to assist the government to enforce the National Mobilization Act and other wartime economic statutes; and to help promote the official policy of price-control in order to consolidate the basis of the economy."[59] A further change came in September 1943 when the PPC resolved, through the recommendation of Chiang Kai-shek, to establish a Commission for the Promotion of Economic Construction. This commission was to absorb and to continue the works of its predecessors and, in addition, it was entrusted with the duty "to investigate the economic conditions, and to draft plans for economic construction to be referred to the government for adoption."[60] Its works included two main areas: first, the immediate problems concerning economic mobilization; second, long-range planning for wartime and postwar economic construction. Five regional offices with enlarged personnel were set up: two in Szechwan, and one each at Sian, Kunming and Hengyang to cover the northwest, the southwest, and the central Yangtze region. During its two-year existence, the Commission made a number of recommendations to the PPC to be considered in the Council's proposals. Some of them were definitely adopted by the government.[61]

If the rural peasant population was not as hard pressed by inflation and material shortage as the town-dwellers, it suffered far worse from the effects of military and labor conscription. According to a reliable estimate, the wartime Chinese government drafted a total of 14 million men to maintain an army between 2.2 and 5.7 million during the war years.[62] Though the areas under Chungking's control had at least 50 million men of military age at any given time, China's military mobilization was inadequate because of the primitive agrarian nature of her economy and the inefficient mechanism for manpower mobilization. Serious deficiency existed in China's wartime military conscription system.

First of all, a centralized office responsible for military recruitment was not established until November 1944. Recruiting was done first by assigning a certain quota to each province, and the province in turn subdivided the quota for each district. As long as the quota was met, the National Government paid little attention to the methods employed by different recruiting authorities, which left much room for abuses. Since the conscription law allowed exemptions to those who could afford to make monetary contributions, the recruiting officials often sold exemptions at a fat profit. The result was that[63]

> . . . the burden of military service was shouldered almost exclusively by the underprivileged peasants. China could not catch the rich or afford to spare the industrially trained for military service. Her draftees were chiefly from the lowest classes, and they were often treated as military coolies.

The raw recruit was subject to all kinds of harsh treatment before he reached the assigned unit. Many recruits were tied together at night or on the march to prevent their desertion. They were seldom adequately fed, clothed, or sheltered in their temporary training camps. Medical attention was virtually non-existent. When the grossly inadequate training period was over, the recruits had to walk hundreds of miles to join their assigned units. Under such miserable conditions, the waste of manpower was tremendous. In 1943, for instance, nearly half of military recruits were lost through sickness, death, and desertion.[64] Those who survived the initial ordeal and became fresh soldiers were not much better off than before. The illiterate peasant soldier was entirely cut off from his family and community and was plunged into a war of which he had little understanding. He would suffer prolonged malnutrition and extremely meagre medical care. The Japanese troops were probably less a threat to his life than disease and epidemic. Expectedly, even in regular army units desertion remained a major problem.[65]

It was only natural that the rural population would fear and resent the system and would try their best to avoid being drafted. In areas where regional sentiment was strong there were outbreaks of armed resistance by the peasants. The sporadic revolts in Kansu and Kweichow in 1943 and the reported riots in many villages in Szechwan through the war years were largely the expression of local discontent toward conscription and tax collection.[66]

In addition to the military conscription, the rural people in China also shouldered the burden of forced labor service during the war. The conscripted labor force was never efficient, yet it was the most economical one for the government because no wage was paid except for food. Some large military construction projects used thousands of conscripted laborers for prolonged periods. The best known ones were the building of the Burma Road in 1938, which used approximately 200,000 peasant laborers for many months, the construction of strategic motor roads and airfields in southwestern provinces in 1943 and 1944 to be used for the direct bombing of the Japanese homeland by the United States Air Force.[67] It is impossible to know the exact total number of conscripted laborers used for the airfield projects, but in a single instance nearly half a million people were mobilized between January and May 1944 for the building of several B-29 bases near Chengtu.[68]

Furthermore, the rural population in areas directly affected by war and the movement of troops was constantly subject to the threat of the army's illegal use of forced labor service. The drafted peasant-coolies were used mainly as porters to carry military provisions or cooking equipment. They were usually kept for a limited time and would be released once the army unit had reached its destination. Such practice, known as "la-fu" (to seize porters), was common in the Chinese army during the war though it never received official sanction. Both the legal and illegal labor conscription inflicted great inconvenience and even terror on the populace, and the peasants looked upon it with apprehension and resentment.

Many PPC Councillors had first-hand knowledge of the working of military and labor conscription at the local level. They naturally expressed their concern over the system. During the first years of the war, the attention of the PPC focused mainly on the abuses of the system by the local authorities, while no serious criticism of the conscription law itself was made. The Councillors urged the government to supervise strictly the practice of military recruitment and to make greater efforts to educate the citizenry in their patriotic duties to defend their own country. Further concern was shown in the treatment of the families of soldiers. The Councillors advised the government to cut down red tape and enforce the regulations providing compensation to families of military personnel adequately. Criticism was also directed at the harsh treatment of new army recruits. The Councillors urged the government to modify and relax the rigid military training imposed on the raw recruits and to provide them with proper care and consideration.[69]

With the prolongation of the war the demand for manpower increased, and so did the abuses of the conscription system. In the PPC, criticism began to be aimed at the faults of the conscription law. During the first session of the Second Council in March 1941 a proposal was passed urging the abolition of the practice of making monetary contribution to buy exemption from military service.[70] In the next two sessions (November 1941 and October 1942) several proposals were made concerning ways to improve the conscription system and the welfare of the enlisted men. The abuses of labor conscription and the army's unlawful seizure of civilians and civilian property also became targets of criticism.[71]

The Council's mounting dissatisfaction with the conscription system seemed to have pressed the government to adopt the Regulations Governing Benefits to the Families of the Officers and Men at the Front in December 1941, a statute aimed to improve the living conditions of the dependents of military personnel.[72] In October 1942, a National Conference on Military Service was convened in Chungking under the auspices of the government. Its purpose was to undertake a full-scale review of the conscription system and to seek improvement. One immediate result of this conference was the promulgation on March 15, 1943, of a Revised Conscription Law.[73]

A major reform of the conscription system was finally adopted by the government with the creation of a Ministry of Conscription on November 16, 1944.[74] Thenceforth the military recruitment was made more equitable and the welfare of the recruits under training or in transfer was much improved. Although this reform in conscription was obviously linked to the military disaster following the Japanese *Ichigo* offensive in that year and was directly attributed to United States pressure, the PPC made no less a contribution by its efforts in pressing the government to look into the matter and by its constant references to the serious deficiencies in the system.

V

Constitutional Movement in the PPC

Aside from the tasks to maintain national unity and to whip up China's war efforts in the mobilization of manpower and resources, the PPC was also involved, throughout the war years, in another important political issue—a movement to bring about a democratic constitutional government. In this movement the moving force came from Councillors belonging to the minor parties and groups as well as some politically active independents in the PPC, the same heterogeneous group that played a principal role in the mediation works between the KMT and the CCP. Their interest in this area seems to have derived mainly from their educational background and the democratic orientation in their political conviction.

Although Sun Yat-sen's program for China's political reconstruction called for the realization of constitutional democracy as the final stage of development, the rule of the National Government during the Nanking decade was politically repressive. Hampered by internal dissension, challenged by the open Communist rebellion, and threatened by Japanese aggression, Nanking clung tenaciously to one-party rule of the KMT. All other political parties were banned, censorship was imposed on all publications, and civil liberty was curtailed. The Party's Fifth

Congress in 1935 had resolved to call a national assembly and elections were actually held in the following year. But without the relaxation of political control and a democratic electoral procedure, the elections of 1936-1937 were one-sided and held without wide public participation. The outbreak of the war brought drastic changes in the country's political situation. The national exigency created by the war forced the government to relax its internal political control in order to achieve maximum unity. Although censorship was retained, its application was liberalized. The country enjoyed an unprecedented freedom of speech, assembly, and the press under this liberal philosophy which was written into the Program of Armed Resistance and National Reconstruction adopted by the KMT and the government in the spring of 1938.

Under the prevailing harmonious atmosphere in the country's political scene in 1937 and 1938, the PPC's main concern was the urgency of China's war and economic dislocation. No serious discussion took place during the first three sessions concerning the constitutional problem, though proposals were made for legal protection of civil liberty and for promotion of self-government and democracy at the local and regional levels.[75] The sudden demand within the PPC for constitutional government came during its fourth session in September 1939. No fewer than seven proposals concerning constitutionalism were made by Councillors. This upsurge of constitutional movement in the Council was obviously the result of the changed military and political conditions in the country. The National Government experienced simultaneously a rapid weakening of its own strength and influence and the fast growth of the power of its principal internal rival, the CCP. Frustration increased the sense of insecurity, and the government became more suspicious and repressive. It was only natural that some PPC Councillors began to question the wisdom of continued one-party rule under the KMT, and to urge a broader participation in the wartime government through the adoption of a constitution.

Of the seven proposals introduced, one was made by the Communist Councillor, Chen Shao-yu, which demanded the recognition and legal protection of all anti-Japanese political parties in the country. It received general support from other non-KMT Councillors who had included a similar demand in their own proposals.[76] Five others were put forth by members of the minor parties and groups. They contained the following main demands:

1) The end of one-party rule by the adoption of a constitution and the creation of a national assembly.
2) The end of discrimination against members of parties other than the KMT, and the practice of forced entry into the KMT.
3) The creation of a wartime, multi-party cabinet responsible to the

PPC as a transitional organ before the establishment of a formal elective national assembly.

The most interesting was the proposal introduced by a group of KMT Councillors. It was the shortest among the seven proposals and yet was received with great enthusiasm within the Council simply because it seemed to indicate the ruling party's sudden interest in constitutionalism. In short, the proposal urged the government to carry out the resolution of the Fifth National Congress of the KMT (1935) for the convening of a national assembly and the adoption of a constitution.[77] Writing with hindsight in 1948, one critic of the KMT interpreted it as "a brilliant tactical move by the Leader of the Party himself . . . (which) would result in the further discrediting of constitutionalism," because the proposal tended to re-affirm the ruling party's determination to revive the assembly elected in 1936-1937 rather than holding new elections.[78] However, at the time when this proposal was made, few, including the critic himself, had come to such a pessimistic and negative view.[79]

These proposals drew a great deal of attention in and out of the Council. They were widely discussed and generated heated debate within the PPC committee.[80] The resolution made from these proposals was divided into two parts, each containing two articles. The first part dealt with fundamental questions: it urged the government to fix a period for the convocation of a national assembly and the adoption of a constitution. It further suggested that the Speaker of the PPC appoint a certain number of Councillors to form an Association for the Promotion of Constitutionalism to assist the government in this regard. The second part was concerned with more immediate issues such as the equal treatment of all people through the rule of law, and the improvement of the quality of administrative offices in the government.[81]

The government's reaction to these proposals was reserved if not hostile. Obviously a wide difference of opinion existed between the government leaders and the non-KMT Councillors concerning the composition of the national assembly and the timetable for its convocation. The Party's CEC in its sixth session in November 1939 had resolved to convene the national assembly in the following November. But the decision was indefinitely postponed by the standing committee of the same CEC. The issue was brought up again by the CEC in its eleventh session in 1943, and it resolved to convene it within a year following the termination of the war. Then the Party's Sixth National Congress passed a resolution in May 1945 calling for the convocation of the assembly on November 12th of the same year.[82] Such frequent change of decisions by the ruling party created confusion and caused the non-KMT Councillors to doubt the government's sincerity. What the government leaders wanted was the national assembly elected in 1936-1937 under the KMT auspices, while the representatives of other parties were adamantly opposed to it. The latter argued that since the election in 1936-1937 was one-sided and unfair, the assembly so elected could not possibly be a popular choice. Moreover, the elections had been held before the war and drastic changes had taken place during the interval. Many elected members were no longer available, and some had even become turncoats. How, they asked, could such an assembly be acceptable to the people and play a vital role in the democratization of the government?[83]

A bitter exchange between the KMT and non-KMT Councillors occurred over this issue during the first session of the Fourth Council in July 1945. Neither side was willing to make concessions. Even the special committee formed to study the problem could not arrive at a decision. It merely suggested that the government carefully consider all expressed opinions in the PPC and make the representation in the proposed assembly satisfactory to all parties concerned![84] This unresolved problem was one of the issues left to the Political Consultative Conference after the end of the war.

Another closely related question was the nature and the content of the constitution. Pursuant to the 1939 PPC resolutions, a 25-man Committee for the Promotion of Constitutionalism was appointed by the Speaker and entrusted with the duty of assisting to draft a constitution. The majority of those appointed to the committee were Councillors of minor parties or independents, including several noted jurists. Yet, from the beginning, the committee was faced with a number of difficulties. First, there were no rules laid down as procedures for the committee to follow. Moreover, the committee members resided in different cities and it was almost impossible to hold frequent meetings with the participation of all. While the opinion of individual members could be expressed through correspondence this was at best a very slow and cumbersome way for the exchange of views. The freedom of the committee was further circumscribed by the government's refusal to permit it to draft a new constitution; instead, the Draft Constitution of May 5, 1936, was to be used as a blueprint from which some deviations would be permitted.[85]

In spite of these handicaps, committee members made a sincere effort to promote constitutionalism. First of all, they sought broad popular participation in the constitutional movement in order to arouse public interest and to emphasize the need for constitutional government in China. In Chungking and several other cities, public meetings were organized to invite interested people to attend and to express their opinions.[86] More important was the committee's exhaustive evaluation of the Draft Constitution of 1936. In a ten-day meeting prior to the convening of the PPC in March 1940, the committee produced a revised draft and submitted it, together with a lengthy supplementary report, to the Council.[87] The revised draft differed from the original in one crucial aspect: the power of the executive branch of the government was reduced and limited by the expanded power given to the national assembly and its recess committee.[88] This revision obviously displeased the top KMT leaders who had been working for years to make the executive branch invulnerable. The result was the government's intentional postponement of its adoption.[89] The question was allowed to rest in the PPC for the next three years.

The decline of PPC's interest in constitutional movement in the next three years (1940-1943) was due partly to the unfavorable attitude of the government leaders and partly to the drastic changes in the domestic and international situation. In the domestic scene, the tension created by the government-CCP frictions in 1941 occupied the primary attention of the nation. All other issues were sidetracked in the PPC by this imminent threat to national unity. Moreover, international developments, notably the outbreak of the Pacific War, so altered the military outlook that the interest of the Council was temporarily occupied by military and diplomatic matters. Only when the excitement passed, and the entrance of the Allies brought no immediate relief to China, were old issues again brought to the fore.

The year 1943 marked the revival of the constitutional movement. By that time, China had been in war for six years, and the end was not yet in sight. War weariness became quite marked and the burdens of the people were further added to by the prevailing apathy and corruption of the government bureaucracy. The Allies were also dissatisfied with China's performance in the war. Increasing criticism of the Nationalist leadership in China was voiced in the American press. To soothe the dissatisfaction expressed both in domestic and foreign quarters, the government was prepared to revive the issue of the constitution and the democratization of the government. In his opening address to the second session of the Third Council in September 1943, Chiang Kai-shek announced the resolution passed by the Party's CEC which was being held simultaneously in Chungking. The resolution stipulated that the convening of the national assembly and the promulgation of the constitution should be completed within a year after the end of the war. Chiang further promised to expedite all preparatory works and urged the PPC Councillors to assist the government in this regard.[90]

Many Councillors were delighted by the announcement, but, remembering their fruitless past efforts, they responded this time in a more cautious manner. Not until the ninth meeting did the PPC promulgate the Organizational Rules of the Association to Assist in the Inauguration of Constitutionalism.[91] The Association so created differed from its predecessor of 1939-1940 in two important ways: first, its membership

(39-49) was not to be chosen exclusively from the PPC, but was to be composed of both Councillors and government leaders, with Chiang Kai-shek serving as its president; secondly, the functions of the association were now more clearly stated in its organizational rules. It was to be a purely advisory body and its proposals had no binding power on the government.[92]

During its two-year existence, the association's main task was to study the Draft Constitution of 1936. Its members were careful to suggest as little modification as possible and generally defended the Draft. It finally produced a report containing thirty-two points and submitted it to the PPC.[93] Yet even this scrupulous work aroused no genuine interest in the government. When the war ended in August 1945, many Councillors who had been engaged in this endeavor came to realize that the problem of constitution-making could never be solved in the PPC; that it must be carried on outside of the Council and must be treated as a part of the general settlement between the government and the CCP. Consequently, the association died a natural death, and its unfinished work was handed over to the Political Consultative Conference which was scheduled to open in the first month of 1946.

VI

Conclusion

To review briefly the main functions and contributions of the PPC during the war years, the most important of these were in the area of national unity. The Japanese invasion had seriously endangered China's survival as a sovereign state and had forced the National Government to appeal to all political, military and popular groups for support and allegiance. The PPC was created "to utilize the best minds in national affairs and to rally all elements in the country in time of war."[94] It is fair to say that both the individual Councillors and the Council as a body strove earnestly to attain the goal of wartime unity. As the only national organization to represent public opinion in wartime China, the Council's unyielding stand on the war issue and its strong support of the Government's policy of total war strengthened the nation's will of resistance and discouraged those officials who still secretly wished to seek a compromising peace during the first years of the war.

From 1939 on, national unity was threatened by the mounting frictions between the National Government and the CCP. The PPC Councillors soon became conscious of the situation. What worried them was the harmful effects of this internal struggle on the conduct of the war. By keeping a watchful eye on each other, the two armed parties would greatly limit their war efforts against the foreign invader. A divided China had less chance to survive.

Another concern was the authoritarian trend that accompanied the changed political situation. The early liberal policies of the government were gradually replaced by political repression which was engendered more by fear of the enemy from within than that of the enemy from without. A group of minor party leaders and independents in the PPC proceeded to offer their service of mediation. Their effort paved the way for a direct negotiation between the two sides.

But before any agreement could be implemented, the country was plunged further into a major crisis by the New Fourth Army Incident of January 1941. Only the pressure of the public opinion, the PPC included, and the fear of international complications convinced the two sides to restrain their actions. Direct KMT-CCP negotiations were soon resumed and armed clash temporarily halted. The negotiations, however, made little progress and were broken off in 1943 following the resumption of armed conflict.

It was the PPC which again pressed the issue and succeeded in re-establishing the contact that led to a series of formal talks in 1944. When the United States mediation began the PPC withdrew from active participation in the proceedings. But when the American effort stalled in the spring of 1945, it was a PPC group that again arranged for the exchange of views and made possible a top-level meeting between the two sides soon after the Japanese surrender. The PPC Councillors did their best to bring the issue to public attention and to press their points to the leaders of both sides. They realized that the Communists were too powerful to be eliminated by military force and that a prolonged civil war could only have adverse effect on China's future development. They therefore urged compromise from both sides in order to bring about a speedy general settlement.

To their disappointment, this viewpoint was not shared by the leaders of the two opposing parties. The CCP leaders were conscious of their rapidly expanding power in the country, and were thus constantly raising their stakes on the bargaining table. They knew that the National Government's popularity was slipping rapidly, and they wanted to make full use of the opportunity to their own benefit. The KMT leaders, on the other hand, failed to make a clear distinction between the group of intellectuals who aspired after liberalism, democracy, and moderate socio-economic reform, and the Communists who desired political power to carry out social revolution by forceful means. The unyielding attitude of the government served only to alienate an increasing number of educated Chinese, and drove them closer to the Communist side.

The attitudes and policies of the two major armed parties were responsible for the polarization of political forces in the country, and made a military showdown between them virtually unavoidable. While the Communists believed that "political power grew out of the barrel of a gun," the conviction of the KMT leaders was not less militant. After 1944, when American military supplies reached China in greater quantity, and when the newly equipped Chinese expeditionary force achieved victory in Burma, many military leaders who dominated the government became overconfident and believed that with sufficient United States material support they could easily crush their internal enemy with the sheer weight of their superior military power. Such a notion, which persisted from 1944 to as late as 1948, was to render the effort of the PPC to bring about a political settlement impossible.

Thus the PPC could not be held responsible for its failure to prevent an eventual civil war. Despite the PPC's persistent strong demand for peaceful settlement of the Communist problem, it was ultimately ignored by the government. The Council's appeals to the CCP for restraint were equally fruitless. Thus the Council was powerless to affect any change of attitude by the two armed rivals. Created as a wartime advisory body to strengthen national unity, the PPC's accomplishment was that it helped to maintain an uneasy truce and limited cooperation between the KMT-controlled government and the Chinese Communists throughout the War of Resistance.

In the area of economic and social affairs, the PPC's accomplishments were more positive. The Council, in response to the government's request, had sent out fact-finding teams to investigate local conditions, and had submitted plans for economic development and social and administrative reforms for Szechwan and other regions in unoccupied China. The government leaders later acknowledged the general adoption of the PPC proposals as guidelines for government policies. The Council participated actively in rationalizing the government's policy of price control and stabilization. It helped to check the abuses in the practice of the forced purchase of grain. Through repeated urgings the Council generated enough pressure to force the government to re-examine the system of military and labor conscription, and to bring about some belated reforms in this area.

The contributions of the PPC in this area were made possible chiefly by the cooperative attitude of some of the government leaders. They themselves were not unaware of the wretched economic conditions of the country in a long war, and the misery of the populace under the burden of material shortage, inflation, heavy taxation, and manpower demands. Perhaps the energy and the expertise of some PPC Councillors could be utilized to study the situation and to suggest ways of improvement. After all, the betterment in the mobilization of manpower and resources could only help strengthen the position of the government and would not endanger the KMT leaders' monopoly of political power.

It would be expedient for the government leaders to show greater willingness to accept the PPC advice in this area in the name of national unity.

Another political issue related to wartime unity was that of the democratization of the government. Once again the PPC occupied an important place in it. The outbreak of the war brought sudden change in the KMT policies and gave new hope for liberalism in the country. The creation of the PPC was indeed the embodiment of this new spirit. Although not treated as a full-fledged parliament, the PPC had all the basic elements of a deliberative representative assembly, and was often referred to as "the wartime parliament" by the news media and government leaders. To the majority of the Councillors, at least during the first few years, the maintenance of national unity and the attainment of democratic principles and institutions were two equally important tasks of the PPC.

The repeated efforts made by the Councillors to promote democracy during the war, however, were largely frustrated. Numerous proposals were passed in the PPC urging the protection of civil liberty, the rule of law, and the early adoption of a constitution. Once these resolutions reached the government, they were permanently shelved. By late 1944, most of the non-KMT Councillors had come to the painful conclusion that the government leaders had no intention of voluntarily giving up their monopoly of political power or even of sharing it with others. Ultimately, they realized only political pressure could force any concession from the leaders of the ruling party. The only choice left for them was whether to take the risk of joining forces with the Communists in order to bring about a coalition government in China, or to give up the fight for democracy and be content with a life of limited freedom and security under the continued KMT rule. Many chose the first road, and pinned their hopes upon the success of a KMT-CCP settlement which would determine the political future of post-war China. When the settlement failed to materialize, the peaceful struggle for democracy under the National Government was, for all practical purposes, ended.

The hasty adoption of a constitution and a national assembly by the government in the midst of the civil war in 1947-1948 could not cover up the political failure of the KMT leadership and the decision it had reached, against the wishes of a large sector of the populace, to settle the Communist problem by force. The constitution and its appearance of democratization were meaningless without peace and the participation of the two strongest opposition groups in the country—the CCP and the Democratic League. The constitution and the assembly were no more than window-dressing to give the battered government a veil of legitimacy.

In retrospect, it must be conceded that, despite its negligence of some vital economic and social problems, the collapse of the National

Government on the mainland was not an inevitable result of its actions in the early 1930's. The Japanese invasion brought havoc to China, yet it also stimulated an unprecedented enthusiasm and vitality among the Chinese people. In the wake of the great national crisis, the people threw their genuine support to the National Government in the hope that the KMT would offer effective leadership to guide the nation through its perils and to rebuild China into a free, modern, and peaceful country. This explains the sudden popularity of the National Government, and for a while it seemed to have been moving in that direction. The creation of the PPC was a triumph for liberalism because the Council mustered probably the best group of "parliamentarians" China could produce at that time, and it became the forum which most accurately reflected the popular will during the war.

On the other hand, the popularity it enjoyed during the early years of the war gave the KMT its final chance, during the years that have passed, to influence the historical development of China. The unwillingness or the inability of the KMT leadership to effect changes in the country in compliance with the popular will during the war years brought not only its own demise on the mainland but the end of any hope of creating a multi-party Western-style democratic government in China for years to come.

NOTES

1. *The Chinese Year Book, 1933* (Shanghai: North China Daily News and Herald, 1934), 254-255.
2. Chien Tuan-sheng, *The Government and Politics of China* (Harvard, 1950), 279.
3. L. E. Eastman, *The Abortive Revolution: China under Nationalist Rule, 1927-1937* (Harvard, 1974), 83.
4. A. Dirlik, "The Ideological Foundations of the New Life Movement: A Study in Counterrevolution," *Journal of Asian Studies*, XXXIV:4 (August, 1975), 945-980. Particularly the concluding remarks.
5. *China Handbook, 1937-1945* (New York: Macmillan, 1947), 66-67, 73-74.
6. The total membership has been mentioned as twenty-four or twenty-five, but may or may not include government representatives. Information on membership can be gathered from Tao Hsi-sheng, "Chi Tso Shun-sheng hsien-sheng" (On Mr. Tso Shun-sheng), *Chuan-chi wen-hsueh*, XV:5 (May, 1969) 陶希聖：「記左舜生先生」（傳記文學）; and Tso Shun-sheng, *The Reminiscences* (Unpublished manuscript, East Asian Institute, Columbia University, March, 1965) 左舜生：「回憶錄」

7. Interview with Carsun Chang, Berkeley, California; June 7, 1966.
8. Kwei Chung-shu (ed.), *The Chinese Year Book, 1938-39* (Shanghai: The Commercial Press, 1939), 336-338, 345-346.
9. *Kuo-min tsan-cheng-hui shih-liao* 「國民參政會史料」 (Taipei, 1962, hereafter cited as *Shih-liao*), 1.
10. *Shih-liao,* 13-18.
11. The Organic Laws of the PPC, April 12, 1938; December 24, 1940; and September 16, 1944. *Shih-liao,* 5, 293, 450.
12. *Shih-liao,* 5. Chien, 288-289.
13. See Appendix 1 for all PPC sessions and membership.
14. "Democracy vs. One-party Rule in Kuomintang China: the 'Little Parties' Organize," *Amerasia* (April 25, 1943), 100-101.
15. Article 12 of the PPC Organic Law of 1938, *Shih-liao,* 5.
16. Chien, 283.
17. Li Huang, *Wo-ti hui-i* 李 璜：「我的回憶」 (*My Memoirs,* unpublished manuscript, East Asian Institute, Columbia University, 1968), 435. A selected list of politically active non-KMT Councillors is presented in Appendix 2.
18. Wang Shih-chieh, "Consolidation of Democracy: the People's Political Council," *China Quarterly,* IV:1 (Winter, 1938-39).
19. Put so bluntly by Japan's War Minister, Sugiyama Gen, in D. J. Lu *From the Marco Polo Bridge to Pearl Harbor* (Washington: Public Affairs Press, 1961), 23. See also Akira Iriye, "The Ideology of Japanese Imperialism: Imperial Japan and China," *Imperial Japan and Asia* (East Asian Institute, Columbia University, 1967), 32-45.
20. J. H. Boyle, *China and Japan at War, 1937-1945: the Politics of Collaboration* (Stanford, 1972), 123-133.
21. Boyle, 134-166.
22. *Shih-liao,* 11-13.
23. *North China Herald,* January 4, 1939. For a detailed account of events leading to Wang's defection see Boyle, 206-228.
24. *Shih-liao,* 11-13.
25. The three Councillors expelled from the PPC were Tao Hsi-sheng, Li Sheng-wu and Pu Tung. For Chang's broadcast speech see *Ta Kung Pao* (Hong Kong) 陶希聖，李聖五， 溥侗：「大公報」 , September 6, 1939.
26. *Shih-liao,* 192-193.
27. Warren Kuo, "The CCP Pledge of Allegiance to the Kuomintang," *Issues and Studies,* IV:11 & 12 (August & September, 1968).
28. *China Handbook,* 76-81.
29. Chiang Kai-shek, *Soviet Russia in China: A Summing-up at Seventy* (New York: Farrar, Straus & Cudahy, 1957), 81-82.
30. The CCP's view of the United Front is amply explained in Mao

Tse-tung, *Collected Works of Mao Tse-tung* (Peking, 1965), II, 23-29, 35-45, 195-211, 213-216.

31. L. P. Van Slyke, *Enemies and Friends: the United Front in Chinese Communist History* (Stanford, 1967), 95.

32. Kao Yin-tsu (ed.), *Chung-hua-min-kuo ta-shih chi*　高陰祖：「中華民國大事記」　(Taipei, 1957), 456. Chiang, 92-93.

33. *Kuo-min tsan-cheng-hui*　「國民參政會」　(Complete Records of the PPC, 1938-1945, hereafter as KMTCH), The 5th meeting of the 5th session, First Council.

34. C. A. Johnson, *Peasant Nationalism and Communist Power: the Emergence of Revolutionary China, 1937-1945* (Stanford, 1962), 136-155.

35. Tsou Tao-fen, *Tao-fen wen chi*　鄒韜奮：「韜奮文集」 (Hong Kong: San-lien, 1959), III, 378-380.

36. The communiques between the Council and the two parties are found in *Tsan-cheng-hui yu yen-lun tzu-yu*　「參政會與言論自由」　(Shanghai, 1941), 2-4.

37. *Shih-liao*, 243. For the Council's telegram to the CCP see Tsou Yang, *Kuo-Kung chih-chien*　鄒　陽：「國共之間」　(n.p., 1945), 51-52.

38. *Shih-liao*, 227.

39. *Foreign Relations of the United States* (hereafter FRUS), 1943, VI: China, 257-258.

40. "Democracy vs. One-party Rule," 101-105.

41. "Democracy vs. One-party Rule," 105-110. Li, 587-588.

42. *Shih-liao*, 291.

43. *China Handbook*, 67-68.

44. *Shih-liao*, 359.

45. *Shih-liao*, 410-413.

46. Chang Chun-mai (Carsun Chang), "Kuo-Kung kung-kai pao-kao chih-hou" (After the Open Reports of the KMT and the CCP), *Min-hsien*, (Chungking　張君勱：「國共公開報告之後」（民憲）　, September, 1944.

47. Van Slyke, 177-180.

48. *Shih-liao*, 388. Wang Yun-wu, *Yu-lu lun kuo-shih*　王雲五：「岫廬論國是」　(Taipei, 1965), 1.

49. For the impasse in the negotiations see *The China White Paper* (Stanford, 1967 reprint), 83-86. The development leading to the top-level meeting is reported in FRUS, 1945, VII: China, 416-417, 426-429. An account of the trip was made by one of the committee members. See Huang Yen-pei, *Yen-an kuei-lai*　黃炎培：「延安歸來」　(Chungking, 1945).

50. *White Paper*, 105-112, 132-140. Wang, *Yu-lu*, 172-173.

51. Chou Kai-chin, *Szechwan Yu tui-Jih kang chan* 周開慶：「四川與對日抗戰」 (Taipei, 1971), 268-269. A. N. Young, *China's Wartime Finance and Inflation, 1937-1945* (Harvard, 1965), 299-310.

52. The armed revolt of Honan peasants in April-May 1944 was a clear case. During the Japanese Ichigo offensive, the peasants attacked the retreating army under the command of Tang En-po and reportedly disarmed and killed 50,000 Chinese troops. FRUS, 1944, VI: China, 193-194. T. H. White & A. Jacoby, *Thunder Out of China* (New York: Sloane, 1946), 177-178.

53. *Shih-liao*, 203, 257, 291-292, 345, 387, 447-448, 505-506.

54. "Tsan-cheng-hui chueh-i-an chi Hsing-cheng-yuan pan-li ching-hsing pao-kao piao" (Reports of the Executive Yuan on the Enforcement of the Resolutions of the PPC), 1938-1944 「參政會決議案及行政院辦理情形報告表」 (Taiwan: the KMT archives, unpublished.)

55. KMTCH, The 4th session, First Council. *Shih-liao*, 112-129.

56. "Tsan-cheng-hui chueh-i-an. . . . ," 19-35.

57. *Shih-liao*, 102-104, 152-156, 228-229.

58. *Shih-liao*, 180-184.

59. *Shih-liao*, 292-295.

60. *Shih-liao*, 347-348.

61. *Shih-liao*, 390-394.

62. F. F. Liu, *A Military History of Modern China, 1924-1949* (Princeton 1956), 135-136. The Province of Szechwan bore the largest share in providing military manpower. During the war years Szechwan contributed a total of 3 million raw recruits, or roughly one-fifth of the total. Chou, *Szechwan*, 245-247.

63. Liu, 137.

64. An eyewitness account of the mistreatment of the conscripts is found in Chiang Meng-ling, "Hsin-chao," Chapter 4, *Chuan-chi wen-hsueh*, XI:2 蔣夢麟：「新潮」（傳記文學）(August, 1967), 89-93.

65. Liu, 137-145.

66. Chou, *Szechwan*, 243-244. FRUS, 1943, China, 232-233, 238-240, 269-270, 316-317, 344-345.

67. A. N. Young, *China and the Helping Hand, 1937-1945* (Harvard, 1963), 51. FRUS, 1938, III: The Far East, 598; 1939, III: The Far East, 753-755; 1944, VI: China, 834.

68. Chou, *Szechwan*, 260-266. FRUS, 1944, VI: China, 866-867. Young, *Helping Hand*, 302.

69. *Shih-liao*, 24, 60, 87, 138, 185, 194.

70. *Shih-liao*, 242.

71. *Shih-liao*, 282-283, 329, 374, 434, 482.

72. *China Handbook,* 275.
73. *China Handbook,* 272.
74. *China Handbook,* 287. Liu, 138.
75. *Shih-liao,* 30-31, 62-63, 91.
76. The individual proposals were reproduced in full and commented on at length in Tsou, III, 226-237.
77. *Shih-liao,* 139.
78. Chien, 307-308.
79. Chien Tuan-sheng, "China's National Unification," *China Quarterly,* V: 3 (Summer, 1940), 409-427.
80. Although not recorded in its minutes, the debate these proposals generated in the PPC is described in detail in Tsou, III, 237-240.
81. *Shih-liao,* 139.
82. Chien, *Government,* 308. *China Handbook,* 118.
83. Tsou, III, 241.
84. KMTCH, The 16th meeting of the 1st session, Fourth Council.
85. Tsou, III, 242.
86. Tsou, III, 251-258.
87. *Shih-liao,* 166-180.
88. An illuminating analysis of the proposed changes in this revised draft and how they differed from the original document is given in Chien, *Government,* 308.
89. Tsou, III, 258-260.
90. *Shih-liao,* 353-355.
91. *Shih-liao,* 351.
92. Chien, *Government,* 309.
93. *Shih-liao,* 518-520.
94. *China Handbook,* 112.

Appendix I
PEOPLE'S POLITICAL COUNCIL
SESSIONS, MEMBERSHIP, AND ATTENDANCE

Session	Date	Place	Membership Categories:				Total	Attendance
			I	II	III	IV		
First Council								
1st	July 6-15, 1938	Hankow	88	6	6	100	200	146
2nd	Oct. 28-Nov. 6, 1938	Chungking					194[a]	140
3rd	Feb. 12-21, 1939	Chungking					194	146
4th	Sept. 9-18, 1939	Chungking					193	141
5th	Apr. 1-10, 1940	Chungking					190	145
Second Council								
1st	Mar. 1-10, 1941	Chungking	90	6	6	138	240(241)[b]	203
2nd	Nov. 17-30, 1941	Chungking					229	173
Third Council								
1st	Oct. 22-31, 1942	Chungking	164	8	8	60	240	218
2nd	Sept. 18-27, 1943	Chungking					240	191
3rd	Sept. 5-18, 1944[c]	Chungking					226	186
Fourth Council								
1st	June 7-20, 1945	Chungking	199	8	8	75	290	238
2nd	Mar. 20-Apr. 2, 1946	Chungking					282	234
3rd	May 20-June 2, 1947	Nanking	227	8	8	119	362	302

[a]The total membership was reduced by death, resignation, or expulsion.
[b]One supplementary member was added to the total membership during the session.
[c]The length of the session was extended from 10 to 14 days.

Appendix II
A SELECTED LIST OF PPC COUNCILLORS
ACTIVE IN POLITICAL AFFAIRS

KMT MEMBERS:

Hsu Hsiao-yen   許孝胡炎中庚   Lin Hu   林虎
Hu Chien-chung   胡建中襄   Liu Po-min   劉閔琳川黃
Kung Keng   孔中棟   Chou Ping-lin   周百炳
Li Chung-hsiang   李上   Tao Po-chuan   陶百飛
Liang Shang-tung   梁   Teng Fei-huang   鄧

CCP MEMBERS

Chen Shao-yu   陳紹禹   Teng Ying-chao   鄧穎超
Chin Pang-hsien   秦邦憲   Tung Pi-wu   董必武
Lin Tsu-han   林祖涵   Wu Yu-chang   吳玉章

MEMBERS OF MINOR PARTIES & GROUPS*:
CHINA YOUTH PARTY:

Chen Chi-tien   陳啟天   Tso Shun-sheng   左舜生
Li Huang   李璜   Yu Chia-chu   余家菊
Tseng Chi   曾琦

DEMOCRATIC-SOCIALIST PARTY (National-Socialist Party):

Chang Chun-mai   張君勱   Hu Shih-ching   胡石青
Chang Sheng-fu   張申府   Liang Shih-chiu   梁實秋
Chang Tung-sun   張東蓀   Lo Lung-chi   羅隆基
Chiang Yung   江庸

NATIONAL SALVATION ASSOCIATION:

Sheng Chun-ju   沈鈞儒   Tsou Tao-fen   鄒韜奮
Shih Liang   史良   Wang Tsao-shih   王造時

---

*With the exception of those deceased all joined the Democratic League
in 1944.

VOCATIONAL EDUCATION SOCIETY:

Chiang Heng-yuan 江恆源   Leng Yu 冷通

Huang Yen-pei 黃炎培

RURAL RECONSTRUCTION ASSOCIATION:

Liang Shu-ming 梁漱溟   Yen Yang-chu 晏陽初

Tao Hsing-chih 陶行知

OTHERS:

Chang Hsi-jo 張奚若   Chien Tuan-sheng 錢端升

Chang Lan 張瀾   Hsu Teh-heng 許德珩

Chang Po-chun 章伯鈞   Liu Wang Li-min 劉王立明

INDEPENDENTS:

Chang Chih-chang 張熾章   Chu Fu-cheng 諸輔成

Chang I-ling 張一麐   Fu Ssu-nien 傅斯年

Chang Po-ling 張伯苓   Hu Ching-i 胡景伊

Chang Shih-chao 章士釗   Hu Lin 胡霖

Chen Chi-yeh 陳嘉業   Hu Wen-hu 胡文虎

Chen Chia-keng 陳嘉庚   Mo Teh-hui 莫德惠

Chen Pao-yin 陳豹隱   Shao Chung-en 邵從恩

Cheng She-wo 成舍我   Tao Meng-ho 陶孟和

Chien Yung-ming 錢永銘   Wang Yun-wu 王雲五

    Wu I-fang 吳貽芳

Comments (1):

BY DISON HSUEH-FENG POE

In preparing myself as the discussant of Dr. Shyu's paper on the People's Political Council (PPC), I have relived many of my wartime Chungking days. This is because, drafted and serving as a counselor in the Supreme National Defence Council, I frequently visited the PPC meetings nearby and listened to many lively debates. Moreover, about one third of its members were my friends, old and new. In fact, some of us did often in private discuss the nation's thorny internal problem the PPC was trying to help solve. Later, as Deputy Director-General of the Chinese Relief and Rehabilitation Administration (CNRRA, counterpart of UNRRA, the United Nations Relief and Rehabilitation Administration), I rendered in the early spring of 1946 a lengthy verbal report to the PPC on our CNRRA programs and problems, including the sensitive and controversial distribution in Communist areas of UNRRA-given materials and commodities. Anyway, I had more than an inkling of what was going on within and without the PPC.

The PPC, though sometimes euphuistically referred to as China's "Wartime Parliament," was a political and consultative body, and not a parliament. There was the Legislative Yuan which held the law-making power. Nonetheless, the PPC, representative in composition and prestigious for arduous work, played its historic role. Dr. Shyu initially points out that the history of the PPC was a part of China's internal political development. That is a keen and valuable observation. Indeed, the establishment of the PPC may be regarded as a significant step in Nationalist China's determined and continuous movement toward constitutional democracy from 1928 to 1947. Here is a brief summary by Prof. Earl H. Pritchard:

> In 1928 the National Government . . . formally proclaimed the end of the military stage and the inauguration of political tutelage. . . . Plans gradually matured for the adoption of a definitive constitution and the inauguration of the constitutional stage in 1937, but the attack of Japan led to the postponement of this action until the end of 1947, when a somewhat modified constitution went into effect.[1]

This chain of events, including the setting up of the PPC, unmistakably demonstrated the Nationalist consistent endeavor to achieve constitutional democracy.

Dr. Shyu's study covers the manifold aspects of the PPC, including its origin and development, its membership and alignment, its sessions and meetings, its functions and contributions, and its expectations and disappointments. It is comprehensive, thoroughgoing and thoughtful. However, I have a few reservations here and there, especially about its conclusion. Perhaps my reservations are due to the way of wording, the degree of emphasis and the manner of appraisal, and not so much to the matter of viewpoint. I choose, therefore, to tackle not the contents of the paper as such but, instead, certain relevant matters implied in the important problems dealt with in the paper. In other words, I propose to introduce for our discussion several questions related to these two main issues: democracy and democratization on the one hand, and on the other unity and unification. In doing so, I shall go beyond Dr. Shyu's paper, beyond in point of scope, so as to examine certain motivations and objectives, and beyond in point of time, so as to include the critical years, 1945-1949.

To be specific, I hereby pose four pertinent questions. First, was there acute and immediate need of furthering democracy and democratization in the midst of the life-or-death struggle against the Japanese invaders? Second, how sincere were the Chinese Communists in their clamor for democracy and democratization? Third, what, after all, remained continuously as the obstacle to national unity? And fourth, who in the last analysis brought about the termination of peaceful unification? Answers to these questions are bound to be controversial. But one has to tread on such treacherous ground if he seeks at all an objective and meaningful assessment of the whole episode. And let me indicate my firm belief: a *fait accompli* cannot claim everything in its favor, and the end does not always justify the means.

Now let us ask first of all: Was there acute and immediate need of furthering democracy and democratization during China's eight years of War of Resistance? History shows that democracy can best develop in times of peace and security, and not in times of war or crisis. Even in advanced constitutional democracies like Great Britain and the United States of America there was during the two World Wars a conspicuous shrinkage of democratic practices. To begin with, the legislature willingly subordinated itself to the executive. In coping with the economic crisis of the early 1930's, the American Congress became a "rubber stamp" under the vigorous leadership of Franklin D. Roosevelt.

For instance, the Emergency Banking Bill was passed by both the Senate and the House in less than eight hours on one and the same day (namely, March 9, 1933) without having to go through the committee stage and without having a printed draft distributed in time to all the members.[2] Naturally, FDR was stigmatized by some critics as a dictator. Then, too, the executive branch of government—the British Cabinet as well as the American President—was literally given law-making power, known as "delegated legislation." Thus, the British Government issued on August 28, 1939, a total of ninety-six "orders-in-Council" as national defense regulations, with the equivalent validity of Parliament-passed laws. Likewise, within ten days after the Pearl Harbor attack the American Congress conferred on President Roosevelt delegated legislative power. President Roosevelt made immediate and full use of this delegated legislation to issue necessary orders in the conduct of war.

Nor is this all. The British "War Cabinet" was composed not of the usual peace-time twenty-odd members but of a very much reduced number, seven, five, and at one time only three. And yet something more startling, almost unthinkable: the term of office of both the legislature and the executive was extraordinarily prolonged. During World War I the British Parliament repeatedly extended its own term, one year at a time, until the end of the war. In World War II FDR was elected to his fourth Presidential term.[3]

Did not these above-mentioned facts constitute a sort of shrinkage in wartime democratic practices? Why? The reason is not far to seek. Of the five possible and actual objectives of government, of any government at any time—namely, security against external aggression, maintenance of domestic order, administration of justice through the courts, promotion of economic welfare, and furtherance of individual freedom— the first two, security and order, are of utmost priority. Without security and order there can be no justice, no welfare and no freedom to be spoken of.

Here is a significant reflection by General Albert C. Wedemeyer, worth our pondering:

> China's real need was for a government with the power to govern. As I saw it the worst ills of China—corruption, maladministration, inefficiency, and the like—were the result not of the dictatorial nature of its government but of its lack of power and authority to get its orders carried out. . . . To call Chiang Kai-shek a fascist dictator, as was the fashion in America, was a ridiculous reversal of the truth, but was tragic in its consequences since it led to U. S. policy being based on a false premise. The powers of the Chinese Nationalist Government, far from being totalitarian, were limited too much. It interfered with the individual too little, not too much. Its sins of omission, not of commission, were the cause of its eventual downfall.[4]

On the other hand, Prof. Lloyd E. Eastman looks at the matter from a different angle. "Because of the nature of Chinese society and of its political traditions, it is perhaps one of China's tragedies during the twentieth century that, in the quest for a viable political system, attempts had been made to erect democratic institutions. In a profound sense, Anglo-American democracy was not suited to China."[5]

Personally I think that, given ample time of peace and order, and with sufficient experience in local self-government, China could attain— as she is now attaining on Taiwan—her own type of "Five-Power" constitutional democracy. For our purpose here it may be safely asserted that there was little, if any, acute and immediate need of furthering democracy and democratization in the midst of a desperate war.

Aside from the question of need, the question of sincerity should be probed. Were the Chinese Communists sincere in their professed faith in democracy and in their adamant urge for democratization? Dr. Carsun Chang has this much to say in his book, *The Third Force*, written during his "exile in India" in the year 1952. "If one studies carefully the subjects which were brought up during the [political consultative] talks in 1945 it appears doubtful that the Communists were really sincere and earnest about democracy and coalition."[6] This brief confession-like passage is very mild but most revealing because Dr. Chang was the founder of the Democratic League, a strong advocate for democratization, and an outspoken critic of the Nationalist leadership. Elsewhere in the book there is another remark: "From now [April 1941] on the Communists announced their own program—land revolution, armed uprising, and the establishment of a soviet government."[7] If Dr. Chang had realized that such a program could be anything but democratic he would have long before regarded the Communists' alleged democratic faith as more than merely "doubtful."

But was the CCP (the Chinese Communist Party) insincere about its demand for a coalition? No, it was not. But then there was a standing directive from Moscow and there was an ulterior motive. To the Communists the world over a coalition is always a temporary foothold, a welcome stepping-stone, to the seizing of complete control of government. The best evidence to support such an interpretation comes from Ambassador Leighton Stuart's report to Washington, dated August 10, 1948:

> Even though at present some form of coalition seems most likely, we believe that from the standpoint of the United States it would be undesirable. We say this because the history of coalitions including Communists demonstrates all too clearly Communist ability by political means to take over complete control of the government and in the process to acquire some kind of international recognition. . . . We would recommend therefore that American efforts be designed to prevent the formation of a coalition government, and our best means to that end is continued and, if possible, increased support of the present government.[8]

Such a *volte face* in point of view, such a warning on the CCP's sinister motive, came altogether too late. Ambassador Stuart's recommendation was totally ignored because the American government had long been misled by a host of diplomatic officials abroad and at home, men like Davies, Service, Ludden, Emerson and Vincent, who represented the Chinese Communists as "so-called Communists," as "agrarian reformers," and as "simply democrats."[9]

As a matter of fact, the National Government did, under increasing American pressure, make successive coalition offers. The one made in December 1944 was to have the Communists represented in the then existing Military Affairs Council.[10] Another formula suggested in January 1945 would have the Communists and other parties participate in a policy-making war cabinet (of 7-9 members) in the Executive Yuan.[11] As to the scheme agreed on at the Political Consultative Conference in January 1946, it was to create an overall State Council (of forty members) with a certain number (yet to be fixed) of seats for the Communists and the Democratic League.[12] All these coalition offers were communicated to the Communist leaders through General Patrick Hurley and later through General George Marshall. They were rejected one after another. At the same time the Communists increased their demands on military and other political matters. In reading over these documentary records, one cannot fail to see that, while the Nationalists showed reluctant but genuine compromise, the Communists aimed at something other than governmental democratization.

There is yet another way to gauge the sincerity of the Communists. Has the Mao regime on the mainland practiced genuine democratization and real democracy? True, Mao Tse-tung did and still does give, as awards for their collaboration, some ministerial and other high posts to members of the Democratic League and some former so-called Independents. But has it been actual power-sharing or mere window dressing? Here are some comments by Dr. Carsun Chang:

> When I speak about democracy I do not mean that brand under which the fellow-travellers cooperate with the Communists. The kind of so-called democracy which thrives . . . in China is a mockery and travesty of a free society, and of the rule of constitutionalism and individual liberty, by which democracy has been known from its very inception. . . . Most of the members of the Democratic League who collaborated with the Communists, like Huang Yen-pei, Chang Lan, Lo Lung-chi, Liang Shu-min, and Chang Pai-chun are either Vice Presidents of the Government at Peking, or Ministers, or members of commissions, or members of the Political Consultative Conference. Sometimes I wonder to myself whether these erstwhile colleagues of mine of the Democratic League are contented with their present lot. I am sure they are not, for they are like birds whose wings have been clipped.[13]

One passage from a writer, none other than Theodore H. White, is worth quoting:

> I asked Mao Tse-tung what their policy was with regard to freedom of the press, and he said they believed in absolute freedom of the press and absolute freedom of speech. It wasn't going to be like Chungking when they won—everybody would have the right to say whatever he felt—there wouldn't be censorship the way Chiang Kai-shek had had in Chungking. I said, "Do you really mean it?" And he said, "Of course we mean it." And I said, "Do you mean that if you come to power, anybody will be able to print anything he wants in a newspaper or publish any newspaper he wants?" And Mao Tse-tung said, "Of course, except for enemies of the people." Nor would he ever define, and I was too young to ask him to define, what he meant by enemies of the people. Obviously now it means anybody who disagrees with him.[14]

It is no exaggeration to say that, having ruled over the mainland for more than one quarter of a century now, the Maoist regime has hardly started the rudiments of democracy. On the other hand, what a contrast may be found on Taiwan today!

Turning to the next issue of unity and unification, let us ask the third question: What after all remained continuously as the obstacle to national unity? Well, the obstacle was huge and conspicuous but in many quarters, within and without China, its recognition was ignored. In the *Book of Mencius* the sage referred to a man who could detect the tiny end-point of a hair but could not see a wagonload of firewood. It was Dr. Hu Shih who pointed out that wagonload of firewood to Mao Tse-tung. These are Dr. Hu's words:

> So naive, indeed, was I that shortly after V-J Day I sent a lengthy radiogram to Chungking to be forwarded to my former student Mao Tse-tung, solemnly and earnestly pleading with him that, now that Japan had surrendered, there was no more justification for the Chinese Communists to continue to maintain a huge private army, and that his Party should now emulate the good example of the British Labor Party which, without a single soldier of its own, had just won an overwhelming victory at the recent election and acquired undisputed political power for the next five years. On August 28, 1945, Mao Tse-tung arrived at Chungking accompanied by the American Ambassador, General Patrick Hurley, another tyro in diplomacy, and my Chungking friend radioed me that my message had been duly forwarded to Mr. Mao in person. Of course, to this day I have never received a reply.[15]

Most likely Dr. Hu would not have sent such a radiogram to his former student if the latter had already started his anti-Confucius campaign.

Furthermore, what use was the Communist army put to? The answer had been provided by Mao himself in his speech to the Red Army in the autumn of 1937. "The Sino-Japanese war affords our party an excellent opportunity for expansion. Our fixed policy should be seventy per cent expansion, twenty per cent dealing with the Kuomintang, and ten per cent resisting Japan. There are three stages in carrying out this fixed policy: the first is a compromising stage . . . the second is a contending stage . . . the third is an offensive stage. . . ."[16] This fixed policy and withal the three successive stages must have been closely followed. This is what General Albert Wedemeyer wrote in his *Reports:*

> The Nationalist Government was trying . . . to defend what was left of Free China. The Chinese Communists were simply engaged in raiding Japanese or *Nationalist Government-controlled areas. (Italics mine)* . . . No Communist Chinese forces fought in any of the major engagements of the Sino-Japanese War. . . . [with the dates and places of the major engagements listed here]. . . . According to the testimony even of Americans who were sympathetic to the Chinese Communist cause, Chinese Communists never challenged any important Japanese garrison post or Japan's control of China's railway system. Thus, for instance, Theodore White admitted in his and Annalee Jacoby's best-selling book, *Thunder Out of China,* that the Chinese Communists fought only "when they had an opportunity to surprise a very small group of the enemy. . . . During the significant campaigns it was the weary soldiers of the Central Government who took the shock, gnawed at the enemy, and died."[17]

At the same time, as observed Prof. Pritchard, "the Japanese armies served, in a sense, as a shield for the Communists."[18] And yet, according to Drew Pearson, "All three of the young Far Eastern experts arrested by the Navy and State Department feel [among other things] that the Northern Chinese Government (sic) . . . has done more fighting against Japan."[19] This is rather a diversion. The point for us to grasp—the wagon-load of firewood for us to see—is that after all it was the huge private, autonomous Communist army that remained all the time as the obstacle to China's unity.

The fourth and last question is this: Who in the last analysis brought about the termination of peaceful unification? A candid examination of the Communists' successive unconscionable actions may reveal that they were responsible for the eventual breakdown. It was the Communists who boycotted the PPC meetings. It was the Communists who, together with the Democratic League, boycotted the constituent National Assembly convened on November 15, 1945, for considering "the constitutional draft which was . . . agreed to by Chou En-lai as the representative of the Communist Party and by the representatives of the Kuomintang and the democratic parties."[20] And, again, it was the Communists who denounced as "illegal" the Constitution adopted in December 1946 and demanded its abrogation. General Marshall declared in his public statement on January 7, 1947:

> In fact, the National Assembly has adopted a democratic Constitution which in all major respects is in accordance with the principles laid down by the all-party Political Consultative Conference of last January (1946). It is unfortunate that the Communists did not see fit to participate in the Assembly, since the Constitution that has been adopted seems to include every major point that they wanted.[21]

Dr. Carsun Chang wrote down his own experience and reflection.

> After the final breakdown of negotiations between the Kuomintang and the Communists, I found, as a man standing for peace and order, that there was no way of working with the Chinese Communists, so I supported the government on condition that the constitutional draft should be adopted and a government on democratic lines organized. The agreement, which Chiang Kai-shek signed, was that after the Constitution was adopted and a government formed on a democratic basis, a policy of truce with the Communists should be continued and negotiations for a coalition government renewed. But the Communist demand that the adopted Constitution be denounced was too much for the government to accept.[22]

Needless to say, these Communist boycottings, denunciations and demands were psychological warfare, carried on to harass, discredit and weaken the National Government in Mao's second stage, "the contending stage" of his "fixed policy."

Finally came the "offensive stage." In the words of Edmund Clubb in his book, *Twentieth Century China,*

> The first report of Japanese readiness to surrender came on August 10 [1945]. Two clashing military orders were issued in China the following day. Generalissimo Chiang, from his headquarters in Chungking, instructed Communist Commander-in-Chief Chu Teh that the Communist forces should maintain their existing positions, refrain from accepting Japanese surrenders, and await orders. From Yenan, Chu Teh ordered that "all anti-Japanese forces of the Liberated Areas" should accept the enemy's surrender in their vicinity, take over enemy arms, and occupy and administer towns and communications previously held by both Japanese and "puppet" troops.[23]

Dr. Wang Yun-wu, a non-party PPC member in all its four Councils, and a participant in the PCC, has this much to say in his book of reminiscences:

Of the agreements arrived at in the Political Consultative Conference what failed most were doubtlessly those related to military matters. This is because the Chinese Communists consistently held rebellion as their final end and so they were unwilling to live up to their promises no matter how reasonable the reached solutions were.[24]

It is not biased or arbitrary to conclude that in the final analysis it was the Communists that brought about the termination of peaceful, democratic unification.

One word is in order here regarding the Marshall Mission. President Truman's main objective, "the unification of China by peaceful, democratic methods," was good and perfect; but the way to "bring to bear in an appropriate and practicable manner the influence of the United States to this end"[25] was eventually ill-advised, one-sided, self-defeating and disastrous in consequences. According to General Wedemeyer,

Hurley, in 1944-45, like Marshall after him, in 1945-46, approached the problem of unifying China on the false supposition that the Chinese Communists were not real Communists under Moscow's command but simply a Chinese faction that could be induced by diplomatic negotiations to come to terms with the Nationalist Government. Unlike Marshall, however, Hurley never wanted or tried to compel Chiang to share power with the Communists.[26]

Let us forego here the question of "false supposition" and consider the way or "manner" "to compel." Dr. Hu Shih did put the matter bluntly:

And what were to be the ways and means by which the Marshall Mission was to "bring to bear the influence of the United States . . . ?" In plain language, the weapon was to be not military pressure and intervention, but the withholding of American aid to China. *But the weapon could only checkmate the Chinese Government and had no effect whatever on the Chinese Communists.*[27]

Nay, the stoppage of American aid was at that critical moment tantamount to giving moral and material aid to the rebellious Party.[28]

Of course, it must be admitted that the National Government had its errors, shortcomings and miscalculations in both political and military matters. But many other things purposely and unwittingly contributed to its debacle on the mainland. "The worst disaster since our victory," stated Winston Churchill on April 1, 1949, "has been the collapse of China under Communist attack and intrigue."[29] The "Communist . . . intrigue" came from Soviet Russia. What a glaring contrast this single remark was to the later voluminous American White Paper, which added insult to injury by blaming the Nationalist Government alone. In retrospect, an American devoted educator and tyro diplomat in China pensively wrote down his conclusion:

> Throughout the years [impliedly, 1927-1949], it [the National Government] had been under the attack from dissident elements in China, especially the Communists, and had been under the pressure of diplomatic and armed assaults from without, especially from Japan. There had been no period in which it could devote itself under circumstances of peace and security to problems of reform and the "people's livelihood." No wonder that when, after eight years of defensive struggle against the Japanese invaders, it was subjected to an all-out attack by the armed forces of the Communist Party in China, which in turn were given encouragement and material aid by the Soviet Union, it had been unable to rally to an effective resistance a war-weary people.[30]

Referring to the American State Department's gathering of "experts" on the Far East in October 1949, immediately after the Communist takeover of the mainland, John Leighton Stuart lamented that "yet in this conference, relatively little was said about China's difficulties within and without and all the onus for the National Government's collapse was placed upon that government itself."[31] Such a verdict, explicit or implicit, then and now, is, I submit, untrue and biased.

NOTES

1. *Annals of the American Academy of Political and Social Science* (Philadelphia, Sept., 1951), p. 7.
2. S. K. Bailey and H. D. Samuel, *Congress at Work* (1953), pp. 231-236.
3. The ideas in this paragraph were part of my discussion with some PPC members like Lo Lung-chi (my Tsing Hua classmate) and Chang Hsi-jo (my Political Science Department colleague at Tsing Hua University). These ideas were embodied in my two wartime articles: (1) "Ta-chan yu cheng-ti hsiang-hu ti ying-hsiang" (Mutual Interaction between World-War and Government-Form), published in the *Hsin ching-chi* (New Economics) magazine, v. 6, issue 12, March 16, 1942; and (2) "Chih-luan ho-chan yu min-chu tu-tsai" (Democracy versus Dictatorship: Relationship with Order and Chaos, Peace and War), published in the *Chun-shih yu cheng-chih* (Military and Political Affairs) magazine, v. 1, issue 5, 1942. These two articles are included in my *Chen-chih lun-tsung* (Collected Political Essays) (Taipei: Cheng Chung Book Co., 1955), pp. 215-234.

4. Albert C. Wedemeyer, *Wedemeyer Reports* (New York: Henry Holt, 1958), p. 377.

5. Lloyd E. Eastman, *The Abortive Revolution, China under Nationalist Rule, 1927-1937* (Harvard, 1974), pp. 179-180.

6. Carsun Chang, *The Third Force* (New York: Bookman, 1952), p. 140.

7. *Ibid.*, p. 76.

8. Quoted in *Wedemeyer Reports*, p. 399.

9. R. D. Buhite, *Patrick Hurley and American Foreign Policy* (Cornell, 1973), pp. 188-189. "Probably in July, 1944," General Joseph W. Stilwell wrote down privately this statement: "The cure for China's trouble is the elimination of Chiang Kai-shek." *The Stilwell Papers* (arr. & ed. by Theodore H. White, New York: Sloane, 1948), p. 321.

10. *Foreign Relations of the United States*, 1944, VI: China 1967, pp. 733-734.

11. Liang Chin-tung, "Heh-erh-li tiao-ting kuo kung ching-kuo" (What Transpired in Hurley's Mediation between the KMT and the CCP) in *Chuan-chi wen-hsueh* (Biographical Literature), v. 26, issue 4 (April, 1975), p. 8. Dr. Liang's research article contains much valuable material from the *Ta-chi tzu-liao* (Documentary Files at Ta-chi).

12. Chang, pp. 148-149.

13. *Ibid.*, pp. 13 & 187.

14. Theodore H. White, *The Roots of Madness* (New York: Norton, 1968), p. 111.

15. Introduction by Hu Shih, in John Leighton Stuart, *Fifty Years in China* (New York: Random, 1954), p. xix.

16. Wedemeyer, p. 283.

17. *Ibid.*, p. 284.

18. *Annals*, article by Pritchard, p. 9.

19. Wedemeyer, pp. 316-317.

20. Chang, pp. 188-189.

21. Stuart, pp. 171-172.

22. Chang, p. 26.

23. Edmund Clubb, *Twentieth Century China* (Columbia, 2nd ed., 1972), p. 255.

24. Wang Yun-wu, *Yu-lu lun kuo-shih* (My Views on National Affairs) (Taipei, 1965), p. 2.

25. See President Truman's Directives and Statement, in Stuart (Appendix), pp. 315-319.

26. Wedemeyer, p. 307.

27. Stuart, Introduction by Hu Shih, p. xviii.

28. Prof. Paul M. A. Linebargar thought "that the fall of Nationalism and the rise of Communism were materially aided by the extreme

psychological pressure from Moscow and Washington." *Annals,* p. 178.

29. Chang, Foreword, p. 5.
30. Stuart, p. 272. One pertinent and provocative passage from Dr. Chang's *The Third Force* is worth quoting. "Two major international issues came to a head. . . . One was the question of Japan, and the other that of the Soviet Union's active support of the Chinese Communists. Chiang was sandwiched between these two enemies. . . . Chiang was then called a traitor because he did not declare war against Japan. . . . If Chiang fought against Japan, as the Communists demanded, he was afraid that the Communists would fish in troubled waters and extend their influence at his expense— which in fact they did from 1937 till the Japanese surrender. . . . In the eyes of the Chinese Communists, Stalin was justified in signing a Mutual Non-Aggression Pact with Nazi Germany, but when Chiang Kai-shek wanted to wait one or two years in order to insure military preparedness before taking on Japan, they called him a traitor. Stalin could sign an agreement for the partitioning of Poland, but Chiang Kai-shek was not granted more time to prepare a war of self-preservation." Chang, p. 96.
31. Stuart, pp. 271-272.

Comments (2):

Comments (2):

BY PAUL K. T. SIH

I wish to offer a few observations on Professor Lawrence Shyu's paper which is very informative and well organized.

While fully agreeing with Professor Poe's comments which are most relevant and revealing as well, I would like to add mine as follows:

Professor Shyu described ably the work of the PPC in three aspects:

(1) wartime national unity;
(2) mobilization of manpower and resources, and
(3) the constitutional movement.

Professor Shyu noted that the PPC made substantial achievements in the second area of operation, that is, mobilization of manpower and resources. It rather failed in the first and third areas, that is, wartime national unity and the constitutional movement. In other words, the PPC succeeded in carrying on its work in the economic and social affairs, but failed in the political area.

Herein lies my question. Why so? To me, the reason is obvious. In the field of economic and social affairs, the PPC had the fullest cooperation of the National Government and therefore it succeeded, while in the political field the PPC required the cooperation of both the KMT and the CCP. But, the PPC lacked this essential factor.

In the field of economic and social affairs, Professor Shyu noted that all recommendations made by the Commission (dealing with investigations of Szechwan and Sikang) were submitted to Chiang Kai-shek, who served concurrently as its Chairman, as Speaker of the PPC, as well as the key leader in the KMT and the government. In this capacity, the Commission became, in effect, a high advisory council to the Supreme wartime leader on the economic policies in the most important province in unoccupied China. Its recommendations were often accepted as a general guideline for the government's economic policies in Szechwan (p. 293).

In another place, Professor Shyu stressed that "during its two-year existence, the Commission made a number of recommendations to the PPC to be considered as part of the Council's (PPC's) proposals. Some of them were definitely adopted by the government" (p. 294). I remember that when I served in the Ministry of Communications, I was put in charge of preparing a monthly report to the Executive Yuan listing all the proposals made by the PPC for implementation in the field of communications. If they were not implemented, reasons had to be given. This is the reason why Professor Shyu could make commendatory remarks on the PPC's positive achievements in the economic and social affairs.

Yet Professor Shyu in his concluding sentences noted that ". . . the Council mustered probably the best group of 'parliamentarians' China could produce at that time, and it became the forum which most accurately reflected the popular will during the war. . . . The unwillingness or the inability of the KMT leadership to effect changes in the country in compliance with the popular will during the war years brought not only its own demise on the mainland but the end of any type of creating a multi-party Western-style democratic government in China for years to come" (p. 306).

Obviously, Professor Shyu's criticism of the KMT's leadership was not in the area of economic and social affairs. It was in the area of political affairs, that is, wartime national unity and the constitutional movement.

It seems to me that it would be most unfair if we put the cause of failure entirely on the side of the KMT. As I stated, success of any political settlement depends upon the concurrence or collaboration of the two parties concerned.

Professor Shyu did point out, however, that: "In the mediation effort, members of the Federation of Democratic Parties in the PPC did their best to press both sides for a political settlement" (p. 288). However, as a matter of fact, the pressure was laid more often on the KMT side, particularly in the latter part of the war by the Federation of Democratic Parties of the PPC, and not on the CCP. To consider that "the Chinese Communist problem is a purely political problem and should be solved by political means" (p. 289) prejudices the whole case.

To explain this point, let me cite a passage from Mr. Li Huang, founder of the China Youth Party and one of the most important leaders of the PPC. In his article, "Chou En-lai's Tactics of United Front and his Diplomatic Strategy," published in *Ta-Cheng Monthly* (Hong Kong), No. 27, Feb. 1, 1976, Mr. Li wrote:

> The KMT originally intended to request the CCP to give up their army as a pre-requisite for political collaboration. For this reason, we, the third party, proposed at the very beginning of the Consultative Conference a policy of: "Nationalization of the Army and Democratization of Political Structure. . . . "

> It was for this purpose that Dr. Carson Chang wrote a letter to Mao Tsetung urging him to relinquish his military power in order to form a coali-

tion government. This was advocated by all the parties concerned including General Marshall. . . . Chou En-lai did not debate the issue positively. He put up a very persuasive argument by maintaining that there shall be first a coalition government and then we may reorganize and nationalize the army. To do this is not only for the benefit of the Communists but for that of all the other parties concerned. If the Communists relinquish their army and the government does not live up to its promise and does not organize a coalition government, what can we do?

Because of this seemingly convincing argument, the Consultative Conference dealt only with political problems and left the military questions entirely to the three-man group consisting of representatives of the Nationalist Government, the CCP, and the United States. None could intervene in its business. The "talk, talk, and fight, fight," show lasted for a year and ten months. General Marshall's mediation began in December 1945 and ended in November 1946. Everybody felt tired and gave up.

General Marshall revealed the fundamental reason why his and the efforts of the PCC (Political Consultative Conference) mediation efforts had failed in his public statement on January 7, 1947:

Most certainly, the course which the Chinese Communist Party has pursued in recent months indicated an unwillingness to make a fair compromise. It has been impossible even to get them to sit down at a conference table with government representatives to discuss given issues. Now the Communists have broken off negotiations by their last offer which demanded the dissolution of the National Assembly and a return to the military positions of January 13th which the government could not be expected to accept.

Professor Shyu criticized in a very general and unsubstantiated way the national government for its corruption and inefficiency. Nobody, of course, can say that any government is perfect. It cannot be perfect in this imperfect world. However, measured by general standards of political morality, at least the high officials in the government were not corrupt. They were efficient. Police irregularities regrettably exist everywhere. Wartime China was no exception. In case any irregularities were found, the government was most severe in punishment, as in the case of correcting malpractice in the military conscription system.

I, myself, lived those eight long years of war attrition in China—Shanghai, Nanking, Hankow, Changsha, Hsiangtan, Hengyang, Kweilin, Kweiyang and, finally, Chungking. With hardship and sufferings, combined with hope and promise, I was one of those who, like Professor Shyu, looked forward to seeing the rise of a united, peaceful and democratic China on the horizon. Yet, this did not materialize. It is with a deep sense of sadness for my homeland that I reviewed Professor Shyu's paper. I believe he will share this sad feeling with me and will give serious consideration to the observations I have stated.

CHAPTER IX

Regional Politics and
the Central Government:
Yunnan and Chungking

BY LLOYD E. EASTMAN

⌐⌐ⒸHINA," JAPANESE WERE wont to say during the War
of Resistance, "is not a nation; it is merely a geographical expression." The arrogance underlying
this assertion infuriated the Chinese. Yet the statement, although grossly misleading, was only partially false. For China
during the war was not a modern nation-state in the sense that the
European states were. Emotionally, it is true, many Chinese had by now
become exceedingly nationalistic. Politically, however, China was not a
modern nation-state, for it lacked a highly articulated, effective system
of control over its military and administrative arms. Nationalist China
during the war may therefore be best understood if it is viewed as a
rather fragile political coalition. This concept, too, does some violence
to the reality, yet it helps us realize that judgments regarding China's
achievements during the war—for example, its ability to marshal the
material and human resources of the nation, or its record of fighting
the Japanese—ought not be made with the same criteria we might use
to judge, say, Germany or the United States.

By the time the war against Japan began in July 1937, the Nationalist
government was dominant in eleven of the eighteen provinces in China
proper and controlled two-thirds of the population. It governed only
one-fourth of the nation's territory, however, for its control was limited
to the central and southern portion of the nation.[1] And by 1939 the
Japanese had occupied the areas which had hitherto served as the political and economic base of the Nationalist government. Now the base of
the government was in west China where the local satraps still viewed
the central government with suspicion, resentment, and foreboding.

In Szechwan, for example, large-scale fighting between provincial
troops and the central-government army had been averted in the spring

of 1937 after sensitive negotiations smoothed over the ruffled relations between Chungking and Nanking. But tensions persisted. In January 1938, for instance, after the provincial chairman, Liu Hsiang, died (presumably of stomach cancer) in a hospital in Nanking, Liu's wife and other Szechwanese partisans loudly charged that central-government agents had murdered him in order to eliminate an obstacle to Nanking's control of the province. And the Szechwanese powers then rejected Nanking's appointment of Chang Chun to replace Liu Hsiang as provincial chairman. Throughout the war, too, the provincial "warlords" in the province, such as Pan Wen-hua, Liu Wen-hui, and Teng Hsi-hou, continued to obstruct central-government control of the capital province of wartime China.[2]

Yen Hsi-shan's relations with Chungking during the war further exemplify how fragile was the political coalition that constituted Nationalist China. When the war began, Yen was named commander of the Second War Zone, and was vice-chairman under Chiang Kai-shek of the Military Affairs Commission. Not once during the war, however, did Yen make an appearance in Chungking nor even meet with Chiang. And he reigned over his province of Shansi almost as though it were an independent kingdom. He maintained his own political party (Democratic Revolutionary Comrades' Association; Min-chu ko-ming tung-chih hui); did not tolerate the presence of national troops within his war zone; viewed Chiang Kai-shek (in the words of a subordinate) with "deep distrust"; and, particularly since 1942, maintained close and amiable relations with the Japanese—even maintaining a liaison office in Japanese-occupied Tai-yuan.

From Yen Hsi-shan's point of view, the Japanese were a lesser threat than was the central government. According to a general in Yen's army, the term "enemy" in the many wall slogans in Yen's war zone referred primarily to the Communists. Ranking second as an enemy of Yen, because it constantly threatened to interfere in local affairs, was the Nationalist government. Next on Yen's list of enemies were the Chinese puppets serving under the Japanese. And finally, lowest on the list, were the Japanese.[3]

Each of the provinces differed in their relations with the center. Some, like Kweichow and Chekiang, were highly loyal to the Chungking authorities. In others, like Kwangtung, the provincial chairman trusted by the Nationalist government (Li Han-hun) was counterbalanced by a military commander (Yu Han-mou) whose loyalties were ambivalent. Yunnan cannot, therefore, be regarded as typifying the relations between all the provinces and the central government. Yet, by examining this one province in some detail, it is possible to discern some of the dynamics affecting Chiang Kai-shek's political coalition during the war.

Yunnan had seldom enjoyed prominence in the national politics of China until the war with Japan. Sequestered deeply in the southwest, it was indisputably part of the Chinese polity. Culturally and ethnically, however, it stood apart. It lay closer to Calcutta than to Shanghai; Burma and French-Indochina were its neighbors; and over half of its sparse and—even by Chinese standards—impoverished population were ethnically non-Chinese. The French-owned Kunming-Hanoi railroad was the province's primary access to the outside world, and over it came French cigarettes, guns, and cultural-economic influences. Kunming, capital of the province, even had something of a French flavor, for numerous French-built offices and homes lay among the crowded, noisy Chinese shops and streets. Indeed, until 1940, the American consulate in Kunming kept its records in French piastres rather than in Yunnanese provincial currency.[4] But the Yunnanese remained suspicious of all outside influences, French or Chinese. They were marked by a deep isolationism, and formidable emotional walls consequently obstructed the inflow of central-government influences throughout the war.

Warlord of Yunnan in the 1930's and 1940's was Lung Yun (1888-1962). Lung Yun was a Lolo, one of the largest minority tribes in the province, and he had had little experience outside his native Yunnan. As a youth, he had participated in the semi-clandestine secret societies that were active in the province. About 1910, at the age of twenty-two, he met Tang Chi-yao, and from then until 1927 their stars were to rise together. Tang was then an instructor at the Yunnan Provincial Military Academy, and he arranged Lung's appointment as a cadet. Subsequent to the revolution against the Manchus, Tang became a major political force in southwest China—and under him Lung Yun took lessons in the rough-and-tumble of warlord and Kuomintang politics. An apt student, Lung led a coup against his mentor and replaced him as chairman of Yunnan in 1927. From then until he was ousted from office by Chiang Kai-shek in 1945, Lung was the dominant personality in Yunnanese politics.[5]

Assessments of Lung Yun vary widely. To some, particularly to partisans of the central government, he was an unregenerate warlord and opium addict, indifferent to all but his personal and provincial interests, and whose administration was backward and corrupt. In fact, however, he was by the standards of his day a relatively dedicated, progressive, and incorrupt provincial militarist. He never succeeded in bringing prosperity to the province, but he eliminated much of the banditry that had long bedeviled the province. Although he was himself hopelessly addicted to opium, he undertook with considerable success after November 1934 to suppress cultivation and trade of the drug. Indeed, during

1936 and 1937, Lung transformed the fiscal basis of his government by making mining and industry, rather than opium, the major source of its revenue. Aside from modern industry, Lung took an active interest in civic improvements and health projects, and he gained a reputation for acting upon as well as talking about these interests. The shocking forms of warlord exploitation that beset neighboring Szechwan were not in evidence in Yunnan, and he seems to have attained genuine popularity with most of his fellow provincials.[6]

Although his province was the largest in China proper (and nearly twice the size of France), Lung Yun never became a major political force during the 1930's.[7] His army before the war numbered only 30-40 thousand men, and the economic base of the province was pathetically small. He therefore moved with circumspection through the shoals of warlord politics. He was not tempted—except for an occasional but fleeting leer at neighboring Kweichow—to become involved in affairs outside his own domain. Caution, restraint, and good sense marked his relations with the other provinces, and the other provincial militarists respected him for it.

To all the provincial militarists in the 1930's, the central government was, of course, the most formidable challenge. Eventually it was to be Lung Yun's undoing, but for eighteen years Lung resisted its centralizing pretensions with consummate skill. Among the regional leaders, Lung during the 1930's stood out as one of the most supportive of the Nationalist government. When a warlord coalition attempted in 1930 to establish a separatist government in Peking, for example, Yunnanese troops moved against the rebellious Kwangsi forces led by Li Tsung-jen and Pai Chung-hsi. During the revolt of Kwangtung and Kwangsi in 1936, Lung again resisted the entreaties for support from the rebel leaders and declared instead his loyalty to the Nanking government. And when Chiang Kai-shek was kidnapped at Sian, Lung offered to lead a punitive expedition against the kidnappers, and he was vituperative in his denunciation of Chang Hsueh-liang. A local newspaper, which reflected Lung's views, called Chang "not only childish but also disloyal and unfilial. He is certainly most stupid and breaks wind."[8]

During the early 1930's, the Nationalist government had been a remote influence and made little difference in the lives of the Yunnanese. The Kuomintang had branches in the province, but, lacking financial and other support from the provincial government, it was virtually moribund. In 1934, the New Life Movement was instituted in government offices, the army, and schools, but thereafter—except on special occasions, such as Chiang Kai-shek's visit to the province in May 1935—it was seldom mentioned and of no consequence. Occasionally, too, an official delegation from Nanking, concerned with geologic surveys or health conditions, would arrive and depart, but these caused little stir in the affairs of the province.

By 1935, however, the central government did begin to make inroads in the province, largely as a result of the Communists' presence in the southwest during their fabled Long March. Some 50,000 national troops entered the province; they spent large sums of national currency, leading to the rumor that soon the Central Bank of China would open a branch in Yunnan. In September 1935, a branch of the Central Military Academy opened in Kunming. Yunnanese army officers attended central-government military schools in Nanking, Hangchow, and Szechwan for advanced technical and, one presumes, political training. And roads were being planned and built, often with subsidies from Nanking.[9]

On the eve of the war with Japan, therefore, the existence of the central government had become a reality for the Yunnanese. And, throughout this process, Lung Yun had moved deftly. As quickly as possible he arranged to have Nanking's anti-Communist troops withdrawn from the province; and he quickly retired the national currency from circulation, thereby preserving the province's monetary autonomy. Even while maximizing the semi-independence of his province, however, he won at least the grudging favor of Chiang Kai-shek. When a group of cadets in the local branch of the Central Military Academy requested that Lung be dismissed from the provincial chairmanship, Chiang supported Lung and imprisoned the cadet agitators.[10] Lung was also rewarded by Chiang in 1935 and 1936 with such prestigious posts as commander-in-chief of the Second-Route Bandit-Suppression Army, Pacification Commissioner of Yunnan and Kweichow, and membership in the Central Supervisory Committee of the Kuomintang.

Despite this considerable evidence that Lung Yun had become a faithful supporter of the Nationalist government, it may be doubted that he ever sensed an emotional or moral commitment to national unity or to the doctrines of the Kuomintang. It appears rather that he pragmatically accepted the fact that the future of China lay with the central government and not with the provincial militarists. It was therefore to his advantage to offer not opposition but at least limited cooperation to the central authorities. As a State Department official observed, his policy toward the central government was marked throughout by "cautious and well-balanced opportunism."[11]

With the outbreak of the war and the Nationalist government's subsequent retreat to the interior, the quality of the relationship between Yunnan and the central government changed fundamentally. Hitherto, Yunnan had been peripheral to the major concerns of the central government, and Nanking had had no need to ensure that the Yunnanese provincial government responded quickly and efficiently to its will.

Now all that was changed. Yunnan now became, second only to Szechwan, the most important province in wartime Nationalist China. Now it became a critical source of men, money, and materiel for the central government. It therefore became a matter of importance to the central government how Yunnan was ruled and how its rulers responded to its wishes.

During the initial months of the war, for example, Chiang Kai-shek was uncertain whether Lung Yun would support the war effort or would revolt against the central government. Chiang therefore felt it insufficient simply to order Lung to dispatch troops to resist the Japanese; he felt it necessary to send an emissary to entreat Lung to do so.[12] In fact, Lung soon sent a reported 160,000 troops to the war zone, seemingly without hesitation. Yet the fact is that Chiang Kai-shek misdoubted Lung's professions of loyalty. And the widespread rumor that Chiang had attempted to oust Lung from the provincial chairmanship in January 1938 may well have been grounded in fact.[13]

When the Japanese invasion began, much of the Yunnanese population enthusiastically supported the cause of resistance. But the war soon imposed strains upon the Yunnanese devotion to the Nationalist cause. Changes came flooding into the province, transforming Yunnan more in three years, perhaps, than it had changed in the preceding thirty years. Central-government influence accompanied these changes, and the Yunnanese authorities—some more than others—attempted to prevent the erosion of local power. By mid-1939, relations with the central government came very close to the breaking-point.

The sources of change were everywhere. Not long after the war began, for example, Yunnan became Nationalist China's chief doorway to the outside world. In October 1938, both Wuhan and Canton fell to the Japanese; fortuitously, the Burma Road, with its terminus in Kunming, had just opened and therefore kept open a line of traffic from external sources of supply. Soon, two all-weather highways connected Yunnan with Szechwan. And Kunming's airport became the busiest in China, servicing flights to Chungking, Hong Kong (until its fall in December 1941), and India (Kunming was the destination for the famed flights over "the Hump" of the United States Air Force).

Suddenly, too, Yunnan was becoming integrated into the cultural and economic life of the nation. By 1938, some 60,000 refugees had moved into the province—not a large number to be sure, but they concentrated in Kunming (pre-war population of which was less than 143,000),[14] and many of them were middle and upper-class sophisticates whose influence was disproportionate to their numbers. Kunming now became an educational center. Prior to the war, the only university in the province had been the undistinguished Yunnan Provincial University. In 1938, however, three of China's leading institutions of higher learning (Peking

National University, Tsinghua University, and Nankai University), together with several lesser universities, were relocated in or near Kunming. Kunming was thus immediately transformed from a cultural backwater into a center of intellectual, cultural, and political ferment.

Yunnan had experienced a modest development of industry since 1935, but with the war a number of new factories were relocated or established in and near Kunming. The National Resources Commission of the central government, whose responsibility it was to develop the nation's defense and heavy industries, particularly sensed the advantages offered by Kunming's access to the Burma Road and its remoteness from the battlefront. It therefore established, for example, the Central Machine Works, which in early 1940 began producing motors, generators, machine tools, etc; and the Electrical Manufacturing Works, which in July 1939 began production of copper and steel wire, light bulbs, batteries, telephones, etc. The Bank of China established a cotton mill in Kunming, and the Ministry of War opened an optical instruments factory.[15]

The Yunnanese had not obstructed these economic and educational incursions upon their placid insularity. The influx of industry created unprecedented prosperity in the province, and the Kunming authorities therefore encouraged further investments that contributed to industrial development and agricultural reconstruction. But the roads, industries and schools also brought in their train the interests and influences of the central government, and during 1938 and 1939 strains in the relationship appeared.

The points of contention during the first several years of the war were, surprisingly, not political or military. In these areas, Chiang Kai-shek moved with a keen awareness of Yunnanese sensitivities. Friction developed, however, in such areas as banking, finance, and foreign trade as Yunnan was drawn inexorably but reluctantly into the economic orbit of the Nationalist government.

One of the pillars of Yunnan's semi-autonomous position, for example, was the provincial government's virtual monopoly of banking and the issue of currency. Despite the central government's currency reforms of November 1935, which had stipulated that *fapi* (the currency of the Nationalist government) was to become the sole legal tender throughout China, Yunnan had continued to use primarily the currency issued by its own government-owned New Futien Bank. In December 1937, a branch of the Central Bank of China was established in Kunming,[16] but it initially restricted its activities to handling the receipts from the customs and from the sales of war bonds. These transactions did not interfere with the New Futien Bank's dominance of the provincial economy, and the Yunnanese authorities consequently sensed little threat from the new bank. In 1938, however, the Central Bank began to issue *fapi* through its Kunming branch. This did threaten the Yunnanese position, and the New Futien Bank attempted to stanch the inflow of *fapi* by manipulating the exchange rates of its notes for *fapi*. For several days in May 1939, it even refused to accept *fapi* at all.[17] It was, however, a losing battle, because *fapi* were now pouring into the province from other sources. The growing numbers of central-government employees, such as workers in the new enterprises of the National Resources Commission and the Central Air Academy (which moved to Yunnan in 1938), were all paid in *fapi*. Refugees and growing numbers of travelers through Yunnan also brought *fapi* in their baggage. By mid-1939, therefore, provincial currency was being accepted only at a discount, and by 1942 *fapi* reigned supreme.[18]

Meanwhile, other national banks sought a foothold in the province. The powerful Bank of China, headed by T. V. Soong, attempted in November 1938 to begin banking and investment operations. The Kunming authorities placed so many obstructions in its way, however, that in December it briefly abandoned the effort and withdrew its personnel to Hong Kong. The withdrawal of the Bank of China, according to an American official in Kunming, was "interpreted here as a recognition of the failure of the possibility of cooperation and also as a kind of declaration of war against the Provincial [New Futien] Bank."[19]

Once again, however, the Yunnanese were unable to hold off the incursions of the central authorities, and by early 1939 all four of the National-government banks, including the Bank of China, had opened branches in Kunming and even in other cities of the province. The Yunnanese economy was now booming, and the New Futien Bank was simply unable to accommodate the growing demands for capital, banking facilities, and foreign-currency exchange. The ascendancy of the central-government banks inevitably reduced Yunnanese control over the provincial economy. But these banks were sufficiently lavish with loans for agricultural reconstruction and with capital for the promotion of specifically Yunnanese industrial undertakings that most opposition was soon mollified.[20]

This tendency of the central government to placate opposition to its encroachments upon Yunnanese independence by remunerating the Yunnanese financially was evident also in a dispute over taxes. Early in the war, for example, the central government proposed that it take over the administration and control the receipts of all "national" taxes in the province, such as the salt tax. The authorities in Kunming initially protested. Finally, however, they acquiesced, but only after the central government agreed to pay a "subsidy" to the Yunnan provincial government that was equivalent to the net revenue from the salt tax. Doubtless this loss of administrative control did not bode well for the long-term autonomy of the province. It was, however, an admirable device for giving face to all parties concerned.[21]

Just when the quarrel with the Bank of China was at its height in December 1938, the defection of Wang Ching-wei heightened the mistrust that permeated relations between Kunming and Chungking.[22] On this self-appointed mission of ending the war through negotiations with the Japanese, Wang's first stop after leaving Chungking on December 18, 1938, was Kunming. Lung Yun was an avowed admirer of Wang,[23] and Wang now hoped to persuade Lung and several of the other militarists in the southwest, such as Chang Fa-kuei, to support his peace movement.

What transpired in that meeting, which lasted into the small hours of December 19, is not known. Lung subsequently claimed that he told Wang that his plan was utterly unrealistic. But Chungking was on tenterhooks, for Lung's conduct during the ensuing months gave ample basis for the fear that he might join in Wang's scheme. On January 10, 1939, for example, Lung was conspicuously absent from a meeting of provincial leaders in Chungking. And wealthy residents of Hong Kong, supporters of Wang, transmitted Y3 million to Kunming, ostensibly to support the provincial program of financial reform, but not improbably a bribe to win Lung Yun's support for Wang.[24]

Lung finally, on February 10, issued a statement to the press. It was, however, ambiguous. He denied that he was associated with Wang Ching-wei's peace movement, and he asserted that he supported the central government's policy of continued resistance to the Japanese. At the same time, he added that he was not opposed to a peace movement as such if Japan would agree to treat with China on a basis of national equality. Meanwhile, Lung remained in contact with Wang, who was now in Hanoi. And he did not issue a formal denunciation of Wang until May 2, a week after Wang had left Hanoi enroute to the Japanese-occupied area of China.[25] The incident of Wang Ching-wei's defection thus passed, but it almost surely left a residue of bitterness that exacerbated the next and most enflamed confrontation between the provincial and national governments.

At issue in this newest dispute was control of Yunnan's extensive foreign trade. Increasingly after the fall of Hankow and Canton, the foreign trade of Nationalist China was channelled through Yunnan. And the Yunnanese government, over the vigorous objections of the central government, levied a likin-type transit tax, euphemistically called the Special Consumption Tax, that was the province's largest single source of revenue.[26] Yunnan itself exported substantial quantities of such goods as tea, raw silk, tung oil, animal skins, and pig bristles. Tin, however, was the province's chief export commodity—one that was a lucrative source of tax income for the provincial government and from which the New Futien Bank derived most of its revenue.[27] So sensitive was the Yunnanese government about tin, in fact, that as early as October 1938 it instituted a monopoly over the export of tin, presumably as a means of forestalling central-government control over the metal.

The encroachments of the central government began during early 1939. In February the National Foreign Trade Commission established an office in Kunming, and the Ministry of Communications informed the provincial government that henceforward it would administer the examination and shipping of all Yunnan's export commodities—except tin. And in April, Chungking banned the local government from imposing the Special Consumption Tax on commodities passing through Yunnan from other provinces.[28]

This was a devastating blow to the provincial government's economic structure, and Lung Yun must have protested with unusual vehemence. In June, the State Department reported that "the Chungking authorities, having lost faith in Chairman Lung's professions of cooperation, are preparing arrangements for a full control of the province." At the same time, the central government was massing troops along the provincial border.[29]

Pushing its advantage, Chungking in July decreed that it was assuming control of all foreign trade throughout the country. This meant that not only would the central government tax all export-import items— now for the first time including also those that originated within Yunnan —but it would also establish monopoly control of the trade of all major export commodities, including tin.

Kunming's response was immediate. It banned the export of any Yunnanese product that did not bear an exchange certificate from the New Futien Bank. And, because that bank refused to issue any certificates, the flow of Yunnanese exports halted completely. In Chungking, a series of long and hard negotiations began, in which the Kunming representatives endeavored to settle not only the disputes over foreign trade and tin, but the whole range of provincial-central government problems. Relations became taut. In August, the attempt by one group of Yunnanese negotiators to reach a settlement was a total failure and they returned home. Chungking watched Yunnanese troop movements with unusually rapt attention. And for four months no tin or other Yunnanese goods moved out of the province.[30]

A second group of Yunnanese negotiators went to Chungking, however, and on October 12, 1939, an agreement was reached. Significantly, the central-government authorities once again avoided running rough-shod over provincial interests, and the settlement was a compromise. The entire export trade of the province was henceforward to be controlled by a branch of the National Foreign Trade Commission, but this branch would be constituted jointly of Yunnanese as well as central-government representatives. The export of tin, tung oil, tea, and pig bristles now became a central-government monopoly, but the central government as compensation agreed to pay the provincial government an annual subsidy of £1,600,000. This sum probably more than repaid Yunnan for relinquishing control of its export trade.[31]

With this agreement in mid-October 1939, peace seemed to have been restored to Nationalist-Yunnanese relations. Lung Yun took the occasion to reaffirm his allegiance to the central government and to announce his determination to kill the traitor Wang Ching-wei.[32] "Politically," reported an American official on October 19, "Yunnan would appear to be now safe for the Nationalist Government."[33]

Thus far during the war, the points of friction between the Yunnan and Nationalist governments had been chiefly economic. The reasons for this are clear enough. The Nationalists had had to create a wartime economic base in the interior, and Yunnan, by dint of its seeming safety from Japanese attack, its vaunted though exaggerated stores of natural resources, and its proximity to Szechwan, the capital province, made it an obvious place to establish strategic enterprises. Moreover, Yunnan's transportation outlets to Hanoi and Burma suddenly transformed Kunming into the nation's leading entrepot for foreign trade—with obvious ramifications in the spheres of banking and taxation.

The process through which the Yunnanese learned to accommodate these economic changes was a painful one, for the foundations of Yunnan's economic autonomy were being eroded. The Nationalist authorities attained their goal of integrating Yunnan into the wartime economic system, however, because of their willingness to reimburse the province financially. Virtually every conflict was ameliorated by grants of subsidies, by promises of loans for provincial reconstruction, or by capital investments in Yunnanese-owned enterprises. And by October 1939, the basic economic differences had been ironed out.

In attaining its economic goals in Yunnan, the Nationalist government had chosen not to challenge the political authority of the Yunnanese leaders nor to alter the political institutions of the province. Certainly, it must have been tempting to do so. There had, of course, been the repeated, almost continual speculation since the war began that Lung Yun would be dismissed from the provincial chairmanship. Yet the Chungking authorities long refrained from challenging the Yunnanese directly on political grounds.

As the relationship with the Nationalist government evolved, however, political and military issues moved to the fore. Progressively Lung Yun was being alienated from the central government, and by late 1944 he was on the verge of open revolt against the Chungking authorities. One source of irritation was the growing presence of national troops in the province. Japanese armies had been active in south China since the latter part of 1939, in November invading southern Kwangsi and occupying the provincial capital of Nanning. Air raids on Yunnan had begun in the fall of 1938, and a Japanese attack on Yunnan was becoming a possibility. When Chiang Kai-shek in late 1939 ordered the first divisions of national troops into the province, however, Lung Yun vigorously protested what he must have regarded as an invasion of his domain. No doubt to appease him, Chiang Kai-shek named him commander of the Generalissimo's Field Headquarters in Yunnan and Kweichow—a position with indefinite military responsibilities, but that carried a Y100,000 monthly stipend, ostensibly for the operation of the new headquarters.[34]

The central government now only had its foot in the door, however, and its demands to admit more national troops into the province were insistent. The parade of Chungking officials traveling to Kunming, including Chen Li-fu, Ho Ying-chin, and Chiang Kai-shek himself, suggested however that Lung Yun was being obstructive. In August 1940, Lung reportedly rejected Ho Ying-chin's request that additional national troops be admitted to the province.[35] He argued, for example, that the growing numbers of soldiers in the province were placing intolerable strains on food supplies.[36] It is probable, too, that he argued that it would be more appropriate to transfer Yunnanese troops, now garrisoned elsewhere, back to the province rather than strengthening the contingent of the national army. By the latter part of 1941, however, national troops virtually had the run of the province, and in March 1943 they outnumbered local troops by a ratio of 4:1.[37]

The central government's efforts to introduce instruments of political control into the province constituted another source of friction. During 1939, the mood of political accommodation resulting from the formation of the united front had begun to dissipate. And the several secret police agencies of the central government—most notably the bureaus of Statistics and Investigation of the party and the army—and the San-min chu-i Youth Corps were progressively employed to enforce an ideological and political uniformity in the Nationalist areas. But Lung Yun, like several of the other provincial militarists, sensed a political advantage in giving refuge to political dissidents—perhaps because these dissidents' criticisms embarrassed the central authority or because, by harboring critics of the "down-river" government, he enhanced his popularity with the highly ethnocentric Yunnanese.

To the intense perturbation of the central authorities, therefore, Kunming became a haven, particularly after 1941 when Hong Kong could no longer provide refuge, for Chinese liberals. Lo Lung-chi, for example, had been a professor at Southwest Associated University and a member of the People's Political Council. He had, however, criticized the Nationalist government so vehemently that the central government had in 1941 ordered his dismissal from both positions. Lung Yun then befriended him. And in 1944 when the Nationalist government insisted that Lo be expelled from the province, Lung refused and merely replied that he would keep Lo under surveillance.[38]

Lo Lung-chi became a leader of the Federation of Democratic Parties when it was formed in 1941. And despite—or because of—the fact that the Federation's doctrinal cornerstone was opposition to the Nationalist's monopoly of government, Lung Yun became its friend and patron. Lung denied that he gave financial aid to the organization, but in fact he employed several of the Federation's leaders, including Pan Kuang-tan (Quentin Pan) and Pan Ta-kuei as well as Lo Lung-chi, in the capacity of "advisors." And he assisted Federation members, when they were financially straitened, to publish their writings. Half of his huge home in Kunming was also reportedly used as a dormitory for faculty at Lienta, and quite possibly liberals among the professors, rather than partisans of the central government, received preference in gaining admittance there.[39]

Thusly disposed, Lung Yun was no friend of the central government's enforcers of political orthodoxy. A preparatory office of the Youth Corps had been established in Yunnan in September 1939,[40] but Lung early the next year denied it permission to establish a branch in Chung-shan University. Lung even ordered several of the leading cadres arrested, and they were released only after Chungking interceded. Indeed, relations between Lung and the Youth Corps were so bad that in April 1940 a Youth Corps extremist incited one of Lung's cooks to poison his food.[41] Although the Youth Corps throughout the war maintained a presence in Yunnan, it was never as vigorous or repressive there as it was in areas more thoroughly subject to Nationalist controls.

It had been impossible for Lung Yun to exclude the central government's secret police from the province, for most central-government enterprises, military units, and Kuomintang branches contained sections concerned with "statistics and investigation." These conducted espionage in the province, and even propagandized within the Yunnanese army. Lung successfully kept these activities to a minimum, however, perhaps because, as was reported in 1944, he had extracted from the Chungking authorities a promise to curtail secret-service activities in the province.[42]

A reflection of the greater political freedom in the province was the relative outspokenness of the local press. The Lienta students and faculty published small periodicals (for example, the *Hsueh-sheng pao* [Student press] and *Min-chu chou-kan* [Democratic weekly]) which, though by any objective criteria would be regarded as restrained in their political comments, would not have lasted a week in Chungking or Sian. And the official organ of the provincial government, the *Yun-nan jih-pao* (Yunnan daily), employed an editorial staff that was sometimes vitriolic in its criticisms of central-government policies.[43]

None who knew Lung Yun believed that his liberalism was more than superficial, embraced for reasons of political advantage. Criticism of Lung himself, for example, probably would not have been tolerated in Yunnan. Nevertheless, Kunming throughout the war enjoyed greater political freedom than anywhere in Nationalist China with the possible exception of Kweilin. And one of the principal complaints of the Nationalist authorities against Lung was that he "harbored leftist elements, causing Kunming to become a hot bed of Communism."[44]

During the years 1939-1942, Yunnan's relations with the Nationalist government had sometimes been tense but had not threatened to snap. From 1943, however, the relationship steadily deteriorated as the strains of the long war began having a telling effect. The inflation which had been relatively moderate until 1942 was by 1943 corroding the economic and social foundations of the government. Corruption was spreading rampantly through the bureaucracy; the industrial economy, beginning about September 1943, turned sharply downward; the army, short of food and weapons, was passive and dispirited.

As the government deteriorated, opposition erupted to the surface. Peasant uprisings, prompted by widespread discontent with conscription and taxation practices of the government, were flaring up in virtually every province of Nationalist China, from Fukien and Kwangtung to Szechwan and Kansu.[45] Even within the government itself, dissatisfaction brewed. One manifestation of this discontent was the plot by several hundred young army officers to remove the high governmental officials and army officers, such as H. H. Kung and Ho Ying-chin, who were believed to be responsible for the corruption and debilitation of the regime. Chiang Kai-shek was not a target of the plot, but the authorities, after discovering the plot in about early December 1943, responded with fury, reportedly executing at least sixteen generals who were leaders in the conspiracy.[46]

Conscious of its deterioration and increasing political vulnerability, the Nationalist government was becoming even more authoritarian—or, as its critics phrased it, dictatorial—as the war dragged on. Chiang Kai-shek was less tolerant of criticism, more remote from even high-level officials, and concentrating ever more power in his own hands. Clarence Gauss, the United States ambassador, observed in December 1943 that "Chiang . . . seems more and more to require that matters of all kinds and degrees be referred to him."[47]

Corresponding to Chiang's attitude was the growth of political repression throughout the Nationalist areas and the mounting influence of reactionary elements within the Kuomintang. The secret services became more active; control over education was tightened; progressives, such as the liberal journalist Sa Kung-liao, were thrown into political prisons.

Censorship, too, now became more oppressive. The CC clique, one of the least liberal of the several factions within the party-government hierarchy, was also in the ascendant, replacing the less ideological and more pragmatic Political Science Clique in the central councils of the regime.[48]

Provincial militarists like Lung Yun partook of the political malaise of this period. They were fearful, because Chiang Kai-shek's heightened authoritarianism implied a determination to repress the regionalists as well as liberals and Communists. They were resentful, because they were convinced that Chiang had used the war to wear down their provincial armies by sending them into battle against the Japanese while he held his own divisions in reserve. And they were jealous, because Chiang's forces had received a lion's-share of American Lend-Lease equipment whereas their provincial armies had to make do with inferior weapons, clothing, food, and training. As a result, Everett F. Drumright reported in April 1943, there was a "bitterness and antagonism that seethes beneath the surface between authorities of the National Government on the one hand and the disappointed yet ever hopeful provincial militarists."[49]

Sensing their individual vulnerability to Chungking's centralizing tactics, provincial leaders at least as early as the spring of 1943 began to sound each other out on the possibility of concerting their opposition to the central government. The Federation of Democratic Parties, likewise discontented with the Nationalist government but for different reasons, also began to participate in the conspiracy.

This conspiracy was still in its formative stages when, in April 1944, the Japanese launched their Ichigo offensive. This was Japan's most formidable military operation of the war in China. It was intended primarily to destroy the Chinese-American air bases in south and east China. But it progressed with such ease—except for six weeks when Hsueh Yueh's land forces and Claire Chennault's Fourteenth Air Force staged a heroic resistance in front of Hengyang—that the Japanese were able to establish a direct, albeit tenuous, link from north China to Indochina. During December 1944, when Ichigo attained its furthest extent, a Japanese attack on Yunnan and Szechwan seemed a certainty.[50]

The political effects of Ichigo were as devastating to the Nationalist government as were the military effects. For the Japanese offensive revealed as never before the corruption, ineptitude, and demoralization of the central government. It revealed more starkly than previously that Chiang Kai-shek willingly threw the provincial armies into decimating combat while his own loyal central-government armies conserved their American-supplied equipment. Moreover, the Ichigo offensive caused the people to lose confidence even in Chiang Kai-shek. Prior to this, Chiang had continued to be regarded as a dedicated, inexpendable leader. Now, however, it burst upon the public consciousness that all of the corruption, factionalism, inefficiency and political repression resulted not just from the shortcomings of Chiang's lieutenants, but from flaws in Chiang himself. Now, it was reported, even liberals who a year earlier had staunchly supported him "see no hope for China under Chiang's leadership."[51]

The anti-Chiang movement in the provinces inevitably picked up momentum in the wake of the Ichigo offensive. To the provincial militarists, it demonstrated—as Li Chi-shen put it—"a deliberate plan on the part of the Central Government to sabotage and destroy the armies of those southern leaders whose loyalty to the ruling clique is considered questionable."[52] Moreover, Ichigo provided the provincial conspirators unprecedented opportunities to act, for the Chungking government was now both militarily threatened and politically weakened.

There were two vortices of the anti-Chiang movement in the provinces, and Lung Yun had been drawn into both of them. One was in Kwangsi, and was headed by that perennial political malcontent, Li Chi-shen.[53] With the support of various military commanders in south China—reportedly including Lung Yun, Chang Fa-Kuei and Yu Han-mou[54]—Li was forming an autonomous, democratic regime in east-central Kwangsi, near the border of Kwangtung. He believed that this regime, which was formally established in early November 1944 as the People's Mobilization Commission, would provide the nucleus of a new national government when Chiang's government disintegrated.[55]

The second center of the anti-Chiang conspiracy was in Kunming, where the prime movers, or at least the most articulate members, of the movement were radicals of the Federation of Democratic Parties, most notably Lo Lung-chi.[56] The Kunming movement was broader and more ambitious in its goals than its counterpart in Kwangsi. By mid-1944, the Federation had established contacts with a broad range of prominent political figures, including the Szechwanese militarists (Pan Wen-hua, Liu Wen-hui, and Teng Hsi-hou), Feng Yu-hsiang and Yen Hsi-shan, a group of Manchurian nationalists supporting Chang Hsueh-liang, military commanders such as Yu Han-mou, and a group of Shensi generals such as Sun Wei-ju. Li Chi-shen was, of course, actively involved. Pai Chung-hsi was virtually the only prominent provincial militarist that was not in some way associated with the movement. And the Communists, who had hitherto remained aloof, had by about May 1944 expressed general approval for the policies of the movement, although they did not commit themselves to participate in it.[57]

This was an extraordinarily disparate group. As the American consul at Kunming aptly remarked, "It would indeed be difficult to imagine a more heterogeneous group of feudal barons and radicals, idealists and practical politicians."[58] Some of the Federation leaders like Lo Lung-chi seem to have held deeply rooted liberal convictions. The militarists and former warlords, however, were probably motivated primarily by the desire to preserve their regional power. Lung Yun, for example, supported the Federation. Federation members apprehended, however, that he did so less from any sense of ideological conviction than from the recognition that his only chance of survival after the war lay in the success of a "democratic" movement which would preserve a federal political structure.[59] In allying with the regional militarists, the Federation leaders displayed more than a little wishful thinking. They convinced themselves, for example, that they could cooperate with these "feudal barons," because China had now progressed to a stage where a return to the anarchy of warlordism was inconceivable. And, in explaining why the democratic protestations of someone like Lung Yun could be relied on, they lamely—and in complete disregard for decades of warlord betrayals—explained that Lung was "enough of a traditionalist" that he would not renege on his promises.[60]

The strategy of this Federation-led movement was formulated on the assumption that the Chungking government was on the verge of collapse. Federation leaders, therefore, thought it possible to abstain from the use of revolutionary violence, and concentrated instead on preparing to fill the void that would be created by the inevitable fall of the Nationalist government. They actively established contacts with the anti-Chiang elements, and attempted to design a political program that would be acceptable to all as a basis for the projected successor regime. The new government was to be a democratic coalition that would guarantee the basic political freedoms of the people. Social revolution was explicitly ruled out. And, clearly a sop to the provincial leaders, the new regime would avoid the excessive centralization of the Chungking government and would encourage greater regional autonomy.

To formalize this political program, a people's congress—comprising representatives 40 per cent of whom were Kuomintang, 20 per cent Communist Party, 20 per cent Federation of Democratic Parties, and 20 per cent other groups—was scheduled to be held in Chengtu on about Double Ten (October 10), 1944. The congress would also lay the groundwork for a Government of National Defense (Kuo-fang cheng-fu) to serve as an interim government between the fall of Chiang Kai-shek and the creation of a permanent government after the defeat of Japan. Although the leaders of the movement anticipated the imminent collapse of the Nationalist government, the congress would precipitate that event by petitioning for Chiang Kai-shek's resignation.[61]

Virtually nothing resulted from all this conspiring and planning. It was naive in the extreme to believe that such a heterogeneous collection of dissidents could work concertedly in the creation of a viable national government. Perhaps because of the mixed character of the participants in the movement, they had not even agreed who would serve as the leader of the new Government of National Defense. Men mentioned as possible leaders included Li Chi-shen, Yen Hsi-shan, and Chang Hsueh-liang. Mao Tse-tung was also suggested as a possibility, though he was dismissed as lacking sufficient stature to attract broad popular support. If a great deal of naiveté and wishful thinking suffused this movement, the fact that it existed and that such a broad spectrum of political elements in the nation associated with it, reveals the extent of opposition to the Chungking government that had developed by 1944.

Certainly during the autumn of 1944, Lung Yun's relations with Chungking had gone from bad to worse. Yunnanese troops in late September had discovered and arrested a messenger who was carrying letters between Chiang Kai-shek and puppet officials in the Japanese-occupied area. Shortly after his arrest, however, military police of the central government seized the messenger. Thereupon Lung Yun sent his troops to surround the headquarters of the military police, and a major clash was avoided only when the agent was returned to the Yunnanese. Subsequently Lung Yun allowed the embattled messenger to proceed to Chungking. Then, however, Lung placed the commander of the central government's military police under arrest.[62]

Shortly after this prickly confrontation, a group of the central government's secret-service agents attempted to break up a mass meeting of several thousand people that was sponsored by the Federation of Democratic Parties—now, after October 10, 1944, known as the Democratic League. Rather than condoning this action, Lung Yun's military police arrested the central-government agents and held them prisoner for several hours.[63]

These incidents were but ripples on the surface. The basic cause of Lung Yun's discontent now was that, despite what was felt to be an imminent attack on the province by the Japanese, Chiang Kai-shek was still rationing out American military supplies only to his own national troops. Lung, and other provincial militarists too, were thus faced with the worrisome prospect of having to defend their provinces with armies that, they knew, were no match for the Japanese. Even if they did successfully resist the Japanese, which they regarded as doubtful, they would be so weakened that they would be powerless to prevent further centralization by the Nationalist authorities.

Lung Yun had appealed to Chungking for American weapons. Indeed, by October 1944 his sense of peril and frustration caused him to speak out in a mass demonstration, demanding that the central government provide American arms for the defense of the province. His newspaper, the *Yun-nan jih-pao,* took up the refrain, its editorials bitterly castigating central-government policies.[64]

Rebuffed by Chungking and with the Japanese armies moving southward and westward, a group of provincial militarists—reportedly consisting of Lung Yun, Pan Wen-hua, Liu Wen-hui, Teng Hsi-hou, Yu Han-mou and a number of Manchurian generals formerly under the command of the now incarcerated Yang Hu-cheng (whose crime had been to kidnap Chiang Kai-shek at Sian)—decided after prolonged negotiations that they would put up no resistance if the Japanese invaded their provinces. Instead, at the critical moment, and without forewarning Chungking, they would withdraw their armies into the security of the mountains. There they would watch as the Japanese destroyed Chiang Kai-shek's armies. After the war had been won by the allies, they would resume their accustomed positions of provincial leadership. If Chiang were not completely defeated by the Japanese, at least his armies would be so weakened that the provincial armies could then easily complete the task.[65]

The conspiring provincial militarists did, however, leave themselves an alternative. Certain that Chiang Kai-shek would not agree to provide them with Lend-Lease arms, they appealed directly to the American authorities. If the United States wished them to continue the resistance against the Japanese, they said, then it must immediately supply their armies with modern weapons. Moreover, they expressed the hope that United States officers would assume full command of their troops. If this were done, they thought, they could both resist the Japanese and emerge from the war in a strengthened position, at least the military equals of Chiang Kai-shek.[66]

This plan to let Chiang Kai-shek suddenly bear the entire brunt of the Japanese attack was as neat a bit of treachery as any that had been conceived in thirty years of warlord struggles and betrayals. Chiang Kai-shek, however, learned of the plot and moved to counteract it. To Lung Yun, who was planning to withdraw his Yunnanese forces to his native area near Chao-tung in the northern panhandle of the province, Chiang sent two of his most trusted emissaries. These were Liu Chien-chun and Ho Ying-chin, natives of neighboring Kweichow, who were respected by Lung but whose loyalty to the central government was unquestioned. Liu Chien-chun warned Lung, for example, that Japan was doomed to be defeated, and that, if Lung went through with this scheme, he would be on the losing side and would be branded as a traitor. Far wiser, Liu told him, would be to resist the Japanese, for, even if Lung's armies were defeated, he would be regarded as a national hero and his control of Yunnan would be correspondingly strengthened. This, Liu Chien-chun said, was a strategy whereby "if you win you will be victorious, and if you are defeated you will also be victorious."[67]

The effect of this argument on Lung is unclear. It is known, however, that Lung, probably during January 1945, negotiated an agreement with the central government. Chungking promised, for example, to allocate sufficient American Lend-Lease materials to fully equip three of Lung's provincial divisions. Lung, for his part, would allow Chiang's secret police greater freedom in the province, he would restrict the activities of the Democratic League, and he would dismiss the editorialists on the *Yun-nan jih-pao* who had been so sharply critical of the Chungking government. Lung also, it may be inferred, promised to abandon his plan of retiring into the mountains in the event of a Japanese invasion.[68]

This compromise did not resolve the contradictions between Chungking and Kunming. Chiang Kai-shek now in the spring of 1945 was looking forward to the postwar situation. And, from the vantage point of Chungking, it appeared probable that a mortal struggle with the Communists was in the offing. If this were true, then Lung Yun's continued rule of Yunnan would be both inconvenient and dangerous. As Chiang Kai-shek put it, "The path of national reconstruction will be hard and long. We must therefore strengthen the central government and reorganize the local governments. For only if we unify will we be strong; then will victory be sure."[69] Lung Yun was an obstacle to that goal of unity, and he had therefore to be eliminated.

Chiang Kai-shek had decided to remove Lung from Yunnan at least as early as April 1945.[70] His first move, so far as is known, was to summon General Tu Yu-ming (customarily referred to in English sources as Tu Li-ming) to Chungking. Tu was commander of the Kunming Defense Headquarters and was one of Chiang's most trusted generals. In their meeting, arranged with the utmost secrecy, Chiang informed Tu of his plan to transfer Lung Yun from Yunnan and to appoint him to the post of chairman of the Military Advisory Council. (This position was an honorific graveyard for Chiang's quondam rivals; the title was prestigious, but carried with it no substantive responsibilities or power.) Chiang Kai-shek feared, however, that Lung Yun would not submit passively to his political demise. He therefore instructed Tu to consolidate control over all key military installations in and around Kunming in the anticipation that Lung would forcefully resist his transfer.[71]

If the Japanese had not suddenly surrendered, Chiang Kai-shek's coup against Lung would have occurred in mid-August 1945. For, in mid-July, he had called in Li Tsung-huang, a Yunnanese but a staunch member of the CC clique, and ordered him to make preparations to assume the chairmanship of Yunnan. And on August 9, Tu Yu-ming was again called to Chungking for a meeting with Chiang, probably with last-minute orders regarding the approaching coup. Just then, however, Chiang learned of Japan's decision to surrender. This postponed the coup for about six weeks.[72]

During this period, the highly efficient Chinese grapevine bore rumors that Chiang was planning to dismiss Lung from his provincial chairmanship. Indeed, in August, Lung even remarked to an American that if Chungking wished to dismiss him, it had merely to issue an order; there was no need for conspiracy because he lacked the power to resist.[73] Perhaps because of this sense of fatalism, Lung fell in with a scheme concocted by Chiang to strip him of effective military support. For, although he had received plenteous hints of Chiang's attitude towards him, he acquiesced in an order from Chungking to send four divisions of his provincial troops, commanded by his half-brother General Lu Han, into Indochina, there to accept the surrender of Japanese forces. After the departure of those troops in mid-September, Lung was virtually denuded of military power. Only 9,000 regular troops and a collection of nondescript *hsien* militia remained to protect him.[74]

The denouement came in early October. At dusk in the evening of October 2, Li Tsung-huang and a select group of other officials flew into Kunming with Chiang Kai-shek's written orders to be delivered to Lung by General Tu Yu-ming, dismissing Lung from all his party and military posts in Yunnan and naming him chairman of the Military Advisory Council.[75] Tu, rather than delivering the order to Lung, set his troops into action. At about four or five o'clock on the morning of October 3, Lung Yun was shocked out of his sleep by the sound of shooting. Dressing quickly, he discovered that a sizable force of the central government's Fifth Army had assembled outside his residence. Lung and two aides, assuming the worst, disguised themselves as civilians, secreted themselves from the grounds by means of a small back door, and stole their way to the fortress-like and heavily defended provincial headquarters, about a half-mile away. Meanwhile, the conflict between the central-government forces and Lung's troops erupted into a mini-war. Throughout that morning and until the early afternoon, the sound of mortar, bazooka, machine-gun, and rifle fire echoed through the streets.

Not until noon, some seven or eight hours after the fighting began, did Tu Yu-ming present the order transferring Lung Yun to Chungking. Lung subsequently claimed that, immediately upon being informed of his transfer, he issued a cease-fire to all his troops. The fighting continued, however, and it is probable that he was personally responsible for the continued resistance. Even if originally he might have acquiesced peacefully in his removal from power, he was now infuriated by Tu's peremptory resort to force. Perhaps too, because of Tu's use of force, Lung was concerned for the safety of himself and his family.[76]

Tu Yu-ming's decision to deploy his army against Lung, before determining what Lung's response to his dismissal would be, was bitterly criticized at the time, and even now one wonders if the bloodshed could not have been avoided if more diplomatic methods had been employed. Both before and after the episode, Lung remarked that he had always been an obedient subordinate of the Generalissimo, and that if Chiang wished him to go to Chungking, he needed only to issue the order.[77]

Lung's protestations of loyalty to Chiang were probably something less than candid, but Chiang Kai-shek himself gave substance to the accusation that Tu had acted improperly when on October 16 he removed Tu from command of the Kunming Defense Headquarters. In punishing Tu, however, Chiang was merely offering a scapegoat to the Yunnanese, who had been infuriated by the central government's use of *force majeure*. In fact, in calling out his army, Tu had acted in full accord with Chiang Kai-shek's wishes. For Chiang, before the coup, had feared that Lung would resist being removed from Yunnan and had discussed those fears with Tu. Moreover, on October 2 Chiang had sent written instructions to Tu to seize control of all airbases in Yunnan "in order to prevent any treacherous disturbances"—clear evidence that Chiang anticipated that Lung Yun might resist his dismissal.[78] The punishment of Tu Yu-ming was therefore only nominal, and he was immediately thereafter rewarded with a new appointment as top commander of Nationalist forces in Manchuria.[79]

If Lung Yun would indeed have complied peacefully with an order from Chiang Kai-shek, then it was a tragic miscalculation to use force. For the resulting fighting fits none of the stereotypes of warlord battles. No love was lost between the Yunnanese and national troops, and they killed each other with a vengeance that might better have been saved for the Japanese. Hundreds died. Prisoners were reportedly shot on the spot. The bodies of Yunnanese soldiers were found to have been bayonetted repeatedly after death. Yunnanese, possibly civilians, served as snipers against the detested national forces; when caught, they were "given a fair trial and shot."[80]

After the first day of fighting, however, Lung was badly outnumbered, and his only hope was to obtain reinforcements from outside the city. He ordered magistrates in nearby *hsien* to dispatch militia to Kunming. And Lung's son, commanding a brigade, was called from Chao-tung, some 200 miles away. Until this help could arrive, Lung parlayed for time. He told his attackers that he would willingly go to Chungking, but that he wished to wait until General Lu Han could arrive from Hanoi to replace him as provincial chairman. But Lung's stalling merely angered Chiang Kai-shek, who feared what impression a protracted resistance might have upon other provincial leaders. Chiang therefore fixed October 5 as the deadline for Lung's departure for Chungking.[81]

Meanwhile, Lung's expected reinforcements did not arrive. The militia did not come, because Tu Yu-ming's forces had cut the telegraph lines. And the relief column headed by his son was badly mauled by the national troops while still some forty miles from Kunming.[82] Learning of this, and after further negotiations with T. V. Soong and Ho Ying-chin (who came to Kunming warning him that Chiang Kai-shek's patience was wearing thin), Lung Yun finally surrendered. On the afternoon of the next day, October 6, he flew to Chungking.[83] This was a notable victory for Chiang Kai-shek and the central government. It was, according to a Chungking newspaper, "equivalent to the recovery of enemy-occupied territory."[84]

Lung Yun, in Chungking, at first lived in trepidation. Chiang did not deign to see him or even go through the formalities of explaining why he had been removed from office in Yunnan. Tai Li's secret police kept him under close surveillance; former friends avoided him; and he was in fear for his life.[85] For the next three years he lived in Chungking and Nanking as a virtual prisoner—although his imprisonment was comfortable and he retained the title of chairman of the Military Advisory Council.

Reverberations from the October coup against Lung Yun were to be felt even years after the event. And, in a marginal way, these contributed to the final overthrow of the Nationalist government in 1949.

The immediate effect of the coup was that, with Lung out of the way, central-government agents were unfettered and unrestrained in their suppression of Kunming's dissident intellectuals. Thus, during November 1945, when it became apparent that negotiations between the Communists and the Nationalists were breaking down, students and faculty in Kunming began protesting the resumption of civil war. Desperately anxious for peace and stability after the long war and intimately familiar with the Nationalists' jealous retention of power, these intellectuals were less critical of the Communists than of the Chungking government. To avoid civil war, they argued, the Nationalists must abandon their "one-man monopoly" of government. Instead, a democratic coalition government must be created that would restore efficiency and morality to government and that would protect the freedoms of the common people. The students were also vehemently critical of the United States which they contended was fostering the trend toward civil war by supporting the Chungking government.[86]

Central-government agents responded to these protests and accompanying demonstrations in their accustomedly heavy-handed fashion. On November 25 they attempted to break up a mass meeting by firing machine guns and rifles over the heads of the crowd. And, in the famous December First Incident, secret police murdered four students with hand-grenades, bayonetted another, and beat up numerous others.[87]

The consequences of these events are difficult to ascertain. Surely the fundamental sources of students' and intellectuals' discontent, that contributed in significant degree to the overthrow of the Nationalist government, lay deep in the political and economic maladies afflicting the nation. Yet this December First Incident did serve as a spark that ignited the student movement which persisted throughout the period 1945-1949. Demonstrations of sympathy for the Kunming martyrs were immediately organized in Canton, Nanking, Shanghai, and other cities of the nation. And progressively thereafter the loyalties of the nation's intellectuals slipped from the Nationalists' grasp.

The repercussions of the overthrow of Lung Yun were also to be felt, somewhat later, in Manchuria. For the Yunnanese provincial troops that had been sent to Indochina in August 1945 perceived, after learning of the coup against Lung, that they had been deceived by the central government and that they had been sent from the province only to clear the way for the elimination of Lung. Moreover, in the eyes of the central government, there was no room in Yunnan for 50,000 or more disaffected soldiers professing loyalty for a commander who was now under virtual arrest in Chungking. After completing their assignment in Indochina, therefore, they were transferred not back to their homes in Yunnan, but to the Northeast to fight the Communists. There the Communists played on the discontents of the Yunnanese troops, stressing in their propaganda that Chiang Kai-shek had used them treacherously, that Yunnan under central-government control had deteriorated so badly that their families "cannot bear to live," and that the counter-revolutionaries in Nanking were laughing up their sleeves at seeing Yunnanese and Communists, both enemies of Chiang Kai-shek, killing each other in Manchuria.[88]

This was effective propaganda, and in March 1946 the entire 184th Division of the Yunnanese Sixtieth Army defected to the Communists— the first defection on such a large scale in the Civil War. Thereafter Nationalist commanders treated the remainder of the Sixtieth Army with suspicion, employing secret agents in its ranks and dispersing its divisions among troops more loyal to the central government. In October 1948, however, during the battle for Chang-chun, this army too surrendered en masse to the Communists. In announcing his defection, the commander, General Tseng Tse-sheng, proclaimed: "After the victory in the War of Resistance, Chiang Kai-shek employed his deceitful schemes, sending our entire army to Hanoi on the pretext of accepting the surrender even while he plotted the Kunming Affair, sacrificing the people of Yunnan in order to eliminate his political rivals."[89] Thus, even three years later and in distant Manchuria, echoes of the coup against Lung Yun were still to be heard.[90]

And, finally, as the Nationalists' house of cards collapsed, the principal leaders of Yunnan during the war opted for Communist rather than Nationalist rule. In December 1948, after over three years of honorific captivity, Lung Yun, in a dramatic and meticulously planned escape, fled from Nanking to Hong Kong. Subsequently, in 1950, he went to Peking, where—until he was charged with being a rightist in 1958—he served as vice-chairman of the National Defense Council.[91]

And Lu Han served from December 1945 to 1949 as provincial chairman of Yunnan and commander of the provincial garrison forces, seemingly a relatively complaisant servant of the Nationalist authorities. When Chiang Kai-shek in late 1949 attempted to establish a final anti-Communist bastion in the southwest, however, Lu Han refused to cooperate. As a result, Chiang had to abandon this last foothold on the mainland and retreated instead to Taiwan. Lu Han remained in China after the Communist victory, and was presented with, among other honors, the Order of Liberation, First Class, in recognition of his contributions in 1949 to the Communist cause.[92]

Nationalist China during the war was not, in the European sense of the term, a nation-state. To marshal material, financial, and military resources for the war, Chungking had to negotiate and compromise, plead and threaten. Not even in the capital province of Szechwan did the sway of the central government extend unobstructed. It might even be said that, to a degree, the Nationalist government was operating in a hostile environment.

Historians should therefore be slow to criticize the Chungking government for not playing a more active role in the war against Japan. Westerners in particular make judgments which ignore that the Chinese Nationalists held only a tenuous control of the state; that Chinese politics had no tradition of pluralism, and that consequently the challenges of the provincial militarists and of the Communists were, perhaps literally, matters of life-and-death; and that it was not an inconsiderable feat, considering the political difficulties and economic resources of the Nationalist government, even to survive the eight years of war. It is a signal fact, for example, that the Nationalist government was able to marshal only about 3 per cent of the nation's gross national product for support of all functions of government during the war.[93] Probably no more than 40 per cent of the divisions in the Nationalist army were "reliable"—i.e., loyal to Chiang Kai-shek.[94] The government had no sizable base of support in the masses. And elements of the population that were politically conscious were progressively withdrawing their support.

The Chungking government was, therefore, extraordinarily weak with only a tenuous hold on the nation's sources of power. And, being weak, Chiang Kai-shek played the politics of weakness. That is, he worked to maintain himself and his government in a position of authority less by increasing his own power than by keeping all other political forces weak. He denied arms to the provincial armies; he kept even medicines from his nominal allies, the Communists; he repressed intellectuals whose ideas seemed to him dangerous; he kept even his supporters weak by balancing them one against the other. For a time this strategy succeeded in the sense that it kept Chiang in power. In a fundamental sense, however, it failed, for by keeping all these elements weak, Chiang prevented the nation from becoming strong. China was therefore the loser, but so also in the long run was Chiang.

Was there an alternative? If we grant that it is a politician's prerogative to perpetuate his power as long as possible, then were there courses of action that might have enabled Chiang both to retain power and to strengthen the Chinese state? Might Chiang, for example, have strengthened the nation by sharing power and weapons with the provincial militarists? This is doubtful, for men like Lung Yun, Liu Wen-hui, and Li Chi-shen were not notably enlightened, modern-minded men. They seem to have been, taken as a group, as hungry for power as Chiang Kai-shek was jealous of preserving his power. And they were little if any more enlightened than he regarding how to wield power for the welfare of the nation. Concessions by Chiang Kai-shek to the provincial militarists would probably, therefore, have resulted sooner or later in his own overthrow, and the rule of the provincial militarists would not have meant greater progress for China.

Or might he better have formed a coalition government containing representatives of all political groups including the Communists? In the short-run this might have been the wise course. But the Communists and the Nationalists could no more mix than could oil and water. Chiang correctly perceived, I think, that the Communists were too well organized, too disciplined, too committed to supra-personal goals, so that they would inevitably dominate any coalition government in which they were included. If one accepted the premise (as did Chiang) that Communist rule would be bad for China, then rejection of this alternative was both logical and necessary.

The only viable and fundamental alternative for Chiang Kai-shek, if he were both to perpetuate his own power and to strengthen China, was to broaden his base of political support. To do this, it would have been necessary to build a mass base among at least the non-Communist elements in the nation. To accomplish this, however, Chiang needed an entirely new concept of political power. His image of power was the traditional one in which elites competed among each other for a share of the political pie, and in which success was to be attained by maximizing one's own power by manipulating and aggregating the support of other elites against one's rivals. Chiang seemed not to comprehend that he could generate new sources of power by mobilizing support from outside the elite structure. He was too traditional and too practiced in the warlord struggles of the 1920's to transcend the politics of weakness. He did, it is true, form the San-min chu-i Youth Corps as a means of broadening his popular support. But he employed that organization largely as yet another instrument of political control rather than as a body that might give expression to popular demands and criticism.

Thus, the Youth Corps degenerated into just another faction in Chiang's constellation of supporters among the political elite. And, to foster national unity at the beginning of the war, he approved the formation of the People's Political Council, which was broadly representative of diverse interests and points of view. Significantly, however, in 1942, after non-Kuomintang elements in the Council became sharply critical of the Nationalists' conduct of government, the Council was reorganized. Non-Kuomintang participation was markedly reduced, and the Council was thereafter an empty showcase of democracy in China, wielding no power that could in a meaningful way alter the policies and practices of the reigning elite.

Chiang, of course, talked a great deal about democracy. His concept of democracy, however, was that the masses should follow him as their leader, punctiliously and unqualifiedly. That concept allowed no room for a loyal opposition, and criticism was tantamount to insubordination. In fact, the political culture of China was assuredly inimical to democracy, and Chiang was blameless for not having transformed China in the image of Britain or the United States. Democracy is not, however, the only means of building political power. What was required was a system of rule in which Chiang and his administrators were responsive to the will and the needs of significant segments of society. Insensitive to all political demands but those of political elites, however, the Nationalist government could not generate new sources of political power. The government and Chiang were accordingly condemned to live and die with the politics of weakness.

NOTES

1. Jürgen Domes, *Vertagte Revolution: Die Politik der Kuomintang in China, 1923-1937* (Berlin: Walter de Gruyter and Co., 1969), facing p. 680. The provinces controlled by Nanking were Anhwei, Chekiang, Fukien, Honan, Hunan, Hupei, Kiangsi, Kiangsu, Kwangtung, Kweichow, and Shantung.
2. Robert A. Kapp, *Szechwan and the Chinese Republic: Provincial Militarism and Central Power, 1911-1938* (New Haven: Yale University Press, 1973), pp. 121-141.
3. Office of Strategic Services Document XL24905, October 29, 1945; *Hsin-min pao* (Chungking), October 28, 1945, in *Chinese Press Review* (United States Consulate-General, Chungking), No. 292, October 29, 1945; *Lost Chance in China: The World War II Dispatches of John S. Service*, ed. Joseph W. Esherick (New York: Random House, 1974), pp. 57-61; and *The Amerasia Papers: A Clue to the Catastrophe of China* (Washington, D.C.: U.S. Government Printing Office, 1970) I: 767-775.

4. Perkins to State, August 31, 1942, State Dept. 893.00 P.R. Yunnan/ 162, p. 8.

5. Howard L. Boorman, ed., *Biographical Dictionary of Republican China* (New York: Columbia University Press, 1967-1970), II: 457-459, III: 223-225; J. C. S. Hall, *The Yunnan Provincial Faction, 1927-1937* (Canberra: The Australian National University Press, 1976), pp. 56-61. I am indebted to John Hall, the author of this latter work, for his knowledgeable comments upon a manuscript of this essay; letter dated December 2, 1976.

6. Hall, pp. 119-169.

7. Szechwan was the largest province of China proper until 1924, when it was divided into the two provinces of Szechwan and Sikang. Despite Yunnan's size, the total population of the province in 1934 was only 12 million. See Chang Hsiao-mei, *Yun-nan ching-chi* (The Economy of Yunnan) (Chungking: 1941), p. A29.

8. State Dept. 893.00 P.R. Yunnan/111, Political Report for December 1937, p. 4. See also Perkins to State, August 31, 1942, State Dept. 893.00 P.R. Yunnan/162, p. 22; and Hall, pp. 179-180.

9. State Dept. 893.00 P.R. Yunnan/84, Political Report for September 1935, p. 5; State Dept. 893.00 P.R. Yunnan/83, Political Report for August 1935, p. 3. On development of roads and railways, see Chang Hsiao-mei, Cps. 7-9.

10. State Dept. 893.00 P.R. Yunnan/91, Political Report for April 1936, p. 7.

11. Perkins to State, August 31, 1942, State Dept. 893.00 P.R. Yunnan/ 162, p. 23.

12. Chin Tien-jung, "Hsi-nan lao-chiang Liu Huan chuan-chi" (Biography of the old general from the southwest, Liu Huan), pt. 8, *Chun-chiu* ("The observation post"), No. 173 (September 16, 1964), pp. 24-25.

13. State Dept. 893.00 P.R. Yunnan/112, Political Report for January 1938, p. 5; Meyer to State, January 29, 1938, State Dept. 893.00/14218, encl. 1, p. 1 and encl. 2, p. 1. Because the Yunnanese prewar army was only 30-40,000 men, there is a question where Lung could have found 160,000 men. John Hall stated in his letter to me, "I suspect they were bandits that Lung found convenient to get rid of. He had tried to palm off 20,000 bandits on Jiang [Chiang Kai-shek] in 1928." See also Hall, p. 73.

14. Perkins to State, August 31, 1942, State Dept. 893.00 P.R. Yunnan/ 162, p. 17. Population figures on Kunming are in Chang Hsiao-mei, p. E12.

15. Perkins to State, August 31, 1942, State Dept. 893.00 P.R. Yunnan/ 162, pp. 4-5; Chang Hsiao-mei, Ch. 15.

16. State Dept. 893.00 P.R. Yunnan/111, Political Report for December 1937, p. 6.

17. Meyer to Johnson, January 29, 1938, State Dept. 893.00/14218, p. 2; State Dept. 893.00 P.R. Yunnan/126, Political Report for May 1939, p. 4.
18. Perkins to State, August 31, 1942, State Dept. 893.00 P.R. Yunnan/162, p. 9. In some outlying areas of Yunnan, however, provincial currency was still being commonly used in 1944. See Ringwalt to State, March 9, 1944, State Dept. 893.5151/990, in *Foreign Relations of the United States, 1944* (Washington, D.C.: U.S. Government Printing Office, 1967), VI: 375.
19. Southard to State, January 12, 1939, State Dept. 893.00/14300, p. 1. See also Perkins to State, August 31, 1942, State Dept. 893.00 P.R. Yunnan/162, p. 8.
20. Perkins to State, August 31, 1942, State Dept. 893.00 P.R. Yunnan/162, pp. 7-8.
21. *Ibid.*, pp. 11-14. A similar but even sharper controversy was waged over Yunnan's totally illegal—in the eyes of the central government—Special Consumption Tax, which was simply a euphemism for the *likin* tax that had been proscribed by Nanking in 1931. This dispute was resolved in an identical way—albeit not until 1942—when the Chungking government agreed to send a subsidy to Yunnan in an amount approximately equal to the previous revenues from that tax.
22. On the defection of Wang, see John Hunter Boyle, *China and Japan at War, 1937-1945: The Politics of Collaboration* (Stanford: Stanford University Press, 1972); and Gerald E. Bunker, *The Peace Conspiracy: Wang Ching-wei and the China War, 1937-1941* (Cambridge, Mass.: Harvard University Press, 1972).
23. Liu Chien-chun, *Yin-ho i-wang* (Memories at Yin-ho) (Taipei: 1966), p. 127.
24. State Dept. 893.00 P.R. Yunnan/123, Political Report for February 1939, pp. 6-7; Boyle, p. 225.
25. State Dept. 893.00 P.R. Yunnan/123, Political Report for February 1939, p. 7; State Dept. 893.00 P.R. Yunnan/126, Political Report for May 1939, p. 4.
26. Chang Hsiao-mei, pp. U32-33, U48-40; Perkins to State, February 12, 1940, State Dept. 893.51/7060, p. 3. See note 21 above.
27. Perkins to State, August 31, 1942, State Dept. 893.00 P.R. Yunnan/162, p. 10.
28. *Ibid.*
29. Peck to State, June 3, 1939, State Dept. 893.00/14381, pp. 1-2.
30. Meyer to Johnson, October 19, 1939, State Dept. 893.00/14457, p. 5; Perkins to State, August 31, 1942, State Dept. 893.00 P.R. Yunnan/162, p. 10.
31. *Ibid.*, pp. 1-5; Perkins to State, August 31, 1942, State Dept. 893.00 P.R. Yunnan/162, pp. 9-11.

32. State Dept. 893.00 P.R. Yunnan/131, Political Report for October 1939, pp. 4-5.

33. Meyer to Johnson, October 19, 1939, State Dept. 893.00/14457, p. 4.

34. Perkins to State, August 31, 1942, State Dept. 893.00 P.R. Yunnan/ 162, p. 20; *Toa nisshi* (East Asia chronological record), Jan.-June 1940, Vol. 1, Pt. 5, p. 84.

35. State Dept. 893.00 P.R. Yunnan/141, Political Report for August 162, pp. 20-21.

36. Perkins to State, August 31, 1942, State Dept. 893.00 P.R. Yunnan/ 162, pp. 20-21.

37. *Ibid.*, Ludden to Gauss, March 5, 1943, p. 2, in Office of Strategic Services 34044.

38. Memorandum by Sprouse, February 27, 1945, State Dept. 893.00/ 2-2745, p. 2.

39. Lawrence Nae-lih Shyu, "The People's Political Council and China's Wartime Problems, 1937-1945" (Ph.D. diss., Columbia University, 1972), p. 149; Chang Wen-shih, *Yun-nan nei-mu* (The inside story in Yunnan) (Kunming: 1949), pp. 16 and 42. John Hall has informed me that the name Chang Wen-shih is a pseudonym for Lung Sheng-wen, Lung Yun's fourth son.

40. State Dept. 893.00 P.R. Yunnan/130, Political Report for September 1939, p. 4.

41. *Toa nisshi*, p. 85.

42. Langdon to State, July 14, 1944, State Dept. 893.00/7-1444, p. 2; Office of Strategic Services L50379, December 12, 1944, p. 1; Office of Strategic Services 355.2/AX1231S/c. 2, p. 3; memorandum by Graham Peck, State Dept. 893.00/15319, encl. 1, pp. 4-5.

43. Memorandum from Sprouse, February 27, 1945, State Dept. 893.00/ 2-2745, pp. 1-3.

44. Li Tsung-huang, *Li Tsung-huang hui-i lu* (Memoirs of Li Tsung-huang) (Taipei: 1972), IV: 215.

45. Vincent to State, April 26, 1943, State Dept. 893.00/15022; Drumright to State, May 19, 1943, State Dept. 893.00/15033; Service to State, June 9, 1943, State Dept. 893.00/15048, encl. 1, p. 1; Acheson to State, July 27, 1943, State Dept. 893.00/15095; Acheson to State, September 18, 1943, State Dept. 893.00/15144, encl. 1, p. 3; *Lost Chance in China*, pp. 20-25.

46. Details of this conspiracy are unusually hazy, and I have seen no reference to it in Chinese sources. The reasons for discontent and the targets of the conspiracy were reported differently by the State Department's several sources. See, e.g., Gauss to State, February 3, 1944, State Dept. 893.00/15273, in *Foreign Relations of the United States*, 1944, VI: 319-326; and memorandum by Service, February 10, 1944, State Dept. 893.00/15279, in *Foreign Relations of the*

United States, 1944, VI: 335-336. Several participants in the Conference on Wartime China, who had served in the government at the time, asserted that stories of this plot have no basis in fact.

47. Gauss to State, December 10, 1943, State Dept. 893.00/15214, Sect. 2, p. 2. See also Gauss to State, July 31, 1944, State Dept. 893.00/7-1344, in *Foreign Relations of the United States*, 1944, VI: 493.

48. The ascendancy of the CC Clique became particularly apparent in May 1944 when its members completely dominated the proceedings of the 12th Plenum of the Central Executive Committee of the Kuomintang. See Gauss to State, June 8, 1944, State Dept. 893.00/6-844.

49. Drumright to Vincent, April 26, 1943, State Dept. 893.105/93, p. 2.

50. Hattori Takushirō, *Dai Tōa sensō* (The Great East Asian War) (Tokyo, 1965), pp. 617-629; Charles F. Romanus and Riley Sunderland, *Stilwell's Command Problems* (Washington, D.C.: U.S. Government Printing Office, 1956), pp. 316-320; Charles F. Romanus and Riley Sunderland, *Time Runs Out in CBI* (Washington, D.C.: U.S. Government Printing Office, 1959), pp. 169-176.

51. Gauss to State, July 31, 1944, State Dept. 893.00/7-1344, in *Foreign Relations of the United States*, 1944, p. 492. See also Langdon to State, July 14, 1944, State Dept. 893.00/7-1444, pp. 3 and 5.

52. Ringwalt to Gauss, July 6, 1944, 893.00/7-644, encl., p. 2.

53. Biographical information on Li Chi-shen is in: Boorman, II: 292-295; *Gendai Chūgoku jimmei jiten* (Biographical Dictionary of Republican China) (Tokyo: 1966), p. 1029; Ringwalt to Gauss, August 28, 1944, State Dept. 893.00/8-2844, pp. 2-4.

54. Lindsey to Hearn, July 21, 1944, Rad #CCA 71, Stilwell Papers Box 4, File #2703. Lung Yun in early 1944 was also negotiating with the Japanese, who hoped to persuade Lung to revolt against Chungking. Lung maintained contact with the Japanese through his messengers and by wireless radio. Nothing came of these contacts. "Statements of Japanese Officers, World War II" (Office of the Chief of Military History, 8-5.1/AD4/vol. 5), Statement No. 516, p. 2.

55. Richard M. Service to Acheson, March 23, 1945, State Dept. 893.00/4-545, encl; Ringwalt to Gauss, July 6, 1944, State Dept. 893.00/7-644; Ringwalt to Gauss, August 28, 1944, State Dept. 893.00/8-2844, p. 8.

56. Not all members of the Federation supported this movement. See Ringwalt to Gauss, August 28, 1944, State Dept. 893.00/8-2844, p. 5; Langdon to State, July 14, 1944, State Dept. 893.00/7-1444, p. 5. Leaders of the Federation who were reportedly privy to the movement, and presumably involved, were Carsun Chang, Tso Shun-sheng, Shen Chun-ju, and Chang Po-chun. See Gauss to State, October 30, 1944, encl. 1, pp. 1-2, OSS 102284.

57. Gauss to State, October 30, 1944, encl. 1, p. 1, OSS 102284. See also Sprouse to State, July 14, 1944, State Dept. 893.00/7-1444, p. 3; Sprouse to Gauss, August 14, 1944, State Dept. 893.00/8-2344, encl. 1, p. 1.
58. Ringwalt to Gauss, May 8, 1944, State Dept. 893.00/15420, p. 3.
59. Sprouse to Gauss, August 14, 1944, State Dept. 893.00/8-2344, encl. 1, p. 3.
60. *Ibid.*; Sprouse to State, July 14, 1944, State Dept. 893.00/7-1444, p. 4; Richard M. Service to Hurley, January 23, 1945, State Dept. 893.00/1-345, p. 2.
61. Ringwalt to Gauss, May 8, 1944, State Dept. 893.00/15420, p. 2; Langdon to State, July 14, 1944, State Dept. 893.00/7-1444, p. 4; Sprouse to Gauss, August 14, 1944, State Dept. 893.00/8-2344, encl. 1, p. 2; Ringwalt to Gauss, August 28, 1944, State Dept. 893.00/8-2844, p. 8.
62. Memorandum by Sprouse, February 27, 1945, State Dept. 893.00/2-2745, p. 1; Office of Strategic Services 108069, November 25, 1944.
63. Memorandum by Sprouse, February 27, 1945, State Dept. 893.00/2-2745, pp. 1-2.
64. *Ibid.*; Langdon to State, October 19, 1944, State Dept. 740-0011 P.W./10-1944, in *Foreign Relations of the United States, 1944*, VI: 175-176.
65. Richard M. Service to Hurley, January 20, 1945, State Dept. 740.0011 P.W./1-2045, p. 2.
66. *Ibid.*, pp. 2-3.
67. Liu Chien-chun, pp. 126, 128.
68. Memorandum by Sprouse, February 27, 1945, State Dept. 893.00/2-2745.
69. Li Tsung-huang, IV: 210.
70. The complicity of the United States in the eventual coup against Lung is mentioned in both Chinese and Western sources, but I have found no conclusive evidence of it. Frank Dorn speaks of "American planning and support . . . to overthrow the scoundrel warlord governor of the province, Lung Yun." Dorn, *The Sino-Japanese War, 1937-41: From Marco Polo Bridge to Pearl Harbor* (New York: Macmillan Publishing Co., Inc., 1974), p. 163. See also Jung Chai, *Chin-ling chiu-meng* (Old Dreams of Nanking) (Hong Kong: 1968), pp. 122-123.
71 Jung Chai, pp. 93-95.
72. Li Tsung-huang, IV: 204-208; Sprouse to State, October 29, 1945, State Dept. 893.00/10-2945; Jung Chai, pp. 95, 105-106. Li Tsung-huang was actually awarded the post of acting chairman; Lu Han subsequently took over the post of provincial chairman.

73. Sprouse to State, October 20, 1945, State Dept. 893.00/10-2045, p. 8.
74. Boorman, II: 446. On the militia, see Li Tsung-huang, IV: 211; and Jung Chai, p. 108.
75. Li Tsung-huang, IV: 210; Sprouse to State, October 20, 1945, State Dept. 893.00/10-2045, p. 3.
76. Sprouse to State, October 20, 1945, State Dept. 893.00/10-2045; Office of War Information, Box 378, C: China 0,1-C (October 11, 1945).
77. Chin Tien-jung, pt. 9, *Chun-chiu*, No. 174 (October 1, 1964), p. 8.
78. Li Tsung-huang, IV: 209.
79. Jung Chai, pp. 93-95 and 115-116. See also Li Tsung-huang, IV: 207-208.
80. Office of War Information, Box 378, C: China 0.1-C (October 11, 1945), 11 p. This report (p. 2) estimated that total casualties in the coup were about 600. See also Robert Payne, *China Awake* (New York: Dodd, Mead and Company, 1947), pp. 183-192.
81. Jung Chai, p. 109; Li Tsung-huang, pp. 211, 217.
82. Jung Chai, p. 108; Payne, p. 188.
83. Li Tsung-huang, IV: 216-217; Sprouse to State, October 20, 1945, State Dept. 893.00/10-2045, p. 4.
84. *Shih-chieh jih-pao* (World Daily) (Chungking), October 5, 1945, in *Chinese Press Review* (Chungking), No. 269 (October 5, 1945), p. 1.
85. Chin Tien-jung, pt. 9, *Chun-chiu*, No. 174 (October 1, 1964), p. 9.
86. Sprouse to State, November 17, 1945, State Dept. 893.00/11-1745, 5 p.; Sprouse to State, December 20, 1945, State Dept. 893.00/12-2045, 18 p.
87. There exist numerous descriptions of the December First Incident in both Chinese and English. See, e.g., *I-erh-i tsan-an te-chi* (Special Collection on the December 1 Massacre; n.p.: n.d.), 50 p.; and Suzanne Pepper, "The Student Movement and the Chinese Civil War, 1945-49," *China Quarterly* 48 (October-December 1971): 701-707.
88. Chang Wen-shih, p. 25.
89. *Ibid.*, p. 58.
90. *Ibid.*, pp. 22-25 and 56-63.
91. Chang Wen-shih, pp. 64-67; Boorman, II: 458-459.
92. Boorman, II: 446-447.
93. In 1939, for example, government expenditures equaled about 9 per cent of the GNP. The budgetary deficit that year, however, was about 70 per cent of expenditures, and this deficit was met primarily by the printing of new, unbacked currency. Hence, for 1939, government revenues were approximately 3.6 per cent of the GNP. In later

years, the fiscal picture seemingly worsened. Indeed, during the entire period of the war, only 6 per cent of expenditures were met by revenues from taxation. See Chang Kia-ngau, *The Inflationary Spiral: The Experience in China, 1939-1950* (Cambridge, Mass.: The M.I.T. Press, 1958), pp. 29, 38, 145-150.

94. F. F. Liu, *A Military History of Modern China, 1924-1949* (Princeton, N.J.: Princeton University Press, 1956), pp. 112, 134. Cf. Charles F. Romanus and Riley Sunderland, *Stilwell's Mission to China* (Washington, D.C.: U.S. Government Printing Office, 1953), p. 35; and Domes, pp. 580 and 584.

Comments (1):

BY WILLIAM L. TUNG

Professor Eastman's paper discusses the relationships between the Central Government and the provincial militarists, with special emphasis on wartime Yunnan. His sources are drawn chiefly from the reports of American diplomats then stationed in China; some of them had long been known to hold a bias against the Kuomintang (Nationalist Party) and its leader, Chiang Kai-shek. Lack of access to the first-hand information from the participants after a lapse of three decades makes it difficult to present balanced views on many controversial issues. Nevertheless, Professor Eastman has ably analyzed the complicated situation in a fairly exhaustive manner.

Since Chiang's ascent to power in 1927, China had made considerable progress toward the implementation of Sun Yat-sen's "Three People's Principles" in the ensuing decade.[1] Unfortunately, as a consequence of successive revolts led by local military commanders, relentless Communist uprisings, and incessant Japanese invasions, the Central Government was indeed in a weak position on the eve of the full-scale war with Japan in July 1937. The adverse circumstances had, however, only hindered but not stopped China's nation-building process. In order to establish an effective system of control over military, financial, and administrative matters throughout free China, the Government, with Chungking as wartime capital, had to take steps to eliminate the regional dominance by remnant warlords. Although the nation's strides toward consolidation were rather slow in comparison with some modern states, its steady efforts to achieve that end enabled China to conduct eight years of war to eventual victory. To the narrow-minded authorities in several regions, any move by the Central Government toward integration was deemed detrimental to their vested interests. This was the attitude held by many provincial leaders.

Before dealing with the major events in Yunnan, Professor Eastman describes the situation in Szechwan to a certain extent. The important figures in the latter province were Liu Hsiang, Liu Wen-hui, Teng Hsi-hou, and Pan Wen-hua, who had engaged in constant struggles for power among themselves. Chiang Kai-shek had long considered Liu Hsiang as the only one who could possibly unify the province behind the Central Government. Upon Chiang's recommendation, Liu was appointed

Chairman or Governor of Szechwan province, Military Commissioner of Szechwan and Sikang provinces, and Commander of the Seventh War Region. Liu died of stomach cancer in a Hankow hospital on January 20, 1938; in his last will, he entreated all Chinese armed forces to fight against the Japanese under the leadership of Chiang Kai-shek.[2] The charge made by certain Szechwanese partisans that central-government agents had murdered Liu was entirely unfounded.

Two days after Liu's death, Chang Chun was appointed Chairman of the Provincial Government of Szechwan. A native of that province and a ranking statesman, Chang Chun commanded Chiang's respect and trust. Several local generals had long coveted that position, but none could win the cooperation of the others. The statement made by Chang Chun about how to reconstruct Szechwan had won for him the confidence and cooperation of many influential quarters.[3] In an evaluation of many Kuomintang leaders, the present discussant once remarked: "Probably there were few figures prominent in the political arena during the Nationalist rule on the mainland whom I have not met or talked with, but none has impressed me more than Chang Chun with respect to broad experience in Chinese politics, as well as unusual ability to win cooperation and support from different interest-groups."[4] Astute and discreet, Chang Chun had got along fairly well with the Szechwanese militarists in carrying out the policies and programs of the Central Government.

Much space of Professor Eastman's paper is devoted to Lung Yun and his rule of Yunnan. However, he cautioned the readers not to regard that province "as typifying the relations between all the provinces and the Central Government." As Chairman or Governor of the Provincial Government of Yunnan, Lung Yun behaved like a traditional warlord and attempted to obstruct the inflow of the influence of the Central Government with consummate skill. Lung's semi-independent status was tolerated before and during the early part of the war. After the government's retreat to the interior, however, Chiang could not permit the continued existence of such a regime in an area second only to Szechwan in importance. In this connection, it should also be pointed out that Yunnan attained national prominence in Chinese politics long before the war, for its expeditionary force led by General Tsai O against Yuan Shih-kai's monarchical scheme in 1916 was vital to the history of modern China.

As a shrewd opportunist, Lung maintained ambiguous relationships with Wang Ching-wei,[5] Chiang's erstwhile rival in the Kuomintang and eventual head of the Japanese-sponsored regime in Nanking. His close association with the dissident intellectuals, such as Lo Lung-chi (Professor of the Southwest Associated University) of the Federation of Democratic Parties or the Chinese Democratic League, heightened Chungking's distrust of him.

At this juncture, a brief explanation of the political nature of this League will perhaps help clarify the existing relationships between the Kuomintang and other political parties. It was first established in 1939, under the name of the Association of Comrades for Unification and Reconstruction (Tung-i Chien-kuo Tung-chih Hui), which was reorganized in 1941 into the League of Chinese Democratic Political Groups (Chung-kuo Ming-chu Chen-tuan Tung-meng). Composed of various political parties and groups, the League advocated the practice of democracy and the abolition of one-party rule. With participating members of diversified political convictions, it could not be expected to become a unified party. After the breakup of the League in 1945, the Chinese Youth Party and the China Democratic Party, two of its members, allied with the Kuomintang. Its other component groups and their leaders, including Lo Lung-chi, went to the Communists.[6]

In those days, there were quite a number of so-called liberals who received special consideration and protection from Lung Yun. Lo Lung-chi was only one of them. After all, who were the liberals and who were the reactionaries? To the Communists and their sympathizers, any uncompromising Kuomintang member was a reactionary and whoever was willing to cooperate with anti-government elements was a liberal. While many Chinese intellectuals then believed in and promoted the practice of democracy, a good number of self-styled liberals were simply opportunists fishing in troubled waters as revealed by later developments. These labels have confused many discerning Western observers of Chinese politics.

Antagonistic to the activities of the Kuomintang and the San-Min Chu-I Youth Corps, while friendly to the student demonstrations against the Central Government, Lung Yun openly defied Chungking's authority in Yunnan, which had become the chief gateway to the outside world during the later period of the Sino-Japanese war. To safeguard this strategic area, reliable forces had been gradually sent there by Chiang. The showdown came on October 3, 1945. Facing political and military pressures, Lung Yun was compelled to relinquish his post in Yunnan for a new assignment as Chairman of the Military Advisory Council in Chungking. Since no modern nation-state would long allow the usurpation of power by local warlords, Lung's removal was inevitable. Some commentators criticized the means used to bring Lung down as too high-handed and having far-reaching repercussions, but this is a matter of opinion. Lung went to Peking in 1950. Eight years later, he was condemned as a rightist, thus ending his political life.

Professor Eastman has mentioned the CC Clique as an important faction within the Kuomintang-government hierarchy. In spite of the rumors to the contrary, there has never been a CC Clique or the "Central Club" in existence. Before and during the period of the Northern Expedition, many Kuomintang members working in different

localities did set up political groups under various names, such as the
Ta Tung Meng (Great Alliance), Hsing Chung Hui (Society for the
Regeneration of China), Shih Chien Che (Institute for Action), F. F.
Group, and A. B. League, which purported to evade the surveillance of
the warlords. After the reunification of China under the Kuomintang,
its Third National Congress adopted a resolution in March 1929 that
all small organizations be abolished. Then anti-Chiang Kai-shek elements
both within and without the party spread rumors that the disbanding
of the small organizations was only a tactic to enhance Chiang's influence and control through the Central Club (C.C.) or Chung Yang
Chu Lo Pu allegedly under the personal direction of the Chen
brothers. Chiang Kai-shek himself was then Director of its Department
of Organization, which was actually administered by his deputy Chen
Kuo-fu, whose younger brother, Li-fu, became Secretary-General of the
Central Party Headquarters. The Communists later applied the term C.C.
to represent the Chen brothers, because their surname begins with the
letter "C". Although Chiang had a large following in the party, with the
Chen brothers in actual charge for a long duration, there was never a
formal organization of CC Clique.[7]

There were, however, two secret organizations or factions fairly
active before the war, namely, the Clean League (Ching Pai Tuan) and
the Regeneration Institute (Fu Hsing She), which were disbanded after
the outbreak of war with Japan. Then the San-Min Chu-I Youth Corps
was openly established for recruiting the young. Because of its frictions
with the Kuomintang, the Youth Corps was eventually merged with the
regular party organization.

In the opinion of Professor Eastman, "Chiang Kai-shek played the
politics of weakness," and he attempted to keep all others weak. By
doing so, he concludes, "China was therefore the loser, but so also in
the long run was Chiang." But what would be the alternative courses of
action that could strengthen the national power? The present discussant
agrees with Professor Eastman that the rule of provincial militarists and
the formation of a coalition government were not good answers. Professor Eastman's constructive suggestion is for Chiang to broaden his
base of political support among the non-Communist elements in the
nation. Actually, Chiang did not fail to realize the importance of recruiting political leaders and talented people outside the Kuomintang.

As early as April 1932, the Central Government convened the National Emergency Conference, attended by many non-Kuomintang leaders.
In December of the same year, the Central Executive Committee of the
Kuomintang adopted a resolution to make necessary preparations for
setting up the People's Political Council. "During the period of its
existence from July 1939 to March 1948, the Council served a useful purpose for national consolidation at the time of war and up to the eve of

the National Assembly in accordance with the provisions of 1946 Constitution."[8] Composed of many prominent individuals in various professions, representatives from different localities, and leaders of the minor political parties and groups, the Council carried out such functions as generally exercised by a national representative body. Among these were: to deliberate on and decide important policies and programs before the execution by the government, to receive government reports and to put interpellations to the government, and to examine the budget prepared by the government. Although the Council later became impotent after the Communist members abstained from its meetings, the ruling party and government did have the sincere intention of maintaining it as a respectable body for the promotion of national unity.[9]

Throughout his paper, Professor Eastman has frankly pointed out many faults of Chiang's conduct of state affairs. As did statesmen in other countries, Chiang and his followers indeed committed mistakes in many respects. But, in his consolidation of national power against the traditional dominance of local militarists, Chiang should not be blamed. Considering Chiang's inherent difficulties and the limited resources at his disposal, "It was not an inconsiderable feat," in the words of Professor Eastman, "even to survive the eight years of war." The present discussant fully shares his view that "historians should therefore be slow to criticize the Chungking government for not playing a more active role" during that eventful period, when it was confronted with a formidable foreign enemy and the challenges of the uncompromising Communists and provincial militarists.

NOTES

1. China's progress during that period is discussed in detail in Paul K. T. Sih (ed.), *The Strenuous Decade: China's Nation-Building Efforts, 1927-1937* 辟光前：艱苦建國的十年 (New York: St. John's University Press, 1970).

2. See Chou Kai-chin, *Min Kuo Chuan Shih Chi Yao (A Brief History of Szechwan Province under the Republican Period)* (Taiwan: Shu Chuan Wen Hsien Yen Chiu She, The Research Institute of the Archives Concerning Szechwan, 1972, 2 vols.), I, pp. 37-38.

3. For Chang's statement, see *ibid.*, I, p. 39.

4. William L. Tung, *Revolutionary China: A Personal Account, 1926-1949* (New York: St. Martin's Press, 1973), p. 131.

5. For details, see Liu Chien-chun, *Yin-ho I-wang (Memories at Yin-ho)* (Taipei: Chuan-chi Wen-hsueh Tsa-chih She, Biographical Literature, 1966), pp. 125-130.

6. For a detailed account of political parties in wartime China, see

William L. Tung, *The Political Institutions of Modern China* (The Hague: Martinus Nijhoff, 1964), pp. 176-179.

7. For further information on the subject, including personal interviews with Chen Li-fu and others, see William L. Tung, *Revolutionary China: A Personal Account, 1926-1949*, pp. 149-151.

8. William L. Tung, *The Political Institutions of Modern China*, p. 190.

9. For details, see Chen Chi-mai, *Chung Kuo Cheng Fu (The Government of China)* (Chungking and Shanghai: The Commercial Press, 1944-45, 3 vols.), II, pp. 259-266; Chien Tuan-sheng, *The Government and Politics of China* (Cambridge: Harvard University Press, 1950), pp. 280-295.

Comments (2):

BY PAUL K. T. SIH

With all due respect and esteem to my beloved colleague and co-worker on this program, Dr. Lloyd Eastman, I wish to offer my remarks on his well-prepared paper on "Regional Politics and the Central Government: Yunnan and Chungking."

Historical study has become easier today than in the past. Things change fast. What happened twenty or thirty years ago can be ascertained and evaluated in terms of actual results right now, without waiting for a longer period of time. Therefore, what we are discussing today about wartime China, 1937-1945, some thirty years ago, can be readily reviewed in a more truthful and objective way in the light of subsequent developments.

First of all, I wish to offer my respect to him for his very candid expression of what he personally has believed. This is particularly true in his evaluation of China's political status during the war, and the immense difficulties China encountered in bearing the sole responsibility for fighting the war in the Far East between 1937 and 1941. This is what he wrote:

> Politically, China was not a modern nation-state, for it lacked a highly articulated, effective system of control over its military and administrative arms. Nationalist China during the war may therefore be best understood if it is viewed as a rather fragile political coalition (p. 329).

In another place (p. 353), he stressed:

> Nationalist China during the war was not, in the European sense of the term, a nation-state. To marshal material, financial, and military resources for the war, Chungking had to negotiate and compromise, plead and threaten . . . the Nationalist government was operating in a hostile environment.

Then he pointed out, with a rather sympathetic tone toward the Nationalist government:

> Westerners in particular make judgments which ignore that the Chinese Nationalists held only a tenuous control of the state; that Chinese politics

369

had no tradition of pluralism, and that consequently the challenges of the provincial militarists and of the Communists were, perhaps literally, matters of life-and-death; and that it was not an inconsiderable feat, considering the political difficulties and economic resources of the Nationalist government, even to survive the eight years of war. It is a signal fact, for example, that the Nationalist government, was able to marshal only about 3 per cent of the nation's gross national product for support of all functions of government during the war. Probably no more than 40 per cent of the divisions in the Nationalist army were "reliable"—i.e., loyal to Chiang Kai-shek.

For all his true understanding of China's situation during the war, he seemed to suggest something which, at least in my personal view, does not reflect entirely the real world in which wartime China lived.

He suggested three alternatives for a better China. He acknowledged that the first two—namely, sharing of power with the provincial militarists, and forming of a coalition government—would be unworkable and that the third alternative might be the only choice. This was to build a mass base among at least the non-Communist elements in the nation.

My observation is this: How could this be done? Where was this non-Communist mass base? The Chinese National leadership initiated and developed the People's Political Council which was the new source of power that Chiang was able to generate from outside the elite structure. What else could he do?

He suggested that Chiang should have a system of rule in which "Chiang and his administrators would be responsive to the will and the needs of significant segments of society." Chiang did have such a system. It was the PPC. Chiang cooperated wholeheartedly with the PPC in social and economic fields, as we read from Professor Lawrence Shyu's paper. The PPC failed to achieve satisfactory results in the other two fields—wartime national unity and the constitutional movement. That was not Chiang's fault. The Chinese Communist Party should share at least equal blame for its failure.

Dr. Eastman's third suggestion appears theoretically sound. Yet it was hard to put it into practice.

There are several points in his paper which are based not on actual facts. Some of them are cited from the reports submitted by the field staff of the American Embassy in Chungking to the State Department. To my understanding, and maybe to the understanding of those reporters themselves, the unverified information or opinions supplied were merely for home consumption and for internal communication. Most of their reports were day-to-day impressions and were not supposed to be cited for factual academic or scholarly research.

For instance, Dr. Eastman noted that there was a plot early in December 1943 to remove some high government officials and army officers, such as H. H. Kung and Ho Ying-chin and, as a result, at least sixteen generals who were leaders in the conspiracy were executed (p. 342). Recently someone asked Ho about this plot, after he read somewhere about it. Ho just dismissed it as sheer gossip.

Dr. Eastman mentioned in other places the widespread rumor of Chiang's attempt to remove Lung Yun (p. 13) and of peasant uprisings in every province, from Fukien and Kwangtung to Szechwan and Kansu. Both are subject to verification. Lung Yun cooperated fully with the central government until 1943, as was reported. Why should Chiang have sought to remove him in the initial months of the war? Chiang needed Lung Yun and Lung Yun needed Chiang. It was Lung Yun who helped the government to build the Burma Road; it was Lung Yun who helped develop Yunnan as the new cultural, economic and industrial center of wartime China, as was noted. Chiang appreciated his cooperation.

If there were such widespread peasant uprisings throughout the nation, as Dr. Eastman mentioned casually, how could China continue to sustain Japanese attacks, particularly in the Ichigo campaign of 1944-1945—the most formidable military operation of Japan during the war? I, for one, lived in Kwangsi, Kweiyang and Szechwan throughout the war. I did not hear anything of this sort with the exception of a few isolated social disorders which were no more serious than those we are witnessing today here in this country.

Before and during the war, on page 330, Yen Hsi-san is identified in Shansi as an enemy of the government, second to Liu Hsiang in Szechwan. This requires further explanation. During the Sian incident, Yen played a very influential part in overcoming the crisis. Without his support, the situation would have been completely different.

On page 343, it is stated that during the Ichigo invasion, "Chiang Kai-shek willingly threw the provincial armies into decimating combat while his own loyal central-government armies conserved their American-supplied equipment." Let us not forget to ask: when did this happen? This was from April 1944 to February 1945. What was the war situation elsewhere in China? What was Chiang Kai-shek's overall war strategy? General Stilwell was in Burma. He demanded that Chiang's troops be sent to fight in Burma. Chiang did this even after Stilwell was gone. He had no army of his own to confront the formidable Japanese attack. He just threw everybody into the fighting when Chungking, the wartime capital, was under immediate threat. General Albert Wedemeyer, Commander of American Forces in China at that time, made no such allegations whatever throughout his current reports or later writings. A serious charge of this nature must be verified by General Wedemeyer to be credible.

Dr. Eastman mentioned that, after 1943, there was increasing discontent toward the government and its leadership and a deterioration of morality. The Chinese people, however, did not feel that way. Instead they felt more confident in the final victory as the international situation became more favorable to the Allied side. However, it is true to say that the same favorable international situation encouraged the dissident elements and political enemies to discredit the Nationalist government and to undermine its power for their subversive purposes.

CHAPTER X

The Sino-Soviet Treaty
of Friendship and Alliance
# of 1945: The Inside Story

BY CHIN-TUNG LIANG

ETWEEN AUGUST 1937 (after the conclusion of the Sino-Soviet Non-aggression Pact) and April 1941 (after the conclusion of the Russo-Japanese Neutrality Agreement) the relationship between China and the Soviet Union was quite friendly. It began to decline after the Soviet Union annexed the Tannuols region in 1940 and to deteriorate further in July 1942 when the Chinese government demanded the U.S.S.R. to withdraw her Eighth Red Army from Tihwa, Sinkiang.[1] After that, the Soviet Union on numerous occasions encouraged the Harchak pastoral tribes to create border disputes between China and Outer Mongolia and, in 1945, its consular agent at Tihwa secretly supplied large amounts of ammunition to the local underground Communists who attacked Ining, occupied it and declared the area to be Eastern Turkestan Republic.[2] Relations between the two countries became worse indeed.

Beginning in 1944, Japan's defeat in the Pacific was almost certain, and Soviet participation in the war against Japan was just a matter of time. The Chinese Communist guerrilla army had already occupied parts of Hopeh, Shantung, Shansi and Honan provinces. In view of such a situation, both Chinese and Western statesmen including President Roosevelt and Henry Wallace[3] were of the opinion that in order to avoid civil war in China the Sino-Soviet relations must first be improved. In fact, Generalissimo Chiang Kai-shek had instructed Premier T. V. Soong to approach Stalin with the same purpose as early as July 1944.[4] Thus, to conclude a friendly treaty with the Soviet Union before the end of the Japanese war was a prime and earnest concern of all Chinese. Unfortunately, the Sino-Soviet Treaty of Friendship and Alliance, negotiated in 1945, was not what the Chinese desired because many items therein had previously been determined and imposed by the secret

373

Yalta Agreement concluded by the three great Powers—the United Kingdom, the Soviet Union, and the United States, without Chinese knowledge and against Chinese interest!

As we all know, the Yalta Agreement was a top secret document. But, strangely enough, this secrecy was broken by the Chinese Communists only two weeks after it was signed, according to Ambassador Patrick Hurley.[5] The Agreement was not known to Nationalist China until one month later, based on two different reports, one from Ambassador V. K. Wellington Koo and the other from Tao-ming Wei. Koo's information, which was sketchy, was obtained from William D. Leahy of the White House,[6] and Wei's information came directly from President Roosevelt himself which runs as follows:

> In my interview with President Roosevelt, I asked him about proposals concerning the Far East made by Stalin at the Yalta Conference. The President replied: "Stalin made three: 1) The recognition of status quo in Outer Mongolia. 2) The Chinese sovereignty over the Chinese Eastern Railway to be recognized, but it should have a mandated operating system. 3) The Soviet Union to have a warm seaport south of Port Arthur, such as Dairen or its nearby port." In Roosevelt's opinion, since *the sovereignty of Outer Mongolia remains with China,* to maintain its status quo would seem to offer no problem. The sovereignty of the Chinese Eastern Railway also belongs to China, but in order to improve its efficiency, a mandated operation system might be organized by three representatives each from China, the United States and the Soviet Union respectively, provided they are railway experts. As for the third proposal concerning a military seaport, this was a new one beyond the previous demand concerning Dairen. . . . The President thought that perhaps Port Arthur could be *leased* to the Soviet Union for a number of years, while its sovereignty still remained China's. With regard to Soviet participation in the war in the Far East, the President assured me that when the right time comes, it will participate. However, this must be kept as a top secret in order to prevent the enemy from strengthening its defense. The President had also discussed the problem of the Chinese Communists with Stalin, and found his general attitude toward the Far East to be quite good.[7]

This report was dispatched on March 12, 1945, exactly one month after the Yalta Conference. Though its contents were brief, they are valuable in the sense that Roosevelt's interpretations of the Soviet original demands on Outer Mongolia, on the Chinese Eastern Railway and on Port Arthur were clearly given. They are particularly important because, as we shall see, after Roosevelt died, Stalin presented the Yalta Agreement in an entirely different light.

While the full text of the Yalta Agreement was officially transmitted to the Chinese government on June 15, 1945,[8] its contents had been confidentially made known to Chiang by Hurley on May 22.[9] This enabled Chiang to cable Soong on May 22 and 23, instructing him to discuss privately counter-measures with delegates Wang Chung-hui and V. K. Wellington Koo, as they were all attending the San Francisco Conference together. On June 3, Chiang received the Soviet Ambassador Petrov in Chungking. During discussion, Chiang urged the Soviet Union to declare war against Japan, and to help China recover the territorial and administrative integrity of Manchuria. He intimated that he had knowledge of the secret Yalta Agreement.[10]

From June 8 to 11, Chiang sent several cablegrams to Soong giving him guidelines in connection with negotiations on Port Arthur:

1. That Port Arthur should be used jointly by Four Powers: China, Great Britain, the United States and the Soviet Union,
2. That Chinese sovereignty and her administrative integrity should be fully maintained, and
3. That under no circumstance should the Soviet Union alone have the sole occupation or lease of Port Arthur.

He also instructed Soong to convey the above points to President Truman, and then to return to Chungking before the end of June, and to proceed afterwards to Moscow for negotiating a treaty with the Soviet Union.[11]

T. V. Soong had been in the United States since April. His mission was to attend the San Francisco Conference as the head of the Chinese Delegation. Before going to San Francisco he had met Harry Hopkins in Washington and had learned from him privately that the attitude of most influential Americans toward China had undergone many changes; that members of the War Department, from General Marshall down, all considered the recall of General Stilwell unfair and that they were still angry about this matter. Although the recent Chinese military situation through the effort of General Wedemeyer had been greatly improved, members of the War Department still deeply hated Chiang, Soong and Hurley.[12]

Since the Secret Agreement of Yalta concerning China was gradually leaked out at the San Francisco Conference and Molotov's attitude towards Soong at San Francisco became more and more friendly every day,[13] Secretary Stettinius strongly urged President Truman to inform China about the Agreement immediately. But Truman, having sent Hopkins to Moscow to sound out Stalin's opinion about China after Roosevelt's death, withheld giving his approval until he received a report from Hopkins. Hopkins' report describing Stalin's favorable attitude toward Chiang did come on June 6. Truman then asked Soong to see him at the White House on June 9.[14]

Two meetings between Truman and Soong were held, first on the
9th of June and second on the 13th.[15] Because Truman was unable to
interpret the meaning of the text of the Yalta Agreement, the result of
these two meetings was insignificant. But a significant meeting did take
place in the afternoon of June 13 between Soong and Hopkins who had
just returned to Washington from Moscow.

> Hopkins reported: "I asked Stalin about this American rumor: 'Once
> the Soviet troops enter Manchuria, he will use the Chinese Communists
> to control this area indirectly.' Stalin replied that 'China at present, includ-
> ing the Chinese Communists, provides no leader who can rule the whole
> country. Since the Soviet Union does not like to negotiate with a divided
> China, Stalin is prepared to support Generalissimo Chiang and his govern-
> ment. Furthermore, the Soviet Union has no intention of invading China's
> sovereignty in Sinkiang or anywhere else. The Soviet Union would like
> to invite voluntarily Chinese representatives to enter and be stationed in
> Manchuria to organize local civil government in cooperation with the
> Soviet Union troops. With respect to the Chinese Communists, the Soviet
> Union considers this as a Chinese domestic matter of no concern to the
> Soviet Union.' "[16]

In the meantime, President Truman instructed Ambassador Hurley
to present the secret Yalta Agreement concerning China to Generalissimo
Chiang on June 15 at Chungking. Although Hurley wondered why this
was to be done on this particular date, he followed the President's
instructions nevertheless. After discussing the matter in general, Chiang
asked Hurley three questions: (1) Has the United States any interest in
sharing the use of Port Arthur? If it does, China would then propose to
the Soviet Union to make it a four-power-operated military port: China,
the United States, the United Kingdom, and the Soviet Union. (2)
Would the United States be willing to participate in concluding the
treaty thus making it multilateral instead of a Sino-Soviet treaty? He
hopes the United States will. (3) The ceding of the Kurile Islands and
the southern part of Sakhalin to Soviet Russia has nothing to do with
China. Why was this included or even mentioned as one of the items
in the Sino-Soviet treaty?

Hurley forwarded Chiang's view to Washington. But the State
Department indicated that the United States had no intention of sharing
the use of Port Arthur, and therefore it would be unsuitable for her to
be involved in the Sino-Soviet treaty. President Truman cabled this to
Hurley on June 18.[17]

Having completed his talks with Truman and Hopkins, T. V. Soong
left the United States on June 16, arriving the following day in Chungking. Meanwhile, Generalissimo Chiang had two more meetings with
Petrov, on June 12 and 16, in which he opposed the lease of Port Arthur

and the discussion about Outer Mongolia.[18] During his ten-day stay in Chungking, Soong kept discussing with government officials about what counter-measures China should take towards the Soviet Union. Soong carried Generalissimo Chiang's personal letter to Stalin on board a borrowed American plane for Moscow on June 27. He was accompanied among others by Victor Hu, Deputy Minister of Foreign Affairs, Chiang Ching-kuo, and Hung-li Shen, Minister of Agriculture, an expert on Manchurian affairs. Soong's party arrived in Moscow on June 30 with a heavy heart.

Six meetings of negotiations were held from June 30 to July 12, and four meetings between August 8 to 18. The Chinese participants for the first six meetings were: T. V. Soong, Pin-chang Fu, Chinese Ambassador to the Soviet Union, Chiang Ching-kuo, and Victor Hu. The Soviet participants were: Stalin, Molotov, Petrov, Soviet Ambassador to China, Lozovsky, Deputy Minister of Foreign Affairs, and Pavlov, an interpreter. For the last four meetings the Chinese delegation added China's newly appointed Foreign Minister Wang Shih-chieh; the Soviet delegation remained unchanged. Whenever a deadlock occurred, Chiang Ching-kuo, as a private citizen, would consult directly with Stalin. Averell Harriman, American Ambassador to the Soviet Union, kept in touch with T. V. Soong throughout the period of negotiations.

The first session took place on June 30, 1945, three hours after the arrival of the Chinese delegation in Moscow, and lasted but fifteen minutes (6:30-6:45 P.M.). It was limited to formal greetings and general announcements about the conference.[19] Soon after his arrival in Moscow, Soong was briefed on secret information concerning Stalin's real attitude and on whether "the Soviet Union will unconditionally support Generalissimo Chiang Kai-shek after the war," as Hurley had reported to President Truman. He found out that what Stalin had really meant was that "in order to unify China it is necessary to compromise with the Chinese Communists." Stalin was merely supporting a unified China.[20]

At the second session on July 2 (8:00-10:30 P.M.), a wide range of topics was discussed including the independence of Outer Mongolia, the status of Dairen, the lease of Port Arthur, the use of railways and seaports, the trusteeship of Korea, and other problems relating to a Sino-Soviet treaty of friendship and alliance. What Stalin had told Hurley and Hopkins concerning his suport to Chiang was also mentioned. With respect to Dairen, Stalin demanded joint ownership and management to be supervised by a Sino-Soviet Commission, with a Chinese as chairman and a Russian as chief executive. Regarding Port Arthur, the Soviet Union was willing to substitute the word "lease" with other appropriate words so long as the navies of the Soviet Union could use the harbor facilities with the Chinese. With regard to the railways, the Soviet Union again suggested Sino-Soviet joint ownership, under Soviet oper-

ation for a period of forty or forty-five years. With regard to the transporting of Soviet troops by the railways, Stalin promised not to do so
during peacetime.

The Soviet Union also agreed to a Korean trusteeship. It was suggested that a treaty of friendship and alliance would be concluded as
soon as agreement on these general principles had been reached. However, Stalin kept insisting on *the independence of Outer Mongolia.* He
said:

> Countries may use Outer Mongolia as a base in the attempt to overthrow
> the Soviet Union's position in the Far East. If the Soviet Union does not
> have Outer Mongolia as a buffer zone, it will lose the whole Soviet Far
> East. Even after Japanese surrender, in five or ten years, she will rise
> again. Since the people of Outer Mongolia will neither join China nor the
> Soviet Union, it should be independent. Furthermore, some people in
> Outer Mongolia are stirring up Inner Mongolia by advocating a Great
> Mongolian Republic. Should this happen, it will threaten North China. In
> China's interest, it would be more advantageous for her to let Outer Mon-
> golia be independent.[21]

T. V. Soong declared that no Chinese government can be allowed
to remain in office if it gives up any of its territory. The Nationalist
Government, ever since Dr. Sun Yat-sen's days, has assured the Chinese
people of its territorial integrity and that includes Outer Mongolia.
Furthermore, should Outer Mongolia be independent, Tibet might follow suit. If England were to control Tibet, it would be disadvantageous
to the Soviet Union.

Stalin seemed to be sympathetic to this idea, but he suggested that
the agreement about the independence of Outer Mongolia might be
concluded secretly, and be made public only after Japan's surrender.
He stressed further that if Outer Mongolia should remain as a part of
Chinese territory, the Soviet Union would not be allowed to station its
troops there. As a result, the defense line of the Soviet Union would be
jeopardized. But T. V. Soong could not commit China to concede the
independence of Outer Mongolia without further instructions from his
home Government, so this matter was referred to Chungking.[22]

In their conversation that evening, Stalin and Soong discussed the
relationship between the Nationalists and Chinese Communists.

> *Stalin:*   Will China accept the participation of some liberal members
> in its government?
> *Soong:*   We attempted to compromise with the Chinese Communists
> last March, at which time we planned to form a wartime cabinet including
> their members, and also I was informed by American Ambassador Hurley

that Your Excellency considered the Chinese Communists as merely land reformers.

Stalin: The Chinese Communists are patriots. As to whether they are real Communists, it is rather doubtful.

Soong: As a Prime Minister, I had planned to go to Yenan to discuss matters on unification of China, but I was not welcome by the Chinese Communists. It is our hope there will be but one army and one Central Government in China. We do not wish to see a divided China with a political party having its own army.

Stalin: Liberal elements which participate in the government are not limited to the Communist Party; other liberal elements may also join in. *China should have only one government under the leadership of the Kuomintang.* But this is China's own problem, I merely express my point of view.

Soong: Exactly as you say, we also hope that the Kuomintang will remain in a position of leadership. Therefore we do not wish to have a coalition government, for if that were to occur, then if one party withdraws, the government will fall.

Stalin: This is a legitimate demand of the Kuomintang.[23]

Reading this record today, it seems that in 1945 Stalin's attitude toward the Nationalists was more reasonable than that of the United States which insisted on a coalition government with the Chinese Communists. But Stalin's manner at the conference was rude, his words insulting and very embarrassing indeed. Chiang Ching-kuo gives a close-up in his book, *Carrying Heavy Burdens Towards the Great Distance:*

> When I saw Stalin on the first day his attitude was very polite. However, during the formal negotiation, he threw a piece of paper in front of Premier Soong with a rude gesture and in an ugly manner, followed by asking him whether he had seen this before? . . . "You may discuss the problems but it should be based upon this paper (the secret Yalta Agreement) which Roosevelt has signed."[24]

Before T. V. Soong left Chungking for Moscow, the Chinese Government had instructed him how to negotiate with the Soviet Union. The problems were focused on two questions: *lease* and the *eminent interest.* As to Outer Mongolia, it was beyond discussion, because what the Soviet Union wanted was *maintaining the status quo.* According to Chinese interpretation, confirmed by Roosevelt, the Chinese suzerainty still remained and therefore it could cause no problem. Now the Outer Mongolian question became a major problem. Soong therefore cabled Chiang with the following alternatives: (1) Should permission be given to the Soviet Union to station its troops in Outer Mongolia for the duration of the treaty? (2) Should Outer Mongolia be given autonomy and the Soviet Union be permitted to station its troops there? (3)

Should Outer Mongolia be allowed to handle its own military and civil affairs independently, but still keep China's suzerainty intact over the country?[25]

When Soong's telegram arrived at Chungking, Chiang was in Sian, making it impossible for him to reply at once. Since Stalin's demands had not only gone beyond the provisions of the Yalta Agreement, but also were against the principle of the American open-door policy, Soong invited Averell Harriman, the American Ambassador, to his residence, and told him what he had gone through in the negotiations with the Soviets. He also requested advice from the U.S. State Department on the correct interpretation of the Yalta Agreement from one of the signatories so that he could use it as a base for further negotiations with Stalin.

The U.S. State Department had then just been reorganized with James F. Byrnes as the new Secretary of State. He was not familiar with Far Eastern affairs. Moreover, the U.S. policy at that time was to avoid any possible friction with the Soviet Union. Therefore, the reply Harriman received from the State Department was that the question was solely a matter between China and the U.S.S.R. Hence no advice would be offered in spite of the fact that the Far Eastern Division of the Department had pointed out that the Soviet Union demands on the Chinese Eastern and South Manchurian Railways, and the preeminent interest at Dairen, were not in conformity with the original meaning of the Yalta Agreement.[26]

In the anxiety of waiting Chungking's new instructions, Soong asked Chiang Ching-kuo to call on Stalin for a private talk. Stalin, while recognizing that China might have her own reason for refusing the cession of Outer Mongolia, persistently maintained his view about defending Siberia and refused to retreat from his position. Furthermore, he said, since China was powerless to drive the invading Japanese troops out of its own territory and had to depend upon the Soviet Union, it was only reasonable for China to concede to the Soviet Union's demands. The Soviet Union's real intention was unwittingly disclosed in Stalin's conversation with Chiang Ching-kuo.

> Stalin said:
> "To tell you the truth, from a strategic point of view, if there were a military Power which attacked the Soviet Union from Outer Mongolia and cut off the trans-Siberian railway, the Soviet Union would be finished. . . . You have said that neither Japan nor China would have strength enough to occupy Outer Mongolia, but you cannot say that there would not be a third power which is capable of doing so."
> "Who is this power? Is it the United States?" asked Chiang Ching-kuo. Stalin emphatically replied: "Certainly."[27]

Historical records show clearly that in 1945 China's weakness, Stalin's craftiness, Roosevelt's naivete, and Truman's ignorance were the main factors causing postwar disaster in the Far East. While the Soviet demands were no doubt interfering with the sovereignty and interest of China, Stalin's real objective was principally to undermine the American position in the Far East.

Since Chungking's new instruction did not come in time as expected and further delay was impossible, T. V. Soong had to offer a counterproposal at the third meeting by granting Outer Mongolia autonomy without giving up China's suzerainty.

The third session took place on July 7 from 11 p.m. to 11:45 p.m. At this session Soong pointed out that the original Yalta Agreement merely stipulated that "the status quo of Outer Mongolia should be maintained," without mentioning about its becoming independent. Stalin declared that Outer Mongolia today is a "People's Republic in fact," therefore, its status quo means "independence." After a lengthy debate, Soong proposed that China was willing to offer Outer Mongolia a high degree of autonomy allowing it to manage its military and foreign affairs, and even conclude a treaty with the Soviet Union for stationing Soviet troops in its territory to defend Siberia. Stalin still argued against this. Finally Stalin presented to the meeting drafts of four Sino-Soviet documents: a treaty of friendship and alliance, an agreement concerning the Chinese Eastern and South Manchurian Railways, an agreement on Port Arthur and Dairen, and a declaration of independence for Outer Mongolia.

Soong insisted that without Chinese agreement on the independence of Outer Mongolia no discussion could be made on the declaration. Stalin, on the other hand, considered that without the declaration of independence for Outer Mongolia there would be no discussion on the Sino-Soviet treaty of alliance. The heated arguments on both sides run as follows:

> *Soong:* We have presented already a realistic proposal on the question of Outer Mongolia.
> *Stalin:* Your proposal is not realistic.
> *Soong:* From our governmental point of view it is realistic.
> *Stalin:* But we cannot agree.
> *Soong:* This is the instruction which I have received.
> *Stalin:* *Let's end here.*
> *Soong:* It is regrettable that Your Excellency cannot understand our position. . . .
> *Stalin:* It is also regrettable that Your Excellency cannot understand our position. *Let's end here.*[28]

Sino-Soviet negotiations at this moment had nearly come to an end. However, new instructions from Chungking were already on the way.

Generalissimo Chiang returned to Chungking on July 5 two days after receiving Soong's cabled report of the second session (July 3), and called a conference of ranking officers to discuss the whole situation. On the same night (July 5) he cabled Soong new instructions. The major points were:

(1) The problem of the independence of Outer Mongolia shall be decided after the unification of our country and complete territorial sovereignty and administrative integrity have been restored.

(2) If the Soviet Union can guarantee the integrity of territorial sovereignty of Manchuria, refrain from supporting the conspiracy of the Chinese Communists, and from encouraging revolt in Sinkiang, then

(3) The Chinese Government will voluntarily propose the independence of Outer Mongolia through plebiscite by its citizens, but this shall not be implemented until after V-J day.

(4) Dairen shall be a free port; Port Arthur shall be a naval base jointly used by China and the Soviet Union; the trunk lines of railways shall be operated jointly by both countries; the management, however, shall be retained by China.

The cable also pointed out that:

This is our *minimum expectation*. If there is no concrete guarantee, then we shall sacrifice for nothing. Under such circumstances negotiation should be *suspended* at the optimum time. The delegate should return to the country first, and after completing the report, then proceed to the Soviet Union.

The wordings of these instructions were firm. On July 7 two similar telegrams mentioned this as one supreme effort to win eternal peace.[29]

These telegrams reached Moscow right after the deadlock at the third session. When Soong compared the Soviet proposals for Port Arthur, Dairen and railways and the Three-Power Yalta Agreement with Chiang's instructions, he immediately saw how far apart they still were:

(1) Respecting Port Arthur and Dairen, the Soviet Union had added these words: "the land and sea adjacent areas."

(2) Although Port Arthur was to be operated jointly by China and the Soviet Union, the Soviet Union was to manage the administration.

(3) Although the Dairen harbor is to be internationalized in name, the Soviet Union insisted that it should be used as a naval base for China and the Soviet Union exclusively.

(4) The city of Dairen was to be jointly administered by China and

the Soviet Union, and the port of Dairen was to be administered solely by the Soviet Union.

(5) The areas surrounding Port Arthur and Dairen could be under Chinese civil administration, but the administrators selected were to have the approval of the Soviet Union.

(6) To recover the properties of the Chinese Eastern and South Manchurian railways, China had to agree that a joint Sino-Soviet Company for forty years be set up to administer all of these enterprises. The director and the manager, as well as a majority of its board of directors, were to be Soviet citizens.[30]

All these demands were not mentioned in the original Three-Power Agreement at Yalta, and therefore the progress of the negotiations was very difficult.

Keeping in close touch with Soong, Ambassador Harriman strongly advised China to concede Port Arthur as a naval base for the Soviet Union, but to insist upon the right of administering Dairen. As to the railways, he suggested that China should only demand ownership. Based upon his own experience, Harriman explained that in negotiating with the Soviet Union one cannot expect to settle all problems in one treaty. And, if the Sino-Soviet negotiations break down, the Soviet Union would start attacking Japan in Manchuria and Inner Mongolia and possibly even invading China Proper. Without a Sino-Soviet treaty at that time it could be more disastrous to China.[31]

In his unofficial contacts with some Soviet leaders, Chiang Ching-kuo was informed that Stalin would never retreat from his insistence on the independence of Outer Mongolia. But if there were any success on this point, the Soviet Union would assist the Nationalist Government in unifying China.[32] With this in mind, Soong asked Stalin for a fourth session.

The fourth session was held on July 9. Although it lasted only a hundred minutes (9:00-10:40 P.M.), it was the turning point of the negotiations. Summarizing the important aspects of his new instructions Soong solemnly addressed Stalin:

> In order to assure good Sino-Soviet relations and to achieve construc-
> tive cooperation between the two countries in accordance with the will of
> the late Sun Yat-sen, the Chinese government is willing to make maximum
> sacrifices. China's most direct need is to attain territorial and administra-
> tive integrity and the genuine unification of its country. It is our hope that
> the Soviet Union will be sympathetic and cooperative and help China by
> giving the following assurances.
>
> 1. *Manchuria:* As assured by Marshall Stalin, the Soviet Union recognizes
>   Manchuria as an integral part of China and will respect its territorial

and administrative integrity, for which the Chinese people are grateful. For mutual benefit, China is prepared to agree that the naval base of Port Arthur shall be made a port to be jointly used by both China and the Soviet Union, and Dairen shall be made an international free port. Both of these arrangements are to be maintained for a period of twenty years. The administration of both ports shall be in the hands of China. The trunk lines of the Chinese Eastern Railway and the South Manchurian Railway shall be placed under a joint operation by China and the Soviet Union but the Soviet Union recognizes China's ownership. It should be understood that all branch lines and enterprises unrelated to the above said two railways would not be included in the joint operation.

2. *Sinkiang:* The Chinese Central Government shall use political means to deal with the recent rebellion in Sinkiang. It is hoped that the Soviet Union will refrain from supplying military arms to the rebels. The area of Altai Mountain, which originally belonged to Sinkiang, shall continue to remain a part of Sinkiang.

3. *Chinese Communists:* The Chinese Central Government finds it impossible to unify China as long as the Chinese Communists maintain their separate military and civilian organizations. It is hoped that the Soviet Government will give *moral as well as material aid solely to the Chinese Central Government.*

4. *Outer Mongolia:* After the Soviet Union has agreed to all the three above mentioned proposals, then the Chinese Government is prepared to grant the independence of Outer Mongolia by a Mongolian plebiscite which should be taken only after the defeat of Japan. And the boundary of Outer Mongolia shall be that of the old Chinese boundary map.

To the above, Stalin replied that he was willing to respect China's sovereign rights and administrative integrity in Manchuria. As to the alleged supplying of armaments to the rebellious group in Sinkiang, he promised to investigate it before further negotiation. He also recognized the right of the Chinese Central Government to suppress the rebels in Sinkiang by force whenever necessary. He further assured the Chinese delegation that he had never supported the Chinese Communists with arms, *and all Russian aid to China, moral or material, would go solely to the Central government.* Moreover, he expressed the hope that China would have one government and one army, pointing out that the merging of the Communist forces with the national army was essential.[33]

Since both parties had come to full agreement on the main issue, the remaining items were left for further discussion. As Stalin and Molotov were very anxious to have the negotiations concluded before their departure for the forthcoming Potsdam Conference, the fifth and sixth sessions were moved along pretty smoothly and swiftly.

At the fifth session held on July 11 (9:00-11:30 P.M.), numerous problems were solved:

(1) Stalin promised to produce written assurances on Manchuria, Sinkiang, and exclusive support of the Chinese Nationalist Government, after completing all other items on the agenda.

(2) Stalin promised to withdraw all Soviet troops from Manchuria within three months after V-J day, to be confirmed by an exchange of notes.

(3) The Chinese Central Government promised to be responsible for the protection of the railways.

(4) China promised to send a military delegation to Manchuria to cooperate with the Soviet occupation troops in establishing a new local civilian government to be confirmed by an exchange of notes.

(5) The Soviet Union promised not to raise any question about ownership of the railways, while reserving the right to transport armaments but not the transportation of Soviet troops in peacetime.

But several items remained to be discussed:

(1) The Soviet Union's insistence on supplying personnel for operating Port Arthur and Dairen, to which the Chinese delegation objected.

(2) The Chinese delegation proposed that under the joint operation of the Chinese Eastern Railway, the president of the board of directors must be a Chinese while the manager could be a Russian; and that under the joint operation of the South Manchurian Railway, the manager must be a Chinese, and the assistant manager a Russian. The Soviet Union objected to both propositions.

(3) The Soviet Union proposed that the sphere of influence of Imperial Russia in Port Arthur be restored, and therefore that the immediate area around Dairen and the South Manchurian Railway be included in the Port Arthur naval base, to which the Chinese delegation objected.[34]

The sixth session was held on July 12 (12:00-12:45 P.M.). Both parties agreed on the draft of the declaration respecting the independence of Outer Mongolia, and on the draft of the Sino-Soviet treaty of friendship and alliance. After objection by the Chinese delegation, no further mention was made concerning the requirement of consent from the Soviet military authority on appointment of Chinese civilian officials in Dairen. The rest of the problems remaining to be solved were:

(1) the operation of the railways;
(2) the administrative authority of Dairen; and
(3) the size of the area to be included in the district of Port Arthur.

Since Stalin and Molotov planned to leave Moscow on July 14 to attend the Potsdam Conference which had been scheduled on July 26,

Soong proposed to take this opportunity to return to Chungking temporarily with Petrov and others to report the results of negotiations to the Chinese government and to come back to Moscow after the Soviet leaders' return. To this, Molotov hesitated but Stalin agreed. Following a cordial and sumptuous entertainment of the Chinese delegation by Stalin on July 13, Soong, Chiang Ching-kuo, and Petrov flew back to Chungking the next day. Victor Hu remained in Moscow to continue the conference with some of the Soviet delegates.[35]

There were significant reasons for Soong's abrupt return to Chungking at the high tide of the negotiations:

(1) While Soong fully realized that a Sino-Soviet treaty of friendship and alliance could only be concluded at China's great sacrifice of certain rights and interests in Manchuria and Outer Mongolia, he was not willing to sign a treaty with those conditions in it. He had in mind to ask Chiang to appoint a new Minister of Foreign Affairs to take his place before he returned to Moscow.[36]

(2) Soong had come to realize that the Soviet demands relating to Outer Mongolia and Manchuria had gone far beyond what was stipulated in the Three-Power Yalta Agreement. Although the independence of Outer Mongolia did not concern the United States, yet the Soviet Union's insistence on the monopoly of numerous rights and interests in Manchuria was definitely contrary to the principle of the open-door policy which the United States government should not overlook.

Harriman had been one of the participants at the Yalta Conference when the Three-Power Agreement was drawn up. He was also going to attend the Potsdam Conference where President Truman would meet Stalin. Soong thought that the American government should be given a chance to reconsider the situation. If the U.S. government would be willing to intercede on China's behalf with respect to the excessive Soviet demands, the chance of success would be better than a counter-measure put up by China alone.

Sino-American source materials verified that Soong arrived in Chungking on July 15 and that Generalissimo Chiang interviewed Petrov on July 19. That same day President Truman was informed of the results of the Sino-Soviet negotiations by the Chinese Government which urged him to advise Stalin not to make excessive demands.[37] Diplomatic strategy was really at work. After arriving at Balealsberg, Harriman submitted three memoranda (dated July 18, 28, and 31) to the State Department urging the United States Government to participate in the Sino-Soviet negotiations dealing with the free port of Dairen.[38] Between July 17 and 23, the Director of the Far Eastern Division of the State Department also submitted four papers urging the Secretary of State to support Soong in order to maintain America's position in Manchuria, one of which argued:

> The commitment taken by us at Yalta in regard to Manchuria and our undertaking to get China to accept these commitments placed us squarely in a position of responsibility which we could not transfer to the Chinese, on the theory that the negotiations were bilateral and that China should get as good terms as it could.[39]

Although it was repeatedly suggested that Soong be invited to Potsdam, Chinese diplomatic strategy lost out because prior to the submitting of these papers, the problem of the Dairen free port had been briefly discussed between Truman and Stalin on July 17.[40] Without realizing the seriousness of this matter, Truman refused Chiang's request for participation.[41] The new Secretary of State, Byrnes, did nothing until August 5 when he sent a telegram to Harriman instructing him to support the Chinese stance and to request that the Soviet government guarantee the open-door policy. Apparently, Byrnes' action came too late.[42]

The Potsdam Conference was ended on August 2. Stalin and Molotov returned to Moscow on August 5. Soong and Wang Shih-chieh, the new Chinese Minister of Foreign Affairs, Soviet Ambassador Petrov, Chiang Ching-kuo, and others including Shih-hui Hsiung, China's newly appointed representative who was going to take charge of Military Affairs of the Northeast provinces, left Chungking on August 6, and arrived in Moscow the next evening at 7:30 P.M.[43] Although only three weeks had passed since the last Sino-Soviet session, the war situation in the Far East had changed dramatically. China, the United Kingdom, and the United States had sent a joint ultimatum to Japan on July 26.[44] The next day Togo Shigenori, the Japanese Foreign Minister, acknowledged that the ultimatum had been received by the Supreme Imperial Conference.[45]

On the day that Soong's party arrived in Moscow, the United States dropped the first atomic bomb on Hiroshima. The Soviet Union had not yet joined the war against Japan, while the latter was already looking for ways to surrender. There were still six outstanding issues to be discussed further between China and the Soviet Union:

(1) *The boundary of Outer Mongolia:* The Soviet Union had suggested that this item should not be mentioned in the treaty, while the Chinese delegation insisted that it must be based upon the Chinese map of Outer Mongolia and that this map be attached to the treaty.

(2) *The administration of Dairen:* The Soviet Union had proposed that a Sino-Soviet joint board of directors be established and that a Russian be the chairman of the board of directors. The Chinese delegation objected to the latter demand.

(3) *Defining the area of the naval base at Port Arthur:* The Soviet

Union proposed to include Ching Chow　　金 州　(Liao Tung Peninsula), whereas the Chinese delegation had suggested that the area between the port of Dairen and the South Manchurian Railway should be excluded.

(4) *The administrative problem of Port Arthur:* The Chinese delegation had proposed that all military problems be referred for solution to a Sino-Soviet joint military commission, to be established, and that all civilian matters be settled solely by the Chinese authorities. With this new proposal the Soviet Union disagreed.

(5) *The operation of the Manchurian Railways:* The Chinese delegation had suggested that the president of the board of directors of both the Chinese Eastern and of the South Manchurian Railways must be a Chinese; that the manager of the Chinese Eastern Railway be a Soviet citizen, while the assistant manager be a Chinese; and that the manager of the South Manchurian Railway be a Chinese and the assistant manager be a Soviet citizen. The Soviet Union, however, had proposed that the managers of both railways must be Soviet citizens.

(6) *Military cooperation in Manchuria:* This matter had been left unsettled, due to the fact that the war against Japan had recently undergone rapid change. Sessions were speeded up, the seventh, eighth, and ninth meetings being held on August 8, 10, and 13 respectively. Final decisions were made at the tenth session held on August 14.[46] The treaty of friendship and alliance consisting of eight articles, four exchange notes, and one memorandum were jointly signed by the Chinese Minister of Foreign Affairs Wang Shih-chieh and by the Soviet Foreign Minister Molotov. The wordings of the treaty and its annex had been examined in early July but the formation of the exchange notes proved to be the most difficult task.[47]

The major aspects of the resultant treaty were:

Concerning the three declarations:

1. The Government of the Soviet Union agrees to grant moral, military and other material aid completely and exclusively to the National Government of China.

2. The Soviet Union recognizes that Dairen, Port Arthur, and the jointly operated Chinese Chang Chun Railway (general name for the trunk lines of the Chinese Eastern and South Manchurian Railways) are an integral part of Manchuria, and respects China's unabridged sovereignty over Manchuria . . . and recognizes the territorial and administrative integrity of the whole area.

3. The Soviet Union declares that it had no intention of interfering with the internal affairs of Sinkiang.

Concerning Outer Mongolia:

After the defeat of Japan the Chinese Government agrees to have a plebiscite held in Outer Mongolia to determine whether its citizens are in favor of independence. If the results of the plebiscite favor independence, China would recognize independence of Outer Mongolia; its boundary would remain unchanged.

Concerning the Chinese Eastern and South Manchurian Railways:

1. Both countries agree that the trunk lines of these two railways are to be merged into one railway system to be called the Chinese Chang Chun Railway, to be owned jointly by China and the Soviet Union which will choose a commercial company to operate it on their behalf.

2. The Sino-Soviet Railway Company is to consist of a joint board of directors, five directors to be Chinese and five Russian. The president of the board of directors is to be a Chinese with two votes, the general manager a Russian, and the assistant manager a Chinese. The appointment of employees of the railway must have the recommendation of the general manager.

3. Policing of the railway and its area is to be China's responsibility. Transporting of Soviet troops in peacetime is prohibited.

Concerning Port Arthur:

1. The precise boundary of the Port Arthur area is to be that shown on the attached map which is to be prepared by the Sino-Soviet military commission.

2. Chinese and Soviet military and commercial vessels are to have free access to Port Arthur. The Soviet Government has the right to maintain its army, navy and air force there for defense purposes.

3. The Sino-Soviet Military Commission, composed of two Chinese and three Soviet representatives, is to be established to supervise the joint use of this base.

4. The civil administration of the port is to remain Chinese. However, in making appointments for leading responsible posts, the Chinese Government is to take into account the interests of the Soviet Union.

Concerning Dairen:

1. Dairen's administration is to be under the aegis of the Chinese Government which has declared Dairen to be a free port open to the commerce and shipping of all nations. The harbor-master is to be a Soviet citizen, the deputy harbor-master a Chinese, both to be appointed by the Soviet manager of the Chinese Chung Chun Railway, subject to the approval of the mayor.

2. Dairen in peacetime is not to be included in the Port Arthur naval base and not to be subject to its regulations. Sections of the Chinese Chang Chun Railway between Dairen and Mukden, lying within the

region of the Port Arthur naval base, are not to be subject to the military supervision or control established in this region.

3. The Soviet Union is to be permitted to lease up to one-half of the installations and equipment of the port.

Concerning Military Cooperation:

1. China will appoint military representatives and staff for the re-covered Manchurian territory, and will establish an administration for the same, in cooperation with the Soviet military forces.

2. This military cooperation is to include the establishment of a Chinese armed force.

3. As soon as any part of the recovered territory ceases to be a zone of immediate military operations, the Chinese National Government is to assume full authority over public affairs and render the Soviet military forces every assistance and support through its civil and military authorities.

Besides these items there was a memorandum reiterating the promise of Stalin to withdraw all Soviet troops from Manchuria within three months following the defeat of Japan.[48]

Although the Soviet demands described above are far in excess of the provisions as agreed upon by the Three Powers at Yalta, China, being a far weaker nation as compared with the Soviet Union after her eight years war against Japan, seems to have done her best in pre-serving her sovereignty and national dignity. Since the contents of the treaty and the exchange notes have already been published by the Chinese government,[49] no details are given here.

It is interesting to note that on August 8, 1945, the very day the Sino-Soviet seventh session was held, the Soviet Union suddenly declared war against Japan without waiting for the conclusion of the Sino-Soviet treaty which had been so earnestly requested by Stalin at the Yalta Conference. On August 10, the day of the eighth session, the second atomic bomb was dropped on Nagasaki. On August 13, the day of the ninth session, the Allied Forces accepted Tokyo's proposal for "uncon-ditional surrender" provided that the Imperial institution be preserved. It is an irony that while the war against Japan had almost come to an end, the conditions for Soviet participation in the war against Japan were still being discussed at the Sino-Soviet negotiating table!

Following the ninth session, Chiang Kai-shek instructed the Chinese delegation to cease negotiating and to insist on a definite agreement on the following: 1) the territorial boundaries of Outer Mongolia; 2) the establishment of a Sino-Soviet military commission for the naval base of Port Arthur; 3) a Chinese harbor-master for Dairen.[50] But members of the Chinese delegation were afraid that, should there be no stipulated restrictions on the movement of the Soviet troops in the treaty, the Soviet Union might take the advantage to invade North China and cause more trouble once they entered Manchuria. The delegation therefore repeatedly requested Chiang for authorization to settle all remaining problems on the spot.[51]

On the last day, the 13th of August, Chiang gave the authorization. So, at the tenth session Soong and Wang reached a compromise with the Soviet delegates on the territorial boundaries of Outer Mongolia and on the Sino-Soviet military commission for the base of Port Arthur. The Sino-Soviet Treaty of Friendship and Alliance was finally signed at Moscow on V-J Day, August 14, 1945. Immediately after the signing of the treaty, Molotov suggested that it become effective at once, but Wang firmly rejected this suggestion. The regular Chinese legal process was duly followed: first examination by the Supreme National Defense Council, then passage by the Legislative Yuan on August 24, 1945, and finally ratification by the Chinese Government.

It is to be further noted that when the Sino-Soviet treaty was finalized, the U.S. open-door policy in Manchuria was doomed. One may recall that when President Truman asked Ambassador Hurley to inform Chiang about the secret Yalta Agreement on June 15, 1945, Chiang's first reaction was: Should the United States be willing to participate in the Sino-Soviet negotiation and conclude a multipartite treaty? If the United States agrees to this, China would be ready for such a meeting. However, when approached, Truman turned down this offer.[52]

During the recess of the negotiations the intention of the Soviet Union was already clear. She tried hard to monopolize the use of the seaports and the railways of Manchuria. On July 14, Chiang called Truman's attention to this fact but Truman did not act. Apparently, he did not realize the significance of this matter.[53] Later, after Harriman briefed the Secretary of State three times at the Potsdam Conference, Secretary Stimson warned Truman too.[54] State Department officers at Potsdam also jointly requested American intervention and even proposed that Soong be invited to come to Germany to discuss this matter.[55]

Secretary Byrnes did not act until after the end of the Potsdam Conference when Stalin had already returned home. On August 5, Byrnes cabled Harriman urging him to negotiate with the Soviet Union on guaranteeing the open-door in Manchuria.[56] His cablegram proposed a four-power multipartite treaty similar to Chiang's original plan although his concern was limited to Dairen only.

Between August 5 and September 20, the State Department called upon Harriman four times urging him to press the Soviet Union for guaranteeing the open door in Manchuria.[57] Harriman negotiated with Stalin twice,[58] corresponded with Molotov twice, and had a face-to-face talk with Molotov once.[59] Although Stalin verbally promised to maintain the open-door policy in Manchuria, efforts to obtain a written document from him proved in vain. During the Sino-Soviet negotiations, Harriman privately told Soong that the United States definitely would not support Soviet excessive demands beyond the Three-Power Yalta Agreement, but when Soong asked him for an assurance of American military backing, if China so insisted towards the U.S.S.R., Harriman made no commitment.[60]

Harriman seemed fully aware that settlement of international disputes depends much upon military strength. When his negotiation with Russia on the open-door policy became deadlocked, he secretly cabled Truman on August 10 suggesting that American troops should enter the Liaotung Peninsula to receive the surrender of the Japanese army in Manchuria.[61] This suggestion was approved and a JCS order to General MacArthur and Admiral Nimitz instructing them to send marines immediately to Dairen before the arrival of Soviet forces was issued, but due to the rapid advance of Soviet troops in this area, the JCS order was soon cancelled.[62] Had this crucial order been carried out, the whole post-war situation of the Far East would have been entirely changed.

We all know that this treaty, though it had been carefully studied, vigorously discussed and solemnly signed and ratified by the two respective governments, was, after all, a mockery. The Soviet promise to observe Chinese sovereignty over Manchuria has never been honored. Neither has her promise to send her aid exclusively to the Nationalist government been carried out. The Chinese Nationalist troops, transported by American Liberty Ships to the Manchurian ports—Dairen, Hulutao or Yinkow— were all denied access.[63] The Chinese Communist guerrillas were armed and equipped with Japanese weapons by the Soviet army before the latter was withdrawn.[64] All this happened before the ink of the signatures on the treaty was dry. This led people to ask why the Soviet Union wanted the treaty, since they could get what they wanted even without it. But Stalin has an explanation. According to a conversation with Stalin by Milovan Djilas, a Yugoslav Communist leader, Stalin said:

> When the war with Japan ended, we invited the Chinese Comrades to reach an agreement as to how a modus vivendi with Chiang Kai-shek might be found. They agreed with us in word, but in deed they did it their way when they got home.[65]

Thus, it seems Stalin wished to shift the responsibility of carrying out the obligation of the treaty to Mao Tse-tung. Whether this statement is justified I shall leave to the reader to ponder. But one thing is certain:

Any treaty signed with Communists, Stalin or anyone else, will have little value unless it can be enforced by your own power. The failure of the Sino-Soviet Treaty of Friendship and Alliance is merely one of the many tragic examples!

NOTES

1. Chiang Kai-shek, *Soviet Russia in China: A Summing-Up at Seventy* (New York: Farrar, Straus & Cudahy, rev. ed. 1958), pp. 76-7; 104-9. Also see *A Disciple of Chiang Kai-shek's Struggle for Freedom, Justice and Peace* 蔣總統為自由正義與和平而奮鬥 述略, pp. 188-202.

2. Chiang Kai-shek, *op. cit.*, pp. 109-10. See also U.S. Department of State, *Foreign Relations of the United States 1945* (Washington, D.C.: Government Printing Office, 1969), Vol. VII, pp. 985-1025. (Hereafter cited as F.R.)

3. Herbert Feis. *The China Tangle: The American Effort in China from Pearl Harbor to the Marshall Mission* (Princeton, N.J.: Princeton University Press, 1953), p. 150. See also U.S. Department of State, *United States Relations with China: With Special Reference to the Period 1944-1949* (Washington, D.C.: Government Printing Office, 1949), p. 550.

4. F.R. 1944, Vol. VII, p. 136.

5. U.S. Senate, 82nd Cong., 1st Ses., *Hearings before the Committee of Armed Services and the Committee on Foreign Relations, Military Situation in the Far East* (Washington, D.C.: Government Printing Office, 1951), Part IV, p. 2886. See also Feis, *op. cit.*, p. 279.

6. In October 1944 while passing through Washington, D.C. on his official duty, Ambassador V. K. Wellington Koo met the White House Chief of Staff, Admiral William D. Leahy. During their conversation Leahy told him about the Soviet demand for the ice-free Port Arthur. Koo exposed this outrageous demand and secretly telegraphed Chiang on October 14. Koo sent another telegram on November 9 and pointed out that in his judgment, the United States desired the Soviet Union to join the war against Japan as soon as possible, and control of Port Arthur was one of its conditions. Leahy's information may have been a trial balloon to find out Chinese reaction. For Koo's telegrams to Chiang, see *Private Papers of President Chiang Kai-shek, Some Aspects of the Secret Yalta Agreement Concerning the Negotiations of the Sino-Soviet Agreements,* unpublished, in Chinese, pp. 37 & 39. (Hereafter cited as *Chinese Yalta Documents.*)

7. For Wei's secret telegram, see *ibid.*, pp. 42-3.

8. U.S., Department of State, *The Conference at Malta and Yalta, 1945* (Washington, D.C.: Government Printing Office, 1955), pp. 897-8. (Hereafter cited as *Yalta Papers.*)

9. See Chiang Kai-shek's telegram to T. V. Soong, *Chinese Yalta Documents*, pp. 50-2.

10. For record of Chiang's conversation with Soviet Ambassador Petrov, see *ibid.*, pp. 53-67.

11. For Chiang's four telegrams to T. V. Soong, see *ibid.*, pp. 72, 73, 74, 75, 82, 84-86.

12. F. R. 1944, VII, p. 136.

13. See T. V. Soong's telegram to Chiang, dated April 15 and April 26, 1945, *Chinese Yalta Documents*, pp. 46-47.

14. F. R. 1945, VII, pp. 893-4 & 896.

15. For T. V. Soong's conversation with President Truman both in Chinese and English, see *Chinese Yalta Documents*, pp. 76-8, 104-7.

16. For Soong's conversation with Hopkins, see *ibid.*, pp. 108-13.

17. See Ambassador Hurley's telegram to Secretary of State Stettinius, and Acting Secretary of State Joseph C. Grew's telegram to Ambassador Hurley: F. R. 1945, VII, pp. 903-4, 906-7.

18. *Chinese Yalta Documents*, pp. 87-102, 119-29.

19. For record of initial conversation between Soong and Marshal Stalin, see *ibid.*, pp. 133-7.

20. See Soong's telegram to Chiang, dated July 1, 1945, *ibid.*, p. 141.

21. See Soong's telegram to Chiang, dated July 2, 1945, *ibid.*, pp. 144-72.

22. See *ibid.*, pp. 144-72, Soong's second conversation with Stalin.

23. *Ibid.*, pp. 144-72, The Record of the Second Stalin-Soong conversation.

24. Chiang Ching-kuo 負重致遠 , *Carrying Heavy Burdens Towards The Great Distance* (Taipei, China, 1960), p. 63.

25. Soong's telegram to Chiang, dated July 3, 1945, see *Chinese Yalta Documents*, p. 175.

26. See Secretary of State Byrnes' telegram to Ambassador Harriman, dated July 4, 1945, and Harriman's reply, dated July 9, 1945; F. R. 1945, VII, pp. 914-5.

27. Chiang Ching-kuo, *op. cit.*, p. 67.

28. *Chinese Yalta Documents*, pp. 197-208. Harriman's telegram to President Truman, dated July 8, 1945, see F. R. 1945, VII, pp. 920-1.

29. See Chiang's five telegrams to Soong, July 6-July 7, *Chinese Yalta Documents*, pp. 181-95. See also Hurley's telegram to Byrnes, July 6, 1945, F. R. 1945, VII, pp. 918-9.

30. See Soong's telegram to Chiang, dated July 9, 1945, *Chinese Yalta Documents*, pp. 217-8.

31. *Ibid.*, pp. 219-20.

32. See Chiang Ching-kuo's telegram to Chiang, August 8, *ibid.*, p. 212.

33. See Soong's telegram to Chiang, dated July 9, 1945, and record of Soong's fourth conversation with Stalin, *ibid.*, pp. 221-43.

34. See Soong's telegram to Chiang, dated July 11, 1945, and record of Soong's fifth conversation with Stalin, *ibid.*, pp. 247-64. See also Harriman's telegram to President Truman and Secretary of State Byrnes, dated July 12, 1945, F. R. 1945, VII, pp. 932-3.

35. See Soong's telegram to Chiang, dated July 12, 1945, and record of Soong's sixth conversation with Stalin, *Chinese Yalta Documents,* pp. 265-74.

36. See Hurley's telegram to Byrnes, dated July 29, 1945, F. R. 1945, VII, pp. 952-3.

37. For record of conversation between Chiang and Ambassador Petrov, see *Chinese Yalta Documents,* pp. 275-93. For Chiang's telegram to President Truman, dated July 19, 1945, see F. R. 1945, VII, pp. 948-9.

38. See F. R. 1945, Vol. VII, pp. 945-8, 950-2, 953-4.

39. According to Feis, the State Department officers who were in Potsdam, namely Dooman and Vincent, had submitted four memos to Secretary Byrnes. See *op. cit.*, pp. 328-9, note 13.

40. According to Byrnes, on July 17, 1945, "President Truman declared that the United States wanted to make sure Dairen was maintained as an open port. Stalin replied that, if the Soviet Union obtained control of the port, it would have that status. I pointed out that, under the agreement President Roosevelt had entered into at Yalta, China was to retain control of Dairen." See James F. Byrnes, *Speaking Frankly* (New York: Harper & Brothers, 1947), p. 205.

41. For President Truman's telegram to Chiang, see *Chinese Yalta Documents,* pp. 294-5.

42. For Byrnes' telegram to Harriman, dated August 5, 1945, see F. R. 1945, VII, pp. 955-6. See also Feis, *op. cit.*, pp. 330-1.

43. *Chinese Yalta Documents,* p. 307.

44. U.S. Department of State, *Occupation of Japan* (Washington, D.C.: Government Printing Office, 1946), pp. 53-5. (See also Feis, *op. cit.*, pp. 326-7.)

45. U.S. Department of State, *Judgment of the International Military Tribunal for the Far East* (Washington, D.C.: Government Printing Office, 1948), pp. 357-85.

46. *Chinese Yalta Documents,* pp. 309-10, 315-6, 336-8, and 341.

47. *Ibid.*, pp. 341-69.

48. *Ibid.*

49. See Republic of China, Ministry of Foreign Affairs, *Treaties Between the Republic of China and Foreign States* (Taipei, China: Commercial Press, 1958), pp. 505-23.

50. Chiang's three telegrams to Soong and Wang, *Chinese Yalta Documents*, pp. 320-5.
51. See various telegrams from Soong, Wang and Chiang Ching-kuo to Chiang Kai-shek, *Ibid.*, pp. 329-33.
52. See *supra*, note 17.
53. See *Chinese Yalta Documents*, pp. 294-5.
54. For Ambassador Harriman's three memos to Secretary of State Byrnes, dated July 18, 28, and 31, 1945, see F. R. 1945, VII, pp. 944-8.
55. See *supra*, note 39.
56. See *supra*, note 42.
57. Secretary of State Byrnes' four telegrams to Ambassador Harriman, dated August 5, 9, 11, and 22, 1945, urging him to negotiate with Stalin, see F. R. 1945, VII, pp. 955-6, 969-70, and 979-80.
58. The first conversation between Ambassador Harriman and Marshal Stalin was on August 8, 1945. Stalin promised to offer a written guarantee, but added that Dairen under Soviet control was not counter to the open-door policy. The Yalta Agreement had not mentioned that a Soviet written guarantee was required. Stalin insisted firmly that Dairen could not be outside the military zone in order to protect Port Arthur.
    The second conversation was on August 27, 1945. Though Stalin again promised a written guarantee yet it was not ever forthcoming. See F. R. 1945, VII, pp. 960-5 and 981.
59. Correspondence from Harriman to Molotov, dated August 9 and 12, 1945. In a face to face talk on August 13, 1945, Molotov said that international trade under the Sino-Soviet treaty was unrestricted; Stalin therefore considered that there was no need for a written guarantee on the open-door policy. See F. R. 1945, VII, pp. 963-5, 972, and 974.
60. Feis, *op. cit.*, p. 344.
61. F. R. 1945, VII, p. 967.
62. See two secret telegrams from JCS to MacArthur and Nimitz, August 11 and August 18, 1945. In the August 11 telegram, JCS instructed MacArthur and Nimitz to make such arrangements as were practicable to occupy the port of Dairen and a port in Korea immediately following the surrender of Japan if those ports had not at that time been taken over by Soviet forces. In the August 18 telegram JCS cancelled the previous order in view of the reported rapid advance of the Russians in Liaotung peninsula. (See JCS message, No. WARK 48004, CCS decimal File 386.2, Japan sec. 3, RG 218, National Archives.)
63. See Feis, *op. cit.*, pp. 384-5.
64. In regard to the Chinese Communist guerrillas entering Manchuria,

see Sin-fu Liao Yuan   星火燎原 , *A Single Spark Can Start a Prairie Fire*   北京人民出版社印，一九六三年 (Jen-min Wen-hsueh Chu-pan-she), Vol. IV. (Peking, 1963). In regard to the equipping of Chinese Communist guerrillas with Japanese weapons, see *Moscow broadcast (in Chinese language)* on September 4, 1967. It publicly admitted that after V-J day, the Soviet Union had supplied a large amount of Japanese ammunition to the Chinese Communists: 700,000 rifles, 11,000 light machine guns, 3,000 heavy machine guns, more than 1,800 cannons, 2,500 coercive cannons, over 700 tanks, 900 planes, and 800 large arsenals. This total amount was much greater than the amount T. F. Tsiang had mentioned in China's formal complaints against the Soviet Union to the United Nations General Assembly, Fourth Session, in September 1949. The complaint charged the U.S.S.R. with aiding the Chinese Communists in their insurrection and with violation of the Sino-Soviet Treaty of Friendship and Alliance of 1945 and of the Charter of the United Nations.

65. See *Vladmir Dedijer (Tito)* (New York: Viking Press, 1953), p. 157. See also Mao Tse-tung's speech at the Moscow airport on November 2, 1957.

Comments:

BY STEVEN I. LEVINE

The Sino-Soviet Treaty of Friendship and Alliance of 1945 was quickly overtaken by events, and its imprint on the historical memory has been slight. Like the Brest-Litovsk Treaty of 1918 between Germany and Bolshevik Russia, called by Sir John Wheeler-Bennett "The Forgotten Peace," the Sino-Soviet Treaty of 1945 has been largely ignored. Yet this fate is undeserved for the treaty was important in several respects.

For the Chinese Government it represented an attempt to stabilize relations with its difficult neighbor to the north in the absence of significant support from the United States or Great Britain. For the Chinese Communists, the treaty raised at least short-term doubts about the willingness of its ideological patron—the USSR—to support the Communist quest for power. The Soviet Union negotiated the treaty as part of a dual policy designed to keep lines open to both the Nationalists and the Communists in a situation of impending civil conflict where the former were perceived as still holding the upper hand. The United States viewed the treaty as the logical culmination of the Yalta Agreement on the Far East, designed to avoid a Soviet-American clash over China.

From the perspective of contemporary students of politics, a reexamination of the treaty is of considerable interest for what it can tell us about the limited capacity of the postwar international system to adjust relations among the major powers. We are indebted to Professor Liang for rescuing the treaty from obscurity.

In the confines of a short paper, Professor Liang has chosen to concentrate on one aspect of the treaty among many—the Sino-Soviet negotiations themselves. His narrative provides an extremely clear review of the main stages in the negotiations and presents intriguing detail from the Presidential Papers of Chiang Kai-shek to which he has been given access. Professor Liang's major contribution, however, is his insistence that the Sino-Soviet negotiations which produced the treaty must be viewed in a broad multilateral perspective reflecting the new structure of the postwar international system.

My own comments will focus upon the issues which Professor Liang presents as well as several additional questions which, in my opinion, deserve further study. I shall proceed from the particular to the general.

Outer Mongolia

Professor Liang's paper confirms that the status of Outer Mongolia was the single most important point of contention between the two sides during the first part of the negotiations. The obvious question we must ask is "why?" Despite the Sino-Soviet Treaty of 1924 which confirmed Chinese suzerainty over Outer Mongolia, the subsequent course of political development there confirmed the territory's de facto separation from China. Under the aegis of the Mongolian People's Revolutionary Party a Soviet-style satellite regime had consolidated its control in Outer Mongolia. Under a bilateral agreement of 1936 Soviet troops were stationed in the Mongolian People's Republic. It was from this base among others that the Red Army (joined by Mongol cavalry) attacked the Japanese in Manchuria in August 1945. In short, the Chinese suzerainty of the 1924 treaty was a dead letter. Unlike Tibet or Sinkiang, Mongolia had undergone a modernizing revolution and was ruled by a revolutionary party closely linked to the USSR.

Was Chinese reluctance to grant Stalin's demands respecting Outer Mongolia merely a negotiating tactic? This seems unlikely. Rather, as T. V. Soong told Stalin, the cession of territory was an explosive political issue in Chinese domestic politics. The outer marches such as Outer Mongolia, I might add, had been a very sensitive area at least since the days of the early republic under Yuan Shih-kai. I would suggest that Chinese leaders sought to maintain a shadowy suzerainty over Outer Mongolia in the long-range hope that when China had recovered her strength she could reabsorb this territory. (This was a hope, incidentally, which the Chinese Communists shared.) Stalin may not only have desired the right to station troops in the MPR and derive the benefit of this strategic buffer vis-à-vis Japan and the United States, but may also have been looking towards a period when a Soviet-controlled Mongolia might deflect pressures from China on his Siberian border. Although Outer Mongolia appears less important than the issues of the Manchurian ports and railways it had more than symbolic significance. Chiang Kai-shek's decision to accept the Soviet demand on Outer Mongolia was not simply an act of *realpolitik*, but a serious concession which may be seen as a token of his desire to achieve a stable Sino-Soviet relationship.

The Internal Politics of the Negotiations

Professor Liang has had a rare opportunity to provide an inside picture of the Sino-Soviet negotiations. Like a good appetizer his narrative serves to whet our desire for additional details. A key question suggested by his paper is what were the politics within the Chinese and Soviet delegations respectively during the course of the negotiations?

We know the names of the participants on both sides, but very little of how their interaction affected the negotiations. Did T. V. Soong and Stalin dominate the proceedings as the senior officials? What role was played by Ambassador Fu on the Chinese side, Molotov and Petrov on the Soviet side? The role of Chiang Ching-kuo is of particular interest. He was obviously something more than a "private citizen" as Professor Liang calls him (p. 377). In addition to his tête-à-tête metings with Stalin, Chiang Ching-kuo, we are told, had unofficial contacts with some Soviet leaders. What were these contacts, at whose initiative, and with what effect? How did Chiang's role affect the course of the negotiations? Did Soong, for example, welcome or resent this private channel to Stalin?

On the Soviet side too it would be interesting to know how the various participants interacted. (Do the Chinese records shed any light on this question?) From the records of Soviet-American negotiations, we know that Molotov and Stalin often played the roles of the tough cop and the sympathetic policeman respectively. When Molotov was un-yielding, Stalin would intervene and make a concession which kept negotiations moving forward. Obviously, this was prearranged to put Stalin in the best possible light from the American perspective and per-petuated the absurd myth that a pragmatic and flexible Stalin was the captive of a doctrinaire and suspicious Soviet politburo. Professor Liang's account suggests that this was not the pattern in Sino-Soviet negotiations.

A related question is the Chungking end of the negotiations. When Generalissimo Chiang convened a meeting of top officials on July 5 to discuss the opening rounds of the Moscow negotiations, just what were the options under discussion? Was there any disagreement with the General-issimo? Did the decision to yield on the issue of Outer Mongolia represent an initiative on Chiang's part or did he endorse a consensus? What transpired at the meetings between the Generalissimo and T. V. Soong during the break in the conference when the latter refused to sign the agreement and a new foreign minister, Wang Shih-chieh, was brought in? How was Dr. Wang prevailed upon to perform this thankless task?

The Setting of the Negotiations

It is clear that negotiating the treaty in Moscow rather than in Chungking or some neutral setting put the Chinese diplomats at a severe disadvantage. For one thing it complicated communications be-tween Chiang Kai-shek and his diplomats on the scene. T. V. Soong apparently lacked the authority to offer any significant concessions with-out referring back to Chungking. It would be interesting to know just what were the instructions Soong carried with him to Moscow, and how much latitude he was given by the Generalissimo to alter these instructions. Did China have a well-thought-out negotiating strategy prepared in advance or did it respond in an ad hoc manner to the Soviet demands? It appears that Professor Liang is suggesting that Chiang held all the negotiating strings firmly in his own hands.

The Moscow setting of the negotiations also facilitated that boorish and overbearing Soviet behavior which was part of the USSR's diplomatic arsenal (p. 379). Did this behavior continue throughout the talks? Was it targeted on T. V. Soong alone? In any case, the Soviets had an important psychological advantage in negotiating in their own capital.

Chiang's Strategy of Multilateralization

It may be objected that all the questions raised thus far relate to fine points and ignore the essence of the situation. As Professor Liang aptly reminds us, the stark truth was that China was far weaker than the Soviet Union and any treaty between the two nations could not but reflect this reality (p. 390). The Generalissimo knew that in bilateral relations between the Soviet Union and China, the latter, lacking sufficient power, would have nothing to fall back upon in resisting Soviet demands except appeals to Soviet good faith and moderation. Therefore, Chiang tried constantly to substitute multilateral arrangements for bilateral ones. If the United States could be brought into the equation on the Chinese side, Stalin would have to moderate his demands. In effect, Chiang's strategy was the old ploy of the fox trying to borrow the prestige of the tiger, as the Chinese saying has it. (Hu chia hu wei 狐假虎威 .) American strength would compensate for Chinese weakness.

Prior to the commencement of Sino-Soviet negotiations, Chiang queried American Ambassador Hurley whether the United States would share in the use of Port Arthur and be a party to a Sino-Soviet treaty. Truman rejected this offer, but the Chinese Government continued to nurture the hope that the United States would intervene decisively. T. V. Soong kept in close contact with the United States Ambassador in Moscow, Averell Harriman, throughout the negotiations. (Harriman, who was an early proponent of a tough line toward Moscow, was personally sympathetic to the Chinese Government position.) Soong hoped that Harriman might trigger at least a strong American diplomatic representation to the Soviets in order to restrict excessive Soviet demands on China. But this hope was frustrated, and the multilateral strategy failed. Spurned by her putative ally, China was left to face a hostile Soviet Union.

The American Policy Perspective

Professor Liang suggests that the United States failure to intervene in the negotiations on the Chinese side was a product of inexperience and/or oversight. This is both too kind and too cutting a view. It is quite true that James Byrnes, the new Secretary of State, had little foreign affairs experience and that Truman himself, for all his bravado, was still feeling his way in foreign affairs during the summer of 1945. But the China policy of the new administration clearly continued that of the preceding Roosevelt era. While we may judge this policy to be mistaken, the President and his Secretary of State knew what they were doing.

Professor Liang skirts the issue of the evolving American perception of Chiang Kai-shek's government during World War II, but this is a crucial part of the picture. In brief, the United States government had very little hope that China would play an important role in the postwar balance of power in Asia. The fictive Great Power status which Roosevelt conferred on China (to the dismay of Churchill and Stalin), was a symbolic payment only and could not conceal the fact that Chinese leaders had been systematically excluded from the key wartime decisions including those which affected Asia and the Pacific. As Professor Liang intimates, the United States was primarily concerned with eliminating China as an arena of Soviet-American postwar conflict. The Yalta Agreement laid the foundation for the structure which the Sino-Soviet negotiations were supposed to erect.

Rightly or wrongly, the United States viewed China as a low priority area in world politics for most of the immediate postwar period. This basic fact explains not only the American refusal to support China in the 1945 negotiations, but also the failure to intervene decisively on the Nationalist side in the civil war of 1946-1949. To be sure, there were persons in the State Department who argued not only that the United States had an obligation to the Chinese Government, but that preservation of the commercial Open Door in Manchuria required an American diplomatic intervention to limit Soviet aggrandizement. But Harriman, Stimson, Vincent and others were unable to convince Truman and Byrnes on this point. Despite all his suspicions of the Soviet Union, Truman believed that a Sino-Soviet treaty was essential to stability in postwar East Asia, and he wasn't going to quibble over what must have seemed like fine points and risk jeopardizing his larger goal.

A curious footnote to American policy which Professor Liang recounts (p. 392) is Truman's eleventh-hour decision to authorize a United States military occupation of the Liaotung peninsula and land troops in Korea. The context of this decision was the massive Red Army

Further Observations:

BY CHIN-TUNG LIANG

After reading Prof. Steven Levine's remarks on my paper, I feel obliged to clarify a few points for the interest of history:

Outer Mongolian Independence

No historian can deny that the suzerainty over Outer Mongolia should remain with China because this was an established fact long before the Manchu Dynasty. What was done by the Soviet Union in connection with the Soviet-Outer Mongolian Alliance has been repeatedly protested by the Chinese government as an infringement of Chinese sovereignty in accordance with the 1924 Sino-Soviet treaty. This treaty was not a "dead letter" even from the Soviet point of view in 1945. If it were, Stalin would not have pressed so hard for the independence of Outer Mongolia at the Yalta and Moscow conferences.

The issue of Outer Mongolia was derived from the interpretation of two words: *Status Quo*. The interpretation of *Status Quo* varied in the minds of Roosevelt and Stalin. Roosevelt informed Chiang through Ambassador Wei Tao-ming that *Status Quo* meant that suzerainty remained in Chinese hands.[1] Stalin, on the other hand, told T. V. Soong that *Status Quo* meant independence of Outer Mongolia. China requested a precise interpretation from Washington. Unfortunately, both the White House and the State Department could not give China a clear answer. It was a very perplexing and difficult affair for China to accept Washington advice on a crucial issue about which Washington itself was unclear. All of the above has been reported in my previous paper which can be checked.

In accepting the Soviet demand on this issue, China had insisted and succeeded in the exchange of guarantees from the USSR. The guarantees were three, viz.:

1. Soviet Union has to assure and respect Chinese territorial sovereignty and administrative integrity in both Manchuria and Sinkiang.
2. No Soviet aid should be given, directly or indirectly, to Chinese rebellions including Chinese Communists.

    3. All Soviet aid, military or civilian, should go only to the Chinese government.

Chairman Chiang Kai-shek's attitude on these guarantees was very firm. In his July 6 instructions to T. V. Soong in Moscow, Chiang stated: "These are the minimum conditions for our considering the independence of Outer Mongolia. Without them, China will have sacrificed in vain, and you should ask the suspension of the negotiations and come home without delay."

These were the facts concerning this issue I found in the Chinese record.

Internal Politics of the Negotiations

In regard to the alleged internal politics played by the Chinese delegation, I did not find any such evidence as the discussant states. However, on the question of "whether T. V. Soong's welcome or resentment of Chiang Chin-kuo's role" was apparent, I did find from the record that they worked in complete harmony. In fact, it was Soong who requested Stalin through Molotov to permit young Chiang to sit in at the conference. Chairman Chiang sent a special instruction to his son asking him to take orders from the Premier but his son had already acted along this line before the instruction was received.[2]

Chungking Conference, July 5

According to the record, there were many voices in that conference, pro and con, over the Soviet demand. Some thought China should reject the demand forthwith and let the Soviet Union be exposed before world public opinion. Others thought a conditional acceptance formula might be found since Stalin had informed President Truman through Hopkins about giving support to Chiang's government and that the USSR had no territorial ambitions in Manchuria and Sinkiang. During the discussion, Ambassador Harriman's advice also carried weight. Harriman warned Soong that if no written accord was obtained before Soviet troops entered Manchuria, China might lose more than Manchuria. Inner Mongolia, Sinkiang and even Peiping itself might also be endangered. After a long debate late at night on July 5, the decision for conditional acceptance finally prevailed, and was executed on July 6 by Chiang's instruction.

It was true that Premier Soong did not like to take responsibility for this thankless duty, in view of his foreseeable difficulty in facing the Legislative Yuan (Chinese Parliament) by which the treaty was to be sanctioned. But after the persuasion of Chairman Chiang, he accepted the arrangement of appointing a new foreign minister to assist his negotiations in Moscow and to share his responsibility in the forthcoming Legislative Yuan.

Chiang Held the Negotiating Strings

I have never suggested that "Chiang held all the negotiating strings." It should be noted that in conducting negotiations for the Sino-Soviet treaty in Moscow, the Chinese position was very, very difficult. While Soong had brought a complete plan and full authority with him to Moscow for the negotiations, the situation changed rapidly on account of Stalin's demand for the independence of Outer Mongolia which was not in the Chungking plan. Rightly and naturally, the Premier and the Chief of State of China had to consult with each other constantly, cautiously and minutely over the new situation in order to avoid any sinister Soviet designs. As a chief of State, Chiang apparently had the duty of making the final decision over such a crucial issue for China.

Strategy of Multilateralization

Multilateral approach in the Sino-Soviet negotiations is by no means a "strategy" but a natural consequence of the Yalta agreement. The Yalta agreement was signed by three Powers: the United States, the USSR and Great Britain. Thus, the Yalta agreement itself was of a multilateral nature. To complete the unfinished Yalta multilateral work, the multilateral negotiation of a Sino-Soviet treaty was a logical and natural procedure. Moreover, the United States was not only a signatory Power of the Yalta agreement but played a role in pressing China to accept the American commitment in Yalta. Thus, she had the obligation and the responsibility towards both the USSR and China to participate in the negotiations in order to see her commitment, no more and no less, exactly fulfilled.

The American participation in the Moscow negotiations was not only suggested by Chairman Chiang and requested by Ambassador Harriman and Secretary Stimson, but also urged by a responsible State Department officer, John C. Vincent, who was usually not so kind to the Nationalist government. In his memo of July 23, 1945, to Secretary Byrnes, Vincent wrote:

> . . . the commitment taken by us at Yalta in regard to Manchuria and our undertaking to get China to accept these commitments *placed US squarely in a position of responsibility which she could not transfer to Chinese on the theory that the negotiations were bilateral.*[3]

In view of the fact that this memo was ignored and that no other positive measures were taken, it has been very difficult to convince historians that "the President of the United States and his Secretary of State did know what they were doing."

We must also realize that in the year 1945, the United States had both the power and the respect to fill in the postwar power vacuum created by the Japanese surrender. What was lacking was the firm American attitude and decisive action which would restrain but not provoke the USSR. Unwilling to fulfill her obligation by participating in the Moscow conference, but at the same time willing to leave a naked and weak China at Soviet mercy in the negotiations, while still believing that this would stabilize the Far East and maintain American interest there, the United States policy-makers were simply unrealistic, as events have proven.

China's Weakness and Its Re-examination

It is a pity to note that China's weakness, due to the exhaustion of fighting seven long years of war against Japan almost single-handed, has not been adequately recognized. During the war, Japan repeatedly approached China for a separate peace. In 1945-46, Stalin approached Chiang three times for a summit talk. China rejected both the Japanese and Russian overtures on the principle that she should be loyal to the Western Allies, particularly to the United States. The outcome of the secret Yalta agreement and of the refusal of the United States to keep the Cairo promise of equipping up to ninety Chinese divisions were certainly terrible blows against China. By these actions alone, China's postwar political prestige and military position were immediately weakened.

Had China accepted Japan's peace offer in 1942-43, the cost in Allied lives and money of defeating Japan would have been far greater. Had Chiang agreed to Stalin's request in 1945-46, the situation of China today might be very much different. The causes of the collapse of Nationalist China were many, but the failure on the American part to maintain its high principles was also, at least, one of the major factors. Twenty-seven years have gone by, and it is high time for us to re-examine the mistakes on both sides so that a lesson might be learned from history.

Contributors
to This Volume

Dennis Chinn 陳興家

Present position
  Assistant Professor of Economics
  Food Research Institute
  Stanford University, Stanford, California, 1974-
Education
  B.A., University of Washington (Economics/Statistics), 1968
  Ph.D., University of California, Berkeley (Economics), 1974
Publications
  "Effects of Income Redistribution on Economic Growth Constraints: Evidence from South Korea," *Economic Bulletin for Asia and the Far East*, United Nations, Vol. 23, No. 1, June 1972, Bangkok.
  "Distributional Equality and Economic Growth: The Case of Taiwan," *Economic Development and Cultural Change*, forthcoming.
  "The Marketed Surplus of a Subsistence Crop: Paddy Rice in Taiwan," *American Journal of Agricultural Economics*, August 1976.
  "Staple Food Control and Industrial Development in Postwar Japan 1950-57: The Role of the Black Market," *Journal of Development Economics*, forthcoming.
  "Land Utilization and Productivity in Prewar Chinese Agriculture: Preconditions for Collectivization," *American Journal of Agricultural Economics*, August 1977.
  "Rural Poverty and the Structure of Farm Household Incomes in Developing Countries: Evidence from Taiwan," *Economic Development and Cultural Change*, forthcoming.

Lloyd E. Eastman 易勞逸

Present Position
  Professor, Department of History
  University of Illinois, 1972-
Education
  B.A., Pacific Lutheran College, 1953
  University of Washington, graduate work, 1953, 1957
  Ph.D., Harvard University, 1963 (at Harvard, 1957-60)
  U.S. Army Language School, Monterey, California;
    Chinese language study, 1954-55
Professional Experience
  Connecticut College, Assistant Professor, 1962-66
  Ohio State University, Associate Professor, 1966-67
  University of Illinois, Associate Professor, 1967-72
  1960-62—Taiwan
  1968-69—Taiwan, Japan, Hong Kong
  1973—Taiwan and Japan

Publications
> *Throne and Mandarins: China's Search for a Policy during the Sino-French Controversy, 1880-1885* (Harvard University Press, 1967).
> *The Abortive Revolution: China under Nationalist Rule, 1927-1937* (Harvard University Press, 1974).
> Articles published in learned and professional journals.

Chi-ming Hou 侯繼明

Present Position
> Charles A. Dana Professor of Economics and Chairman of the Department of Economics at Colgate University, Hamilton, New York (Joined Colgate in 1956.)

Education
> LL.B. (Economics), Fu-Jen University, 1945
> M.A. with Honors (Economics), University of Oregon, 1949
> Ph.D. (Economics), Columbia University, 1954

Professional Experience
> Kazanjian Economics Foundation Scholar, Columbia University, 1950-1951
> Faculty Research Seminar Fellowship, Ford Foundation, 1958 (Yale University)
> Research Fellow in Chinese Economic Studies, East Asian Research Center, Harvard University, Fall of 1959, Fall of 1962, and Summers of 1959-1964
> Brookings Research Professorship, 1965-1966 (University of California, Berkeley)
> Fulbright Lecturer in Economics at National Chengchi University, Taiwan, 1970-1971

Publications
> *Foreign Investment and Economic Development of China: 1840-1937* (Harvard University Press, 1965).
> Some twenty articles, papers and monographs on the Chinese economy and economic development in general.

Chiao-min Hsieh 謝覺民

Present Position
> Professor, Department of Geography, University of Pittsburgh, 1967-

Education
> B.A., National Chekiang University, China (Geography), 1941
> M.A., Syracuse University, Syracuse (Geography), 1950
> Ph.D., Syracuse University (Geography), 1953

Professional Experience
> Honorary Visiting Professor, University of Hong Kong, 1974
> Visiting Professor, Department of Geography, Columbia University, Summer 1967
> Professor, Department of Geography, Catholic University, Washington, D.C., 1964-1967
> Visiting Lecturer, Department of Geography, University of Leeds, England, 1963-1964
> Associate Professor, Department of Geography, Catholic University, Washington, D.C. 1959-1964
> Assistant Professor, Department of Geography, Catholic University, Washington, D.C., 1956-1959

Research Associate, Center of International Studies, M.I.T., Cambridge, Massachusetts, 1954-1956

Instructor, Department of Geography, Dartmouth College, Hanover, New Hampshire, 1953-1954

Lecturer in Geography, National Taiwan Normal University, Taipei, Taiwan, 1946-1947

Research Assistant, China Institute of Geography, Chungking, China, 1941-1946

Publications

Atlas of China, Scholarly Book Division, McGraw-Hill Book Company, New York (1973).

China: Ageless Land and Countless People, Searchlight Series, Van Nostrand Co., Princeton, New Jersey (1967).

Taiwan—Ilha Formosa, Butterworth, Inc., London and Washington, D.C. (1964).

China: The Changing Society, editor and contributor of a chapter on China's boundary changes, with ten other contributors. The book was published by the University of Chicago Press and the Chinese University of Hong Kong Press in 1976.

A Provincial Atlas of China, accepted by Sing-Tao Foundation in Hong Kong, to be printed in color and published in 1976.

Five chapters in books, four monographs and twenty-two articles in learned and professional journals.

Akira Iriye

Present Position

Professor of History, University of Chicago, 1971-

Education

B.A., Haverford College (English History), 1957

Ph.D., Harvard University (U.S. and Far Eastern History), 1961

Professional Experience

Teaching Fellow (History), Harvard University, 1959-1961

Instructor (History), Harvard University, 1961-1964

Lecturer (History) Harvard University 1964-1966

Assistant Professor of History, University of California, Santa Cruz, 1966-1968

Associate Professor of History, University of Rochester, 1968-1969

Associate Professor of History, University of Chicago, 1969-1971

Publications

After Imperialism: The Search for a New Order in the Far East, 1921-1931, Harvard University Press, 1965.

Images in Sino-American Relations (in Japanese), Japan Institute of International Affairs, 1965.

Diplomacy in Japan (in Japanese), Chuokoron, 1966.

Across the Pacific: An Inner History of American-East Asian Relations, Harcourt, Brace, 1967.

U.S. Policy toward China (editor), Little, Brown 1968.

Pacific Estrangement: Japanese and American Expansion, 1897-1911, Harvard University Press, 1972.

The Cold War in Asia: A Historical Introduction, Prentice-Hall, 1974.

Mutual Images: Studies in American-Japanese Relations (editor), Harvard University Press, 1975.

From Nationalism to Internationalism: American Foreign Policy to 1914, Rout-
ledge and Kegan Paul, forthcoming.
Sixteen chapters in books.

John Israel 易社強

Present Position
  Member, Department of History, University of Virginia
Education
  B.S., University of Wisconsin
  M.A. and Ph.D., Harvard University
Professional Experience
  Taught at Claremont Men's College
Publications
  Student Nationalism in China, 1927-1937, Stanford, 1966.
  Rebels and Bureaucrats (co-authored with Donald W. Klein), California, 1976.

Steven I. Levine

Present Position
  Research Associate
  East Asian Institute
  Columbia University, New York
Education
  B.A., Brandeis University
  Ph.D. (Government and Far Eastern Languages), 1972
Professional Experience
  Assistant Professor of Political Science, Columbia University, 1973-1976
  Research Fellow, Research Institute on Communist Affairs, Columbia Univer-
    sity, 1972-1973
  Assistant Professor of History, Merrimack College, 1971-1972
Publications
  "China and the Superpowers: Peking's Policies toward the United States and
    the Soviet Union," *Political Science Quarterly*, Winter 1975-1976.
  Chapters, Chun-tu Hsueh, ed., *Dimensions of China's Foreign Relations*,
    Praeger, 1977; Michel Oksenberg and Gaddis Smith, eds., *Sino-American
    Relations in Historical Perspective* (forthcoming).
  Completing a book on *World Politics and Revolutionary Power in Manchuria,
    1945-49.*

Yun-han Li 李雲漢

Present Position
  Research Fellow, Academia Historica, 1973-
  Associate Professor, Department of History, National Normal University,
    Taiwan, 1973-
Education
  B.A., National Chengchi University, Taiwan, 1954
  M.A., National Chengchi University, Taiwan, 1956
  M.A., St. John's University, New York, 1969
Professional Experience
  Director, Section of Collection, The KMT Archives Commission, 1957-1972
  Visiting Scholar, Columbia University, New York, 1967-1969

Publications

    Admission of the Communists into the Kuomintang and the Purge, 1923-27. Taipei: China Committee for Publication and Prize Awards, 1967.

    National Revolution and the Historical Background of the Recovery of Taiwan. Taipei: The Young Lion Book Company, 1972.

    Yu Yu-jen: the Man and His Life. Taipei: League of Correspondents, 1973.

    Chronological Biography of Huang Ke-kiang. Taipei: The KMT Archives Commission, 1973.

    Sung Che-yuan and Lukouchiao Incident of July 7, 1937. Taipei: Biographical Literature Press, 1973.

Chin-tung Liang (C. T. Liang) 梁敬錞 (和鈞)

Present Position

    Senior Research Fellow, Institute of Modern History, Academia Sinica

    Advisor, Academia Historica, Republic of China

Education

    LL.B., National University of Peking

    M.A., School of Economics, University of London

    LITT.D., The China Academy

Professional Experience

    Professor, National University of Peking

    Justice, Supreme Court, China

    Director, Institute of Modern History, Academia Sinica

Publications

    The Sinister Face of the Mukden Incident, 1969.

    The Chinese Revolution of 1911, 1962.

    General Stilwell in China, 1942-1945: The Full Story, 1972.

    China and the Cairo Conference, 1975.

Hung-hsun Ling (H. H. Ling) 凌鴻勛 (竹銘)

Present Position

    Chairman, T. Y. Lin, Taiwan, Inc., Structural Engineers

Education

    B.Sc. civil engineering, Chiao-tung University, Shanghai, 1915; D.Sc. (Hon.) Chiao-tung University, Hsinchu, 1975

Professional Experience

    American Bridge Company, Pencoyd Plant, and New York Division Office, 1915-1918.

    Chinese National Railways, Cadet Engineer, Engineer, and Bridge Engineer, 1918-1922

    Professor of Civil Engineering, 1923-1925

    President, Chiao-tung University, Shanghai, 1924-1927

    Director and Engineer-in-chief, various Chinese National Railways, responsible for the construction and completion of some 600 miles of new lines and location of some 1,200 miles of projected lines, 1929-1945.

Publications

    A Comprehensive Survey of Railway Development in China.

    Railroad Engineering.

    Seventy Years of Chinese Eastern Railway.

    Biography of Jeme Tien Yew.

Jessie G. Lutz

Present Position
  Professor of History, Douglass College, Rutgers University, 1971-
  Director of Asian Studies, Rutgers University, 1977-
Education
  B.A., University of North Carolina
  M.A., University of Chicago
  Ph.D., Cornell University (Modern Chinese History)
Publications
  Christian Missions in China, Evangelists of What?, edited with an introduction,
    Health Problems in Asian Civilizations, 1965.
  "December 9, 1935: Student Nationalism and the China Christian Colleges,"
    Journal of Asian Studies, XXVI August 1967.
  "The Chinese Student Movement of 1945-49," *Journal of Asian Studies,* XXXI,
    November 1971.
  China and the Christian Colleges, 1850-1950, Cornell, 1971.
  "Education as an Instrument of Change" (review essay), *History of Education
    Quarterly,* Fall 1973.
  "Chinese Nationalism and the Anti-Christian Campaigns of the 1920's," *Modern
    Asian Studies,* Summer 1976.

Chun-fan Mao 毛春帆

Present Position
  Adjunct Assistant Professor of Philosophy, New York University, 1972-
Education
  B.A., The National Southwest Associated University, Political Science, 1944
  M.A., University of Pennsylvania, Political Science, 1947
  Ph.D. matriculated candidate, Public Law and Government, Columbia Uni-
    versity, 1965
Professional Experience
  English Teacher, Second National Middle School, Hochuang, China, 1944-
    1945
  Assistant Professor of International Relations, Chung Hsin University, Taipei,
    1961-1962
  Writer (by special contract), the China Institute in America, New York, 1968-
    1969
  Lecturer in Philosophy and Politics, New York University, 1966-1972
Publications
  Articles, mostly under the *nom de plume* of Yung Meng, have appeared in
    Chinese language journals in Taiwan, including *The Central Daily News,
    The Rambler,* and *China's Women.*
  Special Column entitled "Flying Bird Across the Sea" in *China's Women.*
  Member of the Editorial Board of *Freedom News* and concurrently its New
    York correspondent, January 1976. *Freedom News* is a Chinese language
    periodical published in Hong Kong.

Ou Tsuin-chen (T. C. Ou) 吳俊升 (士選)

Present Position
  Research Professor, New Asia Institute of Advanced Chinese Studies, Hong
  Kong

Education
  B.A., National Southeastern University, Nanking, 1925
  Docteur de l'Université de Paris, 1931
Professional Experience
  Professor and Head of the Department of Education, National Peking University, 1931-1937
  Director of Higher Education, Ministry of Education, 1938-1944
  Professor of Education, National Central University, 1945-1948
  Editor-in-chief, Cheng-chung Book Company, 1946-1948
  Vice Minister of Education, 1949
  Professor of Education, New Asia College, Hong Kong, 1950-1951
  Editor and Editor-in-Chief, Cheng-chung Book Company, 1951-1954
  Vice Minister of Education, 1954-1958
  Professor of Education and Dean of Faculty of Arts, Cheng-chi University, 1958-1959
  Vice President (1960-1964), President (1965-1969), and Director of the Institute of Advanced Chinese Studies and Research (1965-1967), New Asia College
  Delegate of the Chinese Government to the General Conference of UNESCO, 1951, 1954 and 1958
  Senior Specialist, the East-West Center, University of Hawaii, 1964
  Participated in the International Conference on World Crisis in Education, Williamsburg, 1967, and in the Conference on Education for Mankind, University of Chicago, 1968
Publications
  An Outline of Philosophy of Education (in Chinese), revised edition, 1973.
  La Doctrine Pédagogigue de John Dewey, Paris, 1958.
  A Collection of Essays on Education and Culture (in Chinese), 1972.
  Kiang Kao Chi (a collection of poems and essays), 1967.
  Chinese Translation of Dewey's Freedom and Culture, 1953.
  Chinese Translation of A. Laland's Précis Raisonné de la Morale Pratique, 1955.
  John Dewey: Lectures in China 1919-1920 (with Robert W. Clopton as co-editor and translator), 1973.
  "A Chronology of John Dewey" (in Chinese) in *New Asia College Academic Annual*, 1961.
  "A Re-Evaluation of the Educational Theory and Practice of John Dewey" in *Educational Forum*, March 1961.
  "Some Facts & Ideas about Talent and Genius in Chinese History" in the *Yearbook of Education*, London, 1961.
  "Dewey's Lectures and Influence in China" in the *Guide to Works of John Dewey*, Carbondale, 1970.

Dison H. F. Poe 浦薛鳳 (逖生)

Present Position
  Research Professor of Asian Studies, St. John's University
Education
  Graduate, Tsing Hua School, Peking, China, 1921
  B.A., Hamline University, St. Paul, 1923
  M.A., Harvard University, 1925
  LL.D., Hamline University, 1944

Professional Experience

University Teaching:

Professor, Tung-Lu University, Yunnan, 1926-1927
Professor, National Chekiang University, 1927-1928
Professor and Chairman, Department of Political Science, National Tsing Hua University, Peiping, 1928-1937
Professor, Southwest Associated University, Kunming, 1947-1948
Professor, National Central University, Chungking, part-time, 1941-1944, and full-time, Nanking, 1946-1947
Professor, National Chengchi University, Nanking, part-time, 1946-1947
Professor, Dean of Studies, and concurrently Director of the Graduate School of Political Science, National Chengchi University, Taiwan, 1954-1961
Research Chair Professor, National Chengchi University, 1961-1962
John Hay Whitney Foundation Visiting Professor, Hanover College, Indiana, and University of Bridgeport, Connecticut, 1962-1963
Distinguished Professor of Political Science and Philosophy, University of Bridgeport, 1963-1971
Visiting Professor of Asian Studies, St. John's University, New York, 1971-1974

Government Service:

Counselor, Supreme National Defense Council, 1939-1945
Technical Expert, Chinese Delegation to the Dumbarton Oaks Conference, 1944
Technical Expert, Chinese Delegation to the San Francisco Conference, 1945
Deputy Director-General CNRRA (Chinese Relief and Rehabilitation Administration), 1945-1946
Deputy Secretary-General, The Executive Yuan, 1947-1948
Secretary-General, and Council Member, Taiwan Provincial Government, 1948-1954
Head of Chinese Delegation to the UNESCO General Conference, Paris, 1958
Vice-Minister of Education, 1958-1960

Publications

Hsi-yang chin-tai cheng-chih szu-chao (Modern Western Political Theories), Hong Kong, Commercial Press, 1939. Fifth printing, Taiwan, Chung Hua Wen Hua Press, 1965.
Freedom from Fear (on Post-War Peace Organization), New York, Chinese IRP Association, 1944. Reprint with Additional Note, and with Chinese translation, Taipei, Chinese U.N. Association, 1954.
Hsiu-yang kai-mu (Models for Personality Cultivation), a compilation of biographical sketches, Taipei, Chung Hua Wen Hua Press, 1953.
Cheng-chih lun-tsung (Essays on Government and Politics), Taipei, Cheng Chung Book Co., 1955.
Cheng-chih chuan-li chih kou-cheng yu pao-chih (Political Power: Composition and Preservation), a monograph, Taipei, 1958.
Cheng-chih yu fa-lu chih kuan-hsi (Law and Politics—Their Relationship), a monograph, Taipei, 1959.
Hsien-tai hsi-yang cheng-chih szu chao (Contemporary Western Political Theories), Taipei, Cheng Chung Book Co., 1962.
"Imperial Succession and Attendant Crisis," a paper presented at the XXVII International Congress of Orientalists, Ann Arbor, Michigan, August 14,

1967, and published in *The Tsing Hua Journal of Chinese Studies,* v. VIII, Nos. 1 and 2, 1970.

"Political Reconstruction," Chapter 2, in *The Strenuous Decade: China's Nation-Building Efforts, 1927-1937,* New York: St. John's University Press, 1970.

"Naturalism in the *Tao* of Confucius and Lao Tzu," a chapter in *Radical Currents in Contemporary Philosophy,* ed. David DeGrood et al, St. Louis, Green, 1971.

"Confucianism on Violence," a chapter in *Reflections on Revolution* ed. Dale Rieppe et al, 1971.

Chan-shih lun-ping (Wartime Editorials), Taipei, Fu Hsing Book Co., 1973.

"Discussion on Three Conference Papers," in *Sun Yat-sen and China,* ed. Paul K. T. Sih, St. John's University Press, 1974.

"The Laotzian and Confucian *Tao:* Its Origin, Classification, Nature and Function," in *The Tsing Hua Journal of Chinese Studies,* v. XI, Nos. 1 and 2, 1975.

Peter Schran

Present Position

Professor of Economics and Asian Studies, University of Illinois, 1969-

Education

The Free University of Berlin, economics and sociology, 1949-1952

Washington University, St. Louis, Missouri, economics and political science (Fulbright fellowship), 1952-1953

The Free University of Berlin, economics and sociology, 1953-1954

Certificate in economics (Diplom-Volkswirt), 1954

University of California, Berkeley, economics and Chinese (since 1958), 1956-1961

Senior Fellow, Center for Chinese Studies, University of California, Berkeley, 1958-1961

Ph.D. in economics, University of California, Berkeley, 1961

Professional Experience

Teaching Associate, Department of Economics, University of California, 1960-1961

Assistant Professor of Economics, Yale University, 1961-1965

Associate Professor of Economics and Asian Studies, University of Illinois, 1965-1969

Publications

The Development of Chinese Agriculture, 1950-1959, (Urbana, Ill.: University of Illinois Press, 1969), 238 pp.

Guerrilla Economy: The Development of the Shensi-Kansu-Ninghsia Border Region, 1937-1945 (Albany: State University of New York Press, 1976), 323 pp.

More than twenty articles published in learned and professional journals.

Tsung-han Shen (T. H. Shen) 沈宗瀚（海槎）

Present Position

Adviser, Sino-American Joint Commission on Rural Reconstruction, June 1973-

Chairman, Board of Directors, Asian Vegetable Research and Development Center, 1971-

Counselor, Academia Sinica, 1971-

Member, Central Advisory Committee, KMT, 1969-

Education

Graduated from National Peking Agricultural College, Peking, 1918

M.S., State University of Georgia, Athens, 1924

Ph.D., Cornell University, Ithaca, 1928

Professional Experience

Commissioner, Sino-American Joint Commission on Rural Reconstruction, 1948-1964

Chairman, JCRR, 1964-1973

Member, Council for International Economic Cooperation and Development, Executive Yuan (Cabinet), 1964-1973

Chief Technician, Vice Director, and then Director of National Agricultural Research Bureau, 1934-1950

Professor of Plant Breeding, University of Nanking, 1927-1937

Publications

Agricultural Resources of China (New York: Cornell University Press), 1951.

Agricultural Development on Taiwan Since World War II (New York: Cornell University Press), 1964.

Sino-American Joint Commission on Rural Reconstruction: Twenty Years of Cooperation for Agricultural Development (New York: Cornell University Press), 1970.

Agriculture's Place in the Strategy of Development: The Taiwan Experience (Taipei: Joint Commission on Rural Reconstruction), 1974.

Collection of 43 papers on Agriculture (in Chinese) (Taipei: Commercial Press), 1975.

Autobiography (in Chinese) (Taipei: Biographical Literature), 1975.

Lawrence Shyu 徐乃力

Present Position

Associate Professor, Department of History, University of New Brunswick, Fredericton, N.B., Canada, 1944-

Education

B.A., Taiwan Normal University, Taiwan, 1956

M.A., Far Eastern Studies, University of Washington, Seattle, 1960

Ph.D., East Asian History, Columbia University, 1971

Professional Experience

Lecturer in History, Hong Kong Baptist College, Hong Kong, 1960-1963

Escort-Interpreter, Language Services, United States Department of State, Washington, D.C., Summers 1964-1966

Research Assistant, Chinese Oral History Project, East Asian Institute, Columbia University, 1965-1966

Instructor in History, Hobart & William Smith Colleges, Geneva, New York, 1966-1968

Assistant Professor in History, University of New Brunswick, Fredericton, 1968-1973

Publications

"Sino-Soviet Competition in the Mongolian People's Republic," *China Monthly,* June 1961, Hong Kong.

"National Amalgamation and Cultural Blending in Tang China," *Hong Kong Baptist College Journal,* 1962.

"The People's Political Council and China's Wartime Problems, 1937-1945,"

Ph.D. dissertation, Department of History, Columbia University, 1971. Dissertation Abstract No. 72-28, 100, 1972.

"The People's Political Council and China's Unity, 1937-45," a paper presented at the Conference of the Canadian Society for Asian Studies, May 25-26, 1972, Ottawa.

"Prospects of Mainland China-Taiwan Negotiations: A Replay of the Wartime Alliance?", a paper given at the Conference of Asian Studies, June 14-16, 1973, Vancouver.

"Teaching Asian Studies in Canada's Hinterland: the 'Lone Ranger' in New Brunswick," a paper given to the Annual Conference of the Canadian Society for Asian Studies, May 12-14, 1975, Montreal.

Paul K. T. Sih 薛光前

Present Position

Vice President for International Studies and Education, St. John's University, 1974-

Professor of Far Eastern History; Director, Center of Asian Studies, St. John's University, 1959-

Education

LL.B., Soochow University, China, 1933

Doctor of Political Science, University of Rome, Italy, 1935

Professional Experience

Professor of Law, Soochow University, 1940-1941

Professor of Far Eastern History and Politics, Research Director (1951-1956) and Director (1956-1959) of the Institute of Far Eastern Studies, Seton Hall University, 1950-1959

Governmental Service

During the war, 1937-1942, served in the Ministry of Railways and the Ministry of Communications, Republic of China, as Senior Secretary, Division Chief of Research and Publications, Deputy Director General of National Highway Transportation which supervised the Burma Road, and Director General of the Hunan-Szechwan-Shensi Joint Transportation System.

From 1942 to 1948, joined the Ministry of Foreign Affairs, Republic of China, as Technical Counselor, appointed as Advisor to the Chinese Delegation to the Five Foreign Ministers' Council, September 1945 in London, the Peace Conference, April 1946 in Paris, and the Third U.N. General Assembly, November 1948 in Paris, while serving as Chargé d'Affaires with ministerial rank of the Chinese Embassy in Rome, Italy.

From 1948 to 1949, he was China's Delegate to the U.N. Special Committee on the Balkans which was in charge of dealing with the Greek problem.

Publications

From Confucius to Christ, Sheed & Ward, New York, 1952, reprinted in 1974 (also in French and Italian).

Chinese Culture and Christian Spirituality, Chinese Cultural Foundation, 1957.

Democracy in East Asia (ed.), Chinese Cultural Foundation, 1957.

Decision for China, Henry Regnery, Chicago, 1959, reprinted by St. John's University Press, 1971.

The Strenuous Decade: China's Nation-Building Efforts, 1927-1937, ed., St. John's University Press, 1970.

Taiwan in Modern Times, ed., St. John's University Press, 1973.

Sun Yat-sen and China, ed., St. John's University Press, 1974.

The Chinese in America (co-ed. with Leonard Allen), St. John's University Press, 1975.

Some thirty articles and papers published in learned and professional journals.

Anthony M. Tang 唐宗明

Present Position
Professor of Economics, Vanderbilt University
Education
L'Universite L'Aurore, Shanghai, 1941-1942, Civil Engineering
B.B.A., Loyola University of the South, New Orleans, 1949
Ph.D., Economics, Vanderbilt University, 1955
Major undergraduate areas of study: Accounting, International Trade
Major graduate areas of study: Economic Theories, Agricultural Economics, International Economics, International Relations
Professional Experience
Visiting Professor, University of Michigan, 1976-1977
Director, East Asian Studies Program, Vanderbilt University, 1973-1976
Chairman of the Department, Vanderbilt University, 1968-1971
Visiting Professor, Graduate Institute of Economics, National Taiwan University, 1974-1975
Visiting Professor of Economics (concurrently Director of Economic Research Center, Director of University Studies in Economics, and Dean of the Faculty of Commerce and Social Science), The Chinese University of Hong Kong, 1966-1968
Acting Chairman of the Department, June-October 1964
Acting Director, Graduate Program in Economic Development, Vanderbilt University, 1961-1963
Visiting Professor of Agricultural Economics, University of California, Berkeley, 1963-1964
Associate Professor of Economics and Business Administration, Vanderbilt University, 1960-1963
Visiting Lecturer, Institute of Social and Economic Research, Osaka University, Osaka, Japan, 1959-1960
Assistant Professor of Economics, Vanderbilt University, 1956-1960
Assistant Director, Institute on Economic Development, Vanderbilt University, Summer 1956
Instructor in Economics, Vanderbilt University, 1955-1956
Assistant to the Director, Institute on Economic Development, Vanderbilt University, Summer 1954
Research Associate in Economics, Vanderbilt University, 1952-1954
"Ungraded Expert," U.S. War Department, 1945-1946
Captain, Chinese National Army (Bureau of Foreign Affairs), 1943-1945
Publications
Economic Development in the Southern Piedmont, 1860-1950: Its Impact on Agriculture, Chapel Hill: The University of North Carolina Press, 1958.
Some forty articles and papers published in learned and professional journals.

William L. Tung 董 霖（為公）

Present Position
Professor of Political Science, Queens College of the City University of New York, 1962-

Education

B.A., Fuh Tai University, Shanghai, 1928
M.A., University of Illinois, 1937
Ph.D., University of Illinois, 1939
Post-doctoral Research Fellow, Yale University, 1939-1940

Professional Experience

Lecturer of government, Northwestern University, China, 1928-1930
Professor of Political Science, Hangchow University, China, 1940-1942
Professorial Lecturer, Fuh Tai University, China, 1940-1942, 1946-1947
Professor and Chairman of the Department of Political Science, St. John's University, New York, 1957-1962

Publications

China and Some Phases of International Law, London and New York: Oxford University Press, 1940.
Cases and Other Readings in International Law (ed.), Shanghai: Evans Book Co., 1940.
The Political Institutions of Modern China, The Hague: Martinus Nijhoff, 1964.
International Law in an Organizing World, New York: Thomas Y. Crowell Co., 1968.
International Organization under the United Nations System, New York: Oceana Publications, 1969.
China and the Foreign Powers: The Impact of and Reaction to Unequal Treaties, New York: Oceana Publications, 1970.
Revolutionary China: A Personal Account, 1926-1949, New York: St. Martin's Press, 1973.
The Chinese in America, Dobbs Ferry, N.Y.: Oceana Publications, 1974.
V. K. Wellington Koo and China's Wartime Diplomacy, New York: St. John's University, 1977.

William W. Whitson

Present Position

Chief, Foreign Affairs and National Defense Division, Congressional Research Service, Library of Congress, 1976-

Education

U.S. Military Academy, 1948
M.A. and Ph.D., International Relations, Fletcher School of Law and Diplomacy, 1958
Graduate Economics at the Ateneo of Manila, The Littauer School of Public Administration, and The Department of Economics, Harvard University.
Ph.D. dissertation on educational requirements for rational security policy formulation; foreign area and language training in Chinese (Mandarin) and China from 1961 through 1965

Professional Experience

Practical civil and topographic engineering in the Philippines, 1949-1951
General's Aide at the United Nations, 1952
Instructor at West Point, 1954-1957
Advisor to the Dean of the Korean Military Academy, 1958-1959
Served with various engineer, infantry and Ranger troop units including the 82nd Airborne Division, 1948-1961
Political analyst attached to the American Embassy in Taipei, 1965-1967
Political analyst of Mainland China and Far Eastern Affairs, American Consulate General in Hong Kong

Interviewed numerous refugees and senior Chinese business officials

Served on the Policy Planning Staff and the Systems Analysis Staff, Office of the Secretary of Defense, 1969-1970

Senior Social Scientist on China, Rand Corporation, 1970-1974

Director of Policy Research, BDM Corporation, 1974-1976

Publications

Editor, *Doing Business With China,* 1974.

Editor, *The Military & Politics in China,* 1974.

Articles in *Asian Survey* and *China Quarterly.*

Chinese Communist High Command, 1928-71.

Hsiang-hsiang Wu (H. H. Wu) 吳相湘

Present Position

Professor of History, College of Chinese Culture, Yangmingshan, Republic of China, 1969-

Education

B.A., National Peking University, History, 1936

Professional Experience

Assistant, Institute of History and Philology, Academia Sinica, China, 1937

Associate Professor, National Ho-Nan University, China, 1945-1947

Researcher, National Palace Museum of Peiping, China, 1947-1949

Professor, National Taiwan University, 1952-1965

Professor and Head, Department of History, Nanyang University, Singapore, 1966-1969

Publications

The Coup D'etat of 1861, 1942.

Sung Chiao-Jen, 1964.

Biography of One Hundred Renowned Chinese in the Republic of China, four volumes, 1971.

The Second Sino-Japanese War, 1937-1945, two volumes, 1973-1974.

Index

Abend, Hallett, 8, 29
"A. B. League," 366
Academia Historica, xvii
Academia Sinica, x, xxvi, 111
"Agrarian Reformers," 318
Alma Ata, 260
Altai Mountain, 384
Amau Eiji
  author of "Amau Policy," 7
Amau statement, 7, 33
American White Paper, 322, 323
Anami Korechika
  at Changsha, 65, 66
Anhwei, 56, 57, 171, 172, 186, 213
Associated Christian Colleges, 129
Association for Promotion of Constitutionalism, 299
Azerbaijan
  Soviet withdrawal from, xxxii

Bailey, S. K., 323
Baker, Gilbert, 154
Band, Claire and William, 239, 240
"Bandit Extermination Campaigns," 275
Bank of China, 172, 179, 209, 335, 336, 337
Bank of Communications, 209
Barrett, David D., 32
Barry, R. H., 80
Baxter, Glen W., xxiv (Lienta), 123
Beaufre, Andre, 80
Belgium, 254
"Big Four," xxxii, 403
Bisson, T. A., 31
"Blue Shirts," 22, 275
Bodman, Nichols, xxxiv (Lienta), 123
Boorman, Howard L., 80, 356
Borg, Dorothy, 29, 73, 271
Boyle, John Hamilton, 78, 307, 357
Boxer Indemnity Fellowships, 113, 146
Buck, John Lossing, 169, 199, 201
Buhite, R. D., 324
Bunker, Gerald E., 79, 357
Burma, xxvi, 86, 142, 147, 219, 249, 304, 331, 371

defense of, 67
plan to recover, 68
refugees from, 142
Burma Road, 86, 142, 183, 196, 215, 257-260, 267-269, 296, 334, 335, 371
Byas, Hugh, 28
Byrnes, James F., xxxii, 380, 387, 391, 395, 402, 407

Cairo Conference
  promise of ninety divisions, 308
Calcutta, 259, 331
Canada, xxviii
Canton, 61, 86, 156, 205, 215, 244-247, 334, 337, 352
  fall of, 58, 226
Canton-Hankow Railway. *See* Railway Development
Canton-Kowloon Railway. *See* Railway Development
"C C Clique," 343, 348, 365, 366
Central Air Academy, 336
Central Bank of China, 227, 333, 335
Central Daily News, xx, 149
Central Executive Committee (Kuomintang), 276, 279, 288, 299, 301, 366
Central Government (also cited as Chinese Government, National Government), 6, 7, 9-11, 14-17, 23-26, 48, 49, 94, 157, 158, 161, 163, 165
Central Machine Works (Kunming), 335
Central Military Academy, 333
Central Party Headquarters, 366
Central Soviet Government (Yenan), 283
Cha Liang-chao, 137, 165
Cha Liang-cheng, 123, 152
Chahar, 8, 10, 22, 45, 96
Chamber of Commerce (Chinese), 229
Chang, Carsun (Chun-mai), 307, 308, 317, 318, 321, 324, 325, 327
Chang, C. C. (Bank of China), 170, 195
Chang, C. F., 28

423